Frommer's®
Cape Cod, Nantucket
& Martha's Vineyard

My Cape Cod, Nantucket & Martha's Vineyard
by Laura M. Reckford

MOST PEOPLE VISIT CAPE COD, NANTUCKET, AND MARTHA'S VINEYARD

for the beaches. That's understandable. The beaches are wonderful: from the warm waters of Buzzards Bay to the sandy stretches along Cape Cod Bay, where low tide unveils miles of shells and sea life for beachcombers. The calm waters of Nantucket Sound are most popular with families, and the pristine National Seashore beaches, along the rough, unpredictable Atlantic Ocean, are beloved by surfers.

The Cape and Islands have much more to offer, though—centuries of history, for example. Places like the Dexter Grist Mill, in Sandwich, remind us what life was like for Colonial-era Cape residents. And Aquinnah, on Martha's Vineyard, is the ancestral home of Wampanoag, the Native American tribe that first called this region home.

As for outdoor activities, the bike paths, golf courses, and kayaking routes are among the best in New England. But what I like best about the Cape and Islands is the fact that on the busiest, hottest day in August, you can find a secluded place—a favorite walking path, a bike trail, a waterway. You'll stroll, pedal, or paddle a short distance, and miraculously, you'll be the only one there. The following photos offer just a glimpse of why those of us who live on the Cape and the Islands wouldn't live anywhere else.

© Frank Siteman/AGE Fotostock

No trip to Nantucket Island is complete without a stroll around **NANTUCKET HARBOR (left)**. I like to start at the north end of the harbor at the Ropewalk, where yachters meet at the island's only outdoor raw bar—a lively summer scene. Then I wander around the edge of the harbor, gawking at the yachts, until reaching Old South Wharf, where a row of art galleries awaits.

BIKE SHOPS (above) are ubiquitous on Martha's Vineyard, where getting around on two wheels is a great option. My favorite route is an all-day circle-the-island tour that begins in Edgartown, loops through the up-island towns of West Tisbury, Chilmark, and Aquinnah, and passes through Vineyard Haven and Oak Buffs. You can stop along the way for shopping, sight-seeing, picnicking and, of course, relaxing on some of the island's prettiest beaches.

On the Cape and Islands, getting outside is what it's all about. Most people grab a blanket and head for the beach. Whether it's a secluded beach in **BREWSTER** (left), accessed only by a narrow path over the dunes, or a family stroll on a lovely stretch of beach on **NANTUCKET** (below), you'll find a beach for every mood. For more vigorous activity, head for the links. My favorite golf course for scenery is **HIGHLAND LINKS** (above right) in Truro. Playing in the shadow of Highland Lighthouse, on a 50-foot bluff overlooking the Atlantic Ocean, is an undeniable pleasure. If biking is more your speed, the **CAPE COD RAIL TRAIL** (below right) winds past scenic Nauset Marsh, in Orleans. And if you're riding your bike to the nearest ice cream shop, even better.

An overflowing portion of steaming **CHERRYSTONE CLAMS (left)**, some cold beverages, a group of friends—the ingredients of a perfect Cape Cod cocktail hour. The wonderful thing about eating shellfish on the Cape is that the fisherman who hauled it in could very well be sitting at the next table. It's easy to find fresh off-the-boat seafood on the Cape and Islands; it's a specialty of the region.

The colors of the clay **CLIFFS OF AQUINNAH (below)**, on Martha's Vineyard, change depending on the time of day. In the first light of morning, the colors are subdued, but they seem to grow more intense as the sun rises. By sunset, the cliffs appear to glow from within. Making the trek to the far side of the island to see these cliffs is a must.

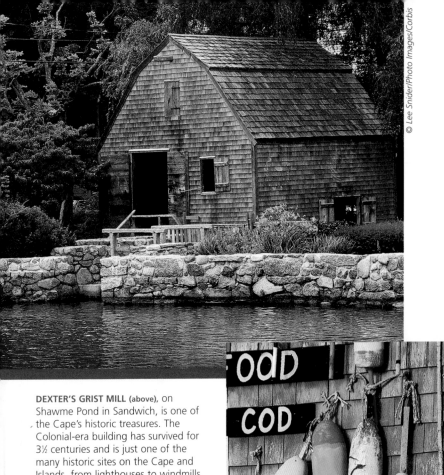

DEXTER'S GRIST MILL (above), on Shawme Pond in Sandwich, is one of the Cape's historic treasures. The Colonial-era building has survived for 3½ centuries and is just one of the many historic sites on the Cape and Islands, from lighthouses to windmills to historic houses, that are open to visitors. The mill still grinds corn, which you can take home with you. It's a bargain—a 2-pound bag costs a few dollars.

Best Cape clam shack? That's a tricky one. For authentic Cape Cod atmosphere, you can't beat **CAP'T CASS ROCK HARBOR SEAFOOD (right),** in Orleans, where the colorful buoys on one exterior wall serve as a beacon to fried-fish aficionados. It's casual here. You just belly up to the counter and order a big plate of fried clams—with bellies, of course.

Of the many places to watch the sunset on the Cape and Islands, nothing comes close to **ROCK HARBOR (left)**, in Orleans, where the ebbing glow of the sunset lights up the trees that were placed in the harbor as channel markers. Rock Harbor is also where to find the Cape's biggest sport fishing fleet—18 boats wait to take you out to snag bluefish, striped bass, tuna, and other big-game fish.

I never get tired of wandering through the Camp Meeting Grounds, in Oak Bluffs on Martha's Vineyard, to see the whimsical **"GINGERBREAD" COTTAGES (above)**. These homes are a prime example of the Victorian architectural style known as Carpenter Gothic, in which craftsmen used their tools to construct intricate scrollwork and other ornamental flourishes. The campgrounds were built for Methodist revival meetings; in the center is the magnificent Trinity Park Tabernacle, an open-sided iron chapel.

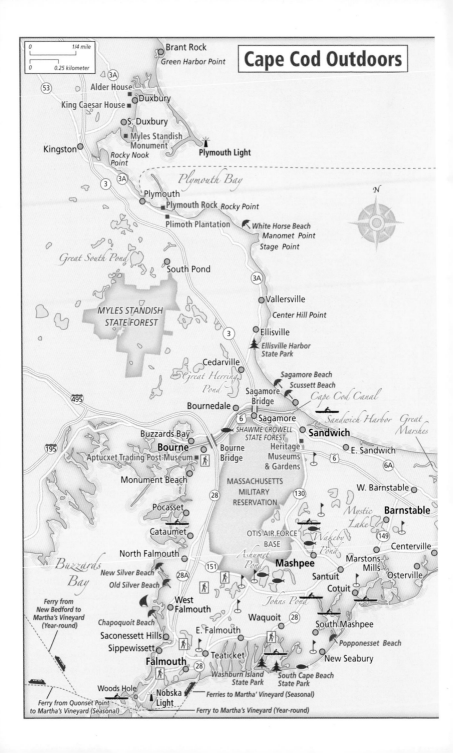

Cape Cod Outdoors

| 0 | 1/4 mile |
| 0 | 0.25 kilometer |

Brant Rock
Green Harbor Point

53
3A
Alder House
King Caesar House
Duxbury
S. Duxbury
Myles Standish Monument
Plymouth Light
Kingston
Rocky Nook Point

Plymouth Bay

N

Plymouth
Plymouth Rock Rocky Point
Plimoth Plantation
White Horse Beach
Manomet Point
Stage Point

Great South Pond
South Pond

3A

Vallersville
Center Hill Point
Ellisville
Ellisville Harbor State Park

MYLES STANDISH STATE FOREST

3

Cedarville

Great Herring Pond

Sagamore Beach
Scussett Beach
Cape Cod Canal

495
Bournedale
Sagamore Bridge
Sandwich Harbor Great Marshes

Buzzards Bay
6 Sagamore
SHAWME CROWELL STATE FOREST
Sandwich

195
Bourne
Aptucket Trading Post Museum
Bourne Bridge
Heritage Museums & Gardens
E. Sandwich
6
6A

Monument Beach
MASSACHUSETTS MILITARY RESERVATION
130
W. Barnstable

28
Mystic Lake
Barnstable

Pocasset
OTIS AIR FORCE BASE
Wakeby Pond
149

Cataumet
Ashumet Pond
Mashpee
Centerville

North Falmouth
151
Marstons Mills
Santuit
Osterville

New Silver Beach
28A
Cotuit

Old Silver Beach
Johns Pond
South Mashpee

Ferry from New Bedford to Martha's Vineyard (Year-round)
West Falmouth
Waquoit
28

Buzzards Bay
Chapoquoit Beach
E. Falmouth
Popponesset Beach

Saconessett Hills
New Seabury

Sippewissett
Teaticket

Falmouth
28

Woods Hole
Washburn Island State Park
South Cape Beach State Park

Ferry from Quonset Point to Martha's Vineyard (Seasonal)
Nobska Light
Ferries to Martha' Vineyard (Seasonal)

Ferry to Martha's Vineyard (Year-round)

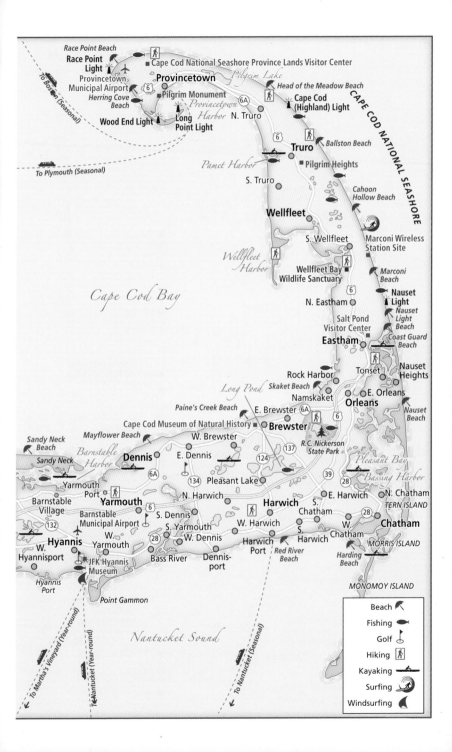

Race Point Beach
Race Point Light
■ Cape Cod National Seashore Province Lands Visitor Center
Pilgrim Lake
Head of the Meadow Beach
Provincetown Municipal Airport
Provincetown
To Boston (Seasonal)
Herring Cove Beach
■ Pilgrim Monument
Provincetown Harbor
N. Truro
▲ **Cape Cod (Highland) Light**
Wood End Light
Long Point Light
To Plymouth (Seasonal)
Pamet Harbor
Truro
Ballston Beach
■ Pilgrim Heights
S. Truro
Cahoon Hollow Beach
Wellfleet
CAPE COD NATIONAL SEASHORE
S. Wellfleet
Marconi Wireless Station Site
Wellfleet Harbor
Wellfleet Bay Wildlife Sanctuary
Marconi Beach
Cape Cod Bay
N. Eastham
▲ **Nauset Light**
Salt Pond Visitor Center
Nauset Light Beach
Eastham
Coast Guard Beach
Rock Harbor
Tonset
Nauset Heights
Long Pond
Skaket Beach
Namskaket
E. Orleans
Orleans
Paine's Creek Beach
E. Brewster
Nauset Beach
Mayflower Beach
Cape Cod Museum of Natural History ■
Brewster
W. Brewster
R.C. Nickerson State Park
Pleasant Bay
Sandy Neck Beach
Barnstable Harbor
Dennis
E. Dennis
Bassing Harbor
Sandy Neck
Yarmouth Port
Pleasant Lake
N. Chatham
TERN ISLAND
Barnstable Village
Barnstable Municipal Airport
N. Harwich
Harwich
S. Chatham
Yarmouth
S. Dennis
Chatham
MORRIS ISLAND
Hyannis
W. Yarmouth
S. Yarmouth
W. Dennis
W. Harwich
S. Harwich
W. Chatham
W. Hyannisport
JFK Hyannis Museum
Bass River
Dennis-port
Harwich Port
Red River Beach
Harding Beach
Hyannis Port
Point Gammon
MONOMOY ISLAND
To Martha's Vineyard (Year-round)
To Nantucket (Year-round)
Nantucket Sound
To Nantucket (Seasonal)

Beach	⚑
Fishing	🐟
Golf	⛳
Hiking	🚶
Kayaking	🛶
Surfing	🏄
Windsurfing	⛵

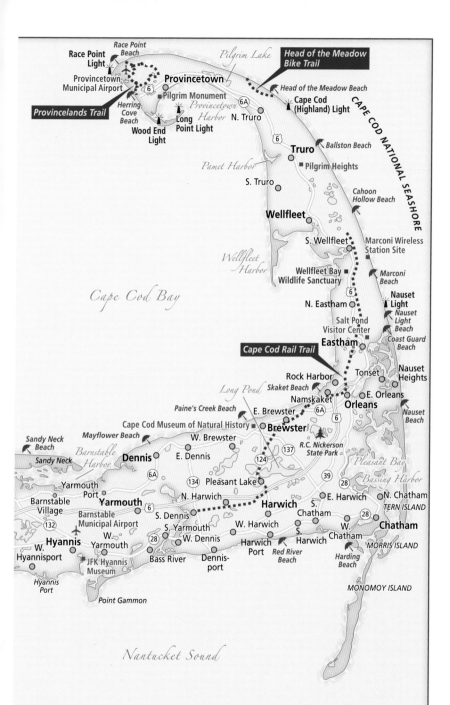

Race Point Beach

Race Point Light

Provincetown Municipal Airport

Pilgrim Lake

Head of the Meadow Bike Trail

Provincelands Trail

Provincetown

6

Pilgrim Monument

Herring Cove Beach

Provincetown Harbor

Long Point Light

Wood End Light

N. Truro

6A

Head of the Meadow Beach

Cape Cod (Highland) Light

CAPE COD NATIONAL SEASHORE

6

Truro

Ballston Beach

Pamet Harbor

Pilgrim Heights

S. Truro

Cahoon Hollow Beach

Wellfleet

Wellfleet Harbor

Cape Cod Bay

S. Wellfleet

Marconi Wireless Station Site

Wellfleet Bay Wildlife Sanctuary

Marconi Beach

6

Nauset Light

N. Eastham

Salt Pond Visitor Center

Nauset Light Beach

Eastham

Coast Guard Beach

Cape Cod Rail Trail

Tonset

Nauset Heights

Rock Harbor

Long Pond

Skaket Beach

Namskaket

E. Orleans

Orleans

Paine's Creek Beach

E. Brewster

6A

6

Nauset Beach

Cape Cod Museum of Natural History

Mayflower Beach

Brewster

R.C. Nickerson State Park

Pleasant Bay

Sandy Neck Beach

W. Brewster

137

Bassing Harbor

Sandy Neck

Barnstable Harbor

Dennis

E. Dennis

124

39

Pleasant Lake

N. Chatham

TERN ISLAND

Yarmouth Port

6A

134

N. Harwich

E. Harwich

28

Barnstable Village

Yarmouth

132

Barnstable Municipal Airport

6

S. Dennis

Harwich

S. Chatham

W.

Chatham

Chatham

Hyannis

W. Yarmouth

28

S. Yarmouth

W. Dennis

W. Harwich

S.

Harwich

W. Chatham

MORRIS ISLAND

W. Hyannisport

JFK Hyannis Museum

Bass River

Dennis-port

Harwich Port

Red River Beach

Harding Beach

Hyannis Port

Point Gammon

MONOMOY ISLAND

Nantucket Sound

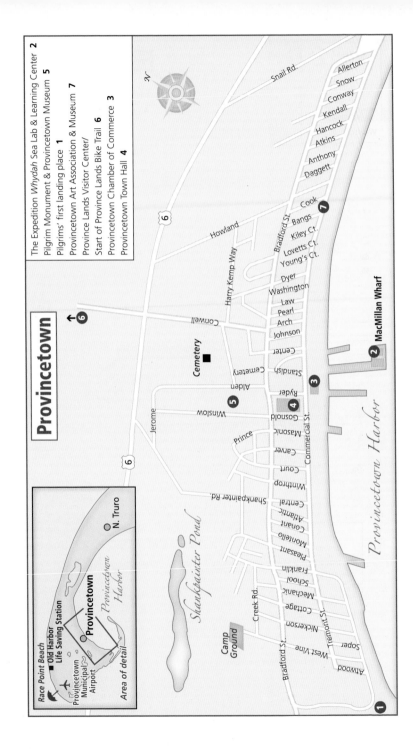

Provincetown

The Expedition *Whydah* Sea Lab & Learning Center **2**
Pilgrim Monument & Provincetown Museum **5**
Pilgrims' first landing place **1**
Provincetown Art Association & Museum **7**
Province Lands Visitor Center/
Start of Province Lands Bike Trail **6**
Provincetown Chamber of Commerce **3**
Provincetown Town Hall **4**

Area of detail

Race Point Beach
Old Harbor Life Saving Station
Provincetown Municipal Airport
Provincetown
Provincetown Harbor
N. Truro

Shankpainter Pond

Camp Ground

Provincetown Harbor

MacMillan Wharf

Nantucket

Beach
Fishing
Golf
Hiking
Kayaking
Windsurfing

Nantucket Sound

Great Point Light

Coskata Beach

Coatue Beach

Wauwinet

Quidnet

Sesachacha Pond

Eel Point

Dionis Beach

Jetties Beach

Coatue Point

Nantucket Cliffs

Children's Beach

Nantucket Town

Eel Point Rd.

Cliff Rd.

Wauwinet Rd.

Squam Rd.

Polpis Rd.

Polpis Rd.

Madaket

Madaket Rd.

Massasoit Rd.

Madaket Beach

Hummock Pond Rd.

Milestone Rd.

Sankaty Head Light

Siasconset Beach

Siasconset

Hummock Pond

SOUTH SHORE

Cisco

Atlantic Ave.

Old South Rd.

Beach Rd.

Cisco Beach

Miacomet Pond

Surfside

Surfside Beach

Nantucket Memorial Airport

New South Rd.

0   3 miles
0   3 kilometers

Atlantic Ocean

Nantucket Harbor

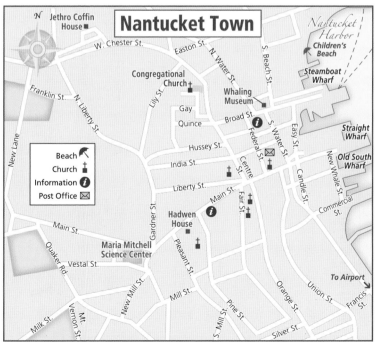

Nantucket Town

Jethro Coffin House

Nantucket Harbor

Children's Beach

W. Chester St.

Easton St.

N. Water St.

S. Beach St.

Steamboat Wharf

Franklin St.

Congregational Church

Whaling Museum

Straight Wharf

New Lane

N. Liberty St.

Lily St.

Gay

Quince

Broad St.

S. Water St.

Easy St.

Old South Wharf

Hussey St.

Federal St.

New Whale St.

India St.

Centre St.

Liberty St.

Main St.

Fair St.

Candle St.

Commercial St.

Hadwen House

Main St.

Gardner St.

Maria Mitchell Science Center

Quaker Rd.

Vestal St.

Pleasant St.

Mill St.

To Airport

Milk St.

Mt. Vernon St.

New Mill St.

S. Mill St.

Pine St.

Orange St.

Union St.

Francis St.

Silver St.

Beach
Church
Information
Post Office

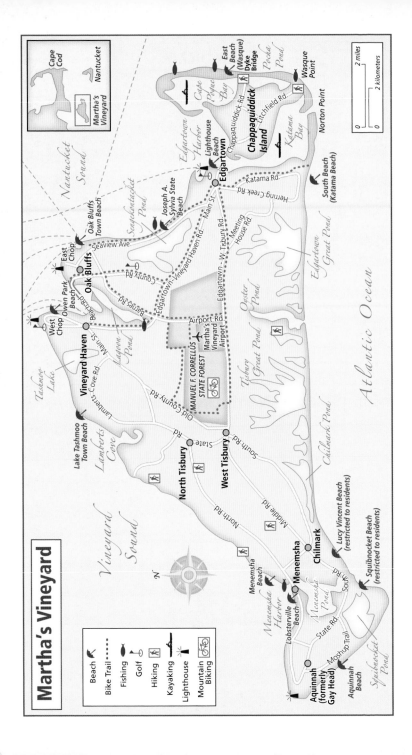

Frommer's®

Cape Cod, Nantucket & Martha's Vineyard 2010

by Laura M. Reckford

WILEY

Wiley Publishing, Inc.

ABOUT THE AUTHOR

Laura M. Reckford is the editor of *The Barnstable Enterprise* newspaper in the town of Barnstable on Cape Cod. Formerly the managing editor of *The Falmouth Enterprise* and *Cape Cod Life* magazine, she has also been on the editorial staffs of *Good Housekeeping* magazine and *Entertainment Weekly.* She co-authored the first edition of *France For Dummies.*

Published by:

WILEY PUBLISHING, INC.

111 River St.
Hoboken, NJ 07030-5774

ISBN 978-0-470-52659-0

Editor: Kathleen Warnock
Production Editor: Jana M. Stefanciosa
Cartographer: Andy Dolan
Photo Editor: Richard Fox
Production by Wiley Indianapolis Composition Services
Front cover photo: Highland Light, Truro, Cape Cod © John Greim / Mira / Alamy Images
Back cover photo: Sunbathing on the beach, Martha's Vineyard © Michael George / Imagestate Media Partners Limited - Impact Photos / Alamy Images

For information on our other products and services or to obtain technical support, please contact our Customer Care Department within the U.S. at 877/762-2974, outside the U.S. at 317/572-3993 or fax 317/572-4002.

Wiley also publishes its books in a variety of electronic formats. Some content that appears in print may not be available in electronic formats.

Manufactured in the United States of America

5   4   3   2   1

CONTENTS

4 SUGGESTED ITINERARIES 62

5 THE UPPER CAPE 74

6 THE MID CAPE 112

7 THE LOWER CAPE 146

8 THE OUTER CAPE 181

9 NANTUCKET 226

10 MARTHA'S VINEYARD 256

11 FAST FACTS, TOLL-FREE NUMBERS & WEBSITES 291

INDEX 301

LIST OF MAPS

HOW TO CONTACT US

In researching this book, we discovered many wonderful places—hotels, restaurants, shops, and more. We're sure you'll find others. Please tell us about them, so we can share the information with your fellow travelers in upcoming editions. If you were disappointed with a recommendation, we'd love to know that, too. Please write to:

Frommer's Cape Cod, Nantucket & Martha's Vineyard 2010
Wiley Publishing, Inc. • 111 River St. • Hoboken, NJ 07030-5774

AN ADDITIONAL NOTE

Please be advised that travel information is subject to change at any time—and this is especially true of prices. We therefore suggest that you write or call ahead for confirmation when making your travel plans. The authors, editors, and publisher cannot be held responsible for the experiences of readers while traveling. Your safety is important to us, however, so we encourage you to stay alert and be aware of your surroundings. Keep a close eye on cameras, purses, and wallets, all favorite targets of thieves and pickpockets.

FROMMER'S STAR RATINGS, ICONS & ABBREVIATIONS

Every hotel, restaurant, and attraction listing in this guide has been ranked for quality, value, service, amenities, and special features using a **star-rating system.** In country, state, and regional guides, we also rate towns and regions to help you narrow down your choices and budget your time accordingly. Hotels and restaurants are rated on a scale of zero (recommended) to three stars (exceptional). Attractions, shopping, nightlife, towns, and regions are rated according to the following scale: zero stars (recommended), one star (highly recommended), two stars (very highly recommended), and three stars (must-see).

In addition to the star-rating system, we also use **seven feature icons** that point you to the great deals, in-the-know advice, and unique experiences that separate travelers from tourists. Throughout the book, look for:

(Finds	Special finds—those places only insiders know about
(Fun Facts	Fun facts—details that make travelers more informed and their trips more fun
(Kids	Best bets for kids, and advice for the whole family
(Moments	Special moments—those experiences that memories are made of
(Overrated	Places or experiences not worth your time or money
(Tips	Insider tips—great ways to save time and money
(Value	Great values—where to get the best deals

The following **abbreviations** are used for credit cards:

AE American Express	**DISC** Discover	**V** Visa
DC Diners Club	**MC** MasterCard	

TRAVEL RESOURCES AT FROMMERS.COM

Frommer's travel resources don't end with this guide. Frommer's website, **www.frommers.com**, has travel information on more than 4,000 destinations. We update features regularly, giving you access to the most current trip-planning information and the best airfare, lodging, and car-rental bargains. You can also listen to podcasts, connect with other Frommers.com members through our active-reader forums, share your travel photos, read blogs from guidebook editors and fellow travelers, and much more.

The Best of Cape Cod & the Islands

Cape Cod is a curling peninsula only 70 miles long that encompasses hundreds of miles of beaches and more freshwater ponds than there are days in the year. The ocean's many moods rule this thin spit of land, and in summer, it has a very sunny disposition indeed. The "arm" of the Cape has beckoned wayfarers since pre-Colonial times. These days more than five million visitors flock from around the world each year to enjoy nature's nonstop carnival, a combination of torrid sun and cool, salty air.

On the Cape, days have a way of unfurling aimlessly but pleasantly, with a round of inviolable rituals. First and foremost is a long, restful stint at the beach (you can opt for either the warmer, gently lapping waters of Cape Cod Bay or the pounding Atlantic surf). The beach is generally followed by a stroll through the shops of the nearest town and an obligatory ice-cream stop. After a desalinating shower and perhaps a nap (the pristine air has a way of inspiring snoozes), it's time for a fabulous dinner. There are few experiences quite so blissful as sitting at a picnic table overlooking a bustling harbor and feasting on a just-caught, butter-dripping, boiled lobster.

Be forewarned, however, that the Cape can be a bit *too* popular at full swing. European settlers waited nearly 3 centuries to go splashing in the surf, but ever since the Victorians donned their bathing costumes, there's been no stopping the waves of sun-, sand-, and sea-worshippers who pour onto this peninsula and the islands beyond every summer.

Experienced travelers are beginning to discover the subtler appeal of the off-season, when the population and prices plummet. For some the prospect of sunbathing with the midsummer crowds on sizzling sand can't hold a candle to the chance to take long, solitary strolls on a windswept beach, with only the gulls as company. Come Labor Day (or Columbus Day, for stragglers) the crowds clear out, and the whole place hibernates until Memorial Day weekend, the official start of "the season." It's in this downtime that you're most likely to experience the "real" Cape. For some it may take a little resourcefulness to see the beauty in the wintry, shuttered landscape (even the Pilgrims, who forsook this spot for Plymouth, didn't have quite the necessary mettle), but the people who do stick around are an interesting, independent-minded lot worth getting to know.

As alluring as it is on the surface, the region becomes all the more so as you become more intimately acquainted with it. One visit is likely to prompt a follow-up. Although you can see all of the Cape, and the islands as well, in a matter of days, you could spend a lifetime exploring its many facets and still just begin to take it all in. Early Pilgrims saw in this isolated spot the opportunity for religious freedom, whaling merchants the watery road to riches, and artists the path to capturing the brilliance of nature's palette. Whatever the incursions of commercialism and overdevelopment, the land is suffused with spirit, and it attracts seekers still.

Narrowing down possible "bests" is a tough call, even for a native of the region. The selections in this chapter are intended merely as an introduction to some of the highlights. They're listed from closest in to farthest out along the Cape, followed by the islands. A great many other outstanding resorts, hotels, inns, attractions, and destinations

PEMBROKE

Marshfield
MARSHFIELD
Brant Rock
Green Harbor

Pembroke

3A

D U X B U R Y

53

Millbrook

3

Duxbury

Silver L.

South
Duxbury

Guret Pt.

27

North
Plympton

Kingston

Plymouth Harbor

K I N G S T O N

North Plymouth

Plympton
PLYMPTON

Plymouth

North
Carver

White Horse
Beach

44

Billington Sea

58

Great South Pd.

Manomet

MIDDLEBOROUGH

Carver

3A

C A R V E R

P L Y M O U T H

Vallerville

C A P E

B A

MYLES STANDISH
STATE FOREST

Sampson Pd.

Long Pd.

Halfway Pd.

Ellisville

495

South
Carver

White
Island
Shores

Cedarville

White
Island Pd.

3

Great Herring Pd.

West
Wareham

25

SCUSSET BEACH S.P.

Town Neck Beach

ROCHESTER

W A R E H A M

Wareham

Sagamore

Sandwich

Buzzards
Bay

East
Sandwich

Sandy Neck Beach

Weweantic

Onset

6

Cape Cod Canal

6

6A

Sandy Neck

Rochester

6

Bourne

MASSACHUSETTS
MIL. RES.

West
Barnstable

M A R I O N

Monument
Beach

S A N D W I C H

149

195

Marion

B O U R N E

Forestdale

Lawrence Pd.

Pocasset

28

130

Mystic L.

Wakeby Pd.

B A R N S T A B

Wequaquet L.

MATTAPOISETT

Wings Neck

Scraggy Neck

Cataumet

OTIS A.N.G.B.

Marstons
Mills

Centerville

Mattapoisett

North Falmouth

Mashpee

28A

Ashumet Pd.

Santuit

North Bay

Craigville
Beach

Old Silver Beach

Cooniamessett Pd.

151

Johns Pd.

Cotuit

Osterville

M A S H P E E

West Falmouth

F A L M O U T H

Waquoit

28

B U Z Z A R D S

West I.

Sippewissett

Teaticket

Grews Pond
Great Pd.

East
Falmouth

South
Mashpee

Waquoit
Bay

Popponesset

New Seabury

SOUTH CAPE BEACH S.P.

Falmouth

Surf Drive Beach

Falmouth
Heights
Beach

Menauhant
Beach

B A Y

Woods Hole

Nobska Pt.

1

are described in the pages of this book. Once you start wandering, you're sure to discover bests of your own.

Basic contact information is given for the places listed below. You'll find more information by referring to the appropriate chapters of the book.

1 THE BEST BEACHES

It is difficult to identify the best beaches without specifying for whom: fearless surfers or timid toddlers, party types or incurable recluses? At the bayside and sound beaches, for instance, the water tends to be much more placid than it is on the ocean, and thus better for little ones who plan only to splash and muck about.

- **Sandy Neck Beach:** This relatively unpopulated, 6-mile barrier beach, extending from the eastern edge of Sandwich to shelter Barnstable Harbor, features pretty little dunes seldom seen on the bayside. Hike in far enough (but avoid the nests of piping plovers), and you're sure to find a secluded spot.

Adventurous types can even camp overnight, with permission (© **508/362-8300**). See p. 77.

- **Old Silver Beach:** This is by far the most popular beach on the Upper Cape, which is why it was the first to raise its prices to $20 a day for day-trippers. On sunny summer days, cars start lining up to get into the parking lot by 9am. Why? It is the closest really good beach to the bridges. It has the widest sandy area and softest sand of the Upper Cape beaches. It is on Buzzards Bay, so it is not too cold. And because there are no large sand bars nearby, you can get into deep water and swim fairly close to shore, instead of having to wade way out. See p. 94.

- **Nauset Beach:** Located along the outer "elbow" of the Cape, this barrier beach descends all the way from East Orleans to a point opposite Chatham—about 9 miles in all, each mile increasingly deserted. The entry point, however, is a body squeeze: It's here that the young crowd convenes to strut their stuff. Administered by the town of Orleans, but still considered part of the Cape Cod National Seashore, Nauset Beach has paid parking, restrooms, and a snack bar. See p. 172.

- **Cahoon Hollow Beach:** Spectacular Cahoon Hollow Beach on the rough, frigid Atlantic Ocean is your reward at the end of a winding trek down a 75-foot dune. See p. 189.
- **Race Point Beach:** Unlike many of the beaches closer to Provincetown, which are tacitly reserved for gays or lesbians, Race Point—another Cape Cod National Seashore beach at the northernmost tip of the Cape—is strictly nondenominational. Even whales are welcome—they can often be spotted with the bare eye, surging toward Stellwagen Bank. The **Province Lands Visitor Center** at Race Point (© 508/487-1256) has particularly good views. See p. 191.
- **Jetties Beach:** Among the region's beaches, Nantucket's have, as a rule, the best amenities; most have restrooms, showers, lifeguards, and food. For families and active types, Jetties Beach (just a half mile from the center of town) can't be beat. Offering boat and windsurfing rentals, tennis courts, volleyball nets, a playground, and great fishing (off the eponymous jetties), it's also scenic (those jetties again) with calm, warm water. See p. 233.
- **Aquinnah Beach** (formerly **Gay Head,** Martha's Vineyard): These landmark bluffs on the western extremity of Martha's Vineyard (call the **Chamber of Commerce** at © 508/693-0085 for directions) are threatened with erosion, so it's no longer politically correct to engage in multicolored mud baths, as hippies once did. Still, it's an incredibly scenic place to swim—come early to beat the crowds. See p. 265.

2 THE BEST BIKE ROUTES

Blessed with many gently rolling hills, the Cape and islands are custom-made for a bike trek—whether as a way to get to the beach or as an outing unto itself.

- **Cape Cod Canal** (© 508/833-9678): On this 14-mile loop maintained by the **U.S. Army Corps of Engineers,** you can race alongside the varied craft taking shortcuts through the world's widest sea-level canal. See p. 78.
- **Shining Sea Bikeway** (© 508/548-8500): Connecting North Falmouth to Woods Hole by way of marshes, cranberry bogs, the Buzzards Bay shoreline, and the picturesque Nobska Lighthouse, this very popular flat and scenic 12-mile path lets you dash to the ferry or dally at the beach of your choice. See p. 94.
- **Cape Cod Rail Trail** (© 508/896-3491): Reclaimed by the Rails-to-Trails Conservancy, this paved railroad bed currently stretches some 25 miles from South Dennis all the way to Wellfleet, with innumerable detours that beckon en route. Several sections of the bike path have recently been rehabilitated to make for an even smoother ride. See chapters 6 through 8.
- **Province Lands Trail** (© 508/487-1256): Offering a rigorous workout, this 7-mile network swoops among the dunes and stunted forests at the very tip of the Cape. Take your time enjoying this moonscape. Be sure to stop off at Race Point Beach for a bracing dip, and at the **Province Lands Visitor Center** (© 508/487-1256) as well. See p. 208.
- **Nantucket Town to Madaket** (© 508/228-1700): Only 3 miles wide and 14 miles long, Nantucket is a snap to cover by bike. The 6-mile Madaket path crosses undulating moors to reach a beach with boisterous surf. See section 2, "Beaches & Recreational Pursuits," in chapter 9.

- **Nantucket Town to Surfside** (© 508/228-1700): An easy, flat few miles from town, Surfside Beach is a perfect mini-excursion for the whole family. There are even benches along the route, if you'd like to stop and admire the scrub pine and beach plums. When you return to town, pause at Brant Point to watch the yachts maneuver in and out of Nantucket Harbor. See section 2, "Beaches & Recreational Pursuits," in chapter 9.

- **Oak Bluffs to Edgartown** (Martha's Vineyard; © 508/693-0085): All of Martha's Vineyard is easily accessible for two-wheel recreationists. This 6-mile path hugs the water almost all the way,

so you're never far from a refreshing dip. See section 3, "Beaches & Recreational Pursuits," in chapter 10.

- **Chilmark to Aquinnah** (Martha's Vineyard; © 508/693-0085): The Vineyard's awe-inspiring vistas of ponds, inlets, and ocean greet you at every turn as you bike along State Road and then turn onto the Moshup Trail, a road that takes you along the coast up to Aquinnah. It's a strenuous ride with perhaps the best views in the region. On the way back, treat yourself to a bike-ferry ride to the fishing village of Menemsha. See section 3, "Beaches & Recreational Pursuits," in chapter 10.

3 THE BEST SMALL TOWNS & VILLAGES

The prettier towns and villages of the Cape and islands combine the austere traditionalism of New England—clusters of well-tended historic houses punctuated by modest white steeples—with a whiff of their own salty history.

- **Sandwich:** For a "gateway" town, Sandwich is remarkably composed and peaceful. Not-too-fussy preservation efforts have ensured the survival of many of this first settlement's attractions, such as the pond that feeds the 17th-century **Dexter Grist Mill** (© 508/888-4910). Generous endowments fund an assortment of fascinating museums including the multifaceted **Heritage Museums and Gardens** (© 508/888-3300), famous for its splendid rhododendrons but interesting to all for its many other exhibits. See p. 74.

- **Woods Hole:** Besides being the Cape's main gateway to Martha's Vineyard, Woods Hole is a world-renowned science community, a charming fishing village, and a bohemian mecca. A

proper tour of the village should include visits to the aquarium and the Woods Hole Oceanographic Institution, a stroll along the bustling harbor, and a drink at the Captain Kidd Bar, the Cape's top tavern. See section 3, "Falmouth," in chapter 5.

- **Yarmouth Port:** It may look somewhat staid on the surface (Hallet's, the local soda fountain, hasn't changed much since 1889, except it now rents videos), but there are a number of quirky attractions here. A museum features the works of author/illustrator Edward Gorey, a Yarmouth Port resident who died in 2000. There's also the gloriously jumbled **Parnassus Books,** owned by vintage bookseller Ben Muse. Stop at **Inaho,** 157 Main St. (© 508/362-5522), all but hidden within an ordinary frame house, for the Cape's best sushi. See p. 129.

- **Chatham:** Only Provincetown offers better strolling-and-shopping options, and Chatham's are G-rated. This is perhaps the Cape's quaintest town. In summer, Friday-night band concerts draw multigenerational crowds by the thousands. For a fun natural-history lesson, take a boat ride to see the hordes of seals on uninhabited Monomoy Island. See p. 161.

- **Wellfleet:** A magnet for creative souls (literary as well as visual), this otherwise classic New England town is a haven of good taste—from its dozens of shops and galleries to its premier restaurant, Aesop's Tables. All is not prissy, however: certainly not the iconoclastic offerings at the **Wellfleet Harbor Actors' Theatre** (✆ **508/349-6835**) or the goings-on at the **Beachcomber,** one of the Cape's best nightclubs. See p. 188.

- **Provincetown:** At the far tip of the Cape's curl, in intensely beautiful surroundings, is Provincetown. Its history goes back nearly 400 years, and in the past century, it's been a veritable headquarters of bohemia—more writers and artists have holed up here than you could shake a stick at. It's also, of course, among the world's great gay and lesbian resort areas—people come here for the pleasure of being "out" together in great numbers. If you're uncomfortable with same-sex public displays of affection, this stop might be best left off your itinerary. More open-minded straights will have a great time—Provincetown has savory food, fun shopping, terrific company, and fascinating people-watching. See p. 204.

- **Nantucket Town:** This former whaling town is so well-preserved it looks as though the whalers left their grand houses and cobblestone streets just yesterday. Tourism may be rampant here,

but it's without the tackier side effects, thanks to stringent preservation measures. A gamut of enticing shops offers luxury goods from around the world. Time has not so much stood still here as vanished. So relax and shift into island time, dictated purely by your desires. See chapter 9.

- **Oak Bluffs, Martha's Vineyard:** This harbor town on Martha's Vineyard evolved from a mid-19th-century Methodist campground. Pleased with the scenic and refreshing oceanside setting (and who wouldn't be?), the faithful started replacing their canvas tents with hundreds of tiny, elaborately decorated and gaudily painted "gingerbread" cottages. Still operated primarily as a religious community, the revivalist village is flanked by a commercial zone known for its rocking nightlife. See chapter 10.

- **Edgartown, Martha's Vineyard:** For many visitors, Edgartown *is* Martha's Vineyard. Its regal captains' houses and manicured lawns epitomize a more refined way of life. Roses climb white picket fences, and the tolling of the Whaling Church bell signals dinnertime. By July a procession of gleaming pleasure boats glides past Edgartown Lighthouse into the harbor, and shops overflow with luxury goods and fine art. Edgartown's old-fashioned Fourth of July parade harkens back to small-town America, as hundreds line Main Street cheering the loudest for the floats with the most heart. It's a picture-perfect little town, a slice of homemade apple pie to go with nearby Oak Bluff's hot-fudge sundae. See p. 263.

---

4 THE BEST LUXURY HOTELS & INNS

- **Wequassett Resort and Golf Club** (Chatham; ✆ **800/225-7125** or 508/ 432-5400): This Chatham institution

occupies its own little peninsula on Pleasant Bay and offers excellent sailing and tennis clinics. It is also next to the

Cape's premier golf course and guests have members' privileges. You'll be tempted to just relax, though—especially if you score one of the clapboard cottages, done in an upscale country mode, right on the water. The on-site restaurant, **28 Atlantic,** is now one of the Cape's best. See p. 158.

- **Captain's House Inn** (Chatham; ✆ **800/ 315-0728** or 508/945-0127): An elegant country inn that positively drips with good taste, this is among the best small inns in the region. Most rooms have fireplaces, elegant paneling, and antiques throughout; the rooms are sumptuous yet cozy. This may be the ultimate spot to enjoy Chatham's Christmas Stroll festivities, but you may need to book your room a couple of years in advance. See p. 168.

- **Brass Key Guesthouse** (Provincetown; ✆ **800/842-9858** or 508/487-9005): The Brass Key Guesthouse, a compound consisting of five historic buildings, is *the* place to stay in Provincetown. With Ritz-Carlton–style amenities in mind, the owners have created a paean to luxury. These are the kind of innkeepers who think of everything: Pillows are goose down, showers have wall

jets, and gratis iced tea is delivered poolside. See p. 215.

- **Cliffside Beach Club** (Nantucket; ✆ **508/228-0618**): Right on the beach and within walking distance (about 1 mile) of town, this is the premier lodging on the island. It may not be as fancy as some, but there's a sublime beachyness to the whole setup: simply decorated rooms; cheerful, youthful staff; a sea of antique wicker in the clubhouse; and of course, the blue, yellow, and green umbrellas lined up on the beach. Every Fourth of July, guests get a front-row seat for the fireworks show at nearby Jetties Beach. See p. 241.

- **Winnetu Oceanside Resort** (Edgartown, Martha's Vineyard; ✆ **866/335-1133** or 508/310-1733): This resort on Katama Beach, just outside Edgartown, has seemingly come out of nowhere in the past few years to become one of the best luxury hotels in the region. The Winnetu stands apart from other luxury resorts because it's also a wonderful place for families, with lots of activities to keep kids busy. The resort's restaurant, **Lure** (✆ **508/627-3663**), complete with a distant water view, is one of the island's best fine-dining options. See p. 277.

5 THE BEST HOTEL DEALS

- **Simmons Homestead Inn** (Hyannis Port; ✆ **800/637-1649** or 508/778-4999): Bill Putman may be the most personable and hospitable innkeeper on Cape Cod. He is determined that his guests have an excellent vacation, a factor that may make the Simmons Homestead Inn one of the best deals around. A former race-car driver/ad exec, Putman has filled his inn with a merry mishmash of animals (stuffed, sculpted, or painted). But his passion is automobiles, and you'll enjoy touring his "museum" of more than 55 red sports cars. See p. 121.

- **Lamb and Lion Inn** (Barnstable; ✆ **800/909-6923** or 508/362-6823): Part B&B, part motel, this historic Cape cottage has been turned into a comfortable lodging with a pool. Hallways have murals, and rooms are creatively decorated. See p. 122.

- **Old Sea Pines Inn** (Brewster; ✆ **508/ 896-6114**): This reasonably priced, large historic inn is a great spot for families. Accommodations range from small singles with shared bathrooms to family suites. In summer, the dining room is the location for weekly dinner theater performances. See p. 153.

1

- **The Orleans Inn** (Orleans; ℂ **800/863-3039** or 508/255-2222): Don't miss this inn, perched right on the edge of Town Cove, and make sure to get a room facing the water. Built in 1875, the inn has been restored to its former grandeur. The water view and great location make this a terrific value. See p. 176.

- **The Inn at Duck Creeke** (Wellfleet; ℂ **508/349-9333**): In one of the Cape's most charming towns, this humble and historic complex offers no-frills rooms, some with shared bathrooms, for bargain prices. With such grandmotherly touches as chenille bedspreads, it will make you feel right at home. A good restaurant and a tavern are also on the property. See p. 195.

- **Beachside at Nantucket** (Nantucket; ℂ **800/322-4433** or 508/228-2241): Although the in-season rates at Nantucket's only motel are about the same as at other B&Bs in town, the off-season rates are a real bargain. Specials could include rooms for less than $110 a night in May. The property is also one of the only lodgings in town with a pool. See p. 242.

- **Edgartown Inn** (Edgartown, Martha's Vineyard; ℂ **508/627-4794**): This quirky, old-fashioned inn is located in the heart of Edgartown. The smells of freshly baked goodies fill the air, and the staff is friendly and helpful. Most important, prices have stayed reasonable, a rarity on the Vineyard. See p. 278.

- **Wesley Hotel** (Oak Bluffs, Martha's Vineyard; ℂ **800/638-9027** or 508/693-6611): This imposing 1879 property, overlooking Oak Bluffs Harbor, is a solid entry in the good-value category, especially with its low off-season rates. It's a no-frills hotel with a great location, just steps from Circuit Avenue, the heart of Oak Bluffs. See p. 279.

6 THE BEST RESTAURANTS

It wasn't long ago that "fancy" food in these parts began and ended with classic French. Now "fancy," when it comes to food, is almost out of style and French food is hard to find. Although one of this year's "bests" is Italian and one is Mexican, most occupy that catchall category of New American, with influences from all over the world. Several aren't even fancy at all, just memorable.

- **Osteria La Civetta** (Falmouth; ℂ **508/540-1616**): It hasn't taken long for locals to realize that what's cooking at the little osteria on Main Street is something very special and authentic. This is the kind of place where the owners, who are from Bologna, send the chefs to Italy in the off-season to learn new skills. From the handmade pasta to the specialty desserts, this is a must try. See p. 103.

- **The Regatta of Cotuit** (Cotuit; ℂ **508/428-5715**): What most distinguishes the Regatta from its competition is the sensational service so rare at local establishments. The Regatta has a quintessential old Cape Cod setting—the building was once a stagecoach inn, and the decor is formal Federal style. Food here is consistently excellent, with fresh ingredients, generous portions, and creative preparations. See p. 127.

- **28 Atlantic** (Chatham; ℂ **508/430-3000**): This superb restaurant at the Wequassett Resort and Golf Club offers the most elegant dining in the region. Floor-to-ceiling plate-glass windows give you a panoramic view of Pleasant Bay. The menu is loaded with delicacies from around the world. In this graceful setting, professional waiters will see to your comfort and thorough satisfaction. See p. 159.

- **Bramble Inn and Restaurant** (Brewster; ⓒ **508/896-7644**): An elegant entry in the Lower Cape dining scene, the Bramble Inn attracts those who don't mind a rather steeply priced, four-course, fixed-price dinner. The five intimate dining rooms are decorated with antique china and fresh flowers. Chef Ruth Manchester is a local favorite for her extraordinary, evolving cuisine. See p. 152.

- **Devon's** (Provincetown; ⓒ **508/487-4773**): The namesake of Devon's is a multi-talented restaurateur with a great attitude. That positive vibe permeates every part of this small fine-dining restaurant, a former fishing shack on Provincetown's far East End. Serving New American cuisine with an emphasis on local provender, this is one of Provincetown's most romantic options, but its teensiness means you do need a reservation. See p. 218.

- **Ross' Grill** (Provincetown; ⓒ **508/487-8878**): Restaurants come and go from this swank seaside town, but Ross' Grill on the second floor of the Whaler's Wharf on Commercial Street looks to be a keeper. Large windows give a view of the harbor as you dine on crispy

Tuscan cod and seafood risotto. With top-shelf service and an intimate atmosphere, this is first class all the way. See p. 220.

- **The Galley** (Nantucket; ⓒ **508/228-9641**): This exquisite beachfront restaurant at the Cliffside Beach Club is the place to go if you want to feel like you are in a spread of *Travel + Leisure* magazine. Delicious food too! See p. 246.

- **Straight Wharf** (Nantucket; ⓒ **508/228-4499**): Talented chef/owners have made this *the* fine-dining restaurant on Nantucket. Make your reservation for 8pm, so you can sit on the outside deck and watch the sun set over the harbor. Whether you opt for one of their specialty seafood dishes (wild striped bass with gazpacho) or choose a land-based entree (filet of Kobe beef), you will not be disappointed. See p. 247.

- **Atria** (Edgartown, Martha's Vineyard; ⓒ **508/627-5850**): This fine-dining venue on Upper Main Street gets rave reviews for its gourmet cuisine and high-caliber service. The menu, featuring produce and meats from local farmers and the daily catch from local fishermen, takes its influences from around the country and around the world. See p. 282.

7 THE BEST CLAM SHACKS

- **The Clam Shack** (Falmouth Harbor; ⓒ **508/540-7758**): The ultimate clam shack sits on the edge of the harbor and serves up reasonably priced fried seafood with all the fixings. Order the fried clams (with bellies, please!), and squeeze into the picnic tables beside the counter to await your feast. See p. 105.

- **Cap't Cass Rock Harbor Seafood** (Orleans; no phone): Take a photo of the family in front of this shack covered with colorful buoys, and then go inside and chow down. Hearty portions of

simply prepared fresh fish keep diners coming back year after year. See p. 178.

- **Arnold's Lobster & Clam Bar** (Eastham; ⓒ **508/255-2575**): Once you get served a heaping plate of fried seafood here, you won't bother with any other clam shack. No one else gives you so much for such a reasonable price on Cape Cod. See p. 187.

- **Moby Dick's Restaurant** (Wellfleet; ⓒ **508/349-9795**): Unfortunately word has spread about this terrific restaurant, and it can get pretty mobbed here around supper time. Still, it's a terrific place to bring the family, screaming kids and all. The clambake special is a 1¼-pound lobster, native Monomoy steamed clams, and corn on the cob. Perfect. See p. 197.

- **Sayle's Seafood** (Nantucket; ℂ **508/228-4599**): Take a 10-minute walk from town on Washington Street Extension, and you'll arrive at this fish store-cum–clam shack. Charlie Sayles is a local fisherman, and everything here is deliciously fresh. Get your fried clams to go and eat them at the beach. See p. 240.

- **The Bite** (Menemsha, Martha's Vineyard; ℂ **508/645-9239**): A travel writer once called it the best restaurant on Martha's Vineyard, perhaps in retaliation for a high-priced meal in Edgartown. Nevertheless this is a top-shelf clam shack, tucked away in a picturesque fishing village. Order your meal to go and stroll over to the beach, which has the best sunset views on the island. The fried clams are delicious; some say the secret is the batter. Of course the fish, unloaded just steps away, couldn't be fresher. See p. 288.

8 THE BEST SHOPPING

No matter how spectacular the scenery or splendid the weather, certain towns have so many intriguing shops that you'll be lured away from the beach, at least temporarily. The inventory is so carefully culled or created that just browsing can be sufficient entertainment, but slip a credit card into your cutoffs just in case.

- **Chatham:** Old-fashioned, tree-shaded Main Street is packed with inviting storefronts, including the **Chatham Glass Company** (ℂ **508/945-5547**), where you can literally look over their shoulders as artisans craft glass treasures.
- **Wellfleet:** The commercial district is 2 blocks long; the art zone is twice that. Pick up a walking map to locate the galleries in town: **Cherrystone Gallery** (ℂ **508/349-3026**) tops the don't-miss list. Seekers of low-key chic will want to check out two designers, **Hannah** (ℂ **508/349-9884**) and **Karol Richardson** (ℂ **508/349-6378**). See p. 194. For designer produce and impeccable seafood, peruse the array at the homey **Hatch's Fish & Produce Market** (ℂ **508/349-2810** for fish, or 508/349-6734 for produce) behind Town Hall. See p. 197.

- **Provincetown:** Overlooking the import junk that floods the center of town, the 3-mile strip of Commercial Street is a shopaholic's dream. It's all here, seemingly direct from SoHo: sensual, cutting-edge clothing (for every sex and permutation thereof), art, jewelry, antiques, and more. And whatever you really need but didn't know you needed can be found at **Marine Specialties** (ℂ **508/487-1730**), a warehouse packed with surplus essentials. See p. 214.
- **Nantucket:** Imagine Martha Stewart cloned a hundredfold, and you'll have some idea of the tenor of shops in this well-preserved 19th-century town. Centre Street—known as "Petticoat Row" in whaling days—still caters to feminine tastes, and the town's many esteemed antiques stores would never deign to present anything less than the genuine article. See section 6, "Shopping," in chapter 10.
- **Oak Bluffs, Martha's Vineyard:** Circuit Avenue, chockablock with such fun stores as **Craftworks** (149 Circuit Ave.; ℂ **508/693-7463**) and **Third World Trading Co.** (52 Circuit Ave.; ℂ **508/693-5550**), has long been a destination for those looking for unique gifts. But

now, a short walk away on Dukes County Avenue, there is a new "gallery district," a cluster of six little shops awaiting exploration. From the **Alison Shaw Gallery,** with walls lined by the well-known photographer's vivid works, to **Pik Nik,** a store full of all manner of art, clothing, and unusual gifts, there is definitely lots here for the discriminating browser.

9 THE BEST BARS & CLUBS

- **Grumpy's** (Falmouth; © **508/540-3930**): Come to Grumpy's to hear some down and dirty blues or local cover bands rocking out. There's live music weekend nights year-round. It's also a friendly bar scene, attracting people of all ages, locals and tourists alike. See p. 107.

- **Embargo** (Hyannis; © **508/771-9700**): Most consider this the best bar in town and, even better, it's for grown-ups. There is live music nightly in the Back Door Bistro and a sizzling Monday-night jazz series popular with locals and those in the know. See p. 128.

- **The Beachcomber** (Wellfleet; © **508/349-6055**): Perched atop the towering dunes of Cahoon Hollow Beach, this bar and dance club is one of the most scenic watering holes on Cape Cod. Although the crowd tends to be on the young and rowdy side, the young at heart are also welcome. See p. 198.

- **Crown & Anchor** (Provincetown; © **508/487-1430**): The specialty bars at this large complex span leather, disco, comedy, drag shows, and cabaret. See p. 223.

- **The Chicken Box** (Nantucket; © **508/228-9717**): The Box is the rocking spot for the 20-something crowd, but depending on the band or theme (reggae, disco, and so on), it can sometimes seem like the whole island is trying to get through the doors here. Jimmy Buffett makes an appearance late at night at least once every summer to jam with the band. See p. 255.

- **Offshore Ale Company** (Oak Bluffs, Martha's Vineyard; © **508/693-2626**): The Vineyard's first and only brew pub features eight locally made beers on tap and entertainment six nights a week in season. See p. 289.

- **Nectar's** (Martha's Vineyard Airport, Martha's Vineyard; © **508/693-1137**): Formerly the Hot Tin Roof, this sprawling club at the airport has been the place to see big names on the Vineyard for decades. See p. 289.

2

Cape Cod in Depth

Cape Cod still resembles the old Patti Page song "Old Cape Cod," with plenty of "sand dunes and salty air," and even "quaint little villages here and there," but it is also a modern destination. Several towns on the Cape are in the process of installing town-wide Wi-Fi (that's wireless Internet for you Luddites), and a number of the region's hotels have top-shelf amenities, including elaborate spas. Sophisticated restaurants abound, along with chic boutiques and cutting-edge art galleries.

Some visitors are surprised that Cape Cod is not one place but many places—15 towns in all and numerous villages, each with its own personality. The nearby islands of elegant Nantucket and quaint Martha's Vineyard also have unique personalities.

Politically the Cape and islands struggle with the usual issues of small-town America, including trying to stay authentic and preserve their ties to history while still embracing modernization. The difference between other small towns and the Cape is that its history and natural beauty—the fact that this is where the Pilgrims actually landed first and that it is home to miles of pristine beaches, for instance—is also its livelihood. People come to see these quaint New England villages and these famous sand dunes—about 75 feet high in places along the Cape Cod National Seashore—and if they pave paradise and put up a parking lot, no one will come to visit. So preservation is prized in all of the Cape's 15 towns, and you will find fascinating historic sites—windmills, historic houses, and lighthouses, to name a few—throughout the region.

The towns of the Cape and the nearby islands of Martha's Vineyard and Nantucket have managed to maintain their special qualities, and visitors still do come by the millions every summer. They bike, hike, kayak, and bask in the sun. They visit historic sites, dine out at refined restaurants, eat in at clambakes, and shop 'til they drop.

Of course, urban and suburban issues of growth, like traffic, wastewater disposal, water quality, and especially traffic—did I mention traffic?—are omnipresent. Writer Kurt Vonnegut, a former Cape Cod resident, once said of Cape traffic, "Traffic to Hyannis Port was backed up through three villages. There were license plates from every state in the republic. The line was moving about 4 miles an hour. I was passed by several groups of 50-mile hikers. My radiator came to a boil four times." The Cape's traffic is notorious, and smart visitors plan their vacations to stay off the roads during prime times and choose a lodging option that is within walking or biking distance of the beach, as well as shops and restaurants (an easy option in many of the Cape's towns).

Cape Cod, Martha's Vineyard, and Nantucket offer what many consider a perfect vacation. There are unforgettable experiences to be had, like the time I saw three minke whales jump out of the water simultaneously, their fluked tails lined up in formation, during a whale watch at Stellwagen Bank, a protected ocean reserve off Provincetown. There are moments of the sublime, like when you chow down on a heaping stack of fried clams (bellies and all) while sitting at a picnic table with a view of the setting sun at Menemsha Harbor on Martha's Vineyard. And there are moments of enrichment, like shooting the breeze with an honest-to-goodness miller while watching him grind corn in a restored 17th-century gristmill in Sandwich. But mostly the Cape and islands are about enjoying a low-key beach vacation, preferably with buckets, shovels, and a trashy novel in tow.

The Cape Cod of today is many things at once: a popular vacationland, a mecca for wealthy second-home owners, a historic fishing village, a hip urban scene, a sleepy retirement community, a suburban subdivision, and even a bedroom community for Boston. Towns wrestle with how to maintain vibrant year-round communities as wealthy second-home owners buy up properties and drive up the cost of living for the average Joe. Towns also struggle to preserve each community's authentic character. As for Martha's Vineyard and Nantucket: the rich are richer, and the struggle is greater. The character of Martha's Vineyard and Nantucket are even more at risk from the dreaded sameness of corporate America, because they are both still so unique.

People on the Cape and islands are talking about the identical issues they are talking about throughout New England, around the country and even around the world: global warming, green energy, water and air quality, drugs and crime, healthcare, immigrants, education, and affordable housing. In classic New England style, the year-round residents of the Cape's villages and towns—there are about 230,000 of us—turn out for town meetings once or twice a year to decide the major issues and spending of the town. Discussions range from school funding to the Patriot Act and everything in between. What's a town meeting like? Show up and see for yourself. Everyone is welcome.

A big issue for all 15 Cape Cod towns in these tough economic times is the lack of funding for general municipal needs, such as schools and sewage. Although school populations are shrinking as working families are allegedly leaving the Cape in droves, expenses, such as the cost of energy, continue to rise. That means big cuts: Teachers are being laid off, programs are being eliminated, and in some districts parents are paying for such things as music programs, sports programs, and even school bus transportation. Water quality is another hot topic at town hall meetings, as the region has an antiquated sewage system that does not prevent wastewater from leaking into the ground and contaminating the bays and estuaries. Several towns are working on sewer plans—systems that probably should have been installed decades ago—while others are embarking on major plans to clean up coastal ponds. In a place where sailing is a lifestyle and the beaches are vital to the economy, there is far too much murky water.

Cape Cod and the islands are tourist destinations, and naturally, their economy rests heavily on the tourism industry. Therefore, the shortage of workers for the Cape's many seasonal minimum-wage jobs presents a problem. Positions for restaurant dishwashers, hotel chamber maids, and landscapers are going unfilled each season as it gets harder and harder to find people to take these jobs. Many large employers used to bring workers in from overseas, from such places as Jamaica, Brazil, and Eastern Europe under the H2B visa program, which is a program that allowed foreign workers sponsored by an

---

(**Fun Facts**) **Old, but Not Feeble**

The Cape has an aging population. We are, by percentage, older than any other county in the commonwealth of Massachusetts. But we are also active, and many senior citizens on Cape Cod bike, kayak, and sail well into their 80s.

employer to work in the U.S. for 6-month periods. Cape Cod businesses would employ these workers during the summer's prime tourist season. However, federal legislation to extend the program has been mired in the larger national debate about immigration in general; for the past two summers, the foreign workers did not come to Cape Cod. Though the Cape and islands are home to a large population of Brazilian immigrants, the region's employers are already contemplating how to handle the shortage in staff for upcoming summers.

One drive past the large, elaborate seaside homes anywhere along the Cape may give some visitors the impression that the region is wealthy, but that is far from true. While the area does have gorgeous second homes that belong to the überwealthy, there are many middle-class neighborhoods and pockets of poverty, and even enclaves of homeless people who sleep in the woods and line up for free meals at the Salvation Army in Hyannis. The Cape's human-service agencies struggle to provide services to all the families that need them, and housing agencies work to create more affordable units, especially rentals, to house the working poor, disabled, and elderly. Some of the housing projects run into problems with neighbors who don't want the units, but many Cape Cod residents acknowledge that more housing must be built. The main question is how and where to do it. The concept of redevelopment (converting unused shops and industrial buildings into affordable housing) is gaining momentum and is also

favored by planners at the Cape Cod Commission, the county land-use agency.

On the islands of Nantucket and Martha's Vineyard the biggest question is: How can locals afford to stay in a place where millionaires, such as Bill Gates of Microsoft, have mansions they visit for 1 week a year? Keeping the character of the islands—and that means the fishermen, carpenters, and shopkeepers, and not just the cobblestoned streets and white picket fences—is critical to islanders of all incomes. The fact that Nantucket still has a character to protect is a tribute to past planners who designated the entire island as a historic district, a legacy that has served it well. Nantucket is the kind of place where the prospect of installing the island's first traffic light can cause an uproar. Residents are right to fight to maintain the island's character, because it is the subtle, incremental growth (a strip mall here, a historic house demolition there) that has altered so much of the character of the Cape's 15 towns. Like Nantucket, Martha's Vineyard also must fight to preserve its history and character. Only here, the problem is mansionization, where bigger and bigger houses are built, replacing cottages and blocking views of the water.

Although the region is fighting to maintain its character, it is also looking to the future. The nation's first off-shore wind project—35 wind turbines in Nantucket Sound—is in the planning stages. The project has been through years of permitting with state and federal agencies weighing in. Although some people object

Destination Weddings in Provincetown

In 2003, when the Massachusetts Supreme Judicial Court ruled that marriage between homosexuals is legal, same-sex couples flocked to all 15 Cape towns, and particularly to Provincetown, one of the country's top gay resorts, to tie the knot among the sand dunes and salt air.

The Wampanoag Tribe

When the Pilgrims first arrived in Cape Cod in 1620, they were greeted by the **Wampanoag Tribe,** a group of Native Americans who lived in the region. The Wampanoags were only officially recognized by the U.S. Government in 2007— 387 years later! Today the Wampanoags hope to build a casino off-Cape, in nearby Middleborough, about 20 miles from the Bourne Bridge. If plans for the casino are accepted, the Wampanoags could use the profits from the casino to fund tribe needs, such as housing and education. Those plans are awaiting decisions by the governor and state legislature, who are debating if and how to allow casinos in the state.

The tribe, which has about 1,500 members today, is in the process of organizing some of its cultural artifacts. The **Indian Museum** on Route 130, in Mashpee (✆ **508/477-0208**), is currently undergoing a renovation.

to the industrialization of Nantucket Sound, many residents are in favor of the project, relishing the chance for the Cape to lead the nation in the construction of sources of alternative energy. Energy conservation is becoming not just smart on the wallet and good for the environment, but absolutely vital to our future. Throughout the Cape and islands, energy-efficient cars, solar panels on buildings, and expanded recycling programs abound. Today the Cape and islands are a sea of "green," surrounded by oceans of blue.

2 LOOKING BACK AT CAPE COD & THE ISLANDS

THE PILGRIMS MEET SQUANTO: ARRIVING IN 1620

In November 1620, a gaunt and exhausted band of Pilgrims traveling on a rickety boat called the *Mayflower* landed on the tip of the Cape in what is now Provincetown. While some people believe that they landed in nearby Plymouth, the Pilgrims actually landed in Provincetown. Plymouth was their second stop. While in Provincetown they put together a little agreement called the **Mayflower Compact,** which was the first governing document of Plymouth Colony. At the far east end of Commercial Street in Provincetown, a rock marks the spot where the Pilgrims are believed to have landed, and a bas-relief on Bradford Street, behind Town Hall, pays tribute to the Mayflower Compact.

The Pilgrims were not the first European explorers to discover the region. Cape Cod was named around 1602 by explorer **Bartholomew Gosnold,** after "the great stoare of codfysshes" he saw offshore. He is also said to have named Martha's Vineyard after his daughter and the large number of grapevines he saw. But many say the area had been visited by Europeans long before Gosnold; and some local historians believe they have evidence, in the form of markings on boulders, that the **Vikings** were here as early as A.D. 1000.

However, the Cape's cultural history really begins with the **Wampanoag Tribe,** a name that translates as "The People of the First Light." This Native American tribe inhabited the northeast coast and used the area that is now the town of

Impressions

With all the known parts of the civilized world behind them, the pilgrims found in this beach not an end but a beginning, whatever it might entail, and that of course is why they went there.

—John Hay, *The Great Beach*, 1963

Mashpee on the Upper Cape as one of their bases. The Pilgrims were greeted by members of the Wampanoag Tribe, among them **Squanto,** who is said to have stayed with the newcomers for the 1½ years that they lived over in Plymouth, teaching them the ways of the New World. The Wampanoags were friendly to the Europeans, offering them food during the cold winter and showing them how to farm crops in the sandy soil. The Pilgrims seem to have repaid them with smallpox and some beaver pelts. The Pilgrims set up one of the first trading posts, at a spot the Native Americans had long been using, at what is now the **Aptucxet Trading Post Museum** (24 Aptucxet Rd., Bourne; ℰ **508/759-9487**).

The Wampanoags were receptive to missionary efforts that led them to be known as "the praying Indians." The 1684 **Indian Meeting House** where they worshiped is one of the oldest churches on Cape Cod and is considered the oldest Indian church in the United States. It is located within an old Indian cemetery on Route 28 in Mashpee, and can be visited by appointment (ℰ **508/477-0208**).

Around 1675, relations between the white man and the Indian soured and **King Phillip's War** was waged by Chief Metacomet (whom the Pilgrims called King Phillip). The 2-year war resulted in the deaths of about 600 settlers and 3,000 Indians.

EARLY TOWNS ON CAPE COD

The Pilgrims continued on to Plymouth, but within a few years other settlers came

from Europe and settled on the Cape. The first town to be incorporated, **Sandwich,** was founded in 1637. The early settlers braved the dangerous cross-Atlantic voyage to escape religious persecution in Europe. Here they formed congregations of religious groups, including Quakers, which are still evident in several Cape Cod towns; the Congregational Church in West Barnstable, founded in 1630, has one of the longest uninterrupted congregations of that denomination in the world. One historian, Henry C. Kittredge, described the early Cape Cod settlers as "zealots and idealists."

The first settlements on the Cape in the early 17th century were compact. The idea was that every member of the community was in close proximity to three crucial places: the mill, the market, and the meeting. They used the large marshlands, particularly those north of Sandwich and Barnstable, as salt hay for grazing sheep and cattle. Most of the Cape was wooded and the early settlers cleared much of the land to raise livestock and used much of the wood to build homes. The first couple of generations of settlers were farmers who were self-sufficient, growing corn and other crops, and raising sheep, pigs, and cattle. For variety, they would indulge in delicacies from the sea, such as clams and lobsters. Corn was the principle crop, and each town soon had a miller to grind the corn. The early mills were operated either through water power or wind power, and the miller was considered one of the most distinguished citizens of the town, because of his prized skill. As there were no stores, any item not grown on the property or made locally had to be purchased from England at great expense. It was easier to buy a parcel of land than an hourglass, noted Kittredge.

As the oldest town in the Cape, Sandwich is a good place to explore the Cape's early history. Evidence of 17th-century life can be found at the **Hoxie House,** built in 1675 (Route 130, Sandwich center; ☎ **508/ 888-1173**), the **Dexter Grist Mill,** built in 1654 on Shawme Pond (Town Hall Square; ☎ **508/888-4910**), the **Sandwich Glass Museum** (129 Main St.; ☎ **08/888-0251**), and the **Heritage Museums and Gardens** (67 Grove St.; ☎ **508/888-3300**).

Some fine examples of historic houses are also on the islands of Nantucket and Martha's Vineyard. In Edgartown on Martha's Vineyard, the **Vincent House,** built in 1672, is the oldest house on the island (off Main St., btw. Planting Field Way and Church St.; ☎ **508/627-8619**). On Nantucket, the **Jethro Coffin House** (☎ **508/ 228-1894**), a 1686 saltbox home, gets the distinction of being the oldest building on the island, though there are countless examples of well-preserved historic structures here,

given that the entire island is designated as a historic district.

FROM PIRATES TO WHALERS: THE CAPE'S RICH MARITIME HISTORY

Before the Cape Cod Canal was dug out and the bridges were constructed in the 1930s, the shipping route around the arm of the Cape carried the reputation as "the graveyard of the Atlantic," for all the shipwrecks that took place among the treacherous shoals and currents off the Cape. Lighthouses were built—the first one was Highland Light in 1797 at Truro—in order to help captains navigate the tricky coastline that often became enveloped in a dense fog. **Highland Light,** also called Cape Cod Light, and the nearby museum run by the Truro Historical Society can be visited (27 Highland Light Rd., Truro; ☎ **508/487-1121**).

There are many tales of shipwrecks at the **Nantucket Shipwreck and Lifesaving Museum** (158 Polpis Rd., Nantucket; ☎ **508/228-1885**) and at the **Old Harbor Lifesaving Museum** in Provincetown

---

The *Whydah:* A Pirate's Treasure Trove

One of the most famous ships that fell prey to the ocean was the *Whydah,* a pirate ship that wrecked near Wellfleet in 1717. The ship was captained by the notorious pirate Samuel (Black Jack) Bellamy. Bellamy and his pirate crew had captured a couple of other vessels in Nantucket Sound, but then the small fleet, manned by what is said to be crews of drunken pirates, was caught in a gale. The two other ships wrecked first, then the *Whydah,* which still had Bellamy aboard, wrecked a couple miles south of Wellfleet's Cahoon's Hollow Beach. Bellamy and 140 of his men drowned. Two men, both of whom had been captured from other ships, made it to shore alive. They alerted the locals who set about to haul in whatever they could that washed ashore from the wrecks. The one thing that the plunderers never did find was the chest of pirate's gold. It took almost 270 years for that loot to be found.

In 1984, local adventurer Barry Clifford began to excavate the site. His findings, including thousands of gold and silver coins, can be viewed at the **Expedition Whydah Sea Lab and Learning Center,** in Provincetown (MacMillan Wharf; ☎ 508/487-8899).

(Race Point Beach; ✆ **508/349-3785**), which both tell the story of the men who risked their lives to save those who would have drowned at sea. Most were lost, but the lifesavers, which later became the **U.S. Coast Guard,** would patrol the coastline ready to assist if need be. A side business (that was quite a bit less noble) was run by those called **"mooncussers,"** who would watch by the full moon for shipwrecks and stand by to pick through any valuable parts of the wreck that came ashore.

Whaling was a prominent and lucrative industry from about 1750 to about 1850, when the industry began to wane. Whalers proved to be some of the most successful seafarers in the Cape's history. In order to make bountiful catches, whalers traveled around the world; when they returned, they inevitably brought souvenirs home with them. Therefore the homes of successful sea captains on the Cape and islands became virtual museums containing treasures from across the globe.

Nantucket became an important whaling port, and its wealth was renowned. The **Nantucket Whaling Museum** (13 Broad St.; ✆ **508/228-1894**) houses exhibits that show the history of whaling and the bounty it allowed seafarers to bring home. The museum displays the interior of an actual candle house, where whale blubber was transformed into candles. Other remnants of whaling life displayed at the museum are the **scrimshaw** (elaborate carvings made from tooth and bone) that sailors would carve to pass the time during the months at sea and **sailor's valentines,** the colorful boxes decorated with hearts made of seashells that crew members purchased from Caribbean ports for their sweethearts.

The **Great Fire of 1846** destroyed Nantucket's town center. After the fire razed the town, much of the town center was rebuilt with the riches from whaling journeys. An economic bust period in the late 19th century meant that nothing was changed for decades and the town has been virtually preserved from that mid-19th-century period, cobblestone streets and all.

Edgartown on Martha's Vineyard also thrived during this period, and there are numerous examples of the majestic sea captains' houses—mostly private homes—along North Water Street. There is also a large concentration of sea captains' houses along Route 6A in **Brewster,** nicknamed the sea captains' town. This is a good place to admire widow's walks, those rooftop porches that were said to allow the wives of sea captains to scan the horizon in anticipation of the return of their men. There are many sea captains' homes that you can visit in the region, but exceptional examples are the **Hadwen House,** on Nantucket (96 Main St.; ✆ **508/228-1894**); the **Dr. Daniel Fisher House,** in Edgartown (99 Main St.; ✆ **508/627-8017**); and the **Julia Wood House,** at the **Falmouth Museums on the Green,** in Falmouth center (at the Village Green; ✆ **508/548-4857**).

Although the fishing industry has been suffering in recent years from over-fishing, the Cape and islands are still the home of many who make their living by harvesting from the sea. In some families, the profession goes back for generations. Stop by the **Fish Pier** in the town of **Chatham** in the Lower Cape after noon to see fishermen unloading their catches. This too is an important part of the history of the region.

THE FIRST TOURISTS: SPIRITUALISTS & SCIENTISTS

The late 19th century brought the beginnings of the tourism industry to the Cape and islands. The first tourists to these shores were looking toward the heavens, but they were not seeking the sun. They came—by the hundreds—for religious retreats.

Impressions

I am not the only person who came here to spend two weeks and remained a lifetime.
—Mary Heaton Vorse, *Time and the Town: A Provincetown Chronicle*, 1991

In Oak Bluffs, on Martha's Vineyard, Methodists would gather in a grove close to the harbor for revivalist camp meetings. The canvas tents they erected for the extended religious revivals were eventually expanded into tiny cottages. Today visitors can stroll around and see these "ginger-bread cottages," a name that has been coined after the elaborate Victorian-era scrollwork and brightly colored details on the houses and also see the **Trinity Park Tabernacle,** the largest wrought-iron structure in the country. Open-air services and concerts are still held here every summer. The **Cottage Museum** (1 Trinity Park; ℂ **508/693-7784**) tells the history of the camp meeting grounds and has early photographs of the visitors, who dressed in modest Victorian garb.

Across Vineyard Sound, in the village of **Woods Hole** in Falmouth, a different kind of summer tourist was discovering the area. Scientists—especially oceanographers—interested in spending their summer vacations surrounded by other scientists were beginning to gather for seminars. Founded as a summer lab in 1888, **Marine Biological Laboratory (MBL)** today is an international center for biological research, education, and training with about 50 Nobel Laureates associated with it. Woods Hole is also home to the **Woods Hole Oceanographic Institution (WHOI),** which was founded in 1930 and is dedicated to ocean research, education, and exploration. The institute runs on about $100 million a year in grants, many from the U.S. Navy. Both **MBL** (100 Water St.; ℂ **508/289-7423**) and **WHOI** (15 School St.; ℂ **508/289-2663**) have visitor centers open to the public. Perhaps drawn by the scientists at MBL and WHOI, several other science organizations have sprouted up in Woods Hole. The village is home to a branch of the **National Oceanic and Atmosphere Administration** and a semester-at-sea school, called **Sea Education Association.** The village is a hub for scientists, fishermen, artists, and bohemians, particularly in the summer.

From around the 1890s to the 1930s, summer cottage communities began to spring up all over the Cape and islands for those who could afford a small second home. Two particularly picturesque summer cottage communities are **Falmouth Heights,** a village along the south shore of Falmouth, where Victorian-era cottages were built on and around a central hill, and **Siasconset**—known as 'Sconset—on Nantucket, where the tiny cottages are all near the ocean, festooned with climbing roses and ringed by white picket fences.

AN ARTISTS COLONY FORMS ON THE OUTER CAPE

Around 1900, a group of artists from New York, led by **Charles Hawthorne,** discovered **Provincetown,** a tiny picturesque fishing village at the tip of the Cape, where the native population of fishermen, many of Portuguese descent, had developed a colorful community. The artists, who set up their easels on the piers and the tiny lanes, made it an even more colorful community. Hawthorne taught his students to

Impressions

In my time here, I have heard it referred as many things: an art colony, a place of tolerance and sexual freedom, a fishing village, an open-air mental hospital, a tourist trap, and a support group for thousands.

—Writer John Skoyles on Provincetown

paint outside—*en plein air*, as the French say—and to give an idea of the figures through broad brush strokes with a palette knife, concentrating on the nuances of shadow, angle, and color rather than getting hung up on detail.

Another famous artist who set up a school decades later in the 1950s was **Hans Hofmann**, a German who favored abstraction, and whose background in art studies reached back to the Paris school of Henri Matisse. New York artists of the **Art Students League,** where Hofmann also taught, began taking summer homes in Provincetown and the nearby towns of Wellfleet and Truro. Some of them even moved there year-round. Visit the **Provincetown Art Association and Museum** (460 Commercial St.; ✆ **508/487-1750**) to understand the rich art history of the town.

As writers and intellectuals followed, the area became a hotbed of bohemia, a kind of Greenwich Village of the north. The liberal, artsy, open-mindedness of the populace made the area a popular spot for gays, and Provincetown is now one of the country's top gay resorts.

JFK & THE CAPE COD NATIONAL SEASHORE

Cape Cod really became well-known when the second-oldest son of a certain family who had been vacationing on the Cape for decades became president. It was the glamour of seeing John F. Kennedy sailing his boat, the *Honeyfitz*, off **Hyannis Port** that gave Cape Cod worldwide panache in the 1960s. Some say the place has never recovered. Hyannis, which is

actually a village in the town of Barnstable, is by far the most built-up part of the Cape. It has a giant mall and numerous plazas surrounded by seas of asphalt. It also has the **John F. Kennedy Hyannis Museum** (397 Main St.; ✆ **508/790-3077**), a large photo display that continues to be one of the Cape's top tourist draws. The Kennedy compound is still in Hyannis Port and is considered "home" for many of the Kennedy clan. Vehicles are warned away from the area by signs, but the curious can still get a good look at the compound, which consists of several homes set closely together, by taking a sightseeing boat trip out of Hyannis Harbor. The Kennedy family's favorite pastimes, such as sailing in Nantucket Sound, continue through the generations.

JFK also did his part to preserve the Cape. In August 1961, he signed a bill designating 27,000 acres from Chatham to Provincetown as a new national park, the **Cape Cod National Seashore.** Visiting the national seashore can mean a trip to one of its spectacular beaches, along 40 miles of coastline from Nauset Beach, in Orleans, to Herring Cove, in Provincetown, or following a ranger on a nature walk through the endangered habitat of an Atlantic White Cedar Swamp, in Wellfleet. There are numerous nature trails offering self-guided tours throughout the seashore, as well as several historic buildings set up as museums. Maps and information can be found at the **Salt Pond Visitor Center,** on Route 6, in Eastham (✆ **508/255-3421**). Standing on this pristine seashore looking out at the churning Atlantic Ocean, putting all America

3 ART & ARCHITECTURE

ART

Artists began coming to the Outer Cape—Provincetown, Truro, and Wellfleet—in the late 19th century when painter **Charles Hawthorne** started teaching classes about painting *en plein air,* with easels set up outside, making use of the famous Cape Cod light, an atmospheric quality local artists prize. Hawthorne soon opened the **Cape Cod School of Art** and later served as one of the founders of the **Provincetown Art Association,** formed as a gathering spot for local artists. Hawthorne's method stressed getting the crux of an image—colors, shapes and nuance—rather than worrying about detail. His students' paintings of local Portuguese children are called "mud heads," as they show the children virtually without facial features, and instead use well-placed shadows or the tilt of a head to reveal the mood of the child.

Hawthorne's protégé, **Henry Hensch,** continued the school, also stressing the Impressionistic style of using soft colors to paint such images as flowers and streetscapes. In the 1950s, **Hans Hofmann,** an intimidating artist who had strong ideas about color and abstraction, came to the Cape. He was known to cut up a student's painting and reorder the pieces as part of his critique. Around the time Hofmann came to the Cape, other abstract expressionist stars of the period, such as Franz Kline, Mark Rothko, and Robert Motherwell, also visited the area and acquired summer homes.

Today the legacy of Hawthorne, Hensch, and Hofman still lives on in the Cape. **John Grillo** is a Wellfleet artist who paints large colorful murals of the opera, circus, and tango; his murals are on

display at Café Heaven, on Commercial Street, as well as the Cove Gallery, in Wellfleet. **The Fine Arts Works Center** (24 Pearl St., Provincetown; ℭ **508/487-9900**), which awards residencies each winter, ensures that a new group of artists and writers are inspired by Provincetown every year. Wellfleet's reputation as an art center is as strong as Provincetown's, and has even been called "the art gallery town," as there are about a dozen interesting galleries along Main Street and Commercial Street. In Falmouth, there are several excellent potters within a few miles of each other along the road to Woods Hole—just look for the signs for "pottery" and pull in to take a look.

The Cape and islands are also a great place to find crafts. On Martha's Vineyard, for example, sculptural iron weather vanes can be found at many local galleries. Historic crafts are also abundant on Martha's Vineyard and Nantucket. Nineteenth-century sailors created crafts to pass the time on their long seafaring trips: **scrimshaw,** elaborate sculptures made of ivory or whale bone; **sailor's valentines,** decorative wood boxes containing colorful shells; and **Nantucket lightship baskets,** handmade reed baskets with mahogany tops and scrimshaw ornamentation, were all popular crafts created by sailors—although sailor's valentines are now thought to have been purchased on Caribbean islands and brought back to New England. Today some artisans are crafting modern examples of these crafts using the old methods.

To find an artist's studio, pick up the invaluable guide *Arts & Artisan Trails of Cape Cod, Martha's Vineyard, and Nantucket* from the Cape Cod Chamber of Commerce. It lists about 200 artists and their studios.

ARCHITECTURE

The Cape's architectural style is best known for its namesake **Cape Cod House,** a simple, wooden, shingled 1½-story cottage with a central chimney. The first Cape Cod–style homes were built in the 17th century by European settlers. Since then, there have been many adjustments to the classic Cape style over the centuries, but you can see early examples of this style, including charming half-capes, along Route 6A, mostly in the village of Yarmouth Port.

A great way to see the history of early American architecture is to drive along the old stagecoach route, Route 6A, formerly known as the Old King's Highway. The narrow road winds along the north side of the Cape from Bourne to Orleans. Here you will see colonial homes of all styles, many of which belonged to wealthy sea captains. **Georgian Colonial** homes were popular in the 1700s, and tend to be two-story square, symmetrical homes that often have two chimneys, one on each side of the roof. You can find several fine examples of Georgian-style homes on Stony Brook Road, near the intersection with Route 6A, in Brewster. Also look for **Federal**-style homes, which have such classical elements as columns at the entryway or a Palladian window (which is shaped like a half oval) above the front door. A good example is the **Julia Wood House,** part of the Falmouth Historical Society Museums on the Green property in Falmouth center.

There are more elaborate homes in the **Greek Revival** style, which was popular in the mid–19th century; these two-story houses typically have a gabled roof, a columned veranda, and other "Greek" architecture elements that mimic temples, such as doorways bounded by carved columns with friezes above. A fine example of Greek Revival is the **Dr. Daniel Fisher House,** on Main Street in Edgartown, on Martha's Vineyard.

Also look for elaborate homes built in the **Second Empire (Mansard)** style, a fancy style inspired by the French houses with mansard roofs and elaborate carvings. A classic example of this style is the **Captain Penniman House** in Eastham, which you can tour in the summer. Homes built in the **Carpenter Gothic** style, or "gingerbread" homes, were popular as well; these Victorian homes tend to be painted playfully in bright colors and adorned with elaborate woodwork carvings and cutouts on the roof and the trim. Examples can be found in the Methodist campground in Oak Bluffs on Martha's Vineyard.

On the Outer Cape and particularly within the bounds of the Cape Cod National Seashore, there is a movement afoot to save **"modern"** 1950s houses from the school of Walter Gropius, one of the leaders of the Bauhaus movement. Think glass boxes, and you'll have an idea of what these houses look like. The jury is out on whether this architectural style will be accepted as suitably historic to qualify for preservation, but there is no doubt as to its aesthetic value or its harmony with the land. Set low into the landscape and looking as though they are all windows, facing toward the ocean, these houses are, without a doubt, classic Cape houses of an entirely different sort.

4 THE LAY OF THE LAND

ONE GIANT SAND BAR

In the beginning, there were the glaciers. The Cape and islands were formed relatively recently, merely 18,000 years ago, during the last episode of global warming, when glaciers receded from the area and left a sandy substrate. In other words, parts of the Cape and islands—particularly the

Outer Cape and Nantucket—are actually just giant sand bars. But what fine sand bars they are.

The best way to explore the geologic and natural essence of Cape Cod is with a visit to the 44,000-acre **Cape Cod National Seashore.** Stretching from Chatham to Provincetown, it covers 40 miles of pristine beach, marsh, kettle ponds, and uplands. There are miles of biking and walking trails, including one in Truro that passes by a wild cranberry bog.

In the geologic scheme of things, Cape Cod is sort of a here-today, gone-tomorrow phenomenon. Cape Cod's outer beach sees an erosion rate of about 4 feet per year. So the place is quite a bit different from when Henry David Thoreau walked from Eastham to Provincetown on the Atlantic side of the coast in the mid–19th century. However, a walk along the shore can still be the setting for a range of surprises. A simple stroll along the beach may present a piece of cloudy sea glass, stones and seashells of all shapes and colors, or even a glimpse of a pod of whales offshore. A great beachcombing site is the shoreline of Brewster, on Cape Cod Bay, where the tide recedes and leaves what seems like miles of ocean floor perfect for exploration.

The terrain of the Outer Cape feels different from the rest of the Cape. Larger trees, such as oaks and elms, are replaced by pitched pine and scrub oak. This is where dune grass, beach plum, and *rosa rugosa*, the hearty beach rose, are sometimes the only thing holding the sandy ground in place. But these fragile and rare habitats, such as the **Atlantic White Cedar Swamp Trail,** near Marconi Beach in Wellfleet, are where many rare and beautiful species, such as the delicate orchid called lady-slippers, can be found.

The salt-marsh habitat, which is found in all parts of the Cape and on both islands, is considered one of the keys to the health of estuaries and ponds. It works like a natural filter, cleaning groundwater before it enters estuaries. It was not too long ago that these areas used to be called swamps, and they were filled and paved for construction of such things as shopping malls. Now they are protected with some of the toughest environmental regulations in the country.

WILDLIFE

The wetlands of the Cape and islands are part of one of the country's greatest annual wildlife spectacles: the passage of thousands of **migratory birds** in spring and fall. Warblers, herons, terns, and oyster-catchers; shorebirds, such as avocets and the endangered Piping Plover; dozens of species of ducks; huge flocks of snow geese, owls, and hawks—these are just a few of the birds that take a rest stop on the Cape as they pass along the Atlantic Flyway, which, for some birds, extends from winter homes in South America to breeding grounds in the vast, marshy tundra within the Arctic Circle.

The Piping Plover, a small, sand-colored shorebird, is a threatened species that nests on Cape Cod. Its populations are so small that each pair that nests is watched closely. The Cape Cod National Seashore is considered one of the most important

---

Impressions

Its geography is simple and explicit. It has the odd flung-out shape of a sand bar, with an excellent but boring canal at one end and at its furthest, wildest shore, Provincetown, the haunt of extroverts and practitioners of the half-arts, such as soap-carving and sandal-making, where women with mustaches stare stonily at men with earrings.

—Paul Theroux

nesting areas for the Piping Plover, and beaches in several parts of the Cape, including Nauset Beach in Orleans and Race Point Beach in Provincetown, are closed every year while the Piping Plovers nest. Ignore the bumper stickers that say, "Piping Plovers taste like chicken," and learn to love these tiny little birds that live on the shore's edge.

The other great wildlife-watching opportunity this region is known for is **whale-watching.** The humpbacks, huge finbacks, and small minkes all cluster to feed around the Stellwagen Bank north of Provincetown from April all the way through November. Monomoy Island is worth a special trip for **seal-watching.** In late winter, thousands of harbor seals take their version of a holiday in the sun, retreating to Monomoy from Maine and points north. Many stay for most of the year. They share the island with thousands of wintering sea ducks, as well as other migrating birds in the spring and fall. For info, call the **Cape Cod Museum of Natural History** (© 508/896-3867).

5 CAPE COD IN POPULAR CULTURE

Over the past 100 years, the Cape and islands have been a very popular place for authors and other creative types. In fact, a selection from authors who have summered here, lived here year-round, or simply enjoyed visiting would fill a weighty tome.

During the 20th century, the Outer Cape was a prime gathering spot for writers and the intelligentsia of the day. Playwright **Eugene O'Neill,** winner of three Pulitzer Prizes and the 1936 Nobel Prize, had his first play, *Bound East for Cardiff,* performed in a shack on a wharf in Provincetown during the summer of 1916. That was long before he became one of the giants of modern drama. In the 1981 film *Reds,* directed by and starring Warren Beatty, the part of Eugene O'Neill is played by Jack Nicholson, and parts of the movie are set in Provincetown. In the 1950s, playwright **Tennessee Williams** was a prominent Provincetown resident, and it's said he wrote parts of *Cat On A Hot Tin Roof* while staying at Captain Jack's Wharf, a bohemian lodging spot on the west end of town. He also shared a house with Carson McCullers in the summer of 1946, when he was writing *Summer and Smoke* and she was transforming her novel *Member of the Wedding* into a play.

Norman Mailer lived in Provincetown for years and filmed his directorial debut, *Tough Guys Don't Dance,* in Provincetown. There's now an artists colony and residencies in Mailer's old house. **Paul Theroux** and **Kurt Vonnegut,** who was a founding member of the still-lively Barnstable Comedy Club, both had houses here and wrote about Cape Cod. **Sebastian Junger,** author of *The Perfect Storm,* has a family home in Truro and is a member of the Provincetown artists club, the Beachcombers.

Any recommended reading list for the Cape and islands starts with the classic *Cape Cod,* by Henry David Thoreau. The famous author traveled to Cape Cod from 1849 to 1857, riding the stagecoach from Boston to Orleans and then walking from Eastham to Provincetown. Another classic book of the region is *The Outermost House,* by Henry Beston, which tells the story of the author's year living in a cabin on the beach in Eastham, recording the seasonal changes. Perhaps my favorite overview of Cape Cod literature can be found in *Cape Cod Stories,* edited by John Miller and Tim Smith, with selections by 26 top writers from Herman Melville to Norman Mailer.

For good beach reading, *Cape Cod,* by William Martin is an entertaining novel with a lot of history thrown in by the best-selling author. There's also *The Great Beach,* by John Hay, a naturalist's history of Cape Cod. For history buffs, *Time and the Town: A Provincetown Chronicle,* by Mary Heaton Vorse, retells the classic history of the town on the Cape's tip in the early part of the 20th century. For two very different takes on Provincetown, both released in 2002, read *Land's End: A Walk in Provincetown,* by Michael Cunningham, the Pulitzer Prize–winning author of *The Hours;* and *Ptown: Art, Sex and Money on the Outer Cape,* by Peter Manso, which provides a bleaker view of Provincetown. *Away Off Shore: Nantucket Island and Its People, 1602–1890,* by Nathaniel Philbrick gives a comprehensive and entertaining history of the island. *Mostly on Martha's Vineyard,* by Henry Beetle Hough, is the entertaining autobiography by the long-time editor of the *Vineyard Gazette.*

True crime novels were practically invented on the Cape with Leo Damore's *In His Garden: The Anatomy of a Murderer,* about a serial murderer in Provincetown and Truro. The tradition of true crime set in the Outer Cape has continued in recent years with *Invisible Eden: A Story of Love and Murder on Cape Cod,* by Maria Flook, about the murder of Christa Worthington, in Truro, in 2002. *The Year We Disappeared,* by Cyline Busby and her father, John Busby, published in 2008, tells the true story of when John Busby was shot in the face while working as a police officer in Falmouth. In the course of telling the story, the book reveals some dark secrets about that town on the Upper Cape.

Although the Cape doesn't receive the same attention from the media as, say, New York City or Los Angeles, Nantucket did get a lot of publicity from *Wings,* a popular television show that ran for 7 years in the 1990s and was set in Nantucket's tiny airport, which, these days, is being expanded to twice the size. Music on Cape Cod must begin and end with Patti Page's classic song, "Old Cape Cod." There's really nothing else that comes close.

6 EATING & DRINKING

Cape Cod's restaurant scene has come a long way from the traditional clam shack, even though those shacks—where you can get lobster with all the fixins' or a steaming, towering plate of fried clams—are still the stuff of which Cape Cod memories are made. Today there are sophisticated restaurants, expensive places serving a sort of generic fine dining, called New American cuisine. Some of these places are quite good, but be prepared to pay for it (on the islands, entrees have hit the $50 mark).

Cape Cod has long been known for its local seafood, and you won't find a restaurant anywhere in the region without seafood on the menu. Fried fish, especially fried clams, are considered the ultimate Cape Cod meal. Another favorite is lobster, broiled with butter sauce. But for more sophisticated fare, look for grilled fish specials, such as striped bass, in midsummer. Raw bars serve local oysters—the ones from Wellfleet are world-famous, and Cotuit oysters are also notable—as well as "steamers," which are steamed clams. The other type of clam you will see on menus is the quahog (pronounced "ko-hog"), which is often served baked, meaning that the meat is cooked and mixed with bread crumbs and then returned to the shell. Steamed mussels are also popular, and are usually served in a garlicky broth. Scallops are another fixture on local menus; look for scallops from Nantucket, which are especially prized.

If you want boiled lobster but don't like to wrestle with it, you can order "lazy man's lobster," a dish that presents lobster meat that has been removed and placed loosely back in the shell. You can also order a lobster roll, which is cold lobster on a hotdog roll, sometimes served with mayonnaise or lettuce. New England clam chowder is another local specialty; it is a creamy, white broth that is served with clams and potatoes (note that it is different from Manhattan clam chowder, which has a red broth). You will sometimes find clam chowder prepared with bacon or Portuguese spicy sausage, such as linguica or chorizo. Portuguese breads also can be found at local markets and on some menus.

Provincetown, Martha's Vineyard, and Nantucket are all considered dining meccas. In Provincetown, the easiest way to decide where to eat is to stroll up and down Commercial Street, checking out the menus. Although there are a number of expensive, fine-dining choices, Province-town also has great inexpensive "street food," such as burritos at the **Aquarium Shops,** burgers at **Mojo's** on Macmillan Wharf, and crepes from the **Outer Crepe,** along with others that come and go with the seasons. You never know what you'll find along Commercial Street, but there are also choices for cheap eats.

On Martha's Vineyard, try **Atria** and **Detente,** in Edgartown, or **Balance** and **Sweet Life,** in Oak Bluffs, for a memorable meal. Trying not to break the bank is the problem on this island.

Nantucket is also well-known for having far too many fine-dining establishments and too few choices for the frugal diner. For that special night out, you could go to **Straight Wharf, Company of the Cauldron,** or the **Galley Beach.** If you are on a budget, you might want to hit Broad Street and take out food from any of the places along what locals call "the strip." There is some pretty good eating here—my favorite is **Stubby's**—for not too much money.

Falmouth has become the place on the Cape to find ethnic cuisine. Besides the typical Chinese fare, there is Indian, Jamaican, and Thai cuisine. There are also several other excellent restaurants in Falmouth, including two Italian places on Main Street that are worth driving from the Mid Cape for (at least that's what my Mid Cape friends tell me).

Dining trends, such as tapas and wine bars, have hit the Cape, and it looks like they may be here to stay. While you can find tapas options in almost every town, the most promising locales are **Embargo,** in Hyannis; **Gracie's Table,** in Dennis; and **Cinco,** on Nantucket.

Ambience is an important part of any dining experience, and the Cape is endowed with numerous waterside restaurants. Great spots with water views are **Falmouth Raw Bar,** on Falmouth Inner Harbor; **Baxter's,** in Hyannis; the **Red Inn,** in Provincetown; **The Home Port,** in Menemsha, on Martha's Vineyard; and **Ropewalk,** on Nantucket. Just be prepared to pay extra for that spectacular water view.

Dining hours on Cape Cod are earlier than in most cities, as befits the many families and seniors who vacation here and call the area home. Most restaurants open for dinner at 5pm and serve until at least

---

Impressions

No one can eat enough steamed clams . . . No meal is more delicious than steamed clams dipped in drawn butter, together with cups of clam broth and Portuguese bread.

—Peter Hunt, *Peter Hunt's Cape Cod Cookbook,* 1954

The Local Brew

Cape Cod Beer (1336 Phinney's Lane, Hyannis; ✆ **508/790-4200**) has two main varieties, Red and IPA, and more than a dozen seasonal brews. Both Martha's Vineyard and Nantucket also have local breweries. On the Vineyard, **Offshore Ale Company** (30 Kennebec Ave., Oak Bluffs; ✆ **508/693-2626**) taps into eight varieties of its own beer. Nantucket's **Cisco Brewers** (5 and 7 Bartlett Farm Rd., Nantucket; ✆ **508/325-5929**) is famous for its brew called Whale's Tale Pale Ale. The brew is also available at many local restaurants.

10pm in season and 9pm off-season. Breakfast places are usually open from about 7 to 11am, and lunch hours are typically 11:30am to 2:30pm. But there are restaurants in every town that serve food throughout the day with no break.

At most restaurants on the Cape and islands, tips are not included on the bill. But there are some exceptions, particularly among the higher-priced restaurants, and generally when you are dining with a party of six or more people. Always check your bill closely to be sure the tip has not been included. If you are unsure, ask your server. In general, a 15% to 20% tip is expected on meals. If you find fault with any aspect of a restaurant, you should ask to speak with a manager immediately, but keep in mind that when a meal goes awry, it often is not the fault of the server.

3

Planning Your Trip to Cape Cod, Nantucket & Martha's Vineyard

The Cape is really many capes: tony in some places, tacky in others; in patches a nature lover's dream, a living historical treasure, or a hotbed of creativity. This chapter will tell you what you need to plan your trip to Cape Cod, Nantucket, and Martha's Vineyard and steer you there smoothly; for international visitors, there is essential information, helpful tips, and advice on the more common problems that you may encounter while vacationing on Cape Cod and the islands. Planning a trip to Cape Cod is a little more complex than packing flip-flops and suntan lotion. But remember, this is a destination that is supposed to be about relaxation, lying on a sun-kissed beach, listening to the lapping surf, or walking along a wildflower-lined path to watch the sun set over the horizon. These simple pleasures are why people have been coming to Cape Cod to vacation for more than a century.

Visiting Cape Cod means traveling over either the Bourne Bridge or the Sagamore Bridge. Most visitors arrive by car, but you can also take a bus or even travel by plane to one of several small airports in the region. You'll need a place to stay in one of the Cape's 15 towns or on one of the islands, and this book is loaded with options. You'll also need a way to get around. Public transportation leaves much to be desired in most Cape Cod towns, although several have good beach shuttles in season. Public transportation on both Martha's Vineyard and Nantucket, on the other hand, is excellent. There is also the option of bringing or renting a bike, a great way to travel from your rental house or hotel to the beach. There's lots more nitty-gritty information below, from information on passports and dates for festivals to weather predications and tips on dining. To pinpoint where you want to go in the area and what you want to do, peruse the region-by-region chapters.

For additional help in planning your trip and for more on-the-ground resources in Cape Cod and the islands, see section 1, "Fast Facts: Cape Cod & the Islands," in chapter 11.

1 WHEN TO GO

Once strictly a warm-weather destination, the Cape and islands traditionally open the season with a splash on Memorial Day weekend and shutter up come Labor Day. The official beginning of summer is heralded by the Figawi sailboat race (see "Calendar of Events," below) on Memorial Day weekend. Traffic all over the Cape is horrendous on this last weekend in May, and ferries are booked solid. It's a rowdy party weekend, but then, strangely, things slow down for a few weeks until late June. The weekend closest to July 4th is another major mob scene, when summer really gets rolling. It's no wonder that July is the second-busiest month of the year, and August is by far the most popular month for visiting the region: You are fairly guaranteed

> **Tips** **Shopping Bargains**
>
> Provincetown's October sales are to die for. Discounts often range from 50% to 70% as merchants clear the shelves before closing for the winter. And remember, Provincetown is not just tacky T-shirt stores. There are excellent men's and women's clothing stores, as well as an abundance of fancy home-accessories stores. See p. 212.

good beach weather these 2 months, and the Atlantic Ocean warms to comfortable swimming temperatures. Summer comes to an end with Labor Day, a heavily trafficked weekend you'll probably want to avoid.

SHOULDER SEASONS

Cape Cod now welcomes more and more tourists to witness the tender blossoms of spring and the fiery foliage of autumn. During these shoulder seasons, lodging tends to cost less, and a fair number of restaurants and attractions remain open. Most important, traffic is manageable. In addition, the natives seem far more accommodating in the off-season, and shopping bargains abound.

In the past few years a number of entertaining town festivals and events have attracted crowds in the spring and fall (see "Calendar of Events," below). Spring brings daffodil festivals and fall brings cranberry, arts, and harvest festivals. Unless your idea of the perfect vacation requires a swim in the ocean, you may be better off with the smaller crowds and better deals of the shoulder months: May, June, September, or October.

OFF-SEASON

November and December don't quite qualify as "off-season" on the Cape and islands. In fact, some say the most crowded time on Nantucket is during the Christmas Stroll in early December; it kicks off a month of holiday events. Martha's Vineyard also rolls out the red carpet in December with events in Edgartown and Vineyard Haven, such as Santa's arrival on

the ferry. Many towns on the Cape, such as Sandwich, Osterville, Falmouth, and Chatham, also have big holiday festivals (see "Calendar of Events," below). The holidays are quite popular for family gatherings on the Cape and islands.

Tourist-oriented establishments on the Cape and islands traditionally close during the coldest months, but some tough out the quietest season—January through March. It's a rare treat to enjoy the region's historic towns and pristine landscapes with almost no one but natives about. To avoid disappointment in the off-season, however, always be sure to call ahead to check schedules.

CLIMATE

The Gulf Stream renders the Cape and islands generally about 10° warmer in winter than the mainland, and offshore winds keep them about 10° cooler in summer (you'll probably need a sweater most evenings). The only downside of being surrounded by water is the other wet stuff: no, not rain, fog! Typically it's sunny about 2 days out of 3—not bad odds. And the foggy days can be rather romantic. Pack some good books for when it pours.

SUMMER The first few weeks of June can be a perfect time to visit the region, but be forewarned: You may need to request a room with a fireplace. Weather this time of year, particularly on the Outer Cape, can be unpredictable at best. At worst, it's cold and rainy. Don't count on swimming in the ocean unless you're a member of the Polar Bear Club. Late June weather is usually lovely. July and August can be perfect—sunny and breezy—or damp, foggy, and humid. Usually it's a combination of the two.

AUTUMN On Cape Cod, it usually starts feeling like fall a week or two after Labor Day. September and October are splendid: Leaves start to change color, roads start to unclog, and everyone seems happier. The ocean retains enough heat to make for bearable swimming during the sunny days of Indian summer, and the subtly varied hues of the trees and moors are always changing, always lovely. Day temperatures are perfect for long hikes along the seashore. By October, you'll need a sweater during the day, and evenings can be downright chilly. But this is a lovely time of year on the Cape and islands.

WINTER It's not supposed to snow on Cape Cod, but it does. In recent years some towns have had more than 100 inches. During a recent winter, the Cape received virtually no snow until a surprise blizzard on April 1. January, February and March tend to be on the bleak side. This is when a lot of locals head south to sunnier climes.

SPRING April is a cheerful time on the Cape and islands, and daffodil festivals abound. In May and June, the entire Cape blossoms. Gardening goes way beyond hobby in this gentle climate, and blooms are profuse from May right through the summer. But springtime weather can be rainy, and the Atlantic Ocean is bone-chillingly cold.

Hyannis's Average Monthly Temperatures

	Jan	Feb	Mar	Apr	May	June	July	Aug	Sept	Oct	Nov	Dec
High Temp (°F)	37	37	44	53	63	72	78	70	71	62	52	42
(°C)	3	3	7	12	17	22	26	21	22	17	11	6
Low Temp (°F)	20	20	28	37	46	56	62	62	53	43	35	25
(°C)	-7	-7	-2	3	8	13	17	17	12	6	2	-4

CALENDAR OF EVENTS

For an exhaustive list of events beyond those listed here, check **http://events. frommers.com**, where you'll find a searchable, up-to-the-minute roster of what's happening in cities all over the world.

APRIL

Daffodil Festival, Nantucket. Spring's arrival is heralded with masses of yellow blooms adorning everything in sight, including a cavalcade of antique cars. Call ✆ **508/228-1700.** April 23 to 25.

Brewster in Bloom, Brewster. You'll find open houses, a crafts fair and flea market, and hot-air balloons. The Old King's Highway (Rte. 6A) is lined with thousands of daffodils. Call ✆ **508/896-3500;** www.brewsterinbloom.org. April 30 to May 3.

MAY

Chatham Maritime Festival, Chatham. A festival to raise awareness of Chatham's fishing industry, with food and events at the Chatham Fish Pier and on Main Street. Call ✆ **508/945-5199.** Early May.

Herb Festival, Sandwich. Activities include exhibits, talks, and garden walks at the Green Briar Nature Center. Call ✆ **508/888-6870.** Mid-May.

Cape Maritime Week, Cape-wide. A multitude of cultural organizations mount special events, such as lighthouse tours, highlighting the region's nautical history. Activities include Coast Guard open houses, lectures, walking tours, and more. The week is sponsored by the

Cape Cod Commission. Call ☎ **508/ 362-3828.** Mid-May.

Nantucket Wine Festival, Nantucket. Vintners from all over converge on Nantucket for wine tastings and cuisine provided by some of the island's top chefs. The Grand Cru is the main event. Call ☎ **508/228-1128,** or visit www.nantucketwinefestival.com. Late May.

Figawi Sailboat Race, Hyannis to Nantucket. This is the largest—and wildest—race on the East Coast. Intense partying in Hyannis and on Nantucket surrounds this popular event. Call ☎ **508/221-6891,** or go online to www.figawi.com. Late May.

Dexter Rhododendron Festival, Sandwich. Heritage Museums and Gardens—at the peak of bloom—sells offshoots of its incomparable botanical collection. Call ☎ **508/888-3300.** Late May.

JUNE

A Taste of the Vineyard, Martha's Vineyard. Island restaurateurs offer samplings of their specialties at Edgartown's Whaling Church to benefit the Martha's Vineyard Preservation Trust. Call ☎ **508/627-8017.** Mid-June.

Harborfest Celebration, Nantucket. It's a chance to sample competing chowders and board tall ships. Call ☎ **508/228-1700.** Mid-June.

Provincetown International Film Festival, Provincetown. Focusing on alternative film, this fete has brought out such celebrities as John Waters and Lily Tomlin. Call ☎ **508/487-FILM** [3456], or see www.ptownfilmfest.org. June 16 to 20.

Nantucket Film Festival, Nantucket. This annual event focuses on storytelling through film and includes showings of short and feature-length films, documentaries, staged readings, panel discussions, and screenplay competitions. Sponsors include *Vanity Fair* magazine, so you may see a celebrity or two. Call ☎ **508/325-6274,** or check online at www.nantucketfilmfestival. org. Mid-June.

Arts Alive Festival, Falmouth. Dozens of artists and performers, including painters, musicians, dancers, filmmakers, and storytellers, give demonstrations, show films, sell artwork, and put on performances at this weekend-long event that opens with a town dance on the library lawn. Call ☎ **508/548-8500,** or visit www.artsfalmouth.org/ artsalive. Mid-June.

St. Barnabas Strawberry Festival, Falmouth. Indulge in strawberry shortcake as well as barbecue and lots of children's games on the grounds of St. Barnabas Church, next to the Village Green. Call ☎ **508/548-8500.** Mid-June.

Aptucxet Strawberry Festival, Bourne. The Aptucxet Trading Post Museum, a replica of the country's first store, hosts crafts demonstrations, accompanied by fresh strawberry shortcake. Call ☎ **508/ 759-9487.** Late June.

Provincetown Portuguese Festival, Provincetown. This cultural event celebrates Provincetown's Portuguese heritage with music, dancing, exhibits, food, a parade, fireworks, and the traditional Blessing of the Fleet. Call ☎ **508/ 487-3424,** or visit www.provincetown portuguesefestival.com. Late June.

Rock 'n' Roll Ramble, Sandwich. Vintage cars from the '50s and '60s converge on Heritage Museums and Gardens for a concert and mutual admiration. Call ☎ **508/888-3300.** Late June.

Brewster Historical Society Antiques Fair, Brewster. This outdoor extravaganza features 80 top dealers. Call ☎ **508/896-9521,** or go to www. brewsterhistoricalsociety.org. Late June.

Hyannis Main Street has a range of free activities in July and August, ranging from concerts at Aselton Park, next to Hyannis Harbor, on Tuesdays, Fridays, and some Sundays; to movies on the Village Green on Wednesday evenings; concerts on the Village Green on Wednesdays; Summer Music Stroll on Thursdays; and Art Stroll on the first Thursday of each summer month. Call the Hyannis Area Chamber of Commerce at **800/4HYNNIS** [449-6647] for details.

Wampanoag Pow Wow, Mashpee. Native American tribes from around the country converge to enjoy traditional dances and games. Call ✆ **508/477-0208,** or visit http://mashpeewampanoag tribe.com. July 4th weekend.

Independence Day, Falmouth. The fireworks at Falmouth Heights Beach are one of the largest shows in the region. Your best bet is to park in town earlier in the evening and walk over to the Heights. Call ✆ **508/548-8500.** July 4th weekend.

Independence Day, Barnstable. A spectacular fireworks display over either Barnstable Harbor or Hyannis Harbor (depending on the nesting of the Piping Plovers). Call ✆ **800/4-HYNNIS** [449-6647]. July 4th weekend.

Independence Day, Provincetown. Festivities include a spirited parade, entertainment, and fireworks over the harbor. Call ✆ **508/487-3424.** July 4th weekend.

Independence Day, Nantucket. The highlight of the island's busiest weekend is fireworks on Jetties Beach. Call ✆ **508/228-0925.** July 4th weekend.

Independence Day, Edgartown. An old-fashioned, small-town parade and fireworks over Edgartown Harbor are the highlights of this beloved event.

Call ✆ **508/693-0085.** July 4th weekend.

Edgartown Regatta, Martha's Vineyard. A highly social sailing event. Call ✆ **508/627-4361,** or go online to www.edgartownyc.org/regatta.php. July 15 to 17.

Mashpee Night at the Pops, Mashpee Commons. A concert by the Cape Cod Symphony Orchestra followed by fireworks. This event attracts about 15,000 pops fans. Call ✆ **508/539-2345** or visit www.mashpeepops.com. July 24.

Barnstable County Fair, East Falmouth. This old-fashioned, 10-day agricultural extravaganza is complete with prize produce and livestock and, of course, rides and a midway. There are concerts nightly. Call ✆ **508/563-3200,** or see www.barnstablecountyfair. org. Mid-July.

Woods Hole Film Festival, Falmouth. A festival that spans 2 weeks and numerous venues and features small independent films. Call ✆ **508/495-FILM [3456],** or go to www.woodsholefilm festival.org. Late July.

AUGUST

Jazz by the Sea and Pops by the Sea, Hyannis. Celebrity "conductors"—such as Olympia Dukakis—enliven these two outdoor concerts. Call ✆ **800/4-HYNNIS** [449-6647]. Early August.

Possible Dreams Auction, Martha's Vineyard. Resident celebrities give—and bid—their all to support the endeavors of Martha's Vineyard Community Services. Call ✆ **508/693-7900,** or visit www.possibledreamsauction.org. Early August.

In the Spirit Arts Festival, Martha's Vineyard. Oak Bluffs celebrates its cultural diversity with food, music, and children's fun. Call ✆ **508/693-0085.** Early August.

Falmouth Road Race, Falmouth. Joggers and world-class runners turn out in droves—10,000 strong—for this annual race that covers just over 7 miles. Entry registration is by lottery and ends in May. Unregistered runners are not allowed to participate. Call ℂ **508/540-7000,** or race to www.falmouthroadrace.com. Mid-August.

Carnival Week, Provincetown. The gay community's annual blowout features performers, parties, and an outrageous costume parade. Call ℂ **508/487-2313.** Mid-August.

Agricultural Society Livestock Show and Fair, Martha's Vineyard. In West Tisbury, you'll find a classic country carnival and a celebration of the Vineyard's agricultural tradition. Call ℂ **508/693-9549,** or see http://mvas.vineyard.net/fair.php. Mid-August.

Sandcastle and Sculpture Day, Nantucket. This fairly serious but fun contest is categorized by age group, which ups the odds of winning. Call ℂ **508/228-1700.** Mid-August.

Festival Days, Dennis. Six days of events, including fun-for-the-family activities such as a kite-flying contest, canoe race, crafts fair, and more. Call ℂ **800/243-9920** or 508/398-3568. Late August.

Illumination Night, Martha's Vineyard. The Oak Bluffs campground is lit with hundreds of Japanese lanterns. Campground officials keep this event a secret until the last minute, so it's hard to plan ahead. Call ℂ **508/693-0085.** Late August.

Oak Bluffs Fireworks and Band Concert, Martha's Vineyard. It's the summer's last blast. Call ℂ **508/693-0085.** Late August.

SEPTEMBER

POP Goes the Summer, Barnstable County Fairgrounds, Falmouth. Experience a Cape Cod Symphony Orchestra concert followed by fireworks. Call ℂ **508/548-8500.** Early September.

Bourne Scallop Festival, Bourne. This annual weekend event features food, crafts, rides, musical entertainment, and more. Call ℂ **508/759-6000,** or visit www.bournescallopfest.com. Early September.

Windmill Weekend, Eastham. This jolly community festival includes a sand-art competition, road races, band concerts, an arts-and-crafts show, a tricycle race, and professional entertainment. The highlight of this weekend is the square dance held under the historic windmill. Call ℂ **508/255-3444,** or see www.easthamwindmillweekend.com. Early September.

Cranberry Festival, Harwich. This is a chance to observe and celebrate the colorful harvest, with 9 days of events ranging from pancake breakfasts to fireworks. Call ℂ **800/441-3199** or **508/430-2811;** or find out more at www.harwichcranberryfestival.org. Mid-September.

Martha's Vineyard Striped Bass and Bluefish Derby, Martha's Vineyard. In its 56th year, the region's premier fishing derby and one of the country's oldest is a month-long classic contest. Call ℂ **508/693-0085,** or see http://mvderby.com. Mid-September to mid-October.

Sandwich Boardwalk Celebration, Sandwich. This community did some serious bonding years ago when its boardwalk was damaged by a storm, and everyone pitched in to build a new one. This festival, with professional kite flying and entertainment for families, has become an annual tradition. Call ℂ **508/833-9755.** Late September.

Harbor Swim for Life, Provincetown. Stalwart swimmers participate in this event to raise money for local AIDS organizations. The race is followed by a festive Mermaid Brunch and a sunset "Festival of Happiness" on Herring Cove Beach. Call ☎ **508/487-1930,** or go to www.swim4life.org. Late September.

Provincetown Arts Festival, Provincetown. Building up to the Provincetown Art Association and Museum Annual Consignment Auction (☎ **508/487-1750**), this festival, which takes place over 4 weekends, is an extraordinary opportunity to collect works spanning the past century. Local artists hold open studios, actors stage readings of Eugene O'Neill, and galleries hold special exhibits. Call ☎ **508/487-3424.** Late September to mid-October.

OCTOBER

Wellfleet OysterFest, Wellfleet. Spend a weekend learning about and tasting Wellfleet's world-famous oysters at this weekend-long street festival, including arts, crafts, and live music. Call ☎ **508/ 349-2510,** or visit www.wellfleet oysterfest.org. Always the weekend (beginning on Fri) after Columbus Day.

Trash Fish Banquet, Provincetown. Unsung, or perhaps undersung, species are creatively cooked to benefit the Center for Coastal Studies. Call ☎ **508/ 487-3622.** Mid-October.

Women's Week, Provincetown. This is a gathering of artists, entertainers, and educators, as well as women who just want to have fun. Call ☎ **508/487-2313,** or go to www.womeninnkeepers. com. Mid-October.

Walking Weekend, Cape-wide. Over 45 guided walks (averaging 2 hr. in length) are sponsored by an organization called Cape Pathways to foster appreciation for the Cape's unique ecology and cultural accomplishments. Call ☎ **508/362-3828.** Mid-October.

Nantucket Harvest Festival, Nantucket. This festival features inn tours

and a big chowder contest, just when the foliage is at its burnished prime. Call ☎ **508/228-1700.** Mid-October.

Nantucket Arts Festival, Nantucket. This weeklong event includes a wet-paint sale, a mini film festival, writers and their works, gallery exhibitions, artist demonstrations, theater, concerts, photography, and more. Call ☎ **508/ 228-1700.** Mid-October.

Yarmouth Seaside Festival, Yarmouth. Enjoy a parade, fireworks, arts and crafts, contests, and sporting events. Call ☎ **800/732-1008** or 508/778-1008; or visit www.yarmouthseasidefestival.com. Mid-October.

NOVEMBER

Lighting of the Pilgrim Monument, Provincetown. The Italianate tower turns into a monumental holiday ornament, as carolers convene below. Call ☎ **508/487-1310.** Thanksgiving Eve (late Nov).

Harbor Lighting, Hyannis. The boats parade by, twinkling with lights, and Santa arrives via lobster boat. Call ☎ **508/362-5230.** Late November.

Fall Festival, Edgartown. Family activities at the Felix Neck Wildlife Sanctuary include a treasure hunt, wildlife walks, and wreath making. Call ☎ **508/ 627-4850.** Late November.

Chatham's Christmas by the Sea, Chatham. A month of town-wide events includes historic-inn tours, carolers, hayrides, open houses, a dinner dance, and Santa. Call ☎ **508/945-5199.** Late November through December.

DECEMBER

Falmouth Christmas by the Sea, Falmouth. A weekend of caroling, tree lighting, Santa, entertainment, and a parade that centers on the historic and lavishly decorated Falmouth Village Green. Call ☎ **508/548-8500.** Early December.

Christmas in Sandwich, Sandwich. Seasonal open houses, exhibits, community caroling, and merchant promotions take place throughout the town. Call ℂ **508/833-9755.** Early December.

Holly Folly, Provincetown. The annual Gay and Lesbian Holiday Festival has events open to all, including guesthouse tours, holiday parties, the Reindeer Run, concerts, and more. Call ℂ **508/ 487-2313,** or see www.ptown.org/ HollyFolly.asp. Early December.

Yarmouth Port Christmas Stroll, Yarmouth Port. Stroll along the Old King's Highway for open houses, visits with Santa, and caroling. Call ℂ **508/778-1008.** Early December.

Christmas Weekend in the Harwiches, Harwich. This town-wide celebration features entertainment, merchant promotions, hayrides, visits with Santa, and more. Call ℂ **800/442-7942** or 508/430-1165. Mid-December.

First Night, Chatham. Following Boston's lead, Chatham puts on a festive evening featuring local performers. Call ℂ **508/945-5199,** or go online to www.firstnightchatham.com. New Year's Eve.

Christmas Stroll, Nantucket. The island briefly stirs from its winter slumber for one last shopping/feasting spree, attended by costumed carolers, Santa in a horse-drawn carriage, and a "talking" Christmas tree. This event is the pinnacle of **Nantucket Noel,** a month of festivities starting in late November. Ferries and lodging establishments book up months before this event, so you'll need to plan ahead. Call ℂ **508/ 228-1700.** Early December.

2 ENTRY REQUIREMENTS

PASSPORTS

Virtually every air traveler entering the U.S. is required to show a passport. All persons, including U.S. citizens, traveling by air between the United States and Canada, Mexico, Central and South America, the Caribbean, and Bermuda are required to present a valid passport. U.S. and Canadian citizens entering the U. S. at land and sea ports of entry from within the Western Hemisphere will need to present government-issued proof of citizenship, such as a birth certificate, along with a government-issued photo ID, such as a driver's license. A passport is not required for U.S. or Canadian citizens entering by land or sea, but it is highly encouraged to carry one.

VISAS

For information on obtaining a visa, please see section 1, "Fast Facts: Cape Cod & the Islands," in chapter 11.

The U.S. Department of State has a **Visa Waiver Program (VWP)** allowing citizens of the following countries to enter the United States without a visa for stays of up to 90 days: Andorra, Australia, Austria, Belgium, Brunei, Denmark, Finland, France, Germany, Iceland, Ireland, Italy, Japan, Liechtenstein, Luxembourg, Monaco, the Netherlands, New Zealand, Norway, Portugal, San Marino, Singapore, Slovenia, Spain, Sweden, Switzerland, and the United Kingdom. Citizens of Czech Republic, Estonia, Hungary, Latvia, Lithuania, Malta, Republic of Korea, and Slovakia are soon to be admitted to the VWP. (*Note:* This list was accurate at press time; for the most up-to-date list of countries in the VWP, consult **http://travel.state.gov/ visa.**) Even though a visa isn't necessary, in an effort to help U.S. officials check travelers against terror watch lists before they arrive at U.S. borders, visitors from VWP countries must register online through the **Electronic System for Travel Authorization** (ESTA) before boarding a plane or a boat to the U.S. Travelers will complete an electronic application providing basic personal and travel-eligibility information. The Department of Homeland Security recommends filling out the form at least 3 days before traveling. Authorizations will be valid for up to 2 years or until the traveler's passport expires, whichever comes first. Currently there is no fee for the online application. *Note:* Any passport issued on or after October 26, 2006, by a VWP country must be an **e-Passport** for VWP travelers to be eligible to enter the U.S. without a visa. Citizens of these nations also need to present a round-trip air or cruise ticket upon arrival. E-Passports contain computer chips capable of storing biometric information, such as the required digital photograph of the holder. If your passport doesn't have this feature, you can still travel without a visa, if it is a valid passport issued before October 26, 2005, and includes a machine-readable zone, or between October 26, 2005, and October 25, 2006, and includes a digital photograph. For more information, go to **http://travel.state.gov/visa**. Canadian citizens may enter the United States without visas; they will need to show passports (if traveling by air) and proof of residence, however.

Citizens of all other countries must have (1) a valid passport that expires at least 6 months later than the scheduled end of their visit to the U.S., and (2) a tourist visa.

CUSTOMS
What You Can Bring Into the U.S.

Every visitor more than 21 years of age may bring in, free of duty, the following: (1) 1 liter of wine or hard liquor; (2) 200 cigarettes, 100 cigars (but not from Cuba), or 3 pounds of smoking tobacco; and (3) $100 worth of gifts. These exemptions are offered to travelers who spend at least 72 hours in the United States and who have not claimed them within the preceding 6 months. It is forbidden to bring into the country almost any meat products (including canned, fresh, and dried meat products such as bouillon, soup mixes, and so forth). Generally, condiments including vinegars, oils, spices, coffee, tea, and some cheeses and baked goods are permitted. Avoid rice products, as rice can often harbor insects.

Bringing fruits and vegetables is not advised, though not prohibited. Customs will allow produce depending on where you got it and where you're going after you arrive in the U.S. International visitors may carry in or out up to $10,000 in U.S. or foreign currency with no formalities; larger sums must be declared to U.S. Customs on entering or leaving, which includes filing form CM 4790. For details regarding U.S. Customs and Border Protection, consult your nearest U.S. embassy or consulate, or **U.S. Customs** (www.customs.gov).

What You Can Take Home from Cape Cod

For information on what you're allowed to bring home, contact one of the following agencies:

U.S. Citizens: U.S. Customs & Border Protection (CBP), 1300 Pennsylvania Ave. NW, Washington, DC 20229 (✆ **877/ 227-5511;** www.cbp.gov).

Canadian Citizens: Canada Border Services Agency (✆ **800/461-9999** in Canada, or 204/983-3500; www.cbsa-asfc. gc.ca).

U.K. Citizens: HM Customs & Excise (✆ **0845/010-9000** outside the U.K., or 020/8929-0152; www.hmrc.gov.uk).

Australian Citizens: Australian Customs Service (✆ **1300/363-263;** www.customs. gov.au).

New Zealand Citizens: New Zealand Customs, The Customhouse, 17–21 Whitmore St., Box 2218, Wellington (© 04/473-6099 or 0800/428-786; www.customs.govt.nz).

Unless you're arriving from an area known to be suffering from an epidemic (particularly cholera or yellow fever), inoculations or vaccinations are not required for entry into the United States.

3 GETTING THERE & GETTING AROUND

GETTING TO CAPE COD & THE ISLANDS
By Plane

Most major carriers offer service to **Boston's Logan Airport,** and from there it's a quick half-hour commuter flight on Cape Air to **Hyannis** or **Provincetown** (about $180–$190 round-trip), or the islands (to **Martha's Vineyard** or **Nantucket,** about $260 round-trip).

It's also easy to shuttle in from New York (from LaGuardia to Hyannis, LaGuardia to Martha's Vineyard, or LaGuardia to Nantucket, all about $500 round-trip). Nonstop flights from either LaGuardia or Newark to Hyannis, Martha's Vineyard, or Nantucket take about 1 hour and 15 minutes. Connections are also available between these airports and to New Bedford, and private charters are easy to arrange.

Comparison-shopping by phone (or computer) can pay off, as preliminary research will help you find the best deal. For example, Continental offers service to Hyannis from LaGuardia Airport and a seasonal service from Newark Airport to Martha's Vineyard and Nantucket. US Airways services Hyannis from LaGuardia; they also service Martha's Vineyard and Nantucket from both Logan and LaGuardia. Cape Air is the only airline currently offering service from Logan Airport to Provincetown.

Among the larger airlines serving Logan Airport are **American Airlines** (© 800/433-7300; www.aa.com), **Continental** (© 800/523-3273; www.continental.com), **Delta** (© 800/221-1212; www.delta.com), **Northwest** (© 800/225-2525; www.nwa.com), **United** (© 800/241-6522; www.united.com), and **US Airways** (© 800/428-4322; www.usairways.com).

Carriers to the Cape and islands include all of the above, plus **Cape Air/Nantucket Airlines** (© 800/352-0714 or 508/771-6944; www.flycapeair.com), **US Airways/ Colgan Air** (© 703/368-8880; www.colganair.com), and **Island Airlines** (© 800/248-7779 or 508/775-6606; www.islandair.net).

To find out which airlines travel to Boston or Providence airports, where you can get connecting flights to the Cape and Islands, see section 2, "Airline, Hotel & Car Rental Websites," in chapter 11.

Flying to Nantucket from Hyannis takes about 20 minutes, depending on the weather, costs about $110 round-trip, and is a great way to avoid the hectic ferry scene. Island Airlines and Cape Air make the most frequent trips from Hyannis to Nantucket, and between these two air carriers alone there are over 50 flights per day. Charter flights are offered by both airlines.

The commuter flights have their own little fare wars, so it's worth calling around. And though flights may lessen in frequency during the off-season, fares sometimes descend as well.

Getting into Town from the Airport

Visitors to the Cape and islands who are flying into Boston's Logan Airport or T.F. Green Airport in Providence, Rhode

Island, can rent a car and drive to Cape Cod in about 1½ hours (from Boston) or an hour (from Providence).

Driving maps are generally available at car rental locations.

The major route from Boston's Logan Airport is I-93 S. to Route 3, which ends at the Sagamore Bridge. The Sagamore Bridge is the bridge to use to access all the Cape towns, except Falmouth and the islands of Martha's Vineyard and Nantucket. For those destinations, plus parts of Bourne, the best route from Logan Airport is I-93 to Route 24 to I-495, which turns in to Route 25 near the Bourne Bridge.

From Providence, Rhode Island, you take I-195 all the way to Route 25 and the Bourne Bridge.

Though cars are not needed for the average visitor to Martha's Vineyard and Nantucket, some visitors choose to rent a car or even a Jeep so that they can drive on certain beaches. Rental establishments on both islands offer ample Jeep rentals in addition to car rentals.

By Car

Similar to the directions above in "Getting into Town from the Airport," visitors from the south (New York, for example) will approach the Cape Cod Canal via I-95 to I-195 to Route 25 and over the Bourne Bridge. Those coming from Boston can either come that way (reaching Rte. 25 via I-93 to Rte. 24 and I-495) or head directly south from Boston on I-93 to Route 3, leading over the Sagamore Bridge.

The bridges are only 3 miles apart, with connecting roads on both sides of the canal, so either bridge will do. The one you choose will most likely depend on where you're going. If you're planning to head south to Falmouth or take a ferry to Martha's Vineyard, you'll want to take the Bourne Bridge and follow Route 28 about 10 miles to Falmouth.

If you're heading farther east of the Sagamore Bridge to any of the other 14

towns on the Cape or to Nantucket, you'll want to travel over the Sagamore Bridge and take Route 6 or its scenic sidekick, Route 6A, which merges with Route 28 in Orleans. From Orleans, the main road is Route 6 all the way to Provincetown.

Those traveling to Nantucket should take the Sagamore Bridge and drive down Route 6 until reaching exit 7. From there you can follow signs to one of the two ferry terminals (Steamship Authority or Hy-Line) in Hyannis.

The big challenge, actually, is getting over either bridge, especially on summer weekends, when upward of 100,000 cars all try to cross at once. Savvy residents avoid at all costs driving onto the Cape on Friday afternoon or joining the mass exodus on Sunday (or Mon, in the case of a holiday weekend), and you'd be wise to follow suit. Call **SmarTraveler** (© 617/ 374-1234, or cellular *1) for up-to-the-minute news on congestion and alternate routes, as well as parking availability in the pay-per-night parking lots that serve the island ferries.

Traffic can throw a major monkey wrench into these projections, but on average, driving time to Hyannis is 5 hours (no traffic) to 7 hours from New York and 1½ to 2 hours from Boston. It'll take about 1 to 1½ hours more to drive all the way to Provincetown.

Traffic can truly be a nightmare on peak weekends. Cars are enough of a bother on the Cape itself: If you're not planning to cover much ground, forego the "convenience" and rent a bike instead (some B&Bs offer "loaners"). On the islands, cars are truly superfluous. Expensive to ferry back and forth ($175 one-way to Nantucket in season, and that's if you manage to make a reservation months, even a year, in advance or are willing to sit in "standby" for many hours), a car will prove a nuisance in the crowded port towns, where urban-style gridlock is not uncommon. Should you change your mind and want

A Word About Traffic

Cape Cod traffic is nothing if not predictable. You do not want to be driving over the Bourne or Sagamore bridges onto the Cape on a summer Friday between 4 and 8pm. Saturday between 10am and 3pm is an equally bad time to arrive. Most of all, you do not want to try to get off the Cape on a Sunday or a holiday Monday between 2 and 8pm. If you find yourself in one of the infamous Cape Cod traffic jams (on Memorial Day in 2000, traffic was backed up 18 miles east from the Sagamore Bridge), there are options. Here are my personal traffic-beating tips. Don't tell anyone.

1. The Bourne Bridge is almost always a less crowded route than the Sagamore Bridge. You can connect to Route 6 from the Bourne Bridge via the canal road, or see number 3 below.
2. When heading off the Cape on Route 6, turn off at exit 5. Take Route 149 south to Route 28. At the Mashpee Rotary, take Route 151 to Route 28 in North Falmouth. Take Route 28 to the Bourne Bridge.
3. To get onto the Cape to points east of Yarmouth, follow step 2 above in reverse.
4. If you are traveling to Nantucket and plan to park your car in Hyannis, watch the signs on Route 6 to see which parking lot is open. If the Brooks Road lot is open, there is no need to drive all the way to the ferry terminal. Instead you will park your car at the lot, which is off Route 28, and take a free shuttle bus to the terminal. Knowing which lot you will park at ahead of time will save you a lot of time in the long run.
5. If you are heading to Martha's Vineyard from points south, such as New York or Connecticut, consider taking a passenger ferry from Rhode Island or New Bedford (see chapter 10). Otherwise be alert to the signs on Route 28 about parking lots. These signs are accurate. If they say the lot is full in Woods Hole, you will not be allowed to park there, so don't bother driving down to check it out. Follow the signs to the open parking lots, and a free shuttle bus will take you to the ferry.

to go motoring once you arrive, you can always rent a car on the islands (see "Getting Around," later in this chapter), usually for *less than the cost of bringing your own vehicle over.*

If you do come by car, have a mechanic check it out beforehand. If you're a member of the **American Automobile Association** (AAA; © 800/222-4357) or another national auto club, call beforehand to ask about travel insurance, towing services, free trip planning, and other services that may be available.

For listings of the national car rental agencies with branches on Cape Cod, Martha's Vineyard, and Nantucket, see section 2, "Airline, Hotel & Car Rental Websites," in chapter 11.

International visitors should note that insurance and taxes are almost never included in quoted rental car rates in the U.S. Be sure to ask your rental agency about additional fees for these. They can add a significant cost to your car rental.

Many rental car agencies have an age requirement of 25 years old. Those who want to rent a car and are 21 to 25 years old pay an additional "age differential" fee each day they are renting the car.

TRAVEL TIMES Please note that traffic is very heavy over the bridges onto the Cape on Friday afternoons and heading off the Cape on Sunday afternoons. Saturday can also have heavy traffic because it is the start and end of the rental cycle at most weekly vacation units. The Bourne Bridge is usually less crowded than the Sagamore Bridge, but unless you are going to Falmouth, you'll have to merge with the Sagamore Bridge traffic on Route 6 anyway. If you are trying to catch a ferry, particularly in Hyannis, always leave plenty of extra time.

By Bus

Greyhound (☎ 800/231-2222; www. greyhound.com) connects Boston with the rest of the country, and **Bonanza Bus Lines/Peter Pan** (☎ 888/751-8800 or 508/548-7588; www.peterpanbus.com) covers a good portion of southern New England. Logan Airport to Falmouth costs about $30 each way.

Bonanza links Boston's Logan Airport and South Station with Bourne, Falmouth, and Woods Hole; its buses from New York reach the same destinations, plus Hyannis. From New York to Hyannis or Woods Hole, the 6-hour ride costs about $73 each way.

Plymouth & Brockton (☎ 508/746-0378; www.p-b.com) offers service from Logan and South Station to Hyannis by way of Sagamore and Barnstable, and offers connections from there to the towns of Yarmouth, Dennis, Brewster, Orleans, Eastham, Wellfleet, Truro, and Provincetown.

From Logan to Hyannis takes about 2 hours on the P&B; to Provincetown it's about 3½ hours (including the transfer in Hyannis).

The proliferation of cheap intercity bus services in the Northeast (**Bolt Bus** [www.boltbus.com], **Megabus** [www. megabus.com], and various **Chinatown bus companies** [www.chinatown-bus. com]) means that you can catch a bus from almost every major city in the Northeast to Boston, sometimes for as little as $15, and from there pick up the P&B to the Cape.

The fare from Logan to Provincetown on P&B is $63 round-trip, $35 one-way; it's $52 and $29 round-trip/one-way from South Station in Boston. To Hyannis, it's $45 round-trip from Logan, $25 one-way; $34 from South Street Station round-trip, and $17 one-way.

Note: If you plan to catch a ferry, don't count on the bus arriving on time (there's no telling what the traffic may do). Plan to take the second-to-last ferry of the day, so you have a backup; and even so, schedule your arrival with an hour to spare.

By Train

Those taking Amtrak and arriving in Boston's South Station will find it easy to take a bus to Cape Cod on Peter Pan Bus to Bourne or Falmouth; or on Plymouth & Brockton to Hyannis/Provincetown. A bus leaves approximately every 1½ hours from Boston to the Cape during high season.

By Boat

Arriving by water to Martha's Vineyard, Nantucket, or even Provincetown gives you a chance to decompress from city worries, while taking in glorious views both coming and going. All the ferries are equipped to carry bikes, for about $12 round-trip.

Bay State Cruise Company (☎ 877/783-3779; www.provincetownfastferry.com) runs a fast ferry to Provincetown from Boston, in addition to a daily round-trip conventional ferry, both from Commonwealth Pier at Boston's World Trade Center. The fast ferry makes three trips a day from May to early October. The trip, which takes 90 minutes, costs $49 one-way, $79 round-trip for adults; $32 one-way,

New York to Hyannis by bus or car	5 to 7 hours, depending on traffic
Boston to Hyannis	1½ hours, with no traffic
Sagamore Bridge to Orleans	1 hour off-season; up to 2 to 3 hours high season
Sagamore Bridge to Provincetown	1½ hours, with little traffic
Hyannis to Sagamore Bridge	30 minutes; Sunday afternoons in season, 3 hours
Bourne Bridge to Woods Hole	35 minutes; Friday afternoons in season, 1¾ hours
Hyannis to Nantucket by plane	12 minutes
Hyannis to Nantucket by Steamship Authority or Hy-Line high-speed catamaran	1 hour
Hyannis to Nantucket by slow Steamship Authority or Hy-Line ferries	2¼ hours
Woods Hole to Martha's Vineyard aboard the Steamship Authority ferries	45 minutes
Falmouth to Edgartown, Martha's Vineyard, aboard the *Pied Piper*	1 hour
Falmouth to Oak Bluffs, Martha's Vineyard, aboard the *Island Queen*	35 minutes

$58 round-trip for children; and $44 one-way, $73 round-trip for seniors. The conventional ferry leaves daily late June through Labor Day, and on weekends late May to late June and mid- to late September. The voyage ($44 round-trip for adults; free for children 4–11) takes about 3 hours each way.

Boston Harbor Cruises (© 877/733-9425 or 617/227-4321; www.bostonharborcruises.com) runs fast ferries from Long Wharf in Boston to Provincetown's Macmillan's Wharf late June to mid-September. It's a 90-minute trip. In high season there are two to three round-trips a day. Ferry tickets cost $79 round-trip for adults. Tickets for seniors cost $69 round-trip; tickets for children cost $58 round-trip. Bikes cost $6 each way. Reservations are a must on this popular boat.

You can also ferry directly to Provincetown from Plymouth, in season, with **Captain John Boats** (© 800/242-2469 or 508/747-2400; www.provincetownferry.com); the trip takes 1½ hours and costs $40 round-trip for adults, $35 for seniors, and $30 for children 12 and under. Bikes cost an extra $5. In July and August, only round-trip tickets are sold. From mid-June to early September, trips leave daily. From late May to mid-June, trips run weekends only.

For detailed information on ferries to the islands, see "Getting There" in chapters 9 and 10.

To Martha's Vineyard

The three "down-island" ports of Martha's Vineyard are hooked up to the Cape and mainland in various ways. **Oak Bluffs** has the busiest harbor in season. It's served by the **Hy-Line** from Hyannis or Nantucket (© 800/492-8082; www.hy-linecruises.com), the *Island Queen* from Falmouth Harbor (© 508/548-4800; www.island queen.com), and the state-run **Steamship Authority** car ferry from Woods Hole (© 508/477-8600; www.steamshipauthority.com, where you can buy tickets online).

Edgartown is serviced by the **Falmouth Ferry Service,** a passengers-only ferry called the *Pied Piper* (© 508/548-9400; www.falmouthferry.com), which leaves from the west side of Falmouth Harbor and makes a 1-hour crossing (six crossings a day in season). It costs about twice as much as the other ferries to the Vineyard. **Vineyard Haven** welcomes **Steamship Authority** car and passenger ferries from Woods Hole year-round (over 20 crossings a day on weekends in season). If you want to bring your car, you'll need a reservation (© 508/477-8600; www.steamshipauthority.com), although there's limited standby space available for those willing to wait around, except during certain peak-demand stretches in summer. Passengers not planning to bring a car do not need a reservation.

From Falmouth, the *Island Queen* makes the quickest crossing, at about 35 minutes. Round-trip fares on all ferry choices to Martha's Vineyard range from about $15 to $40, depending on the distance, and the round-trip rate for cars in season is $135 to $155. Parking costs $10 to $30 per day, depending on the ferry company. Including all of the ferry services, there are dozens of crossings a day from the Cape to the Vineyard in summer.

Hy-Line runs a year-round high-speed ferry to Martha's Vineyard from Hyannis in 55 minutes. In season there are five trips a day, and the round-trip fare is $69 for adults and $48 for children. The traditional ferry makes the trip in season only once per day, takes 1 hour 35 minutes, and costs $43 for adults, $22 for children for round-trip tickets.

From New Bedford, Massachusetts, the fast ferry **MV *Whaling City Express*** travels to Martha's Vineyard in 1 hour. It makes six trips a day in season and is in service year-round, 7 days a week. A ticket costs $70 round-trip for adults; $40 round-trip for children 12 and under; and $62 round-trip for seniors. Contact New England Fast Ferry for details (© 866/683-3779 [toll-free]; www.nefastferry.com).

From **North Kingstown, Rhode Island,** to Oak Bluffs on Martha's Vineyard, the company Vineyard Fast Ferry runs its high-speed catamaran, *Millennium,* two to three round-trips daily from mid-June through October. The trip takes 90 minutes. Rates are $69 round-trip for adults, $46 round-trip for children 4 to 12. The ferry service can also set up shuttle service between Providence Airport or the nearest Amtrak station and the ferry terminal starting at $18 each way. Reservations for the ferry and/or the shuttle can be made by calling © 401/295-4040 or visiting their website at www.vineyardfast ferry.com.

To Nantucket

There are two competing high-speed ferries to Nantucket from Hyannis; both take 1 hour. The passengers-only **MV *Grey Lady*** (© 800/492-8082), Hy-Line's high-speed catamaran, costs $75 round-trip, $39 one-way for adults; $51 round-trip, $29 one-way for children (© 800/492-8082; www.hy-linecruises.com).

The Steamship Authority runs its own high-speed catamaran, the *Iyanough,* which costs $65 round-trip for adults and $49 round-trip for children (© 508/477-8600; www.steamshipauthority.com).

Both the Steamship Authority and Hy-Line also run slow ferries (2¼ hr.) to Nantucket. The Steamship Authority charges $33 round-trip, and Hy-Line charges $43 round-trip. Incidentally, transporting a car costs an astronomical $380 round-trip in season—which makes it pretty silly to bring a car when you consider that the island is only 3 miles wide and 15 miles end to end. A bike (bring your own or rent on-island) will more than suffice.

Ferries also travel to Nantucket from Harwich Port by the **Freedom Cruise Line** (② 508/432-8999; www.nantucket islandferry.com), which makes three trips a day in season and one trip a day in spring and fall. It costs $68 round-trip for adults, $51 for children.

A certain frenzy usually accompanies the ferry departures, but if you arrive about an hour early, you should have plenty of time to drop off your luggage at the pier beforehand, so you won't have to lug it around. Call **SmarTraveler** (see "By Car," above) or listen to radio station 1610 AM to find out what's up and whether traffic is clogged. The Steamship Authority boats offer a luggage trolley, which often fills to capacity a half-hour or more before departure, so it pays to get there early. The Hy-Line staff cheerfully attends to all the loading of luggage and bikes. It's a lot less hassle.

Note: See the note on bus-ferry connections under "By Bus," above. The same holds true for return journeys: Ferry arrival times tend to be more reliable, but give yourself plenty of time, and don't take a chance on the last bus of the day.

GETTING AROUND
By Car

Once you've made it over one of the bridges guarding the Cape Cod Canal—or bypassed the bridges by flying or boating in—getting around is relatively easy. Traveling by car does offer the greatest degree of flexibility, although you'll probably wish no one else knew that. While traffic can often be frustrating, parking is another problem. In densely packed towns, such as Provincetown, finding a free, legal space is like winning the lottery. Parking is also problematic at many beaches. Some are closed to all but residents, and visitors will

almost always have to pay a day rate of about $10 to $20. Renters staying a week or longer can arrange for a discounted week-long or month-long sticker through the local town hall (you'll probably need to show your lease, as well as your car registration). You can usually squeeze into the Cape Cod National Seashore lots if you show up early (by 9am); here the fee is only $15 a day, or $45 per season.

Further complicating the heavy car traffic on the Cape is the seemingly disproportionate number of bad drivers. A few key traffic rules: A right turn is allowed at a red light after stopping, unless otherwise posted. In a rotary (think traffic circle with Boston drivers), cars within the circle have the right of way until they manage to get out. Four-way stops call for extreme caution or extreme courtesy, and sometimes both.

Rental cars are available at the Hyannis Airport and at branch offices of major chains in several towns. The usual maze of rental offers prevails. Almost every rental firm tries to pad its profits by selling Loss-Damage Waiver (LDW) insurance at a cost of $8 to $15 extra per day. Before succumbing to the hard sell, check with your insurance carrier and credit card companies; chances are, you're already covered. If not, the LDW may prove a wise investment. Exorbitant charges for gasoline are another ploy to look out for; be sure to top off the tank just before bringing the car in.

Certain car rental agencies have also set maximum ages or may refuse to rent to those with bad driving records. If such restrictions might affect you, ask about requirements when you book to avoid problems later.

It's worthwhile to call around to the various rental companies to compare prices and to inquire about any discounts available (members of AAA or AARP, for instance, may be eligible for reduced rates). The national companies represented on the Cape and islands include

Avis (© 800/331-1212), **Budget** (© 800/527-0700), **Hertz** (© 800/654-3131), **National** (© 800/227-7368), and **Thrifty** (© 800/367-2277).

Internet resources can make comparison-shopping easier. **Travelocity** (www.travelocity.com) and **Expedia** (www.expedia.com) help you compare prices and locate car rental bargains from various companies nationwide. They will even make your reservation for you once you've found the best deal. Also check out **BreezeNet.com,** which offers domestic car rental discounts with some of the most competitive rates around.

For additional car rental agencies, see section 2, "Airline, Hotel & Car Rental Websites," in chapter 11.

If you're visiting from abroad and plan to rent a car in the United States, keep in mind that foreign driver's licenses are usually recognized in the U.S., but you may want to consider obtaining an international driver's license.

By Bus

To discourage congestion and provide a pleasant experience, a growing number of towns offer free or low-cost in-town shuttles in season. You'll find such services in Falmouth, Woods Hole, Mashpee, Hyannis, Dennis, Yarmouth, Harwich, Martha's Vineyard, and Nantucket. Each town's chamber of commerce can fill you in, or call the **Cape Cod Regional Transit Authority** (© 800/352-7155; www.capecodtransit.org). For commercial bus service between towns, see "Getting to Cape Cod & the Islands," earlier in this chapter.

By Boat

For ferries linking the Cape and islands, see "Getting There," in chapters 9 and 10. Other local water-taxi services and cruise

opportunities are listed by town in the appropriate chapters.

By Bike

The bicycle is the perfect conveyance for the Cape and islands, for distances great and small. The Cape has some extremely scenic bike paths, including the glorious Cape Cod Rail Trail, which meanders through seven towns for over 25 miles. Two wheels are the best way to explore Nantucket's flat terrain, and there are scenic bike routes through all six towns on Martha's Vineyard. You'll find a rental shop in just about every town (see "Bicycling," in subsequent chapters), or better yet, bring your own.

By Moped

They're legal on the islands and can be rented at many bicycle rental shops, but locals loathe them: They're noisy, polluting, traffic-clogging, and a menace both to their riders and to innocent bystanders. In other words, *caveat emptor,* and expect some dirty looks.

By Taxi

You'll find taxi stands at most airports and ferry terminals. The islands also offer jitney services with set rates, such as **Adam Cab,** on Martha's Vineyard (© **800/281-4462** or 508/627-4462), and **Chief's Cab,** on Nantucket (© **508/284-8497**). Several offer bike racks or can arrange for bike transportation with advance notice—call around until you find what you need. Some companies offer sightseeing tours. Among the larger taxi fleets on the Cape are **Falmouth Taxi** (© **508/548-3100**), **Hyannis Taxi Service** (© **508/775-0400**), and Provincetown's **Mercedes Cab** (© **508/487-3333**), which delivers elegance at no extra charge. Other cab companies are listed in the Yellow Pages, as are limousine liveries.

Frommer's lists exact prices in the local currency. The currency conversions quoted above were correct at press time. However, rates fluctuate, so before departing, consult a currency exchange website, such as **www.oanda.com/convert/classic**, to check up-to-the-minute rates.

It's always advisable to bring money in a variety of forms on a vacation: a mix of cash, credit cards, and traveler's checks. You should also exchange enough petty cash to cover airport incidentals, tipping, and transportation to your hotel before you leave home, or withdraw money upon arrival at an airport ATM.

Though the Cape and islands—especially the islands—might seem pricey compared to non–tourist areas, visitors used to city prices will find costs quite reasonable. Basically you can get by on very little if you don't need luxury (rooms in older motels off-season go for as little as $95 a night). Then again, you could spend $1,000 or more on a room—per night. Most of the nicer rooms fall between $250 and $350 a night in summer, half that in off-season.

Restaurant prices offer just as wide a range. You could dine on clam rolls, for instance, at less than $14 a head, or blow that much or more on a mere appetizer. With such a great variety of dining styles available everywhere, the choice is yours.

ATMS

Every town on the Cape has multiple ATMs (automated teller machines), sometimes referred to as "cash machines," or "cashpoints." These are the easiest and best source of cash when you're away from home.

The **Cirrus** (☎ **800/424-7787;** www. mastercard.com) and **PLUS** (☎ **800/843-7587;** www.visa.com) networks span the country; you can find them even in remote regions. Look at the back of your bank card to see which network you're on, and then call or check online for ATM locations on Cape Cod and the islands. Be sure you know your personal identification number (PIN) and daily withdrawal limit before you depart. *Note:* Remember that many banks impose a fee every time you use a card at another bank's ATM. In addition, the bank from which you withdraw cash may charge its own fee. To compare banks' ATM fees within the U.S., use **www.bankrate.com**.

CREDIT CARDS & DEBIT CARDS

You can use your major credit cards pretty much everywhere on the Cape and islands; the exceptions might be some smaller stores or eateries (we indicate in the review of the place whether it's cash only).

Visitors from outside the U.S. should inquire whether their bank assesses a 1% to 3% fee on charges incurred abroad.

It's highly recommended that you travel with at least one major credit card. You must have one to rent a car, and hotels and airlines usually require a credit card imprint as a deposit against expenses.

The Value of United States Currency vs. Other Popular Currencies					
US$	Can$	UK£	Euro (€)	Aus$	NZ$
1	1.10	.60	.71	1.20	1.48

What Things Cost on Cape Cod (High Season)

Taxi from Logan Airport to Falmouth	$200 (includes tip)
Bus ticket from Logan to Falmouth	$27 (one-way)
Bus fare between towns	$3
1-week beach parking pass, Orleans	$50
Bike rental, Cape Cod Rail Trail	$18 (3 hrs.)
1 lb. of taffy from Cape Cod Salt Water Taffy, Yarmouth	$8.99
Cup of coffee at the Corner Store, Chatham	$1.50
Double at Cliffside Beach Club, Nantucket (Very Expensive)	$450–$710
Double at Bay Beach B&B, Sandwich (Expensive)	$245–$345
Double at the Acworth Inn, Hyannis (Moderate)	$149–$169
Double at Old Sea Pines Inn, Brewster (Inexpensive)	$110–$165
Dinner at the Red Inn, Provincetown (Very Expensive)	$75
The Brewster Fish House (Expensive)	$55
Among the Flowers Café, Edgartown, Martha's Vineyard (Moderate)	$35
Marshland Restaurant on 6A, Sandwich (Inexpensive)	$15

5 HEALTH

STAYING HEALTHY

The water is drinkable throughout the Cape and islands, though residents tend to prefer bottled water, available in all grocery stores and convenience stores. Most menus contain a warning to beware of uncooked fish because it can carry diseases. However, considering the amount of fish consumed in the region (fish is a staple in local restaurants), food illness is extremely rare on the Cape and islands. Many restaurants, including fine-dining establishments, include a vegetarian main course on the menu, but kosher foods are difficult to find. When in doubt, it's best to ask.

General Availability of Health Care

You'll find numerous large chain pharmacies on Cape Cod. There's a CVS and Brooks Drugstore in almost every town; a CVS in Hyannis is open 24 hours (see section 1, "Fast Facts: Cape Cod & the Islands," in chapter 11). In the Outer Cape towns of Wellfleet and Truro and in some of the towns up-island on Martha's Vineyard, you might be a half-hour drive from a pharmacy, so it's best to come prepared with everything you need.

COMMON AILMENTS

SUN Even in this northerly clime, **sunburn** is a real hazard—as is, increasingly, **sun exposure,** whatever the latitude. For most skin types, it's safest to start with a lotion with a high SPF and work your way down. Be sure to reapply often, according to the directions, and no matter how thoroughly you slather on lotion, try to stay in the shade during prime frying time—11am to 2pm. Kids should always wear sunscreen with a high SPF number, or a cover-up such as a T-shirt, if they're going to be playing outside for long periods of time (and just try to stop them!). Sunglasses with UVP (ultraviolet protection) lenses will help shield your eyes.

INSECTS The sea breezes keep most **mosquitoes** on the move, but not always (said Thoreau: "I have never been so much troubled by mosquitoes as in such localities"), so pack some bug spray. Birds on the Cape have been diagnosed with **West Nile disease,** so it's a good idea not to let a mosquito bite you if at all possible. Mosquitoes are the carrier of this disease, which just reached the United States a few years ago. However, the chances of catching West Nile are very low.

The most dangerous insect you're likely to encounter may not be so easily dissuaded. Unfortunately, pinhead-size **deer ticks,** which transmit **Lyme disease** (named for the Connecticut community where the malady was diagnosed), are widespread along the Massachusetts coast, and they're especially active just when you're apt to be there: April through October. Nantucket has the dubious distinction of having the highest concentration of Lyme disease in the country. A vaccine tested there is now on the market. Ask your doctor if you should consider the vaccine. If caught in its early stages—symptoms include a ring-shaped rash and flulike achiness—the disease is easily countered with antibiotics; if it's left untreated, however, the effects could eventually prove fatal.

The best protection, so far, is prevention. Avoid walking in brush or high grass—it's bad for the dunes, anyway. If you insist on bushwhacking, cover up in light-colored clothing (the better to spot any clinging ticks), consisting of a long-sleeve shirt and long pants tucked into high white socks. Camping stores such as EMS sell bush pants that are perfect for this purpose—they're actually comfortable in warm weather. For double protection, spray your clothes and hands (but not face) with a DEET-based insect repellent. Check your clothes before removing them, and then check your body; it helps to use a mirror or call upon a significant other. Showering after such an outing is a good safeguard. If, despite your best precautions, you find you've brought home a parasite, remove it with tweezers by pulling directly outward, if you can manage to do so without squeezing the body (that would serve only to inject more bacteria into your bloodstream). Dab the bite with alcohol to help disinfect it, and save the tick in a closed jar. If you're within a few minutes of a medical facility, have a doctor deal with the extraction; if you do it yourself, go for testing and treatment as soon as you can and take the tick with you.

The **Lyme Disease Foundation** (© **860/870-0070;** 24-hour hotline: 800/886-LYME [5963].) distributes brochures to tourist areas and is also able to field questions. Other good sources of information are the **Centers for Disease Control** (© **888/232-3228** or 404/332-4555) and the **Massachusetts Department of Public Health** (© **866/627-7968**).

PLANTS There's one other very good reason not to go in for splendor in the grass: **poison ivy.** The shiny, purplish, three-leafed clusters are ubiquitous and potent; if you so much as brush past a frond, the plant's oil is likely to raise an itchy welt. Clothing that has been in contact with the plant can spread the harmless but irritating toxin to your skin; it's even transmitted by smoke. If you think you've been exposed, your best bet is to wash with soap immediately (otherwise the oil may spread elsewhere on your body). Calamine lotion—available without prescription at all drugstores—should help soothe the itching. You won't spread the rash by scratching, because it's the oil that

> ## Helmets for Your Health!
>
> There's one key health precaution you can take if you plan to do any bicycling while on the Cape and islands: **a helmet.** In Massachusetts, children 12 and under are *required* to wear one. All the good bike shops rent helmets as well, and those few extra bucks could save your life.

does the spreading, but scratches could get infected, so resist the temptation.

WHAT TO DO IF YOU GET SICK AWAY FROM HOME

In a medical emergency, the Falmouth Hospital and Cape Cod Hospital **emergency rooms** are your best bets, but you will be billed for any services performed. There is also the **Community Health Center of Cape Cod** (© **508/477-7090**), in Mashpee Commons, a walk-in clinic that treats even people without insurance.

If you suffer from a chronic illness, consult your doctor before your departure from home. Pack **prescription medications** in your carry-on luggage, and carry them in their original containers, with pharmacy labels—otherwise they won't make it through airport security. Visitors from outside the U.S. should carry generic names of prescription drugs. For U.S. travelers, most reliable health-care plans provide coverage if you get sick away from home. Foreign visitors may have to pay all medical costs up front and be reimbursed later.

For **additional emergency numbers** see section 1, "Fast Facts: Cape Cod & the Islands," in chapter 11.

6 SAFETY

Tourist areas in the United States are generally safe, and the Cape and islands are safer than most. Although a number of towns, particularly the larger ones, suffer their share of crime (much of it drug- and alcohol-related), there's no such thing as a "bad neighborhood" here, per se. However, with crime on the increase everywhere, you need to stay alert and take the usual precautions. Avoid carrying valuables with you on the street or at the beach, and be discreet with expensive cameras and electronic equipment. When milling in crowds (in Hyannis or Provincetown, for example), place your billfold in an inside pocket, and hang on to your purse; anything kept in a backpack should be buried beyond reach. In closely packed places, such as restaurants, theaters, and ferries, keep your possessions in sight, and never sling a bag over the back of your

chair: It's too easy a target. Alas, anything left visible in a car, locked or unlocked, is an open invitation, even in secluded Nantucket.

It would be rare in this region to find security staff screening all those who enter a hotel, especially if there's a restaurant on the premises, so don't relax your guard until your door is securely locked. Many areas are still so countrified that homeowners don't even lock their doors, and you'll find that most B&Bs are fairly laissez-faire; a few lack bedroom door locks altogether. If you're traveling light, it shouldn't matter, but if you're the cautious type, inquire about security measures before setting out.

Women, unfortunately, are no safer here than anywhere else, so avoid visiting deserted areas alone, even during the day. Hyannis can get a bit rowdy when its dance clubs are in full swing, and even more so when they let out. For the most part, though, this is a peaceful place, more like the 1950s, and as long as you keep your wits about you, you should be able to relax, relatively speaking.

DRIVING SAFETY Though Massachusetts is quite strict, drunk driving is a definite hazard: The police logs are full of offenses, from foolish to fatal. The best tactic is to avoid the offenders as much as possible, primarily by staying off the roads late at night. It's probably not a good idea to cover long distances at night, in any case, as there are no 24-hour gas stations to help out in case of emergency. In the event of a breakdown, drivers are usually advised to stay in the car with the doors locked until the police arrive. This is a small and friendly enough place, though, that it would probably be all right to take a chance on the kindness of strangers. Use your judgment, and err, if at all, on the side of caution.

Carjacking has yet to make an appearance on the Cape, but car theft runs high in Massachusetts as a whole, so lock your doors even if the natives never bother.

7 SPECIALIZED TRAVEL RESOURCES

In addition to the destination-specific resources listed below, please visit **Frommers.com** for additional specialized travel resources.

TRAVELERS WITH DISABILITIES

Most disabilities shouldn't stop anyone from traveling in the U.S. Thanks to provisions in the Americans with Disabilities Act, most public places are required to comply with disability-friendly regulations. Almost all public establishments (including hotels, restaurants, museums, and so on, but not including certain National Historic Landmarks), and at least some modes of public transportation provide accessible entrances and other facilities for those with disabilities.

Unfortunately, on Cape Cod and the islands, many of the historic buildings are not ADA-compliant (accessible for travelers with disabilities). Modern construction, however, is generally equipped with such amenities as ramps, and most inns and restaurants have accessible bathrooms.

GLBT TRAVELERS

Gay and lesbian travelers, singly or in pairs, will feel right at home in Provincetown, a world-renowned gay vacation capital. They should also feel comfortable wandering farther afield. This is a sophisticated, semi-urban population, and you'll rarely encounter an overtly bigoted innkeeper, shopkeeper, or restaurateur. If you do, report them to the **Massachusetts Commission Against Discrimination,** 1 Ashburton Place, Room 601, Boston, MA 02108 (© **617/727-3990**).

To avoid unpleasant situations, read between the lines of promotional literature ("fun for the whole family" may mean not much fun for you), or be blunt in stating your expectations (for example, "It will be for me and my partner, [name goes here], and we'd like a queen bed, if possible"). The descriptions of each establishment listed in this book should give some idea of their suitability and compatibility.

SENIOR TRAVEL

With relatively mild winters and splendid summers, Cape Cod and the islands are popular retirement spots. In fact, as of the 2000 U.S. Census, more than a third of the population was 55 or older. Businesses from museums to B&Bs cater to this clientele with attractive discounts, and many restaurants offer early-bird specials (smaller portions at lower prices, offered before the ordinary dinner hour).

Members of **AARP,** 601 E St. NW, Washington, DC 20049 (✆ **888/687-2277;** www.aarp.org), get discounts on hotels, airfares, and car rentals. AARP offers members a wide range of benefits, including *AARP The Magazine* and a monthly newsletter. Anyone older than 50 can join.

FAMILY TRAVEL

Basically a giant sandbox with a fringe of waves, the Cape and islands are ideal family vacation spots. A number of the larger hotels and motels offer deals whereby kids can share their parent's room for free. But beware of the fancier B&Bs: Although it's illegal for them to do so, some actively discriminate against children (see "Tips on Accommodations," later in this chapter). The kind that do are apt to be the kind that children dislike, so it's no great loss. For the most part the local tourism industry is big on serving family needs, so there's not much you'll need to do by way of advance preparation.

A Frommer's guide that provides in-depth info for families visiting the region is *Frommer's Family Vacations in the National Parks* (Wiley Publishing, Inc.), which has a large section on the Cape Cod National Seashore.

To locate accommodations, restaurants, and attractions that are particularly kid friendly, refer to the "Kids" icon throughout this guide.

STUDENT TRAVEL

Check out the **International Student Travel Confederation (ISTC;** www.istc. org) website for comprehensive travel-services information and details on how to get an **International Student Identity Card (ISIC),** which qualifies students for substantial savings on rail passes, plane tickets, entrance fees, and more. It also provides students with basic health and life insurance and a 24-hour helpline. The card is valid for a maximum of 18 months. You can apply for the card online or in person at **STA Travel** (✆ **800/781-4040** in North America; ✆ 134-782 in Australia; ✆ 087/1230-0040 in the U.K.; www. statravel.com), the biggest student travel agency in the world; check out the website to locate STA Travel offices worldwide.

If you're no longer a student but are still under 26, you can get an **International Youth Travel Card (IYTC)** from the same people, which entitles you to some discounts. **Travel CUTS** (✆ **800/592-2887;** www.travelcuts.com) offers similar services for both Canadians and U.S. residents. Irish students may prefer to turn to **USIT** (✆ **01/602-1906;** www.usit.ie), an Ireland-based specialist in student, youth, and independent travel.

TRAVELING WITH PETS

Families love to bring their pets to Cape Cod. Usually they bring dogs, but one pet-friendly cottage colony owner told me about a guest who showed up with two horses. A number of inexpensive motels on the Cape welcome dogs or set aside a few rooms for guests who bring their dog. Some of these charge a pet fee.

The most deluxe pet accommodations in the region are surely the Woof Cottages, also known as the Wharf Cottages, at Nantucket's **The Cottages at the Boat Basin** (✆ **866/838-9253;** www.the cottagesnantucket.com). You can stay with your dog or cat in specially designated units that come with plush pet beds, toys, and treats, plus a bandanna to make your dog as stylish as a Nantucket native.

In Provincetown, perhaps the Cape's dog-friendliest community, dozens of people walk their dogs down Commercial Street every day. Many motels allow pets, and dogs are welcome at several outdoor cafes.

Every town has good hiking trails where people exercise their dogs—sometimes off-leash, even though the law forbids it. Most towns don't permit dogs on the beach in peak daytime hours and/or in summer, but you can take your dog onto many beaches in early morning and evening and/or off-season. Check with the local chamber of commerce for the local rules.

Dogs are not allowed on many trails in Cape Cod National Seashore, though you may walk your dog on-leash on some of its beaches; look for signs posted with the dog rules.

Wherever you go with your pet, don't forget to clean up. Some beaches and trails have plastic-bag dispensers and trash cans for that purpose.

8 SUSTAINABLE TOURISM

Nature's beauty is one of the great assets of Cape Cod and the islands. Besides Cape Cod National Seashore, there are numerous protected areas run by state and local authorities—that's why sustainable tourism is so important to this area. You will find that many lodging establishments, particularly those on Martha's Vineyard and Nantucket, include information in each hotel room about steps the hotel is taking to be more environmentally responsible and how you can help. Typical steps are to hang up towels if you do not need them to be changed every day. Water is precious on Cape Cod and the islands because of the limits of the region's sole source aquifer. For that reason, major attempts are made to conserve water. Many towns go into voluntary water restrictive measures every summer. For the visitor, that means that unless you request water in a restaurant, you might not be served it automatically. The water saved is not just the water in the glass but also the amount of water it takes to wash the glass.

Several towns on Cape Cod take great measures to educate their citizens about not using too much fertilizer and pesticides on lawns. A true "Cape Cod" lawn does not use any fertilizer at all. You will see examples of **xeriscaping** around Cape Cod, particularly in Falmouth, in front of the town hall. Xeriscaping is a method of landscaping that uses little to no water or fertilizer. You will see a colorful mélange of beach grasses and other sustainable plants that require little to no care. This type of landscaping is also popular in the Outer Cape towns, where water is also at a premium.

Very little of the Cape is sewered, and the towns are all engaged in discussions about how to hook more homes up to sewers in order to protect the water quality in the region's bays and estuaries. This will likely be the largest issue in the region in the coming years.

Sustainable tourism is conscientious travel. It means being careful with the environments you explore, and respecting the communities you visit. Two overlapping components of sustainable travel are **ecotourism** and **ethical tourism. The International Ecotourism Society (TIES)** defines ecotourism as responsible travel to natural areas that conserves the environment and improves the well-being of local people. TIES suggests that ecotourists follow these principles:

- Minimize environmental impact.
- Build environmental and cultural awareness and respect.
- Provide positive experiences for both visitors and hosts.
- Provide direct financial benefits for conservation and local people.
- Raise sensitivity to host countries' political, environmental, and social climates.
- Support international human rights and labor agreements.

You can find some eco-friendly travel tips and statistics, as well as touring companies and associations—listed by destination under "Your Travel Choice"—at the **TIES**

General Resources for Green Travel

In addition to the resources for the Cape and islands listed above, the following websites provide valuable, wide-ranging information on sustainable travel. For a list of even more sustainable resources, as well as tips and explanations on how to travel greener, visit www.frommers.com/planning.

- **Responsible Travel** (www.responsibletravel.com) is a great source of sustainable travel ideas; the site is run by a spokesperson for ethical tourism in the travel industry. **Sustainable Travel International** (www.sustainable travelinternational.org) promotes ethical tourism practices and manages an extensive directory of sustainable properties and tour operators around the world.

- In the U.K., **Tourism Concern** (www.tourismconcern.org.uk) works to reduce social and environmental problems connected to tourism. The **Association of Independent Tour Operators** (**AITO;** www.aito.co.uk) is a group of specialist operators leading the field in making holidays sustainable.

- In Canada, **www.greenlivingonline.com** offers extensive content on how to travel sustainably, including a travel and transport section and profiles of the best green shops and services in Toronto, Vancouver, and Calgary.

- In Australia, the national body that sets guidelines and standards for ecotourism is **Ecotourism Australia** (www.ecotourism.org.au). **The Green Directory** (www.thegreendirectory.com.au), **Green Pages** (www.thegreen pages.com.au), and **Eco Directory** (www.ecodirectory.com.au) offer sustainable travel tips and directories of green businesses.

- **Carbonfund** (www.carbonfund.org), **TerraPass** (www.terrapass.com), provides info on "carbon offsetting," or offsetting the greenhouse gas emitted during flights.

- **Greenhotels** (www.greenhotels.com) recommends green-rated member hotels around the world that fulfill the company's stringent environmental requirements. **Environmentally Friendly Hotels** (www.environmentally friendlyhotels.com) offers more green accommodation ratings. The **Hotel Association of Canada** (www.greenkeyglobal.com) has a Green Key Eco-Rating Program, which audits the environmental performance of Canadian hotels, motels, and resorts.

- **Sustain Lane** (www.sustainlane.com) lists sustainable eating and drinking choices around the U.S.; also visit **www.eatwellguide.org** for tips on eating sustainably in the U.S. and Canada.

- For information on animal-friendly issues throughout the world, visit **Tread Lightly** (www.treadlightly.org). For information about the ethics of swimming with dolphins, visit the **Whale and Dolphin Conservation Society** (www.wdcs.org).

- **Volunteer International** (www.volunteerinternational.org) has a list of questions to help you determine the intentions and the nature of a volunteer program. For general info on volunteer travel, visit **www.volunteer abroad.com** and www.idealist.org.

website, **www.ecotourism.org.** While much of the focus of ecotourism is about reducing impacts on the natural environment, ethical tourism concentrates on ways to preserve and enhance local economies and communities, regardless of location. You can embrace ethical tourism by staying at a locally owned hotel or shopping at a store that employs local workers and sells locally produced goods.

9 SPECIAL INTEREST TRIPS AND TOURS

A number of organizations, outfitters, and tour companies offer special trips to Cape Cod, Nantucket, and Martha's Vineyard.

BIKING

Several biking tour companies offer bike trips on Cape Cod and the islands. My favorite, **Bike Riders** (② **800/473-7040;** www.bikeriderstours.com), offers a 6-day "island-hopping" trip to Martha's Vineyard and Nantucket in which you stay at top hotels on the islands and eat at terrific restaurants. After biking all day, you've earned the pampering! Trips are in June, July, and August and cost about $2,500.

FISHING

Orvis Fly-Fishing School, based at the Chatham Bars Inn in Chatham (② **800/235-9763;** www.orvis.com), offers 2-day fly-fishing seminars on the Cape for about $430.

HIKING

Every town on Cape Cod has open space with excellent hiking trails. The local chapter of Audubon, at **Wellfleet Bay Wildlife Sanctuary,** in South Wellfleet (② **508/349-2615;** www.massaudubon.org), offers hikes of all lengths, including a half-day trip to Monomoy, an island and bird sanctuary off Chatham.

KAYAKING

Kayaking has become almost as popular as biking on the Cape and islands. Depending on your skill level, there are dozens of estuaries and inlets to explore, as well as more challenging waterways to conquer. For example, you might enjoy a meandering paddle trip through the estuaries of Nauset Marsh or a trip across Vineyard Sound from Woods Hole to Martha's Vineyard, which is a 4-mile trip through sometimes choppy waters. You'll need a sea kayak for that trip. A number of outfits based on Cape Cod offer kayaking trips and lessons. **Eric Gustafson** runs guided kayak tours (② **508/349-1429;** www.funseekers.org) of kettle ponds and tidal rivers from Chatham to Truro. **Cape Cod Kayak** (② **508/563-9377;** www.capecodkayak.com) offers ecotours on waterways mainly on the Upper Cape. **Eastern Mountain Sports,** in Hyannis (② **508/362-8690;** www.ems.com), sponsors trips mainly in the Mid Cape area. **Goose Hummuck,** in Orleans (② **508/255-2620;** www.goose.com), runs kayak trips mainly in the Lower Cape. **Cape Outback Adventures,** in Wellfleet (② **508/349-1617**), runs kayak trips in the Lower and Outer Cape. Day-long trips cost anywhere from $40 to $70.

For more information on escorted general-interest tours, including questions to ask before booking your trip, see **www.frommers.com/planning.**

CELLPHONES

Verizon seems to have the best cellphone coverage of all the carriers, but you will see numerous cellphone towers and most of the Cape has pretty good cellphone service. Exceptions are Woods Hole and the Outer Cape, particularly Truro and Provincetown.

Just because your cellphone works at home doesn't mean it'll work everywhere in the U.S. (thanks to our nation's fragmented cellphone system). It's a good bet that your phone will work in major cities, but take a look at your wireless company's coverage map on its website before heading out; T-Mobile, Sprint, and Nextel are particularly weak in rural areas. If you need to stay in touch at a destination where you know your phone won't work, **rent** a phone that does from **InTouch USA** (© 800/872-7626; www.intouch global.com) or a rental car location, but beware that you'll pay $1 a minute or more for airtime.

If you're not from the U.S., you'll be appalled at the poor reach of the **GSM (Global System for Mobile Communications) wireless network,** which is used by much of the rest of the world. Your phone will probably work in most major U.S. cities; it definitely won't work in many rural areas. To see where GSM phones work in the U.S., check out www.t-mobile. com/coverage. And you may or may not be able to send SMS (text messaging) home.

TELEPHONES

Generally hotel surcharges on long-distance and local calls are astronomical, so you're better off using your **cellphone** or a **public pay telephone.** Many convenience groceries and packaging services sell **prepaid calling cards** in denominations up to $50; for international visitors these can be the least expensive way to call home.

Many public pay phones at airports now accept American Express, MasterCard, and Visa credit cards. **Local calls** made from pay phones in most locales cost either 25¢ or 35¢ (no pennies, please).

Most long-distance and international calls can be dialed directly from any phone. **For calls within the United States and to Canada,** dial © 1 followed by the area code and the seven-digit number. **For other international calls,** dial © 011 followed by the country code, city code, and the number you are calling.

Calls to area codes **800, 888, 877,** and **866** are toll-free. However, calls to area codes **700** and **900** (chat lines, bulletin boards, "dating" services, and so on) can be very expensive—usually a charge of 95¢ to $3 or more per minute, and they sometimes have minimum charges that can run as high as $15 or more.

For **reversed-charge or collect calls,** and for person-to-person calls, dial © 0 (the digit), then the area code and number; an operator will come on the line, and you should specify whether you are calling collect, person-to-person, or both. If your operator-assisted call is international, ask for the overseas operator.

For **local directory assistance** ("information"), dial © **411;** for long-distance information, dial © **1,** then the appropriate area code and 555-1212.

VOICE-OVER INTERNET PROTOCOL (VOIP)

If you have Web access while traveling, consider a broadband-based telephone service (in technical terms, **Voice-over Internet protocol,** or **VoIP**), such as Skype (www.skype.com) or Vonage (www.vonage. com), which allows you to make free international calls from your laptop or in a cybercafe. Neither service requires the people you're calling to also have that service or islands. There is usually a half-hour maximum limit for use.

INTERNET & E-MAIL

You won't have trouble finding a place to log on and get Internet access anywhere on the Cape and islands. Two towns, Falmouth and Orleans, have set up Wi-Fi zones in their downtown areas, so anyone can log on in a moment's notice.

Many lodgings either have Wi-Fi or a computer that their guests can use to surf the Web. If all else fails, you will be able to log on from any local library on the Cape

Without Your Own Computer

To find cybercafes, check **www.cyber captive.com** and **www.cybercafe.com**. Though they are rare on the Cape and islands, you will find good ones in Provincetown and on Nantucket. And, as mentioned above, almost every library on the Cape has free Internet access.

We list some of the Cape's cybercafes; see section 1, "Fast Facts: Cape Cod & the Islands," in chapter 11.

11 TIPS ON ACCOMMODATIONS

The listings in this book feature a range of summer rates for a room with double occupancy. Keep in mind that this figure does not take into account the state and local tax, which is 9.7%. Prices off-season are typically discounted by about 20% to 30%, sometimes more.

Virtually every town on the Cape has lodgings to suit every taste and budget. The essential trick is to secure reservations months in advance for the peak season of July through August (June and Sept are getting crowded, too). You can't count on luck; in fact, unless you're just planning a day trip, you probably shouldn't even visit at the height of summer unless you've prearranged a place to stay.

Accommodations range from sprawling, full-facility resorts to cozy little B&Bs with room for only a handful of guests. The price differential, surprisingly enough, may not be that great. A room at a particularly exquisite inn might run more than a modern hotel room with every imaginable amenity.

Because there are hundreds of lodging establishments of every stripe throughout the Cape and islands, I've focused only on those with special qualities: superb facilities, for example, or especially friendly and

helpful hosts. I've personally visited every place listed in this guide, but worthy new inns—as well as resurrected old ones—are constantly popping up.

For tips on surfing for hotel deals online, visit **www.frommers.com/planning.**

Reservations Services Several reservations services cover the region, but do your due diligence: it's "buyer beware" when it comes to such terms as "water view" or "beachfront" (Provincetown's in-town beach, for instance, is quite scenic for strolls, but a bit too close to an active harbor to make for pleasant swimming).

Some inns and hotels offer special packages, which they may or may not list, so always inquire. Most require a 2-night minimum on weekends, 3 or even 5 if it's a holiday weekend. All provide free parking, although in a congested area such as Provincetown you may have to play musical spaces.

FAMILY-FRIENDLY CHOICES Although all lodgings in the state are prohibited by law from discriminating on the basis of age, a lot of the fancier, fussier B&Bs will be none too happy if you show up with a young child or infant in tow. You might not be too happy either, spending your entire vacation attending to damage control. It can't hurt to inquire—perhaps anonymously, before calling to book—about an establishment's attitude toward children and its suitability for their needs. If you get the impression that your child won't be welcome, there's no point in pushing it: The child, sensing correctly that he/she is not wanted, is likely to exceed your worst expectations. If, on the other hand, you know your child to be a reliable model of "company behavior," you might want to risk an unannounced arrival.

It's probably easier from the outset, though, to seek out places that like having kids around. Motels are always a safe bet (it's what they're designed for), and the descriptions provided in this book should indicate other likely spots.

A popular family option—but again, you must make plans as much as a year in advance—is to rent a cottage or house by the week, or even month (see below).

RENTING A COTTAGE OR HOUSE

Families planning a Cape Cod vacation, especially families with young children, should consider renting a cottage or house rather than choosing an inn or hotel. The trick to finding a great rental can be summed up in two words: *Book early.* Start calling Realtors in January and February (if not sooner—some vacationers who return every summer book a year in advance). If you can visit earlier in the year to check out a few places, that helps, but if not, you may be able to view choices on a Realtor's website or see photos that the Realtor can mail to you.

Believe it or not, there are parts of Cape Cod that are not close to a beach. When talking to a Realtor, ask specifically for rentals on the water, with views of the water, or within a half-mile of a beach. You'll have a better Cape Cod vacation if you are within walking distance of a beach.

Prices on rentals vary, but they are always much lower off-season. Depending

on the rental, off-season could mean late June or even late August, so ask what the cutoff dates are for high-season prices. Location is the single biggest factor in determining price: A two-bedroom cottage could cost $800 a week in Dennis or $8,000 a week on Nantucket. Tell your Realtor your price range and what you are looking for, and he or she will select appropriate listings for you to choose from.

Each town's chamber of commerce can put you in touch with local Realtors. You can also call the **Cape Cod & Islands Association of Realtors** (© **508/442-0006;** www.cciaor.com) for a complete list of Realtors in the area.

Here is a list of good Realtors with rentals in different regions of the Cape and on the islands: **Real Estate Associates,** in North Falmouth (© **508/563-7173**); **Kinlin/Grover Realtors,** in Sandwich (© **508/362-2723**); **Bay Village Realty,** in Brewster (© **508/896-6200**); **Duarte/Downey Real Estate,** in Truro (© **508/349-7588**); **Linda R. Bassett Vacation Rentals,** on Martha's Vineyard (© **508/627-9201**); and **Nantucket Real Estate Co.,** on Nantucket (© **800/228-4070** or 508/228-2530).

CAMPING A number of state parks and recreation areas maintain campgrounds; for a full listing for the state, contact the **Department of Conservation and Recreation,** Division of Forests and Parks (© **617/727-3180**).

The largest such area on the Cape is the 2,000-acre **Nickerson State Park** (© **508/896-3491**), offering over 400 campsites. The Massachusetts Audubon Society offers limited tenting at its 1,000-acre **Wellfleet Bay Wildlife Sanctuary** (© **508/349-2615**).

Note: Camping is expressly forbidden within the Cape Cod National Seashore (with the exception of a few "grandfathered" commercial campgrounds) and on Nantucket. Seashore camping is not allowed on

House-Swapping

House-swapping is becoming a more popular and viable means of travel; you stay in their place, they stay in yours, and you both get an authentic and personal view of the area, the opposite of the escapist retreat that many hotels offer. Try **HomeLink International** (www.homelink.org), the largest and oldest home-swapping organization, founded in 1952, with over 11,000 listings worldwide ($75 for a yearly membership). **HomeExchange.com** ($50 for 6,000 listings) and **InterVac.com** ($70 for over 10,000 listings) are also reliable.

Martha's Vineyard either. The Vineyard has one campground, called **Martha's Vineyard Family Campground,** on 92 Edgartown Road (© **508/693-3772**), which is in the middle of the island and far from a beach.

A partial list of private campgrounds that belong to the **Massachusetts Association of Campground Owners** appears in the Massachusetts Office of Travel and Tourism's free *Getaway Guide* (© **800/227-MASS** [6277] or 617/973-8500).

SURFING FOR HOTELS

In addition to the online travel booking sites **Travelocity, Expedia, Orbitz, Priceline,** and **Hotwire,** you can book hotels through **Hotels.com, Quikbook.com**, and **Travelaxe** (www.travelaxe.net).

HotelChatter.com is a daily webzine offering smart coverage and critiques of hotels worldwide. Go to **TripAdvisor.com** or **HotelShark.com** for helpful independent consumer reviews of hotels and resort properties.

It's a good idea to **get a confirmation number** and **make a printout** of any online booking transaction.

SAVING ON YOUR HOTEL ROOM

The **rack rate** is the maximum rate that a hotel charges for a room. Hardly anybody pays this price, however, except in high season or on holidays. To lower the cost of your room:

- **Ask about special rates or other discounts.** You may qualify for corporate, student, military, senior, frequent-flier, trade-union, or other discounts.
- **Dial direct.** When booking a room in a chain hotel, you'll often get a better deal by calling the individual hotel's reservation desk rather than the chain's main number.
- **Book online.** Many hotels offer Internet-only discounts or supply rooms to Priceline, Hotwire, or Expedia at rates much lower than the ones you can get through the hotel itself.
- **Remember the law of supply and demand.** Resort hotels are most crowded and therefore most expensive on weekends, so discounts are usually available for midweek stays. Business hotels in downtown locations are busiest during the week, so you can expect big discounts over the weekend.
- **Look into group or long-stay discounts.** If you come as part of a large group, you should be able to negotiate a bargain rate. Likewise, if you're planning a long stay (at least 5 days), you might qualify for a discount. As a general rule, expect 1 night free after a 7-night stay.
- **Sidestep excess surcharges and hidden costs.** Many hotels have the unpleasant practice of nickel-and-diming their guests with opaque surcharges. When you book a room, ask what is

3

Value   Hostel Hospitality on the Cape & Islands

Hostelling International/Cape Cod (📞 617/718-7990; http://capecod.hiusa.org/index.php) offers low-cost seasonal accommodations in dorms (and a few private rooms), generally from late spring to sometime in September, at four sites on the Cape and Islands: Martha's Vineyard, Mid Cape (Eastham), Nantucket, and Truro. Rates vary but range from $25 to $35 per person per night in a dorm room for nonmembers. The private rooms (when available) cost from $125 to $200 per night. HI membership is $28 a year for adults, $18 for adults 55 and over, and free for 17 and under. Note that there's a limit on the length of stay. You can also buy daily memberships at the Cape Cod hostels for $3.

HI/AYH properties are in Eastham, just off the bike trail; in a former Coast Guard station overlooking Ballston Beach in Truro; adjoining the 4,000-acre Manuel F. Correllus State Forest in West Tisbury on Martha's Vineyard; and in an 1874 lifesaving station on Surfside Beach on Nantucket.

If you haven't been to a hostel before (or it's been awhile since you did the backpack/Eurailpass adventure), here's some basic info about the Cape Cod hostels:

- Continental breakfast is included with the room rate.
- Each hostel has a fully equipped kitchen so you can prepare meals.
- Linens, pillows, and blankets are provided free of charge (sleeping bags are not permitted).
- There is no minimum stay required.
- Check-in is between 3 and 10pm.
- No smoking or alcohol is permitted.
- Nonmembers may either buy a daily membership for $3 or become a Hostelling International member.
- Once checked in, there is 24-hour access.

included in the room rate, and what is extra. Avoid dialing direct from hotel phones, which can have exorbitant rates. And don't be tempted by the room's minibar offerings. Finally, ask about local taxes and service charges, which can increase the cost of a room by 15% or more.

- **Book an efficiency.** A room with a kitchenette allows you to shop for groceries and cook your own meals. This is a big money saver, especially for families on long stays.
- **Consider enrolling in hotel "frequent-stay" programs,** which are upping the ante lately to win the loyalty

of repeat customers. Frequent guests can now accumulate points or credits to earn free hotel nights, airline miles, in-room amenities, merchandise, tickets to concerts and events, and discounts on sporting facilities. Perks are awarded not only by many chain hotels and motels (Hilton HHonors, Marriott Rewards, Wyndham ByRequest, to name a few), but also some individual inns and B&Bs.

LANDING THE BEST ROOM

Somebody has to get the best room in the house. It might as well be you. You can start by joining the hotel's frequent-guest program, which may make you eligible for upgrades. Always ask about a corner room. They're often larger and quieter, with more windows and light, and they often cost the same as standard rooms. When you make your reservation, ask if the hotel is renovating; if it is, request a room away from the construction. If you're a light sleeper, request a quiet room away from vending or ice machines, elevators, restaurants, bars, and discos. Ask for a room that has most recently been renovated or redecorated.

If you aren't happy with your room when you arrive, ask for another one. Most lodgings will be willing to accommodate you.

In resort areas, particularly in warm climates, ask the following questions before you book a room:

- What's the view like? Cost-conscious travelers may be willing to pay less for a back room facing the parking lot, especially if they don't plan to spend much time in their room.
- Does the room have air-conditioning or ceiling fans? Do the windows open? If they do, and the nighttime entertainment takes place alfresco, you may want to find out when show time is over.
- What's included in the price? Your room may be moderately priced, but if you're charged for beach chairs, towels, sports equipment, and other amenities, you could end up spending more than you bargained for.
- How far is the room from the beach and other amenities? If it's far, is there transportation to and from the beach, and is it free?

4

Suggested Itineraries

You can easily see a sampling of the highlights on the Cape and islands in a week, and you'll still have many hours for lounging around on the beach, a don't-miss activity. Two weeks will enable you to see all the most interesting attractions in the region plus have even more time to spend with your family. It's best to plan a leisurely visit that allows plenty of opportunities to try a different beach every day, to poke around antiques shops, or to explore marshes by kayak.

Cape Cod does not have a very convenient public transportation system, so you will have to drive your own car to see the sites. Take traffic into account when planning your itineraries. Getting an early start on the road is critical if you are staying in Falmouth, say, and want to drive to the Outer Cape to check out the Cape Cod National Seashore. Avoid midday drives on such roads as Route 28 from Falmouth to Dennis; it tends to be loaded with traffic.

Both Martha's Vineyard and Nantucket have excellent public transportation systems, and when you visit the islands you can leave your car behind. On both islands, and occasionally on Cape Cod, you can explore on bicycle; I'll include the must-ride bike paths.

Staying in a central area on the Cape is a good strategy for exploring the peninsula. Spending a couple of nights in Provincetown or on the islands of Nantucket and Martha's Vineyard is also a real treat.

There are 15 towns on Cape Cod, six towns on Martha's Vineyard, and one main town on Nantucket. The itineraries below do not include visits to every town, but you may find yourself stopping between recommended attractions for, say, refreshment at a quaint ice-cream parlor. The Cape is full of discoveries for those who wander off the beaten track.

No matter which itinerary you choose, you'll want to include some unstructured time on the beach or at one of the Cape's many freshwater ponds, because enjoying the outdoors is really what the Cape is all about.

1 THE REGIONS IN BRIEF

Newcomers—known locally as "wash-ashores"—invariably struggle with the terms "Upper" and "Lower," used to describe, respectively, the westernmost and easternmost sections of the Cape. The distinction is thought to allude to the longitude, which decreases as you head east.

Many find it helpful to use the analogy of the "arm" of Cape Cod, with the Upper Cape towns of Sandwich, Falmouth, Bourne, and Mashpee forming the upper arm; Chatham the elbow of the Lower Cape; and Provincetown the "fist." On Martha's Vineyard, similar confusion reigns over what's meant by "up-island" and "down-island." Down-island consists of the touristy port towns of Vineyard Haven, Oak Bluffs, and Edgartown. In the summer months, locals try to stay up-island, avoiding down-island at all costs.

Even the term "land" may be a bit misleading; the Cape and islands are actually just heaps of sand, without bedrock. Described geologically as "terminal moraine," they're what remains of the grit heaved and dumped by the motion of massive glaciers that finally receded some 12,000 years ago, leaving a legacy of "kettle ponds"—steep-sided freshwater pools formed when sharp fragments of the glacier were left to melt in place. Under the relentless onslaught of storms and tides, the landmass's outlines are still subject to constant change and eventual erasure.

The modern landscape is vastly different from what was visible a century ago. Virtually all the trees represent new growth. The settlers, in their rush to build houses and ships and to fuel hearths and factories, plundered all the lumber. Were it not for the recession during the late 19th century, you'd be looking at turnip fields and "poverty grass"—so called because it will grow anywhere, needing next to nothing to survive. Instead the Lower Cape and Mid Cape are now lushly forested, and if the tree cover gets spindly along the Outer Cape, it's the result of battery by salt winds rather than human depredation.

The islands also show the effects of the ocean winds—predominantly those out of the southwest. Harbor towns and down-island areas enjoy a canopy of trees, and the more exposed portions consist primarily of grassy sand plains and moors.

The 15 towns on Cape Cod have quite distinct personalities to match the varied landscape. Few similarities exist, for instance, among rural Truro, rowdy Hyannis, and historic Sandwich Village.

Most frequent vacationers to Cape Cod return to the same village every year, rarely venturing beyond their chosen town's lines. But the resourceful visitor who explores the

The shoreline has eroded about a full mile since Colonial times, and current scientific predictions give the Cape and islands a projected life span of as much as 5,000 more years—or as little as 500. Not to make light of the situation, but this is all the more reason to enjoy them while you can!

region, perhaps driving the Old King's Highway (Rte. 6A), shopping in Chatham, beaching it at the National Seashore, and checking out an island or two, will get an eyeful of the area's diversity.

Visitors may be confused by the similar names of towns on the Cape, particularly in the Mid Cape area. When you book a room, it may be helpful to understand these distinctions. Barnstable County consists of the 15 towns on Cape Cod, all of which are made up of individual villages. The largest town on Cape Cod is called Barnstable, and it is made up of eight villages: Cotuit, Osterville, Marstons Mills, Centerville, Hyannis, Hyannis Port, West Barnstable, and (is there an echo in here?) Barnstable Village.

Despite the similar names, towns and even villages on the Cape retain their distinct characters. For instance, picturesque little Barnstable Village (along Rte. 6A, the historic Old King's Hwy.) couldn't be more different from Hyannis (off Rte. 28), transportation hub and home of the mall. Both are villages in the town of Barnstable. In the same vein, the sleepy, rural village of West Barnstable (off Rte. 6A) doesn't have much in common with wealthy, preppy Osterville (off Rte. 28 on the coast). Other notable villages in Barnstable include Cotuit (off Rte. 28; historic and quaint), Marstons Mills (off Rte. 28, but inland; mainly residential), Centerville (off Rte. 28; beachy, yet with some commercial sprawl), and Hyannis Port (off Rte. 28, on the coast; a residential neighborhood made famous by the Kennedys).

A number of other villages and towns are notable for their unique characteristics. Woods Hole—where bohemians and scientists coexist in a bustling ferry port—is a village in the town of Falmouth, whose downtown has a pleasant Main Street and picture-postcard town green. Chatham and Osterville both have main streets that are destinations for shoppers seeking expensive, quality wares. Gay-friendly Provincetown has a colorful main street with great people-watching opportunities. Sandwich may well be the quaintest town; Wellfleet, the most artsy. West Barnstable, Barnstable, Yarmouth Port, Dennis, and Brewster are all prototypical New England villages along the historic Old King's Highway. Of these, Dennis Village has the most going on, with a museum, cinema, and playhouse all in one historic complex. The Outer Cape towns (Eastham, Wellfleet, Truro, and Provincetown) have the National Seashore beaches, but many families prefer the accessibility of the villages on Nantucket Sound: West Dennis and Harwich Port offer pretty beaches with calm surf and warmer waters.

On the islands, location is also an important factor. Most visitors to Nantucket choose lodging in town, where everything is within walking distance. On Martha's Vineyard, down-island towns (Vineyard Haven, Oak Bluffs, and Edgartown) host the majority of the action—shops, restaurants, and multitudes of tourists. If a serene escape from the grind is what you seek, you may want to be up-island (West Tisbury; Chilmark, including the village of Menemsha; or Aquinnah), but you'll need a car—or a passion for biking—to enjoy these locations.

Socially the towns of the Cape and islands have their differences, too. Older, more protected communities, such as Sandwich, Falmouth, and Edgartown, appeal to traditionalists, while 20-somethings and adventurous types of all ages seem to feel more at home in open-minded, forward-thinking settings such as Wellfleet or Provincetown. Families are sure to have a fabulous time everywhere on the Cape and islands, because splashing surf and expanses of sand are ubiquitous.

Route 28 east of Hyannis, an eyesore of tacky strip-mall development, represents a warning of what the future holds unless residents continue to clamp down on zoning. Though the pressures of development are unrelenting, Cape lovers have done a pretty good job, so far, of fending off more egregious offenders. The Cape Cod National Seashore—though hotly protested when it was instituted in 1961—serves as a living reminder of the glory that could have been lost, or perhaps reserved solely for the enjoyment of the ultrarich.

Today it is the unspoiled natural beauty and historical charm of the area that attracts visitors. Cape Cod's yearly haul of 17 million visitors infuses the region with more than $700 million in revenues. Tourism has been the leading business sector since the late 19th century and is likely to remain so for centuries to come.

2 CAPE COD & THE ISLANDS IN 1 WEEK

This route gives you an overview of the highlights of the Cape, Nantucket, and Martha's Vineyard. You'll see the major attractions, such as the Heritage Museums and Gardens, in Sandwich; the Shining Sea Bikeway, in Falmouth; and Commercial Street, in Provincetown; plus the islands. It's a whirlwind tour, but builds in some downtime for relaxing. See p. 66 for a map of this itinerary.

Day ❶: Arrive in Falmouth

After arriving in **Falmouth** ★★★, the second largest of Cape Cod's 15 towns, take a bike ride down the 4-mile **Shining Sea Bikeway** ★★★ (p. 94) from Falmouth center to the village of Woods Hole to get a feel for the coastline. The bike path offers views of Martha's Vineyard and passes saltwater ponds and marshland. **Woods Hole** ★★★ (p. 91) is the home of several world-renowned science institutions, including **Woods Hole Oceanographic Institution.** Check out the fishing fleet on the Woods Hole dock, the houseboats in Great Harbor, and the free **aquarium** ★, where you can watch seals being fed.

Day ❷: Day Trip to Martha's Vineyard

Hop a ferry from Woods Hole or Falmouth Inner Harbor for the 30- to 45-minute trip to Vineyard Haven or Oak Bluffs on **Martha's Vineyard.** While on the Vineyard, you can take a quick stroll around the three down-island towns of

Oak Bluffs ★★★, Edgartown ★★★, and Vineyard Haven ★★, which are connected by frequent shuttle buses. In Oak Bluffs, you'll want to see the **gingerbread houses** ★★★ (p. 256), which are Carpenter othic–style homes, built in the late 19th century when the area was the site of frequent revival meetings. The cottages surround the **Trinity Park Tabernacle** ★★ (p. 290), an elegant open-air church.

Day ❸: Sandwich ★★★

You'll need a full day to explore the town of **Sandwich,** and you'll need an early start. In the morning, visit the **Heritage Museums and Gardens** ★★★ (p. 79), near **Shawme Pond,** a short drive from the center of town. After taking a few hours to enjoy Heritage's unique collections and extensive gardens, stop at the **Sandwich Glass Museum** ★★ (p. 80), in the center of town, to learn about this fascinating industry and to watch glass artisans in action. End your day at **Sandy**

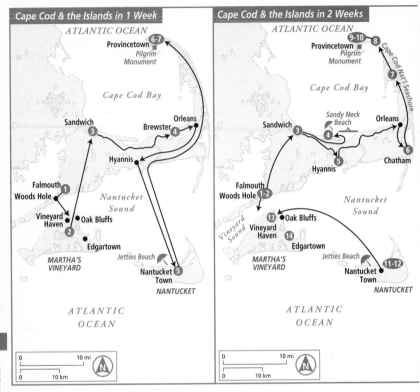

Neck Beach ★★★ (p. 77), one of the Cape's most beautiful beaches.

Day ❹: The Old King's Highway (Rte. 6A), Brewster & Orleans

Drive up the **Old King's Highway/Route 6A** from Sandwich to Brewster, checking out interesting stores along the way, particularly the fine antiques shops. Spend the rest of the morning visiting one of Brewster's bay beaches, such as **Breakwater Beach** ★★ (p. 147), during low tide, and explore the flats, the miles of exposed beach left when the tide recedes. In the afternoon, head out from **Rock Harbor** in **Orleans** ★★ on an afternoon charter fishing trip (p. 173).

Day ❺: A Day Trip to Nantucket

Take the 1-hour fast ferry from Hyannis, either the Hy-Line or the Steamship Authority, to arrive in Nantucket by lunchtime. Buy sandwiches in town, and bike to **Jetties Beach** ★★★ (p. 233) for a picnic lunch. Explore several historic sites on foot. The **Whaling Museum** ★★★ is a must. Other interesting sites are the **Jethro Coffin House** ★★ (p. 235), Nantucket's oldest house, and the **Hadwen House** ★★ (p. 235), an example of the town's 19th-century prosperity.

Day ❻: Whale-Watching

It's tough to take in everything **Provincetown** ★★★ has to offer in 1 day, so I've

An Outdoor Lover's Tour of Cape Cod

ATLANTIC OCEAN

Provincetown ⑦

Wellfleet

Audubon's Wellfleet Bay
Wildlife Sanctuary ⑥

Cape Cod Bay

Great
Marsh ④
Barnstable

S. Dennis ③ R. C.
Nickerson
State Park

Falmouth ①
Woods Hole ② Washburn
Island

Monomoy Island ⑤
Wildlife Refuge

Nantucket Sound

MARTHA'S
VINEYARD

NANTUCKET

ATLANTIC
OCEAN

0   10 mi
0   10 km

Cape Cod for Families

ATLANTIC OCEAN

Provincetown

Cape Cod Nat'l Seashore ⑦

Cape Cod Bay

③ ② Sandwich
Cape Cod Museum
of Natural History

⑥ Brewster

Mashpee ④
Cape Cod Children's
Museum

⑤ Yarmouth

Falmouth ①

Nantucket Sound

0   5 mi
0   5 km

Nantucket & Martha's Vineyard Tour

Falmouth

Oak Bluffs ④ MARTHA'S
VINEYARD Nantucket Sound

Menemsha ⑦ ⑤ Edgartown

Aquinnah ⑥ South
Beach

Wauwinet

Nantucket ① ②
Town
③ Sconset

Surfside
Surfside NANTUCKET

0   5 mi
0   5 km

ATLANTIC
OCEAN

given it 2. Staying overnight for a couple of nights will give you enough time to take in this multifaceted and unique town. One must is a **whale-watch** on the **Dolphin Fleet** ★★ (p. 210), a half-day adventure out to **Stellwagen Bank** to see the magnificent ritual of whales feeding in their natural habitat. You'll be tired and hungry after the boat ride. Wander down **Commercial Street,** stopping at shops along the way, to choose a restaurant for dinner, preferably one on the water with a sunset view.

Day ⑦: Provincetown

Your second day in Provincetown should include a trip to the **Pilgrim Monument**

& Provincetown Museum ★★ (p. 211). Climb the 116 steps of the monument to get a bird's-eye view of the tip of the Cape, the curling spit of sand bordered by marshes and massive dunes. The museum gives a great overview of the history of the town. Adventurous bike riders will want to take a couple of hours to bike the **Province Lands Trail** ★★, which winds its way past marshland and over dunes. Take a sunset sail on the **Bay Lady II** ★ (p. 209), a handsome schooner, before settling in for another good meal at one of Provincetown's fine restaurants.

Two weeks on the Cape and islands gives you ample time for a relaxing family vacation that takes in a number of the sites. You'll get to take a leisurely drive down the Old King's Highway, explore art galleries in Provincetown, listen to a town band concert in Chatham, and even take a kayak trip in Barnstable's Great Marsh. See p. 66 for a map of this itinerary.

Day ❶: Falmouth ★★★

Start your tour of the Cape and islands in **Falmouth,** where you'll need a couple of days to see all the sites. Bike down the **Shining Sea Bikeway** ★★★ (p. 94) to the village of **Woods Hole** ★★★, a fishing village and world-renowned science center. Visit the aquarium and take a 90-minute discovery cruise aboard **OceanQuest** ★★ (p. 87), a fun, science-filled boat cruise. Wander through the free **Spohr Gardens** (p. 96), in Quissett, near Woods Hole.

Day ❷: Sailing in Vineyard Sound

Spend the morning at **Falmouth Heights Beach** ★★★ (p. 92), and then head to **Grews Pond** ★★ (p. 93), a fresh-water pond in **Goodwill Park,** for swimming and a picnic lunch. Take a sunset cruise around Vineyard Sound on the *Liberte* ★★ (p. 94), a 74-foot, three-masted schooner out of **Falmouth Inner Harbor.**

Day ❸: Sandwich ★★★

Spend several hours exploring the **Heritage Museums and Gardens** ★★★ (p. 79), in Sandwich. Check out **Sandy Neck Beach** ★★★ (p. 77), one of the Cape's best beaches. On the way home, stop for ice cream at **Twin Acres Ice Cream Shoppe** (p. 85), an ice-cream shop out of another century.

Day ❹: Kayak Trip to Sandy Neck

Exploring estuaries of the Cape by kayak is a great way to get away from the crowds. A trip around the **Great Marsh** in Barnstable and over to **Sandy Neck** (p. 77), the 7-mile peninsula that extends from Sandwich, can take a couple of hours or most of a day, depending on how much you want to do. Experienced kayakers will want to paddle out to the tip of Sandy Neck, where there's an isolated 19th-century summer community, complete with a lighthouse and a couple dozen simple cottages.

Day ❺: A Drive up Route 6A, a Trip to Hyannis

The **John F. Kennedy Hyannis Museum** (p. 119) is one of the most popular attractions on the Cape. Visit it first thing in the morning, and then walk around **Hyannis Harbor,** which, as part of a new renovation, has a number of small crafts shacks where artists demonstrate and sell their wares. Drive over to the north side of the Cape to explore the **Old King's Highway/ Route 6A,** which stretches from Sandwich to Orleans. The road hasn't changed much since the 19th century, when it was a stagecoach route. There's great shopping, especially antiquing, on Route 6A, as well as restaurants in all price ranges.

Day ❻: Chatham ★★★

Spend the day in **Chatham,** one of the Cape's most charming towns. Stroll down **Main Street** to check out the shops. Stop at the **Chatham Fish Pier** (p. 162) to watch the fishermen bring in the daily catch. Drive to **Morris Island,** part of the **Monomoy National Wildlife Refuge** ★★ (p. 164), to hike trails and do some bird-watching. Have a drink on the porch of the Chatham Bars Inn and then head over for a band concert (every Fri night in summer) at Kate Gould Park.

Day ❼: Cape Cod National Seashore

A visit to **Cape Cod National Seashore** (p. 190) is not just a day on the beach. There are visitor centers, numerous trails, and several historic sites. The first stop is **Fort Hill,** which has one of the best scenic vistas on the Cape. Your next stop is the **Salt Pond Visitor Center** ★★ (p. 185), in Eastham. In Truro, you can visit the **Highland House Museum and Highland Lighthouse** (p. 201). A climb to the top of the lighthouse will give you a great view of the coastline. Continue on to **Province-town** ★★★ for a visit to the **Province Lands Visitor Center** ★ (p. 211) and the **Old Harbor Lifesaving Museum** ★ (p. 211).

Day ❽: Whale-Watching Off Provincetown

You'll need several days in **Provincetown** to take in all that this unique place has to offer. A trip to **Stellwagen Bank** on a **whale-watch** takes half a day, but it's an experience you'll always remember. See p. 210.

Day ❾: Provincetown History & Arts

The **Pilgrim Monument & Province-town Museum** ★★ (p. 211) are musts for an overview of the history of the town and a bird's-eye view of the geography from the top of the monument. You'll want to leave yourself plenty of time for strolling along Commercial Street and stopping at galleries, especially the **Provincetown Art Association & Museum** ★★ (p. 212). For those who enjoy biking, pedaling through the Provincetown dunes on the Province Lands Trail is heaven.

Day ❿: A Sail Off the Coast of Provincetown

A hike along the **West End breakwater** ★★ is a temptation for most visitors, but only the truly hearty hike all the way out to

Long Point at the tip of the Cape Cod peninsula. A less vigorous way to get there is by boat; Flyer's Boatyard runs frequent shuttles. End your day with a sunset sail on the *Bay Lady II* ★ (p. 209), a 73-foot schooner.

Day ⓫: Exploring Nantucket

It's worth it to spend a couple of nights on **Nantucket** to see the whole island and to have time to try out some of the fabulous fine-dining restaurants. The island is perfect for casual bikers. You can crisscross the entire island on well-maintained bike paths. You may want to try all the major paths, to 'Sconset, to **Madaket,** and to **Surfside Beach.** For history buffs, the first stop is the **Whaling Museum** ★★★ (p. 236). A Nantucket Historical Association ticket will get you into several other interesting historic sites. Leave plenty of time to wander the cobbled streets of Nantucket for shopping.

Day ⓬: Nantucket Tours

Two terrific tours on Nantucket will give you special insight on the island: around the **harbor** and out to **Great Point.** Several companies offer a cruise around the harbor, including *Endeavor* **Sailing Excursions** ★★ (p. 238), or you can rent your own motorboat to check it out. The Trustees of Reservations offers tours through the **Coskata-Coatue Wildlife Refuge** and out to **Great Point Lighthouse.**

Day ⓭: Arrive on Martha's Vineyard

Whether you decide to explore by shuttle bus, by guided bus tour, or by bicycle, you'll have time to see the major sites on the island of **Martha's Vineyard** in a couple of days. Start your visit in **Vineyard Haven,** which has, arguably, the best shopping on the island. With your gift shopping completed, you can head over to **Oak Bluffs** to check out the "gingerbread houses," the turn-of-the-20th-century Victorian cottages clustered around the **Trinity Park Tabernacle** ★★ (p. 290).

Before leaving Oak Bluffs, take a ride on the **Flying Horses Carousel** ★★ (p. 272).

Day ⓮: Edgartown & Aquinnah
Next head to **Edgartown,** a quintessential New England town of sea captains' houses and white picket fences. Take the 5-minute ferry over to **Chappaquiddick** to stroll

through **Mytoi,** a 14-acre Japanese garden. Head "up-island," by bike or shuttle bus, to **West Tisbury,** to check out the interesting art galleries. In **Chilmark,** you'll want to stop in **Menemsha,** a traditional, weathered fishing village. In **Aquinnah,** you'll visit the red-clay **Gay Head Cliffs.**

4 AN OUTDOOR LOVER'S TOUR OF CAPE COD

Many people visit Cape Cod because of its natural beauty. If you are one of those who enjoy getting outside, whether to hike, bike, or kayak, this itinerary is for you. You'll bike along the coastline, paddle through marshes, and watch seals and whales frolic offshore. This is the real Cape Cod, far from the traffic and T-shirt shops. See p. 67 for a map of this itinerary.

Day ❶: A Bike Ride & a Sail
One of the Cape's best bike trails is the **Shining Sea Bikeway** in **Falmouth.** Rent a bike at Corner Cycle on the Queen's Byway and ride 4 miles on the beachfront path, all the way to **Woods Hole.** In Woods Hole, have lunch at an outdoor table at one of the fine restaurants. After exploring the village of Woods Hole, bike back to Falmouth. On the way you can check out the osprey nest on **Oyster Pond,** near Surf Drive Beach. In the afternoon or early evening, take a 2-hour sailboat ride on the three-masted *Liberte,* a custom schooner. The sunset cruise is the most popular.

Day ❷: Washburn Island in Falmouth
A 40-minute paddle by canoe or kayak will land you on **Washburn Island** (p. 96), a state-owned sanctuary in **Waquoit Bay** containing nature trails and pristine beaches. There are 10 primitive campsites on the island, most located close to the beach. The island feels wonderfully isolated, though you are only a stone's throw

from densely populated summer communities in Falmouth.

Day ❸: Biking the Rail Trail ★★★
Biking the 25-mile **Cape Cod Rail Trail** (p. 137) from **South Dennis** to **Wellfleet** is a great way to take in the Cape's diverse ecosystems, past woods, dunes, ponds, marshes, and cranberry bogs. Most people bike just a section of the trail. The portion within **Nickerson State Park** in **Brewster** is a popular spur. You'll pass places to purchase snacks, drinks, and sandwiches along the way, so it's possible to make a day of it, stopping for a picnic at the halfway point.

Day ❹: Kayaking Barnstable's Great Marsh
One of the best all-day kayak trips on the Cape is through **Barnstable's Great Marsh** and out to the tip of **Sandy Neck.** After launching in **Barnstable Harbor,** you can spend hours exploring the marsh, paddling deep up into **Scorton Creek** at high tide. Paddle out of the marsh before low tide, and then parallel the shore of Sandy Neck all the way out to the little

summer colony on the tip. You can check out the lighthouse and picnic on the beach before paddling back to Barnstable Harbor.

Day ❺: The Seals of Monomoy

Several companies run boat tours out to the island of **South Monomoy,** off the coast of Chatham, to view the enormous **gray seal colony.** Boats leave out of Stage Harbor. Both islands of North Monomoy and South Monomoy together make up a 2,750-acre **wildlife sanctuary** favored by migrating birds. Audubon runs bird-watching tours to the islands in season.

Day ❻: Audubon Sanctuary in Wellfleet

You could spend all day (and the night if you're an Audubon member) exploring the trails at **Audubon's Wellfleet Bay Wildlife Sanctuary** (p. 192). The 1,000-acre refuge features a butterfly garden and numerous trails in addition to a visitor center whose design is on the cutting edge of environmentally friendly architecture.

Day ❼: Watching Whales in Stellwagen Bank

Whale-watching (p. 210) is an activity the whole family can enjoy. It takes a couple of hours for the boat to get out to **Stellwagen Bank,** the prime fishing ground for whales in the area. Once there, you're bound to see several different types. The onboard naturalist will help you identify them.

---

5 CAPE COD FOR FAMILIES

Cape Cod really is perfect for families. Numerous attractions are designed to entertain, and tire out, the little ones. Want to do more than build sand castles at the beach? This tour contains a number of fun and educational activities all over the Cape. See p. 67 for a map of this itinerary.

Day ❶: A Day at the Beach

Ease your way into the laid-back Cape Cod lifestyle by spending the morning at the beach. Beaches most suitable for children include **Old Silver Beach** ★★★ (p. 94), in **Falmouth.** Spend the afternoon at one of the Cape's pristine ponds, such as **Grews Pond** ★★ in Falmouth.

Day ❷: Sandwich ★★★

Sandwich offers several attractions that are big hits with children and that adults will also enjoy. **Heritage Museums and Gardens** ★★★ (p. 79) contains several buildings with collections as diverse as antique cars and baseball memorabilia. **Dexter Grist Mill** ★ (p. 79) offers a fascinating history lesson at a gristmill that still functions. **Green Briar Nature Center &**

Jam Kitchen ★ (p. 78) has walking trails and, yes, a jam kitchen.

Day ❸: Cartwheels 2 & Cape Cod Canal Bike Path

Spend the morning riding the **Cape Cod Canal Bike Path** ★★★, a flat, easy trail. Another way to see the canal is by boat. **Cape Cod Canal Cruises** offers an inexpensive family cruise. In the afternoon, head to **Cartwheels 2** (p. 89). Kids can't resist the go-carts, bumper boats, and minigolf.

Day ❹: A Museum for Kids

Particularly fun for the younger kids is the **Cape Cod Children's Museum** ★ (p. 109) in **Mashpee,** where you can spend the morning. The perfect afternoon activity is a discovery cruise organized by **Ocean-Quest** (p. 87), which leaves from Great Harbor in **Woods Hole** and treats your kids like mini scientists. End the day in **Falmouth** with a **free outdoor concert** at Peg Noonan Park (Fri) or Bigelow Marine Park (Thurs), or a free outdoor children's movie (Wed).

Day ❺: Kids Stuff in Yarmouth

There are several children's activity sites in Yarmouth along Route 28. If the **trampolines, go-carts,** and **minigolf** (p. 132) don't tire them out, you can take them to the **ZooQuarium** ★ (p. 132) to hang out at the petting zoo and catch a sea lion show.

Day ❻: Cape Cod Museum of Natural History

Your kids will be having so much fun they might not realize they are learning something at the **Cape Cod Museum of Natural History** ★★★ (p. 149, in Brewster.

Don't forget to explore the paths behind the beach, especially the **John Wing Trail,** which leads all the way out to Cape Cod Bay. Look closely as you walk; you may spot a turtle or even a rare bird. The museum keeps lists of all the birds spotted in recent days.

Day ❼: Cape Cod National Seashore

Kids love the huge dunes and big waves at the **Cape Cod National Seashore.** Just be sure you stay near the lifeguards and keep an eye on the little ones. There are a number of terrific walking trails from **Eastham** to **Provincetown** within the national seashore that are fun to explore, especially the **Pilgrim Spring Trail,** in Truro (p. 201). After a morning at the beach, don't forget to stop at **Ben & Jerry's Scoop Shop** ★ (p. 187), in Eastham. Spend the afternoon on a **whale-watch** (p. 210) out of **Provincetown** ★★★.

6 NANTUCKET & MARTHA'S VINEYARD

The islands of Nantucket and Martha's Vineyard are as distinct as two neighboring islands can be. This tour lets you explore both of them in a week. You'll see the highlights of both islands—the beaches and historic sites of Nantucket and the scenic landscapes and quaint towns on the Vineyard. See p. 67 for a map of this itinerary.

Day ❶: Arrive on Nantucket

Explore the cobbled streets of historic **Nantucket,** which has some of the best shopping in the region. Walk, bike, taxi, or take a shuttle bus down to **Jetties Beach** ★★★ (p. 233), a beautiful expanse of sand that has the added benefit of numerous amenities, including tennis courts, volleyball nets, a playground, and a skate park. After the beach, bike or drive out to **Madaket Beach** ★★★ on the west side of the island to watch the sunset.

Day ❷: Biking the Island

Spend your second day on the island taking a bike tour. From town, take the

Milestone Road path out to 'Sconset, where you can marvel at the tiny rose-covered cottages. Bike back to town on the **Polpis Road bike path,** passing the red-striped **Sankaty Head Lighthouse** along the way. On the Polpis path, you can take a side trip to **Wauwinet,** where it's possible to hike or four-wheel drive out to **Great Point Lighthouse.**

Day ❸: Beaching & Boating

In the morning, bike to **Surfside Beach** ★★★, just 3 miles south of town. In the afternoon, take a cruise around **Nantucket Harbor,** checking out the multimillion-dollar yachts and the worka-day fishing boats.

Day ❹: Arrive on Martha's Vineyard

Take the seasonal ferry from Nantucket to **Oak Bluffs,** the most boisterous town on **Martha's Vineyard.** Wander through the camp meeting grounds to see the elaborate 19th-century **"gingerbread cottages,"** in the island's first summer community. Ride the **Flying Horses Carousel** (p. 272) and duck into **Mad Martha's** ★ to buy an ice cream cone, which you can eat while watching the world go by on **Circuit Avenue.** At night, head to **Vineyard Haven** to see a play at the **Vineyard Playhouse** (p. 290).

Day ❺: Edgartown

Bike or drive to **Edgartown,** where you can wander past white picket fences in front of grand sea captains' houses. Numerous gift shops, clothing stores, and art galleries are in the center of town. Take a bike ride to **Katama** ★★★, also called South Beach (p. 267), which fronts the Atlantic Ocean.

Day ❻: Aquinnah

Drive, bike, or take the shuttle bus out to **Aquinnah,** the homeland of the Vineyard's Native American community. Walk out to the viewing spot where you can see both the majestic red-clay **Gay Head Cliffs** and the picturesque red-brick **Gay Head Lighthouse** (p. 290). A long path leads down to the beach itself, a pristine beauty.

Day ❼: An Arboretum & a Fishing Village

Visit Chilmark's **Polly Hill Arboretum** (p. 270) in the morning. It's a delight to wander past stone walls, and through the dogwood alley and the "tunnel of love," an arbor of bleached hornbeam. Spend the afternoon in the tiny fishing village of **Menemsha,** part of the town of **Chilmark.** Wander down the dock to watch the fishing boats unloading the catch of the day, which will be served in the island's restaurants that night. The waters of **Menemsha Beach** ★★ (p. 266), in Vineyard Sound, are surprisingly warm in the summer. Watching the sunset over a picnic dinner in Menemsha is a Vineyard tradition.

The Upper Cape

Just over an hour from Boston by car, the Upper Cape towns have become bedroom as well as summer communities. They may not have the let-the-good-times-roll feel of towns farther east, but they're spared the seasonal changeability of the more resorty towns. Shops and restaurants—many catering to an older, affluent crowd—tend to stay open year-round.

The four Upper Cape towns are all quite different. Bourne straddles the Cape Cod Canal; a few of its villages (Bournedale, Buzzards Bay, and Sagamore Beach) are on the mainland side, and the others (Cataumet, Pocasset, Bourne, Monument Beach, and Sagamore) are on the Cape side. The Canal provides this area with most of its recreational opportunities: biking, fishing, canal cruises, and the herring run.

Sandwich ★★★ is the Cape's oldest town. At its core sits a lovely historic village, offering lots of unique shops and charming inns. Still, the town is primarily a pastoral place, with several working farms. In East Sandwich, miles of conservation land lead out to Sandy Neck, a barrier beach extending into Barnstable. The Old King's Highway (Rte. 6A) winds its way through Sandwich past a number of fine gift shops, galleries, and specialty stores.

Falmouth ★★★, the site of Cape Cod's first summer colony, is one of the larger towns on the Cape; it has a year-round population of 32,000. Main Street—with a number of high-quality boutiques, restaurants, and galleries, in addition to the usual touristy T-shirt shops—offers prime strolling and shopping. Falmouth's Village Green is quintessential New England, with two imposing historic churches: St. Barnabas, a sturdy, reddish stone building; and the First Congregational, a white-clapboard, steepled church boasting a Paul Revere bell. Just north of Falmouth center, along Route 28A, lies West Falmouth; it has several good antiques stores, a fine general store, and a picture-perfect little harbor.

The most scenic drive in Falmouth leads to the beach at Falmouth Heights, a bluff covered with grand, shingled Victorians built during the first wave of tourist fever in the late 1800s. Falmouth's southernmost village is Woods Hole, which is the main ferry port for Martha's Vineyard. Home at any given time to several thousand research scientists, it has a certain neo-Bohemian panache, lively bars, and an air of vigorous intellectual inquiry. It's also a working fishing village and one of the most picturesque spots on the Cape.

Mashpee is the ancestral home of the Cape's Native American tribe, the Wampanoags. Much of the town's coastline is occupied by a huge resort called New Seabury; inland, the Mashpee National Wildlife Refuge offers frequent walking tours through its thousands of woodland acres.

1 SANDWICH ★★★

3 miles E of Sagamore; 16 miles NW of Hyannis

Sandwich is both the oldest town on the Cape and, arguably, the quaintest. Towering oak trees and historic houses line its winding Main Street. Two early-19th-century churches and the columned Greek Revival Town Hall, in service since 1834, surround the town

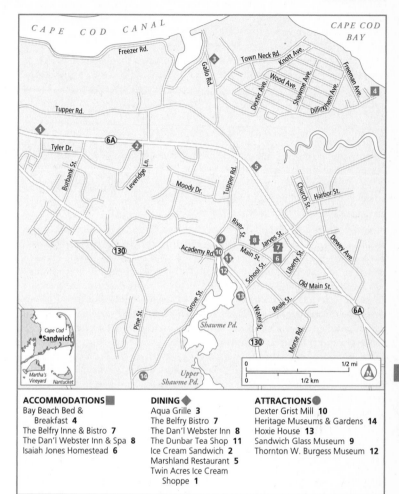

ACCOMMODATIONS ■
Bay Beach Bed &
  Breakfast **4**
The Belfry Inne & Bistro **7**
The Dan'l Webster Inn & Spa **8**
Isaiah Jones Homestead **6**

DINING ◆
Aqua Grille **3**
The Belfry Bistro **7**
The Dan'l Webster Inn **8**
The Dunbar Tea Shop **11**
Ice Cream Sandwich **2**
Marshland Restaurant **5**
Twin Acres Ice Cream
  Shoppe **1**

ATTRACTIONS ●
Dexter Grist Mill **10**
Heritage Museums & Gardens **14**
Hoxie House **13**
Sandwich Glass Museum **9**
Thornton W. Burgess Museum **12**

square. A 1640 gristmill still grinds corn beside bucolic Shawme Pond, which is frequented by swans, geese, ducks, and canoeists. To the north, villagers have built a boardwalk over the extensive salt marsh. Farther east, Sandy Neck, one of the Cape's most beautiful beaches, reaches into Cape Cod Bay.

Sandwich was founded in 1637 by a contingent of Puritans looking for a quiet place to worship. There is still an element of peacefulness in this little town located just a few miles from the Sagamore Bridge.

Sandwich's claim to fame is its prominence as the home to the nation's first glass factories in the early to mid–19th century. The famous Boston and Sandwich Glass Company and others employed more than 500 craftspeople in town. In fact, the town still supports a number of highly skilled glassmakers. Sandwich is fortunate to have two very well-endowed museums—the **Heritage Museums and Gardens** ★★★ and the **Sandwich Glass Museum** ★★—as well as quirkier sites, such as the **Green Briar Nature Center & Jam Kitchen** ★ and the **Thornton W. Burgess Museum** ★.

Many historic homesteads have been converted into charming bed-and-breakfasts that welcome guests year-round. There are also excellent antiques shops in the area. The town is a convenient base for exploring other parts of the Cape that may offer more lively activities, like the nightlife of Hyannis or the ocean beaches of Wellfleet.

ESSENTIALS

GETTING THERE   If you're driving, take Route 6A east toward Sandwich after crossing either the Bourne Bridge or the Sagamore Bridge. The Sagamore Bridge will get you closer to your destination. You can also fly into Hyannis (see section 3, "Getting There & Getting Around," in chapter 3).

There is free on-street parking readily available on Main Street and Jarves Street in the center of town. In addition, each inn has sufficient parking for guests and most inns are located walking distance to Sandwich center.

VISITOR INFORMATION   Contact the **Cape Cod Chamber of Commerce,** routes 6 and 132, Hyannis, MA 02601 (✆ **888/332-2732** or 508/362-3225; www.capecod chamber.org), open year-round, mid-April to mid-November daily 9am to 5pm; mid-November to mid-April Monday to Saturday 10am to 4pm. Stop in at the **Route 25 Visitor Center** (✆ **508/759-3814;** fax 508/759-2146), open daily, 9am to 5pm; call for off-season hours. The **Sandwich Chamber of Commerce** (✆ **508/833-9755;** www. sandwichchamber.com) and **Sandwich Visitor Services Board** (www.sandwichmass.org) put out a handy Sandwich booklet. The Cape Cod Canal Region Chamber of Commerce's **Sandwich Information Center** (✆ **508/833-1632**) is on Route 130 (exit 2, off Rte. 6, the Mid-Cape Hwy.). It is open daily 10am to 5pm. The **Cape Cod Canal Region Chamber of Commerce,** 70 Main St., Buzzards Bay, MA 02532 (✆ **508/759-6000;** fax 508/759-6965; www.capecodcanalchamber.org), open year-round, Monday to Friday 9am to 5pm, can provide literature on both Sandwich and Bourne. A consortium of Sandwich businesses has put together an excellent walking guide (with map) available at most inns in town.

A GET-ACQUAINTED STROLL

This walk starts at the Sandwich Glass Museum, ends at the Dunbar Tea Shop, and takes 2 to 4 hours, depending on the number of stops you make; you'll cover about 1¼ miles. Your best bet is to explore the village on any midsummer day between 10am and 4pm, except Sunday, when some spots are closed.

You may park (free with admission) at the **Sandwich Glass Museum,** 129 Main St. (✆ **508/888-0251;** www.sandwichglassmuseum.org), a well-curated collection tracing the town's history with an emphasis on glass made in Sandwich from 1825 to 1888.

Farther down Grove Street is **Old Cemetery Point,** overlooking peaceful Shawme Pond, about one-third mile down the road. Read the historic headstones and keep an eye out for box turtles. Head back through the center of town and observe the exterior of **Old Town Hall,** on Main Street—a magnificent Greek Revival edifice, complete with Doric columns. It still houses some town offices. Continue down Main Street, past the **First Church of Christ,** which is topped by an impressive spire. Built by a colleague of renowned Boston architect Charles Bulfinch in 1847, it was reportedly modeled on Sir

Christopher Wren's St. Mary-le-Bow, in London. The next church you'll pass, to your left, is an **1833 meetinghouse,** now privately owned, which has been used in years past as a doll museum and a bed-and-breakfast.

Make a left-right zigzag along Main and School streets to reach Water Street, which skirts the eastern edge of Shawme Pond. Directly opposite, on the shore side of Water Street, you'll spot the **Hoxie House,** at 18 Water St. (© **508/888-1173**), one of the oldest houses on the Cape. The interior is spare—not out of any aesthetic ideal but because resources were so hard to come by in Colonial New England. The settlers didn't even have closets because they were taxed as an additional room, windows were tiny to avoid the tax on glass, and pockets were considered a waste of good material. Docents explain all the details in frequent tours.

After the Hoxie House tour, head northward along Water Street, passing (on the same side) the **Thornton W. Burgess Museum,** 4 Water St. (© **508/888-6870;** www.thornton burgess.org), which celebrates the life and work of native son Burgess (1874–1965). He was a highly successful author of children's books and creator of such still-beloved characters as Jimmy Skunk and Grandfather Frog. Just past the Burgess Museum is the **Dexter Grist Mill** (© **508/888-4910;** www.dexterhistoricalsociety.com/gristmill.html), a lovingly restored water mill (ca. 1640). The millstones still grind corn; buy a bag of meal to go, but only if you'll have a chance to whip up something later in the day (it doesn't keep well). Now that you're back at the center of town, this is a good time to pause for a spot of tea. The **Dunbar Tea Shop,** 1 Water St. (© **508/833-2485;** www.dunbartea.com), serves hearty lunches, teas, and breakfasts. The attached shop features British imports and antiques, including vintage books. It's a pleasant place to while away a good portion of the afternoon.

BEACHES & RECREATIONAL PURSUITS

BEACHES   For the Sandwich beaches listed below, nonresident parking stickers—$90 for the length of your stay—are available at **Sandwich Town Hall Annex,** 145 Main St. (© **508/833-8012**). *Note:* No swimming is allowed within the Cape Cod Canal because the currents are much too swift and dangerous. The Army Corps' **Cape Cod Canal Visitors Center,** at the Sandwich Marina (© **508/833-9678;** www.nae.usace.army.mil/recreati/ccc/recreation/recreation.htm), is open 10am to 5pm in season. It displays exhibits about the canal, and rangers lead walks in the area.

- **Sandy Neck Beach** ★★★, off Sandy Neck Road, in East Sandwich (sandyneckbeach park.com): This 6-mile stretch of silken barrier beach with low, rounded dunes is one of the Cape's prettiest and most unspoiled. It is somewhat isolated, with no commercial businesses or accommodations on the beach. Because it is a Cape Cod Bay beach, the water tends to be warmer than the open ocean, and the waves are never too high. That makes it popular with families. The fact that the beach stretches out for miles makes it popular with endangered Piping Plovers—and their nemesis, off-road vehicles (ORV). That means that the ORV trails are closed for much of the summer while the Piping Plover chicks hatch. ORV permits ($140 per season for nonresidents) can be purchased at the gatehouse (© **508/362-8300**). ORV drivers must be equipped with such supplies as a spare tire, jack, shovel, and tire-pressure gauge. Parking for the beach in the upper parking lot costs $15 per day in season. Up to 4 days of camping in self-contained vehicles is permitted at $10 per night, plus an ORV permit.

- **Town Neck Beach,** off Town Neck Road, in Sandwich: A bit rocky but ruggedly pretty, this narrow beach offers a busy view of passing ships, plus restrooms and a snack bar. Parking costs $10 per day, or you could hike from town (about 1½ miles) via the community-built boardwalk spanning the salt marsh.

- **Wakeby Pond,** Ryder Conservation Area, John Ewer Road (off South Sandwich Rd., on the Mashpee border): The beach, on the Cape's largest freshwater pond, has lifeguards, restrooms, and parking ($10 per day).

BICYCLING　The **U.S. Army Corps of Engineers** (recreation hot line, with weather, tides, and current info: ☎ **508/759-5991;** or visit the website listed above) maintains a flat, 14-mile loop along the **Cape Cod Canal** ★★★, equally suited to bicyclists, skaters, runners, and strollers. The most convenient place to park (free) is at the Bourne Recreation Area, north of the Bourne Bridge, on the Cape side. You can also park at the Sandcatcher Recreation Area at the end of Freezer Road in Sandwich.

BOATING　If you want to explore under power of your own paddle, you can rent canoes and kayaks in Falmouth and float around Old Sandwich Harbor, out to Sandy Neck, or through the salt-marsh maze of Scorton Creek, which leads out to Talbot Point, a wooded spit of conservation land.

FISHING　Sandwich has eight fishable ponds; for details and a license, inquire at **Town Hall** in the center of town (☎ **508/888-0340**). Permits cost nonresidents $39 for the season, $25 for a 3-day pass. Children, seniors, and Massachusetts residents receive discounts. No permit is required to fish from the banks of the Cape Cod Canal. Here your catch might include striped bass, bluefish, cod, pollock, flounder, or fluke. Call the **U.S. Army Corps of Engineers** (☎ **508/759-5991;** or visit their website listed above) for Canal tide and fishing information.

FITNESS　The local fitness center is the **Sportsite Health Club,** at 315 Cotuit Rd., in Sandwich (☎ **508/888-7900**). It offers 15,000 square feet of Nautilus and other fitness equipment, along with steam baths, saunas, racquetball, classes, and free child care. A 1-day pass costs $12, plus $5 extra per person for racquetball.

GOLF　The **Sandwich Hollows Golf Club,** on 1 Round Hill Road, in East Sandwich (☎ **508/888-3384;** www.sandwichhollows.com), is a 6,200-yard, par-71 town-owned course. In season, a round costs $30 to $40, depending on the day and time. The 18-hole, par-3 **Holly Ridge Golf Course,** at 121 Country Club Road, in South Sandwich (☎ **508/428-5577;** www.hollyridgegolf.com), is, at 2,900 yards, shorter and easier. A round costs $34 in season, with afternoon discounts.

NATURE & WILDLIFE AREAS　The **Shawme-Crowell State Forest,** off Route 130, in Sandwich (☎ **508/888-0351;** www.mass.gov/dcr/parks/southeast/schr.htm), offers 298 campsites and 742 acres to roam. Entrance is free. Camping costs $12 for Massachusetts residents, $14 for nonresidents.

The **Sandwich Boardwalk** ★★, which the community rebuilt in 1991 after Hurricane Bob blew away the 1874 original, links the town and Town Neck Beach by way of salt marshes that attract many birds, including great blue herons.

As if to signify how oddly enchanted this little corner of the world is, there's a sweet little (57-acre) nature center here—and within it is an even sweeter kitchen, where local ladies have been cooking up jams and jellies since 1903. The **Green Briar Nature Center & Jam Kitchen** ★ is at 6 Discovery Hill Rd., East Sandwich (off Rte. 6A, about 1½ miles east of town center; ☎ **508/888-6870;** www.thorntonburgess.org); once you've caught a whiff of the jam, you'll want to take some home. (Try the local delicacy, beach-plum jelly.) Jam-making workshops are offered for adults and children in the summer and fall. Prices are $38 per person for adult classes, usually Wednesday evening or Saturday during the day (members of the Thornton Burgess Society pay $28). You will end up with four to six jars of jam. Children will be intrigued by the expansive kitchen, as well as some old-fashioned nature exhibits on such animals as rabbits, turtles, iguanas, and snakes. The center is open mid-April to December, Monday through Saturday 10am to 4pm, Sunday 1 to 4pm; January to mid-April Tuesday through Saturday 10am to 4pm. Admission is by donation; the suggested donation is $1 per child and $5 for families. Summer story time is at 10:30am on Monday, Wednesday, and Saturday, costing $1 per person.

TENNIS   Sandwich has public courts at the Wing School, Oak Ridge School, Forestdale School, and Sandwich High School. Contact the **Sandwich Recreation Department** (✆ **508/888-4361**) for details.

SANDWICH HISTORICAL SIGHTS

Dexter Grist Mill ★ (Kids)   This charmingly weathered building has survived some 350 years and at least as many lives. At present it serves its original purpose, grinding corn with turbine power; you can watch the wooden gears in action and buy a bag to take home and cook up into Colonial "johnnycakes" (short for "cakes for the journey") or trendy polenta. Fresh cornmeal costs $3.50 for a 2-pound bag, $9 for three bags. During the glassmaking boom of the 1800s, this mill was but one of many pressed into service to keep the factory workers well fed. When the laborers dispersed, the mill sat useless until a local entrepreneur thought to convert it into a tearoom to serve the new tide of tourists arriving by motorcar. The mill was fully restored in 1961 and will probably be good for a few more centuries of stalwart service.

Water St. (on Shawme Pond, behind Town Hall). ✆ **508/888-4910;** www.dexterhistoricalsociety.com/gristmill.html. Admission $3 adults, $2 children 6–12; combination ticket for Dexter Mill and Hoxie House ($5 adults, $3 children) available from the Hoxie House (see below). July–Aug daily 10am–4:45pm; call for off-season hours. Closed mid-Oct to mid-June.

Heritage Museums and Gardens ★★★ (Finds)(Kids)   This is one of those rare museums that appeals equally to adults and the children they drag along; the latter will leave clamoring for another visit. All ages have the run of 76 beautifully landscaped acres, crisscrossed with walking paths and riotous with color in late spring, when the towering rhododendrons burst forth in blooms that range from soft pink to gaudy orange. Scattered buildings house a wide variety of collections, from Native American artifacts to Cape Cod Baseball League memorabilia. The art holdings, especially the primitive portraits, are outstanding. The high point for most children will be a ride on the 1912 carousel (safely preserved indoors). Also sure to dazzle is the replica Shaker round barn packed with gleaming antique automobiles, including some once owned by celebrities (don't miss Gary Cooper's Duesenberg). Next door is the **Carousel Cafe,** good for a restorative snack, including soups, sandwiches, and salads. The gift shop at the gatehouse is also worth checking out. Call ahead for a schedule of the outdoor summer concerts usually held Sundays around 2pm, free with admission.

67 Grove St. (about ¹⁄₂ mile southwest of the town center). ✆ **508/888-3300.** www.heritagemuseumsandgardens.org. Admission $12 adults, $10 seniors 65 and over, $6 children 4–16, free for children 3 and under. Apr–Oct daily 10am–5pm. No tickets sold after 4:15pm. Closed Nov–Mar.

Hoxie House ★   Once a contender for the title of the Cape's oldest house (a couple of privately owned Provincetown houses appear to have a stronger claim), this saltbox (ca. 1680) is nonetheless a noteworthy beauty, with its diamond-pane windows and broad interior planking—made of "king's wood," so called because England's king had, under pain of severe penalty, reserved the larger trees for his warships. The house was occupied pretty much as is, with neither electricity nor plumbing, into the 1950s, which explains how it remained so remarkably intact. Even so, it had to be taken apart and reassembled to serve as the model Colonial home you see today. Fortunately restorers opted not for the cluttered Colonial Revival look but a stark austerity that's much more historically accurate and shows off to advantage a handful of antiques on semipermanent loan from Boston's Museum of Fine Arts.

18 Water St. (on Shawme Pond, about ¹/₄ mile south of the town center). © **508/888-1173.** Admission $3 adults, $2 children 5–15, free for children 5 and under; combination ticket ($5 adults, $3 children) available here for Hoxie House and Dexter Grist Mill (see above). Mid-June to mid-Oct Mon–Sat 10am–5pm; Sun 1–5pm. Closed mid-Oct to mid-June.

Sandwich Glass Museum ★★ (**Finds**)   Even if you don't consider yourself a glass fan, make an exception for this fascinating museum, which captures the history of the town. A 20-minute video introduces Deming Jarves's brilliant endeavor, which flourished from 1828 to 1888, bringing glassware—a rare commodity available only to the rich—within reach of the middle classes. Jarves picked the perfect spot, surrounded by old-growth forest, to fuel the furnaces, with a harbor handy for shipping in fine sand from farther up the coast and salt-marsh hay with which to pack outgoing orders. All went well until Midwestern glass factories started using coal; unable to keep up with their level of mass production, he switched back to hand-blown techniques.

A multimillion-dollar renovation and expansion has freshened up the entire museum, and glass is displayed in light and airy rooms. Highlights of the renovation include a furnace, where glass-blowing demonstrations are featured, and a multimedia theater. Since the museum is run by the Sandwich Historical Society, one room is given over to changing exhibits highlighting other eras in the town's history, such as its stellar seafaring days. An excellent gift shop stocks Sandwich-glass replicas, as well as original glassworks by area artisans.

Note: Arrive by 3:30pm to allow yourself time to see glass-blowing demonstrations (10am–4:30pm) and presentations in the theater.

129 Main St. (in the center of town). © **508/888-0251.** www.sandwichglassmuseum.org. Admission $5 adults, $1.25 children 6–14, free for children 5 and under. Apr–Dec daily 9:30am–5pm; Feb–Mar Wed–Sun 9:30am–4pm. Closed Jan, Thanksgiving, and Christmas.

Thornton W. Burgess Museum ★ (**Kids**)   Prominent in the early half of the 20th century, this locally bred children's-book author racked up 170 tomes to his credit, as well as 15,000 stories. His somewhat simple texts, featuring anthropomorphic animals prone to preaching, may seem a bit dated, but they still go over big with little listeners, especially at the summer-morning story hours. The gift shop carries reissues of his work, should they desire a memento. It's also worth a peek inside to see Harrison Cady's spirited illustrations and exhibits attesting to Burgess's other life work, conservation. He may have inherited this interest from his aunt (the original inhabitant of this 1756 cottage), who gained a certain notoriety for claiming that she could communicate directly with the animal and plant worlds. The museum offers walking tours of Victorian Sandwich on Thursday mornings in June, July, and August. Tours start on the museum grounds at 10:30am. Animal story times take place Monday, Thursday, and Saturday mornings at 10:30am in July and August, weather permitting.

4 Water St. (on Shawme Pond, near the center of town). ⓒ **508/888-6870.** www.thorntonburgess.org. **81**
Suggested donation $2 adults, $1 children. Mid-Apr to Oct Mon–Sat 10am–4pm; Sun 1–4pm. Closed Nov
to mid-Apr.

KID STUFF

The venerable 18-hole **Sandwich Mini Golf,** 159 Rte. 6A, at the corner of Main Street
(ⓒ **508/833-1905**), is a grassy 1950s classic that encapsulates Cape Cod history. Built
on a former cranberry bog, it boasts an unusual floating green. Hours are Monday to
Saturday from 10am to 8pm and Sunday from noon to 8pm. Admission is $7 for adults,
$6 for children 12 and under. Add $4 and play two rounds, or 36 holes.

OTHER ACTIVITIES

Hemisphere   This beachfront restaurant and club with views of Cape Cod Bay is fine
for a drink or a bite to eat. Head out to the second-floor deck and grab one of the tables
along the railing, where the views are sensational. Closed November to March. 98 Town
Neck Rd. ⓒ 508/888-6166; www.hemispherecapecod.com. Rte. 6A to Tupper Rd.; ¹/₂ mile to
Town Neck Rd.

Sandwich Auction House   Do you have the guts—not to mention the funds—to
be a player? You'll find out soon enough as the bidding grows heated over an ever-
changing parade of antique goods, from chests to portraits to spinning wheels. Antique-
rug auctions take place once a month. Sit on your hands if you must. Auctions are held
the first and third Saturday of every month, year-round; previews start at 2pm the same
day. MasterCard and Visa are accepted. 15 Tupper Rd. (at Rte. 6A). ⓒ 508/888-1926. www.
sandwichauction.com. Free admission.

SHOPPING

Small as it is, Sandwich has a handful of appealing shops—some with items you're
unlikely to find anywhere else. Most of the shops are concentrated in the center of town.
Several of the museums listed above (see "Sandwich Historical Sights," above) also have
worthwhile gift shops.

ANTIQUES & COLLECTIBLES   The **Sandwich Antiques Center,** 131 Rte. 6A, at
Jarves Street (ⓒ **508/833-3600**), showcases wares from over 100 dealers in 6,000 square
feet of rooms. It's headed by a congenial auctioneer and offers virtual one-stop shopping
for the likes of Sandwich glass, primitives, country furnishings—you name it. The center
is open daily year-round.

ARTS & CRAFTS   The **Giving Tree Gallery,** 550 Rte. 6A, East Sandwich, about 4
miles east of the town center (ⓒ **888/246-3551;** www.givingtreegallery.com), is an art
and fine-crafts gallery with something extra: a nature walk through bamboo trails.
Intriguing sculptures are placed strategically around the property. The path through a
bamboo forest is for those who appreciate a Far Eastern aesthetic. In fact, there's something very Zen about the whole Giving Tree experience. It's closed January to late May.

For the finest in art glass and the perfect souvenir of your Sandwich vacation, visit **The
Glass Studio** ★★, 470 Rte. 6A, East Sandwich (ⓒ **508/888-6681;** www.capecodglass.
net), where master glass blower Michael Magyar crafts such one-of-a-kind pieces as his
"sea bubbles" series and Venetian-style goblets. Watch glass blowing Thursday through
Sunday from 10am to 1pm and 2 to 5pm.

At **McDermott Glass Studio & Gallery** ★★, 272 Cotuit Rd., Sandwich (ⓒ **508/
477-0705;** www.mcdermottglass.com), Dave McDermott creates exquisite hand-blown

THE UPPER CAPE

5

SANDWICH

art glass, from vases to stemware. Glass blowing takes place Thursday to Saturday from 10am to 5pm.

BOOKS   **Titcomb's Bookshop** ★ (Finds), 432 Rte. 6A, East Sandwich, about 4 miles east of the town center (✆ 508/888-2331; www.titcombsbookshop.com), has a terrific selection of books (both new and used) relating to Cape Cod and much more. Look for the life-size statue of Ben Franklin out front.

FOOD & WINE   **Crow Farm** ★, 192 Rte. 6A, one-quarter mile east of the town center (✆ 508/888-0690; www.crowfarm.net), is a picture-perfect farm stand purveying superb local produce such as sweet corn, tomatoes, peaches, and apples, as well as flowers. It's closed Sunday in summer but open daily in spring and fall. It's closed late December through April. **The Brown Jug,** 155 Main St., in Sandwich (✆ 508/888-4669; www. thebrownjug.com), is stocked with delicacies from around the corner and around the world, from fine cheeses and olive oils to rich baked goods and hearty homemade breads.

GIFTS/HOME DECOR   **The Weather Store** ★, 146 Main St. (✆ 800/646-1203; www.theweatherstore.com), has a fascinating collection of meteorological paraphernalia, old and new, ranging from antique instruments to coffee-table books. Although technically open year-round, from January through April, it's open by chance or appointment.

SEAFOOD   **Joe's Lobster & Fish Market,** off Coast Guard Road, near Sandwich Marina (✆ 508/888-2971; www.joeslobstermart.com), is the place to go for the freshest fish and shellfish to prepare at your cottage rental.

WHERE TO STAY

Sandwich has a number of motels along Route 6A, but the one with the best location is **Sandy Neck Motel,** at 669 Rte. 6A, East Sandwich (✆ 800/564-3992 or 508/362-3992; www.sandyneck.com), which sits at the entrance to the road leading to Sandy Neck, the best beach in these parts. Rates are $129 double, and $199 to $299 for one- and two-room efficiencies. It's closed November to mid-April.

Expensive
The Dan'l Webster Inn and Spa ★★   This large lodging and dining spot in the center of Sandwich village is a dependable bet for a comfortable stay or a hearty meal. The inn encompasses a modern main building, designed to look historic, as well as several historic homes nearby that have been outfitted with modern amenities. The main building sits on the site of a Colonial tavern favored by Daniel Webster, the famous orator who enjoyed fishing on the Cape. The suites located in nearby historic houses are especially appealing; they feature fireplaces and canopy beds. There are also eight deluxe one-room suites in the main building, with such amenities as balconies, gas fireplaces, oversize whirlpool baths, and heated tile floors in the bathrooms. The inn's common spaces are bustling; sometimes tour buses stop here. The **restaurant** is quite good, especially considering the high volume of customers (see "Where to Dine," below). An on-site spa offers massages, facials, and other body treatments.

149 Main St. (in the center of town), Sandwich, MA 02563. ✆ 800/444-3566 or 508/888-3622. Fax 508/888-5156. www.danlwebsterinn.com. 46 units. Summer $199–$249 double; $289–$399 suite. Rates include full breakfast Mon–Fri and off-season only. AE, DC, DISC, MC, V. **Amenities:** Restaurant, tavern/bar; access to health club (2 miles away); small outdoor heated pool; room service; spa. *In room:* A/C, TV, hair dryer.

Moderate
The Belfry Inne & Bistro ★★ (Finds)   This lodging option consists of three historic buildings in the center of Sandwich village. The turreted 1879 **rectory** has romantic

rooms with queen-size retrofitted antique beds, a claw-foot tub (or Jacuzzi) for every room, and a scattering of fireplaces and private balconies. Next door is **the Abbey,** a former church that owner Chris Wilson has converted into six unique deluxe guest rooms, several with fireplaces and whirlpool baths, and a very fine restaurant (see "Where to Dine," below). The abbey rooms are painted vivid colors and tucked cleverly into sections of this old church. One room features a stained-glass window; another has angel windows. All of the Abbey rooms have Jacuzzis. Mr. Wilson also owns the **Village House,** located next door, with six rooms decorated in a French country style within an 1860 Federal-style house.

8 Jarves St. (in the center of town), Sandwich, MA 02563. ☎ **800/844-4542** or 508/888-8550. Fax 508/888-3922. www.belfryinn.com. 22 units (in 3 properties). Summer $149–$315 double. Rates include full breakfast. AE, MC, V. **Amenities:** Restaurant. *In room:* AC, TV, hair dryer, Wi-Fi.

Isaiah Jones Homestead Bed & Breakfast ★ (**Value**) Of the many B&Bs in Sandwich Center, this one is a particularly good value. The innkeepers have appointed this courtly 1849 Victorian with fine antiques and reproductions. Many rooms have additional romantic touches such as fireplaces and oversize whirlpool baths. Two minisuites in the carriage house have sitting alcoves with sleeper sofas. The three-course breakfast, served with fine china and crystal, is highly refined.

165 Main St. (in the center of town), Sandwich, MA 02563. ☎ **800/526-1625** or 508/888-9115. Fax 508/888-9648. www.isaiahjones.com. 7 units. Summer $175–$275 double. Rates include full breakfast. AE, DISC, MC, V. No children under 12. *In room:* A/C, TV/DVD, hair dryer, no phone.

Wingscorton Farm Inn ★★ (**Finds**) (**Kids**) This 7-acre farmhouse inn, located a 5-minute walk from a small and quiet bay beach, will delight youngsters and animal lovers of all ages. It's been a working farm since 1758 and still houses a cheerful brood of sheep, goats, dogs, cats, chickens, a pet turkey, and a potbellied pig on its tree-shaded grounds. The main house is a classic Colonial with a "keeping room" boasting a 9-foot-long hearth. Upstairs are two paneled bedrooms with canopy beds, working fireplaces, braided rugs, and antiques. The carriage house has a loft bedroom, kitchen, and private deck.

11 Wing Blvd. (off Rte. 6A, about 5 miles east of the town center), East Sandwich, MA 02537. ☎ **508/888-0534.** Fax 508/888-0545. 4 units, carriage house, cottage. Summer $225 suite; $250 carriage house; $1,100 weekly cottage. Rates for suites and carriage house include full breakfast. AE, MC, V. Pets welcome. *In room:* A/C, TV, fridge, no phone.

Inexpensive

Spring Garden Inn ★ (**Value**) (**Kids**) This well-maintained, beautifully landscaped motel overlooks acres of conservation land known as the Great Sandwich Salt Marsh. Every room comes with a south-oriented patio or porch that takes in the lush view. Barbecue grills and picnic tables are available outside on the mahogany deck. With its spacious, tree-shaded backyard and pool, the reasonably priced motel is understandably popular with families. Guests will also appreciate the complimentary homemade continental breakfasts.

578 Rte. 6A (P.O. Box 497; about 5 miles east of the town center), East Sandwich, MA 02537. ☎ **866/345-5641** or 508/888-0710. www.springgarden.com. 11 units, 9 with tub/shower, 2 with shower only. Summer $105–$115 double; $130 efficiency. Rates include continental breakfast. DISC, MC, V. Closed Dec–Mar. **Amenities:** Outdoor pool. *In room:* A/C, TV/DVD, fridge.

Spring Hill Motor Lodge ★ This motel boasts all sorts of amenities, such as an outdoor heated pool and a night-lit tennis court, and the owners keep it in top condition.

The interiors are cheerfully contemporary, the grounds verdant. In addition to the motel rooms, there are three cottages that are light, airy, and comfortable. The cottages have full kitchens (microwave ovens instead of standard ovens) as well as two televisions and a VCR.

351 Rte. 6A (about 2½ miles east of the town center), East Sandwich, MA 02537. © **800/647-2514** or 508/888-1456. Fax 508/833-1556. www.springhillmotorlodge.com. 24 units, 20 with tub/shower, 4 with shower only. Summer $135–$185 double; $250 1-bedroom cottage; $350 2-bedroom cottage. AE, DC, DISC, MC, V. **Amenities:** Elegantly landscaped heated outdoor pool; night-lit tennis court. *In room:* A/C, TV, fridge.

WHERE TO DINE
Expensive
The Belfry Bistro ★★ ⟨Finds⟩ NEW AMERICAN   Sandwich's most romantic dining option is located in a renovated abbey. Portions are generous. The menu changes seasonally, but among the appetizers, you might find a Thai-crab-and-baby-shrimp cake or mini barbecue pork empanadas, which are braised and wrapped in pastry. The entrees run the gamut from the unusual black grouper roasted in a banana leaf to the traditional grilled filet of beef over whipped potatoes with green beans. Because this restaurant hosts many weddings and other events, it is sometimes closed to the public, so be sure to call ahead. While the Belfry Bistro serves dinner only, the more casual **Painted Lady Cafe** next door serves lighter, less expensive ($8–$25) fare, such as brie cheeseburgers and chicken potpie, from 11:30am to 3pm and 4 to 8:30pm. The Painted Lady serves lunch only on Sunday and is closed Monday.

8 Jarves St. (in the center of town). © **508/888-8550.** Reservations recommended. Main courses $20–$32. AE, MC, V. Feb–Dec Tues–Sun 5–10pm (last seating at 8:30pm). Closed Jan.

The Dan'l Webster Inn ★★ AMERICAN   You have a choice of four main dining rooms—from a casual, Colonial-motif tavern to a skylight-topped conservatory fronting a splendid garden. The atmospheric Tavern at the Inn, with its own pub-style menu, is perhaps the most popular. All of the dining rooms are served by the same kitchen. Appealing high-season specials are the sugar-cane-skewered shrimp and the sesame-encrusted striped bass. For lighter appetites, half-portions are available. There is also a children's menu.

149 Main St. (in the center of town). © **508/888-3622.** Reservations recommended. Main courses $18–$29; tavern menu $7–$14. AE, DC, DISC, MC, V. June–Aug daily 7:30–11am, 11:30am–3pm, and 4:30–9pm; call for off-season hours.

Moderate
Aqua Grille ★ SEAFOOD   Overlooking Sandwich's picturesque marina and not-so-picturesque power plant, this dining spot, owned by the respected Zartarian family of the Paddock Restaurant in Hyannis, wants to be the premier place for fish in Sandwich. All the elements are in place: a spacious, attractive dining room decorated in pleasing aqua shades; a glass-enclosed harbor-view deck; and a long, curving bar. The food is delicious and plentiful, with fish (grilled or fried) the obvious choice, plus lots of pasta dishes. The towering lobster salad with green string beans, tomato, avocado, chives, and crème fraîche is the perfect antidote to a steamy summer night. Try to get a table that doesn't face the power plant.

14 Gallo Rd. (next to Sandwich Marina). © **508/888-8889.** www.aquagrille.com. Reservations recommended. Main courses $8–$24. AE, DC, MC, V. Late Apr–Oct Mon–Fri 11:30am–8:30pm; Sat–Sun noon–9pm. Closed Nov–late Apr.

The Bee-Hive Tavern ★ AMERICAN   A cut above the rather characterless restaurants clustered along this stretch of road, this modern-day tavern offers atmospheric old-time touches without going overboard. Green-shaded banker's lamps, for example, illuminate the dark wooden booths, and vintage prints and paintings convey a clubby feel. The food is good if not spectacular, and well priced for what it is. The menu features steaks, chops, and fresh-caught fish among the pricier choices; burgers, sandwiches, and salads cater to lighter appetites (and wallets). This is a great option for lunch, when you should try one of the Cape's best lobster rolls.

406 Rte. 6A (about ¹/₂ mile east of the town center), East Sandwich. (✆ **508/833-1184.** Main courses $7–$16. MC, V. Mon–Sat 11:30am–3pm and 5–9pm; Sun 9–11:30am, noon–3pm, and 5–9pm.

The Dunbar Tea Shop ★★ (Finds) BRITISH   Whether you choose the cozy confines of the Tea Room on a crisp autumn day or the shady outside grove in summer, you'll enjoy the hearty English classics served here. Lunch begins at 11am and features homemade soups, salads, and such sandwiches as the Farmer's Lunch (crusty warm bread, roast beef, horseradish sauce, and English mustard). The Tea Room also serves tea, of course, with all the traditional fixings and accompaniments you'd expect. A tea-themed gift shop is attached.

1 Water St. (in the center of town). (✆ **508/833-2485.** www.dunbartea.com. Main courses under $10. DISC, MC, V. June–Sept daily 11am–4:30pm; Oct–May Wed–Mon 11am–4:30pm.

Marshland Restaurant on 6A (Value) (Kids) DINER   Locals have been digging this diner for 2 decades. This is home-cooked grub, slung fast and cheap. You'll gobble up the hearty breakfast and be back in time for dinner, when fried seafood plates are a specialty.

109 Rte. 6A. (✆ **508/888-9824.** www.marshlandrestaurant.com. Most items under $10. No credit cards. Daily 6am–8:30pm.

Sweets

Sweet tooth acting up? Stop by Sandwich's appropriately named **Ice Cream Sandwich** ★, at 66 Rte. 6A, across from the Stop & Shop (✆ **508/888-7237;** www.icecreamsandwich. net), for a couple of scoops of the best local ice cream. Try the Cape Cod chocolate chunk. It's closed November through March. Sandwich's most classic ice-cream shop is **Twin Acres Ice Cream Shoppe** ★, 21 Rte. 6A, Sandwich (✆ **508/888-0566**), which specializes in soft serve. With its red, white, and blue bunting, this place is right out of a Norman Rockwell illustration.

---

2 BOURNE

4 miles W of Sagamore; 16 miles NW of Hyannis

Bourne, with seven villages, hugs Buzzards Bay on both sides of the Cape Cod Canal. The town has changed quite a bit since President Grover Cleveland moved to Bourne more than 100 years ago. Evidently attracted by the trout, he decided to set up his summer White House at Monument Beach in the 1890s. That house is long gone, but one vestige—his personal train station—is on view at the Aptucxet Trading Post Museum, a reconstructed version of this country's first place of commerce, where Pilgrims traded with Native Americans and the Dutch. Also visible from here—and from the Cape Cod Canal bike path, which runs right past the post—is the intriguing **Vertical Lift Railroad**

Bridge (built in 1935); its track moves up or down to permit the passage, respectively, of ships or trains. Cataumet, with its winding roads, is the most upscale village in Bourne. The village of Buzzards Bay, its somewhat dingy Main Street paralleling the canal, has most of the shops.

ESSENTIALS

GETTING THERE The villages in the town of Bourne are on both sides of the Cape Cod Canal. To get to Buzzards Bay, take exit 1 off Route 25, before crossing the Bourne Bridge. To get to Cataumet, Pocasset, Monument Beach, and Bourne Village, cross the Bourne Bridge. Follow Route 28 S., a limited access highway, and watch the signs for the appropriate exit. You can also fly into Hyannis (see section 3, "Getting There & Getting Around," in chapter 3).

VISITOR INFORMATION Contact the **Cape Cod Chamber of Commerce** (see "Visitor Information," under "Sandwich," earlier in this chapter), or stop at the **Route 25 Visitor Center.** The **Cape Cod Canal Region Chamber of Commerce,** 70 Main St., Buzzards Bay (© **508/759-6000;** www.capecodcanalchamber.org), can provide literature on Bourne.

BEACHES & RECREATIONAL PURSUITS

BEACHES Bourne has only one public beach: **Monument Beach** ★, off Shore Road. Half the parking lot is free (this fills up fast), and the other half requires a sticker from **Bourne Town Hall,** at 24 Perry Ave., in Buzzards Bay (© **508/759-0623**). Though the beach is small and pebbly, it's picturesque. Full public-beach facilities accompany the relatively warm waters of Buzzards Bay.

BICYCLING See "Bicycling," under "Sandwich," earlier in this chapter. The **Cape Cod Canal bike path** ★★★, 14 miles on both sides of the Canal, is one of the best on the Cape. On the mainland side of the Canal, on Main Street in Buzzards Bay, access is at the far end of Buzzards Bay Park. On the Cape side of the Canal, access is at the Bourne Recreation Area, just north of the Bourne Bridge, along Canal Road.

BOATING If you have your own canoe or kayak or want to rent one in Falmouth, you'll enjoy exploring Back River and Phinney's Harbor at Monument Beach. **Cape Cod Kayak** (© **508/563-9377;** www.capecodkayak.com) rents kayaks (free delivery locally) by the day or week and offers lessons and ecotours on local waterways. Canoe and kayak rentals are $35 to $60 for a full day. Lessons are $45 per hour. Two- or 3-hour trips are $45 to $65.

FISHING So plentiful are the herring making their spring migration up the **Bournedale Herring Run** ★★ (© **508/759-5991;** Rte. 6 in Bournedale, about 1 mile southwest of the Sagamore Bridge rotary) that you can net them once they've reached their destination, Great Herring Pond. You can obtain a shellfish permit from **Bourne Town Hall,** at 24 Perry Ave., Buzzards Bay (© 508/759-0600). Also plentiful here are pickerel, white perch, walleye, and bass. For freshwater fishing at Flax Pond and Red Brook Pond in Pocasset, you'll need a license from the Bourne Town Hall (see above). You can also obtain a freshwater fishing license at **Red Top Sporting Goods,** at 265 Main St., in Buzzards Bay (© **508/759-3371;** www.redtoptackle.com). Surf-casting along the Cape Cod Canal requires no permit.

ICE-SKATING The **John Gallo Ice Arena,** 231 Sandwich Rd., in Bourne (© **508/759-8904;** www.galloarena.com), is open to the public daily from September to March, with reduced hours in the summer. Rates are $3 for adults, $2 for children.

(Kids) OceanQuest

No visit to the Cape would be complete without some type of seafaring excursion on the Atlantic. If you're not a sailor or if you don't have the time or budget for an all-day boat trip, consider a unique, hands-on discovery cruise with **OceanQuest** ★★, Water Street (in the center of town), Woods Hole (© **800/ 376-2326** or 508/385-7656; www.oceanquest.org). Departing from Woods Hole, these 1¹⁄₂-hour harbor cruises are perfect for families, as real marine research is conducted with passengers serving as bona fide data collectors.

Here's how it works: Participants are split into two teams. Up in the bow, company founder Kathy Mullin, or a scientist borrowed from one of the revered local institutes, trains the new crew in the niceties of reading water temperature, assessing turbidity, and taking other key measurements. In the stern, passengers get to examine the specimens hauled up by the dredger. Midway into the trip the teams switch stations, so that everyone gets to contemplate topics such as the sex life of a spider crab or why the water looks a particular shade of blue or green. Kids get a real kick out of being addressed as "Doctor," and even adults who think they know it all will probably come away much better informed.

The 90-minute cruise costs $22 for adults, $17 for children 4 to 12, $5 for children 3 and under; boats shove off four times a day Monday through Friday from mid-June to October. Trips depart at 10am, noon, 2pm, and 4pm. Reservations are strongly recommended.

NATURE & WILDLIFE AREAS   The Bourne Conservation Trust has managed to get hold of a handful of small plots; for information, contact the town **Conservation Commission** (© **508/759-0615**). The largest tract is the **Four Ponds Conservation Area/ Town Forest,** which consists of 280 acres off Barlows Landing Road in Pocasset. The 40-acre **Nivling-Alexander Reserve** (off Shore Rd., at Thaxter Rd.) has three walking trails and flanks Red Brook Pond, where fishing is permitted (see above); it offers a half-mile wooded walk past several cranberry bogs. The **U.S. Army Corps of Engineers** (© **508/759-5991**), which is in charge of the **Cape Cod Canal,** gives free naturalist-guided nature walks and slide shows about the Canal. Visit the **Cape Cod Canal Visitor Center,** 60 Ed Moffitt Dr. (at the northeast corner of the canal; take Rte. 130 to Tupper Rd. to Town Neck Rd. to Coast Guard Rd.), Sandwich (© **508/833-9678**), for more details about this interesting waterway. There are several exhibits, as well as free public programs and canal guide booklets. Open daily 10am to 5pm in season.

TENNIS   In the Bourne area, public courts are located near the old schoolhouse on County Road in Cataumet, and in Chester Park, opposite the railroad station in Monument Beach. For information, call the **Bourne Memorial Community Center,** on Main Street in Buzzards Bay (© **508/759-0650**), which also has courts.

VISIT A MUSEUM

Aptucxet Trading Post Museum   Long before the Canal was a twinkle in Myles Standish's (and later, George Washington's) eye, Native Americans had been portaging goods between two rivers, the Manomet and Scusset, that once almost met at this site; its name in Algonquian means "little trap in the river." The Pilgrims were quick to notice that Aptucxet made an ideal trading spot, especially because, as Gov. William Bradford pointed out, it would allow them to trade with the Dutch to the south without "the compassing of Cape-Codd and those dangerous shoulds [shoals]." In 1627, the Pilgrims built an outpost here, hoping to cash in as conduits for native-caught pelts. The present building is a replica, built after a pair of local archaeologists, using ancient maps, uncovered the original foundation in 1926. The other detritus they dug up (arrowheads, pottery shards, and so on) is displayed in a roomful of rather dim, crowded display cases. Also be sure to have a look at the **Bournedale Stone,** which was discovered serving as a threshold for a Native American church built in the late 17th century. Overturned, it revealed strange, runelike inscriptions—fueling the legend (unsubstantiated as yet) that Vikings roamed the Cape around A.D. 1000.

Even though the building is not authentic, the curator does a very good job of conjuring up the hard, lonely life led by the pair of sentinels assigned here. Several other odd artifacts are scattered about the grounds, such as **President Grover Cleveland's personal train station** from his estate at Gray Gables.

The **Cape Cod Canal bike path** ★★★ runs right behind the museum. This is a good spot from which to observe the **Vertical Lift Railroad Bridge** ★, which represented state-of-the-art technology for its time (1935, when it cost $1.5 million). Rush hour, between 5 and 6pm, is your best chance to catch the bridge lowering its trestle (for the garbage cars headed off-Cape). In the off-season, you might get a colorful sunset thrown in for good measure.

24 Aptucxet Rd., off Perry Ave. (about 1/2 mile west of the town center), Bourne Village. © **508/759-9487;** www.bournehistoricalsoc.org/aptucxettradingpost.html. Admission $4 adults, $3.50 seniors, $2 children 6–18, free for children 5 and under. Families do not pay more than $10 in total. July–Aug Tues–Sat 10am–4pm, Sun 3–5pm; June and Sept Tues–Sat 10am–5pm. Closed Oct–May.

5 ## TAKE A CRUISE

Cape Cod Canal Cruises ★★ (Value)(Kids) Get an underbelly view of the Cape's two swooping car bridges and its unusual railroad bridge as a narrator fills you in on the Canal's history. It was the brainchild of New York financial wizard Augustus Perry Belmont, who completed it in 1914 at a cost of $16 million and never saw a penny of profit. Found to be too narrow and perilous (the current reverses with the tides, roughly every 6 hr.), the waterway was handed over to the U.S. Army Corps of Engineers for expansion in 1928 at the discount price of $11.5 million. It continues to serve as a vital shortcut, sparing some 30,000 boats yearly the long, dangerous circuit of the Outer Cape.

The 4pm **family cruise,** offered Monday to Saturday, is a real bargain, at $14 per adult and free for children 12 and under. The Sunday-afternoon trip is accompanied by New Orleans–style jazz, and the sunset entertainment cruises on Friday and Saturday (21 and older only) feature live bands.

Onset Bay Town Pier (on the northern side of the Canal, about 2 miles west of the Bourne Bridge), Onset. © **508/295-3883.** www.hy-linecruises.com. Tickets $14–$19 adults, children 12 and under half-price or free. Mid-June to Sept departures Mon 10am, 1:30pm, and 4pm; Tues–Thurs 10am, 2pm, 4:30pm, and 7pm; Fri–Sat 10am, 1:30pm, 4pm, and 8pm; Sun 10am and 2pm. Call for off-season schedule. Closed mid-Oct to Apr.

TAKE YOURSELF OUT TO A BALLGAME

Sports fans of all ages will enjoy taking in nine innings of the Grand Old Game. Part of the elite-amateur **Cape Cod Baseball League** (© **508/432-6909;** www.capecodbaseball.org),

KID STUFF

Stuck with a gray day? Pack the family off to **Cartwheels 2,** at 340 Macarthur Blvd./Rte. 28, about 2 miles south of the Bourne Bridge (© **508/743-9930;** www.cartwheels2. com). As far as entertaining kids goes, this place is probably the best bargain on the Cape. Older kids will like the go-carts and whiffle-ball cages. Little kids have a moonwalk, bumper boats, and minigolf. It's $6 per ride, but you'll definitely want to buy a 2-hour unlimited-rides pass for $21 to save money.

SHOPPING

Instead of the usual cutesy Cape Cod shops, Bourne is known for its factory outlets. **Cape Cod Factory Outlet Mall,** just off Route 6, exit 1, Sagamore (© **508/888-8417;** www.capecodfactoryoutlet.com), has 20 stores, including Van Heusen, L'Eggs/Hanes/ Playtex/Bali, Osh Kosh B'Gosh, and Samsonite.

GIFTS   You can observe artisans continuing the tradition of the Boston & Sandwich Glass Company at **Pairpoint Glass Works** ★, 851 Sandwich Rd. (Rte. 6A, near the foot of the Sagamore Bridge), Sagamore (© **800/899-0953;** www.pairpoint.com). Thomas J. Pairpoint was a leading designer in the 1880s. The output includes skillful replicas. Glass-blowing takes place Monday to Friday from 9am to 4pm. Bargain-lovers flock to the **Christmas Tree Shops** at the Sagamore Bridge, Sagamore (© **508/888-7010**). The stock here is not just holiday-related. Housed in an oversize thatch-roofed Tudor cottage, complete with spinning windmill (you can't miss it), the array is Woolworthian in scope. There are six more branches of Christmas Tree Shops in other towns on the Cape.

SEAFOOD   You couldn't hope for a fresher catch than what you'll find at **Cataumet Fish,** 1360 Rte. 28A, Cataumet (© **508/564-5956**). Buy a whole fish or cart home a couple of lobsters.

WHERE TO STAY

The Beachmoor ★ (**Value**   Quite a bit off the beaten track, this property, located right at the mouth of the Cape Cod Canal, next to the Massachusetts Military Academy, offers bargain rates and a pleasant ambience. There are views of the Cape Cod Canal from the suite, the commons room, and the superb casual **restaurant** on the first floor (see "Where to Dine," below). Rooms are decorated individually and with flair, and there's loving attention to detail throughout. For instance, iron bedsteads are romantically draped with gauzy fabric, and curtains are handmade with lacy netting. A tiny private beach in front of the hotel is perfect for sunning.

11 Buttermilk Way (south on Main St., left on Academy Dr., right on Tower Lane), Buzzards Bay, MA 02532. © **508/759-7522.** www.beachmoor.com. 6 units. Summer $95–$105 double; $135 suite. Rates include continental breakfast. AE, DC, DISC, MC, V. Closed Jan to mid-Feb. **Amenities:** Restaurant (see below). *In room:* TV/VCR, no phone.

WHERE TO DINE

Expensive

The Beachmoor ★★ NEW AMERICAN   If you happen to be anywhere near the Bourne Bridge and in need of dinner, you'll want to head over to the Beachmoor in Buzzards Bay. They serve up terrific food along with a wonderful view of the Cape Cod

Canal. Specialties at dinner include Beachmoor Stew (shrimp, clams, scallops, lobster, and fish in a saffron broth) and the daily trilogy, which might include poached salmon with béarnaise sauce, grilled swordfish with basil butter, and broiled scallops in lemon butter. Save room for dessert, and if baked pear is on the menu, don't hesitate. It's a heavenly concoction of crisp-on-the-outside, doughy-on-the-inside pastry surrounding delicate baked pears, served with vanilla ice cream and raspberry sauce. Evening entertainment is offered on Friday (Nick Lombardo sing-along) and Saturday (Al "Fingers" Russo at the piano bar). On Sunday there's a brunch buffet for $15.

11 Buttermilk Way, Buzzards Bay. *C* **508/759-7522.** Reservations recommended. Main courses $16–$30. AE, DC, DISC, MC, V. Apr–Sept Wed–Sat 5–10pm, Sun 11:30am–8pm; Oct–Dec Thurs–Sat 5–10pm, Sun 11:30am–8pm. Closed Jan–Mar.

Moderate

The Chart Room ★★ SEAFOOD

Great sunset views over Red Brook Harbor and fresh fish are reason enough to visit this dockside restaurant, housed in a former railroad barge at a busy marina. A piano bar lends a bit of elegance, as does the well-heeled clientele. The only downside is due to this restaurant's ongoing popularity; it can get very loud here. The younger crowd likes to gather at the bar for the mudslides, said to be the best in the region.

1 Shipyard Lane (in the Kingman Yacht Center, off Shore Rd.), Cataumet. *C* **508/563-5350.** Dinner reservations required. Main courses $12–$25. AE, MC, V. Mid-June to early Sept daily 11:30am–10pm; mid-May to mid-June and early Sept to mid-Oct Thurs–Sat 11:30am–10pm, Sun 11:30am–3pm. Closed mid-Oct to mid-May.

Quahog Republic ★ (Finds) SEAFOOD

You'll impress all your friends if you can actually find this classic Cape Cod restaurant, surrounded on three sides by water. Sitting on the large deck of this restaurant is the quintessential summer experience. What started out as a run-down beach bar is now a terrific place for lunch on a sunny summer day. The house favorite is the fish and chips, made with a large piece of fresh cod encased in crunchy batter. Perhaps even more popular are the burgers, either the Mashnee Island burger with pineapple, bacon, cheese, and shrimp or the Aussie with bacon, cheese, and a fried egg on top. There's live entertainment Sunday from 4 to 7pm in season.

162 Leeward Rd., Bourne. *C* **508/759-9390.** http://quahogrepublic.com. Reservations not accepted. Main courses $6–$19. MC, V. June–Aug daily 11:30am–10pm; Sept–Dec and May Thurs 4–10pm, Fri–Sat 11:30am–10pm, Sun 4pm–sunset. Closed Jan–Apr. At the Bourne Bridge rotary, take the first right onto Trowbridge Rd. At the VFW Post stay right and follow signs to Mashnee Island; cross causeway to Mashnee Island and take 1st left for restaurant.

Parrot Bar and Grille NEW AMERICAN

This upbeat casual family restaurant specializes in seafood and pasta. Try the lobster pie or the blackened swordfish with Southwestern salsa. Local bands entertain Thursday to Saturday, with no cover charge.

1356 Rte. 28A, Cataumet. *C* **508/563-2117.** www.parrotbargrille.com. Reservations recommended in season. Main courses $10–$15. MC, V. Daily 11:30am–10pm.

An Internet Cafe

The best Web cafe on the Cape is the **Daily Brew Coffee Bar and Café** ★, Cataumet Square, 1370 Rte. 28A, Cataumet (*C* **508/564-4755;** www.thedailybrewcoffeehouse.com), where you can get awesome espressos, cappuccinos, and baked goods, as well as soups, salads, and sandwiches. Several computers are located upstairs if you want to log on. There is outside seating on a covered patio in back. The cafe is open 5am to 3pm year-round.

On weekends, local bands draw a crowd of young adults to the **Courtyard Restaurant and Pub,** 1337 County Rd., Cataumet (© **508/563-1818;** www.courtyardcapecod. com). Cover charge varies. From here you can barhop to the **Parrot Bar and Grille,** 1356 Rte. 28A (see "Where to Dine," above), which has live music Thursday to Saturday in season.

3 FALMOUTH ★★★

18 miles S of Sagamore; 20 miles SW of Hyannis

Falmouth is a classic New England town, complete with historic churches alongside the Village Green and a bustling Main Street. The town offers a variety of activities and summer events for vacationers, from beautiful beaches and bike paths to weekly outdoor band concerts and summer theater. Founded in 1660 by Quakers from Sandwich, Falmouth proved remarkably arable territory: By the 19th century, it reigned as the strawberry capital of the world. Today, with over 32,000 year-round residents, it's the second-largest town on the Cape, after Barnstable.

With more than a century of catering to summertime guests (it was the first "fashionable" Cape resort, served by trains from Boston starting in the 1870s), Falmouth residents have hospitality down to an art. The area around the historic **Village Green ★★** (used for military exercises in the pre-Revolutionary days) is a veritable hotbed of B&Bs, with each vying to provide the most elaborate breakfasts and solicitous advice. Listen to your hosts, and you'll soon feel like a native.

Officially a village within Falmouth (one of eight), tiny **Woods Hole ★★★** has been a world-renowned oceanic research center since 1871, when the U.S. Commission of Fish and Fisheries set up a primitive seasonal collection station. Today the various scientific institutes crowded around the harbor—principally, the National Marine Fisheries Service, the Marine Biological Laboratory (founded in 1888), and the Woods Hole Oceanographic Institute (a newcomer as of 1930)—have research budgets in the tens of millions of dollars and employ thousands of scientists. Woods Hole's scientific institutions offer a unique opportunity to get in-depth—and often hands-on—exposure to marine biology.

Belying the stereotype of the nerdy scientist, the Woods Hole community is far from uptight; in fact, it's one of the hipper communities on the Cape. There are a number of agreeable restaurants and shops, making the small, crowded gauntlet of Water Street a very pleasant place to stroll. Don't even think of parking here in summer; take the shuttle bus from Falmouth, or bike down on the Shining Sea Bikeway.

West Falmouth ★★ (which is really more north of town, stretched alongside Buzzards Bay) has held on to its bucolic character and makes a lovely drive, with perhaps an occasional stop for the more alluring antiques stores. **Falmouth Heights ★★★**, a cluster of shingled Victorian summer houses on a bluff east of Falmouth's harbor, is as popular as it is picturesque; its narrow ribbon of beach is a magnet for all, especially families. The **Waquoit Bay** area ★, a few miles east of town, has thus far eluded the over-commercialization that blights most of Route 28, and with luck and foresight will continue to do so. Several thousand acres of this vital estuarine ecosystem are now under federal custody.

GETTING THERE After crossing either the Bourne or Sagamore bridge, take Route 28 or 28A south. Crossing the Bourne Bridge will get you closer to your destination. Or fly into Hyannis (see section 3, "Getting There & Getting Around," in chapter 3).

Falmouth's bus station near the center of town is serviced by **Peter Pan Bus Lines** (59 Depot Ave.; ✆ **888/751-8800** or 508/548-7588; www.peterpanbus.com). Daily express buses run to and from Boston's Logan Airport ($30 one-way, $55 round-trip), as well as Boston's South Station train and bus terminal ($26 one-way, $50 round-trip). There are also daily buses to Providence, Rhode Island ($29 one-way, $56 round-trip); T. F. Green Airport in Providence ($32 one-way, $58 round-trip); and New York City ($73 one-way, $121 round-trip). Off-season, there are discounts for 7- and 14-day advance purchases.

To get around Falmouth and Woods Hole (where parking in summer is impossible due to ferry traffic to Martha's Vineyard), use the seasonal (late June–Labor Day) **Whoosh Trolley** (✆ **800/352-7155;** www.thebreeze.info), which makes a circuit every 20 minutes down Falmouth's Main Street to Woods Hole from 9:30am to 7:10pm Monday to Friday, and until 9:30pm on weekends from late May to late September and later in midsummer. You can pick up the trolley at the Falmouth Mall on Route 28, where there is plenty of parking. You can also flag down the trolley anywhere along the route. The trolley fare is $1 per trip or $3 for a 1-day pass.

Tip: The **Whoosh Trolley**'s extended hours (until 10:30pm Fri–Sat in July and Aug) means you can use it to go down to Woods Hole in the summer for dinner. Otherwise, parking in Woods Hole in high season can be a major challenge.

The **Sealine Shuttle** (✆ **800/352-7155**) connects Woods Hole, Falmouth, and Mashpee with Hyannis year-round (except holidays). The fare ranges from $1 to $4, depending on distance; children 4 and under ride free.

VISITOR INFORMATION Contact the **Falmouth Chamber of Commerce,** 20 Academy Lane, Falmouth, MA 02540 (✆ **800/526-8532** or 508/548-8500; www.falmouth chamber.com), which is open year-round Monday to Friday 9am to 5pm, Saturday 9am to 4pm, and Sunday 9am to 2pm, or the **Cape Cod Chamber of Commerce** (see "Visitor Information," under "Sandwich," earlier in this chapter).

WINDING DOWN For a well-earned pick-me-up, take a biscotti break at **Coffee Obsession** ★ (✆ **508/540-2233**), a hip and friendly coffee bar in the Queens Buyway, at the corner of North Main and Palmer Avenue.

BEACHES & RECREATIONAL PURSUITS

BEACHES Although Old Silver Beach, Surf Drive Beach, and Menauhant Beach will sell a 1-day pass, most other Falmouth public beaches require a parking sticker. Day passes to Old Silver are $20, and day passes to Surf Drive and Menauhant are $10. Renters can obtain temporary beach parking stickers, for $60 per week or $70 for 2 weeks, at **Falmouth Town Hall,** 59 Town Hall Sq. (✆ **508/548-7611**), or at the **Surf Drive Beach bathhouse** in season (✆ **508/548-8623**). The town beaches for which a parking fee is charged all have lifeguards, restrooms, and concession stands. Some of Falmouth's more notable public shores are as follows:

- **Falmouth Heights Beach** ★★★, off Grand Avenue, in Falmouth Heights: Once a rowdy spot, this is primarily a family beach these days. Parking is sticker-only, and some local inns will provide stickers to guests. This neighborhood supported the Cape's first summer colony; the grand Victorian mansions still overlook the beach. The beach has lifeguards and bathroom facilities.

ACCOMMODATIONS ■
Baileys by the Sea **26**
Beach Breeze Inn **29**
Coonamessett Inn **1**
Inn on the Sound **25**
Palmer House Inn **4**
Red Horse Inn **19**
Seaside Inn **23**
Tides Motel **27**

ATTRACTIONS ●
Falmouth Museums on
the Green **5**

DINING ◆
Bangkok Cuisine
Thai Restaurant **18**
Ben & Bill's Chocolate
Emporium **8**
Betsy's Diner **16**
The Boat House
Restaurant & Lounge **21**
Box Lunch **17**

The British Beer Company **23**
Cape Cod Bagel Co. **2**
Casino Wharf Fx **24**
The Clam Shack **28**
Coffee Obsession **3**
Falmouth Raw Bar **20**
The Flying Bridge **22**
Golden Swan Indian Cuisine **12**
La Cucina Sul Mare **10**

Laureen's **7**
Molly's Tea Room **9**
Osteria La Civetta **6**
Peking Palace **15**
Pies A La Mode **13**
RööBar **11**
Steve's Pizzeria & More **14**

- **Grews Pond** ★★, in Goodwill Park, off Palmer Avenue, in Falmouth: This freshwater pond in a large town forest stays fairly uncrowded, even in the middle of summer. While everyone else is experiencing beach rage, trying to find parking at Falmouth's popular saltwater beaches, here you park for free and can wander shady paths around the pond. You'll find picnic tables, a playground, barbecue grills, a lifeguard, and restrooms.
- **Menauhant Beach** ★, off Central Avenue, in East Falmouth: A bit off the beaten track, Menauhant is a little less mobbed than Falmouth Heights Beach and better protected from the winds. There are lifeguards, bathroom facilities, and a bathhouse. A 1-day parking pass costs $10.

- **Old Silver Beach** ★★★, off Route 28A, in North Falmouth: Western-facing (great for sunsets) and relatively calm, this warm Buzzards Bay beach is a popular, often crowded, choice. This is the chosen spot for the college crowd and other rowdy young folk. Mothers and their charges cluster on the opposite side of the street, where a shallow pool formed by a sandbar is perfect for toddlers. The beach boasts several amenities, including a bathhouse with showers and bathrooms, food concessions, and lifeguards. Sailboards are available to rent in season. A 1-day parking pass costs $20.
- **Surf Drive Beach** ★★★, off Shore Street in Falmouth: About a half-mile from downtown, and appealing to families, this is an easy-to-get-to choice (it's a 10-min. walk from Main St.) but with limited parking. The area between the jetties is a shallow, calm area called "the kiddie pool." You'll find an outdoor shower, bathrooms, a food concession, and lifeguards. A 1-day parking pass costs $10.

BICYCLING The **Shining Sea Bikeway** ★★★ (✆ **508/548-8500**) is a 12-mile beauty that travels on an old railroad right-of-way from North Falmouth past cranberry bogs, farmland, and the Great Sippewissett Marsh, then skirts Vineyard Sound from Falmouth center to Woods Hole. This is one of the Cape's most scenic bike paths and one of the few that travels alongside a beach. There is free parking on Locust Street; on Depot Avenue; in West Falmouth, on Old Dock Road; and at the trail head on County Road, in North Falmouth. The Falmouth Chamber of Commerce offers a map and brochure about the bike path.

The path's name is a nod to Falmouth's own Katharine Lee Bates, who wrote the lyrics to "America the Beautiful," with its verse, "And crown thy good with brotherhood, from sea to shining sea!"

The closest bike shop—convenient to the main cluster of B&Bs, some of which offer "loaners"—is **Corner Cycle,** at 115 Palmer Avenue, at North Main Street (✆ **508/540-4195;** www.cornercycle.com). A half-day bike rental is $17 ($12 for children), a 24-hour rental $26 ($18 for children). For a broad selection of vehicles—from six-speed cruisers to six-passenger "surreys"—and good advice on routes, visit **Holiday Cycles,** at 465 Grand Ave., in Falmouth Heights (✆ **508/540-3549**), where a half-day bike rental is $20, a 1-day rental $25, and a week rental $65. The surreys rent for $20 to $30 an hour. Holiday Cycles does not accept credit cards.

BIRD-WATCHING The **Shining Sea Bikeway** (see above) is a great spot to bird-watch, especially near Oyster Pond, where there's an osprey nest. Keep an eye out for yellow-breasted chats and orange-crowned warblers, as well as such waterfowl as mallards and buffleheads. You may also see herons and egrets.

BOATING **Patriot Party Boats,** 227 Clinton Ave. (at Scranton Ave., on the harbor), Falmouth (✆ **800/734-0088** or 508/548-2626; www.patriotpartyboats.com or www.the liberte.com), offers one-stop shopping for would-be boaters. The Patriot fleet includes a poky fishing vessel, the *Patriot Too;* and a 74-foot, three-masted schooner, the ***Liberte*** ★★ (2-hr. sails; $20–$30 adults, $15–$20 children 11 and under). On the *Liberte,* Chris Tieje hauls up the sails and regales passengers about his custom-made schooner, while the impressive vessel cruises the sound. The most expensive trip and the most popular is the sunset sail at 6:30pm. Other trips leave at 10:30am and 2pm. For info on fishing trips, see "Fishing," below.

Cape Cod Kayak (✆ **508/563-9377;** www.capecodkayak.com) rents kayaks (free delivery) by the day or week, and offers lessons and ecotours on local waterways. Canoe and kayak rentals are $35 to $60 for 8 hours. Lessons are $49 per hour. Four-hour trips are $45 to $65.

If you want to explore on your own, a great area for exploring is Waquoit Bay (see "Nature & Wildlife Areas," below). **Washburn Island** ★★★, a protected reserve with wooded trails and pristine beaches, is about a 45-minute paddle from the town boat ramp near Edward's Boat Yard on Route 28 in East Falmouth.

FISHING Falmouth has six fishable ponds. A complimentary fishing map and guide are available from the Falmouth Chamber of Commerce. Freshwater fishing and shellfishing licenses can be obtained at **Falmouth Town Hall,** 59 Town Hall Sq. (𝒞 508/548-7611). Freshwater fishing licenses ($29 for Massachusetts residents, $39 for nonresidents) can also be obtained at **Eastman's Sport & Tackle,** 150 Main St. (𝒞 **508/548-6900**).

Surf Drive Beach is a great spot for surf-casting, once the crowds have dispersed. Other good locations are the jetties off Nobska Point, in Woods Hole, and Bristol Beach, on Menauhant Road, in East Falmouth.

To go after bigger prey, head out with a group on one of the **Patriot Party Boats,** based in Falmouth's Inner Harbor (𝒞 **800/734-0088** or 508/548-2626; www.patriot partyboats.com). Boats leave twice daily, at 8am and 1pm, in season. The *Patriot Too,* with an enclosed deck, is ideal for family-style "bottom fishing" (4-hr. trips $40 adults, $25 children 12 and under; sportfishing trips $70 adults, $40 children; equipment and instruction provided).

For deep-sea fishing enthusiasts, there are about a half-dozen sportfishing outfits that operate out of Falmouth Inner Harbor, cruising around Nantucket Sound, Vineyard Sound, and the Elizabeth Islands for bass, blues, tuna, and shark. Trips cost about $500 for a half-day, $700 for a full day. Call the chamber (𝒞 **508/548-8500**) for info.

FITNESS If you're jonesing for time in the gym, the **Falmouth Sports Center,** at 33 Highfield Dr. (𝒞 **508/548-7433**), offers weight-training facilities for $9 per day. Racquetball costs an extra $12 per person, per hour. Tennis is $26 per person, per hour.

GOLF Falmouth abounds in golf courses—six public ones at last count. Among the more notable is the challenging 18-hole championship course at **Ballymeade Country Club,** 125 Falmouth Woods Rd. (𝒞 **508/540-4005;** www.ballymeade.com). Greens fees are $60 (Mon–Fri) and $75 (Sat–Sun) and include carts.

ICE-SKATING Public skating ($5 per person; rental skates $4) is offered year-round at the **Falmouth Ice Arena,** 9 Skating Lane, off Palmer Avenue (𝒞 **508/548-7080;** www. falmouthicearena.com), the home rink of Colleen Coyne, who was part of the gold-medal 1998 Olympic hockey team; call for information and hours.

NATURE & WILDLIFE AREAS **Ashumet Holly and Wildlife Sanctuary** ★★, operated by the Massachusetts Audubon Society, at 186 Ashumet Rd., off Route 151, in East Falmouth (𝒞 **508/362-1426**), is an intriguing 49-acre collection of more than 1,000 holly trees spanning 65 species culled from around the world. Preserved by the state's first commissioner of agriculture, who was concerned that commercial harvesting might wipe out native species, they flourish here, along with over 130 species of birds and a carpet of Oriental lotus blossoms, which covers a kettle pond come summer. The trail fee is $3 for adults and $2 for seniors and children 15 and under.

Close to the center of Falmouth (just follow Depot Rd. to the end) is the 650-acre **Beebe Woods** ★★, a treasure for hikers and dog walkers. From here you can wend your way to the **Peterson Farm** ★★ (entrance off Woods Hole Rd.; take a right at the Quissett farm stand), purchased by the town of Falmouth in 1997. The 90-acre farm has paths through woods and fields, as well as a flock of sheep grazing in a meadow near historic farm buildings. Bluebird boxes (special birdhouses for bluebirds) line the path on the way to a quiet pond. There is no charge to walk in Beebe Woods.

Tiny but dazzling, the privately owned **Spohr Gardens** ★★, on Fells Road, off Oyster Pond Road in Woods Hole, invites visitors to explore 6 magical acres beside Oyster Pond. In the spring, thousands of daffodils bloom, followed by rhododendrons and day lilies. Paths wind past a collection of nautical treasures, such as huge anchors and millstones. Remarkably, this private garden is free and open to the public. Donations for garden maintenance are accepted.

Named for its round shape that sticks out into the harbor, **The Knob** ★★ (13 acres of trails at Quissett Harbor, at the end of Quissett Road), provides a perfect short walk and lovely views of Buzzards Bay. There's very limited parking at this small, secluded harbor, so try it early or late in the day. The Knob is owned by the nonprofit group Salt Pond Areas Bird Sanctuaries and is free and open to the public.

The 2,250-acre **Waquoit Bay National Estuarine Research Reserve (WBNERR),** at 149 Waquoit Hwy., in Waquoit (© **508/457-0495;** www.waquoitbayreserve.org), maintains a 1-mile, self-guided nature trail. The reserve also offers a number of walks and interpretive programs, including the popular "Evenings on the Bluff," on Tuesday nights at 6:30pm, which is geared toward families. The visitor center is open Monday to Friday from 10am to 4pm. You'll find several interesting exhibits especially appropriate for children. On Saturday in season, WBNERR hosts a free 20-minute cruise over to **Washburn Island** ★★. Once on the island, visitors can explore its wooded trails or relax on its pristine beaches. The 12-passenger motorboat leaves at 9am and returns by 12:30pm. The reserve also manages 11 primitive campsites on Washburn Island. Permits cost a mere $10 a night. Advance reservations for the cruise and camping are required and can be made by calling © **877/422-6762.** (The campsites book up 6 months in advance for summer weekends, but you'll have better luck with a late-spring or early-fall booking.)

TENNIS   Among the courts open to the public are those at the **Falmouth High School,** 874 Gifford Rd., Falmouth Recreation Department; and at the **Lawrence School,** on Lakeview Avenue, a few blocks from the center of town. Call the Falmouth Chamber of Commerce (© **508/548-8500**) for information. Both are first-come, first-served. Among the commercial enterprises offering outdoor courts—clay, Har-Tru, and hard—are **Ballymeade Country Club** (see "Golf," above) and the **Falmouth Sports Center** (see "Fitness," above), which has six indoor courts in addition to three outside. Rates are $52 an hour for singles.

WATERSPORTS   Falmouth is something of a sailboarding mecca, prized for its unflagging southwesterly winds. Although Old Silver Beach in North Falmouth is the most popular spot for windsurfing, the sport is allowed there only prior to 9am and after 5pm. The Trunk River area on the west end of Falmouth's Surf Drive Beach and a portion of Chapoquoit Beach are the only public beaches where windsurfers are allowed during the day. Concessions rent windsurfing equipment at Surf Drive Beach. Windsurfing races are held at Trunk River Beach, about a mile west from Surf Drive Beach, Saturday mornings in the summer.

SEA SCIENCE IN WOODS HOLE

Marine Biological Laboratory   The small Robert W. Pierce Visitors Center and Gift Shop offers visitors who are short on time a chance to gain some insight into the goings-on at this preeminent scientific facility, part of which is housed in an 1836 candle factory. Visitors can peer into a microscope, like the scientists on staff here, to observe marine organisms. A guided tour requires a little more forethought—the MBL prefers that reservations be made a week in advance—but will definitely reward the curious. After a slide presentation, a retired scientist leads visitors through the holding tanks and then to the lab to observe actual research in progress. The MBL's area of inquiry is not limited to the aquatic but encompasses the "biological process common to all life forms."

7 MBL St., Woods Hole. ☏ **508/289-7423** (to schedule tours). www.mbl.edu. Free admission. Visitors Center July–Aug Mon–Sat 10am–4:30pm, Sun noon–4:30pm; call for off-season hours. Closed Jan–Apr. 1-hr. tours by reservation (no children under 5) late June–Aug Mon–Fri 1, 2, and 3pm.

Woods Hole Oceanographic Institution Exhibit Center and Gift Shop   This world-class research organization—locally referred to by its acronym, WHOI (pronounced *hoo-ey*)—is dedicated to the study of marine science. And with some $80 million in annual funding at stake, there's serious science going on here. This is a small but interactive exhibit center. Kids might enjoy looking through microscopes at organisms or listening to sounds of marine animals on a computer. *Titanic* fans will enjoy the brief video, displays, and a life-size model of the submersible that discovered the wreck. You can climb into the model and flick switches if you like. One-hour **walking tours** of WHOI are offered twice a day on weekdays in July and August; reservations are required and can be made by calling ☏ **508/289-2252.**

15 School St. (off Water St.), Woods Hole. ☏ **508/289-2663.** www.whoi.edu. $2 donation requested. Late May–early Sept Mon–Sat 10am–4:30pm; call for off-season hours. Closed Jan–Mar.

Woods Hole Science Aquarium ★ **Kids**   A little beat up after 1¼ centuries of service and endless streams of eager schoolchildren, this aquarium—the first such institution in the country—may not be state of the art, but it's a treasure nonetheless. The highlight is the recently renovated state-of-the-art seal tank out front that houses LuSeal and Bumper, grey seals that are too injured to be released in the wild. The displays, focusing on local waters, might make you think twice before taking a dip. Children show no hesitation, though, in getting up to their elbows in the "touch tanks"; adults are also welcome to dabble. A key exhibit that everyone should see concerns the effect of plastic trash on the marine environment.

166 Water Street at Albatross St. (off the western end of Water St.), Woods Hole. ☏ **508/495-2001.** http://aquarium.nefsc.noaa.gov. Free admission; donations accepted. Mid-June to early Sept Tues–Sat 11am–4pm; early Sept to mid-June Mon–Fri 10am–4pm. Adults need a picture ID to enter.

FALMOUTH HISTORICAL SIGHTS

Falmouth Museums on the Green ★★   These three buildings contain fascinating vestiges of Falmouth's colorful history and are definitely worth a visit. The 1790 Julia Wood House was built by Revolutionary physician Dr. Francis Wicks; a simulacrum of his office, complete with terrifying tools, is not for the faint of heart. Next door, past an authentic Colonial garden, is the mid-18th-century **Conant House,** which evolved from a half-Cape built to accommodate the town's minister; it now houses nautical collections, including intricate "sailor's valentines" made of shells, and whaling exhibits. A china hutch in the dining room displays romantic Staffordshire china. A special room chronicles the life of Katharine Lee Bates, Falmouth-born author of "America the Beautiful." Also on the grounds is the **Dudley Hallett Barn,** which contains vintage farm tools and the sleigh that Dr. Wicks used for house calls.

In the summer, the museum sponsors guided strolls, gallery talks, trolley tours, and afternoon teas. The free 90-minute guided strolls take place every Tuesday at 10am in

July, August, and September. Trolley tours—for $15—take place every Wednesday at 10:30am and 2pm, in September and October.

55–65 Palmer Ave. (at the Village Green). © 508/548-4857. www.falmouthhistoricalsociety.org. Admission $5 adults, free for children 12 and under. Late June–early Oct Tues–Fri 10am–4pm, Sat 10am–1pm; by appointment only early Oct–late June.

Woods Hole Historical Museum ★　Exhibits change at this small but charming museum. The permanent 1895 diorama of the town should give you the former flavor of this combination seaport/scientific community and tourist destination. The neighboring barn shelters a Small Boat Museum, which displays artifacts including an Old Town canoe, a Cape Cod "knockabout," a Herreshoff 12½, and a fine example of a "spritsail" boat. There's also the reconstructed 1893 hobby workshop of a local doctor. To delve into town lore in more detail, reserve a place on one of the free **walking tours** offered Tuesdays at 4pm in July and August.

579 Woods Hole Rd. (on the eastern edge of town), Woods Hole. © 508/548-7270. www.woodshole museum.org. Free admission; donations welcome. Mid-June to mid-Sept Tues–Sat 10am–4pm; off-season by appointment.

BASEBALL

Part of the elite-amateur **Cape Cod Baseball League** (© 508/432-6909; www.capecod baseball.org), the Falmouth Commodores play at Guv Fuller Field behind the Gus Canty Community Center, off East Main Street, in July and August. Admission is free, though a donation of $5 is requested. Call the **Falmouth Chamber of Commerce** (© 508/548-8500) to check the schedule, or pick one up at the **Gus Canty Community Center,** 790 E. Main St. (© 508/457-2567).

SHOPPING

Falmouth's spiffy Main Street has a number of good clothing, home-goods, and gift stores. There are also several good arts-and-crafts galleries in West Falmouth and Woods Hole.

ARTS & CRAFTS　Joan Lederman creates and sells her one-of-a-kind ceramics at the **Soft Earth** ★, in Woods Hole (© 508/540-5237; www.thesoftearth.com). Lederman glazes her pottery with sediment found on ocean floors all over the world. She obtains much of her material from the oceanographic scientists based in Woods Hole. The colors and patterns created by the sediment make each of her practical pieces, which include bowls, platters, mugs, vases, and the like, utterly unique works of art. Her studio/gallery is open to visitors from 11am to 1pm weekdays or by appointment.

BOOKS　**Booksmith,** 33 Davis Straits (in Falmouth Plaza), Falmouth (© 508/540-6064; www.booksmithfalmouth.com), is a terrific all-around bookstore, with a good selection of novels and nonfiction paperbacks for beach reading. The very appealing **Eight Cousins Children's Books,** 189 Main St., Falmouth (© 508/548-5548; www. eightcousins.com), offers books, games, and toys for children of all ages. The town's largest repository of books is **Inkwell Bookstore,** at 199 Main St., Falmouth (© 508/540-0039; www.inkwellbookstore.com), where you'll find a good mix of beach reading and nonfiction, plus the town's biggest magazine rack.

FASHION　Don't be too intimidated to browse in **Maxwell & Co.,** 200 Main St. (in the center of town), Falmouth (© 508/540-8752; www.maxwellandco.com), which may be the highest-end clothier on the Cape. Comfortable Italian fashions are displayed here in an elegant setting. Its end-of-summer sale in mid-August offers up to 70% off the prices of these exquisite goods.

The clothing at **Caline for Kids,** 149 Main St. (in the center of town), Falmouth (© **508/548-2533;** www.calineforkids.com), ranges from practical to elegant, and sometimes manages to be both. Sizes from newborn to 14 are available.

FOOD & WINE   People drive from all over the region for the wine selection (and prices) at **Kappy's,** 21 Spring Bars Rd., off Route 28 (© **508/548-2600;** www.kappys.com), the Cape's largest liquor, beer, and wine store. "Pick your own" is the password at the long-established **Tony Andrews Farm and Produce Stand ★★** 394 Old Meeting House Rd. (about 1½ miles north of Rte. 28), East Falmouth (© **508/548-4717;** www.tony andrewsfarmstand.com), where it's strawberries early in the summer, and tomatoes, sweet corn, squash, sunflowers, and more as the season progresses. Of course, you can just buy them here without picking, though the Puritans wouldn't have approved. Open daily 10am to 6pm. **Coonamessett Farm ★★**, 277 Hatchville Rd. (about 1 mile east of Sandwich Rd.), East Falmouth (© **508/563-2560;** www.coonamessettfarm.com), has a full farm stand of vegetables grown in the fields out back. You can pick your own vegetables, look at the farm animals (including two cute llamas), or rent a canoe for a paddle in the pond out back. A **Vegetarian Buffet Dinner** is served Friday nights in season (5–8pm; $19 adults, $9.95 children, free for children 5 and under) at the farm's cafe. The popular **Jamaican Buffet Dinner** on Wednesday nights in summer (5–8pm; $20 adults, $11 children) features jerk chicken and live reggae music.

GIFTS   **Bojangles,** 239 Main St. (© **508/548-9888.** www.bojanglesintl.com), is a high-end gift shop/women's clothing boutique. Stop here for fun gifts and fine crafts, including exceptional hand-painted glassware.

SPA   **Bellezza Day Spa,** 221 Main St. (© **508/299-8300;** www.spabellezza.com), is perhaps the most luxurious beauty shop on Cape Cod. Set in a high-ceilinged storefront on Falmouth's Main Street, the spa offers all manner of facials, waxings, massages, manicures, haircuts, and other services.

WHERE TO STAY

For a basic motel with a great location, try the **Tides Motel** (© **800/628-3811** or 508/548-3126; www.tidesmotelcapecod.com), on Clinton Avenue, at the far west end of Grand Avenue in Falmouth Heights. The 1950s-style no-frills (no air-conditioning, no phone) motel sits on the beach at the head of Falmouth Harbor facing Vineyard Sound. Rates in season are $165 to $175 double, $220 suite. It's closed late October to mid-May.

The **Red Horse Inn ★**, at 28 Falmouth Heights Rd., Falmouth (© **508/548-0053;** www.redhorseinn.com), is a family-friendly option just a short walk from Falmouth Inner Harbor. The 22 rooms are priced from $195 to $215. Open year-round.

The **Seaside Inn,** at 263 Grand Ave., Falmouth Heights (© **800/827-1976;** www. seasideinnfalmouth.com), is a reasonably priced motel in a superb location, across the street from Falmouth Heights Beach and next to the British Beer Company, a family-style restaurant. The 23 rooms, with air-conditioning, TVs, phones with free calls, and some with kitchenettes and decks, are priced at $144 to $199 for a double, $234 to $304 for a deluxe room. Open year-round.

Expensive

Inn on the Sound ★★ (Finds)   The ambience here is as breezy as the setting, high on a bluff beside Falmouth's premier sunning beach, with a sweeping view of Vineyard

Sound from the large front deck. There's none of the usual frilly/cutesy stuff in these well-appointed guest rooms, most of which have ocean views, several with their own private decks. Many of the bathrooms have been renovated with large, luxurious tiled showers. The focal point of the inn's living room is a handsome boulder hearth (nice for those nippy nights). Most guests enjoy having their breakfast, which features lots of home-baked goodies, served on the front deck.

313 Grand Ave., Falmouth Heights, MA 02540. ✆ **800/564-9668** or 508/457-9666. Fax 508/457-9631. www.innonthesound.com. 10 units, 8 with tub/shower, 2 with shower only. Summer $195–$345 double; Off-season $135–$195. Rates include full breakfast. AE, DISC, MC, V. No children 11 and under. *In room:* TV, hair dryer, no phone.

Moderate

Baileys by the Sea ★ (Finds)   If you love the beach, the location of this charming bed-and-breakfast, a few steps from Falmouth Heights Beach, is liable to make you swoon. Bailey's has a casual feel, with whitewashed walls and views of Vineyard Sound from all seven of the inn's rooms. Everything about this inn feels very summery, from the sheer curtains, full with breezes; the rocking chairs; even the waffle robes provided in each room. Falmouth Heights, one of the Cape's first summery communities, is a wonderful place to stroll and gaze at Victorian homes, or simply walk for miles along the beach, with views of Martha's Vineyard in the distance. Besides the beach just out the door, there are also two restaurants, a family-style tavern and a fine-dining establishment, both a short walk away.

321 Grand Ave., Falmouth, MA 02540. ✆ **866/548-5748** or 508/548-5748. Fax 508/548-6974. www. baileysbythesea.com. 6 units. Summer $205–$310 double; off-season $155–$235. Rates include full breakfast. MC, V. *In room:* A/C, TV, hair dryer.

Beach Breeze Inn ★   This inn has a great location, just steps from Surf Drive Beach and a short and pleasant stroll to Main Street, with its many shops and restaurants. Guests here beat the summer traffic blues, because with beach and town within walking distance, you never need to use your car! Rooms are sunny and spacious with motel-style privacy; many of them have separate entrances. The inn was built in 1858, and spent many years as a run-down boardinghouse. It has been thoroughly freshened up and is now a terrific lodging option, particularly for families.

321 Shore St. (about ¼ mile south of Main St.), Falmouth, MA 02540. ✆ **800/828-3255** or 508/548-1765. www.beachbreezeinn.com. 20 units. Summer $179–$289 double; $1,500–$1,700 weekly efficiencies. MC, V. **Amenities:** Unheated pool. *In room:* TV, fridge.

Coonamessett Inn ★★   A gracious inn built around the core of a 1796 homestead, the Coonamessett Inn is Falmouth's most traditional lodging choice. The original inn was a few miles away and flanked the namesake river. Set on 7 lushly landscaped acres overlooking a pond, it has the feel of an attractive country club. Some of the rooms, decorated in reproduction antiques, can be a bit somber, so try to get one with good light (rooms nos. 1–6, plus the "village rooms" that face the pond). Most have a separate sitting room attached. On-site is a **restaurant** featuring a very comfortable tavern room as well as a more formal dining room. The extensive buffet brunch here on Sundays brings out people from all over town.

Jones Rd. and Gifford St. (about ½ mile north of Main St.), Falmouth, MA 02540. ✆ **508/548-2300.** Fax 508/540-9831. www.capecodrestaurants.org. 27 units, 1 cottage. Summer $170–$250 double; $220 2-bedroom suite; $280 cottage. Rates include continental breakfast. AE, MC, V. **Amenities:** Restaurant. *In room:* A/C, TV, hair dryer.

Palmer House Inn ★   Located just steps from the historic Falmouth Village Green and a bike-rental shop, and a short stroll to Main Street's shops and restaurants, the Palmer House Inn, a vintage Queen Anne Victorian, has a terrific location. Innkeepers Bill and Pat O'Connell are most welcoming. Rooms are decorated to highlight the inn's 19th-century heritage with pretty floral wallpaper, curtains, and bedding. Rooms feature majestic beds, including a canopied mahogany beauty in a turret room. The Henry James Room on the third floor has a romantically draped four-poster bed and a whirlpool tub under a skylit cathedral ceiling. The living room is a fine place to curl up with a book in front of the fireplace or to gather before dinner with a glass of wine, provided by your hosts. Breakfasts in the sunny dining room are elaborate, with such options as Swiss eggs in puff pastry or chocolate-stuffed French toast.

81 Palmer Ave. (on Falmouth Village Green), Falmouth, MA 02540. ☎ **800/472-2632** or 508/548-1230. Fax 508/540-1878. www.palmerhouseinn.com. 17 units. Summer $199–$249 double. Rates include full breakfast. AE, MC, V. *In room:* A/C, TV, hair dryer.

Sands of Time Motor Inn & Harbor House ★★   This property, which is across the street from the Woods Hole ferry terminal, consists of two buildings: a two-story motel in front of a shingled 1879 Victorian mansion. The motel rooms feature crisp, above-average decor, plus private porches overlooking the harbor. The rooms in the Harbor House are more lavish and romantic—some with four-posters, working fireplaces, wicker furnishings, and harbor views. There is a small heated pool on the grounds. All rooms are equipped with computer jacks.

549 Woods Hole Rd., Woods Hole, MA 02543. ☎ **800/841-0114** or 508/548-6300. Fax 508/457-0160. www.sandsoftime.com. 35 units, 2 with shared bathroom. Summer $160–$225 double. Rates include continental breakfast. AE, DC, DISC, MC, V. Closed Nov–Mar. **Amenities:** Small outdoor heated pool. *In room:* A/C, TV.

Woods Hole Inn ★★   This newly opened inn in the heart of Woods Hole is the place to stay for people who want to be in the thick of it. The ferry terminal is just steps from the back door, so expect to hear the horn announcing its departure beginning at the crack of dawn. But in addition to the noise and hurly-burly of this urban setting, there are the beautiful views of Vineyard Sound and Martha's Vineyard from the rooms and the unique charm of this seafaring port at every turn. Rooms are beautifully decorated with high-end amenities, and the innkeepers live up to a commitment to stay "green" in a range of ways. There is a burrito shack, called **Quick's Hole,** in the building.

28 Water Street Ave., Woods Hole, MA 02540. ☎ **508/495-0248.** www.woodsholeinn.com. 5 units. Summer $150–$275 double; off-season $130–$180 Rates include continental breakfast. MC, V. **Amenities:** Restaurant (burrito shack); bikes. *In room:* TV/DVD, Wi-Fi.

WHERE TO DINE

Expensive

The Boat House Restaurant and Lounge ★ NEW AMERICAN/SEAFOOD Set harborside, the large plate-glass windows of this casual restaurant overlook mainly powerboats stacked high in a marina on Falmouth Inner Harbor. Service is very friendly here and the atmosphere, especially from the large bar area, tends to be quite jovial. The food, though pricey, is very good. Standouts are bouillabaisse and garlic-oil-rubbed sirloin. There are also a number of pasta and fried-fish choices on the menu. This place turns into a rowdy club with live music on summer evenings (see "Falmouth After Dark," later in this chapter). It's particularly appealing at lunchtime, when prices are lower and the bar scene is quieter.

88 Scranton Ave. (on Falmouth Inner Harbor), Falmouth. ✆ **508/548-7800.** Reservations accepted. Main courses $18–$26. AE, MC, V. Mid-June to mid-Sept daily 11:30am–10pm; call for off-season hours. Closed mid-Oct to mid-May.

Casino Wharf FX ★ SEAFOOD   This new high-end two-story restaurant replaced the infamous Casino, a rowdy nightclub with legendary wet T-shirt contests. Although its beachfront location is sublime, the Marriott-style decor is better suited to a Boston hotel than a Cape restaurant. Both levels of the restaurant have soaring ceilings and large outdoor decks set above the beach. The top-level deck is open to the weather (and rather high up at the equivalent of three floors above the beach). Both floors also have large bars positioned for beach views out the restaurant's floor-to-ceiling windows. I recommend coming here for lunch and ordering either the delicious Cape Cod Reuben—a fried cod sandwich with cheese—or yummy swordfish kabobs. Dinner is somewhat pricey, with traditional grilled seafood and steak entrees.

286 Grand Ave. (next to Falmouth Heights Beach), Falmouth Heights. ✆ **508/540-6160;** http://casino wharf.weebly.com. Reservations accepted. Main courses $18–$40. AE, MC, V. Daily Mon–Thurs 11:30am–3pm and 5:30–10pm, Fri–Sun 8:30–11am, 11:30am–3pm, and 5–10pm; call for off-season hours.

Falmouth Raw Bar ★ SHELLFISH   If what you crave is a giant lobster roll, which consists of chunks of lobster and mayo on a big hotdog roll, this stylish bar overlooking Falmouth Inner Harbor is the place to get it—for $25. There are also steamed lobster dinners, Wellfleet oysters, local steamers, local little necks, and shrimp, and that's about it. The drinks menu is about twice as long as the food menu, with frozen drinks a specialty.

56 Scranton Ave. (at the corner of Robbins Rd, next to Falmouth Inner Harbor), Falmouth. ✆ **508/548-7RAW** [7729]. www.falmouthrawbar.com. Reservations not accepted. Main courses $17–$45. AE, MC, V. Daily 11:30am–10pm; call for off-season hours. Closed mid-Oct through April.

The Fishmonger Cafe ★ VEGETARIAN/NATURAL FOODS   A cherished carry-over from the early 1970s, this sunny, casual cafe attracts local young people and scientists, as well as Bermuda-shorted tourists, with an ever-changing array of imaginatively prepared dishes. Prices have risen substantially over the past couple of years, making dinner in this casual setting feel like a splurge. The eclectic dinner menu changes every few days with some exotic fare, such as Thai entrees. Regulars sit at the counter to enjoy a bowl of the Fisherman's Stew while schmoozing with staff bustling about the open kitchen. Newcomers usually go for the tables by the window, where you can watch boats come and go from Eel Pond. The menu ranges widely (lunch could be a tempeh burger made with fermented soybeans, or ordinary beef), and longtime customers look to the blackboard for the latest innovations, which invariably include delectable desserts such as pumpkin-pecan pie.

56 Water St. (at the Eel Pond drawbridge), Woods Hole. ✆ **508/540-5376.** www.fishmongercafewoods hole.com. Reservations not accepted. Main courses $15–$25. AE, MC, V. Mid-June to Oct daily 7:30–10pm; call for off-season hours. Closed mid-Dec to mid-Feb.

La Cucina Sul Mare ★★ (Finds) ITALIAN   Locals and tourists alike line up outside this popular Main Street restaurant, one of Falmouth's best, craving its hearty Italian fare. The interior features cheerful murals and a tin ceiling, and large picture windows overlook Main Street. A new outside deck in the back is a setting on warm nights. Chef/owner Mark Ciflone's signature dishes include such classic Italian specialties as lasagna, braised lamb shanks, *osso buco*, lobster *fra diavlo* over linguine, chicken Parmesan, and veal piccata, among others. The desserts here are homemade and delicious. Service is often excellent.

Osteria La Civetta ★★★ Ⓕ Finds NORTHERN ITALIAN   This authentic and intimate restaurant is run by the Toselli family of Bologna, Italy. This is European-style dining and service: Courses are ordered a la carte, meat is not served on the same plate as pasta, and even vegetables are ordered separately. Because diners are expected to have multiple courses, servings are smaller than at the average American restaurant. But diners can share courses for a moderately priced fine-dining experience. The food here is exquisite. With homemade pasta, the *lasagna alla Bolognese* is a great choice. Another favorite is the handmade *tagliatelle al funghi e tartufo nero,* which has porcini mushrooms and black truffle oil. Desserts are also made on-site: My favorite is the chocolate salami; don't ask, just order and eat.

133 Main St. (across from the post office), Falmouth. ℰ **508/540-1616.** www.osterialacivetta.com. Reservations recommended. Main courses $15–$25. MC, V. Wed–Sun noon–2:30pm and 5:30–10pm.

Phusion Grille ★★ NEW AMERICAN   This restaurant has a terrific location on Eel Pond in Woods Hole. The interior is all blond wood and Asian screens, but nothing blocks the views of the wraparound floor-to-ceiling windows. The food can be inconsistent here, though it is frequently very good and served by skilled waitstaff. Favorites are filet mignon on a wild-mushroom risotto cake, and diver scallops with fresh herbed pasta. The dessert menu features a very special fresh-fruit strudel. There is live music at Sunday brunch and weekend evenings in summer.

71 Water St., Woods Hole. ℰ **508/457-3100.** www.phusiongrille.com. Reservations not accepted. Main courses $21–$27. AE, MC, V. Tues–Sat 11:30am–2:30pm; Sat and Sun 8am–11pm; daily 5–10pm. Closed mid-Oct to mid-May.

RoöBar ★★ NEW AMERICAN   RoöBar is the top restaurant in town for service, food, and atmosphere. With hand-blown glass lamps over the bar and metal sconce sculpture on the walls, it's an arty and hip setting. The food is exceptionally yummy, if pricey. Creative appetizers include Thai wontons with ginger chicken, and a crispy tuna stick with a spicy dipping sauce. Good main-course choices include the snapper pie, which is a braised snapper in a puff pastry, and coriander-crusted day-boat cod with fried coconut polenta. Pizzas ($11–$15) from the wood-fired oven come with unusual toppings such as scallops, prosciutto, and beef satay. For dessert, go for the crème brûlée. They don't take reservations, but if you call a half-hour ahead, you can put your name on the waiting list. There's another RoöBar in Plymouth, and the owners also run a restaurant called Del Mar in Chatham.

285 Main St. (at Cahoon Court, in the center of town), Falmouth. ℰ **508/548-8600.** www.theroobar.com. Main courses $11–$26. AE, MC, V. Fri–Sun 11:30am–3pm; daily 5–10pm; call for off-season hours.

Moderate
The Captain Kidd Bar ★★ Ⓕ Finds SEAFOOD/PUB FARE   This atmospheric pub is a good place to come for a drink and a pizza, appetizers, or a light meal. The semiofficial heart of Woods Hole, Captain Kidd really comes into its own once the tourist hordes subside. It's then that the year-round scientists and fishing crews can huddle around the fireplace, congregate on the glassed porch overlooking Eel Pond, or belly up to the hand-carved mahogany bar (thought to date from the early 1800s) and drink to their heart's content. Although the Kidd shares a kitchen with a fancier and more expensive seasonal

restaurant next door, called **The Waterfront,** the fare at the Kidd is pub grub and some seafood. Homemade clam chowder is thick as paste, with large chunks of potato and clam; stuffed quahogs are piled high, and french fries are the real deal, thickly sliced. Another attraction here is wireless Internet access along with several computers, set up for free Internet use.

77 Water St. (west of the Eel Pond drawbridge), Woods Hole. ✆ **508/548-8563.** www.thecaptainkidd. com. Reservations not accepted. Main courses $15–$20; pizzas $7–$11. AE, MC, V. Daily 11am–4pm and 5–9pm. Pizza served to 11pm in summer.

Chapoquoit Grill ★★ NEW AMERICAN   One of the few worthwhile dining spots in sleepy West Falmouth, this little roadside bistro has Californian aspirations: wood-grilled slabs of fish accompanied by trendy salsas, and crispy personal pizzas delivered straight from the brick oven. People drive here from miles around for the flavorful food. A no-reservations policy means long waits nightly in season and weekends year-round.

410 Rte. 28A, West Falmouth. ✆ **508/540-7794.** www.chapoquoitgrill.com. Reservations not accepted (but call ahead to be put on a wait list). Main courses $10–$18. MC, V. Daily 5–10pm.

The Flying Bridge ★★ Kids AMERICAN/CONTINENTAL   Seafood, appropriately enough, predominates at this shipshape harborside megarestaurant (capacity: nearly 600). With three bars tossed into the mix and live music upstairs on weekends, things can get a bit crazy; you'll find comparative peace and quiet—as well as tiptop nautical views—out on the deck. In addition to basic bar food (Buffalo chicken wings and the like), you'll find hefty hunks of protein and fish in many guises, from fish and chips—with optional malt vinegar—to appealing blackboard specials. This is a great place to bring the kids because they'll enjoy wandering onto the attached dock to watch the ducks in the harbor.

220 Scranton Ave. (about ¹⁄₂ mile south of Main St., on Falmouth Inner Harbor). ✆ **508/548-2700.** www. capecodrestaurants.org. Reservations not accepted. Main courses $8–$20. AE, MC, V. Mid-Apr to mid-Oct daily 11:30am–9pm. Closed mid-Oct to mid-Apr.

Landfall ★★ Kids AMERICAN   A terrific harbor setting, Cape Cod-y cuisine, and good service make this Woods Hole seafood restaurant stand out. This is the type of place where you'll see the owner busing tables on busy nights. Besides the usual fish and pasta dishes, there's "lite fare" such as burgers and fish and chips for under $15. This is a great place to bring the kids; a children's menu comes with games and crayons. Or come for a drink at the half-dory bar to enjoy this massive wooden building constructed of salvage, both marine and terrestrial. The "ship's knees," on the ceiling, are the ribs of an old schooner that broke up on the shores of Cuttyhunk Island; the big stained-glass window came from a mansion on nearby Penzance Point. A large bank of windows looks out onto the harbor, and the Martha's Vineyard ferry, when docking, appears to be making a beeline straight for your table.

Luscombe Ave. (¹⁄₂ block south of Water St.), Woods Hole. ✆ **508/548-1758.** www.woodshole.com/ landfall. Reservations recommended. Main courses $7–$26. AE, MC, V. Mid-May to Sept daily 11:30am–9:30pm; call for off-season hours. Closed late Nov to mid-Apr.

Laureen's ★ MIDDLE EASTERN/NEW AMERICAN   This attractive cafe, with indoor and outdoor tables in the center of town, is ideal for a quick bite or sip. It specializes in vegetarian and Middle Eastern fare. Try one of the feta pizzas. Everything is available to go, or you can eat here. Service is a little on the leisurely side, so relax into a lengthy and entirely enjoyable meal.

Inexpensive

Betsy's Diner ★ (Finds)(Kids) AMERICAN   I once had the best piece of baked scrod ever at this vintage 1950s diner. It was breaded with cornflakes. This is hearty food like your mother used to make, if your mother was a variation of June Cleaver. The menu features turkey dinner, breakfast all day, and homemade soups. Some say the fried clams here are the best in town. Many people come for the large selection of scrumptious homemade pies, which may be the best on Cape Cod. Each red vinyl booth is equipped with its own jukebox with retro hits.

457 Main St. (a couple blocks east of the center of town), Falmouth. ℂ **508/540-0060.** Reservations not accepted. All items under $11. AE, MC, V. Mon–Sat 6am–8pm; Sun 7am–2pm; call for off-season hours.

The British Beer Company ★ PUB FARE/PIZZA   The view is great at this faux British pub across the street from Falmouth Heights Beach. The food quality, though, is inconsistent. Stick with the fish and chips and you'll be fine. The lobster bisque is also good and has won local awards. Of course, there is beer; 23 drafts are available, such as Guinness and John Courage, as well as bottled selections.

263 Grand Ave. (across from the beach), Falmouth Heights. ℂ **508/540-9600.** www.britishbeer.com/local/falmouth. Reservations not accepted. All items under $15. AE, DC, DISC, MC, V. Daily 10:30–11:30pm.

The Clam Shack (Kids) SEAFOOD   This classic clam shack sits at the head of Falmouth harbor and offers steaming plates of fried seafood that you carry to a picnic table inside, outside, or up on the roof deck with the best view in town. The food is basic clam-shack fare, but the fish is fresh and you can't beat the view. Kids will love the casual atmosphere and the outdoor dining on the roof deck. Do note that prices are a little higher here than at clam shacks in town without the harbor view.

227 Clinton Ave. (off Scranton Ave., on Falmouth Inner Harbor, about 1 mile south of Main St.), Falmouth. ℂ **508/540-7758.** Reservations not accepted. Main courses $5–$25. No credit cards. Daily 11:30am–7:30pm. Closed early Sept–late May.

Moonakis Cafe ★★ DINER   The place serves the best breakfast in town, with a large list of special omelets and pancakes every morning. Many people rave about the homemade corned-beef hash. There is counter seating as well as tables. If you're lucky, owner Paul Rifkin will wander over to your table and strike up a conversation, or even better, a debate. Lunch highlights are the quahog chowder and pastrami sandwich, among many others.

460 Waquoit Hwy./Rte. 28, Waquoit. ℂ **508/457-9630.** Reservations not accepted. All items under $10. MC, V. Mon–Sat 7am–1:30pm; Sunday 7am–noon.

Peking Palace ★★ CHINESE/JAPANESE/THAI   This popular, well-kept Chinese restaurant has an extensive menu that includes Japanese and Thai food. There are also three regional Chinese cuisines (Cantonese, Mandarin, and Szechuan), as well as Polynesian. The decor is modern and sophisticated. Sip a fancy drink to give yourself time to take in the menu, and be sure to solicit your server's opinion: That's how I encountered some heavenly spicy chilled squid. This is the only place in town that serves dinner until midnight.

452 Main St. (a few blocks east of the center of town), Falmouth. ℂ **508/540-8204.** www.pekingpalacefalmouth.com. Reservations for parties of 6 or more only. Main courses $5–$15. AE, MC, V. Daily 11:30am–midnight.

★ SANDWICHES/BURRITOS   Just steps from the Woods Hole ferry terminal, this is a great place for a quick sandwich. Named after a nautical landmark off the Elizabeth Islands nearby, this is high quality fast food—especially the burritos, which are spicy enough to have one patron report, "my eyes are sweating."

6 Luscombe Ave., Woods Hole. ℂ **508/495-0742.** www.quicksholewickedfresh.com. Reservations not accepted. Main courses $5–$15. Cash only. Daily 10am–10pm. Closed mid-Oct to late May.

Multicultural Dining in Falmouth

If you crave authentic spicy Indian food, head to **Golden Swan Indian Cuisine** ★, 323 Main St. (in the center of town), Falmouth (ℂ **508/540-6580**). For better or for worse, this place kept the name, the waitstaff, and most of the decor (including the pilgrim plates on the bathroom doors) of the old Golden Swan, which served '50s-style "Continental cuisine" since the 1970s. But don't be fooled. This is the real thing: curries, lamb stews, and mouthwatering fried breads. A number of delicious vegetarian entrees are also available. You can choose from several different levels of heat; choose the hottest and have a hose ready. Main courses are $9 to $18. Open daily 4:30am to 10pm; reservations and credit cards are accepted.

   Bangkok Thai Cuisine Restaurant, 809 Main St., at the east end of Main Street, just west of Falmouth Heights Road (ℂ **508/495-3760**), serves delicious Thai cuisine, including all the traditional dishes, such as pad thai, mee siam, and various curries. Wash your meal down with a frothy and sweet Thai-style iced tea. Main courses are $9 to $14. Open daily 11:30am to 3pm and 4 to 9:30pm. Reservations and credit cards accepted.

Takeout & Picnic Fare

Cape Cod Bagel Co., 419 Palmer Ave., Falmouth (ℂ **508/548-8485**), carries the usual bagel sandwiches, soups, coffee, and other beverages, but the bagels here, made on the premises, are definitely the best in town. Open 6am to 5:30pm. **Box Lunch,** 781 Main St., Falmouth (ℂ **508/457-7657;** www.boxlunch.com), is one of a number of franchises on the Cape that carry the pita "rollwiches." These are excellent sandwiches (over 50 selections) made fast, and they're perfect for picnics. Open 8am to 7pm. **Steve's Pizzeria & More,** 374 Main St., Falmouth (ℂ **508/457-9454**), has good pizza and subs, and quick service. Open 11am to 10pm.

Coffee & Tea

Coffee Obsession, 110 Palmer Ave., in the Queen's Buyway Shops (ℂ **508/540-2233;** www.coffeeobsession.com), is a hip coffee bar where everyone goes for a cuppa joe. It's open from 6am to 7pm Monday through Saturday and 7am to 6:30pm on Sunday. You'll see slackers, suits, and surfers all lined up for the best coffee in town. **Coffee O.,** as it's known to locals, has a branch in **Woods Hole,** at 38 Water St. (ℂ **508/540-8130**). The Woods Hole location has several computers with Internet access and a play area for children; it's open daily 6:30am to 9pm.

   Molly's Tea Room, 227 Main St. (ℂ **508/457-1666;** www.mollystearoom.com), is the place to get an authentic cup of tea and a light meal, perhaps a sandwich or a salad. A full case of baked goodies beckons. It's open year-round, daily 11am to 6pm.

Sweets

Locals know to get to **Pie in the Sky Dessert Café and Bake Shop** ★★, 10 Water St., Woods Hole (ℂ **508/540-5475**), by 9am for sticky buns, the best anywhere. Those bound for Martha's Vineyard stop at this small bakery near the ferry terminal for treats before hopping on the boat.

Falmouth residents are the beneficiaries of a struggle for ice-cream bragging rights: **Ben & Bill's Chocolate Emporium** ★, at 209 Main St., in the center of town (ⓒ **508/548-7878;** www.benandbills.com), draws crowds even in winter, late into the evening. They come for the homemade ice cream, not to mention the hand-dipped candies showcased in a wraparound display—a chocoholic's nightmare or dream come true, depending. Those who can trust themselves not to go hog-wild might enjoy watching the ice cream being made. Open 9am to 11pm.

Pies A La Mode ★★, 352 Main St., unit 4, Falmouth (ⓒ **508/540-8777;** www. piesalamode.com), has delicious homemade ice cream and gelato, a lighter blend than ice cream, as well as wonderful baked goods, including homemade quiches. Open Monday to Saturday 10am to 10pm and Sunday noon to 9pm in season; call for off-season hours.

There's also **Smitty's Homemade Ice Cream** ★, at 326 E. Falmouth Hwy., East Falmouth (ⓒ **508/457-1060**), whose proprietor, the cheerful blond Smitty, is an ice-cream man from central casting.

FALMOUTH AFTER DARK

DRINKS   Ever since the close of the famous nightclub, The Casino-By-The-Sea, in Falmouth Heights, those looking for a fun waterfront drinking establishment have frequented the **Boat House,** at 88 Scranton Ave., on Falmouth Inner Harbor (ⓒ **508/548-7800;** www.boathousefalmouth.com). The Boathouse features live bands in season, from classic rock to jazz, and dancing is popular here. Cover for live shows varies; the place is closed September to mid-May.

Grab a stool at the **British Beer Company** ★, 263 Grand Ave., Falmouth Heights (ⓒ **508/540-9600;** www.britishbeer.com/local/falmouth), and choose from a revolving selection of over 18 drafts from the British Isles as you ponder views of the beach across the street.

God knows whom you'll meet in the rough-and-tumble old **Captain Kidd Bar** ★, 77 Water St., in Woods Hole (ⓒ **508/548-9206;** www.thecaptainkidd.com): maybe a lobsterwoman, maybe a Nobel Prize winner. Good grub, too—see "Where to Dine," earlier.

Everyone heads to **Liam Maguire's Irish Pub** ★, at 273 Main St., in Falmouth (ⓒ **508/548-8563;** www.liammaguire.com), for a taste of the Emerald Isle. Live music on weekends year-round, often by Liam himself. No cover.

Grumpy's Pub, at 29 Locust St. (ⓒ **508/540-3930;** www.grumpyspub.net), is a good old bar/shack with live music (rock, blues, and jazz) Thursday to Saturday nights. Cover is free to $5. Look for free passes on the counter at Coffee Obsession nearby.

The great menu with lots of intriguing appetizers at **RoöBar,** 285 Main St., in Falmouth (ⓒ **508/548-8600;** www.theroobar.com), draws a hip crowd.

FILM   The Upper Cape's only year-round art-house cinema is **Regal Cinemas Nickelodeon,** 742 Rte. 151, East Falmouth (ⓒ **508/563-6510**). With six small screens, this is a great alternative to the usual mall movies. **Falmouth Cinema Pub** (ⓒ **508/495-0505**), located at the Falmouth Mall, on Teaticket Highway, has the unusual concept of sitting at tables while watching the movie. The menu consists of pub-style fare such as pizza and burgers. Standard mall fare on the screens.

PERFORMANCE   Off-season, **The Woods Hole Folk Music Society** ★ (ⓒ **508/540-0320;** www.arts-cape.com/whfolkmusic) mounts biweekly concerts October through May (first and third Sun of each month), attracting a real grassroots crowd to Community Hall on Water Street, by the Eel Pond drawbridge. General admission is $8; discounts are available for members, seniors, and children.

The **Cape Cod Theatre Project** (© **508/457-4242;** www.capecodtheatreproject.org) is a playwrights' workshop open to the public. These staged play readings are performed for just a few weeks in July, usually at the Falmouth Academy Theatre, on Depot Avenue. The play choices tend to be provocative and elicit strong opinions. The rest of the year the talent behind these productions are most likely strutting the boards in New York City. Call for a schedule. Admission is $20.

Starting at about 7:30pm on Thursday evenings in July and August, the spirited volunteers of the **Falmouth Town Band** swing through big-band numbers as small fries (and some oldsters) dance about. Concerts are held at the Band Shell, on Scranton Avenue, next to Falmouth Inner Harbor, and are free. On Friday nights in summer, **free concerts** are held in Peg Noonan Park, on Main Street, from about 6 to 7:30pm; you might hear anything from a jazz quartet to a folk singer. On Wednesday nights in summer, also in Peg Noonan Park, there are **free children's movies** shown on a big screen at dusk. On Monday nights, it's **Lobster on the Lawn,** at St. Barnabas Church, next to the Village Green. For $15, you get a lobster roll, drink, chips, and dessert; a great deal. Call the Falmouth Chamber of Commerce at © **508/548-8500** for details.

The top talent from college drama departments across the country form the **College Light Opera Company** ★ (© **508/548-0668;** www.collegelightopera.com), which puts on a fast-paced summer repertory from late June through August. So winning is the work of these 32 young actors and 17 musicians (some of them ultimately Broadway-bound) that the house is usually booked solid, so call well ahead or keep your fingers crossed for a scattering of singles. Its venue, the Highfield Theatre, on the Depot Avenue Extension, off North Main Street, in Falmouth, is a former horse barn and for the past half-century has been a terrific straw-hat theater. Performances are held Tuesday to Saturday at 8pm; there's also a Thursday matinee at 2pm. Tickets are $30.

4 MASHPEE

11 miles SE of Sagamore; 12 miles W of Hyannis

Mashpee is a study in contrasts. This is the location of South Cape Beach State Park, a beautiful stretch of unspoiled coastline on Nantucket South, but the major portion of Mashpee's shoreline has been claimed by the New Seabury Resort development. Further housing developments are rapidly carving up the inland woods, leaving less and less room for the region's original residents, the Mashpee Wampanoags, whose nomadic ancestors began convening in summer camps by these shores millennia ago. In 1660, concerned by the natives' rapid disenfranchisement and heartened by their willingness to convert, missionary Richard Bourne got the Plymouth General Court to grant his "praying Indians" a 10,500-acre "plantation" in perpetuity. The provision proved far from perpetual, as settlers—and much later, developers—began chipping away at the holdings.

After lengthy litigation in the 1970s and early 1980s, the Mashpee Wampanoags—whose tribal roster now numbers about 1,000—were denied tribal status (unlike the Gay Head Wampanoags of Martha's Vineyard) and were stymied in their efforts to preserve the land. It was only in 1995, with the backing of local legislators, that the sizable—5,871 acres—Mashpee National Wildlife Refuge was carved out of the disputed territory.

ESSENTIALS

GETTING THERE   After crossing the Sagamore Bridge, take Route 6 to exit 2, and Route 130 S. Or you can cross the Bourne Bridge and take Route 28 S. about 6 miles to

VISITOR INFORMATION Contact the **Mashpee Chamber of Commerce,** at 520 Main St., P.O. Box 1245, Mashpee, MA 02649 (© **508/477-0792;** fax 508/477-5541; www.mashpeechamber.com); or the **Cape Cod Chamber of Commerce.** (See "Visitor Information," under "Sandwich," earlier in this chapter.)

BEACHES & RECREATIONAL PURSUITS

BEACHES The small part of the shoreline not reserved for the New Seabury Resort is an under-sung sleeper: **South Cape Beach** ★★★, off Great Oak Road (5 miles south of the Mashpee rotary). Mashpee is set amid the 450-acre **South Cape Beach State Park** (© **508/457-0495**). This lengthy stretch of beach has miles of hiking trails. Parking costs $7 per day.

BOATING **Cape Cod Kayak** (© **508/563-9377;** www.capecodkayak.com) rents kayaks (free delivery) by the day or week and offers lessons and ecotours on local waterways. Call for a schedule and more information, or see "Beaches & Recreational Pursuits," under "Falmouth," earlier in this chapter.

If you'd rather explore on your own, you can rent a canoe in Falmouth (see "Falmouth," earlier in this chapter) and paddle around the Mashpee River, Popponesset Bay, and Mashpee/Wakeby Pond.

FISHING **Mashpee/Wakeby Pond** (boat landing off Rte. 130, Fisherman's Landing.) is considered one of the top 10 bass-fishing lakes in the country. Saltwater fishing licenses can be obtained at Sandwich, Falmouth, or Barnstable town halls. South Cape Beach in Mashpee (see "Beaches," above) is a prime spot for surf-casting.

NATURE TRAILS The **Mashpee Conservation Commission** (© **508/539-1400,** ext. 540) sponsors free naturalist-guided nature tours throughout Mashpee from May through December. Call for a schedule. A shady peninsula jutting into the Cape's largest body of fresh water (the adjoining Wakeby/Mashpee Pond), the 135-acre **Lowell Holly Reservation** off South Sandwich Road in the northern corner of the township harbors some 500 holly trees and a number of magnificent centennial beeches. The stewards of this enchanted place, the **Trustees of Reservations** (© **978/921-1944**), charge $6 per day for the 2-mile trail loop on summer weekends; weekday admission is free. **South Cape Beach State Park** (see "Beaches," above) also offers a network of sandy trails.

WATERSPORTS The town of Mashpee offers swimming lessons at **Attaquin Park** at Mashpee/Wakeby Pond, off Route 130, and also at South Cape Beach; call the **town leisure services department** (© **508/539-1400,** ext. 519) for details.

FOR KIDS The **Cape Cod Children's Museum** ★, 577 Great Neck Rd. S. (© **508/539-8788;** www.capecodchildrensmuseum.org), has a toddler castle and a 30-foot pirate ship, among other kid pleasers. It also sponsors many special events. The museum is open Monday through Saturday 10am to 5pm and Sunday noon to 5pm. Admission is $6 for ages 1 to 59, $5 for seniors.

SHOPPING

Shopping in Mashpee is pretty much limited to the **Mashpee Commons,** at the Mashpee rotary, routes 151 and 28 (© **508/477-5400;** www.mashpeecommons.com). Designed to resemble an ideal New England village (right down to the sidewalk measurements, modeled on Woodstock, Vermont), Mashpee Commons is a gussied-up shopping complex with a facadelike feel. This is where you'll find such chains as **Gap, Talbots, Banana Republic,** and **Starbucks.** There's also **M. Brann** for retro accessories and the **Signature Gallery** for superb American crafts. For book hounds, there's **Market Street Bookshop,** 20 Steeple St. (🕿 **508/539-6985**), a fine independent bookstore. For **movies** playing at Mashpee Commons 6, call 🕿 **800/FANDANGO** [326-3264].

WHERE TO STAY

New Seabury Resort ★★ (**Kids**)   Only 26 of the 1,600 condos in this 2,300-acre resort are available for vacationers to rent by the night. Those lucky enough to get one of them can enjoy a 3½-mile private beach on Vineyard Sound. The tastefully decorated condos are clustered into "villages" of varying personalities: Maushop, for instance, with its crushed-shell walkways and clambering roses, is meant to mimic Nantucket. The Popponesset Marketplace with restaurants and gift shops on the premises also sponsors concerts and other family events.

20 Red Brook Rd. (about 4 miles south of the Mashpee rotary), New Seabury, MA 02649. 🕿 **800/999-9033** or 508/539-8322, ext. 6. Fax 508/477-9790. www.newseabury.com. 28 units. Summer $347 1-bedroom villa; $523 2-bedroom villa. AE, DC, MC, V. **Amenities:** 5 restaurants (including the Popponesset Inn, an upscale venue; and the Raw Bar); bike trails (w/rentals); scheduled children's activities; 2 18-hole golf courses; health club; 2 outdoor pools; 16 all-weather tennis courts; miniature golf. *In room:* TV.

WHERE TO DINE

Expensive

Bleu ★★ FRENCH BISTRO   A sophisticated menu awaits diners at Bleu, the funky French bistro at bustling Mashpee Commons. Chef Frederic Feufeu (no kidding) brings a delicacy to dishes such as white-truffle honey-glazed duck breast with mission figs, and roasted filet mignon on sautéed potatoes. There are also fish and vegetarian choices. A bistro menu, available all evening, lists less expensive, lighter choices. The wine list offers numerous vintages by the glass and many well-priced choices. As you would expect for a French restaurant, the desserts are especially appealing.

10 Market St., Mashpee Commons (at the intersection of rtes. 151 and 28). 🕿 **508/539-7907.** www.bleurestaurant.com. Reservations recommended. Main courses $16–$29. AE, MC, V. Daily 11:30am–4pm and 5–10pm.

Simmer ★★ NEW AMERICAN   This first-class restaurant is full of surprises. The first is the space, all curving walls and cozy sitting areas. The second surprise is the excellent service, something unusual to find on the Cape. The third and perhaps best surprise is the food: Every dish is a triumph of creativity. The menu varies with the seasons. There are always seafood delights, such as lobster and scallop ravioli, but also unexpected choices, such as escargots. As for main courses, there could be a crispy duckling with a mango glaze, or a dish from local waters such as pan-roasted cod with sautéed spinach. Such desserts as the Key lime cheesecake are all house-made.

36 South St. (off Rt. 28, in South Cape Village plaza across from Mashpee Commons), Mashpee. 🕿 **508/539-0025.** Reservations recommended. Main courses $19–$32. AE, MC, V. Tues–Sun 4:30–11:30pm.

Trevi Café and Wine Bar MEDITERRANEAN   This restaurant brings a dash of European style to the Mashpee Commons open-air mall. The lunch menu features wonderful paninis and salads; dinner offerings, besides salads and sandwiches, come mainly from an interesting *tapas* menu, offering small servings of such delectables as grilled

asparagus or homemade buttery pasta in a white-wine and garlic sauce. A few regular-size
entrees are available nightly as specials. This is a terrific place to come for either a light
bite, perhaps something quick before a movie, or a big meal. The main seating area is a
large sunny patio. Inside is taken up mostly by a large bar area where patrons can choose
from the extensive wine list or cocktail menu.

25 Market St., Mashpee Commons. ℂ **508/477-0055.** www.trevicafe.com. Reservations accepted. Main
courses $11–$32. MC, V. Daily 11:30am–10pm.

Moderate

Siena Italian Bar and Grill NORTHERN ITALIAN   This large, loud, and popular
restaurant serves tasty Italian fare next to the movie theater in Mashpee Commons. Specialties include the brick-oven pizzas and the creative pasta dishes. Some find the portions
on the small side, but the quality is usually quite good.

11A Steeple St., Mashpee Commons. ℂ **508/477-5929.** www.siena.us. Reservations accepted. Main
courses $9–$26. MC, V. Mon–Sat 11:30am–3:30pm and 4:30–10pm; Sun noon–9pm.

Wicked Fire Kissed Pizza ★★ PIZZA   Fantastic gourmet pizzas and such casual
fare as salads and burgers are on the menu at this very stylish pizzeria. The pizza is made
from organic ingredients, including organic flour and yeast, and is cooked in a 700° stone
hearth oven. These are old-world Neapolitan-style pizzas but with the modern flair of
such ingredients as lobster and brie; steak and onions; and scallops and bacon. Traditional toppings are also available.

36 South St., South Cape Village. ℂ **508/477-7422.** www.wickedrestaurant.com. Reservations accepted
for parties of 8 or more. Main courses $9–$26. MC, V. Daily 11:30am–10pm.

The Mid Cape

If the Cape had a capital, Hyannis would be it. The Kennedy mystique, peaking with the 1960s Camelot era of John and Jackie, triggered development that over the decades has created a sprawling concrete jungle on routes 132 and 28 and has nearly doubled the Cape's year-round population. At over 200,000, the number of people living on the Cape year-round is still climbing. The summer population is about three times that, and you'd swear every single person had daily errands to run in Hyannis. That said, this teeming town has many pockets of charm. The waterfront area, where the islands' ferries dock, has been spruced up by the Walkway to the Sea, a path and park area. Main Street, in Hyannis, long eclipsed by the megastores along Route 132, is a pleasant place to stroll.

The town of Barnstable, the seat of Cape Cod's Barnstable County government, is made up of seven villages: Hyannis, Barnstable Village, West Barnstable, Osterville, Centerville, Cotuit, and Marstons Mills. Some of those villages have their own "villages": for instance, the famous Hyannis Port is a section of Hyannis. Along the north side of the Cape on Route 6A (the Old King's Hwy.) is Barnstable Village, its compact Main Street anchored by an imposing granite county courthouse. West Barnstable, also on 6A, has a handful of delightful specialty stores and views of acres of salt marsh leading out to Cape Cod Bay. Along the Mid Cape's south coast (off Rte. 28) are Cotuit, Marstons Mills, Osterville, and Centerville, all with gracious residential sections. Osterville has a charming strollable Main Street, and Centerville has Barnstable's best public beach, at Craigville.

While Barnstable is an ideal base from which to explore the rest of the Cape and

islands, there's also fun to be had nearby. If you are staying in the vicinity of Hyannis, you'll certainly want to head over to the north side of the Cape for a drive along the Old King's Highway, but you'll also want to stroll around Hyannis Harbor, stopping for lunch at Tugboat's or Baxter's, where seagulls will compete for a bite of your lobster roll. You'll find a number of interesting shops and galleries on Main Street, in Hyannis (see "Shopping," later in this chapter, as well as cafes and bars (see "Hyannis & Environs After Dark," later in this chapter).

Some of the finest seaside mansions on the Cape are in the old-money villages of Cotuit, Osterville, Centerville, and Hyannis Port. To explore this "Gold Coast" by car, take some detours off Route 28, driving south toward Nantucket Sound. These winding country roads are also good for biking (see "Bicycling," below).

The towns of Yarmouth and Dennis straddle the Mid Cape from north to south, with the north-side villages along the historic Old King's Highway and the south-side villages along commercialized and overdeveloped Route 28. That's not to say there aren't some nice enclaves along the south shore. Some of the beaches along this stretch of Nantucket Sound (West Dennis Beach and Parker's River Beach, in South Yarmouth) are popular with families, but the villages themselves (Dennisport and South and West Yarmouth) have definitely seen better days. Developers in the past 30 years have gotten carried away. In stark contrast, Yarmouth Port and Dennis Village on the north side are perfect little time capsules, loaded with old-fashioned New England charm, an encyclopedic array of historic homes, galleries, and terrific small shops.

15 miles E of Sagamore; 44 miles S of Provincetown

As the commercial center and transportation hub of the Cape, hyperdeveloped Hyannis—officially a "village"—grossly overshadows the actual seat of town government in the bucolic community of Barnstable. The two locales couldn't be more dissimilar. As peaceful as Hyannis is hectic, the bay area along historic Route 6A unfolds in a blur of greenery and well-kept colonial houses. The downtown Hyannis area, on the other hand—sapped by the strip development that proliferated at the edges of town after the Cape Cod Mall was built in 1970—has made a remarkable comeback, particularly in the lively Main Street area, with attractive banners and a pretty public park flanking the wharf where frequent ferries depart for the islands. If you were to confine your visit to this one town, however, you'd get a warped view of the Cape. Along routes 132 and 28, you could be visiting Anywhere, U.S.A.: They're lined with the standard chain stores, restaurants, and hotels, and mired with maddening traffic.

Hyannis has more beds and better room rates than anywhere else on the Cape, but there's little rationale for staying along the highways of route 28 and 132—unless you happen to have missed the last ferry out to Nantucket. Even elaborate resort facilities can't begin to compensate for the lack of local color.

The best strategy is to stay somewhere peaceful near the edge of town, in one of the moneyed villages, such as Hyannis Port or Centerville to the west, or in one of the bayside villages of Barnstable and West Barnstable due north, and just go into Hyannis to sample the restaurants and nightlife. Hyannis and environs can offer plenty of both to suit every palate and personality.

ESSENTIALS

GETTING THERE   After crossing either the Bourne or Sagamore bridge, head east on Route 6 or 6A. The Sagamore Bridge will get you closer to your destination. Route 6A passes through West Barnstable and Barnstable Village; exit 6 (Rte. 132) off Route 6 leads to Hyannis.

You can fly into Hyannis, and there is good bus service from Boston and New York (see section 3, "Getting There & Getting Around," in chapter 3).

The **Sealine** (© 800/352-7155) makes a circuit of Barnstable, Mashpee, and Falmouth, Monday through Saturday, and the fare is a reasonable $1 to $4 (depending on the distance); children 5 and under ride free. The **Hyannis Area Trolley** (© 800/352-7155 or 508/385-1430) covers two loops—the Route 132 malls and the Main Street/waterfront area—every half-hour from 10am to 9pm from late June to early September. Rates are $1 for adults, 50¢ for seniors, and free for children 5 and under.

VISITOR INFORMATION   For information contact the **Hyannis Area Chamber of Commerce,** 387 Main St., Hyannis, MA 02601 (© 508/362-5230; fax 508/362-9499; www.hyannis.com), which is open Monday through Saturday 9am to 5pm, Sunday 10am to 2pm; or the **Cape Cod Chamber of Commerce,** routes 6 and 132 (just off the exit 6 eastbound ramp), Hyannis, MA 02601 (© 888/332-2732 or 508/362-2156; fax 508/362-2156; www.capecodchamber.org), open year-round, mid-April to mid-November daily 9am to 5pm; mid-November to mid-April Monday through Saturday 10am to 4pm.

BEACHES Barnstable's primary bay beach is Sandy Neck Beach, accessed through East Sandwich (see "Beaches & Recreational Pursuits" under section 1, "Sandwich," in chapter 5). Most of the Nantucket Sound beaches are fairly protected and thus not big in terms of surf. Beach parking costs $15 a day, usually payable at the lot; for a weeklong parking sticker ($50), visit the Recreation Department at 141 Bassett Lane, at the new **Hyannis Youth & Community Center** (© **508/790-6345**).

- **Craigville Beach** ★★★, off Craigville Beach Road, in Centerville: Once a magnet for Methodist "camp" meetings (conference centers still line the shore), this broad expanse of sand boasts lifeguards and restrooms. A destination for the bronzed and buffed, it's known as "Muscle Beach."

- **Kalmus Beach** ★★, off Gosnold Street, in Hyannis Port: This 800-foot spit of sand stretching toward the mouth of the harbor makes an ideal launching site for windsurfing enthusiasts, who sometimes seem to play chicken with the steady parade of ferries. The surf is tame, the slope shallow, and the conditions ideal for little kids. There are lifeguards, a snack bar, and restrooms.

- **Orrin Keyes Beach** ★★ (also known as Sea Beach), at the end of Sea Street, in Hyannis: This little beach at the end of a residential road is popular with families.

- **Veterans Beach,** off Ocean Street, in Hyannis: A small stretch of harborside sand adjoining the John F. Kennedy Memorial (a moving tribute from the town), this spot is not tops for swimming, unless you're very young and easily wowed. Parking is usually easy though, and it's walkable from town. The snack bar, restrooms, and playground will see to a family's needs.

BICYCLING Although there are no paved bike paths in Barnstable (the Rail Trail in Dennis is the closest), the winding roads in Marstons Mills and Osterville make for pleasant scenic rides. There's free public parking at the Marstons Mills millpond at the intersection of routes 28 and 149 or behind the stores in Osterville Center. From the intersection of routes 28 and 149, bear right on Route 149 where it turns into Main Street. Main Street soon intersects with Route 28; cross Route 28 (carefully), and then cruise down South County Road into Osterville. Several roads here afford wonderful bay views, not to mention views of some of the finest homes on Cape Cod. For the best views, bike to the ends of Bay Street, West Bay Road, and Eel River Road to Sea View Avenue. A leisurely bike ride through this area is perhaps the best way to see some of the most impressive seaside mansions on the Cape.

BOATING You can rent a kayak from Eastern Mountain Sports (see "Watersports," below) for $50 a day or $100 for 3 days and paddle around **Scorton Creek, Sandy Neck,** and **Barnstable Harbor** on the north side of the Cape. On the south side of the Cape, paddlers enjoy the waters around **Great Island** in Osterville. In Centerville, you can navigate the **Centerville River.** For experienced paddlers, **Barnstable's Great Marsh—** one of the largest in New England—offers beautiful waterways out to Sandy Neck.

FISHING The township of Barnstable has 11 ponds for freshwater fishing; for information and permits, visit **Town Hall,** at 367 Main St., Hyannis (© **508/862-4044**); or **Sports Port,** 149 W. Main St., Hyannis (© **508/775-3096**). Shellfishing permits are available from the **Department of Natural Resources,** at 1189 Phinneys Lane, Centerville (© **508/790-6272**). Surf-casting, sans license, is permitted on Sandy Neck (see "Beaches & Recreational Pursuits," under section 1, "Sandwich," in chapter 5).

ACCOMMODATIONS ■

Cape Cod Resort &
  Conference Center
  at Hyannis **4**
Heritage House Hotel **22**
Hyannis Inn Motel **11**
Simmons Homestead Inn **2**

DINING ◆

Alberto's Ristorante **16**
Baxter's Boat House **21**
Ben & Jerry's **17**
Bistro 586 **7**
The Black Cat **20**
Colombo's Cafe **8**
Common Ground Café **14**
The Daily Paper **1**
Eclectic Café **6**
Harry's **5**
Lambert's Rainbow Fruit **1**
Le Petite France Café **17**

The Naked Oyster Bistro & Raw Bar **23**
The Original Gourmet Brunch **10**
The Paddock **3**
Palio Pizzeria **11**
Roadhouse Café **8**
The Steak House & Sports Bar **13**
Wianno Grille **23**

ATTRACTIONS ●

Cape Cod Maritime Museum **19**
John F. Kennedy Hyannis Museum **14**

Among the charter boats berthed in **Barnstable Harbor** is Capt. Justin Zacek's
Drifter (© **508/398-2061**), a 36-foot boat offering half- and full-day trips costing $550
to $775, depending on the length of the trip and the number of people. **Hy-Line
Cruises** offers seasonal sonar-aided "bottom" or blues fishing from its Ocean Street dock
in Hyannis (© **508/790-0696**). The cost for a half-day trip is $34 to $38 per adult, $22
to $33 for kids. **Helen H Deep-Sea Fishing,** at 137 Pleasant St., Hyannis (© **508/790-
0660**), offers two daily expeditions aboard a 100-foot boat with a heated cabin and full
galley. Adults pay $35, children $24.

GOLF   Open year-round, the **Hyannis Golf Club,** 1840 Rte. 132 (© **508/362-2606**),
offers a 46-station driving range, as well as an 18-hole championship course. High-season

greens fees are $60. Smaller but scenic, the 9-hole **Cotuit High Ground Country Club** is at 31 Crockers Neck Rd., Cotuit (© **508/428-9863;** www.cotuithighground.com). An 18-hole round costs $15.

HARBOR CRUISES   For a fun and informative introduction to the harbor and its residents, take a leisurely, 1-hour, narrated tour aboard one of Hy-Line Cruises' 1911 steamer replicas, **MV *Patience*** or **MV *Prudence.*** There are five 1-hour family cruises a day in season, but for a real treat take the Sunday 3pm "Ice Cream Float," which includes a design-your-own Ben & Jerry's ice-cream sundae. Hy-Line Cruises depart from the Ocean Street Dock (© **508/790-0696;** www.hy-linecruises.com), and you should call for a reservation and schedule. Tickets are $16 for adults and free to $8 for children 12 and under. There are 16 departures daily from late June to September; it's closed November to mid-April. Credit cards are accepted. Parking is $5 per car.

NATURE   **Long Pasture Wildlife Sanctuary** ★★, 345 Bone Hill Rd., Barnstable Village (© **508/362-7475;** www.massaudubon.org), a 110-acre Audubon sanctuary, offers easy-to-walk trails out to a meadow with a view of Barnstable Harbor. Wildlife spottings are likely to include numerous butterflies, dragonflies, and red-tailed hawks. Admission $4 for nonmember adults, $3 nonmember children.

WATERSPORTS   **Eastern Mountain Sports,** 1513 Iyannough Rd./Rte. 132 (© **508/ 362-8690;** www.ems.com), offers rental kayaks—tents and sleeping bags, too—and sponsors free clinics and walks, such as a full-moon hike. Kayaks rent for $50 a day, $100 for 3 days.

WHALE-WATCHING   Although Provincetown is about an hour closer to the whales' preferred feeding grounds, it would take you at least an hour (possibly hours on a summer weekend) to drive all the way down-Cape. If your time and itinerary are limited, hop aboard **Hyannis Whale Watcher Cruises,** Barnstable Harbor (about ½ mile north of Rte. 6A, on Mill Way), Barnstable (© **800/287-0374** or 508/362-6088; fax 508/362-9739; www.whales.net), for a 4-hour voyage on a 100-foot high-speed cruiser. Naturalists provide the narration, and should you fail to spot a whale, your next trek is free. Tickets cost $45 for adults, $40 for seniors (62 and older), and $26 for children 4 to 12 from April through mid-October; call for a schedule and off-season rates. No trips mid-October through March.

BASEBALL

The two locally based **Cape Cod Baseball League** (© **508/432-6909.** www.capecod baseball.org) elite amateur teams are the **Hyannis Mets** (who play at McKeon Field, on Old Colony Blvd.) and the **Cotuit Kettleers** (Lowell Park). For a schedule, contact the **Hyannis Area Chamber of Commerce** (© **508/362-5230**) or the **Barnstable Recreation Division** (© **508/790-6345**).

KID STUFF

The **Lightning Falls** minigolf course, 455 W. Main St. (© **508/771-3194**), offers a nice diversion for young children or for the young at heart. A round costs $7 for adults, $6 for children. Open in season 10am to 11pm. About a mile north, off Route 132, the **Cape Cod Potato Chips factory,** 100 Breed's Hill Rd., at Independence Drive, off Rte. 132, in Hyannis (© **508/775-7253;** www.capecodchips.com) offers free 15-minute tours that end with a tasting. Tours are held in July and August, Monday to Friday from 9am to 5pm. Call for off-season hours. On Wednesday mornings in summer, the **Cape Cod Melody Tent,** at the West End rotary (© **508/775-5630;** www.melodytent.com),

SHOPPING

Although Hyannis is undoubtedly the commercial center of the Cape, the stores you'll find there are fairly standard for the most part; you could probably find their ilk anywhere else in the country. It's in the wealthy enclaves that are west of Hyannis, such as Osterville, and along the Old King's Highway (Rte. 6A) to the north, that you're likely to find the real gems. On weekends from late May to mid-June, and daily from mid-June through September, art enthusiasts may want to visit **Harbor Your Arts Artist Shanties** ★, Ocean Street, along Hyannis Harbor; (www.harboryourarts.com). In its seven artists' shacks, you can watch the artists at work and buy directly from them. Nearby on **Pearl Street,** the town of Barnstable is beginning to set up a small arts district. There are several art galleries and studios clustered together, giving a chance for the public to see artists at work. The first Thursday of the month in the summer is an **Arts Stroll** in Hyannis, in which galleries offer open houses and musicians serenade strollers.

ANTIQUES/COLLECTIBLES Of the hundreds of antiques shops scattered through the region, perhaps a dozen qualify as destinations for well-schooled collectors. **Harden Studios,** 3264 Rte. 6A (in the center of town), Barnstable Village (📞 **508/362-7711;** www.hardenstudios.com), is one. Owner Charles M. Harden used to supply to-the-trade-only dealers in the Boston Design Center. An architect by training, he renovated this antique house, built around 1720, to display his finds. Some items, such as primitive portraits and mourning embroidery, are all but extinct outside of museums. Other sturdy, serviceable pieces, such as colonial corner cabinets and slant-top desks, are competitively priced, as are the antique Oriental carpets underfoot. An adjoining barn gallery features nature-centered works by area artists, including Harden's son, an accomplished etcher.

ARTS & CRAFTS The caliber of the shows at the **Cape Cod Art Association,** 3480 Rte. 6A (about ⅓ mile west of Hyannis Rd.), Barnstable (📞 **508/362-2909;** www.cape codartassoc.org), may vary—this is, after all, a nonprofit community venture—but it's worth visiting just to see the skylit studios, designed by CCAA member Richard Sears Gallagher in 1972. Everyone raves about "Cape light," and here you'll see it used to optimal advantage. If the setting fires up artistic yearnings, inquire about classes and workshops, which are held year-round.

Ex-Nantucketer Bob Marks fashions the only authentic Nantucket lightship baskets crafted off-island; as aficionados know, they don't come cheap (a mere handbag typically runs in the thousands). The other handmade furnishings found at **Oak and Ivory,** 1112 Main St. (about 1 mile south of Rte. 28), Osterville (📞 **508/428-9425;** www.oakand ivory.com), from woven throw rugs to pared-down neo-Shaker furniture, fit the country-chic mode at more approachable prices.

At 374 Main St., in Hyannis, **Red Fish, Blue Fish** (📞 **508/775-8700;** http://redfish bluefish.com) wins the funky-gallery award, hands down. Owner Jane Walsh makes jewelry in the front window, but inside this closetlike space, every inch is covered with something unusual and handmade. There is usually a teenager or two hanging out here.

Tao Water Art Gallery, 1989 Rte. 6A, West Barnstable (📞 **508/375-0428;** www. taowatergallery.com), is a former garage converted into a very Zen-like space. It features paintings by Chinese artists as well as museum reproductions of Chinese antiques and jade.

Camelot on Cape Cod: The Kennedys in Hyannis Port

It's been nearly 50 years since those days of Camelot, when JFK was in the White House and America seemed rejuvenated by the Kennedy style, but the Kennedy sites on Cape Cod still attract record numbers of visitors every summer. The Hyannis compound was often seen in the media in the late summer of 2009 as Senator Edward Kennedy spent his final days there. And in July 1999, when John Jr.'s plane crashed into Vineyard Sound, thousands visited the Kennedy Hyannis Museum to mourn the loss by viewing classic photos of the family in Hyannis Port.

Images of Jack Kennedy sailing his jaunty *Wianno Senior* on Nantucket Sound, off Hyannis Port, form part of this nation's collective memory. The vacationing JFK was all tousled hair, toothy grin, earthy charisma, and attractive *joie de vivre*. Remember Jackie sitting beside him, wearing a patterned silk scarf around her head and looking like she'd rather be in Newport, where no one had ever heard of touch football?

The Kennedys always knew how to have fun, and they had it in Hyannis Port. And ever since Hyannis Port became JFK's summer White House, Cape Cod has been inextricably linked to the Kennedy clan. Although the Kennedys spend time elsewhere—working in Washington or wintering in Palm Beach—when they go home, they go to Cape Cod. Generations of Kennedys have sailed these waters, sunned on these beaches, patronized local businesses, and generally had a high old time.

Meanwhile much has changed since the early 1960s on Cape Cod, especially in the Mid Cape area. In those 40-plus years, the mall was built in Hyannis, and urban sprawl infested routes 132 and 28. Yet much, thankfully, remains the same. The Kennedy compound, with its large, gabled Dutch Colonial houses, still commands the end of Scudder Avenue in Hyannis Port. Nearby is the private Hyannisport Golf Club, where Rose loved to play a short round on the foggy oceanfront course. The beaches here are still pristine.

Richard Kiusalas and Steven Whittlesey salvage antique lumber and turn it into cupboards, tables, and chairs, among other things; old windows are retrofitted as mirrors. Most of their stock at **West Barnstable Tables** ★, 2454 Meetinghouse Way (off Rte. 149, near the intersection of Rte. 6A), West Barnstable (© **508/362-2676;** www.west barnstabletables.com), looks freshly made, albeit with wood of unusually high quality. Pieces are priced accordingly: A dining-room set—pine trestle table with six bow-back chairs—runs more than $4,000. When the wood still bears interesting traces of its former life, it's turned into folk-art furniture.

BOOKS & EPHEMERA   Named for the revolutionary printer who helped foment the War of Independence, **Isaiah Thomas Books & Prints,** 4632 Falmouth Rd./Rte. 28 (near Rte. 130), Cotuit (© **508/428-2752;** www.isaiahthomasbooks.com), has a 60,000-volume collection, housed in an 1850 home. The shop is full of treasures, clustered

To bask in the Kennedys' Cape Cod experience, visit the **John F. Kennedy Hyannis Museum** ★, 397 Main St., Hyannis ((C) **508/790-3077;** http://jfk hyannismuseum.org). Admission is $5 for adults, $2.50 for children 10 to 16, and $3 for seniors; hours are from mid-April through October Monday to Saturday 9am to 5pm, and Sunday and holidays from noon to 5pm. Last admission is at 3:30pm. Call for off-season hours. The museum shows a documentary on Kennedy, narrated by Walter Cronkite, and contains several rooms' worth of photos of the Kennedys on Cape Cod. The candid shots included in this permanent display capture some of the quieter moments, as well as JFK's legendary charm. Most of us have seen some of these photos before, but here they are all blown up, mounted, and neatly labeled; if you get confused about lineage, consult the family tree on the wall at the end of the exhibit. The last 3 years of JFK's life were a bit chaotic (some 25,000 well-wishers thronged the roads when the senator and president-to-be returned from the 1960 Democratic Convention), but he continued to treasure the Cape as "the one place I can think and be alone."

Busloads of tourists visit the **Kennedy Memorial** just above Veterans Beach on Ocean Avenue; it's a moving tribute, beautifully maintained by the town, but crowds in season can be distracting. Finally, you may want to drive by the simple white clapboard church, St. Francis Xavier, on South Street; Rose attended Mass daily, and Caroline Kennedy and several other cousins got married here.

Spend your day in the Mid Cape recreating like a privileged Kennedy scion. Rent a windsurfer at Kalmus Beach. Play a round of golf at the **Hyannis Golf Club** ((C) **508/362-2606**), a public course on Route 132. **Four Seas Ice Cream** ((C) **508/775-1394**), at 360 S. Main St., in Centerville, is a must. For lodging right in Hyannis Port, stay at **Simmons Homestead Inn,** 288 Scudder Ave., Hyannis Port ((C) **800/637-1649** or 508/778-4999).

Rose Kennedy once told a reporter, "Our family would rather be in Hyannis Port in the summer than anyplace else in the world." And yours?

by topic. Owner/expert James S. Visbeck is happy to show off his first editions, rare miniatures, and maps; you get the sense that sales are secondary to sheer bibliophilic pleasure.

You should be able to find just about any book you're looking for at the big chain bookstores: **Borders,** 990 Iyannough Rd./Rte. 132, Hyannis ((C) **508/862-6363**); and **Barnes & Noble,** 769 Iyannough Rd. (at the Cape Cod Mall, on Rte. 132), Hyannis ((C) **508/862-6310**).

FOOD   Cape Cod Potato Chips, 100 Breed's Hill Road (at Independence Way, off Rte. 132), Hyannis ((C) **508/775-7253;** www.capecodchips.com), really are the world's best. Long a local favorite—they're chunkier than the norm—they originate right here. Free 15-minute factory tours are offered Monday to Friday from 9am to 5pm in July and August. Call for off-season hours. **Cape Cod Beer** ((C) **508/790-4200;** www.capecod

beer.com), at 1336 Phinney's Lane, Hyannis, gives free tours of its brewery on Saturdays at 1pm and Tuesdays at 11am.

HOME DECOR   As a Nantucket innkeeper whiling away the winter, Claire Murray took up hooking rugs and turned her knack into an international business. At **Claire Murray,** 867 Main St. (in the center of town), Osterville (© **508/420-3562;** www.clairemurray.com), and at her store at 770 Rte. 6A, in West Barnstable (© **508/375-0331**), hobbyists can find all the fixings for various needle crafts, including kits, and advice as needed. Those of us with little time on our hands can just buy the finished goods, from sweaters and quilts to the signature folk-motif rugs.

Flowery pastels are the hallmark of **Joan Peters,** 885 Main St. (in the center of town), Osterville (© **508/428-3418;** www.joanpeters.com), favored by the *Town & Country* set. She designs a wide array of compatible fabrics and ceramics—right down to the bathroom sink, if need be—so that it's easy to achieve a pervasive, light-splashed look that doesn't appear too overtly matched and mixed.

SEAFOOD   The best place to buy fresh seafood in the vicinity of Hyannis is **Cape Fish & Lobster,** at 406 W. Main St., in Centerville (© **508/771-1122**). This is where the top restaurateurs in Hyannis get their seafood. The prices are reasonable, and the catch is the freshest in town.

TWO MARITIME MUSEUMS

The **Cape Cod Maritime Museum** ★, at 135 South St., in Hyannis, on the eastern end of Aselton Park (© **508/775-1723;** www.capecodmaritimemuseum.org), is small but interesting. The museum displays artifacts from ships that wrecked off the shore of Cape Cod and exhibits a collection of items from the United States Lifesaving Service, the precursor to the Coast Guard. The museum is open Tuesday through Saturday 10am to 4pm, Sunday noon to 4pm. Admission is $5 for adults, $4 for students and seniors, and free for children 6 and under. On the north side of town, the **Coast Guard Heritage Museum** ★ (© **508/362-8521;** www.coastguardheritagemuseum.org) is located at a former U.S. Custom House, which is also the former Trayser Museum building (3353 Main St./Rte. 6A, Barnstable Village). The main museum building houses displays of pre–Coast Guard groups, such as the lighthouse service, the lightship service, and the lifesaving service. The village blacksmith shop gives demonstrations daily. Also on the property is the oldest wooden jail in the country, built in the 1600s. The museum is open May through October, Tuesday through Saturday, 10am to 3pm. Admission is $5.

WHERE TO STAY

In Hyannis, Hyannis Port & Centerville

There are a variety of large, generic, but convenient hotels and motels in Hyannis.

Heritage House Hotel, 259 Main St. (in the center of town), Hyannis (© **508/775-7000;** www.heritagehousehotel.com), is ideally located on Main Street, walking distance from restaurants, shops, and the ferries to Nantucket and Martha's Vineyard. There is an indoor and an outdoor pool, hot tub and saunas, and a restaurant/lounge on-site. During the high season, the 130 rooms are priced at $129 on weekdays and $149 on weekends for double occupancy.

Also centrally located on Main Street, within strolling distance of restaurants, shopping, and the ferries, is the 77-room **Hyannis Inn Motel,** 473 Main St., Hyannis (© **800/922-8993** or 508/775-0255; www.hyannisinn.com). Summer rates are $117 to $144 double—a real value. During the Kennedy administration, this motel served as the press headquarters. It has an indoor pool, a breakfast restaurant (the meal is not included with room rates), and a cocktail lounge. It's closed late October to mid-March.

If you prefer more amenities, there's the **Resort and Conference Center at Hyannis,** at 35 Scudder Ave., at the West End Circle just off Main Street (© **866/828-8259;** www.capecodresortandconference.com). Summer rates are $200 to $230 double. Out the back door is an 18-hole, par-3 executive golf course. There are also an indoor and an outdoor pool, two restaurants, and a fitness center.

A great choice for families is the **Cape Codder Resort & Spa,** 1225 Iyannough Rd./Rte. 132 (at the intersection of Bearse's Way), Hyannis (© **888/297-2200** or 508/771-3000; www.capecodderresort.com). It features two restaurants (Grand Cru Wine Bar, and Hearth 'n Kettle for families) and a spa (massage and other body treatments). Kids love the indoor wave pool with two water slides. Summer rates in the 260 rooms are $159 to $198 double, $350 to $382 suite. Rooms have all the usual amenities, plus high-speed Internet access and video games.

Moderate

Long Dell Inn ★★ (Value) This handsome 1850s former sea captain's home, which is on the National Register of Historic Places, has been welcoming guests for 80 years. The current innkeepers are the types with real know-how, serving up three-course gourmet breakfasts and providing great advice on things to do. Rooms are comfortable and charmingly decorated in classic New England style, with antiques; two have private decks and one has a minifridge and microwave. But perhaps the best part about the inn is its location, just a short walk to one of the best beaches on Cape Cod, Craigville Beach.

436 S. Main St., Centerville, MA 02632. © **508/775-2750.** www.longdellinn.com. 7 units. Summer $155–$180. Rates include full breakfast. AE, MC, V. *In room:* AC, TV, hair dryer, Wi-Fi.

Simmons Homestead Inn ★★ (Finds) The first things passersby notice are all the classic red sports cars: 56 at last count. A former ad exec and race-car driver, innkeeper Bill Putman likes to collect. He's made his sports-car collection into a small **museum** open to the public (admission $8 adults, $4 children 10–16; free for inn guests) called **Toad Hall** (© **508/778-4934;** www.toadhallcars.com), from *The Wind in the Willows.* Inside the inn is his animal collection. The stuffed toys, sculpture, needlepoint, and wallpaper differentiate the rather traditional rooms in this rambling 1820s captain's manse. This is an inn where you'll find everyone around the hearth sipping complimentary wine (served at "6-ish") while they compare notes and nail down dinner plans. To help his guests plan their days and evenings, Putman has typed up extensive notes on day trips, bike routes, and his own quirky restaurant reviews. Guests who prefer privacy may book the spiffily updated "servants' quarters," a spacious, airy wing with its own private deck. Rooms vary in size, but all are decorated with comfort and a sense of humor in mind. Four hammocks swing from trees in the shady backyard of this homey establishment.

288 Scudder Ave. (about ¼ mile west of the West End rotary), Hyannis Port, MA 02647. © **800/637-1649** or 508/778-4999. Fax 508/790-1342. www.simmonshomesteadinn.com. 14 units. Summer $180–$240 double; $300 2-bedroom suite. Rates include full breakfast. AE, DISC, MC, V. Dogs welcome. **Amenities:** Bikes; billiards parlor. *In room:* A/C ($10/night charge), hair dryer, no phone.

In Barnstable Village

To check on availability at 17 bed-and-breakfasts along Route 6A from Sandwich to Brewster, check out **www.historiccapecodbay.com.** Being on Route 6A means most of these inns are walking distance to a bayside beach and shops and restaurants in Barnstable Village.

The Acworth Inn   Anyone looking to avoid the excess of Victorian furnishings in many B&Bs will delight in the simple, fresh, immaculate decor here. A couple of rooms have such extra amenities as TVs, minifridges, and whirlpool tubs. Two rooms in the carriage house have been combined into one romantic luxury suite with a whirlpool tub, TV/VCR, working fireplace, air-conditioning, and minifridge. The three-course breakfasts include such favorites as cranberry pie, quiches, and stuffed French toast. The inn is close to Barnstable Village and popular Cape Cod Bay beaches, so the complimentary bikes may be all you need in the way of wheels.

4352 Rte. 6A/Old King's Hwy. (near the Yarmouth Port border), Cummaquid, MA 02637. (¢ **800/362-6363** or 508/362-3330. Fax 508/375-0304. www.acworthinn.com. 5 units. Summer $149–$169 double; $229 suite. Rates include full breakfast. AE, DISC, MC, V. **Amenities:** Bikes. *In room:* A/C, hair dryer, no phone.

Ashley Manor Inn   A lovely country inn along the Old King's Highway, this house is a much-modified 1699 colonial mansion that retains many of its original features, including a hearth with beehive oven, built-in corner cupboards in the wainscoted dining room, and wide-board floors, many of them brightened with Nantucket-style splatter paint. The rooms, all but one of which boast a working fireplace, are spacious and inviting: true retreats. A deluxe room in its own wing has a separate entrance, whirlpool tub, glass-enclosed shower, canopy bed, and fireplace. All bathrooms are supplied with luxury towels of 100% Egyptian cotton. The 2-acre property itself is shielded from the road by an enormous privet hedge, and fragrant boxwood camouflages a Har-Tru tennis court. (You'll find loaner bikes beside it, ready to roll.) Romantics can sequester themselves in the flower-fringed gazebo. Breakfast on the brick patio is worth waking up for.

3660 Rte. 6A (just east of Hyannis Rd.), Barnstable, MA 02630. (¢ **888/535-2246** or 508/362-8044. Fax 508/362-9927. www.ashleymanor.net. 6 units. Summer $175 double; $235 suite. Rates include full breakfast. AE, DISC, MC, V. No children 13 and under. **Amenities:** Bikes; Har-Tru tennis court. *In room:* A/C, TV, hair dryer.

Beechwood Inn ★★ (Finds   Look for a butterscotch-colored 1853 Queen Anne Victorian all but enshrouded in weeping beech trees. Admirers of late-19th-century decor are in for a treat: The interior remains dark and rich, with a red-velvet parlor and tin ceilings in the dining room, where innkeeper Debbie Traugot serves a three-course breakfast featuring home-baked delights such as applesauce pancakes and raspberry bread. Two of the upstairs bedrooms embody distinctive period styles: The Cottage Room contains furniture painted in an 1860s mode; and the Eastlake Room is modeled on the aesthetic precepts of William Morris that flourished in the 1880s. Each affords a distant view of the sparkling bay. All rooms have Sealy Posturepedic Plush mattresses. Rooms range from quite spacious (Lilac) to romantically snug (Garret); some have a fireplace and TV/VCR. The Traugots breed golden retrievers and guests are free to play with puppies, if they so desire. The fact that this inn is walking distance to a Cape Cod Bay beach and to Barnstable Village where there are several restaurants is also a plus.

2839 Rte. 6A (about 1½ miles east of Rte. 132), Barnstable Village, MA 02630. (¢ **800/609-6618** or 508/362-6618. Fax 508/362-0298. www.beechwoodinn.com. 6 units, 4 with tub/shower combination, 2 with shower only. Summer $185–$210 double. Rates include full breakfast. AE, DISC, MC, V. No children 12 and under. *In room:* A/C, TV/VCR, Wi-Fi, fridge, hair dryer, no phone.

Lamb and Lion Inn ★   This is an unusual property: part B&B, part motel. From the roadside, it's one of those charming old Cape Cod cottages (ca. 1740) along the Old

King's Highway (where charming "Capes" are ubiquitous), set up on a knoll with a slop- **123**
ing lawn full of colorful flowers. Inside it's a motel-like space with units encircling a pool
and hot tub. The rooms are all individually decorated, and six rooms have kitchenettes.
All rooms in the main inn building are air-conditioned. The multilevel barn suite, with
three loft-type bedrooms, is a funky historic space (built in 1740), filled with rustic nooks
and crannies. There's also an outdoor shower, a true Cape Cod tradition.

2504 Main St./Rte. 6A, Barnstable, MA 02630. ✆ **800/909-6923** or 508/362-6823. Fax 508/362-0227. www.lambandlion.com. 10 units, 6 with tub/shower combination, 4 with shower only. Summer $189–$275 double. Rates include continental breakfast. MC, V. Well-behaved pets allowed (40-lb. limit). **Amenities:** Hot tub; pool. *In room:* A/C, TV.

WHERE TO DINE
In Hyannis
Expensive
Alberto's Ristorante ★★★ ITALIAN   What makes this place a sure bet is consistency. You always know you'll get a great meal here. Owner/chef Felisberto Barreiro's most popular dishes are his treatments of lobster, rack of lamb, and beef tenderloin. Hand-cut pasta is also a specialty, including the ultrarich seafood ravioli cloaked in saffron-cream sauce. Though the atmosphere is elegant, with sconces shedding a warm glow over well-spaced, linen-draped tables, it is not one of hushed reverence: People clearly come here to have a good time, and the friendly service and fabulous food ensure that they do. Locals who appreciate a bargain know to come between 3 and 6pm, when a full dinner, with soup, salad, and dessert, costs as little as $10 to $15. There's live jazz or piano music daily year-round.

360 Main St., Hyannis. ✆ **508/778-1770.** www.albertos.net. Reservations recommended. Main courses $11–$27. AE, DC, DISC, MC, V. Daily 11:30am–11pm.

The Black Cat Tavern ★ NEW AMERICAN   Conveniently located on Hyannis Harbor less than a block from the Hy-Line ferries, this is a fine place to catch a quick bite or full meal while you wait for your boat to come in. The menu is pretty basic—steak, pasta, and, of course, fish—but attention is paid to the details; the onion rings, for instance, are made fresh. The dining room, with its bar of gleaming mahogany and brass, will appeal to chilled travelers on a blustery day; in fine weather, you might prefer the porch. There's live jazz on the weekends in season.

165 Ocean St. (opposite the Ocean St. Dock), Hyannis. ✆ **508/778-1233.** http://blackcattavern.com. Reservations not accepted. Main courses $15–$29. AE, DC, DISC, MC, V. Apr–Oct daily 11:30am–9pm; call for off-season hours. Closed Jan.

Eclectic Cafe ★★ (Finds) NEW AMERICAN   After being closed for several years, this small restaurant, hidden down an alley off Hyannis's Main Street, is back in business and creating quite a buzz. A short time after opening, Chef Jeff Dunn won a competition for best seafood dish: striped bass with chutney (if it's on the menu, order it). This is an intimate place; most of the seating is on the outdoor patio, but there is a small bar room in addition to the cozy dining room. This is the place to be adventurous in your ordering. Try the roasted vegetable tower, which is topped with mozzarella. As a main course (if the striped bass is not on the menu), try the halibut stuffed with horseradish butter or any of the other wonderful seafood concoctions.

606 Main St. (the west end of town), Hyannis ✆ **508/771-7187.** http://eclecticcafecapecod.com. Reservations recommended. Main courses $19–$28. AE, DISC, MC, V. Apr–Oct daily 5–10pm; call for off-season hours.

The Naked Oyster Bistro & Raw Bar ★ NEW AMERICAN   Overlook the fact that this fun bistro restaurant is located in an office complex and enjoy the experience. The specialty here is fresh local seafood, and oyster fans will be fascinated by the selection of "dressed oysters," from the traditional Rockefeller to a more exotic baked *oishi*, with wasabi and soy. The main courses feature such spicy options as sautéed Thai shrimp and blackened Cajun swordfish, as well as hearty dishes such ass grilled filet mignon with garlic mashed potatoes. Portions are large and service is professional and cheerful. In the evenings, there is a young-professionals bar scene; and some say the bartenders serve the best martinis in town.

20 Independence Dr. (just off Rte. 132, at Park Place), Hyannis. ✆ **508/778-6500.** www.nakedoyster. com. Reservations accepted. Main courses $14–$24. AE, MC, V. June–Aug daily 4–9:30pm; Sept–May Mon–Fri 11:30am–3pm, daily 4–9:30pm.

The Paddock ★★★ CONTINENTAL   In the more than 3 decades the Paddock has been open, it has maintained a solid reputation with consistently good food and service. The dining room is candlelit and romantic; on clear nights you can sit on the plant-filled summer porch. The menu combines creative options with traditional choices (you can still order extra béarnaise sauce on the side). For appetizers, there's chicken-liver pâté, but also polenta crab cakes with chipotle-chili cream and sweet mango salsa. Main courses include filet mignon—yes, this is the place to come for steak in the Mid Cape—and sesame-encrusted yellowfin tuna served rare with Asian greens. There is free valet parking, and a pianist entertains nightly in the pub area. *Note:* Those attending a Melody Tent performance can leave their car in the Paddock lot during the performance if they eat here first.

20 Scudder Ave. (West End rotary, at the intersection of W. Main and Main sts.), Hyannis. ✆ **508/775-7677.** www.paddockcapecod.com. Reservations recommended. Main courses lunch $7–$13; dinner $17–$28. AE, DC, DISC, MC, V. Apr to mid-Nov Mon–Sat 11:30am–2:30pm and 5–10pm; Sun noon–8:45pm. Closed mid-Nov to Mar.

The Steak House and Sports Bar ★★ STEAKHOUSE   One of the few places in town where you can count on getting a good steak, the Steakhouse has an upscale sports-bar-type atmosphere. The appetizer menu is loaded with such hearty fare as ribs. There are also big juicy burgers and pastrami sandwiches. But the steak menu is all about the cut: porterhouse, filet mignon, T-bone, sirloin. After you choose your cut, you choose your potato (fried, baked, mashed, garlic) and vegetable. The sports-bar part of this place is recognizable from the 32 high-def TVs that can be seen from virtually anywhere in the room. There is a large bar downstairs and a more intimate bar upstairs.

72 North St. (just off the West End rotary), Hyannis. ✆ **508/775-7100.** Reservations recommended. Main courses $10–$27. AE, DC, MC, V. Daily 4:30–11pm; call for off-season hours.

Roadhouse Café ★★ AMERICAN/NORTHERN ITALIAN   This is neither a roadhouse nor a cafe, but it is a solid entry in the Hyannis dining scene. The extensive menu is pretty much split between American standards, such as steak (not to mention oysters Rockefeller), and real Italian cooking, unstinting on the garlic. A less expensive, lighter-fare menu, including what some have called "the best burger in the world," is served in the snazzy bistro in back. Among the appetizers are such delicacies as beef carpaccio with fresh-shaved Parmesan, and vine-ripened tomatoes and buffalo mozzarella drizzled with balsamic vinaigrette. The vinaigrette also makes a tasty marinade for native swordfish headed for the grill. The signature dessert, a distinctly non-Italian cheesecake nights for the live jazz in the bistro (see "Hyannis & Environs After Dark," below).

488 South St. (off Main St., near the West End rotary), Hyannis. (C) **508/775-2386.** www.roadhousecafe.com. Reservations recommended. Main courses $15–$26. AE, DC, DISC, MC, V. Daily 4–9:30pm.

Five Eighty Six Bistro and Bar ★ BISTRO   For a hopping bar scene and good, reasonably priced eats, this is a solid choice. Your best bet on the small menu is the selection of wood-fire-grilled gourmet pizzas, though there is also standard bistro fare such as steak frites, as well as pasta, meat, and seafood dishes (see "Hyannis & Environs After Dark," below). There is live music in season Mondays, Thursdays, Fridays, and Saturdays from 9:30pm on.

586 Main St., Hyannis. (C) **508/778-6515.** www.fiveeightysixbistro.com. Reservations recommended. Main courses $13–$24. AE, DC, MC, V. Daily 5–10pm.

Wianno Grille ★ PUB/SEAFOOD   When you're in the mood for a nothing-fancy meal in sleek surroundings, this new restaurant near the Barnstable Airport may be just the ticket. Calling itself an "upscale pub," the Wianno Grille offers straightforward fare, such as fish and chips, burgers, sandwiches, and salads, as well as heartier dishes such as barbecue ribs, sirloin, and lamb chops. The main floor has an almost-room-length bar and cozy booths. Downstairs you'll find larger tables more suitable for families. Sunday brunch is popular here.

380 Barnstable Rd. (Staples Plaza, just off the airport rotary), Hyannis (C) **508/778-5587.** www.wiannogrille.com. Reservations accepted. Main courses $8–$25. AE, MC, V. Daily 11:30am–10pm.

Moderate

Colombo's Café & Pastries ★ ITALIAN   This traditional Italian cafe was opened in recent years by Dave Columbo, who owns the Roadhouse Café nearby. The place to go for old-fashioned Italian food like you would find in Boston's Old North End, this restaurant fills a gap for a style of cuisine that is not found too often in these parts. Forget nouvelle cuisine and twirl some of this hearty pasta around a fork and dig in.

544 Main St. (on the west end of town), Hyannis. (C) **508/790-5700.** www.colomboscafe.com. Reservations not accepted. Main courses $12–$22. MC, V. Daily 5–10pm.

Harry's Blues Bar & Cajun Restaurant ★★ CAJUN   Seemingly transported from the French Quarter, this small restaurant/bar—park benches serve as booths—has added some Italian and French options to its menu, but it's the authentic Cajun cooking that keeps customers coming back: baby back ribs, jambalaya, hoppin' johns, and red beans and rice. On the weekends, get set for a heaping serving of R&B (see "Hyannis & Environs After Dark," below). This place hops until 1am. *Tip:* Arrive for a late dinner around 8:30pm, and you'll have yourself a great table once the music starts.

700 Main St. (at Stevens St., near the West End rotary), Hyannis. (C) **508/778-4188.** www.harrysbluesbar.com. Reservations not accepted. Main courses $10–$19. MC, V. Restaurant daily 11:30am–10pm. Bar daily 11:30am–1am.

Inexpensive

Baxter's Boat House ★ (Value) (Kids) SEAFOOD   A shingled shack on a jetty jutting out into the harbor, Baxter's has catered to the boating crowd since the mid-1950s, with such Cape classics as fried clams and fish virtually any way you like it, from baked to blackened, served on paper plates at picnic tables. This is a good place to bring a brood of kids. If you sit out on the deck, be wary of swooping seagulls looking to spirit away your lunch.

177 Pleasant St. (near the Steamship Authority ferry), Hyannis. ☎ **508/775-7040;** www.baxterscapecod. com. Main courses $8–$14. AE, MC, V. Late May–early Sept daily 11:30am–9pm; hours may vary at the beginning and end of the season. Closed mid-Oct to early Apr.

Common Ground Cafe ★ (Value) AMERICAN   Talk about an out-of-body experience: Step off Main Street Hyannis into this New Age-y sandwich shop run by a commune. The barn-board walls and wide-plank floors surround alcoves with private booths containing amorphous tree-stump tables. You can see straight up to the second-floor juice-and-smoothie bar, where they also sell some health and beauty products. But enough about atmosphere; this place makes the best iced tea on Cape Cod (the house blend is a mixture of mint teas and lemon). Everything is made from scratch here. The sandwiches and salads are, as you'd expect, wholesome and delicious. Though the menu is small, it also has some south-of-the-border choices: The burrito with turkey is a winner. If I understand correctly from their literature (available at the door), the "Common Ground" is love. Count me in.

420 Main St., Hyannis. ☎ **508/778-8390.** Most items under $6. AE, DC, DISC, MC, V. Mon–Thurs 10am–9pm; Fri and Sun 10am–3pm.

The Daily Paper ★ (Value) DINER   The newest diner in town has all the expected accoutrements, such as red banquets and a long diner counter with plenty of swivel stools, but there is also excellent grub here, including what one diner called, "the best toast I've ever had." Breakfast is served until 11:30am Monday through Saturday and all day on Sunday. There is also a kids menu.

644 W. Main St., Hyannis. ☎ **508/790-8800.** www.dailypapercapecod.com. Most items under $10. MC, V. Mon–Sat 6am–2pm; Sun 7am–1pm.

The Original Gourmet Brunch ★ (Finds) AMERICAN   Though the name feels very 1970s, this classic breakfast joint hearkens back to the 1950s, when small, quirky, family-owned restaurants were all that Cape Cod had to offer. When you travel the narrow redbrick path off Main Street into this humble low-ceilinged establishment, you may first notice the oddly slanted floors. Next you'll see the walls covered with autographed photos of celebrities who have rubbed elbows with owner Joe Cotellessa, the man who probably seated you. The menu offers over 100 combinations of omelets, from peanut butter and jelly to bacon and asparagus. There are also Belgian waffles, quiche, and award-winning chili.

517 Main St., Hyannis. ☎ **508/771-2558.** Reservations not accepted. All items under $11. MC, V. Daily 7am–2pm.

Palio Pizzeria ★ PIZZA   This is the place to get the best brick-oven pizza in Hyannis. It is located on Main Street, in a central location a short walk from the harbor, ferries, parks, and museums. They also have homemade pasta here, in addition to homemade cannoli and biscotti.

435 Main St., Hyannis. ☎ **508/771-7004.** www.paliopizzeria.com. Most items under $10; pizzas $14–$19. MC, V. Mon–Sat 11am–10pm.

Coffee & Desserts

La Petite France Cafe, 349 Main St., Hyannis, in the center of town (☎ **508/775-1067;** www.lapetitefrancecafe.com), serves scrumptious croissants, breads, and pastries, all baked on-site. For lunch there are homemade soups, quiches, and crepes, as well as sandwiches and salads. Open Monday to Friday 7am to 3pm, Saturday 8am to 3pm. Closed January to mid-March.

Vermont's favorite sons, **Ben & Jerry,** have one of their playful ice-cream parlors at 352 Main St., Hyannis (© **508/790-0910**). Open daily from 10:30am to midnight.

A modest luncheonette may make an unlikely shrine, but since 1934, several generations of summer-goers—including enthusiastic Kennedys—have fed their ice-cream cravings at **Four Seas Ice Cream** ★★, 360 S. Main St., at Main Street, in the center of Centerville (© **508/775-1394;** http://fourseasicecream.com). Founder Richard Warren was into exotic flavors long before they became the norm. The parlor's specialties include rum-butter toffee, cantaloupe, and—at the height of the season—Cape Cod beach plum. Closed early September to late May.

Takeout & Picnic Fare

Another branch of the popular **Box Lunch** (© **508/790-5855;** www.boxlunch.com), serving pita "rollwiches," is right on Main Street (no. 357) in Hyannis. These are the best—and fastest—sandwiches in town. Open Monday to Saturday 9am to 6pm, Sunday 9am to 4pm.

Lamberts Rainbow Fruit ★★ (© **508/790-5954**), at 1000 W. Main St., Centerville, has the best produce selection, bar none, in the area. Also, this is the place to pick up such picnic fixings as breads and spreads.

In Barnstable Village, Osterville & Cotuit
Very Expensive

The Regatta of Cotuit ★★★ NEW AMERICAN   Under chef/owner Weldon Fizell, the Regatta continues to be one of the best fine-dining spots on Cape Cod. It now also boasts one of the best bistro menus served in the new **Tap Room Bar.** This 1790 Cape was once a stagecoach inn, and some have found the Federal-era atmosphere a tad formal. So the new bar area makes this a more casual place to dine. Either way, food and service are always top-notch. Menu items revolve around local provender, such as caramelized sea scallops from Georges Bank, with goat-cheese risotto; or Atlantic halibut with a basil pasta flan. Buffalo tenderloin has been on the menu for years, as has the crispy half duck. The cuisine is exquisitely prepared and presented, fortified by herbs and vegetables plucked fresh from the kitchen garden. There is live jazz Tuesdays, Thursdays, and Sundays. On Wednesdays, a four-course $45 prix-fixe meal, including wine, is offered in addition to the regular menu.

4631 Rte. 28 (near the intersection of Rte. 130), Cotuit. © **508/428-5715.** www.regattarestaurant.com. Reservations recommended. Main courses $28–$39; tap-room menu $12–$20. AE, MC, V. Apr–Dec daily 5–9pm; Jan–Mar Wed–Sun 5–9pm.

Expensive

The Barnstable Restaurant and Tavern ★★ NEW AMERICAN/PUB   Located in a 200-year-old stagecoach stop on the Old King's Highway, Barnstable Tavern has long been a sought-after destination. In recent years, chef/owner Rob Calderone has put together a menu of sophisticated options such as roast lamb with mustard sauce, roast duck with orange liqueur sauce, and sole piccata. A raw bar spotlights local oysters and clams. Families looking for a reasonably priced meal will be pleased by the pub fare— burgers, sandwiches, pasta, fried seafood—that's still served amid the atmosphere of the olden days. The wine list is notable for its large number of well-priced bottles.

3176 Main St./Rte. 6A (in the center of Barnstable Village). © **508/362-2355.** www.barnstablerestaurant. com. Reservations accepted. Main courses $9–$25. AC, DC, MC, V. Daily 11:30am–9pm.

Dolphin Restaurant ★ NEW AMERICAN   It looks like just another run-of-the-mill roadside eatery, so it's easy to miss from the road. Never mind the corny decor (pine paneling and clunky captains' chairs) or the little plate of crackers and cheese dip that greets you at the table, both carry-overs from the restaurant's 1953 debut. The finesse is to be found in the menu, where amid the more typical fried fish, you'll find such delicacies as Chilean sea bass with roasted corn salsa and lime vinaigrette, roast duck with mango glaze and toasted coconut, or arctic char with caramelized onions and citrus butter. The signature dessert is amaretto bread pudding.

3250 Rte. 6A (in the center of town), Barnstable. ℭ 508/362-6610. Reservations not accepted. Main courses $17–$23. AE, MC, V. May–Oct daily 5–9:30pm, Mon–Sat 11:30am–3pm; call for off-season hours.

The Islander ★ CARIBBEAN   You'll really feel like an insider as you wind your way through the fancy neighborhoods of Osterville to this small restaurant set in the old Crosby boatyard. In the mid–19th century, the Crosby brothers invented a new kind of sailboat that came about "quick like a cat." You can still see wooden Crosby Cat sailboats in the boatyard, as well as million-dollar yachts. The catch of the day, prepared with a Caribbean twist, is the specialty of the house.

72 Crosby Circle (at the end of West Bay Rd., on the harbor at the Crosby Boat Yard), Osterville. ℭ 508/428-6719. www.theislandercapecod.com. Reservations highly recommended. Main courses $17–$25. MC, V. June–Aug daily 11:30am–2:30pm and 5:30–9:30pm; call for off-season hours. Closed late Sept to mid-May.

Mattakeese Wharf ★ SEAFOOD   This water-view fish house, with broad decks jutting out into the Barnstable harbor, gets packed in season; don't even bother on summer weekends. The outdoor seating fills up first, and no wonder, with Sandy Neck sunsets to marvel over and fish so fresh it could have flopped on deck. There's a Mediterranean subtext to the extensive menu. The bouillabaisse is worthy of the name, and the varied combinations of pasta, seafood, and sauce—from Alfredo to *fra diavolo*—invite return visits. There's live piano music most nights in season.

273 Millway Rd. (about ½ mile north of Rte. 6A), Barnstable. ℭ 508/362-4511. www.mattakeese.com. Reservations recommended. Main courses $14–$28. AE, DC, DISC, MC, V. June to mid-Oct daily 11am–9:30pm; call for off-season hours. Closed mid-Oct to Apr.

HYANNIS & ENVIRONS AFTER DARK
Low-Key Evenings
Baxter's Boat House   This congenial little lounge, with map-topped tables and low-key blues piano, draws an attractive crowd, including the occasional vacationing celebrity. See "Where to Dine," above. 177 Pleasant St, Hyannis. ℭ 508/775-7040. www.baxterscapecod.com.

Embargo ★★   Attracting an urbane crowd of singles in the 30-to-50 age group, this upbeat Spanish-themed bar is well worth a stop for some tapas and a drink—make mine sangria!—before dinner. It is making a name for itself for the tapas menu, which includes such mouthwatering offerings as Serrano-ham-wrapped dates stuffed with brie, and Kobe beef sliders. Half-price tapas are served daily 4:30 to 6pm. 453 Main St, Hyannis. ℭ 508/771-9700.

Roadhouse Café   Duck into this dark-paneled bar, decorated like an English gentlemen's club in burgundy leather, if you're looking for sophisticated entertainment and company. The bar stocks 48 boutique beers, in addition to all the usual hard, soft, and sweet liquors, and you won't go hoarse trying to converse over the soft jazz. The bistro area next to the bar has live jazz piano nightly. See "Where to Dine," above. Insiders

know to show up Monday nights to hear local jazz great Dave McKenna. 488 South St,
Hyannis. ℭ **508/775-2386.** www.roadhousecafe.com.

Live & Loud

Harry's Blues Bar & Cajun Restaurant There's hardly room to eat here, let alone rock out, but the cramped dance floor makes for instant camaraderie. The classic blues music heard here, such as Rick Russell and the Cadillac Horns, really demands to be absorbed in such an intimate space. Live performance reigns nightly in season and about 5 nights a week year-round. See "Where to Dine," above. 700 Main St. (at Stevens St, Hyannis.). ℭ **508/778-4188.** www.harrysbluesbar.com. Thurs–Sat cover $10 or less.

The Island Merchant This hip cafe on Main Street, in Hyannis, has a great Greenwich Village atmosphere. Live entertainment nightly, with jazz, rock, and blues. From 10pm to 1am, burgers are $2. Mondays, Wednesdays, and Thursdays, half-price appetizers are served at the bar from 5:30 to 7:30pm. Closed Tuesdays. 302 Main St, Hyannis. ℭ **508/771-1337.** www.theislandmerchant.com. No cover.

Performances, Movies, Readings & Lectures

The Barnstable Comedy Club A local favorite since 1922, the oldest amateur theater group in the country offers a mix of old chestnuts and original farces off-season. Call for a schedule. 3171 Rte. 6A (in the center of town), Barnstable. ℭ **508/362-6333.** Tickets $12–$15, students and seniors $10–$14.

The Cape Cod Melody Tent ★ Built as a summer theater in 1950, this billowy, blue big-top proved even better suited to variety shows. A nonprofit venture since 1990 (proceeds fund other cultural initiatives Cape-wide), the Melody Tent has hosted the major performers of the past half-century, from jazz greats to comedians, crooners to rockers. Every seat is a winner in this grand oval, only 20 banked aisles deep. Curtain 8pm nightly July to early September. There's also a children's theater program Wednesday mornings at 11am; tickets are $8. Call for a schedule. 21 W. Main St., Hyannis (West End rotary). ℭ **508/775-5630,** or Ticketmaster ℭ **800/745-3000.** www.melodytent.org. Tickets $18–$45.

---

2 YARMOUTH ★

---

19 miles E of Sandwich; 38 miles S of Provincetown

This cross section represents the Cape at its best—and worst. Yarmouth Port, on Cape Cod Bay, is an enchanting town, clustered with interesting shops and architectural pearls, whereas the sound-side "villages" of West to South Yarmouth are an object lesson in unbridled development run amok. This section of Route 28 is a nightmarish gauntlet of tacky accommodations and "attractions." Yet even here, you'll find several spots of interest.

Legend has it that Leif Eriksson found the region very attractive indeed, and set up what was meant to be a permanent camp by the Bass River around A.D. 1000. No trace has yet been found—other than the puzzling "Bournedale stone," with its vaguely runic inscriptions, now housed at the Aptucxet Trading Post Museum in Bourne (see p. 87). Why Eriksson left—and whether, in fact, he came to Cape Cod at all, and not some similar spot—are mysteries still unanswered. We do know that Yarmouth, most likely named for an English port, was the second Cape town to incorporate, following closely on the heels of Sandwich, and that at the height of the shipping boom, Yarmouth Port boasted a "Captain's Row" of 50 fine houses, most of which remain showpieces to this day.

So you've got the north shore for culture and refinement, and the south shore for kitsch. Take your pick, or enjoy the best of both worlds.

ESSENTIALS

GETTING THERE   After crossing the Sagamore Bridge, head east on Route 6 or 6A. The section of Route 6A, north of Route 6's exit 7, passes through the village of Yarmouth Port. The villages of West Yarmouth, Bass River, and South Yarmouth are located along Route 28, east of Hyannis; to reach them from Route 6, take exit 7 south (Yarmouth Rd.) or exit 8 south (Station St.); or fly into Hyannis (see section 3, "Getting There & Getting Around," in chapter 3).

If you need to get around the area without a car, the Yarmouth Easy Shuttle circles Route 28 from Hyannis's bus terminal; for details contact the Yarmouth Area Chamber of Commerce (see below).

GETTING AROUND   The **H2O Line,** run by the Cape Cod Regional Transit Authority (© **800/352-7155;** www.capecodtransit.org), runs from Hyannis to Orleans, making stops in Yarmouth on six round-trips daily. Trips from Dennisport to Hyannis cost $2.50. The **Yarmouth Shuttle,** also called **The Breeze** and also run by the Cape Cod Regional Transit Authority, travels down Route 28 (from Hyannis to the Bass River) and down Old Main Road in South Yarmouth, and makes stops at Seagull and Bass River beaches. Flag it down anywhere along the route. Fares start at $1 and increase depending on the length of your ride.

VISITOR INFORMATION   Contact the **Yarmouth Area Chamber of Commerce,** 424 Rte. 28, West Yarmouth, MA 02673 (© **800/732-1008** or 508/778-1008; fax 508/778-5114; www.yarmouthcapecod.com) or the **Cape Cod Chamber of Commerce** (see "Visitor Information," under "Hyannis, Barnstable & Environs," earlier in this chapter). The Yarmouth chamber is open Monday through Friday 9am to 5pm and Sunday 10am to 3pm, in season. Off-season, the hours are Monday through Friday 9am to 5pm.

BEACHES & RECREATIONAL PURSUITS

BEACHES   Yarmouth boasts 11 saltwater and 2 pond beaches open to the public. The body-per-square-yard ratio can be pretty intense along the sound, but so is the social scene, so no one seems to mind. The beachside parking lots charge $15 a day and sell weeklong stickers ($70).

- **Bass River Beach** ★, off South Shore Drive, in Bass River (South Yarmouth): Located at the mouth of the largest tidal river on the eastern seaboard, this sound beach offers restroom facilities and a snack bar, plus a wheelchair-accessible fishing pier. The beaches along the south shore (Nantucket Sound) tend to be clean and sandy with comfortable water temps (kids will want to stay in all day), but they can also be crowded during peak times. You'll need a beach sticker or a day pass to park here.
- **Gray's Beach,** off Center Street, in Yarmouth Port: This isn't much of a beach, but tame waters make this tiny spit of dark sand good for young children; it adjoins the **Callery-Darling Conservation Area** ★ (see "Nature & Wildlife Areas," below). The **Bass Hole boardwalk** ★★ offers one of the Mid Cape's most scenic walks. Parking is free here, and there's a picnic area with grills.
- **Parker's River Beach,** off South Shore Drive, in Bass River: The usual amenities are available, such as restrooms and a snack bar, plus a 20-foot gazebo for the sun-shy. A beach sticker or day pass is required.

- **Seagull Beach** ★, off South Sea Avenue, in West Yarmouth: Rolling dunes, a board-walk, and all the necessary facilities—such as restrooms and a snack bar—attract a young crowd. Bring bug spray, though: Greenhead flies get the munchies in July. You'll need a beach sticker or day pass to park here.

BICYCLING The **Cape Cod Rail Trail** ★★★ (© 508/896-3491; www.mass.gov/dcr/parks/southeast/ccrt.htm) is a few miles away, on Route 134 (near the entrance to Rte. 6), in South Dennis. Rent a bike at the trail head, and if you are feeling Olympian, bike all the way to Wellfleet (25 miles).

BOATING You can rent a canoe or kayak at **Cape Cod Waterways,** 16 Rte. 28, Den-nisport (© 508/398-0080; www.capecodwaterways.com), and paddle along the Bass River, which flows between South Yarmouth and West Dennis on the south side of the Cape. Canoe or kayak rental for 1½ hours costs $20 to $32.

FISHING Of the five fishing ponds in the Yarmouth area, Long Pond near South Yar-mouth is known for its largemouth bass and pickerel; for details and a license (shellfishing is another option), visit **Town Hall,** at 1146 Rte. 28, in South Yarmouth (© 508/398-2231); or **Riverview Bait and Tackle,** at 1273 Rte. 28, in South Yarmouth (© 508/394-1036). Full-season licenses for Massachusetts residents cost $29; for out-of-staters, $39. You can cast for striped bass and bluefish off the pier at Bass River Beach (see "Beaches," above).

FITNESS The **Mid-Cape Racquet Club** (see "Tennis," below) doubles as a fitness center.

GOLF The township maintains two 18-hole courses: the seasonal **Bayberry Hills,** off West Yarmouth Road, in West Yarmouth (© 508/394-5597; www.golfyarmouthcape cod.com/Bayberry.htm), and the **Bass River Golf Course,** off High Bank Road, in South Yarmouth (© 508/398-9079; http://bassrivergolfcourse.com). The Bass River course is one of the Cape's most famous courses. It was founded in 1900 and redesigned by Don-ald Ross. It is open year-round. A round at Bayberry costs $85; at Bass River, it costs $58. Prices are reduced in the afternoon. Another 18-holer open to the public is the par-54 **Blue Rock Golf Course,** off High Bank Road, in South Yarmouth (© 508/398-9295); it's open year-round, and a round costs $49.

NATURE & WILDLIFE AREAS For a pleasant stroll, follow the 2 miles of trails main-tained by the **Historical Society of Old Yarmouth** ★★ on 53 acres. Park behind the post office and check in at the gatehouse, whose herb garden displays a "Wheel of Thyme." The in-season trail fee (50¢ adults, 25¢ children) includes a keyed trail guide: Look for—but do not pick—the endangered pink lady-slipper, a local orchid. Your path will cross the transplanted 1873 Kelley Chapel, said to have been built by a Quaker grandfather to comfort his daughter after the death of her child.

In Yarmouth Port, follow Centre Street about a mile north and bear northeast on Homers Dock Road; from here a 2.5-mile trail through the Callery-Darling Conserva-tion Area leads to Gray's Beach, where you can continue across the Bass Hole boardwalk for a lovely view of the marsh.

TENNIS There are four public courts at Flax Pond, off North Main Street, in South Yarmouth; four more at Sandy Pond, on Buck Island Road, off Higgins Crowell Road; plus 10 at Dennis-Yarmouth High School, at Station Avenue, in South Yarmouth. For details, contact the **Yarmouth Recreation Department** (© 508/398-2231). **The Mid-Cape**

Racquet Club, 193 Whites Path, South Yarmouth (© **508/394-3511;** www.mid caperacquet.com/home), has nine indoor courts ($22 per person, per hr.), racquetball and squash courts, and health-club facilities ($15 per day).

BASEBALL & SOCCER

The **Dennis-Yarmouth Red Sox,** part of the Cape Cod Baseball League (www.capecod baseball.org), play at Dennis-Yarmouth Regional High School's Red Wilson Field, off Station Avenue, in South Yarmouth. For a schedule, contact the **Yarmouth Chamber of Commerce** (© **508/778-1008**), the **Yarmouth Recreation Department** (© **508/398-2231**), or the **League** (© **508/432-6909**).

The **Cape Cod Crusaders** soccer team takes on a dozen other Atlantic-coast teams from mid-May to early August, also at the Dennis-Yarmouth Regional High School. For details contact the **Yarmouth Chamber of Commerce** (© **508/778-1008**).

KID STUFF

Children tend to crave the "junk" we adults condemn, so they're likely to be enthralled by the rainy-day enticements of Route 28, which include trampolines, batting cages, pitch and putt, and bumper cars. Among the more enduringly appealing miniature golf courses clamoring for attention is **Pirate's Cove,** at 728 Main St./Rte. 28, South Yarmouth (© **508/394-6200;** www.piratescove.net/location/9; daily 10am–10pm in season, closed Nov to mid-Apr), where the trap decor is strong on macabre humor and there are two 18-hole courses. A round is $7.95 for those 13 and older, $6.95 for children 12 and under.

ZooQuarium ★ (**Kids**) This slightly scruffy wildlife museum has made great strides in recent years toward blending entertainment with education. It's a little easier to enjoy the seal and sea lion show once you've been assured that the stars do, in fact, like performing. They have been trained with positive reinforcement only and arrived with injuries that precluded their survival in the wild. The aquarium is arranged in realistic habitats, and the "zoo" consists primarily of indigenous fauna, both domesticated and wild (the pacing bobcat is liable to give you pause). Children will be entranced by the Zoorific theater (a live-animal education program) and the children's discovery center with hands-on activities. The exhibit "A Walk Through the Cape Cod Woods" features some of the little creatures that inhabit the woodland floor. A very creditable effort is made to convey the need for ecological preservation.

674 Rte. 28 (midway btw. West Yarmouth and Bass River), West Yarmouth. © **508/775-8883.** www.zooquariumcapecod.net. Admission $10 adults, $7 children 2–9. June–Aug daily 9:30am–5pm; Sept–Nov Wed–Mon 9:30am–4pm; Dec–Feb Sat-Sun only 9:30am–3pm. Closed March–May.

SHOPPING

Driving Route 6A, the Old King's Highway, in Yarmouth Port, you'll pass a number of antiques stores and fine shops for the home. Unless you have children in tow, you may want to bypass Route 28 entirely and stay on the pretty north side of Yarmouth.

BOOKS The most colorful bookshop on the Cape (if not the whole East Coast) is **Parnassus Books** ★, 220 Rte. 6A (about ¼ mile east of the town center), Yarmouth Port (© **508/362-6420;** www.parnassusbooks.com). This jam-packed repository—housed in an 1858 Swedenborgian church—is the creation of Ben Muse, who has been collecting and selling vintage tomes since the 1960s. Relevant new stock, including the Cape-related reissues published by Parnassus Imprints, is offered alongside the older treasures.

Don't expect much handholding on the part of the gruff proprietor. You'll earn his respect by knowing what you're looking for or, better yet, being willing to browse until it finds you. The outdoor racks, maintained on an honor system, are open 24 hours a day, for those who suffer from abibliophobia—fear of lacking for reading material.

GIFTS/HOME DECOR   To emulate that Cape look—breezy chic—study the key ingredients artfully assembled at **Design Works,** 159 Rte. 6A (in the center of town), Yarmouth Port (𝓒 **508/362-9698**): stripped-pine antiques, crisp linens, and colorful majolica.

The design approach at **Peach Tree Designs,** 173 Rte. 6A (in the center of town), Yarmouth Port (𝓒 **508/362-8317**), is much more adventurous and eclectic. A bold hand is evident in the juxtaposition of disparate elements, from hunting prints to beribboned hats, model ships to hand-woven throws. The gift pickings are superlative as well—especially if you're shopping for yourself.

MUSEUMS

Captain Bangs Hallet House Museum ★   Typical of the sumptuous tastes of the time, this 1840 Greek Revival house is named for the China trade seafarer who lived here from 1863 to 1893. The Historical Society of Old Yarmouth, which oversees the property, has filled its beautifully proportioned rooms with the finest furnishings of the day, from Hitchcock chairs to a Hepplewhite sofa. The rustic kitchen in back belongs to the 1740 core around which this showy edifice was erected. Note the nearly 200-year-old weeping beech tree and the herb garden beyond, which lead to a scenic 2-mile walking trail (see "Nature & Wildlife Areas," above).

11 Strawberry Lane (off Rte. 6A, about ¹/₂ mile east of the town center; park behind the post office at 231 Rte. 6A), Yarmouth Port. 𝓒 **508/362-3021.** www.hsoy.org. Admission $3 adults, 50¢ children 12 and under. June–Oct Thurs–Sun tours at 1, 2, and 3pm. Groups by appointment. Closed Nov–May.

The Edward Gorey House ★★   At this museum devoted to the life and works of Edward Gorey, you can peek into the artist's whimsically mischievous world. Perhaps most widely known for the animated opening to the television series *Mystery!* on PBS, Gorey died in 2000, and his home on the Yarmouth Port Common has been converted into an intimate museum. On display are original artworks, photographs, and first editions from his career as an author, playwright, illustrator, and costume and set designer. Gorey's passion for animals is also a focus of the collection.

8 Strawberry Lane (off Rte. 6A, on the Common), Yarmouth Port. 𝓒 **508/362-3909.** www.edwardgorey house.org. Admission $5 adults, $3 students and seniors, $2 children 6–12, free for children 5 and under. Wed–Sat 11am–4pm; Sun noon–4pm. Closed Feb.

Winslow Crocker House ★★   The only property on the Cape currently preserved by the prestigious Society for the Preservation of New England Antiquities, this house, built around 1780, deserves every honor. Not only is it a lovely example of the shingled Georgian style, it's packed with outstanding antiques—Jacobean to Chippendale—collected in the 1930s by Mary Thacher, a descendant of the town's first land grantee. Anthony Thacher and his family had a rougher crossing than most: Their ship foundered off Cape Ann in 1635 (near an island that now bears their name), and though their four children drowned, Thacher and his wife were able to make it to shore, clinging to the family cradle. You'll come across a 1690 replica in the parlor.

250 Rte. 6A (about ¹/₂ mile east of the town center), Yarmouth Port. 𝓒 **617/227-3957,** ext. 256. www. historicnewengland.org. Admission $4, free to Yarmouth Port residents and SPNEA members. June–Oct 1st Sat of each month, tours hourly 11am–5pm (last tour at 4pm). Closed Nov–May.

So many hotels and motels line Route 28 and the shore in West and South Yarmouth that it may be hard to make sense of the choices. The following are some that offer clean rooms and cater to families looking for a reasonably priced beach vacation. All are within a few miles of the beach or right on the beach. For those staying on Route 28, the town runs frequent beach shuttles in season.

The **Tidewater Inn,** 135 Main St./Rte. 28, West Yarmouth (© **800/338-6322** or 508/775-6322; www.tidewater-capecod.com), is a short walk (½ mile) from a small beach on Lewis Bay, and a not-so-short walk (about a mile) from Hyannis's Main Street and the ferries to Nantucket. Summer rates are $140 to $160 for double occupancy. One of the more attractive motels along this strip, it's a white clapboard double-decker motel with green shutters and doors. The Tidewater also has an indoor pool, an outdoor pool, and a breakfast restaurant.

Clarion Inn, 1199 Main St./Rte. 28, South Yarmouth (© **800/527-0359** or 508/394-7600; www.clarioncapecod.com), is popular with families. The summer rate for the 114 guest rooms is $169 to $189 double. It has indoor and outdoor heated pools, a breakfast restaurant, and exercise and game rooms.

Ocean Mist Motor Lodge ★, 97 S. Shore Dr., South Yarmouth (© **508/398-2633;** www.innseasonresorts.com), is a large motel right on the beach. There's also an indoor pool, just in case it rains. Summer rates are $209 double, $289 suite. It's a good choice if you have kids.

Very Expensive

Red Jacket Resort ★★ (Kids) Of the huge resort motels lining Nantucket Sound in South Yarmouth, Red Jacket has the best location and activities. Some of the activities include kayaking, paddleboat and sailboat rentals, catamaran cruises, a daily summertime children's program of supervised sports and activities (which may take advantage of the playground), minigolf, shuffleboard, horseshoes, badminton, and basketball and volleyball (one court of each). All rooms have a balcony or private porch; you'll want one overlooking the private beach on Nantucket Sound or looking out toward Parker's River.

1 S. Shore Dr. (P.O. Box 88), South Yarmouth, MA 02664. © **800/672-0500** or 508/398-6941. Fax 508/398-1214. www.redjacketresorts.com. 170 units, 14 cottages. Summer $285–$450 double; $550–$1,025 cottages. A $15 resort fee per day is added to all bills. MC, V. Closed Nov to mid-Apr. **Amenities:** Free parking, restaurant, bar/lounge; concierge, exercise room; ice-cream shop; indoor and outdoor heated pools; putting green; sauna; tennis court; whirlpool. *In room:* A/C, TV/VCR, fridge, hair dryer.

Expensive

Captain Farris House ★★ Sumptuous is the only way to describe this 1845 inn, improbably set amid a peaceful garden, a block off bustling Route 28. A skilled interior decorator has combined fine antiques and striking contemporary touches to lift this inn's interiors way above the average homey B&B decor. Some suites are apartment-size, containing sitting rooms equipped with a fireplace and whirlpool-tub bathrooms bigger than the average bedroom. Next door, the 1825 Elisha Jenkins House contains an additional large suite with its own sundeck.

308 Old Main St. (just west of the Bass River Bridge), Bass River, MA 02664-4530. © **800/350-9477** or 508/760-2818. Fax 508/398-1262. www.captainfarris.com. 10 units, 9 with tub/shower combination, 1 with shower only. Summer $175–$215 double; $225 suite. Rates include full breakfast, free parking. AE, DISC, MC, V. Closed Dec to mid-Feb. *In room:* A/C, TV/VCR, hair dryer.

The Inn at Cape Cod ★ You can't miss this captain's house/bed-and-breakfast; it's the one that looks like a tall, thin Southern plantation manor with four towering Ionic columns. Upon entering the elegant foyer with its grandly curving staircase, you are led into a comfortable seating-and-breakfast area. My favorite guest room is the romantic front room with a sitting room and large private balcony overlooking the scenic Old King's Highway. The owners are continually remodeling and updating the inn. Behind the property are miles of wooded walking trails open to the public.

4 Summer St. (P.O. Box 96), Yarmouth Port, MA 02675. © **800/850-7301** or 508/375-0590. www.innat capecod.com. 9 units, 2 with tub/shower combination, 7 with shower only. Summer $180–$295 double; $260–$335 suite. Rates include full breakfast, free parking. MC, V. Closed Dec–Feb. No children 8 and under. *In room:* A/C, TV/DVD, Wi-Fi.

Liberty Hill Inn ★ This 1825 Greek Revival captain's house is set high on a knoll in charming Yarmouth Port, just off Route 6A, the Old King's Highway, which, with its majestic captains' houses and century-old elm trees, hasn't changed much in the last 100 years. Rooms in the main house, with its narrow stairways, have colonial antiques and wicker furniture. The carriage house with four rooms is suitable for families with children. The inn stands out for its breakfasts, with such delectables as baked blueberry French toast and crab scramble. One room is accessible for visitors with disabilities.

77 Main St./Rte. 6A (1 mile from the village center), Yarmouth Port, MA 02675. © **800/821-3977** or 508/362-3976. Fax 508/362-6485. www.libertyhillinn.com. 9 units. Summer $150–$230 double. Rates include full breakfast and afternoon tea, free parking. AE, MC, V. *In room:* A/C, TV/DVD, hair dryer, Wi-Fi, no phone.

WHERE TO DINE
Expensive

Lyric ★★ NEW AMERICAN This new restaurant is gearing up to be one of the top fine-dining establishments on the Cape. The atmosphere and creative cuisine are there, but consistency is still an issue. Yet attention should be paid to a place that makes its own foie gras, tops a potato and leek bisque with a scallop, and puts a half lobster over home-made pasta. All entrees are served with organic vegetables. There is a very reasonably priced wine list with a number of interesting choices by the glass. Diners have also commented favorably on the service and the size of the portions. A singer and piano player add to the ambience.

43 Main St./Rte. 6A (take exit 7 off Rte. 6), Yarmouth Port. © **774/330-0000.** www.lyriccapecod.com. Reservations recommended. Main courses $18–$34. AE, MC, V. Thurs–Sat lunch 11:30am–2:30pm; Thurs–Tues dinner 4:30–10pm; Sun brunch 11:30am–3pm.

Moderate

Inaho ★★ (Finds) JAPANESE What better application of the Cape's oceanic bounty than fresh-off-the-boat sushi? You can sit in awe at the sushi bar and watch chef/owner Yuji Watanabe perform his legerdemain, or enjoy the privacy afforded by a gleaming wooden booth. From the front, Inaho is a typical Cape Cod cottage, but park in the back so you can enter through the Japanese garden. The decor is minimalist with traditional shoji screens and crisp navy-and-white banners softened by tranquil music and service.

157 Main St./Rte. 6A (in the village center), Yarmouth Port. © **508/362-5522.** www.inahocapecod.com. Reservations recommended. Main courses $13–$23; sushi rolls $3–$7. MC, V. Mon–Sat 4:30–10pm.

Old Yarmouth Inn ★ NEW ENGLAND   If a traditional Cape Cod atmosphere is what you're looking for, you can't do much better than this. It's an old stagecoach inn, serving such Yankee basics as prime rib and baked scrod. The food is fresh, hearty, and tasty. People are catching on that this is good food at reasonable prices, so it can be crowded on weekends in season. One of the most requested dishes is the deluxe lobster roll, with huge chunks of fresh lobster. The Sunday brunch, a combination buffet and a la carte meal, is popular. A lighter-fare menu is also available.

223 Rte. 6A (in the center of Yarmouth Port). ✆ **508/362-9962.** www.oldyarmouthinn.com. Reservations recommended. Main courses $14–$25. AE, DC, DISC, MC, V. June–Oct Tues–Sat 11:30am–2:30pm; Sun 10am–1pm; daily 4:30–9pm. Call for off-season hours.

---

3 DENNIS ★

---

20 miles E of Sandwich; 36 miles S of Provincetown

If Dennis looks like a jigsaw puzzle piece snapped around Yarmouth, that's because it didn't break away until 1793, when the community adopted the name of Rev. Josiah Dennis, who had ministered to Yarmouth's "East Parish" for close to 4 decades. His 1736 home has been restored and now serves as a local-history museum.

In Dennis, as in Yarmouth, virtually all the good stuff—pretty drives, inviting shops, and restaurants with real personality—are in the north, along Route 6A. Route 28 is chockablock with more typical tourist attractions, RV parks, and family-oriented motels—some with fairly sophisticated facilities but nonetheless undistinguished enough not to warrant even a drive-by (the few exceptions are noted below). What the south side does have is very fine beaches and several very good restaurants and clubs. In budgeting your time, be sure to allocate the lion's share to Dennis Village. It's as stimulating and unspoiled today as it was when it welcomed the Cape Playhouse, the country's oldest surviving straw-hat theater, during the anything-goes 1920s.

ESSENTIALS

GETTING THERE   After crossing the Sagamore Bridge, head east on Route 6 or 6A. The Sagamore Bridge will get you closer to your destination. Route 6A passes through the villages of Dennis and East Dennis (which can also be reached via northbound Rte. 134 from Rte. 6's exit 9). Route 134 S. leads to the village of South Dennis; if you follow Route 134 all the way to Route 28, the village of West Dennis will be a couple of miles to your west, and Dennisport a couple of miles east. Or fly into Hyannis (see section 3, "Getting There & Getting Around," in chapter 3).

GETTING AROUND   The **H2O Line,** run by the Cape Cod Regional Transit Authority (✆ **800/352-7155;** www.capecodtransit.org), runs from Hyannis to Orleans, making stops in Dennis on six round-trips daily. Trips from Dennisport to Hyannis cost $2.50.

VISITOR INFORMATION   Contact the **Dennis Chamber of Commerce,** 238 Swan River Rd., West Dennis, MA 02670 (✆ **508/398-3568;** www.dennischamber.com), or the **Cape Cod Chamber of Commerce** (see "Visitor Information," under "Hyannis, Barnstable & Environs," earlier in this chapter). The Dennis chamber is open May to October Monday through Friday 10am to 4pm; November to April Monday through Friday 10am to 2pm.

BEACHES   Dennis harbors more than a dozen saltwater and two freshwater beaches open to nonresidents. The bay beaches are charming and a big hit with families, who prize the easygoing surf, so soft it won't bring toddlers to their knees. The beaches on the sound tend to attract wall-to-wall families, but the parking lots are usually not too crowded, as so many beachgoers stay within walking distance. The lots charge $15 to $20 per day; for a weeklong permit ($60), visit **Town Hall,** at 485 Main Street, in South Dennis (© **508/394-8300**).

- **Chapin Beach** ★★, off Route 6A, in Dennis: This is a nice, long bay beach pocked with occasional boulders and surrounded by dunes. There is no lifeguard, but there are restrooms.
- **Corporation Beach** ★★, off Route 6A, in Dennis: Before it filled in with sand, this bay beach—with wheelchair-accessible boardwalk, lifeguards, snack bar, restrooms, and a children's play area—was once a packet landing owned by a shipbuilding corporation comprised of area residents.
- **Mayflower Beach** ★★, off Route 6A, in Dennis: This 1,200-foot bay beach has the necessary amenities, plus an accessible boardwalk. The tide pools attract lots of children.
- **Scargo Lake,** in Dennis: This large kettle-hole pond (formed by a melting fragment of a glacier) has two pleasant beaches: Scargo Beach, accessible right off Route 6A, and Princess Beach, off Scargo Hill Road, where there are restrooms and a picnic area.
- **West Dennis Beach** ★★, off Route 28, in West Dennis: This long (½-mile) but narrow beach along the sound has lifeguards, a playground, a snack bar, restrooms, and a special kite-flying area. The eastern end is reserved for residents; the western end tends, in any case, to be less packed.

BICYCLING   The 25-mile **Cape Cod Rail Trail** ★★★ (© **508/896-3491**) starts—or, depending on your perspective, ends—here, on Route 134, a half-mile south of Route 6's exit 9. Once a Penn Central track, this 8-foot-wide paved bikeway extends all the way to Wellfleet (with a few on-road lapses), passing through woods, marshes, and dunes. Sustenance is never too far off-trail, and plenty of bike shops dot the course. At the trail head is **Barb's Bike Shop,** 430 Rte. 134, South Dennis (© **508/760-4723.** www. barbsbikeshop.com), which rents bikes and does repairs. Rates are $12 for 2 hours, and up to $24 for the full day. Another paved bike path runs along Old Bass Road, 3½ miles north to Route 6A.

BOATING   Located on the small and placid Swan River, **Cape Cod Waterways,** 16 Rte. 28, Dennisport (© **508/398-0080;** www.capecodwaterways.com), rents canoes, kayaks, and paddleboats, for exploring 200-acre Swan Pond (less than a mile north) or Nantucket Sound (2 miles south). A full-day kayak rental costs $58 for a single, $74 for a tandem.

   Bass River Cruises, located at Bass River Bridge (at Rte. 28), in West Dennis (© **508/ 362-5555;** www.capecodrivercruise.com), explores the Bass and Weir rivers the way Leif Eriksson might have—by boat. This one, a poky but stable custom minibarge, the MV *Starfish,* is motorized, so the whole circuit takes only 1½ hours. If some of the tales strike you as rather tall, there's still plenty of wildlife and prime real estate to ogle. Trips are offered four times a day mid-May through mid-October; tickets are $18 for adults and $7 for children ages 1 to 11. Call for the schedule.

FISHING   Fishing is allowed in Fresh Pond and Scargo Lake, where the catch includes trout and smallmouth bass; for a license (shellfishing is also permitted), visit **Town Hall,**

at 485 Main Street, in South Dennis (☏ **508/394-8300**); or **Riverview Bait and Tackle,** at 1273 Rte. 28, in South Yarmouth (☏ **508/394-1036**). Plenty of people drop a line off the Bass River Bridge along Route 28, in West Dennis. Several charter boats operate out of the Northside Marina, in East Dennis's Sesuit Harbor, including the *Albatross* (☏ **508/385-3244**), which charges $32 for adults, $28 for seniors and children 11 and under. It makes two 4-hour trips per day.

FITNESS/JOGGING   For joggers, and fitness freaks in general, the 1.5-mile **Life-course trail,** located at Old Bass River and Access roads in South Dennis, features 20 exercise stations along its tree-shaded path.

GOLF   The public is welcome to use two 18-hole championship courses: the hilly, par-71 **Dennis Highlands,** on Old Bass River Road, in Dennis, and the even more challenging par-72 **Dennis Pines,** on Golf Course Road, in East Dennis. For information on either course, call ☏ **508/385-8347;** www.dennisgolf.com. Both charge $60 for a round, less in the afternoons.

NATURE & WILDLIFE AREAS   Behind the town hall parking lot on Main Street in South Dennis, a half-mile walk along the **Indian Lands Conservation Trail** leads to the Bass River, where blue herons and kingfishers often take shelter. Dirt roads off South Street, in East Dennis, beyond the Quivet Cemetery, lead to **Crow's Pasture,** a patchwork of marshes and dunes bordering the bay; this circular trail is about 2.5 miles round-trip.

TENNIS   Public courts are located at the Dennis-Yarmouth Regional High School, in South Yarmouth, and at Wixon Middle School, on Route 134, in South Dennis; for details contact the **Dennis Recreation Department** (☏ **508/760-6162**). Or you may be able to book time at the **Mashantum Tennis Club,** at 11 Forehand Dr., off Nobscusset Road, in Dennis Village (☏ **508/385-7043;** www.mashantumtennis.com), which has clay courts for $10 per person. Also try **Sesuit Tennis Centre,** at 1389 Rte. 6A, in East Dennis (☏ **508/385-2200;** www.sesuittennis.com). At Sesuit, singles and doubles are $25 per person.

MUSEUMS

Cape Cod Museum of Art ★★   Part of the prettily landscaped Cape Playhouse complex, this museum has done a great job of acquiring hundreds of works by representative area artists dating back to the turn of the 20th century. The large galleries upstairs display special exhibits, sometimes a single artist, sometimes groups. The downstairs rooms show works from the permanent collection, including many works from Provincetown artists going back to the early years of the 20th century. There's also an outdoor sculpture garden. Call ahead for a schedule of special shows, lectures, concerts, and classes. *Note:* Admission is free (donation requested) on Thursday from 10am to 8pm.

60 Hope Lane (off Rte. 6A, in the center of the village), Dennis Village. ☏ **508/385-4477.** www.cmfa.org. Admission $8 adults, free for children 18 and under. Tues–Sat 10am–5pm (till 8pm Thurs); Sun noon–5pm. From Rte. 6, take exit 8 and make a right on Rte. 6A; museum is 3 miles down Rte. 6A.

Josiah Dennis Manse and Old West Schoolhouse (Kids)   This compact 1736 saltbox housed Rev. Josiah Dennis, the town's first minister. Though not necessarily original, the furnishings are fascinating, as is a diorama of the Shiverick Shipyard, which was the source in the mid-1800s of the world's swiftest ships. Costumed guides lead guests through a maritime room and a children's room. There is also a Native American exhibit. Don't miss the 1770 schoolhouse, where a comprehensive (if strict) approach to learning is beautifully preserved.

77 Nobscusset Rd. (north of Rte. 6A, about ½ mile west of the town center). ✆ **508/385-2232.** www. **139**
dennishistsoc.org/historical/manse.htm. Donations accepted. Late June to mid-Sept Tues 10am–noon;
Thurs 2–4pm. Closed mid-Sept to late June.

Scargo Tower **Moments**   All that remains of the grand Nobscusset Hotel, this 28-foot
stone observatory looks out from its 160-foot perch over the entire Outer Cape, including the tightly furled tip that is Provincetown. In the foreground is Scargo Lake—the
legacy, native legend has it, of either the giant god Maushop or perhaps a princess who
bid her handmaidens to scoop it out with clamshells.

Scargo Hill Rd. (off Old Bass River Rd., south of Rte. 6A, in the center of town), East Dennis. No phone. Free
admission. Daily 6am–10pm.

BASEBALL

The Dennis-Yarmouth Red Sox, part of the **Cape Cod Baseball League** (www.capecod
baseball.org), play at Dennis-Yarmouth High School's Red Wilson Field, off Station Avenue, in South Yarmouth. For a schedule, contact the **Yarmouth Area Chamber of
Commerce,** 424 Rte. 28, West Yarmouth, MA 02673 (✆ **508/778-1008**); the **Yarmouth
Recreation Department** (✆ **508/398-2231,** ext. 284); or the **League** (✆ **508/432-
6909**).

KID STUFF

If kids get sick of all the miscellaneous go-carts and minigolf concessions on Route 28,
they can take in a show. On Thursday and Friday mornings in season, at 9:30 and
11:30am, the **Cape Playhouse,** at 820 Rte. 6A, in Dennis Village (✆ **508/385-3911;**
www.capeplayhouse.com), hosts various visiting companies that mount children's theater
geared toward kids 4 and older; at only $9, tickets go fast.

SHOPPING

You can pretty much ignore Route 28. There's a growing cluster of antiques shops in
Dennisport, but the stock is flea-market level and requires more patience than most mere
browsers—as opposed to avid collectors—may be able to muster. Save your time and
money for the better shops along Route 6A, where you'll also find fine contemporary
crafts.

ANTIQUES/COLLECTIBLES   More than 136 dealers stock the co-op **Antiques Center of Cape Cod,** 243 Rte. 6A (about 1 mile south of Dennis Village center), Dennis
(✆ **508/385-6400;** www.antiquecenterofcapecod.com); it's the largest such enterprise
on the Cape. You'll find all the usual "smalls" on the first floor; the big stuff—from
blanket chests to copper bathtubs—beckons above.

Eldred's, 1483 Rte. 6A (about ¼ mile west of Dennis Village center), East Dennis
(✆ **508/385-3116;** www.eldreds.com), where the gavel has been wielded for more than
40 years, is the Cape's most prestigious auction house. Specialties include Asian art,
American and European paintings, marine art, and Americana. Call for a schedule.

ARTS & CRAFTS   The creations of **Ross Coppelman Goldsmith,** 1439 Rte. 6A
(about ¼ mile west of the town center), East Dennis (✆ **508/385-7900;** www.ross
coppelman.com)—mostly fashioned of lustrous 22-karat gold—have an iconic drama to
them: They seem to draw on the aesthetics of some grand, lost civilization.

Scargo Pottery, 30 Dr. Lord's Rd. S. (off Rte. 6A, about 1 mile east of the town center), Dennis (✆ **508/385-3894;** www.scargopottery.com), is a magical place. Harry Holl
set up his glass-ceilinged studio here in 1952; today his work, and the output of his four

THE MID CAPE

6

DENNIS

grown daughters, fills a sylvan glade overlooking Scargo Lake. Much of it, such as the signature birdhouses shaped like fanciful castles, is meant to reside outside. The other wares deserve a place of honor on the dining-room table or perhaps over a mantle. Hand-painted tiles by Sarah Holl are particularly enchanting.

WHERE TO STAY
Very Expensive

Lighthouse Inn ★★ (**Kids**) Set on placid West Dennis Beach on Nantucket Sound, this popular resort has been welcoming families for more than 60 years. In 1938, Everett Stone acquired a decommissioned 1855 lighthouse and built a charming inn and cottage colony around it. With a private beach, heated outdoor pool, tennis courts, and miniature golf and shuffleboard right on the premises, there's plenty to do. The rooms aren't what you'd call fancy, but some have great Nantucket Sound views. Four rooms are fully accessible to travelers with disabilities.

The **dining room**—with state flags rippling from the rafters—is open to the general public and serves breakfast, lunch, and dinner. Lunch is also served under umbrellas on the deck overlooking Nantucket Sound. At the entrance to the complex, **The Sand Bar,** a classic bar with cabaret-style entertainment, serves as an on-site nightspot (see "Dennis After Dark," later).

1 Lighthouse Inn Rd. (off Lower County Rd., 1/2 mile south of Rte. 28), West Dennis, MA 02670. © 508/398-2244. Fax 508/398-5658. www.lighthouseinn.com. 44 units, 24 cottages. Summer $255–$280 double; $305–$335 1-bedroom cottage; $500–$600 2-bedroom cottage; $543–$624 3-bedroom cottage. Rates include full breakfast and all gratuities and parking.. MC, V. Closed mid-Oct to mid-May. **Amenities:** 2 restaurants (large dining room, pool snack bar), bar w/entertainment; InnKids, a free supervised play program (ages 3–11) offered July–Aug; minigolf; outdoor heated pool w/ample sunning deck, chairs, umbrellas, and pool house/changing rooms; shuffleboard; outdoor tennis court; volleyball. *In room:* A/C, TV, fridge, hair dryer.

Expensive

Corsair & Cross Rip Resort Motels ★ (**Kids**) Of the many family-oriented motels lining this part of Nantucket Sound, these two neighbors are among the nicest, with fresh contemporary decor, two beach-view pools, and their own chunk of sand, a 200-foot long private beach. As a rainy-day backup, there's an indoor pool, a game room, and a toddler playroom equipped with toys. Some rooms have kitchenettes. All rooms have access to barbecue grills.

41 Chase Ave. (off Depot St., 1 mile southeast of Rte. 28), Dennisport, MA 02639. © 800/345-5140 or 508/398-2279. Fax 508/760-6681. www.corsaircrossrip.com. 47 units. Summer $225–$300 double; $325–$390 suites, including parking. Special packages and family weekly rates available. AE, MC, V. Closed mid-Oct to Apr. **Amenities:** Toddler playroom and kids' playground; outdoor Jacuzzi; 2 outdoor pools and 1 indoor pool. *In room:* A/C, TV, fridge, hair dryer.

Moderate

Isaiah Hall B&B Inn ★★ A short walk to the Cape Playhouse complex, which includes a movie theater and art museum, this inn is the perfect place to stay for culture buffs. The "great room" in the carriage-house annex seems to foment late-night discussions, to be continued over home-baked breakfasts at the long plank table that dominates the 1857 country kitchen. Room styles range from 1940s knotty pine to spacious and spiffy. They are quaint, countrified, and spotlessly clean. Four have balconies or decks. Two of the rooms have minifridges, and one has a fireplace. The inn's location on a quiet side street in a residential neighborhood bodes well for a good night's sleep, but it's also just a short walk to Corporation Beach on Cape Cod Bay.

508/385-9928. Fax 508/385-5879. www.isaiahhallinn.com. 12 units, 6 with tub/shower combination, 6 with shower only. Summer $150–$199 double; $375 suite. Rates include full breakfast and free parking. AE, DISC, MC, V. No children 7 and under. *In room:* A/C, TV/DVD/VCR, hair dryer.

WHERE TO DINE
Expensive
Blue Moon Bistro ★★ MEDITERRANEAN   Beautiful presentations of innovative cuisine are the hallmarks at this Dennis Village venue, one of the newer entries in the Cape's fine-dining roster. The restaurant's deep-blue ceiling and dark wood floors contribute to the warm and inviting atmosphere; crisp white tablecloths hint at the elegant dining to come. Chef/owner Peter Hyde, who was trained in Europe, gives a twist to traditional recipes. Instead of a crab cake, his is a crab-and-cod cake with spicy red peppers. His Mediterranean fish soup includes the Portuguese sausage, chorizo, for added pizzazz. One of our favorites is the luscious grilled beef tenderloin wrapped in house-smoked bacon. There are also always a couple of vegetarian options on the menu. Don't miss the homemade desserts.

605 Main St./Rte. 6A (in the center of Dennis Village), Dennis Village. ℂ **508/385-7100.** www.bluemoon bistro.net. Reservations recommended. Main courses $16–$30. AE, MC, V. June–late Aug Wed–Sat 5–10pm; Tues and Sun 5–9:30pm; Apr–May and late Aug–Nov Wed–Sun 4–11pm. Closed Dec–Mar.

Gracie's Table ★ Ⓕⓘⓝⓓⓢ SPANISH TAPAS   Just steps from the Cape Playhouse and Cape Cinema, Gracie's Table offers something different on Cape Cod: Spanish-style dining. Preparations by chef/owner Ann Austin are inspired by cuisine from the Basque region, as well as southwest France. Although there are plenty of full meals to choose from, the specialty here is *tapas,* unusual small dishes. The best way to enjoy tapas is for each diner to choose several dishes and share the different tastes with their dining companions. Tapas choices include hot lobster roll, potato-and-chorizo tortilla, and tuna carpaccio with horseradish sorbet. The dining room is sleek and sophisticated, and is staffed by professional servers who are always willing to recommend their favorite tapas.

800 Main St./Rte. 6A (at Theatre Marketplace, in front of the Cape Playhouse complex), Dennis Village. ℂ **508/385-5600.** www.graciestablecapecod.com. Reservations recommended. Tapas $5–$15; main courses $18–$30. AE, MC, V. Thurs–Mon 5–9pm; call for off-season hours.

The Ocean House New American Bistro and Bar ★★★ Ⓕⓘⓝⓓⓢ NEW AMERI-CAN   This restaurant set on the beach overlooking Nantucket Sound has long had a stellar reputation, and, under Chef Anthony Sylvestri and a menu of fusion cuisine, it's better than ever. There's a buzz around this creative cuisine, making this oceanfront restaurant a must-go location. One appealing thing about the Ocean House is that you can come for a multicourse fine-dining meal or just some appetizers. Favorites here are the lemongrass-battered gray sole and the grilled beef tenderloin with Maytag blue cheese. With the dining room's large arches framing the beach beyond, this is a wonderful place to spend the evening.

3 Chase Ave. (at Depot St., on the beach), Dennisport. ℂ **508/394-0700.** Reservations strongly recommended. Main courses $18–$34. MC, V. June–Sept Tues–Sun 5–10pm; call for off-season hours.

The Red Pheasant Inn ★★★ NEW AMERICAN   An enduring Cape favorite since 1977, this handsome space—an 18th-century barn turned chandlery—has managed not only to keep pace with trends but also to remain a front-runner. Favorites from chef/owner Bill Atwood include roast rack of lamb, boneless roast duckling, and sole meunière. In the fall, expect game specials such as venison and ostrich. His signature cherrystone-and-scallop chowder gets its zip from fresh-plucked thyme. Two massive brick fireplaces tend to be the focal point in the off-season, drawing in the weary—and delighted—wanderer. In fine weather you'll want to sit out in the garden room.

905 Main St. (about ¹/₂ mile east of the town center), Dennis Village. ℂ **508/385-2133.** www.redpheasant inn.com. Reservations required. Main courses $18–$30. DISC, MC, V. Jan–Mar Wed–Sun 5–9:30pm; Apr–Dec daily 5–9pm.

Scargo Cafe ★ INTERNATIONAL   A richly paneled captain's house given a modernist reworking, this lively bistro—named for Dennis's scenic lake—deftly spans old and new with a menu neatly split into "traditional" and "adventurous" categories. Traditionalists will find surf and turf, and the popular grilled lamb loins served with mint jelly (talk about traditional!); adventurous dishes include the likes of "wildcat chicken" (a sauté of sausage, mushrooms, and raisins, flambéed with apricot brandy). The menu here is pricey, but lighter and less expensive nibbles ($11–$14), such as burgers or "Scallop Harpoon"—a bacon-wrapped skewerful, served over rice—are available throughout the day, a boon for beachgoers who tend to return ravenous. Serving food until 11pm makes this an option after a show at the Cape Playhouse across the street.

799 Main St./Rte. 6A (opposite the Cape Playhouse), Dennis. ℂ **508/385-8200.** www.scargocafe.com. Reservations accepted for parties of 6 or more. Main courses $19–$31. AE, DISC, MC, V. Mid-June to mid-Sept daily 11am–3pm and 4:30–11pm; mid-Sept to mid-June daily 11am–10pm.

Moderate

Clancy's of Dennisport ★ SEAFOOD   Every Cape Cod town has its own version of the "fish place with a fantastic view." Here the vista is relatively low-key: The eatery overlooks the placid Swan River. When looking for a not-too-fancy meal, this is a place where both families and couples can go for consistently good, inexpensive food. The menu features homemade meatloaf, turkey dinners, sandwiches, salads, burgers, and pasta, in addition to fish, chicken, and steak. Clancy's is also a good choice for Sunday brunch, and it has a kids menu. A short drive away there is the summer-only restaurant **Clancy's Fish 'n Chips and Beach Bar,** 228 Lower County Rd., Dennisport (ℂ **508/ 394-6900**). It is open daily mid-May to Labor Day and has a great casual summer-time ambience.

8 Upper County Rd. (east of Rte. 134), Dennisport. ℂ **508/394-6661.** www.clancysrestaurant.com. Reservations accepted. Main courses $7–$24. AE, DISC, MC, V. June–Aug daily 11:30am–10pm; call for off-season hours.

Gina's by the Sea ★★ SOUTHERN ITALIAN   A landmark amid Dennis's "Little Italy" beach community since 1938, this intimate little restaurant has a few tricks up its sleeve, such as homemade ravioli stuffed with smoked mozzarella. Most of the fare here is the traditional Italian food of our youth, but nonetheless tasty: The ultra-garlicky shrimp scampi, for instance, needs no updating. Save room for Mrs. Riley's Chocolate Rum Cake, made daily by owner Larry Riley's mother; it's scrumptious. This popular place fills up fast, so if you want to eat before 8:30pm, arrive before 5:30pm. Take a sunset or moonlight walk on the beach (just over the dune) to round out the evening.

134 Taunton Ave. (about 1¹/₂ miles northwest of Rte. 6A). ℂ **508/385-3213.** www.ginasbythesea.com. Reservations not accepted. Main courses $10–$23. AE, MC, V. Apr–Nov Thurs–Sun 5–10pm. Closed Dec–Mar. Turn north across from the Dennis Public Market and follow the signs.

Norabella ★ SOUTHERN ITALIAN   This charming chef-owned establishment is a slice of Olde Cape Cod. It is a tiny hole-in-the-wall shack that you would drive right by if we didn't tell you about. Chef Jeff Wilson's specialty is authentic Italian—similar to what you might find in Boston's North End—but without the overwhelming garlic. There are such favorites as penne Bolognese and veal Milanese, and there are always interesting specials. This is also the type of place where the chef pokes his head out of the kitchen and asks you how the meal was and you tell him with all honesty that it was perfect. The chef's special dessert is the chocolate hazelnut fritters, which are very distinct, but I prefer the tiramisu, light and sumptuous.

702 Rte. 28 (take exit 9 off Rte. 6), West Dennis. ℰ 508/398-6672. http://norabella.com. Reservations recommended. Main courses $15–$22. MC, V. Daily 4:30–10pm.

Inexpensive

Captain Frosty's ★ (Kids) SEAFOOD Here you won't find the typical, tasteless, deep-fried seafood seemingly dipped in greasy cement. The breading is light (thanks to relatively healthy canola oil), and the fish itself is the finest available—fresh off the local day boats and hooked rather than netted (the maritime equivalent of clear-cutting a forest). You won't find a more luscious lobster roll anywhere, and the clam-cake fritters seem to fly out the door.

219 Rte. 6A (about 1 mile west of the town center). ℰ 508/385-8548. www.captainfrosty.com. Most items under $15. No credit cards. June–Aug daily 11am–9pm; call for off-season hours. Closed late Sept–early Apr.

The Dog House ★★ (Finds) HOTDOG STAND This just might be the ultimate hot-dog stand, housed in a tiny peaked-roof hut about a half-mile from Nantucket Sound. Hot dogs, cheese dogs, and chili dogs with all the fixings are the specialty here, but there's also chili and hamburgers. For noncarnivores, there's the Surf Burger (salmon). French fries are thickly cut, and onion rings are hand-battered. Fresh lemonade is on hand to wash it all down. Down your dog at one of the dozen picnic tables in this pine glade.

189 Lower County Rd., Dennisport. ℰ 508/398-7774. All items under $10. No credit cards. Mid-May to mid-Sept daily 11am–8:30pm; call for off-season hours. Closed mid-Oct to mid-May.

Joey's Pizzeria ★ (Finds) PIZZA Joey says he tried dozens of recipes before perfecting his pizza dough—and it shows. These flavorful old-style Italian thin-crust pies may just be the best pizza on Cape Cod. The menu also has subs and pasta dishes.

197 Lower County Rd., Dennisport. ℰ 508/398-7437. All pizzas under $17. MC, V. Mid-May to mid-Sept daily 11:30am–10pm; call for off-season hours. Closed mid-Oct to mid-May.

Marathon Seafood SEAFOOD Family-owned and operated for over 15 years, this place holds its own among the Route 28 fast-food/clam-shack competition. You should order a heaping, steaming platter of fried fish, clams, scallops, or shrimp, or a combo served with french fries and onion rings. Wash it down with a chocolate milkshake. It's hard on the heart but easy on the wallet.

231 Rte. 28, West Dennis. ℰ 508/394-3379. http://marathonseafoodcapecod.com. Main courses $7–$15. MC, V. June–Sept daily 11am–11pm; call for off-season hours. Closed Dec–Feb.

Sesuit Harbor Cafe ★ SEAFOOD Right on the beach in a busy boatyard, this clam shack promises one of those authentic Cape Cod experiences that are becoming harder and harder to find. It's worth seeking out the family-owned establishment for its picture-postcard views and tasty food. Specialties include clam chowder, lobster rolls, and fried clams. Good breakfasts, too. Order from the counter and find a seat at one of the picnic tables outside.

357 Sesuit Neck Rd., Dennis. ✆ **508/385-6134.** Reservations not accepted. Main courses $7–$17. MC, V. June–Sept daily 7am–8:30pm; call for off-season hours. Closed mid-Oct to late Apr. Rte. 6A to Bridge St.; take a right on Sesuit Neck and follow to the harbor.

Sweets

Ice Cream Smuggler ★   A noteworthy stop on any Cape-wide ice-cream crusade, this cheerful parlor dispenses terrific custom homemade flavors, as well as seductive sundae concoctions and fudge-bottom pies.

716 Rte. 6A, Dennis Village. ✆ **508/385-5307.** www.icecreamsmuggler.com. July–Aug daily 11am–10:30pm; Apr–June and Sept to mid-Oct noon–9pm. Closed mid-Oct to Mar.

Stage Stop Candy ★   Considered by some to be Cape Cod's best chocolates, this is a must-visit for candy fanatics.

411 Main St./Rte. 28, Dennisport. ✆ **508/394-1791.** www.stagestopcandy.com. July–Aug Mon–Sat 9am–8:30pm, Sun 10:30am–8:30pm; call for off-season hours. Closed for 2 weeks in Jan.

Sundae School ★   For a time-travel treat, visit this spacious barn retrofitted with a turn-of-the-20th-century marble soda fountain and other artifacts from the golden age of ice cream. Homemade flavors include Milky Way, Kahlúa Chip, and Grapenut. Local berries and real whipped cream make for especially tasty toppings.

381 Lower County Rd. (at Sea St., about ¹/₃ mile south of Rte. 28), Dennisport. ✆ **508/394-9122.** www. sundaeschool.com. Summer daily 11am–11pm; Sat–Sun only in spring and fall. Closed mid-Sept to mid-Apr.

DENNIS AFTER DARK
Performances

Cape Playhouse ★★ Finds   The oldest continuously active straw-hat theater in the country and still one of the best, this way-off-Broadway enterprise was the 1927 brainstorm of Raymond Moore, who'd spent a few summers as a playwright in Provincetown and quickly tired of the strictures of "little theater." Salvaging an 1838 meetinghouse, he plunked it amid a meadow and got his New York buddy, designer Cleon Throckmorton, to turn it into a proper theater. Even with a roof that leaked, it was an immediate success, and a parade of stars—both established and budding—have trod the boards in the decades since, from Ginger Rogers to Jane Fonda (her dad spent his salad days there, too, playing opposite Bette Davis in her stage debut), Humphrey Bogart to Tab Hunter. Not all of today's headliners are quite as impressive (many hail from the netherworld of TV reruns), but the theater can be counted on for a varied season of polished work. Performances are held mid-June to early September, Monday to Saturday at 8pm; matinees take place Wednesdays and Thursdays at 2pm, and Saturdays at 4pm. On Friday mornings, performances of children's theater are at 9:30 and 11:30am. 820 Rte. 6A (in the center of town), Dennis Village. ✆ **877/385-3911** or 508/385-3911. www.capeplayhouse.com. Tickets $25–$55, children's theater $9.

Live Music & Entertainment

Compass Rose Summer Shanty   This small bar and restaurant in the middle of a marina is a great little place to have a drink overlooking the harbor. Food is just so-so, though they do make a delicious lobster roll, which is big enough to split between two people. Seating is outside on the deck overlooking the Bass River, or inside where a pianist entertains nightly except Tuesdays, in season. One of the musicians plays Jimmy Buffett–style tunes, which seems about right for the atmosphere at this place. Bass River Marina (off Rt. 28), West Dennis. ✆ **508/394-0400.** www.summershanty.com.

O'Shea's Olde Inne (Finds) This authentic Irish bar offers the best "sessions" or traditional Irish music-making, on Cape Cod. A walk through the doors of the modest old Cape cottage is a step back in time. Late in the evenings someone is bound to take out a guitar or a fiddle, and everyone will sing along. The sessions are Wednesday 7:30 to 9pm, Saturday 2:30 to 5:30pm, and Sunday 6:30 to 9pm. There's live music from 9pm 'til midnight 7 nights a week, in season. 348 Main St./Rte. 28, West Dennis. © **508/398-8887.** www. osheasoldeinne.com.

The Sand Bar This homey cabana was built in 1949, the year Dennis went "wet." Rock King, a combination boogie-woogie pianist and comedian, still rules the evening and wows the crowd on Thursdays and Saturdays. At the Lighthouse Inn (see "Where to Stay," earlier in this chapter), West Dennis. © **508/398-7586.** Tues–Sun 8pm–close. Closed mid-Sept to mid-June. Cover varies. Free admission for guests of the Lighthouse Inn.

Sand Dollar Bar and Grill This is the place where the young, collegiate, preppy crowd hangs out. On summer nights, there is often a long line to get in. Friday, Saturday, and Sunday, there is a 99¢ raw bar and live music starting at 4pm. For families, kids karaoke is Tuesday and Wednesday nights from 6 to 9pm. Entertainment begins nightly at 9pm. 244 Lower County Rd., Dennisport. © **508/398-4823.** http://sanddollarbg.com. Closed mid-Sept to mid-June. Cover varies. Free admission for guests of the Lighthouse Inn.

Sundancers This club that overlooks the Bass River attracts a young crowd for music and dancing. This is also a popular restaurant serving lunch and dinner. Among the entertainment offerings are karaoke, '80s night, and reggae nights. Open daily. Entertainment begins after 5pm. 116 Main St./Rte. 28, West Dennis. © **508/394-1600.** www. sundancerscapecod.com.

A Retro Movie Theater

Cape Cinema ★★ (Moments) In 1930, Raymond Moore—perceiving of motion pictures as a complement rather than a threat to live theater—added a movie house, modeled on Centerville's Congregational Church, to the Cape Playhouse complex. The interior decoration is an Art Deco surprise, with a Prometheus-themed ceiling mural and folding curtain designed by artist Rockwell Kent and Broadway set designer Jo Mielziner. The art-house programming makes this one of the few places on Cape Cod where you can see movies that are not standard mall fare. That, plus the setting and seating—black leather armchairs—may spoil you forever for what passes for cinemas today. It's open year-round, with three shows daily. Purists will love that this movie theater is commercial-free. 36 Hope Lane (off Rte. 6A, on the grounds of the Cape Playhouse). © **508/385-2503** or 385-5644. www.capecinema.com. Tickets $8.50.

The Lower Cape

The four towns on the Lower Cape are primarily family-oriented summer communities. In the quaint village of Harwich Port, the beach is a mere block off Main Street, so the eternal summer pastime of a barefoot stroll capped off by an ice-cream cone can still be easily observed. To get to Chatham at the Cape's elbow requires an intentional detour, which may have helped preserve that town as a charming and more upscale locale than some of the other towns along the Nantucket Sound. With its Main Street a gamut of appealing shops and eateries, Chatham approaches an all-American, small-town ideal—complemented nicely by a scenic lighthouse and plentiful beaches nearby.

Occupying the easternmost portion of historic Route 6A, Brewster still enjoys much the same cachet that it boasted as a high roller in the maritime trade. But for a relatively recent incursion of condos and, of course, the cars, it looks much as it might have in the late 19th century; its general store still serves as a social center. For some reason—perhaps because excellence breeds competition—Brewster has spawned several fine restaurants and has become something of a magnet for gourmands.

As the gateway to the Outer Cape, where all roads merge, Orleans offers more variety in the way of shops and entertainment than some of its neighbors. Its nearby cousin, East Orleans, is in itself a destination, offering a couple of fun restaurants and—best of all—a chunk of magnificent, unspoiled Cape Cod National Seashore.

1 BREWSTER ★★

25 miles E of Sandwich; 31 miles S of Provincetown

One of the "youngest" of the Cape towns, Brewster—named for the Pilgrim leader William Brewster—dissociated itself from Harwich in 1803, the better to enjoy its newfound riches as a hotbed of the shipping industry. All along the winding curves of the Old King's Highway (now Rte. 6A), successful captains erected scores of proud houses—99 in all, according to the local lore. When Henry David Thoreau passed through in the mid-1850s, he remarked: "This town has more mates and masters of vessels than any other town in the country."

The Greek/Gothic Revival First Parish Church, built in 1834, embodies many of those mates' and masters' stories. Among the more dramatic tales conjured by the gravestones in back is that of Capt. David Nickerson, who is said to have rescued an infant during the French Revolution—possibly the son of Louis XVI and Marie Antoinette. Whatever his origins, "René Rousseau" followed in his adoptive father's footsteps, ultimately drowning at sea. His name was incised on the back of Nickerson's headstone, according to the custom of the day. Nickerson's name also appears on a pew in the white clapboard church.

Brewster still gives the impression of setting itself apart, mostly free of the commercial encroachments that have plagued the Cape's southern shore. The 380-acre condo-and-golf complex known as Ocean Edge, on what was once a huge private estate, is a premier resort destination. Brewster also welcomes the tens of thousands of transient campers and day-trippers who arrive each summer to enjoy the nearly 2,000 wooded acres of Nickerson State Park.

ESSENTIALS

GETTING THERE After crossing either the Sagamore Bridge or the Bourne Bridge (see section 3, "Getting There & Getting Around," in chapter 3), head east on Route 6 or 6A. Crossing the Sagamore Bridge will get you closer to your destination. Route 6A, on the north side of the Cape, passes through the villages of West Brewster, Brewster, and East Brewster. You can also reach Brewster by taking Route 6's exit 10 north, along Route 124. Or fly into Hyannis (see section 3, "Getting There & Getting Around," in chapter 3).

VISITOR INFORMATION Contact the **Brewster Chamber of Commerce Visitor Center,** behind Brewster Town Hall, 2198 Main St./Rte. 6A, Brewster (© **508/896-3500;** fax 508/896-1086; www.brewstercapecod.org); or the **Cape Cod Chamber of Commerce,** routes 6 and 132, Hyannis, MA 02601 (© **888/332-2732;** www.capecod chamber.org). The Brewster Visitor Center is open from mid-June to early September daily from 10am to 3pm and is closed from mid-October to late April. The Cape Cod Chamber of Commerce visitor center is open year-round Monday to Saturday from 9am to 5pm and Sundays and holidays from 10am to 4pm.

BEACHES & RECREATIONAL PURSUITS

BEACHES Brewster's eight lovely bay beaches have minimal facilities. When the tide is out, the "beach" enlarges to as much as 2 miles, leaving behind tide pools to splash in and explore, and vast stretches of rippled, reddish "garnet" sand. On a clear day, you can see the whole curve of the Cape, from Sandwich to Provincetown. That hulking wreck midway, incidentally, is the USS *James Longstreet,* pressed into service for target practice in 1943, and used for that purpose right up until 1970; it's now a popular dive site. You can purchase a beach parking sticker ($15 per day, $50 per week) at the **Brewster Visitor Center,** behind Brewster Town Hall, at 2198 Main St./Rte. 6A, a half-mile east of the General Store (© **508/896-4511**).

- **Breakwater Beach** ★★, off Breakwater Road, Brewster: A brief walk from the center of town, this calm, shallow beach (the only one with restrooms) is ideal for young children. This was once a packet landing, where packet boats would unload tourists and load up produce—a system that worked until the railroads came along.
- **Flax Pond** ★★, in Nickerson State Park (see "Nature & Wildlife Areas," below): This large freshwater pond, surrounded by pines, has a bathhouse and offers watersports rentals. The park contains two more ponds with beaches—Cliff and Little Cliff. Access and parking are free.
- **Linnells Landing Beach** ★, on Linnell Road, in East Brewster: This is a half-mile, wheelchair-accessible bay beach.
- **Paines Creek Beach** ★, off Paines Creek Road, West Brewster: With 1½ miles on which to stretch out, this bay beach has something to offer sun lovers and nature lovers alike. Your kids will love it if you arrive when the tide's coming in—the current will give an air mattress a nice little ride.

BICYCLING The **Cape Cod Rail Trail** ★★★ (www.mass.gov/dcr/parks/southeast/ ccrt.htm) intersects with the 8-mile **Nickerson State Park** trail system at the park entrance, where there's plenty of free parking; you could follow the Rail Trail back to

Dennis (about 12 miles) or onward toward Wellfleet (13 miles). **Idle Times** (✆ **508/255-8281;** www.idletimesbikes.com) provides rentals within the park in season. Another good place to hop on the trail is Underpass Road, about a half-mile south of Route 6A. Here you'll find **Brewster Bicycle Rental,** 442 Underpass Rd. (✆ **508/896-8149;** www.brewsterbike.com), and Brewster Express, which makes sandwiches to go. Both shops offer free parking. Bicycle rentals start at around $14 for 4 hours and go up to about $28 for 24 hours.

BOATING You can rent a canoe at **Jack's Boat Rental** (✆ **508/349-9808;** www.jacksboatrental.com), located on either Cliff Pond or Flax Pond, within Nickerson State Park. Canoes cost $25 a half-hour and $15 for each additional half-hour. There are also kayaks, paddleboats, surf bikes, and Sunfish sailboats to rent. You can rent a kayak by the day or the week from **Goose Hummock,** on Town Cove, in Orleans (✆ **508/255-2620;** www.goose.com), and paddle around Paines and Quivett creeks, as well as Upper and Lower Mill ponds. Renting a kayak to paddle around Town Cove for 3 hours will cost you $25 to $45. A 24-hour kayak rental costs $50 for a single, $75 for a tandem.

FISHING Brewster offers more ponds for fishing than any other town: 14 in all. Among the most popular are Cliff and Higgins ponds (within Nickerson State Park), which are regularly stocked. For a license, visit the town clerk at **Town Hall,** at 2198 Rte. 6A (✆ **508/896-3701**). Brewster lacks a deep harbor, so would-be deep-sea fishers will have to head to Barnstable or, better yet, Orleans.

GOLF One of the most challenging courses in Brewster is **Captain's Golf Course** at 1000 Freemans Way (✆ **508/896-1716;** www.captainsgolfcourse.com). In season, a round at Captain's course is $66, with discounted afternoon rates.

NATURE & WILDLIFE AREAS Admission is free to the three trails maintained by the **Cape Cod Museum of Natural History** (see below). The **South Trail,** covering a .75 mile round-trip south of Route 6A, crosses a natural cranberry bog beside Paines Creek to reach a hardwood forest of beeches and tupelos; toward the end of the loop, you'll come upon a "glacial erratic," a huge boulder dropped by a receding glacier. Before heading out on the .25-mile **North Trail,** stop in at the museum for a free guide describing the local flora, including wild roses, cattails, and sumacs. Also accessible from the museum parking lot is the **John Wing Trail,** a 1.5-mile network traversing 140 acres of preservation land, including upland, salt marsh, and beach. (*Note:* This can be a soggy trip. Be sure to heed the posted warnings about high tides, especially in spring, or you might very well find yourself stranded.) Keep an eye out for marsh hawks and blue herons.

As it crosses Route 6A, Paines Creek Road becomes Run Hill Road. Follow it to the end to reach **Punkhorn Park Lands,** an undeveloped 800-acre tract popular with mountain bikers; it features several kettle ponds, a "quaking bog," and 45 miles of dirt paths composing three marked trails (you'll find trail guides at the trail heads).

Though short, the .25-mile jaunt around the **Stony Brook Grist Mill** (see below) is especially scenic. In spring, you can watch the alewives (freshwater herring) vaulting upstream to spawn; and in the summer, the millpond is surrounded and scented by honeysuckle. Also relatively small, at only 25 acres, the **Spruce Hill Conservation Area** behind the Brewster Historical Society Museum (see below) includes a 600-foot stretch of beach, reached by a former carriage road reportedly favored by Prohibition bootleggers.

Just east of the museum is the 1,955-acre **Nickerson State Park** at Route 6A and Crosby Lane (✆ **508/896-3491;** www.mass.gov/dcr/parks/southeast/nick.htm), the legacy of a vast, self-sustaining private estate that once generated its own electricity (with a horse-powered plant) and attracted notable guests, such as President Grover Cleveland, with its own golf course and game preserve. Today it's a nature preserve encompassing 420 campsites (reservations pour in a year in advance to **Reserve America** at © 877/ 422-6762, which charges $15 for Massachusetts residents, $17 for out-of-staters), eight kettle ponds (stocked year-round with trout), and 8 miles of bicycle paths. The rest is trees—some 88,000 evergreens, planted by the Civilian Conservation Corps. This is land that has been through a lot but, thanks to careful management, is bouncing back.

TENNIS   Five public courts are located behind the police station; for details, contact the **Brewster Recreation Department** (© 508/896-9430).

WATERSPORTS   Various small sailboats, kayaks, canoes, and even aqua bikes (also known as sea cycles) are available seasonally at **Jack's Boat Rentals** (© 508/349-9808), located on Flax Pond within Nickerson State Park (see "Boating," above). Canoe or kayak rentals for a couple of hours cost $40.

BREWSTER HISTORIC SIGHTS & MUSEUMS

Brewster Historical Society Museum   This somewhat scattershot collection offers glimpses of Brewster's past. It includes a model of the town's first house (built in 1660), vestiges of an old post office and barbershop, and various relics of the China trade—the import business that made the town's fortune.

3341 Rte. 6A (about 1 mile east of the town center). © **508/896-9521.** www.brewsterhistoricalsociety. org. Free admission; donations accepted. July–Aug Thurs–Sat 1–4pm; call for off-season hours. Closed early Oct–May.

Brewster Ladies' Library   So inviting is the buttercup-yellow facade of this Victorian library, built in 1868, that curiosity will undoubtedly draw you inside. The two young ladies who started up this enterprise in 1852 with a shelf full of books had the right idea. The original pair of reading rooms remains intact, with facing fireplaces and comfy armchairs. A major addition houses meeting rooms, an auditorium, and a Brewster history room. The library hosts special exhibits, lectures, and concerts.

1822 Rte. 6A (about ⅛ mile southwest of the Brewster Store). © **508/896-3913.** www.brewsterladies library.org. Free admission. Tues and Thurs 10am–8pm; Wed and Fri–Sat 10am–5pm.

Cape Cod Museum of Natural History ★★★ (Kids)   Long before "ecology" had become a buzzword, noted naturalist writer John Hay helped found a museum that celebrates—and helps preserve—Cape Cod's unique landscape. Open since 1954, the museum was also prescient in presenting interactive exhibits. The display on whales, for instance, invites the viewer to press a button to hear eerie whale songs; the children's exhibits include an animal-puppet theater. All ages are invariably intrigued by the "live hive"—like an ant farm, only with busy bees. Four marine-room tanks (one 125-gal. tank and three 55-gal. tanks) contain freshwater and saltwater fish, turtles, frogs, crabs, lobsters, starfish, and a variety of mollusks. The bulk of the museum, naturally, is outdoors, where 85 acres invite exploration (see "Nature & Wildlife Areas," above). Visitors are encouraged to log their bird and animal sightings upon their return. A true force in fostering environmental appreciation, the museum sponsors all sorts of activities, such as lectures, concerts, marsh cruises, bike tours, and "eco-treks"—including a sleepover on uninhabited Monomoy Island, off Chatham. Other activities include evening astronomy cruises, seal cruises, and Pleasant Bay excursions. Call for a schedule.

869 Rte. 6A (about 2 miles west of the town center). © **508/896-3867.** www.ccmnh.org. Admission $8 adults, $7 seniors 65 and over, $3.50 children 3–12. June–Sept daily 9:30am–4pm; Feb–Mar Thurs–Sun 11am–3pm; Apr–May and Oct–Dec Wed–Sun 11am–3pm. Closed major holidays.

Harris-Black House and Higgins Farm Windmill   Most Cape towns can still boast a windmill or two, with a few of them even functioning, but this no-longer-working model is especially handsome. Built in 1795 in the "smock" style that can be traced back to Colonial days, it boasts an unusual cap shaped like a boat's hull. A few steps away is a classic half-Cape house, built that same year, consisting of one square room, 16 feet to a side. Here one of the poorer members of the community—a blacksmith who doubled as barber—lived simply, yet apparently happily, with his wife and 10 children.

785 Rte. 6A (about 2 miles west of the town center, on the Drummer Boy grounds), West Brewster. Ⓒ **508/896-9521.** Free admission. July–Aug Thurs–Sat 1–4pm; call for off-season hours. Closed Nov–Apr.

Stony Brook Grist Mill and Museum ★ Ⓚ𝐢𝐝𝐬   It may be hard to believe, but this rustic mill beside a stream was once one of the most active manufacturing communities in New England, cranking out cloth, boots, and ironwork for over a century, starting with the American Revolution. The one remaining structure was built in 1873, toward the end of West Brewster's commercial run, near the site of a 1663 water-powered mill, America's first. After decades of producing overalls and, later, ice cream (with ice dredged from the adjoining pond), the factory was bought by the town and fitted out as a corn mill, with period millstones. Volunteers now demonstrate and urge onlookers to get in on the action in the restored gristmill. A bag of cornmeal costs $2. The second story serves as a repository for all sorts of Brewster memorabilia, including some ancient arrowheads. Archaeological excavations in this vicinity, sponsored by the Cape Cod Museum of Natural History, have unearthed artifacts dating back some 10,000 years. As you stroll about the millpond (see "Nature & Wildlife Areas," above), be on the lookout—who knows what you'll stumble across?

830 Stony Brook Rd. (at the intersection of Satucket Rd.), West Brewster. Ⓒ **508/896-9521** Free admission. July–Aug Sat 10am–2pm; call for off-season hours. Closed Sept–Apr.

BASEBALL

The Brewster Whitecaps of the **Cape Cod Baseball League** (www.capecodbaseball.org) play at the Cape Cod Tech field, off Route 6's exit 11. For a schedule, contact the **Brewster Chamber of Commerce** (Ⓒ **508/896-3500**), the **Brewster Recreation Department** (Ⓒ **508/896-9430**), or the **League** (Ⓒ **508/432-6909**).

KID STUFF

For an educational experience that's also fun, take the kids to the **Cape Cod Museum of Natural History** ★★★ and the **Stony Brook Grist Mill** ★ (see above for both). Both have walking trails, and the museum has extensive exhibits geared toward children, including a number of interactive exhibits.

SHOPPING

ANTIQUES/COLLECTIBLES   Brewster's stretch of Route 6A offers the best antiquing on the entire Cape. Die-hards would do well to stop at every intriguing shop; you never know what you might find. There are several consistent standouts.

Deborah Rita, proprietor of **Countryside Antiques,** 2052 Main St./Rte. 6A (Ⓒ **508/896-1444**), roams the world in search of stylish furnishings, mostly old, though age—and price—are evidently no object.

ARTS & CRAFTS   Clayton Calderwood's **Clayworks,** 3820 Main St./Rte. 6A, East Brewster (Ⓒ **508/255-4937;** www.claytonsclayworks.com), is always worth a stop, if only to marvel at the famous mammoth urns. There's also a world of functional ware here such as bowls, pots, and lamps, in porcelain, stoneware, and terra cotta.

At **The Spectrum,** 369 Rte. 6A, about 1 mile east of the Dennis border (© **800/221-2472** or 508/385-3322; www.spectrumamerica.com), you'll find the kind of crafts that gave crafts a good name: fun stuff, with a certain irony to it, but unmistakably chic. In 1966, two young RISD (Rhode Island School of Design) grads opened shop in a rural schoolhouse. Bob Libby and Addison Pratt now oversee six stores: three on the Cape and islands (the other branches are in Hyannis and on Nantucket), and one each in Newport, Troy (Mich.), and Palm Beach. Their taste is top-of-the-line, as you'll see in a quick tour of this split-level, country-modern shop.

Collectors from around the world converge at **Sydenstricker Glass,** 490 Main St., Brewster (© **508/385-3272;** www.sydenstricker.com), in which a kiln-fired process developed in the mid-1960s that uses concepts from the art of enameling yields unique glassware, especially dishes and stemware.

GIFTS/HOME DECOR   Though quite a bit spiffier than a "real" general store, the **Brewster Store,** 1935 Main St./Rte. 6A, in the center of town (© **508/896-3744;** www. brewsterstore.com), an 1866 survivor that was fashioned from an 1852 Universalist church, is a fun place to shop for sundries and catch up on local gossip. The wares are mostly tourist-oriented these days but include some handy kitchen gear (cobalt glassware, for example) and beach paraphernalia. Give the kids a couple of dimes to feed the Nickelodeon piano machine, and relax on a sunny church pew out front as you pore over the local paper.

You don't have to be a foodie—though it helps—to go gaga over the exhaustive collection of culinary paraphernalia, from esoteric instruments to foodstuffs, at the **Cook Shop,** 1091 Rte. 6A, about 1½ miles west of the town center (© **866/561-COOK [3665]** or 508/896-7698; www.cookshopcapecod.com). If you're stuck cooking up a practical yet unusual house gift, look no further.

SEAFOOD   **Breakwater Fish and Lobster Market,** at 235 Underpass Rd., in Brewster (© **508/896-7080**), stocks the freshest fish in town and also sells smoked fish.

AN INTERNET CAFE & HERB SHOP

Stop at **Great Cape Herbs,** 2624 Main St./Rte. 6A (about 2 miles east of town center), in Brewster (© **800/427-7144** or 508/896-5900; www.greatcape.com), to pick up all manner of herbs or to use the Internet. This is one of the few places on the Cape that provides computers and Internet access on Sundays. The store is open daily in summer.

WHERE TO STAY

All the lodgings in this section provide onsite or nearby parking as part of their rates.

Very Expensive

Ocean Edge Resort & Club ★★   Evocative of a country club or a private seaside estate, Ocean Edge is replete with New England–style charm—lovely quilts, sliding glass doors that lead to patios or balconies—hotel rooms off the mansion are extremely large and comfortable. Spread out across the 400-acre property, one- to three-bedroom villas offer the freedom of a private residence (full kitchens, washer/dryers, and fireplaces in some) and the convenience of not having to drive anywhere (shuttle buses run all over the property). However, you might want to go out for groceries or to a local restaurant once in a while; the food served here is fine but not impressive. Whether you go for a getaway with your family or friends, or even for a romantic escape, you won't lack for things to do. Relax on the private 700-foot beach; go swimming; play golf or tennis; or rent a bike and ride the Rail Trail.

2907 Main St., Brewster, MA 02631. © 508/896-9000. Fax 508/896-9123. www.oceanedge.com. 335 units. Summer $265–$445 double hotel room; $800–$1,800/night or $2,400–$7,500/week 2- to 3-bed-room villa. AE, DISC, MC, V. **Amenities:** 4 restaurants; babysitting; bike trail and bike rentals; children's program for ages 4–12; concierge; fitness center; 18-hole championship golf course; 8 pools (2 indoor, 4 outdoor, 2 for toddler); room service; 11 tennis courts; conference/banqueting facilities. *In room:* A/C, TV, hair dryer, full kitchen or kitchenette (in villas), Wi-Fi.

Expensive

Captain Freeman Inn ★★   Donna and Peter Amadeo are the owners of this mint-green 1866 Victorian, one of the best B&Bs in the area. The "luxury rooms" each have a fireplace and private porch with a two-person hot tub. Delectable yet healthy breakfasts are served in the elegant parlor or on a screened porch overlooking the outdoor pool and a lush lawn set up for badminton and croquet. A wine-and-beer **bar** stands at your service for an afternoon or evening refreshment. Breakwater Beach is a 5-minute walk away.

15 Breakwater Rd. (off Rte. 6A, in the town center), Brewster, MA 02631. © 800/843-4664 or 508/896-7481. Fax 508/896-5618. www.captainfreemaninn.com. 12 units, all with tub/shower combinations. Summer $200–$240 double. Rates include full breakfast and afternoon tea. MC, V. No children 10 and under. **Amenities:** Loaner bikes; outdoor heated pool. *In room:* A/C, hair dryer.

Moderate

The Bramble Inn and Restaurant ★★ ⓥ Value   Cliff and Ruth Manchester oversee this rambling mid-19th-century home, decorated in a breezy, country-casual manner. The inn building, constructed in 1861, houses one of the Cape's best restaurants (see "Where to Dine," below) on the first floor. The rooms are small and spare, but quaint, with antique touches such as canopy beds with crocheted bedspreads. Cliff makes crea-tive breakfasts, such as mixed-fruit Swedish pancakes, which are served outside in the courtyard garden. The inn is about a half-mile from calm beaches on Cape Cod Bay.

2019 Rte. 6A (about ⅓ mile east of the town center), Brewster, MA 02631. © 508/896-7644. Fax 508/896-9332. www.brambleinn.com. 5 units, 2 with tub/shower combination, 3 with shower only. Sum-mer $158–$178 double. Rates include full breakfast. AE, DISC, MC, V. Closed Dec 31–Apr 1. **Amenities:** Restaurant. *In room:* A/C, TV, hair dryer.

Candleberry Inn ★   Innkeepers Stuart and Charlotte Fyfe graciously welcome guests to their restored 18th-century Federal-style home. These spacious accommodations fea-ture wide-board floors, wainscoting, and windows with original glass. The decor is country but not cutesy. Some rooms have working fireplaces and canopy beds. Extras include terry-cloth robes in every room as well as down pillows and feather beds. Three rooms in the carriage house are decorated in a more contemporary style; two share an outside deck, one is a deluxe suite, and all have TVs. In season, the three-course full breakfast is frequently served on the sunny porch overlooking the 2 acres of landscaped grounds, which have colorful flower beds throughout. Guests love the view of Main Street from the "glider" rocking benches on the lawn. Breakwater Beach is about a mile north.

1882 Main St./Rte. 6A, Brewster, MA 02631. © 800/573-4769 or 508/896-3300. Fax 508/896-4016. www.candleberryinn.com. 8 units, 1 with tub/shower combination, 7 with shower only. Summer $145–$160 double; $195 suite. Rates include full breakfast and afternoon tea. AE, DISC, MC, V. From Rte. 6, take exit 9B; take a right on 6A, inn is 4½ miles on left. Children 10 and over welcome. *In room:* A/C, hair dryer.

Michael's Cottages and Bed & Breakfast ★ (Value) These cottages on an immacu- lately groomed compound are small yet centrally located. Across the street is Brewster's Drummer Boy park, which has a playground, historic windmill, and antique house; Brewster's summer band concerts are held there as well. The closest beach is Paines Creek, about 1 mile away. There are three one-bedroom cottages, one three-bedroom cottage, one efficiency, and two B&B rooms. The cottages have screened porches, fireplaces, and microwaves. The three-bedroom cottage also has a dishwasher and washer/dryer. In July and August, rentals are available by the week only.

618 Main St./Rte. 6A, Brewster, MA 02631. ✆ **800/399-2967** or 508/896-4025. Fax 508/896-3158. www. michaelsinbrewster.com. 7 units, 2 with tub/shower combination, 5 with shower only. Summer $150–$160 double; $850–$915 double weekly; $1,200–$2,100 3-bedroom weekly. B&B rooms include continental breakfast. AE, DISC, MC, V. *In room:* A/C, TV, fridge, hair dryer.

Inexpensive

Old Sea Pines Inn ★★ (Value) (Kids) This reasonably priced, large historic inn is a great spot for families. In the main house, a handful of rather minuscule boarding-school-scale rooms on the second floor recall the inn's days as the Sea Pines School of Charm and Personality for Young Women. This is one of the few places on the Cape where solo travelers can find a single room for substantially less than a double. There are two other buildings, one of which is fully wheelchair-accessible (another rarity among historic inns). Whereas the main house has an air of exuberance muted by gentility, the annex rooms are downright playful, with colorful accouterments, including pink TVs. Sunday evenings from mid-June through mid-September, Old Sea Pines is the site of a dinner-theater performance by the Cape Cod Repertory Theatre Company (see "Brewster After Dark," below).

2553 Main St. (about 1 mile east of the town center), Brewster, MA 02631. ✆ **508/896-6114.** Fax 866/444-4552 www.oldseapinesinn.com. 24 units, 5 with shared bathroom. Summer $85 double with shared bathroom; $110–$165 double; $155–$175 suite. Rates include full breakfast and afternoon tea. AE, DC, DISC, MC, V. Closed Jan–Mar. *In room:* TV, hair dryer.

WHERE TO DINE

Very Expensive

The Bramble Inn and Restaurant ★★★ NEW AMERICAN Often named among the best restaurants on Cape Cod, this intimate restaurant consists of five small rooms each imbued with its own personality, from the Tack Room to the elegant parlor. Antique table settings add to the charm. Such niceties fade to mere backdrop, though, beside Ruth Manchester's extraordinary cuisine. A menu that evolves every few weeks gives her free rein to follow seasonal delicacies. She has a solid grounding in Mediterranean cuisines and a gift for improvising exotic influences. Her assorted seafood curry (with lobster, cod, scallops, and shrimp in a light curry sauce with grilled banana, toasted almonds, coconut, and chutney) and her rack of lamb (with deep-fried beet-and-fontina polenta, pan-seared zucchini, and mustard port cream) have been written up in the *New York Times.* A new bar area also has its own menu of lighter and less expensive fare that is also served in the courtyard garden.

2019 Main St./Rte. 6A (about ¹/₃ mile east of Rte. 124), Brewster. ✆ **508/896-7644.** www.brambleinn. com. Reservations required for fine dining, but not accepted for bistro. Main courses $24–$51. AE, DISC, MC, V. June to early Sept daily 6–9pm; call for off-season hours. Closed Jan–Mar.

Chillingsworth ★★★ FRENCH This longtime contender for the title of fanciest restaurant on the Cape now has two dining options: the formal dining room, and the more casual bistro. The dining room boasts antique appointments reaching back several centuries and a seven-course *table d'hôte* menu that will challenge the most shameless gourmands. Specialties include steamed lobster over spinach and fennel with sea beans and lobster-basil butter sauce; and seared and roasted boneless rib-eye of veal with fresh morels, mushroom torte, and asparagus. Finish it off with warm chocolate cake with pistachio ice cream and chocolate drizzle. Or try the moderately priced a la carte bistro, which serves lunch and dinner daily in season, in the adjoining greenhouse or under huge umbrellas on the shady lawn. There are also three deluxe inn rooms ($110–$150, double occupancy) on the premises.

2449 Main St./Rte. 6A, Brewster. (C) **508/896-3640**. www.chillingsworth.com. Reservations required for fine dining at dinner, recommended for bistro and lunch. Fixed-price meals $60–$70; bistro $17–$32. AE, DC, MC, V. Mid-June to Aug Thurs–Sun 11:30am–2:30pm, Mon–Sun 6–9:30pm (bistro opens for dinner at 5:30pm; on Mon one seating only for fine-dining 7–7:30pm); call for off-season hours. Closed Dec to mid-May. From Rte. 6, take exit 10; take a right on 6A, 1¹/₂ miles on left.

Expensive

The Brewster Fish House ★★ NEW AMERICAN Many locals and visitors alike swear this small, intimate eatery humbly occupying an old house on the side of Route 6A is the Cape's best restaurant. The approach to seafood is nothing if not inspired. Consider, for instance, an appetizer: day-boat sea scallop ceviche with bell pepper, jalapeño, and basil; or, as a main course: crisp-skin wild striped bass with Stony Island mussels. These are two examples of summer menu items devised to take advantage of the latest haul. Besides seafood there are always beef and vegetarian dishes on the menu. No wonder the place is packed. Better get here early (before 7pm) if you want to get in.

2208 Main St./Rte. 6A, Brewster. (C) **508/896-7867**. http://brewsterfish.com. Reservations not accepted. Main courses $17–$29. MC, V. May–Aug Mon–Sat 11:30am–3pm and 5–9:30pm, Sun noon–3pm and 5–9:30pm; call for off-season hours. Closed Dec–Apr. From Rte. 6, take exit 12 toward Brewster.

Moderate

Brewster Inn & Chowder House ★ SEAFOOD/AMERICAN To really get the gist of the expression "chow down," just observe the early-evening crowd happily doing so at this plain century-old restaurant known mostly by word of mouth. The draw is hearty, predictable staples—the homemade chowder; various fried, broiled, or baked fish—at prices geared to ordinary people rather than splurging tourists. Check the blackboard for interesting variations—maybe mussels steamed in cream and curry. If you like to indulge in a martini before your meal, this place makes the best ones in town. There's also a good old bar, the Woodshed (see "Brewster After Dark," below), out back.

1993 Rte. 6A (in the center of town). (C) **508/896-7771**. Reservations not accepted. Main courses $12–$18. AE, DISC, MC, V. Late May to mid-Oct daily 11:30am–3pm and 5–10pm; call for off-season hours.

Inexpensive

Cobie's ★ (Kids) AMERICAN Accessible to cars whizzing along Route 6A and within collapsing distance for cyclists exploring the Rail Trail, this picture-perfect clam shack has been dishing out exemplary fried clams, lobster rolls, foot-long hot dogs, black-and-white frappés, and all the other beloved staples of summer since 1948.

3260 Rte. 6A (about 2 miles east of Brewster center). (C) **508/896-7021**. www.cobies.com. Most items under $15. No credit cards. Late May–early Sept daily 10:30am–9pm. Closed early Sept–late May.

Sweets

How unusual to find a bake shop tucked away in a sweet little country gift shop. **Hopkins House Bakery,** 2727 Main St. ((C) **508/896-3450**), is an especially good one, with hermit cookies (molasses, raisins, and nuts) a standout. Heather Baxter also bakes breads and terrific muffins, including what she calls "the best corn muffin ever." Homemade fruit pies and sticky buns are also a specialty. Open Thursdays through Sundays 8am to 5pm in July and August, weekends only in June and September. Closed October to May.

BREWSTER AFTER DARK

Performances at the **Cape Cod Repertory Theatre,** 3299 Rte. 6A, Brewster, about 2½ miles east of Brewster center (© **866/811-4111** or 508/896-1888; www.caperep.org or www.theatermania.com), are given Tuesday to Saturday at 8pm from early July to early September. In summer, this shoestring troupe tackles the Bard, as well as serious contemporary fare, at a 200-seat outdoor theater on the old Crosby estate (now state-owned and undergoing restoration). Tickets for outdoor performances are $28. In season, they also put on a Broadway musical-dinner revue Sunday and Monday nights at the **Old Sea Pines Inn** ($55 four-course fixed-price meal; see "Where to Stay," above). Off-season they perform at various locales. Call for off-season hours.

Hot local bands take the tiny stage seasonally at **The Woodshed,** at the Brewster Inn & Chowder House, 1993 Rte. 6A (© **508/896-7771**), a far cry from the glitzy discos on the southern shore. If your tastes run more to Raitt and Buffett than techno, you'll feel right at home in this dark, friendly dive. Cover charge $5.

---

2 HARWICH ★

24 miles E of Sandwich; 32 miles S of Provincetown

Harwich Port, the village in the town of Harwich, where most vacationers find themselves, is the quintessential sleepy seaside village, not too mucked up—as yet—by the creeping commercialization of Route 28. The town's main claim to fame is as the birthplace, in 1846, of commercial cranberry cultivation: The "bitter berry," as the Narragansetts called it, is now Massachusetts's leading agricultural product. The curious can find elucidating displays on this and other local distinctions at the Brooks Academy Museum in the inland town of Harwich. The incurious, or merely vacation-minded, can loll on the beach.

ESSENTIALS

GETTING THERE After crossing the Sagamore Bridge (see section 3, "Getting There & Getting Around," in chapter 3), head east on Route 6 and take exit 10 south along Route 124. Harwich is located at the intersection of Route 39, where the two routes converge. Head southwest to Harwich Port and West Harwich, both located on Route 28. East Harwich (more easily reached from Rte. 6's exit 11) is inland, a few miles northeast. Or fly into Hyannis (see section 3, "Getting There & Getting Around," in chapter 3).

VISITOR INFORMATION Contact the **Harwich Chamber of Commerce,** 1 Schoolhouse Rd., Harwich Port, MA 02646 (© **508/430-1165;** fax 508/430-2105; www.harwichcc.com), open late May to late September daily from 9am to 5pm; call for off-season hours. You can also contact the **Cape Cod Chamber of Commerce** (see "Visitor Information," under "Brewster," earlier in this chapter).

BEACHES & RECREATIONAL PURSUITS

BEACHES The Harwich coast is basically one continuous beach punctuated by the occasional harbor. Harwich Port is so close to the sound that it's a snap to walk the block or two to the water—provided you find a parking place in town (try the lot near the chamber of commerce booth in the center of town). Parking right at the beach is pretty much limited to residents and renters, who can obtain a weekly sticker for $55 at the **Community Center,** 100 Oak St., Harwich (© **508/430-7568.**

- **Bank Street Beach** ★★, at the end of Bank Street, in Harwich Port: This is one of the few sound beaches in Harwich Port that has parking, but you will need a sticker. The sound beaches are generally warm and calm and very good beaches for swimming. This is a pretty (and popular) stretch, where you'll see lots of families as well as the self-conscious college crowd. As for amenities, there are lifeguards and restrooms.
- **Hinckleys Pond** ★ and **Seymours Pond** ★, west of Route 124, and right off the Rail Trail; and **Bucks Pond** ★★, off Depot Road, at Route 39, northeast of Harwich: Although Hinckleys and Bucks have limited parking, no parking sticker is required. At Seymours, however, you will need a sticker. Lifeguards are on staff in season, but you won't find any restrooms here.
- **Red River Beach** ★, off Uncle Venies Road, south of Route 28, in South Harwich: This is the only sound beach in town offering parking for day-trippers (they still have to get here early to nab a spot); the daily fee is $10. Marked off with stone jetties, this narrow, 2,700-foot beach has full facilities, with bathrooms. It also has lifeguards.
- **Sand Pond** ★, off Great Western Road, near Depot Street: This beach honors the weekly beach sticker, as do the two parking lots at Long Pond (btw. routes 137 and 124). The beach has restrooms and lifeguards.

BICYCLING Transecting Harwich for about 5 miles, the Cape Cod Rail Trail skirts some pretty ponds in the western part before veering north and zigzagging toward Brewster along Route 124. For rentals and information, contact the **Bike Depot,** 11 Pleasant Lake Ave./Rte. 12, Harwich (© **508/430-4375**), which is on the bike trail. A 24-hour bike rental costs $30.

BOATING You can rent a canoe by the day or the week at **Goose Hummock,** in Orleans (© **508/255-2620;** www.goose.com), and paddle down the Herring River, in West Harwich. Meandering from a reservoir south to the sound, the river is a natural herring run framed by a cattail marsh.

FISHING There are six ponds available for fishing in the Harwich area, as well as extensive shellfishing in season; for details and a license, visit **Town Hall,** at 732 Main St., in Harwich Center (© **508/430-7514**). For supplies and instruction, visit **Fishing the Cape,** at the Harwich Commons, routes 137 and 39 (© **508/432-1200;** www. fishingthecape.com); it's the official Cape headquarters for the **Orvis Saltwater Fly-Fishing School and Guides** (© **800/235-9763;** www.orvis.com). Instruction for 2 days costs $470. Several deep-sea fishing boats operate out of Saquatucket Harbor (off Rte. 28, about ½ mile east of Harwich Port), including the 33-footer *Fish Tale* (© **508/432-3783**), which charges $650 for 6 hours and $800 (includes lunch) for 8 hours. The 65-foot *Yankee* (© **508/432-2520**) is a party boat out of Saquatucket Harbor offering two 4-hour trips per day (8am–noon and 12:30–4:30pm) Monday through Saturday and one trip on Sunday in season. Off-season there's one trip per day. Trips cost $35 for adults and $33 for seniors and children 9 and under.

GOLF Both the championship 18-hole **Cranberry Valley Golf Course,** at 183 Oak St., in Harwich (© **508/430-5234;** http://cranberrygolfcourse.com), which wends its way among cranberry bogs, and the 9-hole **Harwich Port Golf Club,** at 51 South St., in Harwich Port (© **508/432-0250;** www.harwichportgolf.com), are open to the public.

Cranberry Valley charges $62 for a round, and Harwich Port Golf Club charges $30 for 18 holes.

NATURE & WILDLIFE AREAS   The largest preserve in Harwich is the 245-acre **Bells Neck Conservation Area,** north of Route 28, near the Dennis border. It encompasses the Herring River, ideal for birding and canoeing (see "Boating," above).

TENNIS   Public courts are available on a first-come, first-served basis at the Cape Cod Technical High School, on Route 124; and Brooks Park, on Oak Street, about one-quarter mile east of Harwich Center, off Route 39; for details, contact the **Harwich Recreation Department** (✆ 508/430-7553). Open late May through September, the **Wychmere Harbor Tennis Club,** at 792 Main St., in Harwich Port (✆ 508/432-1000; www.wychmereharbor.com) comprises nine Har-Tru courts and two hard courts; lessons can be scheduled. Court time is $50 for the day.

HISTORICAL HARWICH

Brooks Academy Museum ★   Gathered in an 1844 Greek Revival academy that offered the country's first courses in navigation, the collections of the Harwich Historical Society are good for a rainy afternoon's worth of wonderment. On permanent display is an extensive exhibition chronicling the early days of the cranberry industry, when harvesting was a backbreaking chore performed on hands and knees with a wooden scoop, mostly by migrant workers. (It simplified matters enormously once someone figured out that the bogs could be flooded and threshed so that the berries bob to the surface.) Other holdings include Native American tools, paintings by local artist C. D. Cahoon, nautical items of historical interest, and extensive textiles, imaginatively presented. The complex also includes a Revolutionary powder house and—kids might get a kick out of this—a nicely restored 1872 outhouse.

80 Parallel St. (at the intersection of Sisson Rd. and Main St., about 1 mile north of Harwich Port center). ✆ **508/432-8089.** www.harwichhistoricalsociety.org. Free admission, but donations accepted. Museum mid-June to mid-Oct Thurs–Sat 1–4pm. Closed mid-Oct to mid-June. Research library and photo archive by appointment only year-round.

BASEBALL

The **Harwich Mariners,** part of the **Cape Cod Baseball League** (www.capecodbaseball. org), play at Whitehouse Field, behind the high school in Harwich. For a schedule, contact the **Harwich Chamber of Commerce** (✆ 800/442-7942 or 508/430-1165), the **Harwich Recreation Department** (✆ 508/430-7553), or the **League** (✆ 508/432-6909).

KID STUFF

West Harwich gets some spillover from Dennis's overdevelopment, including such junior-tourist attractions as **Harbor Glen Miniature Golf,** at 168 Rte. 28 (✆ 508/432-8240), which costs $6 for those 13 and over, $4 for those 6 to 12, and $2 for those 5 and under; the **Trampoline Center,** at 296 Rte. 28 (✆ 508/432-8717), which costs $5 for 10 minutes; and **Bud's Go-Karts,** at the intersection of routes 28 and 39 (✆ 508/432-4964), which welcomes hot-rodders as young as 8, provided they meet the height requirement (54 in.). The go-carts are $6 per ride. All three are open until 10 or 11pm in summer. For free self-entertainment, visit **Castle in the Clouds,** a community-built playground behind the Harwich Elementary School, on South Street, in Harwich. Young culture mavens might want to take in a performance at the **Harwich Junior Theatre,** at 105 Division St., in West Harwich (✆ 508/432-2002; www.hjtcapecod.org), which has been satisfying summer customers since 1952; if you plan to stick around for a while, your youngsters could even take classes and possibly work their way onstage. Tickets cost $12 to $22 adults, $16 seniors 65 and over, $12 youths 20 and under.

SHOPPING

Route 28 harbors lots of mini malls and shops, big on gifts (on the trite side) and unsensational art. With a few exceptions, save your power shopping for Chatham.

ANTIQUES/COLLECTIBLES **The Barn at Windsong,** 245 Bank St., a half-mile north of Harwich Port center, midway between routes 28 and 39 (© **508/432-8281**), is the kind of archetypal shop antiquers crave: a lovely old barn in the country, packed with premium goods. Offerings include furniture, glass, china, and rugs. Closed November through April.

WHERE TO STAY

There are several above-average motels in Harwich. **The Tern Inn,** 91 Chase St., West Harwich (© **800/432-3718** or 508/432-3714; www.theterninn.com), is in a quiet residential neighborhood. Summer rates are $149 to $189 for a double, and $995 per week for a one-bedroom cottage, $1,295 for a three-bedroom cottage. The Tern has a small, unheated pool. Rooms do not have phones, but all have TVs, minifridges, and air-conditioning. Just 75 yards from a wide Nantucket Sound beach, the **Commodore Inn** ★, 30 Earle Rd., West Harwich (© **800/368-1180** or 508/432-1180; www.commodore inn.com), has 27 lovely rooms resembling upscale condos with cathedral ceilings and an outdoor heated pool. It's a short walk to the beach. Rates are $225 to $245 double and include a full buffet breakfast in season. All rooms have microwave ovens and minifridges, as well as air-conditioning, TVs, and phones with dataports. Some have Jacuzzis and fireplaces. Closed mid-October to March. **Sandpiper Beach Inn** ★★, 16 Bank St., Harwich Port (© **800/433-2234** or 508/432-0485; www.sandpiperbeachinn.com), is plunked right on a lovely Nantucket Sound beach. All rooms have air-conditioning, phones, TVs, hair dryers, and fridges. Summer rates (including continental breakfast) are $220 to $440 double, $370 to $440 for suites. Closed November to mid-April.

Very Expensive

Wequassett Resort and Golf Club ★★★ This 22-acre resort set on placid but pretty Pleasant Bay has long been the place to go for vacationing tennis, golf, and sailing enthusiasts, and recent renovations adding more luxury rooms have made it even more deluxe. Inn guests enjoy exclusive nonmember privileges to Cape Cod National Golf Club. The restaurant on-site, **28 Atlantic,** is one of the Cape's top dining spots (see "Where to Dine," below). Rooms are spread out in a half-dozen buildings and are spacious and comfortable, with 15 beachfront units. All rooms have either a balcony or a patio, and rooms for guests with disabilities are available. The calm private bay beach, just steps from the rooms, is called Clam Point. Chatham's North Beach is a 15-minute ride via the inn's Power Skiff ($12 adults, $5 children).

2173 Rte. 28 (about 5 miles northeast of Chatham center, on Pleasant Bay), Harwich, MA 02633. © **800/225-7125** or 508/432-5400. Fax 508/432-5032. www.wequassett.com. 120 units. Summer $525–$825 double; $795–$2,800 suites. $15 per day resort charge. AE, DC, DISC, MC, V. Closed Dec–Mar. **Amenities:** 2 restaurants (28 Atlantic for fine dining, see review below; Outer Bar and Grille for casual fare, both open to the public); babysitting; bike rentals ($20–$40 per day); Children's Fun Club ($25 for half-day; $45 for full day); concierge; fitness room; golf course next door ($105 a round; $20 for a cart); heated outdoor pool; room service; 4 all-weather Plexipave tennis courts ($15 an hr. per person), plus a pro shop; watersports equipment/rentals (sailboards, Sunfish, Daysailers, and Hobie Cats for about $40

Winstead Inn and Beach Resort ★★   This property is composed of two buildings set about a mile apart: the 14-room Beach House Inn, on a private Nantucket Sound beach and a short walk from Harwich Port, and the remodeled seven-room Winstead Inn, near Harwich Center. The Beach House is an antiques-filled 1920s inn. The Winstead is a handsome colonial-style building with a pool. Both inn buildings are within walking distance of shops and restaurants, so you don't have to contend with summer traffic. Those staying at the Winstead can take a free shuttle to the beach in a 1949 Pontiac Woody.

4 Braddock Lane, Harwich, MA 02646. (*) **800/870-4405** or 508/432-4444. Fax 508/432-9152. www. winsteadinn.com. 21 units. Summer $325–$525 double. Rates include continental breakfast. MC, V. **Amenities:** Outdoor heated saltwater pool at in-town property. *In room:* A/C, TV, fridge, hair dryer.

WHERE TO DINE
Very Expensive

L'Alouette Bistro ★★ CONTEMPORARY FRENCH   If you're looking for a romantic spot with candlelit dining, you'll find it at this cozy old Cape cottage, where owners Alan and Gretchen Champney give classic French cuisine a shot in the arm. Such choices as escargot and seared foie gras are authentically presented, but there are also surprises, such as pistachio-crusted lamb with Bordeaux sauce. The pasta with poached lobster and truffled cognac and tarragon sauce is a pleasing twist on a traditional favorite.

787 Rte. 28 (about 1/2 mile east of the town center), Harwich Port. (*) **508/430-0405.** www.lalouette bistro.com. Reservations highly recommended. Main courses $22–$34. AE, DISC, MC, V. Late May to mid-Oct daily 5–9pm (last reservation at 8:30pm); mid-Oct to late May Tues–Sun 5–9pm.

28 Atlantic ★★★ NEW AMERICAN   This restaurant on the grounds of the Wequassett Resort is one of the top places to eat on Cape Cod. The elegant spacious dining room overlooks Pleasant Bay through immense floor-to-ceiling glass panels. The food stands out as superb, from the *amuse bouche* (a little taste teaser) to the exceptional desserts. Menu items use local provender, but there are also delicacies from around the world. You might start with the Cape lobster and roasted corn bisque with sherried Devonshire cream; move on to the composed salad of mâche, melon, prosciutto, grapes, goat-cheese mousse, and tawny port syrup; and then get to your main course, perhaps skillet-seared local bluefish with saffron-smoked mussel risotto, wilted Swiss chard, and lobster oil. For more casual dining, the Wequassett poolside cafe is the stylish **Outer Bar ★★**, with views of Pleasant Bay. It's open to the public from 11:30am to 10pm.

2173 Rte. 28 (at the Wequassett Resort and Golf Club, about 5 miles northwest of Chatham center, on Pleasant Bay). (*) **508/430-3000.** www.wequassett.com. Reservations recommended. Main courses $21–$44. AE, DC, DISC, MC, V. May–Nov daily 7–11am and 6–10pm; call for off-season hours. Closed Dec to mid-Apr.

Expensive

Buca's Tuscan Roadhouse ★★ (Finds) NORTHERN ITALIAN   No wonder this place is so popular: an atmosphere that's somehow romantic and festive at the same time, wonderful food, and superior service. The only problem is getting a reservation, even in January. But once you do land a table, you can relax into this most enjoyable dining experience. Homemade pastas, off-the-boat fish, tender cuts of meat—it doesn't get much better than this. From basics such as eggplant parmigiana to *cacciucco*, a mélange of seafood in a garlicky broth, the food is delicious. Wines by the glass are also exceptional.

4 Depot Rd. (on the corner of Rte. 28, close to the Chatham border), Harwich. ☎ **508/432-6900.** www. bucasroadhouse.com. Reservations recommended. Main courses $18–$25. AE, MC, V. June–Aug daily 5–9:30pm; call for off-season hours.

The Cape Sea Grille ★★ NEW AMERICAN   Chef/owner Doug Ramler is the new power behind the stove at this upscale enterprise occupying a peach-toned 19th-century beach house, a former sea captain's home. The dining rooms tend toward the impersonal side, perhaps the restaurant's only weak link. The food is excellent. The specialty of the house is the pan-seared lobster with pancetta, potatoes, grilled asparagus, and a Calvados-saffron reduction, but other enticing choices on the menu include seafood *tapas* and duck confit. City sophisticates who insist on creativity and innovation will find this the most consistently rewarding source in town. The restaurant is also a short walk to a neighborhood beach, the perfect place for an after-dinner moonlight stroll.

31 Sea St. (south of Rte. 28, in the center of town), Harwich Port. ☎ **508/432-4745.** www.capeseagrille. com. Reservations recommended. Main courses $19–$33. AE, MC, V. June–Aug daily 5–10pm; call for off-season hours. Closed mid-Nov to early Apr.

Moderate

The Port ★ NEW AMERICAN   With a big-city vibe, this hip venue, with a sleek, contemporary feel, tends to attract a younger crowd in the bar, but the dining room is gaining a reputation for consistent fine dining. Specializing in local seafood, this is the place to go for local shellfish and such dishes as Portuguese stew, a spicy blend of shrimp, scallops, mussels, and calamari. Basic options are a step above: The hamburger, for example, is a Kobe beef burger, and the best pasta choice is Chatham littlenecks (clams) over linguini.

541 Main St./Rte. 28 (in the center of town), Harwich Port. ☎ **508/430-5410.** www.theportrestaurant. com. Reservations recommended. Main courses $19–$32. AE, MC, V. Apr–Dec daily 5–10pm. Closed Jan–Mar.

Villa Roma ★ (**Finds**) ITALIAN   If you didn't know about this perfect little roadhouse, you'd drive right by. Walk into the dimly lit bar area, and then head back to one of the comfortably snug dining rooms. This old house retains the charm of Olde Cape Cod, something that is becoming harder and harder to find. On the menu is classic Italian fare, nothing fancy. There's lasagna with homemade meatballs, shrimp scampi, and a wonderfully light veal piccata. The prices are very reasonable, even cheap, considering your meal comes with a salad or soup. But the best thing about this place is the atmosphere and the friendly staff.

278 Rte. 28, West Harwich. ☎ **508/432-6868.** www.villaromaonthecape.com. Reservations for 6 or more only. Main courses $10–$20. AE, MC, V. Daily 5–9:30pm.

Inexpensive

Seafood Sam's (**Kids**) SEAFOOD   Strategically located within a big bounce of the Trampoline Center, this McDonald's-style clam shack—part of a Cape-wide chain—dishes out deep-fried seafood, fast.

302 Rte. 28 (about ¹/₂ mile east of the town center), Harwich Port. ☎ **508/432-1422.** www.seafoodsams. com. Most items under $12. DISC, MC, V. Mid-Feb to late Nov daily 11am–9pm. Closed late Nov to mid-Feb.

Sweets

Sundae School ★ ICE CREAM   Another branch of the local chain (also in Dennis Port and East Orleans), this is homemade ice cream and a sure crowd pleaser with the

kids. Real whipped cream and real cherries will keep the parents happy, too. Fresh-fruit
sundaes are a popular choice here, and everyone likes to admire the 1938 ice-cream truck.

606 Main St. (in the center of town), Harwich Port. (℃ **508/430-2444.** www.sundaeschoolicecream.com. Mid-May to early Oct daily 11am–10:30pm. Closed early Oct to mid-May.

HARWICH AFTER DARK

The Irish Pub ★   For years, this has been the premier Irish bar on the Cape. It feels authentic because it is. A variety of live entertainment (it could be Irish music, karaoke, or anything in between), Thursday to Saturday in season, is usually rollicking good fun. 126 Main St./Rte. 28, West Harwich. (℃ **508/432-8808.** www.capecodsirishpub.com. Cover under $5.

3 CHATHAM ★★★

32 miles E of Sandwich; 24 miles S of Provincetown

Sticking out like a sore elbow (and out of the way of much of the Cape's tourist flow), Chatham was one of the first spots to attract early explorers. Samuel de Champlain stopped by in 1606 but got into a tussle with the prior occupants over some copper cooking pots; he ended up leaving in a hurry. The first colonist to stick around was William Nickerson, of Yarmouth, who befriended a local sachem (tribal leader) and built a house beside his wigwam in 1656. One prospered; the other—for obvious reasons—didn't. To this day, listings for Nickersons still occupy a half-page in the Cape Cod phone book.

Chatham, along with Provincetown, is the only area on the Cape to support a sizeable commercial fishing fleet—against increasing odds. Overfishing has resulted in closely monitored limits to give the stock time to bounce back. Boats must now go out as far as 100 miles to catch their fill. Despite the difficulties, it's a way of life few locals would willingly relinquish. As in Provincetown, there's surprisingly little animosity between the hardworking residents and the summer vacationers at play, perhaps because it's clear that discerning tourist dollars are helping to preserve this lovely town for all.

ESSENTIALS

GETTING THERE   After crossing the Sagamore Bridge (see section 3, "Getting There & Getting Around," in chapter 3), head east on Route 6, and take exit 11 south (Rte. 137) to Route 28. From this intersection, the village of South Chatham is about a half-mile west, and West Chatham is about 1½ miles east. Chatham itself is about 2 miles farther east on Route 28. To fly to Chatham, take a commercial flight into Hyannis (see section 3, "Getting There & Getting Around," in chapter 3).

VISITOR INFORMATION   Visit the **Cape Cod Chamber of Commerce** (see "Visitor Information," under "Brewster," earlier in this chapter); the **Chatham Chamber of Commerce,** 2377 Main St., South Chatham, MA 02659 (℃ **800/715-5567** or 508/ 945-5199; www.chathaminfo.com); or the **Chatham Chamber booth** (no phone), at 533 Main St., in Chatham. Hours for both the Chatham chamber and the booth are July and August Monday to Saturday 10am to 5pm, Sunday noon to 3pm; closed late October to April. Call for off-season hours.

A STROLL AROUND CHATHAM

A stroll around Chatham, taking you from one end of Main Street to the other, and to interesting sites nearby, can give you a great feel for this picturesque town. The walk covers a distance of approximately 2½ miles and takes 2 to 3 hours, depending on how many stops you make along the way. Parking on Main Street can be a challenge at the height of summer, so pretend you're a turn-of-the-20th-century traveler and start out at the **Chatham Railroad Museum** ★, on 153 Depot St. (closed mid-Sept to mid-June), 1 block north of Main Street, at the western end of town. You can't miss it: It's a gaudy 1887 Victorian station in the "Railroad Gothic" style, painted yellow with fanciful russet ornamentation. The building itself is full of railroading memorabilia, and the big exhibits—antique passenger cars—are out back.

If you've got children along, they'll surely want to stretch their legs (and imaginations) at the **Play-a-Round Park** ★★, opposite the Railroad Museum. Dreamed up by prominent playground designer Robert Leathers, it's a marvelous maze of tubes, rope ladders, slides, and swings. The only way you'll get going again is to promise to come back.

Head west to the end of Depot Street, and turn right on Old Harbor Road, which, if followed past Main Street, becomes State Harbor Road. About a mile farther along, past Oyster Pond, you'll encounter the **Atwood House Museum** ★, at 347 Stage Harbor Rd. (© **508/945-2493;** www.chathamhistoricalsociety.org); closed Oct to mid-June. The 1752 house itself shelters the odds and ends collected by the Chatham Historical Society over the past 7 decades; piece by piece, they tell the story of the town. The Society even managed to save an entire 1947 "fishing camp," a run-down cottage that looks as if the occupant just stepped out to check a line.

Heading back toward Main Street, bear right on Cross Street and look for **Chase Park and Bowling Green,** presided over by the Old Grist Mill, built in the late 18th century. You might actually try some lawn bowling along the lovingly tended greens before returning to Main Street, where the shops are too prolific and special to pass up. Then head eastward toward the shore, but be sure to duck into the **Mayo House,** at 540 Main St. (© **508/945-4084**), a sweet little three-quarter Cape built in 1818. Entrance is free, and—if you've studiously avoided lengthy historical house tours so far—it can give you, in just a couple of minutes, a good sense of what life might have been like here in centuries past.

Main Street veers right when it reaches the shore. Continue along for about one-quarter mile to view the **Chatham Light** ★★, an 1876 beacon not open to the public but still in operation: Its light shines 15 miles out to sea. This is a good vantage point from which to marvel over the "break" that burst through Chatham's barrier beach in 1987. In the years since, the newly created island, South Beach, has already glommed onto the coastline, becoming a peninsula. This is one landscape that rarely stays put for long.

Retrace your steps northward along the shore. In about ¾ mile, you'll pass the grand **Chatham Bars Inn** ★★★, at 297 Shore Rd. (© **800/527-4884** or 508/945-0096), which started out as a private hunting lodge in 1914. Passersby are welcome to look around the lobby, restored to reflect its original Victorian splendor. Linger on the porch over coffee or a drink, if you like, before pressing on to the **Chatham Fish Pier,** about a quarter-mile farther along Shore Road. If you've timed your visit right (from noon on), the trawlers should just now be bringing in the catch of the day. You can observe the haul from an observation deck. Also have a look at *The Provider,* an intriguing outdoor sculpture by Woods Hole artist Sig Purwin.

WINDING DOWN When you've had enough, or the insects insist that you head on home, go back to Main Street, down Seaview Street, past the Chatham Seaside Links golf course. One long block later (about ½ mile), you're back in the center of town. You can

DINING ◆
The Blue Coral **9**
Carmine's Pizza **5**
Chatham Candy Manor **7**
Chatham Squire **8**
Chatham Wayside Inn **6**
Del Mar Bar & Bistro **1**
The Impudent Oyster **10**

Nickerson Fish & Lobster **13**
Red Nun Bar & Grill **3**
Vining's Bistro **5**

ATTRACTIONS ●
Chatham Railroad Museum **2**
The Old Atwood House
　Museum **4**

ACCOMMODATIONS ■
Captain's House Inn **15**
Chatham Bars Inn **12**
Chatham Wayside Inn **6**
The Hawthorne **11**
Moses Nickerson House **14**

THE LOWER CAPE

7

CHATHAM

relax and unwind at the **Chatham Wayside Inn** ★, at 512 Main St. (© **508/945-5550**). Secure a table on the greenery-curtained patio and watch the world go by, as you fortify yourself with regionally inspired snacks and sweets on the large screened porch.

BEACHES & RECREATIONAL PURSUITS

BEACHES　Chatham has an unusual array of beach styles, from the peaceful shores of the Nantucket Sound to the treacherous, shifting shoals along the Atlantic. For information on beach stickers ($15 per day, $60 per week), call the **Permit Department,** at 283 George Ryder Rd., in West Chatham (© **508/945-5180**).

- **Chatham Light Beach** ★★: Located directly below the lighthouse parking lot (where stopovers are limited to 30 min.), this narrow stretch of sand is easy to get to: Just walk down the stairs. Currents here can be tricky and swift, though, so swimming is discouraged.
- **Cockle Cove Beach, Ridgevale Beach,** and **Hardings Beach** ★★: Lined up along the sound, each at the end of its namesake road, south of Route 28, these family-pleasing beaches offer gentle surf suitable for all ages, as well as full facilities, including lifeguards. Parking stickers are required.

• **Forest Beach** ★: With limited parking and no lifeguard, this sound landing near the Harwich border is still popular, especially among surfers.

- **North Beach** ★★: Extending all the way south from Orleans, this 5-mile barrier beach is accessible from Chatham only by boat; if you don't have your own, you can take the **Beachcomber**, a water taxi, which leaves from Chatham Fish Pier on Shore Road. Call ✆ 508/945-5265 (www.sealwatch.com) to schedule your trip, though reservations are not necessary. Round-trip costs $30 for adults, $20 for children 12 and under. The water taxi makes the trip from 10am to 5pm daily in season on sunny days. Inquire about other possible drop-off points if you'd like to beach around.

- **Oyster Pond Beach,** off Route 28: Only a block from Chatham's Main Street, this sheltered saltwater pond (with restrooms) swarms with children. It's free to park here, and there is a lifeguard.

- **South Beach** ★★: A former island jutting out slightly to the south of the Chatham Light, this glorified sand bar can be dangerous, so heed posted warnings and content yourself with strolling or, at most, wading. A sticker is not required to park here.

BICYCLING Though Chatham has no separate recreational paths per se, a demarcated bike/blading lane makes a scenic, 8-mile circuit of town, heading south onto "The Neck," east to the Chatham Light, up Shore Road, all the way to North Chatham, and then back to the center of town. A descriptive brochure prepared by the **Chatham Chamber of Commerce** (✆ 800/715-5567 or 508/945-5199) shows the suggested route, and there are lots of lightly trafficked detours worth taking.

BIRD-WATCHING In summer, the Wellfleet Bay Wildlife chapter of the **Audubon Society** (✆ 508/349-2615) offers bird-watching trips to the **Monomoy National Wildlife Refuge** ★★ on North Monomoy Island (monomoy.fws.gov). On the tour of North Monomoy, after a 15-minute boat ride from Chatham, you'll embark on a 4-hour guided tour, where you'll encounter a variety of species—from herring gulls and sandpipers to black-bellied plovers and willets. Tours cost around $35 adults, $30 children 12 and under, and are recommended not just for avid bird-watchers, but for anyone who enjoys the outdoors. Reservations are required.

BOATING You can rent a kayak (see below) and paddle down the Oyster River, past Hardings Beach, and over to Morris Island. You can also explore Pleasant Bay, the Cape's largest, and reach the inside shore of the Outer Beach. For those with sufficient experience, Pleasant Bay is the best place to sail; if the winds don't go your way, try Forest Beach, on the South Chatham shore.

    Nauti Jane's Boat Rental, at 337 Rte. 28, in Harwich Port (✆ **508/430-6893;** www.nautijanesboatrentals.com), also offers kayak and sailboat rentals at the Wequassett Inn, on Pleasant Bay, and on Ridgevale Beach, in Chatham (✆ **508/432-4339**): Available crafts include kayaks, Sunfish, surf bikes, and sailboats up to 16 feet. Kayaks rent for $30 per hour or $42 for 2 hours; sailboats rent for $65 to $99 for 2 hours or $115 to $185 for half-day.

FISHING Chatham has five ponds and lakes that permit fishing; Goose Pond off Fisherman's Landing is among the top spots. For saltwater fishing sans boat, try the fishing bridge on Bridge Street, at the southern end of Mill Pond. First, though, get a license at **Town Hall,** at 549 Main St., in Chatham (✆ **508/945-5100**) or at **Goose Hummock,** in Orleans (✆ **508/255-2620**). If you hear the deep sea calling, sign on with *The Headhunter* (✆ **508/430-2312;** www.capecodfishingcharters.com), a 33-foot sportfishing boat. Sportfishing rates average around $650 for 5 hours. Shellfishing licenses are available at the **Permit Department,** at 283 George Ryder Rd., in West Chatham (© **508/945-** 5180**

GOLF Once part of the Chatham Bars Inn property and now owned by the town, the scenic 9-hole, par-34 **Chatham Seaside Links,** at 209 Seaview St., in Chatham (© **508/ 945-4774**), isn't very challenging but is fun for neophytes; inquire about instruction. A 9-hole round costs $19.

NATURE & WILDLIFE AREAS Heading southeast from the Hardings Beach parking lot, the 2-mile round-trip **Seaside Trail** offers beautiful parallel panoramas of Nantucket Sound and Oyster Pond River; keep an eye out for nesting pairs of horned lark. Access to 40-acre Morris Island, southwest of the Chatham Light, is easy: You can walk or drive across and start right in on a marked .75-mile trail. Heed the high tides as advised, though—they can come in surprisingly quickly, leaving you stranded.

Chatham's natural bonanza lies southward: The uninhabited **Monomoy Islands** ★★, 2,750 acres of brush-covered sand favored by some 285 species of migrating birds, is the perfect pit stop along the Atlantic Flyway. Harbor and gray seals are catching on, too: Hundreds now carpet the coastline from late November through May. If you go out during that time, you won't have any trouble seeing them—they're practically unavoidable. **Wellfleet Bay Wildlife Sanctuary,** operated by the Audubon Society (© **508/349-2615;** www.massaudubon.org), offers guided trips. The Audubon's 3-hour trips take place April through September, and they cost $35 per person. The boat to Monomoy leaves from Chatham, and the trip includes a naturalist-guided nature hike.

SEAL-WATCHING The **Beachcomber** ★★ (© **508/945-5265;** www.sealwatch.com) runs **seal-watching cruises** out of Stage Harbor from mid-May to late September daily in season, weekends in the shoulder seasons. Parking is on Crowell Road, at Chatham Boat Company, near the bakery. The 90-minute cruises cost $27 for adults, $25 for seniors, $23 for children 3 to 15, and free for children 2 and under.

Outermost Adventures (© **508/945-5858;** www.outermostharbor.com) runs boat shuttle service to South Beach. The ride takes 10 minutes; and, once on the beach, passengers can walk for 2 minutes to the far side of the spit to see seals gathered along the coast. The shuttle begins at 8am, goes every 20 minutes, and is first-come, first-served. The last pick-up is at 4:30pm. The cost is $20 adults, $10 children 12 and under. Trips run from Memorial Day to Columbus Day.

TENNIS Free public courts are located near the Railroad Museum, on Depot Street, and at Chatham High School, on Crowell Road; for details, contact the **Chatham Recreation Department** (© **508/945-5175**). In addition, you may be able to rent one of the three courts at the **Chatham Bars Inn,** on Shore Road (© **508/945-6759**), which cost $35 an hour.

CHATHAM HISTORICAL SIGHTS

Chatham Railroad Museum ★ (**Kids**) Even if you're not a railroad fanatic, it's worth visiting this beautiful 1887 depot to imagine the sights that would greet a Victorian visitor. To begin, the building itself is a "Railroad Gothic" work of wooden art, topped by a tapering turret. Inside you'll find volunteers dispensing lore and explaining the many displays. The museum's major holding is lined up in back: a "walk-through" 1918 New York caboose.

153 Depot Rd. (off Main St., 1 block north of the rotary). No phone. Donations accepted. Mid-June to mid-Sept Tues–Sat 10am–4pm. Closed mid-Sept to mid-June.

THE LOWER CAPE / 7 / CHATHAM

The Old Atwood House Museum ★   For further glimpses of Chatham's past, visit this gambrel-roofed 1752 homestead, divided (rather awkwardly) into assorted wings celebrating different phases and products of the local culture. The house harbors all sorts of odd collections, from seashells to the complete works of early-20th-century author Joseph C. Lincoln, a renowned Cape writer whose hokey books are avidly collected by locals. One room definitely worth a visit is the New Gallery, featuring admirably direct portraits of crusty sea-goers by local artist Frederick Stallknecht Wight. His work, unfortunately, was always overshadowed by the *oeuvre* of his mother, Alice Stallknecht Wight, who executed pretend-primitive murals of villagers enacting religious scenes (a contemporary Christ-as-fisherman, for instance, celebrating the Last Supper). Her work occupies an adjoining barn; see if you think she deserves it. By far, the most enchanting exhibit on hand is an entire 1947 fishing "camp"—a one-room old-boys' club salvaged, complete with shabby furnishings, from the onslaught of the winter storms that brought about the "break" of 1987.

347 Stage Harbor Rd. (about ²/₃ mile south of Main St.). © **508/945-2493.** www.chathamhistorical society.org. Admission $5 adults, $3 students. Mid-June to Oct Tues–Sat 10am–4pm. Closed Nov to mid-June.

BASEBALL

The Chatham Athletics (or "A's"), part of the **Cape Cod Baseball League** (www.cape codbaseball.org), play at Veterans Field, off Depot Street. Admission is free, though donations are requested. For a schedule, contact the **Chatham Chamber of Commerce** (© **800/715-5567** or 508/945-5199), the **Chatham Community Center** (© **508/945-5175**), or the **League** (© **508/432-6909**).

KID STUFF

The **Play-a-Round Park ★★**, on Depot Street (see "A Stroll Around Chatham," above), will suffice to keep kids entertained for hours on end. The weekly **band concerts ★★** (© **508/945-5199**), at Kate Gould Park, held Friday nights in summer, are perfectly gauged for underage enjoyment: There's usually a bunny-hop at some point in the evening. Junior connoisseurs get a chance, once a year in late July, to enjoy some really fine music, when the Monomoy Chamber Ensemble puts on a free morning children's performance at the **Monomoy Theatre** (© **508/945-1589;** www.monomoytheatre.org), and musicals there are always fun.

SHOPPING

Chatham's tree-shaded Main Street, lined with specialty stores, offers a terrific opportunity to shop and stroll. The goods tend to be on the conservative side, but every so often, you'll happen upon a hedonistic delight.

ARTS & CRAFTS   Headed for such prestigious outlets as Neiman Marcus, the hand-blown glassworks of James Holmes originate at **Chatham Glass Company,** 758 Main St., just west of the Chatham rotary (© **508/945-5547;** www.chathamglass.com), where you can literally look over their shoulders as the pieces take shape. Luscious colors are their hallmark; the intense hues, combined with a purity of form at once traditional and cutting-edge contemporary, add up to objects that demand to be coveted.

At **Chatham Pottery,** 2058 Rte. 28, east of the intersection with Route 137 (© **508/430-2191;** http://store.chathampottery.com), striking graphics characterize the collaborative work of Gill Wilson (potter) and Margaret Wilson-Grey (glazer). Their work consists primarily of blue block-print-style designs set against off-white stoneware. The most popular design may be the etched pair of swimming fish, based on sketches over

100 years old. It's a look that's somewhat addictive. Luckily it's available in everything from platters and bowls to lamps and tiles.

BOOKS　**Yellow Umbrella Books,** 501 Main St., in the center of town (✆ **508/945-0144**), offers both new and used books (from rare volumes to paperbacks perfect for a disposable beach read). This full-service, all-ages bookstore invites protracted browsing.

FASHION　Catering to fashionable parents and their kids, ages newborn well into the teens, the **Children's Shop,** 515 Main St., in the center of town (✆ **508/945-0234;** www.chathamchildrenshop.com), is the best children's clothing store in a 100-mile radius. While according a nod to doting grannies with such classics as hand-smocked party dresses, Ginny Nickerson also stays up-to-speed on what kids themselves prefer.

The flagship store of **Puritan Clothing Company** is at 573 Main St., Chatham (✆ **508/945-0326;** www.puritancapecod.com). This venerable institution, with stores all over the Cape, has updated its clothing considerably in the past 10 years. You'll find a wide range of quality men's and women's wear, including Polo, Nautica, Eileen Fisher, and Teva, at good prices.

WHERE TO STAY

Chatham's lodging choices tend to be more expensive than those of neighboring towns because it's considered a chichi place to vacation. But for those allergic to fussy, fancy B&Bs and inns, Chatham has several good motel options.

Practically across the street from the Chatham Bars Inn, the **Hawthorne** ★, 196 Shore Rd. (✆ **508/945-0372;** www.thehawthorne.com), is a motel with one of the best locations in town: right on the water, with striking views of Chatham Harbor, Pleasant Bay, and the Atlantic Ocean. An additional perk here is free phone calls (local and long distance) and Internet access. Rates for the 26 rooms are $290 to $320 double. The more expensive rooms are efficiencies with kitchenettes. Closed mid-October to mid-May.

Chatham Seafarer, 2079 Rte. 28 (about ½ mile east of Rte. 137), Chatham (✆ **800/786-2772** or 508/432-1739; www.chathamseafarer.com), is a lovely, personable, well-run motel on Route 28. It's only about a half-mile from Ridgevale Beach, but there is also a pool here. Rates are $165 to $215 double.

The least expensive option is the **Chatham Motel,** 1487 Main St./Rte. 28, Chatham (✆ **800/770-5545** or 508/945-2630; www.chathammotel.com), 1½ miles from Hardings Beach. Look for the shingled motel with yellow shutters. There's an outdoor pool, shuffleboard, and plenty of barbecue grills. Summer rates in the 32 rooms are $165 double, $225 suite.

Very Expensive

Chatham Bars Inn ★★★ (Kids)　The grand historic Chatham Bars Inn, which is located on a private beach overlooking a barrier beach and the Atlantic Ocean, is one of the premier properties on Cape Cod. The main inn building is surrounded by 26 shingled cottages on 25 acres. Most rooms are tastefully up-to-date, and many have private balconies with views of the beach or the prettily landscaped grounds. A deluxe **spa** and 12 spa rooms have luxurious amenities, including Jacuzzi tubs and in-room saunas. The inn is walking distance to Chatham center's fine shops and restaurants, but the hotel's proximity to the beach and other activities on-site may mean you may never leave the property.

297 Shore Rd. (off Seaview St., about ¹/₂ mile northwest of the town center), Chatham, MA 02633. ✆ **800/527-4884** or 508/945-0096. Fax 508/945-5491. www.chathambarsinn.com. 205 units. Summer

$455–$725 double; $995–$1,050 1-bedroom suite; $790–$2,625 2-bedroom suite. AE, DC, MC, V. **Amenities:** 4 restaurants (the formal Main Dining Room, the Chef's Table & Wine Cellar, the Tavern, and the seasonal Beach House Grill located on the beach); babysitting; complimentary children's program for ages 4 and over, available morning–night in summer; concierge; putting green (Seaside Links, a 9-hole course open to the public, adjoins the resort; guests play for $18 fee); outdoor heated pool; room service; 3 all-weather tennis courts ($15 an hour); Health & Wellness Center offering spa and massage services and fitness equipment. *In room:* A/C, TV/VCR/DVD, fridge, hair dryer, Wi-Fi.

Expensive

Captain's House Inn ★★★ (Finds) This 1839 Greek Revival house—along with a cottage and a carriage house—set on 2 meticulously maintained acres is a shining example of its era and style. The hospitality and amenities here make this one of the top B&Bs on Cape Cod. The inn provides a wonderful array of extras, such as robes, bottled water, newspapers, early-morning coffee, and room service. The breakfast room is also the site of a **traditional tea.** Be sure to book your room well in advance.

369–377 Old Harbor Rd. (about ½ mile north of the rotary), Chatham, MA 02633. © **800/315-0728** or 508/945-0127. Fax 508/945-0866. www.captainshouseinn.com. 16 units, 14 with tub/shower combinations, 2 with shower only. Summer $260–$475 double. Rates include full breakfast and afternoon tea. AE, DISC, MC, V. **Amenities:** Exercise room; outdoor heated pool; room service. *In room:* A/C, TV/VCR, hair dryer.

Chatham Wayside Inn ★★ Centrally located on Chatham's Main Street, this former stagecoach stop, dating from 1860, has undergone a thoroughly modern renovation. Don't expect any musty antique trappings: It's all lush carpeting, a warehouse worth of Waverly fabrics, and polished reproduction furnishings, including four-posters. There's an outdoor heated pool in the back. This is one of the few inns on the Cape with rooms and a restaurant fully accessible to travelers with disabilities.

512 Main St. (in the center of town), Chatham, MA 02633. © **800/242-8426** or 508/945-5550. Fax 508/945-3407. www.waysideinn.com. 56 units. Summer $265–$325 double; $400–$475 suite. Off-season packages available. DISC, MC, V. **Amenities:** Restaurant/bar (see review below); outdoor heated pool. *In room:* A/C, TV/VCR, hair dryer.

Pleasant Bay Village ★★ Across the street from Pleasant Bay, a few minutes' walk from Pleasant Bay Beach, this is one fancy motel (with prices set accordingly). The 6-acre complex has an array of rooms and cottages, done in restful pastels. Many bathrooms feature marble countertops and stone floors. In summer, you can order lunch from the **grill** without having to leave your place at the heated pool.

1191 Orleans Rd./Rte. 28 (about 3 miles north of Chatham center), Chatham, MA 02633. © **800/547-1011** or 508/945-1133. Fax 508/945-9701. www.pleasantbayvillage.com. 58 units. Summer $185–$265 double; $265–$525 1- or 2-bedroom suite (for 4 occupants). AE, MC, V. Closed Nov–Apr. **Amenities:** Restaurant (breakfast May–Oct; lunch and dinner July–Aug only); 8-person hot tub; heated pool. *In room:* A/C, TV, fridge, hair dryer.

Moderate

Moses Nickerson House ★ (Value) Your host George "I am not Moses" Watts and his wife, Linda, run this gem of a B&B with a sense of humor mixed with gracious hospitality. A grand captain's home in the classicist style, this 1839 manse's every inch is devoted to stylish comfort.

364 Old Harbor Rd. (about ½ mile north of Main St.), Chatham, MA 02633. © **800/628-6972** or 508/945-5859. Fax 508/945-7087. www.mosesnickersonhouse.com. 7 units, 1 with tub/shower combination, 6 with shower only. Summer $209–$259 double. Rates include full breakfast and afternoon tea. AE, DISC, MC, V. *In room:* A/C, TV, hair dryer.

Expensive

The Blue Coral ★ NEW AMERICAN   "Seaside cuisine" starts on an outdoor court-yard just off Main Street. Specialties include the 3-pound lobster dinner with all the fixins' and sushi-grade bluefin tuna pan-seared with balsamic demi-glace. One of the most popular dishes is the lobster ravioli served with a brandy cream sauce. There's live entertainment in the form of jazz and blues on Thursday through Sunday nights in season. This place gets a big crowd on clear nights, so come early or late.

483 Main St. © 508/348-0485. www.thebluecoral.com. Reservations recommended. Main courses $18–$40. AE, DISC, MC, V. Early June–early Sept daily 11:30am–4pm and 5:30–10pm. Closed mid-Sept to early June.

Del Mar Bar & Bistro ★★ BISTRO   Wood-fired thin-crust pizza—try the fig and prosciutto—is a specialty at this urban-flavored bistro not far from Chatham center. Pasta choices include lobster and shrimp ravioli. Menu standouts are usually on the blackboard. That's where you'll find dishes incorporating freshly caught fish. The only downside to this restaurant is it's not on Chatham's main drag with all the other shops and restaurants. It's a short drive (about 1 mile) away. There is entertainment—reggae, steel drums, jazz—Wednesday to Sunday in season.

907 Main St. © 508/945-9988. http://delmarchatham.com. Reservations accepted for parties of 6 or more. Main courses $17–$28. AE, MC, V. Daily 5–10pm.

Moderate

Chatham Squire ★★ (Finds) AMERICAN   The Chatham Squire is the unofficial center of Chatham, where generations of summer residents mix with the year-rounders: fishermen and landed gentry. The surprise is that this quintessential Cape Cod pub has the best clam chowder in these parts. It turns out the Squire gets its clams from the elite clam beds off Monomoy, cultivated in pristine water and considered the freshest around. The menu also features pasta (zebra ravioli is filled with lobster meat) and barbecued baby back ribs (with the Squire's secret sauce), among other dishes.

487 Main St. (in the center of town). © 508/945-0945. http://thesquire.com. Main courses $11–$23. AE, DISC, MC, V. May–Oct Sun–Thurs 11:30am–10pm; Fri–Sat 11:30am–10:30pm. Call for off-season hours.

Chatham Wayside Inn ★ NEW AMERICAN   The Wayside's central location on Main Street makes it a good spot for a reasonably priced meal in Chatham. Diners have several seating choices depending on their mood (and the weather): the clubby tavern with gleaming wood tables surrounded by comfy Windsor chairs, the front room with cozy booths, or the large screened terrace, perfect during summer's dog days. More important, perhaps, is what's on the plate. Wayside specialties include crab cakes, or such entrees as rack of lamb and pesto cod. For something a little different, try the chowder; it's prepared Portuguese-style with double-smoked bacon, fresh quahogs, and red bliss potatoes. Whether it's summer or winter, you'll want to end your meal with the apple-and-cranberry crisp; the secret is the oatmeal-and-brown-sugar crust. The Wayside is an even better choice at lunchtime, when the terrace is the perfect spot to watch Main Street's parade of shoppers.

512 Main St. (in the center of town). © 508/945-5550. http://waysideinn.com. Reservations accepted. Main courses $16–$26. DISC, MC, V. May–Oct daily 11:30am–4pm and 5–10pm; Nov–Dec and Feb–Apr Tues–Sun 8–11am, 11:30am–4pm, and 5–9pm. Closed Jan.

The Impudent Oyster ★ INTERNATIONAL   All but hidden off the main drag, this perennially popular 1970s-era eatery—complete with decorative stained glass—continues to cook up fabulous fish in exotic guises, ranging from Mexican to Szechuan, but mostly Continental. The flavorful specialties of the house are the sole piccata (native sole with lemon, fresh herb, and caper butter sauce), the steak au poivre, and the *pesca fra diavolo* (local littlenecks, lobster, and other seafood simmered in a spicy sauce over fettuccine). A tavern menu is served at the bar from 3 to 5pm, with soup, salads, raw bar, chicken fingers, and burgers. There is also a children's menu. This place is very busy in the summer, so make a reservation.

15 Chatham Bars Ave. (off Main St., in the center of town). (C) 508/945-3545. Reservations recommended. Main courses $14–$20. AE, MC, V. Mon–Sat 11:30am–3pm and 5–9:30pm; Sun noon–3pm and 5–9:30pm.

Vining's Bistro ★★ (Finds) FUSION   If you're looking for cutting-edge cuisine in a sophisticated setting, venture upstairs at Chatham's innocuous-looking mini mall and into this ineffably cool cafe. The film-noirish wall murals suggest a certain bohemian abandon, but the food is up-to-the-minute and priced to suit young people. The menu offers compelling juxtositions such as the warm lobster tacos with salsa *fresca* and crème fraîche, or the spit-roasted chicken suffused with *achiote*-lime marinade and sided with a salad of oranges and jicama.

595 Main St. (in the center of town). (C) **508/945-5033.** http://viningsbistro.net. Reservations not accepted. Main courses $16–$24. AE, DC, MC, V. June to mid-Oct daily 5:30–9:30pm; call for off-season hours. Closed Jan–Mar.

Inexpensive

Carmine's Pizza ★ ITALIAN   A new-wave pizzeria that pays homage to the old ways with checkered tablecloths and soda-parlor chairs, this little eatery takes a bold approach to toppings—for example, pineapple, jalapeños, and pesto. A favorite is the Californian, with garlic, feta cheese, spinach, sautéed mushrooms and onions, plum tomato, artichoke, and Kalamata olives. Cool down after with their creamy gelato.

595 Main St. (in the center of town). (C) **508/945-5300.** Pizzas $10–$19. MC, V. May–Sept daily 10am–11pm; call for off-season hours. Closed Jan–Mar.

Red Nun Bar & Grill (Value) DINER   There used to be lots of casual little hole-in-the-wall places like this on the Cape. Now there are precious few. With just five tables and some bar seats, this is a good place to go early, late, or off-season. They serve comfort food, such as Mama's meatloaf, cheeseburgers, and a fish sandwich made from this morning's catch that was probably brought in by one of the guys bellied up to the bar. A good selection of beers is on tap, too.

746 Main St. (near Monomoy Theatre and Veterans Field). (C) **508/348-0469.** www.rednun.com. Main courses under $11. MC, V. May–Sept daily 11:30am–10pm; call for off-season hours. Closed Jan 15–Apr 1.

A Pie Shop

Marion's Pie Shop ★ (Finds)   Nearly a half-century's worth of summer visitors have come to depend on this bakery for dinner and dessert pies, from sea clam to lemon meringue. Load up on the fruit breads and sweet rolls, and you can pretend you're having a four-course B&B breakfast—on the beach.

2022 Rte. 28 (about ½ mile east of Rte. 137). (C) **508/432-9439.** http://marionspieshopofchatham.com. Mon–Sat 8am–6pm; Sun 8am–4pm.

Sweets

Chatham Candy Manor ★ (Kids) (Finds)   Normally I cross the street to avoid this type of temptation, but Naomi Turner's hand-dipped chocolates (her mother opened the shop in the 1940s) are just too good to pass up. Surely there can't be anything too terribly harmful in an occasional "cranberry cordial" or chocolate-dipped strawberry, right? But once you start perusing the old-fashioned oak cases, it can be very hard to stop. Turtles, truffles, and the homemade fudge are tops. Children line up to watch them make candy canes here at Christmas time.

484 Main St. (in the center of town). © **508/945-0825.** www.candymanor.com. June–Aug daily 9am–10pm; Sept–May daily 9am–6pm.

CHATHAM AFTER DARK

Although most towns boast some comparable event, Chatham's free **band concerts**—40 players strong—are arguably the best on the Cape and attract crowds in the thousands. This is small-town America at its most nostalgic, as the band, made up mostly of local folks, plays those standards of yesteryear that never go out of style. Held in **Kate Gould Park** (off Chatham Bars Ave., in the center of town) from July to early September, it kicks off at 8pm every Friday. Better come early to claim your square of lawn (it's already a checkerboard of blankets by late afternoon), and be prepared to sing—or dance—along. Call © **508/945-5199** for information.

Performance Arts

Monomoy Theatre   Every summer since 1958, the Ohio University Players have commuted to this jewel box of a 1930s theater to put on a challenging play a week, from musicals to Shakespeare. In late July they take a well-earned week off to cede the stage to the highly accomplished Monomoy Chamber Ensemble. Performances take place mid-June to August, Tuesday to Saturday at 8pm and Thursday matinee at 2pm. Closed September to mid-June. 776 Rte. 28 (about ¼ mile west of the rotary). © **508/945-1589.** www.monomoytheatre.org. Tickets $15–$25.

Bars & Live Music

The Chatham Squire   A great leveler, this local institution attracts patrons from all the social strata in town. CEOs, seafarers, and college students alike convene to kibitz over the roar of a jukebox or band (Fri–Sat off-season only) and their own hubbub. Good pub grub, too (see "Where to Dine," above). 487 Main St. (in the center of town). © **508/945-0945.** http://thesquire.com.

4 ORLEANS ★★

31 miles E of Sandwich; 25 miles S of Provincetown

Orleans is where the *Narrow Land* (the early Algonquin name for the Cape) starts to get very narrow indeed: From here on up—or "down," in paradoxical local parlance—it's never more than a few miles wide from coast to coast; in some spots, it's as little as 1 mile. All three main roads (rtes. 6, 6A, and 28) converge here, too, so on summer weekends, traffic can be fierce.

But this is also where the oceanside beaches open up into a glorious expanse some 40 miles long, framed by dramatic dunes and blessed—from a swimmer's or boarder's perspective—with serious surf. The thousands of ship crews who crashed on these shoals over the past 4 centuries could hardly be expected to assume so sanguine a view. Shipwrecks may sound like the stuff of romance, but in these frigid waters, hitting a sand bar usually spelled a death sentence for all involved. So enamored were local inhabitants by the opportunity to salvage that some improved their odds by becoming "mooncussers"—praying for cloudy skies and luring ships toward shore by tying a lantern to the tail of a donkey, so as to simulate the listing of a ship at sea.

Such dark deeds seem very far removed from the Orleans of today, a sedate town that shadows Hyannis as a year-round center of commerce. Lacking the cohesiveness of smaller towns, and somewhat chopped up by the roadways coursing through, it's not the most ideal town to hang out in, despite some appealing restaurants and shops. The village of East Orleans, however, is fast emerging as a sweet little off-beach town with allure for both families and singles. About 2 miles east is seemingly endless (nearly 10 miles long) **Nauset Beach** ★★★, the southernmost stretch of the Cape Cod National Seashore preserve and a magnet for the young and the buff.

ESSENTIALS

GETTING THERE   After crossing the Sagamore Bridge (see section 3, "Getting There & Getting Around," in chapter 3), head east on Route 6 or 6A, which converges with Route 28 in Orleans. Or fly into Hyannis (see section 3, "Getting There & Getting Around," in chapter 3).

VISITOR INFORMATION   Contact the **Orleans Chamber of Commerce,** 44 Main St. (P.O. Box 153), Orleans, MA 02653 (① **800/865-1386** or 508/255-1386; www.capecod-orleans.com), open year-round Monday through Friday from 10am to 3pm; or the **Cape Cod Chamber of Commerce** (see "Visitor Information," under "Brewster," earlier in this chapter). There's an **information booth** at the corner of Route 6A and Eldredge Parkway (① **508/240-2484**). Its hours are mid-May to mid-October, Monday through Saturday from 9am to 5pm and Sunday from 11am to 3pm. Closed mid-October to mid-May.

BEACHES & RECREATIONAL PURSUITS

BEACHES   From here on up, on the eastern side, you're dealing with the wild and whimsical Atlantic, which can be kittenish one day and tigerish the next. While storms may whip up surf you can actually take a board to, less-confident swimmers should definitely wait a few days until the turmoil and riptides subside. In any case, current conditions are clearly posted at the entrance. Weeklong parking permits ($50 for renters) may be obtained from **Town Hall,** at 19 School Road, Orleans (① **508/240-3700**). Day-trippers who arrive early enough—better make that before 10am on weekends in July and August—can pay at the gate (① **508/240-3780**).

- **Crystal Lake** ★, off Monument Road, about ¾ mile south of Main Street: Parking—if you can find a space—is free, but there are no facilities.
- **Nauset Beach** ★★★, in East Orleans (① **508/240-3780**): Stretching southward all the way past Chatham, this 10-mile-long barrier beach, which is part of the Cape Cod National Seashore but is managed by the town, has long been one of the Cape's gonzo beach scenes—good surf, big crowds, lots of young people. Full facilities, including a snack bar serving terrific fried fish, can be found within the 1,000-car parking lot; the in-season fee is $15 per car, which is also good for same-day parking at Skaket Beach (see below). Substantial waves make for good surfing in the special section reserved for that purpose, and boogie boards are ubiquitous. In July and August, there are concerts every Monday from 7 to 9pm in the gazebo.

- **Pilgrim Lake** ★, off Monument Road, about 1 mile south of Main Street: A beach parking sticker is necessary for this small freshwater beach, which has lifeguards.
- **Skaket Beach** ★, off Skaket Beach Road to the west of town: This peaceful bay beach is a better choice for families with young children. When the tide recedes (as much as 1 mile), little kids will enjoy splashing about in the tide pools left behind. Parking costs $15, and you'd better turn up early.

BICYCLING   Orleans presents the one slight gap in the 25-mile off-road **Cape Cod Rail Trail** ★★★ (© **508/896-3491;** www.mass.gov/dcr/parks/southeast/ccrt.htm): Just east of the Brewster border, the trail merges with town roads for about 1½ miles. The best way to avoid vehicular aggravation and fumes is to zigzag west to scenic Rock Harbor. Bike rentals are available at **Orleans Cycle,** at 26 Main St., in the center of town (© **508/255-9115;** www.orleanscyclecapecod.com), which charges $24 for a 24-hour rental, and there are several good places (see "Takeout & Picnic Fare," later in this chapter) to grab some snacks.

BOATING   You can rent a canoe (see below) and paddle around Town Cove, Little Pleasant Bay (to Sampson, Hog, and Pochet islands), and the body of water called simply The River. Experienced paddlers can paddle through Pleasant Bay to the inside shore of the Outer Beach.

Arey's Pond Sailing School, off Route 28, in South Orleans (© **508/255-0994;** www.areyspondboatyard.com), offers sailing lessons on Daysailers, Catboats, and Rhode 19s in season on Little Pleasant Bay. Individual lessons are $65 per hour; weekly group lessons are around $189. The **Goose Hummock Outdoor Center,** at 15 Rte. 6A, south of the rotary (© **508/255-2620;** www.goose.com), rents out canoes, kayaks, and more, and the northern half of Pleasant Bay is the place to use them; inquire about guided excursions. Canoe and kayak rentals are $50 to $75 per day.

FISHING   Fishing is allowed in Baker Pond, Pilgrim Lake, and Crystal Lake; the latter is a likely spot to reel in trout and perch. For details and a license, visit **Town Hall,** at 19 School Road (Post Office Square), in the center of town (© **508/240-3700,** ext. 305), or **Goose Hummock** (see "Boating," above). Surf-casting—no license needed—is permitted on Nauset Beach South, off Beach Road. **Rock Harbor** ★★, a former packet landing on the bay (about 1¼ miles northwest of the town center), shelters New England's largest sportfishing fleet: some 18 boats at last count. One call (© **508/255-9757**) will get you information on them all. Or go look them over. Rock Harbor charter prices range from $550 for 4 hours to $750 for 8 hours. Individual prices are also available ($140 per person for 4 hr.; $150 per person for 8 hr.).

FITNESS   If you're here for a while and need a place to stay in shape on rainy days, check out **Willy's Gym, Fitness, and Wellness Center,** at 21 Old Colony Way, at Orleans Marketplace (© **508/255-6826;** www.willysgym.com). The Cape's biggest (21,000 sq. ft.) exercise facility is air-conditioned and open year-round. Dozens of classes are offered weekly, from basic aerobics to tai chi and Indonesian martial arts. Willy's also provides child care. Day passes are $17.

ICE-SKATING   Orleans boasts a massive municipal rink, the **Charles Moore Arena** at 23 O'Connor Way, off Eldredge Park Way, about 1 mile southwest of the town center (© **508/255-5902;** www.charlesmoorearena.org). In season, it's open to the public Monday to Friday from 11am to 1pm. From September through March, it's open to the public Monday and Wednesday from 11am to 1pm, Thursday from 3:30 to 5pm, and Sunday from 2 to 4pm. Friday night is "Rock Nite" for party animals ages 9 through 14. The cost is $5 adults, $4 children 12 and under; skate rentals run $2.

NATURE & WILDLIFE AREAS   Inland there's not much, but on the Atlantic shore is a biggie: **Nauset Beach.** Once you get past the swarms of people near the parking lot, you'll have about 9 miles of beach mostly to yourself. You'll see lots of birds (take a field guide) and perhaps some harbor seals off-season.

TENNIS   Hard-surface public courts are located at the Nauset Middle School in Eldredge Park on a first-come, first-served basis; for details, contact the **Orleans Recreation Department** (© **508/240-3785**).

WATERSPORTS   The **Pump House Surf Shop,** at 9 Cranberry Hwy./Rte. 6A (© **508/240-2226;** http://pumphousesurf.com), rents and sells wet suits, body boards, and surfboards, while providing up-to-date reports on where to find the best waves. Surfboards rent for $20 to $30 a day. **Nauset Surf Shop,** at Jeremiah Square, Route 6A, at the rotary (© **508/255-4742;** www.nausetsports.com), also rents surfboards, boogie boards, skim boards, kayaks, and wet suits.

HISTORICAL MUSEUMS

French Transatlantic Cable Station Museum ★   This ordinary-looking house
was, from 1890 to 1940, a nexus of intercontinental communications. Connected to France via a huge cable laid across the ocean floor, local operators bore the responsibility of relaying stock-market data, keeping tabs on World War I troops, and receiving the joyous news of Lindbergh's 1927 crossing. Service was discontinued with the German invasion of France in 1940, and resumed briefly between 1952 and 1959, when it finally closed down; newer, automated technologies having rendered the facility obsolete. The exhibits, prepared with the assistance of the Smithsonian, are a bit technical for nonscientists, but docents on hand will patiently fill in the blanks.

41 Rte. 28 (corner of Cove Rd., north of Main St.). © **508/240-1735.** www.frenchcablestationmuseum. org. Free admission. July–Aug Thurs–Sun 1–4pm; June and Sept Fri–Sun 1–4pm. Closed Oct–May.

Jonathan Young Windmill (Kids)   The majestic old windmill in Cove Park (next to
Town Cove) has been authentically restored and is open for guided tours in season. Though it is no longer grinding corn and barley, the mill's works are fully operable. Most mills on the Cape have been moved many times from town to town, and the Orleans mill has certainly seen more than its share of relocations. The mill was built in the early 1700s in South Orleans. In 1839, it was moved to Orleans center and then to Hyannis Port. In 1983, it was moved back to Orleans and donated to the Orleans Historical Society. Some

of the guides at the mill are actual millers, who give visitors an entertaining spiel about **175** the millwrights (the men who built the mills and kept the gears in working order) and millers (who ground the corn) who have worked at this mill over the centuries.

Rte. 6A (just south of the rotary). ✆ **508/240-1329**. www.orleanshistoricalsociety.org/JYW.html. Free admission; donations accepted. Late June–Aug daily 11am–4pm; call for off-season hours.

Orleans Historical Society at The Meeting House Museum ★ Few Cape towns have quite so colorful a history as Orleans—the only town on the Cape with a non-English, non–Native American name. Upon separating from Eastham in 1797, Orleans assumed the name of an honored guest: future king Louis-Philippe de Bourbon, duke of Orleans, who safely sat out the Revolution abroad, earning his living as a French tutor. Orleans suffered British naval attacks during the War of 1812 and German submarine fire in 1918. You'll find a great many mementos in this 1833 Greek Revival church, along with assorted artifacts—from arrowheads to hand-hewn farm tools—and a thinly veiled terrorist threat, dated 1814, from a British captain offering to spare the town's saltworks in Rock Harbor for a paltry $1,000. The townspeople balked, a warship struck, and the home team triumphed in the Battle of Orleans.

3 River Rd. (at Main St., about 1 mile east of the town center). ✆ **508/240-1329**. www.orleanshistorical society.org/MHM.html. Donation $2. July–Aug Thurs–Sat 10am–1pm; off-season by appointment only.

BASEBALL

The **Orleans Cardinals,** the easternmost team in the **Cape Cod Baseball League** (www. capecodbaseball.org), play at Eldredge Park (off Eldredge Park Way, btw. rtes. 6A and 28). For a schedule, call the **Orleans Chamber of Commerce** (✆ **800/865-1386** or 508/255-1386), the **Orleans Recreation Department** (✆ **508/240-3785**), or the **League** (✆ **508/432-6909**).

KID STUFF

The **Charles Moore Arena** (see "Ice-Skating," above) offers respite from a rainy day. Young skaters—and anxious parents—might be interested to know that the Nauset Regional Middle School, in Eldredge Park, has its own **skateboard park,** with four ramps and a "fun box"; helmets are required.

SHOPPING

Though shops are somewhat scattered, Orleans is full of great finds for browsers and grazers.

ANTIQUES/COLLECTIBLES Got an old house in need of illumination, or a new one in want of some style? You'll find some 400 vintage light fixtures at **Continuum Antiques,** 7 S. Orleans Rd./Rte 28, south of the junction with Route 6A (✆ **508/255-8513**), from Victorian on down, along with a smattering of old advertising signs and venerable duck decoys.

ARTS & CRAFTS Stop by **Kemp Pottery,** 9 Cranberry Hwy./Rte. 6A, about one-quarter mile south of the rotary (✆ **508/255-5853;** www.kemppottery.com), and check out Steve Kemp's turned and slab-built creations. From soup tureens to fanciful sculptures, they're remarkably colorful and one of a kind.

Tree's Place, Route 6A, at the intersection of Route 28, Orleans (✆ **888/255-1330** or 508/255-1330; www.treesplace.com), is considered the premier gallery for contemporary realist work in the region. There is also an extensive fine-crafts, gift, and tile shop here.

BOOKS   In the Skaket Corners shopping center, on Route 6A, is a branch of the large retailer **Booksmith/Musicsmith** (✆ **508/255-4590;** http://booksmithmusicsmith.net).

FASHION   **Karol Richardson,** 47 Main St., in the center of town (✆ **508/255-3944;** www.karolrichardson.com), is a preview of Richardson's main showroom in Wellfleet; stop in to see the latest from this gifted ex-Londoner.

GIFTS   Birders will go batty over **Bird Watcher's General Store,** 36 Rte. 6A, south of the rotary (✆ **800/562-1512;** www.birdwatchersgeneralstore.com). The brainchild of local aficionado Mike O'Connor, who'd like everyone to share his passion, it stocks virtually every bird-watching accessory under the sun, from basic binoculars to costly telescopes, modest birdhouses to birdbaths fit for a tiny Roman emperor; there's also a good selection of CDs and field guides.

For something a little different, check out **Weekend,** 217 Main St., East Orleans (✆ **508/255-9300;** www.capeweekend.com), a boutique opened by former set designer Mari Pocari, in a historic building that used to be a general store. It sells one-of-a-kind colorful jewelry, art, women's fashions, baby apparel, and home design and spa products.

WHERE TO STAY

Expensive

A Little Inn on Pleasant Bay ★★ (Finds)   Set back from a winding road that follows the coast between Orleans and Chatham, A Little Inn on Pleasant Bay sits on a hill next to a cranberry bog and overlooks the water (Pleasant Bay, naturally). The four rooms in the peaceful main house, which dates to 1798, have been completely renovated in warm tiles, light woods, and subtle colors that reflect a sort of Zen–Pottery Barn aesthetic. An adjacent building has three additional rooms. There is also a carriage house with two rooms.

654 S. Orleans Rd., South Orleans, MA 02662. ✆ **888/332-3351** or 508/255-0780. www.alittleinnon pleasantbay.com. 9 units. $245–$315 double. Extra person $30 per night. Rates include continental breakfast and evening sherry. AE, MC, V. No children under 10. *In room:* A/C, hair dryer, no phone.

Moderate

The Cove ★   This well-camouflaged motel complex on busy Route 28 also fronts placid Town Cove, where guests are offered a free minicruise in season. The interiors are adequate, if not dazzling, and a small heated pool and restful gazebo overlook the waterfront. Some rooms have kitchenettes (complete with microwave). Be sure to request one with a balcony and a cove view.

13 S. Orleans Rd./Rte. 28 (north of Main St.), Orleans, MA 02653. ✆ **800/343-2233** or 508/255-1203. Fax 508/255-7736. www.thecoveorleans.com. 47 units. Summer $157–$196 double; $207–$234 suite or efficiency. AE, DC, DISC, MC, V. **Amenities:** Small heated pool. *In room:* A/C, TV/VCR, fridge, hair dryer.

Nauset Knoll Motor Lodge ★★ (Value)   Overlooking Nauset Beach, one of Cape Cod's most popular beaches, this nothing-fancy motel with picture windows will suit beach lovers to a T. The simple, clean rooms are well maintained; and, by staying here, you'll save on daily parking charges at Nauset Beach. The whole complex is owned by Uncle Sam and is under the supervision of the National Park Service.

237 Beach Rd. (at Nauset Beach, about 2 miles east of the town center), East Orleans, MA 02643. ✆ **508/255-2364.** www.capecodtravel.com/nausetknoll. 12 units. Summer $175 double. MC, V. Closed late Oct–early Apr. *In room:* TV, no phone.

The Orleans Inn ★   You can't miss this mansard-roofed beauty, perched right on the edge of Town Cove. Absolutely get one of the rooms facing the water. Built in 1875, the inn has been lovingly restored and maintains its central place in the community. The simple rooms, some with twin beds or sleeper sofas, are cheerful, with modern amenities and such extra touches as a box of chocolates on the bureau. Downstairs is a bar and restaurant with wonderful views of the cove.

3 Old Country Rd./Rte. 6A (P.O. Box 188, just south of the Orleans rotary), Orleans, MA 02653. © **800/863-3039** or 508/255-2222. Fax 508/255-6722. www.orleansinn.com. 11 units. Summer $175–$250 double; $250–$325 suite. Rates include full breakfast. AE, MC, V. Dogs allowed. **Amenities:** Restaurant/bar. *In room:* TV, fridge.

Ship's Knees Inn The rooms here aren't fancy—more like "homey" with quilts and nautical decor—but the proximity to Nauset Beach (a 5-minute walk from the inn) makes this restored sea captain's home a fine choice for those interested primarily in hitting the beach.

186 Beach Rd., East Orleans, MA 02643. © **888/744-7756** or 508/255-1312. Fax 508/240-1351. www. shipskneesinn.com. 16 units, 2 with shared bathroom. Summer $125–$130 double with shared bathroom; $175–$235 double. Rates include continental breakfast. AE, MC, V. **Amenities:** Pool. *In room:* A/C, TV, fridge, Wi-Fi.

Inexpensive

Nauset House Inn ★★ (Value) Just a half-mile from Nauset Beach, this reasonably priced country inn is a cozy setting for those seeking a quiet retreat. Several of the rooms in greenery-draped outbuildings feature such romantic extras as a sunken tub or private deck. The most romantic hideaway here, though, is a 1907 conservatory appended to the 1810 farmhouse inn.

143 Beach Rd. (P.O. Box 774; about 1 mile east of the town center), East Orleans, MA 02643. © **800/771-5508** or 508/255-2195. Fax 508/240-6276. www.nausethouseinn.com. 14 units, 6 with shared bathroom, 4 with tub/shower combination, 4 with shower only. Summer $80 single; $89–$99 double with shared bathroom; $120–$185 double with private bathroom. Rates include full breakfast. DISC, MC, V. Closed Nov–Mar. No children under 12. *In room:* No phone.

The Parsonage Inn ★ (Value) Blessed with charming British innkeepers, this 1770 full Cape—whose name describes its original function—offers a unique, personalized experience. Elizabeth Browne is an accomplished pianist who might, if the evening mood is right, take flight in a Chopin mazurka or Mozart sonata.

202 Main St. (P.O. Box 1501), East Orleans, MA 02643. © **888/422-8217** or 508/255-8217. Fax 508/255-8216. www.parsonageinn.com. 8 units, 3 with tub/shower combination, 5 with shower only. Summer $135–$180 double. Rates include full breakfast. AE, MC, V. *In room:* A/C, TV, hair dryer, Wi-Fi, no phone.

WHERE TO DINE

Expensive

Abba ★★★ INTERNATIONAL Abba, a local favorite, is a fresh take on fine dining in the Lower Cape. Tables are closely packed inside, so we prefer the covered outdoor-dining area behind the restaurant. Chef/co-owner Erez Pinhas of Israel creates what can be described only as fusion cuisine, a little Middle Eastern, a little European, a little New American, plus some Thai and New England thrown in. Where else can you start with a falafel, then try a steaming plate of shrimp pad thai, and end with chilled melon soup?

90 Old Colony Way, at West Rd. (2 blocks from Main St., toward Skaket Beach). © **508/255-8144.** www.abbarestaurant.com. Reservations highly recommended. Main courses $18–$27. AE, MC, V. June–Aug daily 5–10pm; call for off-season hours.

Joe's Beach Road Bar & Grille ★ NEW AMERICAN   This 1857 captain's house with adjoining tavern is a favorite with locals. While the front room has a more traditional ambience, the tavern space features a huge fieldstone fireplace and World War II posters. With denim tablecloths and bandannas serving as napkins, the atmosphere is casual. The 28-foot mahogany bar is a popular meeting place. The menu varies from fancy dishes such as grilled Atlantic salmon filet with a red-pepper *coulis* and basil vinaigrette to Joe's pizza (with goat cheese, roasted peppers, and spinach) or high-falutin' fish and chips—beer-battered, with saffron aioli.

At the Barley Neck Inn, 5 Beach Rd. (about ¹/₂ mile east of the town center), East Orleans. © 508/255-0212. www.barleyneck.com. Reservations accepted. Main courses $10–$25. AE, DC, MC, V. June–early Sept daily 5–10pm; call for off-season hours.

The Lobster Claw Restaurant ★ SEAFOOD   This family-owned-and-operated business has been serving up quality seafood for almost 30 years. There's plenty of room for everyone in this sprawling restaurant, where booths spill over with boisterous families, and the usual flotsam and jetsam hang artfully from the ceiling. Get the baked stuffed lobster here with all the fixings. There's a children's menu, as well as early-bird specials served daily from 4 to 5:30pm.

42 Rte. 6A (just south of the rotary). © 508/255-1800. www.lobsterclaw.com. Reservations not accepted. Main courses $10–$19. AE, DC, DISC, MC, V. Apr–Oct daily 11:30am–9pm. Closed Nov–Mar.

Mahoney's Atlantic Bar & Grill ★ NEW AMERICAN   Seafood is the specialty at this casual bar/restaurant on Main Street. Such dishes as tuna sashimi, grilled sea bass, and pan-seared lobster explain why you came to Cape Cod. The menu also offers poultry, meat, pasta, and vegetarian dishes. Sixteen wines are available by the glass for those who like to sample. Grab a booth and stay awhile. Thursday and Saturday nights in season, there's live jazz and blues with no cover.

28 Main St. (in the center of town). © 508/255-5505. www.mahoneysatlantic.com. Reservations not accepted. Main courses $16–$25. AE, MC, V. May–Sept daily 5–10pm; closed Mon Oct–Apr.

Inexpensive

Cap't Cass Rock Harbor Seafood ★ SEAFOOD   Most tourists figure that a silvered shack sporting this many salvaged lobster buoys has an inside track on the freshest of seafood. The supposition makes sense, but the stuff here is about par for the area and the preparations are plain. Nevertheless, it's fun to eat in a joint left untouched for decades as time—and dining fads—marched on.

117 Rock Harbor Rd. (on the harbor, about 1¹/₂ miles northwest of the town center). No phone. Reservations not accepted. Most main courses under $12. No credit cards. Late June to mid-Oct Tues–Sun 11am–2pm and 5–9pm. Closed mid-Oct to late June.

Land Ho! ★★ AMERICAN   A longtime hit with the locals (who call it, affectionately, "the Ho"), this rough-and-tumble pub attracts its share of knowledgeable tourists as well, drawn by the good prices and relaxed feeling. The food may be nothing to write home about, but it's satisfying and easy on the budget. Light fare, such as soup, pizza, and burgers, is served until midnight. Just being there (provided you can find the door; it's around back) will make you feel like an insider.

Rte. 6A and Cove Rd. © 508/255-5165. www.land-ho.com/orleans/home.html. Reservations not accepted. Main courses $9–$22. AE, DISC, MC, V. Mon–Sat 11:30am–10pm; Sun noon–10pm.

The Yardarm ★ PUB GRUB   This rowdy joint serves the best chowder in town. It's a delectable seafood concoction that comes in three sizes: little predicament, big predicament, and huge dilemma. Locals also flock to Prime Rib Night (Mon and Thurs), Mexican Night (Tues–Wed), and Steak Night (Fri–Sat). But you'll go to watch the colorful characters bellying up to the bar for a burger and a brew.

48 Rte. 28 (just east of Main St.). ✆ **508/255-4840.** www.yardarmrestaurant.com. Reservations not accepted. Most items under $15. AE, DC, MC, V. Daily 11:30am–3pm and 5:30–9:30pm.

Takeout & Picnic Fare

Fancy's Farm ★   Rarely are vegetables rendered so appealing, and many of them are grown locally. The charming barnlike setting contributes to this place's appeal, as do the extras—fresh breads, pastries, juices, sandwiches, and exotic salads and soups to go. This is a great stop on the way to Nauset Beach for picnic supplies.

199 Main St., East Orleans. ✆ **508/255-1949.** July–Aug Mon–Sat 6am–8pm, Sun 6am–6pm; Sept–June Mon–Sat 7am–6pm, Sun 6:30am–7pm. Closed Feb.

Nauset Fish & Lobster Pool ★   The area's premier spot for fresh seafood; the selection is extensive and bountiful.

38 Rte. 6A (just south of the rotary), Orleans. ✆ **508/255-1019.** July–Aug daily 9am–8pm; call for off-season hours.

Orleans Whole Food   The largest health-food store on the Cape, this bright and cheerful porch-fronted grocery offers all sorts of freshly made snacks and sandwiches to take out—or to tear into during an impromptu picnic in the adjoining garden.

46 Main St. (in the center of town), Orleans. ✆ **508/255-6540.** www.orleanswholefoodstore.com. Mon–Sat 8:30am–8pm; Sun 9am–6pm.

Sweets

Cottage Street Bakery ★   One of the Cape's best bakeries, this one specializes in homemade breads, cookies, and Danish. There are also homemade soups and tasty sandwiches.

5 Cottage St., Orleans. ✆ **508/255-2821.** www.cottagestreetbakery.com. Daily 6am–5pm; call for off-season hours.

The Hot Chocolate Sparrow ★★   This is the place to come for coffee and treats in Orleans. Real fudge flavors the hot chocolate and all mocha derivatives thereof. Frozen hot chocolate and frozen mochas are summer specialties. It's a good place to stop in, casually check the posters announcing local happenings, and then dive in for a remorseless pig-out.

5 Old Colony Way, Orleans. ✆ **508/240-2230.** www.hotchocolatesparrow.com. Apr–Oct daily 6:30am–11pm; Nov–Mar Sun–Thurs 6:30am–9pm, Fri–Sat 6:30am–11pm.

Sundae School ★   A smaller branch of the local chain (also in Dennis Port and Harwich Port), this little ice-cream shop offers some mighty sophisticated flavors.

210 Main St., East Orleans. ✆ **508/255-5473.** www.sundaeschoolicecream.com. Mid-May to early Oct daily 11am–10:30pm. Closed early Oct to mid-May.

ORLEANS AFTER DARK

Joe's Beach Road Bar & Grille (✆ **508/255-0212;** see "Where to Dine," above) is a big old barn of a bar that might as well be town hall: It's where you'll find all the locals exchanging juicy gossip and jokes. Live music ranges from jazz to rock to blues. There's never a cover charge.

There's often live music at **Land Ho!** (© **508/255-5165;** see "Where to Dine," above), the best pub in town. Performers are on the bill on Monday and Tuesday nights in season, and Thursday and Saturdays off-season. There's usually no cover charge.

The Academy Playhouse, 120 Main St., about ¾ mile southeast of the town center (© **508/255-1963;** www.apacape.org), makes a fine platform for local talent in the form of musicals and drama, recitals, and poetry readings. The 162-seat arena-style stage is housed in the town's old town hall (built in 1873). Tickets are $20. Shows take place July through August Tuesday to Sunday at 8pm; call for off-season hours. A children's theater series runs from late June to early September on Friday and Saturday mornings. Cost is $10.

The Outer Cape

The rest of the Cape may have its civilized enticements, but it's only on the Outer Cape that the landscape and even the air feel really beachy. You can smell the seashore just over the horizon—in fact, you can smell it everywhere you go because you're never more than a mile or two away from sand and surf.

You won't find any high-rise hotels along the shoreline here. No tacky amusement arcades either. Just miles of pristine beaches and dune grass rippling in the wind. You'll also see the occasional cottage inhabited by some lucky soul who managed to get his or her hands on it before the coastline became the federally protected Cape Cod National Seashore in the early 1960s.

Henry David Thoreau witnessed virtually the same peaceful panorama when he roamed here in the 1850s. With luck and determination on the part of current inhabitants and visitors, the landscape will remain intact. The Outer Cape, after all, is a place to play—in the sand, and in the delightful, unconventional towns that have flourished here, far from the rest of civilization.

While they share the majestic National Seashore, Outer Cape towns are quite diverse. Eastham, as the official gateway to the National Seashore, certainly gets its share of visitors, yet there is also a sleepy quality to this town, which used to have the distinction of being the turnip capital of the country. Grab a stool at a locals' joint, such as Flemings Donut Shop, on

Route 6, for a taste of Olde Cape Cod before there was ever any talk of a National Seashore.

Wellfleet, called the art-gallery town, is in my view one of the nicest towns on Cape Cod. The very strollable Main Street is lined with intriguing shops in historic buildings. Commercial Street, which leads to the harbor, has the art galleries, filled with work by mainly local artists inspired by this region. Wellfleet was for years one of the premier fishing villages on Cape Cod, and it still has a bustling and picturesque harbor. There are also freshwater ponds and National Seashore beaches; some of Cape Cod's finest swimming holes and most spectacular beaches line the coast of Wellfleet.

Tiny Truro is the least developed of the Cape's towns; it has the smallest population and the highest proportion of acreage reserved for the National Seashore. The center of town is one of those blink-and-you-miss-it affairs, though the fact that Truro has four libraries should tell you something about its residents.

Provincetown is a former Portuguese fishing village turned into an internationally famous art and gay colony with a flamboyant nightlife. The main drag (so to speak) is Commercial Street, with the best shopping on Cape Cod. Families come for the strolling, museums, and whale-watching; bon vivants for the restaurants, cafes, and entertainment; and gays for the camaraderie. And the beaches? Seemingly endless.

35 miles E of Sandwich; 21 miles S of Provincetown

Despite its optimal waterside location (the distance from bay to ocean is as little as 1 mile in spots), Eastham is one of the least pretentious locales on the Cape—and yet highly popular as the gateway to the magnificent Cape Cod National Seashore.

The downside—or upside, depending on how you look at it—is that there aren't many shops or attractions worth checking out. Even Eastham's colorful history, as the site of the Pilgrims' first encounter with hostile natives, has faded with time. A mock-1680s windmill in the center of town serves as a reminder of the days when, according to Cape historian Arthur Wilson Tarbell, Eastham served as "the granary of eastern Massachusetts." Few take the trouble to track down the graves of three "First Comers" in the Old Cove Burying Ground, on Route 6, a mile past the Orleans rotary, on the right (park at Corliss Way).

Mostly, though, this is a place to kick back and let the sun, surf, and sand dictate your day.

ESSENTIALS

GETTING THERE After crossing the Sagamore Bridge, head east on Route 6 or 6A. Once you pass straight through the Orleans rotary, you are in Eastham. Or fly into Hyannis or Provincetown (see section 3, "Getting There & Getting Around," in chapter 3).

Where to pahk the cah becomes somewhat of an issue on the Outer Cape: Lodgings in Eastham, Truro and Wellfleet all have ample free parking. Provincetown can be more of a challenge. Most inns there have space for one car per room.

VISITOR INFORMATION An information booth run by the town of Eastham is located at 1700 Rte. 6, at Governor Prence Road (✆ 508/255-3444), and is open Memorial Day to late September daily from 9am to 6pm, with reduced hours in the shoulder season. Call or write the **Eastham Chamber of Commerce** for an informational brochure: P.O. Box 1329, Eastham, MA 02642 (✆ 508/240-7211; www.easthamchamber.com). You may also contact the **Cape Cod Chamber of Commerce,** routes 6 and 132, Hyannis, MA 02601 (✆ 888/332-2732 or 508/362-3225; www.capecodchamber.org), open year-round Monday to Saturday from 9am to 5pm, Sunday and holidays from 10am to 4pm.

BEACHES & RECREATIONAL PURSUITS

BEACHES From here on up, the Atlantic beaches are best reserved for strong swimmers: Waves are big (often taller than you), and the undertow can be treacherous. The flat, nearly placid bay beaches, on the other hand, are just right for families with young children. The sand slopes so gradually that you won't have to worry about them slipping in over their heads. When the tide recedes (twice daily), it leaves a mile-wide playground of rippled sand full of fascinating creatures, including horseshoe and hermit crabs. Stickers for town beaches can be purchased ($55 for a weeklong pass) at the Department of Public Works office at 555 Old Orchard Rd. (✆ 508/240-5973), near the town dump. A day pass for $15 can be purchased at most town beaches and at the ocean-side National Seashore beaches ($15 per day, $45 for the season).

- **Coast Guard & Nauset Light beaches** ★★★, off Ocean View Drive: These pristine and popular National Seashore ocean beaches have lifeguards and restrooms. Coast Guard Beach, with its steep sand dunes, consistently ranks as one of the best beaches in the U.S. in national surveys. Though National Seashore beaches can be chilly (this is the Atlantic Ocean, after all), the water is clean and clear. Big waves attract lots of boogie boarders. Similar to all National Seashore beaches, the vistas are lovely (just 30 miles of beach). At Coast Guard Beach, the old white Coast Guard building is scenically perched on a bluff. At Nauset Light Beach, the red-striped lighthouse, having moved back from its oceanfront perch, looks over the parking lot. A short walk away are the Three Sisters Lighthouses, three squat structures that have been set in a parklike enclave. Parking either at the beach or the shuttle lot at the Salt Pond Visitor Center is $15 per day, $45 per season. Parking lots at these two beaches and the shuttle lot tend to fill up between 10am and 1pm. The shuttle runs every 5 to 10 minutes. Drop-off and pick-up at the beach is prohibited. Coast Guard Beach has a boardwalk that provides access to the beach and is convenient for people in wheelchairs.

- **First Encounter, Campground & Sunken Meadow beaches ★★:** All three offer the calm waters of Cape Cod Bay. The water is significantly warmer than at the ocean beaches listed above. At low tide, there are miles of flats, where youngsters might enjoy searching for sea creatures such as crabs. To get to First Encounter Beach, take Samoset Road, opposite town hall (on Route 6), and follow signs. To get to Campground Beach and Sunken Meadow Beach, follow Route 6 to the intersection of Brackett Road and turn onto Old County Road, then take a right on Massasoit Road. These town-operated bay beaches charge $15 a day; $55 per week. First Encounter Beach's name comes from the fact that it is thought to be the site of the first encounter between Pilgrims and Native Americans after the Pilgrims landed in Provincetown. No snack bar, but an ice-cream truck makes the rounds.

- **Great Pond & Wiley Park ★:** These two town-run freshwater beaches are also open to the public, on the same terms as the bay beaches. Both are off Samoset Road.

BICYCLING With plenty of free parking available at the **Cape Cod National Seashore's Salt Pond Visitor Center ★★** (✆ **508/255-3421;** www.nps.gov/caco/planyour visit/visitorcenters.htm), Eastham makes a convenient access point for the **Cape Cod Rail Trail ★★★** (✆ **508/896-3491;** www.mass.gov/dcr/parks/southeast/ccrt.htm). Northward, it's about 5 wildflower-lined miles to Wellfleet, where the trail ends; Dennis is about 20 miles southwest. A 1.5-mile spur trail, winding through locust and apple groves, links the visitor center with glorious Coast Guard Beach; it's for bikes only (no blades). Rentals are available at the **Little Capistrano Bike Shop** (✆ **508/255-6515;** http://capecodbike.com), at 30 Salt Pond Rd., just west of Route 6, and across the street from the Salt Pond Visitor Center. Bikes rent for about $23 per day. The best trailside eatery—fried clams, lobster, and the like—is **Arnold's** (✆ **508/255-2575;** http:// arnoldsrestaurant.com), on Route 6, about 1 mile north of the visitor center.

BOATING The best way to experience Nauset Marsh is by kayak or canoe. Rentals are available in neighboring towns: The closest source would be the **Goose Hummock Outdoor Center,** at 15 Rte. 6A, in Orleans (✆ **508/255-2620;** www.goose.com).

Jack's Boat Rental (✆ **508/349-9808;** www.jacksboatrental.com) is on Route 6, next to the Cumberland Farms store, in Wellfleet. Canoes rent for $55 a day, kayaks for $50 to $65 a day. Jack's also rents Sunfish sailboats and paddleboats. If you rent for 2 days, the third day is free. They have a seasonal outlet, from mid-June to early September, on **Wellfleet's Gull Pond** (✆ **508/349-7553).** Kayak and canoe rentals at Gull Pond cost $20 to $25 for a half-hour and $10 to $15 for each additional hour. After 3 hours, the fourth hour is free.

FISHING   Eastham has four ponds open to fishing; Herring Pond is stocked. Fresh-water-fishing licenses can be purchased at **Goose Hummock,** 15 Rte. 6A, Orleans (℃ **508/255-0455;** www.goose.com), or from the town clerk at Town Hall, 2500 Rte. 6 (℃ **508/240-5900**). For a shellfishing license, visit the **Natural Resources Department,** at 555 Old Orchard Rd. (℃ **508/240-5972**). Surf-casting is permitted at Nauset Beach North (off Doane Rd.) and Nauset Light Beach (off Cable Rd.).

FITNESS   Willy's Gym, Fitness and Wellness Center, 4730 Rte. 6, North Eastham (℃ **508/255-6370;** www.willysgym.com), offers racket sports, plus Nautilus and free weights, various classes, an Olympic pool, saunas, steam rooms, and whirlpools. Non-members pay $20 a day.

NATURE TRAILS   There are five self-guided nature trails with descriptive markers—for walkers only—within this portion of the Cape Cod National Seashore. The 1.5-mile **Fort Hill Trail,** off Fort Hill Road (off Rte. 6, about 1 mile south of the town center), takes off from a free parking lot just past the **Captain Edward Penniman House** ★, a fancy, multicolored 1868 Second Empire manse, maintained by rangers from the Cape Cod National Seashore. Seashore rangers lead occasional tours of the house's interior in season. You can visit the house in July and August, Tuesday to Friday from 1 to 4pm. Call the visitor center at ℃ **508/255-3421** (www.nps.gov/caco/index.htm). But the exterior far outshines the interior, and more interesting sights await outside. Check out the huge whale-jawbone gate before walking across the street to the trail. Following the trail markers, you'll pass "Indian Rock" (bearing the marks of untold generations who used it to sharpen their tools) and enjoy scenic vantage points overlooking the channel-carved marsh—keep an eye out for egrets and great blue herons—and out to sea. The Fort Hill Trail hooks up with the .5-mile **Red Cedar Swamp Trail,** offering boardwalk views of an ecology otherwise inaccessible.

Three relatively short trails fan out from the Cape Cod National Seashore's Salt Pond Visitor Center by Eastham. The most unusual is the .25-mile **Buttonbush Trail** ★, specially adapted for the sight-impaired, with a guide rope and descriptive plaques in both oversize type and Braille. The **Doane Loop Trail** ★, a .5-mile woodland circuit, about 1 mile east of the visitor center, is graded to allow access to wheelchairs and strollers. The 1-mile **Nauset Marsh Trail** ★ skirts Salt Pond to cross the marsh (via board-walk) and open fields before returning by way of a recovering forest. Look both ways for bike crossings!

SURFING   Hitting the surf is a popular pastime at the National Seashore beaches, such as Cahoon's Hollow, on the Outer Cape. For surfing, windsurfing, and kitesurfing lessons, contact Eric Gustafson of **Funseekers** (℃ **508/349-1429;** www.funseekers.org), which charges $120 for a 2-hour surfing lesson for one person. A 2-hour lesson for two people is $180, and for three people, it's $240. Kitesurfing lessons are $250 for 3 hours.

TENNIS   Five public courts are located at the **Nauset Regional High School** in North Eastham and can be used on a first-come, first-served basis; for details, contact the Nauset Regional High School (℃ **508/255-1505**). **Willy's Gym,** 4730 Rte. 6, North Eastham (℃ **508/255-6370;** www.willysgym.com), offers six indoor courts at a fee of $20 per person.

TWO MUSEUMS

The 1869 Schoolhouse Museum   Run by the volunteers of the Eastham Historical Society, this former one-room schoolhouse—with separate entrances for boys and girls—encapsulates the town's accomplishments. Exhibits range from early Native American

> ## ⓘ Tips   Drive with Caution
>
> There have been many serious accidents on Route 6 in Eastham, and as a result, the speed limit here declines rather abruptly from 55 to 40 mph. Eastham police are vigilant about enforcement.

tools to mementos of author Henry Beston's yearlong stay on Coast Guard Beach, which resulted in *The Outermost House,* as compelling a read today as it was back in 1928. And in case you were wondering—yes, that strange garden gate is in fact the washed-up jawbones of a rather large whale.

Nauset Rd. (off Rte. 6, opposite the Salt Pond Visitor Center). ⓒ **508/255-0788.** www.easthamhistorical. org. Free admission. July 4–Labor Day Mon–Fri 1–4pm; Sept Sat 1–4pm. Closed Oct–June.

Salt Pond Visitor Center at the Cape Cod National Seashore ★★   Begin your exploration of the seashore by taking a look at the center's excellent exhibits about this unique environment. After all, since you're undoubtedly going to spend a fair amount of time on the beach, you might as well find out how it came to be, what other creatures you'll be sharing it with, and how not to harm it or them.

Occupying more than half the landmass north of Orleans and covering the entire 30-mile oceanfront, the 44,000-acre Cape Cod National Seashore is a free gift from legislators who had the foresight to set it aside as a sanctuary in 1961. Take advantage of the excellent educational exhibits and continuous film loops offered here; particularly fascinating is a video about the 1990 discovery of an 11,000-year-old campsite amid the storm-ravaged dunes of Coast Guard Beach, which was about 5 miles inland when these early settlers spent their summers here. After absorbing some of the local history, be sure to take time to venture out—on your own or with a ranger guide—to the surrounding trails (see "Nature Trails," above).

Note: For more information about the Cape Cod National Seashore, journey up to Race Point, in Provincetown, where another visitor center is tucked into the dunes.

Corner of Nauset Rd. and Rte. 6. ⓒ **508/255-3421.** www.nps.gov/caco. Free admission. Late May to mid-Oct daily 9am–5pm; mid-Oct to late May daily 9am–4:30pm.

KID STUFF

No one will look askance if you let your kids try the **Buttonbush Trail ★** (see "Nature Trails," above) in a blindfold: In fact, it's encouraged, not only as a good way to foster empathy for the blind but also to heighten multisensory awareness. You'll find more pastimes, such as miniature golf, along Route 6, and, of course, at the beaches.

WHERE TO STAY

Expensive

Fort Hill Bed and Breakfast ★★   Overlooking Nauset Marsh in the scenic Fort Hill area is the delightfully sophisticated Fort Hill Bed and Breakfast. Built in the Greek Revival style of the mid-1800s, this former farmhouse-turned-B&B offers three suites, all of which have queen-size beds. The spacious and pleasant Emma suite includes a living area complete with a piano and a library of excellent books. The bathroom is plenty roomy and has a large bay window. The Nantucket cottage is perfect for those looking for that extra bit of privacy or space, and the separate kitchen and large living area with working fireplace make for comfortable digs for a longer stay. The warm and amiable innkeepers, Jean and Gordon Avery, serve up a creative and delicious breakfast.

75 Fort Hill Rd., Eastham, MA 02642. ℰ **508/240-2870.** www.forthillbedandbreakfast.com. 3 units. Memorial Day–Columbus Day $235–$325. Rates include full breakfast. Ask about weekly discounts for the Nantucket cottage. No credit cards. No children under 18. Closed Thanksgiving and Christmas. **Amenities:** Wi-Fi in main living area. *In room:* A/C, TV/VCR, kitchen (Nantucket cottage only), hair dryer, no phone.

The Whalewalk Inn & Spa ★★ (Finds) This is where you stay if you are looking for a deluxe B&B in the Outer Cape. Regularly hailed as one of the Cape's prettiest inns, this 1830 Greek Revival manse fully deserves its reputation. Located in a quiet residential area just a few blocks off the Rail Trail, the inn is decorated in a tasteful, mostly pastel, palette. A six-room carriage house sports deluxe rooms with antique four-poster beds, fireplaces, and private decks, and several have whirlpool tubs for two. An on-site **spa** makes this inn even more noteworthy.

220 Bridge Rd. (about ¾ mile west of the Orleans rotary), Eastham, MA 02642. ℰ **800/440-1281** or 508/255-0617. Fax 508/240-0017. www.whalewalkinn.com. 16 units, 11 with tub/shower combination, 5 with shower only. Summer $310–$365 double; $420 suite. Rates include full breakfast. AE, DISC, MC, V. No children 11 and under. Closed Jan–Feb. **Amenities:** Resistance pool; hot tub; spa w/massage; sauna; weight machines. *In room:* A/C, TV/DVD/VCR, hair dryer.

Moderate

Inn at the Oaks ★ This 1869 Queen Anne Victorian, across the street from the Salt Pond Visitor Center and about a mile from Coast Guard Beach, is one of the few bed-and-breakfasts on Cape Cod with a billiard room. The large, colorful house is set well back from the road on a woodsy property. Rooms range from cozy to spacious; some have brass beds and claw-foot tubs. The carriage house in back has three large family suites.

3085 County Rd./Rte. 6 (opposite Salt Pond Visitor Center), Eastham, MA 02642. ℰ **877/255-1886** or 508/255-1886. Fax 508/240-0345. www.innattheoaks.com. 10 units, 7 with tub/shower combination, 3 with shower only. Summer $155–$195 double; $245–$270 suite. Rates include full breakfast and afternoon tea. AE, DISC, MC, V. Pets allowed in certain suites. **Amenities:** Billiard room; spa w/massage services and 2-person hot tub. *In room:* A/C, TV/DVD, hair dryer, Wi-Fi.

The Penny House Inn & Spa Whizzing past on Route 6, you'd scarcely suspect there's a peaceful inn tucked away behind a massive hedge. The rooms vary widely in size and price. Many rooms have fireplaces; a couple have whirlpool tubs. Five deluxe rooms are equipped with bathrobes, phones, TVs, and minifridges.

4885 Rte. 6, Eastham, MA 02642. ℰ **800/554-1751** or 508/255-6632. Fax 508/255-4893. www.penny houseinn.com. 12 units, 8 with tub/shower combination, 4 with shower only. Summer $215–$260 double; $335–$395 suite. Rates include full breakfast. AE, DISC, MC, V. **Amenities:** Heated outdoor saltwater pool; day spa w/hydro tub and massage. *In room:* A/C, TV/VCR (in some), fridge (in some), hair dryer, no phone (in some).

Inexpensive

Beach Plum Motor Lodge (Value) Look for the riot of flowers that Gloria Moll cultivates each year around her tiny front-yard pool, which is just big enough for a cool dip and fragrant sunning. The rooms—in classic little cabins out back—are also smallish, but they're more than adequate for most people's needs and very generously priced, especially when you take into account the home-baked breakfast treats.

2555 Rte. 6 (about ¼ mile north of the town center), Eastham, MA 02642. ℰ/fax **508/255-7668.** www. beachplummotorlodge.com. 5 units; 2 with shared, shower-only bathrooms. Summer $76–$82 double.

HI-Mid Cape Eastham Hostel (Value) Though nowhere near as picturesque as the Hostelling International–Truro, 14 miles north (see "Where to Stay," under "Truro," later in this chapter), this inland cluster of cabins makes a good stopover along the almost adjacent Rail Trail, and the bay is a quick glide away.

75 Goody Hallet Dr. (off Bridge Rd., about ¹/₂ mile west of the Orleans rotary), Eastham, MA 02642. (✆ **888/901-2085** or 508/255-2785. http://capecod.hiusa.org. 48 beds. $25–$35 per bunk for members; $28–$38 per bunk for nonmembers; $128–$175 private rooms. MC, V. Closed mid-Sept to mid-May. *In room:* No phone.

WHERE TO DINE
Moderate
Arnold's Lobster & Clam Bar ★★ (Finds)(Kids) AMERICAN Some consider this the best clam shack on the Cape for its fresh fish, hearty portions, and reasonable prices. Offering a takeout window on the Rail Trail and a picnic grove for those who hate to waste vacation hours sitting indoors, this popular eatery dishes out all the usual seashore standards, from rich and crunchy fried clams (cognoscenti know to order whole clams, not strips) to foot-long chili dogs. There's a good kids menu, too.

3580 Rte. 6 (about 1¹/₄ miles north of the town center), Eastham. (✆ **508/255-2575.** www.arnolds restaurant.com. Main courses $3–$34. No credit cards. Mid-June to mid-Sept daily 11:30am–9:30pm; call for off-season hours. Closed mid-Sept to late May.

Takeout & Picnic Fare
Box Lunch ★ (Finds) This is yet another source of the popular, Cape-invented pita "rollwiches."

4205 Rte. 6, North Eastham. (✆ **508/255-0799.** www.boxlunch.com. May–Oct daily 7am–8pm; call for off-season hours. Closed Jan.

Sweets
Ben & Jerry's Scoop Shop ★ (Kids) This premium ice-cream parlor is just about all most Eastham residents need in the way of evening entertainment.

50 Brackett Rd. (at Rte. 6), North Eastham. (✆ **508/255-2817.** www.benjerry.com/northeastham. July–Aug 8am–10pm; call for off-season hours. Closed Nov–Apr.

Hole-in-One Donut Shop Old-timers convene at the counter of this shop to ponder the state of the world. You can join in, or scurry home with your haul of hand-cut donuts and fresh-baked muffins and bagels.

4295 Rte. 6 (about ¹/₄ mile south of the town center), Eastham. (✆ **508/255-9446.** www.theholecapecod. com. Daily 5am–4pm.

EASTHAM AFTER DARK
Most Saturday nights in season (the schedule is somewhat erratic), the **First Encounter Coffee House,** Chapel in the Pines, 220 Samoset Rd., off Rte. 6, one-quarter mile west of town center; (no phone; **www.firstencounter.org**), a tiny 1899 church in Eastham, hosts some very big names on the folk and rock circuit, such as Livingston Taylor and Patty Larkin. Tickets are $15 to $20; call for a schedule. Closed May and September.

The **Salt Pond Visitor Center,** on Salt Pond Road, in Eastham, east of Rte. 6; ((✆ **508/255-3421;** www.nps.gov/caco/planyourvisit/visitorcenters.htm), puts on a varying schedule of entertainment, including concerts and guest presentations, in season. A nominal fee ($2–$3) may apply. Call for a schedule.

2 WELLFLEET ★★★

42 miles NE of Sandwich; 14 miles S of Provincetown

Wellfleet—with the well-tended look of a classic New England village—is the favored destination of artists, writers, off-duty psychiatrists, and other contemplative types. Distinguished literati, such as Edna St. Vincent Millay and Edmund Wilson, put the rural village on the map in the 1920s, when Provincetown's bohemian heyday was fading. In her brief and tumultuous tenure as Wilson's wife, Mary McCarthy pilloried the pretensions of the summer population in her novel, *A Charmed Life,* but had to concede that the region possesses natural beauty: "steel-blue freshwater ponds and pine forests and mushrooms and white bluffs dropping to a strangely pebbled beach."

To this day, Wellfleet remains remarkably unspoiled. Once you depart from Route 6, commercialism is kept to a minimum, though the town boasts plenty of appealing shops—including a number of distinguished galleries—and a couple of excellent New American restaurants. It's hard to imagine any other community on the Cape supporting so sophisticated an undertaking as the Wellfleet Harbor Actors' Theatre, or hosting such a wholesome event as public square dancing on the Town Pier. And where else could you find, right next door to an outstanding nature preserve (the Wellfleet Bay Wildlife Sanctuary), a thriving drive-in movie theater?

ESSENTIALS

GETTING THERE After crossing the Sagamore Bridge, head east on Route 6. Pass through the Orleans rotary, and continue on Route 6 to Wellfleet. Or fly into Provincetown or Hyannis (see section 3, "Getting There & Getting Around," in chapter 3).

VISITOR INFORMATION Contact the **Wellfleet Chamber of Commerce** (off Rte. 6), P.O. Box 571, Wellfleet, MA 02667 (© **508/349-2510;** fax 508/349-3740; www. wellfleetchamber.com), or the **Cape Cod Chamber of Commerce** (see "Visitor Information," under "Eastham," earlier in this chapter). The Wellfleet information center is open mid-June to mid-September 9am to 6pm daily. Call for off-season hours.

BEACHES & RECREATIONAL PURSUITS

BEACHES Though the distinctions are far from hard and fast, Wellfleet's fabulous ocean beaches tend to sort themselves demographically: LeCount Hollow is popular with families, Newcomb Hollow with high-schoolers, White Crest with the college crowd (including surfers and off-hour hang gliders), and Cahoon Hollow with 30-somethings. Only the latter two beaches permit parking by nonresidents ($15 per day). To enjoy the other two, as well as Burton Baker Beach, on the harbor, and Duck Harbor, on the bay, plus three freshwater ponds, you'll have to walk or bike in, or see if you qualify for a sticker ($35 for 3 consecutive days, $70 per week). Bring proof of residency to the seasonal Beach Sticker Booth, on the Town Pier, or call the **Wellfleet Recreation Department** (© **508/349-0314**). Parking is free at all beaches and ponds after 4pm.

- **Marconi Beach ★★**, off Marconi Beach Road, in South Wellfleet: A National Seashore property, this cliff-lined beach (with restrooms) charges an entry fee of $15 per

day, or only $45 for the season. *Note:* The bluffs are so high that the beach lies in
shadow by late afternoon.

- **Mayo Beach,** Kendrick Avenue (near the Town Pier): Right by the harbor, facing south, this warm, shallow bay beach (with restrooms) is very central but will please young waders and splashers. This is one of the few beaches on the Cape with free parking. Make sure you go at high tide; at low tide, oyster farmers take over. You could grab a bite (and a paperback) at the Bookstore Restaurant across the street, which serves three meals a day and sells used books around back.

- **White Crest & Cahoon Hollow beaches** ★★★, off Ocean View Drive, in Wellfleet: These two town-run ocean beaches—big with surfers—are open to all. Like all the oceanside beaches on the Outer Cape, there are large sand dunes bordering the beach, which is a wide-open and beautiful expanse. Both have snack bars and restrooms. What makes Cahoon Hollow Beach unique is that there is a restaurant/nightclub, The Beachcomber, in the beach parking lot. So you can go straight from your day at the beach to an evening of listening to live music and dancing, if you choose. Parking costs $15 per day.

BICYCLING   The end (to date) of the 25-mile (and growing) **Cape Cod Rail Trail** ★★★ (© 508/896-3491; www.mass.gov/dcr/parks/southeast/ccrt.htm), Wellfleet is also among its more desirable destinations: A country road off the bike path leads right to LeCount Hollow Beach. Located near the bike-path terminus, **South Wellfleet General Store** (© 508/349-2335) can see to your snacking needs and, next door, **Little Capistrano Bike Shop** (© 508/349-2363; http://capecodbike.com) rents bikes for $26 per day.

BOATING   **Jack's Boat Rentals,** on Gull Pond, off Gull Pond Road, about a half-mile south of the Truro border (© 508/349-7553; www.jacksboatrental.com), rents out canoes, kayaks, sailboards, and Sunfish, as well as sea cycles and surf bikes. Gull Pond connects to Higgins Pond by way of a placid, narrow channel lined with red maples and choked with yellow water lilies. Needless to say, it's a great place to paddle. Renting a kayak or canoe at Gull Pond for a couple of hours costs about $50. If you'd like a canoe for a few days, you'll need to go to the Jack's Boat Rentals location on Route 6 in Wellfleet (next to the Cumberland Farms). There a kayak rents for $50 for a single, and $65 for a tandem for 24 hours. Sunfish sailboats are $200 for 3 days. Rentals come with a roof rack if you need it. There are many wonderful places to canoe in Wellfleet—for example, a trip across the harbor from Wellfleet's Town Pier to Great Island.

For information about other excellent naturalist-guided tours, inquire about trips sponsored by the **Cape Cod Museum of Natural History** (© 508/896-3867; www.ccmnh.org) and the **Wellfleet Bay Wildlife Sanctuary** (© 508/349-2615).

The **Chequessett Yacht & Country Club,** at 680 Chequessett Neck Rd., in Wellfleet (© 508/349-3704; www.cycc.net), offers group sailing lessons. Call for rates. For experienced sailors, **Wellfleet Marine Corp.,** 25 Holbrook Ave., Wellfleet (© 508/349-6417; www.wellfleetmarine.com), rents 14- and 19-foot sailboats in season. The cost is $45 to $55 for the first hour, $16 to $19 for each additional hour, or $125 to $150 for the day. They also rent 14- to 16-foot motorboats for $45 to $70 for the first hour and $16 to $30 for each additional hour, plus a 20% fuel surcharge on all rentals.

FISHING   For a license to fish at Long Pond, Great Pond, or Gull Pond (all stocked with trout and full of native perch, pickerel, and sunfish), visit **Town Hall,** at 300 Main St. (© 508/349-0301). Massachusetts residents pay $14 for a 3-day pass or $29 for a season pass; nonresidents pay $25 for a 3-day pass or $39 for a season pass. Surf-casting,

Cape Cod National Seashore

No trip to Cape Cod would be complete without a visit to **the Cape Cod National Seashore,** on the Outer Cape, and an afternoon barefoot stroll along "The Great Beach," where you see exactly why the Cape attracts artists and poets. On August 7, 1961, President John F. Kennedy signed a bill designating 27,000 acres in the 40 miles from Chatham to Provincetown as the Cape Cod National Seashore, a new national park. Unusual in a national park, the Seashore includes 500 private residences, the owners of which lease land from the park service. Convincing residents that a National Seashore would be a good thing for Cape Cod was an arduous task back then, and Provincetown still grapples with Seashore officials over town land issues.

The Seashore's claim to fame is its spectacular beaches—in reality, one long beach—with dunes 50 to 150 feet high. This is the Atlantic Ocean, so the surf is rough (and cold), but a number of the beaches have lifeguards. Seashore beaches include **Coast Guard** and **Nauset Light** beaches, in Eastham; **Marconi Beach,** in Wellfleet; **Head of the Meadow Beach,** in Truro; and Provincetown's **Race Point** and **Herring Cove** beaches. A $45 pass will get you into all of them for the season, or you can pay a daily rate of $15.

The Seashore also has a number of walking trails—all free, all picturesque, and all worth a trip. In Eastham, **Fort Hill** (off Rte. 6) has one of the best scenic views on Cape Cod and a popular boardwalk trail through a red-maple swamp. The **Nauset Marsh Trail** is accessed from the Salt Pond Visitor Center, on Route 6, in Eastham. **Great Island,** on the bay side in Wellfleet, is surely one of the finest places to have a picnic; you could spend the day hiking the trails. On **Pamet Trail,** off North Pamet Road, in Truro, hikers pass the decrepit old cranberry-bog building (restoration is in the works) on the way to a trail through the dunes. Don't try the old boardwalk trail over the bogs here; it has flooded and is no longer in use. The **Atlantic White Cedar Swamp Trail** is located at the

which doesn't require a license, is permitted at the town beaches. Shellfishing licenses—Wellfleet's oysters are world-famous—can be obtained from the **Shellfish Department,** 35 Kendrick Avenue (✆ **508/349-0325**). Shellfish licenses are $50 per season for residents, $75 per season for nonresidents. Also heading out from here, in season, is the 60-foot party fishing boat *Naviator* (✆ **508/349-6003;** www.naviator.com), which charges $40 for adults, $35 for seniors, and $30 for children for a 4-hour trip, gear and bait provided. Charter boats include the *Erin-H* (✆ **508/349-9663;** www.virtualcape cod.com/erinh), charging about $575 for a half-day and $775 for a full day.

GOLF   Hugging a pretty cove, the **Chequessett Yacht & Country Club,** on 680 Chequessett Neck Rd. (✆ **508/349-3704;** www.cycc.net), has one of the loveliest 9-hole courses on the Cape; nonmembers need to reserve at least 3 days ahead. Greens fees are $33 for 9 holes, $44 for 18 holes; prices are lower in the afternoon.

NATURE & WILDLIFE AREAS   You'll find 6 miles of very scenic trails lined with lupines and bayberries—Goose Pond, Silver Spring, and Bay View—within the **Wellfleet Bay Wildlife Sanctuary,** in South Wellfleet (see below). Right in town, the short, picturesque

Marconi Station site; **Small Swamp** and **Pilgrim Spring** trails are found at Pilgrim Heights Beach; and **Beech Forest Trail** is located at Race Point, in Provincetown. The best bike path on Cape Cod is the Province Lands Trail, 5 swooping and invigorating miles, at Race Point Beach. If that's not enough in the way of sports, surf-casting is allowed from the ocean beaches—Race Point is a popular spot.

The Seashore also includes several historic buildings that tell their part of the region's history. At Race Point Beach, in Provincetown, the **Old Harbor Lifesaving Station** serves as a museum of early lifesaving techniques. **Captain Edward Penniman's 1868 house,** at Fort Hill, in Eastham, is a grandly ornate Second Empire home; and the 1730 **Atwood-Higgins House,** in Wellfleet, is a typical Cape-style home; both are open for tours. Five lighthouses dot the Seashore, including **Highland Light,** in Truro, and **Nauset Light,** in Eastham, both of which have been moved back from precarious positions on the edges of dunes.

Most of the Seashore beaches have large parking lots, but you'll need to get there early (before 10am) on busy summer weekends. If the beach you want to go to is full, try the one next door—most of the beaches are 5 to 10 miles apart. Don't forget your beach umbrella; the sun exposure here can get intense.

Getting There: Take Route 6, the Mid-Cape Highway, to Eastham (about 50 miles). Pick up a map at the Cape Cod National Seashore's **Salt Pond Visitor Center,** in Eastham (© **508/255-3421;** www.nps.gov/caco). Another visitor center is at **Race Point.** Both centers have ranger activities, maps, gift shops, and restrooms. Seashore beaches are all off Route 6 and are clearly marked. Additional beaches along this stretch are run by individual towns, and you must have a sticker or pay a fee.

boardwalk known as **Uncle Tim's Bridge,** off East Commercial Street, crosses Duck Creek to access a tiny island crisscrossed by paths. The Cape Cod National Seashore maintains two spectacular self-guided trails. The 1.25-mile **Atlantic White Cedar Swamp Trail,** off the parking area for the Marconi Wireless Station (see "Wellfleet Historical Sights," below), shelters a rare stand of the lightweight species of cedars prized by Native Americans as wood for canoes; red maples are slowly crowding out the cedars, but meanwhile, the tea-tinted, moss-choked swamp is a magical place, refreshingly cool even at the height of summer. A boardwalk will see you over the muck (these peat bogs are 7 ft. deep in places), but the return trip does entail a calf-testing half-mile trek through deep sand. Consider it a warmup for magnificent **Great Island,** jutting 4 miles into the bay (off the western end of Chequessett Neck Rd.) to cup Wellfleet Harbor. Before attaching itself to the mainland in 1831, Great Island harbored a busy whaling post; a 1970 dig turned up the foundations of an early-18th-century tavern. These days the "island" is quite uninhabited and a true refuge for those strong enough to go the distance. Just be sure to cover up, wear sturdy shoes, bring water, and venture to Jeremy Point—the very tip—only if you're sure the tide is going out.

A spiffy, eco-friendly visitor center serves as both introduction and gateway to the **Wellfleet Bay Wildlife Sanctuary,** off Route 6, a couple hundred yards north of the Eastham border, in South Wellfleet (© **508/349-2615;** fax 508/349-2632; www.wellfleet bay.org), a 1,000-acre refuge maintained by the Massachusetts Audubon Society. Passive solar heat and composting toilets are just a few of the waste-cutting elements incorporated into the seemingly simple $1.6 million building, which nestles in its wooded site like well-camouflaged wildlife. You'll see plenty of the latter—especially lyrical red-winged blackbirds and circling osprey—as you follow 5 miles of looping trails through pine forests, salt marsh, and moors. To hone your observation skills, avail yourself of the naturalist-guided tours offered during the day and sometimes at night (see "Wellfleet After Dark," later in this chapter); you'll see and learn much more. Also inquire about special workshops for children (some, like the Japanese "fish-printing" session, are truly ingenious), and about canoeing and birding trips. A listing of all Wellfleet Bay Wildlife Sanctuary events, with dates and times, is posted in the main building.

Trail use is free for Massachusetts Audubon Society members; the trail fee for non-members is $5 for adults and $3 for seniors and children. Trails are open July through August from 8am to 8pm, and September through June from 8am to dusk. The visitor center is open Memorial Day to Columbus Day daily from 8:30am to 5pm; during the off-season, it's closed Monday.

Note: It's worth joining the Massachusetts Audubon Society just for the chance—afforded only to members—to camp out here.

TENNIS   Public courts are located at Mayo Beach, on Kendrick Avenue, near the harbor; for details and exact fees, contact the **Wellfleet Recreation Department** (© **508/ 349-0314**). Also for a fee, book one of the five clay courts at the **Chequessett Yacht & Country Club,** on 680 Chequessett Neck Rd. (© **508/349-3704;** www.cycc.net), or one of the eight at **Oliver's Clay Courts,** at 2183 Rte. 6, about 1 mile south of town (© **508/ 349-3330;** www.oliversredclaytennis.com). Oliver's, which is notable for being shady, charges $16 an hour for court time. At Chequessett, 1 hour of singles play costs $22, doubles $24.

WATERSPORTS   Surfing is restricted to White Crest Beach, and sailboarding to Burton Baker Beach, at Indian Neck, during certain tide conditions; ask for a copy of the regulations at the Beach Sticker Booth on the Town Pier.

Eric Gustafson (© **508/349-1429;** www.funseekers.org) offers windsurfing and surfing lessons ($120 for 2 hr.) and, for the most adventurous, kite-boarding ($250 for 3 hr.). He also now teaches stand-up paddleboarding ($60 per hour) in the ocean and estuaries of Wellfleet. Stand-up paddleboarding, which comes from an ancient Hawaiian form of transport and uses a surfboard and paddle, is gaining popularity in the United States as a full-body workout.

WELLFLEET HISTORICAL SIGHTS

Marconi Wireless Station   It's from this bleak spot that Italian inventor Guglielmo Marconi broadcast, via a complex of 210-foot cable towers, the world's first wireless communiqué: "Cordial greetings from President Theadore [sic] Roosevelt to King Edward VII in Poldhu, Wales." It was also here that news of the troubled *Titanic* first reached these shores. There's scarcely a trace left of this extraordinary feat of technology (the station was dismantled in 1920); still, the displays convey the leap of imagination that was required.

Marconi Site Rd. (off Rte. 6, about ³/₄ mile south of the town center). © **508/771-2144.** www.nps.gov/ caco. Free parking and admission. Open dawn–dusk, year-round.

Wellfleet Historical Society Museum   Every last bit of spare Wellfleet memora- **193**
bilia seems to have been crammed into this old storefront. The volunteer curators have
taken pains to arrange the surfeit of artifacts so that visitors can follow up on a particular
interest—the United Fruit Company (now Chiquita Brands International, Inc.), say,
which got its start here in 1870 when one of Lorenzo Dow Baker's swift clipper ships
delivered a cargo of exotic bananas, or Marconi's mysterious transoceanic experiments.
Even restless children are likely to find something of interest, particularly among the
antique toys in the attic. The museum hosts fascinating speakers and sponsors a chowder
supper once a summer. Historical walking tours around town take 1¼ hours, cost $3, and
leave at 10:15am.

266 Main St. (in the center of town). ✆ **508/349-9157.** www.wellfleethistoricalsociety.org. Free admission. Late June–early Sept Tues and Fri 10am–4pm; Wed, Thurs, and Sat 1–4pm. Closed early Sept–late
June.

KID STUFF
No conceivable nocturnal treat beats an outing to the **Wellfleet Drive-In Theater**—
unless it's a double feature prefaced by a game of on-site minigolf while you're waiting
for the sky to darken. The restaurant on-site is the **Dairy Bar and Grill** (✆ **508/349-
0278;** www.wellfleetdrivein.com), which specializes in fried seafood and is open from
11:30am to 10pm daily in season. There's minigolf next to the restaurant. During the
day, check out what's up at the Wellfleet Bay Wildlife Sanctuary. (See "Beaches & Recreational Pursuits," above.)

SHOPPING
Boasting more than a dozen arts emporia, Wellfleet has begun hailing itself as "the art-
gallery town." Though it may lag behind Provincetown in terms of quantity, the quality
does achieve comparable heights. Crafts make a strong showing, too, as do contemporary
women's clothing and eclectic home furnishings. There's just one drawback: Unlike
Provincetown, which has something to offer virtually year-round, Wellfleet pretty much
closes up come Columbus Day, so buy while the getting's good.

ANTIQUES/COLLECTIBLES   Wheeler-dealers should head for the **Wellfleet Flea
Market,** 51 Rte. 6, north of the Eastham-Wellfleet border (✆ **800/696-3532** or 508/
349-2520; www.wellfleetdrivein.com/flea_market.htm). A few days a week in summer
and during the shoulder seasons, the parking lot of the Wellfleet Drive-In Theater "daylights" as an outdoor bazaar featuring as many as 300 booths. Though a great many
vendors stock discount surplus, there are usually enough collectibles dealers on hand to
warrant a browse through. An added bonus: Kids can kick loose in the little playground
or grab a quick bite at the snack bar. Lookers are charged $2 to $3 per carload. Open
weekends and Monday holidays, from mid-April through June, September, and October,
from 8am to 4pm; Wednesdays, Thursdays, weekends, and Monday holidays in July and
August, from 8am to 4pm.

   Farmhouse Antiques, Route 6, at Village Lane, Wellfleet (✆ **508/349-1708;** www.
farmhouseantiques.com), is a large storehouse filled with a variety of goods, including a
wide array of furniture, stacks of books and ephemera, and the antique chandeliers that
didn't fit in the Orleans shop, Continuum (Farmhouse is a dealer for Continuum's
wares).

ARTS & CRAFTS   **Cherrystone Gallery,** 70 E. Commercial St., about one-quarter
mile south of East Main Street (✆ **508/349-3026**), is slightly off the main arts drag and

THE OUTER CAPE

8

WELLFLEET

intentionally out of step, but this tiny gallery is probably more influential than all the others put together. It got a head start by opening in 1972 and showing such luminaries as Rauschenberg, Motherwell, and, more recently, Wellfleet resident Helen Miranda Wilson. Closed late September to mid-June.

One of the more distinguished galleries in town, the smallish **Cove Gallery,** 15 Commercial St., by Duck Creek (© **508/349-2530;** www.covegallery.com)—with a waterside sculpture garden—carries the paintings and prints of many well-known artists, including Barry Moser and Leonard Baskin. John Grillo's work astounds every summer during his annual show, which has featured boldly painted tango-themed paintings, watercolors, and prints. Alan Nyiri, whose dazzling color photographs are collected in the coffee-table book *Cape Cod,* shows regularly, as does Carla Golembe, whose lively Caribbean-influenced tableaux have graced several children's books. Closed mid-October through April.

Crafts make a stronger stand than art at **Left Bank Gallery,** 25 Commercial St., by Duck Creek (© **508/349-9451;** www.leftbankgallery.com). A 1933 American Legion Hall, it's an optimal display space. Whereas the paintings occupying the former auditorium sometimes verge on hackneyed, the "Potter's Room" overlooking the cove is packed with sturdy, handsome, useful vessels, along with compatible textiles. Also worth hunting out are the curious collages of Kim Victoria Kettler. The **Left Bank Small Works & Jewelry Gallery,** 3 W. Main St., in the center of town (© **508/349-7939**), features the spillover from the Left Bank Gallery, and in some ways, it's superior. There's also an irresistible sampling of new-wave jewelry designs, collected from over 100 noted artisans across the nation and arrayed in clever thematic displays.

FASHION At **Hannah,** 234 Main St. (© **508/349-9884**), Susan Hannah shows her own private label in this nicely rehabbed house, along with other designers' works. The emphasis is on flowing lines and relaxed fabrics—slinky rayon, soft cotton jersey, and nubby linen. Closed mid-September to late May.

Slightly more citified is **Off Center,** 354 Main St. (© **508/349-3634**), where the clothes are neither traditional nor trendy, but right-on, go-anywhere chic. Closed January through March.

Somewhat to the left of—and across the street from—its parent shop, Off Center, is **Eccentricity,** 361 Main St., in the center of town (© **508/349-7554**), which lives up to its name with dramatic antique kimonos and artifacts from Japan, India, and Africa. Closed January through March.

Karol Richardson, 11 W. Main St. (© **508/349-6378;** www.karolrichardson.com), is owned and operated by its namesake, an alumna of the London College of Fashion and a refugee from the New York rag trade. She has a feel for sensual fabrics and a knack for fashions that, in her own words, are "wonderfully comfortable but sophisticated at the same time and very flattering to the less-than-perfect body." The lovely clothes that are seasonally displayed in this barn showroom, and slavered over by several generations, bear out the claim. Closed mid-October through April.

GIFTS **Jules Besch Stationers,** 15 Bank St. (© **508/349-1231**), specializes in stationery products, including papers, ribbon, gift cards, handmade journals and albums, desktop pen sets, guest books, and unusual gift items. This is an exquisite store in a mansard-roofed former bank building and is certainly worth a browse. Closed January through March.

Moderate

Aunt Sukie's Bayside Bed & Breakfast ★   Sue and Dan Hamar's house is perched on a bluff in an exclusive residential neighborhood overlooking Cape Cod Bay. Behind the house, a boardwalk path leads to a private bay beach. The Nickerson Suite is in the old part of the house and has wide-board wood floors and a fireplace. The Chequessett and Billingsgate rooms are more contemporary, as befits the addition completed in 1993. All rooms have sweeping bay views. In the back is a large deck where guests eat breakfast and can sunbathe during the day.

525 Chequessett Neck Rd., Wellfleet, MA 02667. ℭ **800/420-9999** or 508/349-2804. www.auntsukies. com. 3 units, 1 with tub/shower combination, 2 with shower only, 1 cottage. Summer $195–$270 double; cottage $1,600 per week. Room rates include continental breakfast. MC, V. Closed mid-Oct to mid-May. *In room:* Fridge.

Even'tide ★ (**Kids**)   Set back from the road in its own roomy compound, complete with playground, this motel on the main highway of the Outer Cape feels more like a friendly village centered around a 60-foot, heated indoor pool—a godsend in inclement weather and a rarity in this part of the Cape. Besides the main motel building, there are seven cottages on the property with one, two, and three bedrooms. The Rail Trail goes right by the motel, and a 1-mile footpath through the woods leads to Marconi Beach.

650 Rte. 6 (about 1 mile north of the Eastham border), South Wellfleet, MA 02663. ℭ **800/368-0007** or 508/349-3410. Fax 508/349-7804. www.eventidemotel.com. 40 units, 39 with tub/shower combination, 1 with shower only. Summer $155–$180 double; $185–$220 efficiency. There is a $25 surcharge here Sat– Sun for a 1-night stay. AE, DISC, MC, V. Closed Dec to mid-Apr. **Amenities:** Playground; large heated indoor pool. *In room:* A/C, TV, fridge.

Surf Side Cottages ★★ (**Kids**)   This is where you want to be: just steps from a spectacular beach with 50-foot dunes, within biking distance of Wellfleet Center, and a short drive from Provincetown for dinner. The beach is LeCount's Hollow, and a path through the pines takes you to the sand. These cottages, fun and modern in a 1960s way, have one, two, or three bedrooms. All cottages have kitchens including microwaves, as well as fireplaces, barbecues, outdoor showers, and screened porches. Some have dishwashers and (most important) roof decks. From mid-May to mid-October, the cottages rent weekly. It's best to bring your own sheets and towels; renting a set costs $10 per person. Reserve early.

Ocean View Dr. (at LeCount Hollow Rd.; P.O. Box 937), South Wellfleet, MA 02663. ℭ/fax **508/349-3959.** www.surfsidecottages.com. 18 cottages, showers only. Summer $1,200–$2,500 weekly; off-season $95– $175 per day. MC, V. Closed mid-Nov to early Apr. Pets allowed in some cottages off-season. *In room:* Fridge.

Inexpensive

The Inn at Duck Creeke (**Value**)   This historic complex consists of four buildings set on 5 woodsy acres overlooking a tidal creek and salt marsh. Three lodging buildings include the main building, an 1880s captain's house, with charming but basic rooms, many with shared bathrooms; the carriage house, with cabin-style rooms; and the 1715 saltworks building, with smaller, cottage-type rooms with antique decor. In the main building, the shared bathrooms adjoin two rooms, so there's an intimacy here those in search of privacy might not desire. There's definitely a no-frills quality to this lodging option—towels are thin, and so are walls. There are two restaurants (see "Where to

Dine," below) on-site: **Sweet Seasons,** the more expensive, and the **Duck Creeke Tavern,** with a publike atmosphere and live entertainment in season.

70 Main St. (P.O. Box 364), Wellfleet, MA 02667. ⓒ **508/349-9333.** Fax 508/349-0234. www.innatduck creeke.com. 26 units, 8 with shared bathroom, 13 with tub/shower combination, 5 with shower only. Summer $95–$115 double with shared bathroom; $125–$140 double with private bathroom. Rates include continental breakfast. AE, MC, V. Closed Nov–Apr. **Amenities:** 2 restaurants (seafood restaurant and tavern). *In room:* No phone, Wi-Fi.

WHERE TO DINE
Expensive

Sweet Seasons Restaurant/Duck Creeke Tavern ★ NEW AMERICAN   Chef/owner Judith Pihl's Mediterranean-influenced fare is still appealing after 20-plus years, as is this mullion-windowed dining room's peaceful pond view. Some of the dishes can be a bit heavy by contemporary standards, but there's usually a healthy alternative: Wellfleet littlenecks and mussels in a golden, aromatic tomato-and-cumin broth, for instance, as opposed to Russian oysters with smoked salmon, vodka, and sour cream. Specialties of the house include creamy sage-and-asparagus ravioli, swordfish with artichoke tapenade, and Seasons shrimp with feta and ouzo. Lighter fare is served in the adjoining Duck Creeke Tavern, with main courses costing $9 to $17.

At the Inn at Duck Creeke, 70 Main St. (about ¼ mile west of Rte. 6). ⓒ **508/349-6535.** www.innatduck creeke.com. Reservations recommended. Main courses $17–$30. AE, MC, V. July–Sept Tues–Sun 5:30–9:30pm. Closed Oct–June.

Moderate

The Lighthouse (**Kids** AMERICAN   Nothing special in and of itself, this bustling, nearly year-round institution on Main Street is an off-season haven for locals and a beacon to passing tourists year-round. The casual, bustling atmosphere means it's a good place to bring kids. People might not notice right away that they are misbehaving. Except on Thursday's Mexican Night, the menu is all-American normal, from the steak-and-eggs breakfast to the native seafood dinners. Appreciative patrons usually keep up a dull roar throughout the day, revving up to a deafening roar as the Bass and Guinness flow from the tap.

317 Main St. (in the center of town). ⓒ **508/349-3681.** www.mainstreetlighthouse.com. Main courses $10–$25. DISC, MC, V. May–Oct daily 7am–midnight; call for off-season hours. Closed Mar.

The Wicked Oyster ★★ NEW AMERICAN   This old warehouse-style building on the way to Wellfleet Center has been converted into a cool and casual year-round restaurant. Several restaurants have come and gone from this spot, but this one looks like a keeper. There are several sections of the restaurant: an enclosed front porch, an ample dining room, and a large bar area. With a busy to-go area for coffee and pastries, this place definitely has a bustling atmosphere. You'll see families with small children, 20-something couples, and older folks enjoying this comfortable and convenient restaurant. Breakfast is popular here and features a multitude of omelets plus very strong coffee. For lunch, sandwiches and fried fish are on the menu. Dinner choices range from burgers to more refined options, such as pan-fried sole with lemon-caper butter; spring risotto with mushrooms and asparagus; or, for large appetites, grilled Angus tenderloin.

50 Main St. (just off Rte. 6, close to Wellfleet Center). ⓒ **508/349-3455.** www.thewickedo.com. Reservations recommended. Main courses $16–$26. MC, V. June–Aug daily 7am–noon and 5–9:30pm; call for off-season hours.

Winslow's Tavern ★★ BISTRO   This upscale bistro offers summertime treats, such as grilled lobster, along with such bistro classics as steak frites. Of course they have Wellfleet oysters, the town's world-famous bivalve. But they also have wonderful salads and light meals. With an alert waitstaff and contemporary setting, this is a very pleasant dining experience. On sunny afternoons, sit out on the front lawn here, the perfect perch for people-watching on Wellfleet's Main Street.

316 Main St. (in the center of town). © 508/349-6450. www.winslowstavern.com. Reservations for parties of 6 or more only. Main courses $13–$23. AE, MC, V. Mid-June to Aug daily noon–3pm and 5:30–9:30pm; call for off-season hours. Closed late Oct to mid-May.

Inexpensive

Mac's Shack ★ **Kids** SEAFOOD   Mac and Alex Hay are brothers on a mission: They want to run the best darn clam shack on Cape Cod. In 2006, they rehabbed the landmark Lobster Hutt building (it's the large building with the boat and fisherman on the roof) and opened to the raves of the summer crowd. Come here for Wellfleet's world-famous oysters from an expert shucker at the extensive raw bar. Standard clam-shack fare, such as lobster dinners and fried clams, is served, and there's a sushi bar. The large picnic tables and paper plates make this an indestructible place to bring kids.

91 Commercial St. (a few blocks north of Wellfleet Center). © 508/349-6333. www.macsseafood.com. Reservations not accepted. Main courses $8–$20. MC, V. Mid-June to early Sept daily 4:30–9:30pm; call for off-season hours. Closed mid-Oct to mid-May.

Moby Dick's Restaurant ★ **Kids** SEAFOOD   This is your typical clam shack, with the requisite netting and buoys hanging from the ceiling, but it just happens to be about the most popular one on Cape Cod. That's because of the consistent high quality of the food and fair pricing. This is how it works: You order your meal at the register, sit at a picnic table, and a cheerful college student brings you your meal. Fried fish, clams, scallops, and shrimp are all good here; try the Moby's Seafood Special—a heaping platter of all of the above, plus coleslaw and fries. The lobster bisque is quite popular. There's also a kids menu. Portions are huge; bring the family and chow down.

3225 Rte. 6. © 508/349-9795. www.mobydicksrestaurant.com. Reservations not accepted. Main courses $8–$20. MC, V. Mid-June to early Sept daily 11:30am–9:30pm; call for off-season hours. Closed mid-Oct to Apr.

Takeout & Picnic Fare

Box Lunch ★   With a porch usually hemmed in by bicycles, this is the original source of the Cape's signature "rollwiches": rolled pita sandwiches with unusual fillings, such as stuffing included in the turkey sandwich.

50 Briar Lane (north of Main St., in the town center). © 508/349-2178. www.boxlunch.com. Mid-June to mid-Sept daily 7am–4pm; mid-Sept to mid-June daily 7am–2:30pm.

Hatch's Fish & Produce Market **Finds**   This former fishing shack is the unofficial heart of Wellfleet. You'll find the best of local bounty, from fresh-picked corn and fruit-juice popsicles to steaming lobsters and home-smoked local mussels and pâté. Virtually no one passes through without picking up a little something, along with the latest talk of the town.

310 Main St. (behind Town Hall). © 508/349-2810 (fish) or 508/349-6734 (produce). www.hatchsfish market.com. June to mid-Sept 9am–7pm. Closed mid-Sept to May.

Mac's Seafood Market and Harbor Grill Restaurant ★ **Finds Kids**   Located on the town pier, this takeout shack with picnic tables features fresh local seafood unloaded from the boats just steps away. Besides grilled fish dinners, there are homemade chowders, seafood salads, sushi, and a raw bar. Perfect for families, you can sit on the picnic tables overlooking the harbor or take your meal over to Mayo Beach nearby. Wellfleet Town Pier. ℂ **508/349-9611.** www.macsseafood.com. Daily 11:30am–9:30pm. Closed Oct–late May.

Sweets

The Chocolate Sparrow ★ This closet-size outlet of a local chocolatier is hard to pass by once you've happened upon it. There's also a room full of penny candy.

326 Main St. (in the center of town). ℂ **508/349-1333.** Daily 10:30am–9:30pm. Closed early Sept–late May.

A Nice Cream Stop (Kids) This is Wellfleet's premier premium ice-cream parlor, scooping Emack & Bolio's, a luscious Boston boutique brand.

326 Main St. (in the center of town). ℂ **508/349-2210.** Mid-June to early Sept daily 11am–10pm. Closed early Sept to mid-June.

WELLFLEET AFTER DARK
Clubs & Watering Holes

The Beachcomber ★(Finds) Arguably the best dance club on Cape Cod, the 'Comber—housed in an 1897 lifesaving station—is definitely the most scenic, and not just in terms of the youthful clientele. It's right on Cahoon Hollow Beach—so close, in fact, that late beachgoers on summer weekends can count on a free concert: reggae, perhaps, or a local band covering Toots and the Maytals. Other nights, you might run into blues, ska, or rock. Parking is tricky here because the restaurant is on a busy beach, where parking costs $15. If you park in the Beachcomber lot before 5pm, the $15 cost can be put toward food or a T-shirt at the restaurant. After 5pm, parking is free. Open late June to early September daily noon to 1am; call for off-season hours. Closed early September to late May. 1220 Old Cahoon Hollow Rd. (off Ocean View Dr., at Cahoon Hollow Beach). ℂ **508/349-6055.** www.thebeachcomber.com. Cover varies $10–$25.

Duck Creeke Tavern Live music featuring local talent—jazz, pop, folk, blues, and various hybrids—is on the bill Thursday through Sunday nights in the summer. A good light-fare menu is also available. Check out the bar itself, fashioned from old doors. There is usually no cover. Closed mid-October to late May. At the Inn at Duck Creeke, 70 Main St. (about ¼ mile west of Rte. 6). ℂ **508/349-7369.** www.innatduckcreeke.com.

From Belfries to Bats & Other Entertainment

The **First Congregational Church of Wellfleet,** 200 Main St., about one-quarter mile west of Route 6 (ℂ **508/349-6877;** www.wellfleetchurch.org), hosts organ concerts Sundays at 8pm during July and August on its elaborate 1873 instrument. They're a good excuse to stop in and take a look around—the soaring 1850 Greek Revival church has the world's only bell tower ringing ship's time (an innovation introduced in 1952). Admission is free.

Wednesday nights in July and August, Wellfleet's workaday fishing pier (off Kendrick Ave.) resounds to the footfalls of avid amateur **square dancers** of every age. Call the Wellfleet Recreation Department at ℂ **508/349-0314** for more information.

How about a night hike or bat walk? Both are offered at the **Wellfleet Bay Wildlife Sanctuary** (ℂ **508/349-2615;** see "Beaches & Recreational Pursuits," earlier in this chapter). Rates vary; call for schedule and reservations. Just don't take in any vampire movies at the drive-in beforehand.

The **Wellfleet Drive-In Theater,** 51 Rte. 6, just north of the Eastham border
(✆ **508/349-7176;** www.wellfleetdrivein.com), clearly deserves National Landmark
status: Built in 1957, it's the only drive-in left on Cape Cod and one of a scant half-dozen
surviving in the state. The rituals are unbending and every bit as endearing as ever: the
playtime preceding the cartoons, the countdown plugging the allures of the snack bar,
and finally, two full first-run features. The drive-in is open daily from late May through
mid-September; show time is at dusk. Call for off-season hours. Admission is $7.50 for
adults and $4.50 for seniors and children 5 to 11.

The principals behind the **Wellfleet Harbor Actors' Theatre (WHAT),** 2357 Rte. 6
(next to the post office), or 1 Kendrick Ave. (next to the town pier; ✆ **508/349-9428;**
www.what.org), aim to provoke—and usually succeed, even amid this very sophisticated,
seen-it-all summer colony. WHAT's newer 200-seat space, the Julie Harris Stage, which
opened in June 2007 on Route 6, is up and running. Smaller shows are still done in the
90-seat harbor theater. WHAT for Kids shows are performed in a tent on the Route 6
property. What makes this theater stand out is that they go to great lengths to secure
original work, some local and some by playwrights of considerable renown, with the
result that the repertory rarely suffers a dull moment. Performances at the harbor and on
the Julie Harris Stage are given Wednesday to Sunday, with afternoon and evening shows
from late May through October; call or check their website for a schedule. Tickets are
$29 to $32. WHAT for Kids performances cost $9 for open seating in the tent, Mondays
through Thursdays at 7:30pm.

3 TRURO ★★

46 miles E of Sandwich; 10 miles S of Provincetown

Although Truro is one of those blink-and-you'll-miss-it towns, the location is great: a
tranquil village between charming Wellfleet and rowdy Provincetown. With only 1,600
year-round residents (fewer than in 1840, when Pamet Harbor was a whaling and shipbuilding port), the town amounts to little more than a smattering of stores and public
buildings, and lots of low-profile houses hidden away in the woods and dunes. As in
Wellfleet, writers, artists, and vacationing psychotherapists are drawn to the quiet and
calm. Painter Edward Hopper lived in contented isolation in a South Truro cottage for
nearly 4 decades.

The natives manage to entertain themselves with get-togethers at the Truro Center for
the Arts or, more simply, among themselves. There are free concerts on the village green,
across from the post office, on Thursday evenings in summer, and locals play croquet on
the green Sunday mornings. A lot of money may be circulating in this rusticated community, but inconspicuous consumption is the rule of the day. The culmination of the
social season, tellingly enough, is the late-September "dump dance," held at Truro's recycling center. For bigger kinds of excitement or cultural stimulation, Provincetown is only
a 10-minute drive away (you'll know you're getting close when you spot the wall-to-wall
tourist cabins lining the bay in North Truro).

ESSENTIALS

GETTING THERE After crossing the Sagamore Bridge, head east on Route 6 or 6A to
Orleans, and north on Route 6. Or fly into Provincetown (see section 3, "Getting There
& Getting Around," in chapter 3).

Contact the **Truro Chamber of Commerce,** Route 6A (at Head of the Meadow Rd.), Truro, MA 02666 (© **508/487-1288;** www.trurochamberof commerce.com); or the **Cape Cod Chamber of Commerce** (see "Visitor Information," under "Eastham," earlier in this chapter). The Truro Chamber office is open Monday through Friday 10am to 4pm in season.

BEACHES & RECREATIONAL PURSUITS

BEACHES   Parking at all of Truro's exquisite Atlantic beaches, except for one Cape Cod National Seashore access point, is reserved for residents and renters. To obtain a sticker ($30 per week), inquire at the beach-sticker booth, next to the North Truro Post Office (© **508/487-6983**). Walkers and bikers are welcome to visit such natural wonders as Ballston Beach, where all you'll see is silky sand and grass-etched dunes. Parking is free at all beaches after 4pm.

- **Corn Hill Beach** ★★, off Corn Hill Road: Offering restrooms, this bay beach—near the hill where the Pilgrims found the seed corn that ensured their survival—is open to nonresidents for a parking fee of $10 per day. The enormous parking lot ensures most visitors will get a spot. Be aware of the tide schedule; at low tide the water is too shallow for swimming unless you venture far from shore.

- **Head of the Meadow Beach** ★★★, off Head of the Meadow Road: Among the more remote National Seashore beaches, this spot (equipped with restrooms) is known for its excellent surf. Sand dunes bordering the beach are about 100 feet tall. Half of the beach is considered a town beach, and the other half is National Seashore; the latter section has the lifeguard. A colony of seals has taken to hanging out on an offshore sand bar on the south end of the beach. A parking lot connected by a short boardwalk to the beach makes this beach more easily accessible than other National Seashore beaches. It is also connected by a short bike path to Pilgrim Heights (see "Bicycling," below). Parking costs $10 per day or $30 per season in the town section of the lot, $15 per day or $45 per season in the National Seashore section of the lot.

- **Long Nook and Ballston beaches** ★★★, off Long Nook Road and off Pamet Road: These beautiful town-run ocean beaches are less crowded than the Wellfleet and Provincetown beaches and just as pretty. You need town beach stickers to park here.

BICYCLING   Although it has yet to be linked up to the Cape Cod Rail Trail, Truro does have a stunning 2-mile bike path of its own: the **Head of the Meadow Trail** ★, off the road of the same name (look for a right-hand turn about ½ mile north of where rtes. 6 and 6A intersect). Part of the old 1850 road toward Provincetown—Thoreau traveled this same route—skirts the bluffs, passing Pilgrim Heights (where the Pilgrims found their first drinking water) and ending at High Head Road. Being fairly flat as well as short, this stretch should suit youngsters and beginners. You can rent a bike in Provincetown or Wellfleet.

BOATING   The inlets of Pamet Harbor are great for canoeing and kayaking; when planning an excursion, study the tides so you won't be working against them. The closest rentals are in Wellfleet, at **Jack's Boat Rental** (© **508/349-9808;** www.jacksboatrental. com), on Route 6, next to the Cumberland Farms store.

FISHING   Great Pond, Horseleech Pond, and Pilgrim Lake—flanked by parabolic dunes carved by the wind—are all fishable; for a freshwater fishing license, visit **Town Hall,** at 24 Town Hall Road (© **508/349-7004**). You can also call town hall for a shell-fishing license. Surf-casting is permitted at Highland Light Beach, off Highland Road.

North Truro boasts the most scenic—and historic—9-hole course on the Cape.
Created in 1892, the minimally groomed, Scottish-style **Highland Links,** at 10 Lighthouse Rd., off South Highland Road (© **508/487-9201;** www.truro-ma.gov), shares a
lofty bluff with the 1853 Highland Light, where Thoreau used to stay during his Outer
Cape expeditions. Greens fees at the federally owned, town-run Highland Links are
reasonable ($33 for 9 holes, $55 for 18 holes).

NATURE TRAILS   The Cape Cod National Seashore, comprising 70% of Truro's land,
offers three self-guided nature trails. The .5-mile **Pamet Trail** ★, off North Pamet Road,
leads you past an old cranberry-bog building and bogs that have reverted to marshland.
Park in the lot to the left of the Hostelling International–Truro (see "Where to Stay,"
below) and walk back to the fire-road entrance about 500 feet down North Pamet Road.
The **Pilgrim Spring Trail** ★ and **Small Swamp Trail** ★ (each a .75-mile loop) head out
from the National Seashore parking lot just east of Pilgrim Lake. Pilgrim Spring is where
the parched colonists sipped their first fresh water in months. Small Swamp is named for
Thomas Small, a rather overly optimistic 19th-century farmer who tried to cultivate fruit
trees in soil more suited to salt hay. Both paths overlook Salt Meadow, a freshwater marsh
favored by hawks and osprey.

TENNIS   Courts are available at the **Pamet Harbor Yacht and Tennis Club,** 7 Yacht Club
Rd. (© **508/349-3772;** www.phytc.com). Hourly fees are $20 singles and $30 doubles.

A MUSEUM & AN ARTS CENTER

Highland House Museum and Highland Lighthouse   Built as a hotel in 1907,
the Highland House is a perfect repository of the odds and ends collected by the Truro
Historical Society: ship's models, harpoons, primitive toys, a pirate's chest, and so on. Be
sure to visit the second floor, set up as if still occupied by 19th-century tourists. In 1996,
Highland Lighthouse was moved back from its perilous perch above a rapidly eroding
dune. Now the lighthouse is within 800 feet of the museum and is also operated by the
Truro Historical Society. Seasonal lighthouse tours run May through October. There is a
48-inch height requirement, so little ones can't climb up the tower.

27 Highland Light Rd. (off S. Highland Rd., 2 miles north of the town center on Rte. 6). © **508/487-1121.**
www.trurohistorical.org. Admission to both museum and lighthouse $5 adults, free for children 12 and
under; admission to lighthouse $4 for all, with height requirement of 48 in. Museum June–Sept daily
10am–4:30pm (last tickets sold at 3:30pm); lighthouse May–Oct daily 10am–6pm. Closed Nov–Apr.

Truro Center for the Arts at Castle Hill   Send ahead for a brochure, and you
could work some learning into your vacation. A great many celebrated writers and artists—from poet Alan Dugan to painter Edith Vonnegut—emerge from their summer
hideaways to offer courses, lectures, and exhibits at this bustling little complex, an 1880s
horse barn with windmill (now home to the administrative offices). The roster changes
slightly from year to year, but you can rest assured that the stellar instructors will be at
the top of their form in this stimulating environment. The center also offers lots of children's workshops for artists age 7 and older. Castle Hill Evenings, which are $10 lectures
and readings, take place Tuesdays in July and August at 8pm at the Wellfleet Library.

10 Meetinghouse Rd. (at Castle Rd., about ³/₄ mile northwest of the town center). © **508/349-7511.**
www.castlehill.org. Admission varies. Call for schedule. Closed Oct–May.

A GALLERY WITH A SENSE OF HUMOR
The Susan Baker Memorial Museum, 46 Shore Rd./Rte 6A, one-quarter mile northwest of Route 6, North Truro (© **508/487-2557;** www.susanbakerart.com), showcases

Ms. Baker's creative output, from fanciful/functional papier-mâché objets to brightly colored European landscapes. Despite the place's name, Baker has not passed on; it seems that she herself has exaggerated rumors of her death so as to rate her own museum without actually croaking. You might guess that she is definitely a character, as original as her work. Her main stock in trade—here and at her Provincetown outlet—is humor displayed in various media, from artist's books to very atypical T-shirts (among the more popular slogans in Provincetown: "Too Mean to Marry"). Open June to September daily 10am to 5pm. Call ahead October through May.

A VINEYARD IN THE DUNES ★

Truro Vineyards of Cape Cod, 11 Shore Rd./Rte. 6A, North Truro (© **508/487-6200;** http://trurovineyardsofcapecod.com), is one of the last working farms in the Outer Cape and the site of an honest-to-goodness vineyard. The vineyard uncorked its first home-grown chardonnay and cabernet franc in the fall of 1996, the Muscadet in 1997, the merlot in 1998. Inside the main house on this pastoral property, the living room, with its exposed beams, is decorated with interesting oenological artifacts. Late May through October, free wine tastings are held Monday to Saturday from 11am to 5pm, Sunday noon to 5pm. Guided tours of the property take place at 1 and 3pm.

WHERE TO STAY
Moderate

Days' Cottages ★ (Value) These are the famous tiny cottages you always see in local paintings and photos. Lined up along the bay beach in North Truro, these absolutely identical cottages—named after flowers—are all white clapboard with sea-foam-green shutters. Although lacking frills, each has a living room, two small bedrooms, a kitchen, and a bathroom. The downside is that these accommodations are somewhat rough: The bedrooms are minuscule, and in some of the cottages, the fireplace has about 10 years' worth of graffiti written on the brick chimney. There is also the noise of passing cars on this busy stretch of road to contend with. The upside is miles of bay beach for walking and swimming, with views of Provincetown's quirky skyline in the distance. In season, beginning June 1, the cottages are rented only by the week, and they usually book up far in advance.

271 Rte. 6A (a couple miles south of the Provincetown border), North Truro, MA 02652. © **508/487-1062.** Fax 508/487-5595. www.dayscottages.com. 23 cottages, all shower only. Summer $150–$180 per night; $1,250 weekly. No credit cards. Closed mid-Oct to Apr. *In room:* Kitchen.

Kalmar Village ★★ (Value) (Kids) Spiffier than many of the motels and cottages along this spit of sand, this 1940s complex has little white cottages with black shutters. Cottages have picnic tables, grills, and daily maid service. Some cottages have air-conditioning. The clientele—mostly families—can splash the day away in the 60-foot freshwater pool or on the 400-foot private beach. This place books up early and by the week only in July and August.

674 Shore Rd./Rte. 6A (about ¼ mile south of the Provincetown border), North Truro, MA 02652. © **508/487-0585.** Fax 508/487-5827. www.kalmarvillage.com. 16 units, 40 cottages. Summer $125–$300 double; $655–$1,065 efficiencies weekly; $1,485–$2,600 cottages weekly. DISC, MC, V. Closed mid-Oct to mid-May. **Amenities:** Outdoor pool. *In room:* TV, fridge.

Outer Reach Resort (Value) This motel, set high on a bluff on Route 6 (the Mid Cape Hwy.), is where you stay if you are looking for a cheap, no-frills motel room and you don't plan to spend much time there. Rooms are clean and surprisingly spacious, some with king-size beds. Many rooms have distant ocean views, and some have balconies and views of Provincetown. But the complex is a bit run-down in places, and the staff is unusually surly (even by Cape Cod standards). In addition to the outdoor pool and tennis court, there's a basketball hoop and shuffleboard. The ocean is 1 mile east. There's a mediocre restaurant, Adrian's, within the complex. You're better off driving to Provincetown for dinner.

535 Rte. 6 (midway btw. North Truro center and the Provincetown border), North Truro, MA 02652. ☎ **800/942-5388** or 508/487-9090. Fax 508/487-9007. www.outerreachresort.com. 58 units. Summer $139–$189 double. MC, V. Closed late Oct to mid-May. Dogs allowed in some rooms for a fee. **Amenities:** Restaurant; outdoor pool; concrete tennis court. *In room:* A/C, TV, fridge, no phone.

Inexpensive

Hostelling International–Truro (Value) By far, the most scenic of the youth hostels on the Cape, this Hopperesque house on a lonely bluff a short stroll from Ballston Beach was once a Coast Guard station; these days it winters as an environmental-studies center. During the summer, it's a magnet for hikers, cyclists, and surfers.

111 N. Pamet Rd. (1¼ miles east of Rte. 6), Truro, MA 02666. ☎ **508/349-3889.** http://capecod.hiusa.org. 42 beds. $32–$35 bed in dorm room; $125–$150 private room. MC, V. Closed early Sept–late June.

WHERE TO DINE

Babe's Mediterranean Bistro ★ MEDITERRANEAN/MIDDLE EASTERN Formerly a humble little breakfast diner a stone's throw from the dunes of the Outer Cape, Babe's is now the Outer Cape's newest place for ethnic cuisine. Chef/owner Peter Thrasher takes his inspiration from the Eastern Mediterranean and North Africa in preparing his cuisine. The menu, which uses vegetables from the chef's garden, changes often. Flavors taste wonderfully different, making this a perfect place for diners unafraid to explore. Dishes to try include *Muhammara,* a hummuslike spread, served as an appetizer, with special bread; chickpea and asparagus soup; Turkish lamb kabobs; *Izmiri Krofte,* a type of meatball dish, with figs and peppers; and Moroccan chicken, served in a clay pot.

69 Shore Rd./Rte. 6A, North Truro. ☎ **508/487-9955.** www.babestruro.com. Reservations recommended. Main courses $14–$20. MC, V. June–Sept daily 5:30–10pm. Closed Oct–May.

Blackfish Restaurant ★★ NEW AMERICAN If you hear people whispering about a restaurant in Truro, it is probably this one, considered a secret place that only insiders know about. Set in the town's old Blacksmith Shop Restaurant, this place still has the rustic, casual feel of the old restaurant, but the cuisine—featuring such delicacies as foie gras, duck prosciutto, and Wellfleet mussels—gives it away as a spot for fine dining. Stick with the lovely fish dishes, such as panko-crusted sole with cauliflower mash, though the more adventurous will enjoy the rabbit ragu over fresh pasta. Burgers are also a specialty and come with such fancy toppings as goat cheddar and Worcestershire aioli.

17 Truro Center Rd./Rte. 6A, Truro. ☎ **508/349-3399.** Reservations recommended. Main courses $19–$24; burgers $9–$13. AE, MC, V. Late May to mid-Oct daily 5–10pm. Closed mid-Oct to late May.

Terra Luna ★ FUSION People come from miles around to sample the outstanding breakfasts at this modest restaurant. The muffins and scones emerge fresh from the oven, and entrees such as the breakfast burrito or strawberry mascarpone-cheese pancakes call for a hearty appetite. You can start in again in the evening, on well-priced Pacific Rim and/or neo-Italian fare, such as penne prosciutto sautéed with garlic, black pepper, and a splash of vodka. Main courses include local seafood and lobster dishes, such as lobster risotto with asparagus and saffron. There's even a creative children's menu here.

104 Shore Rd./Rte. 6A, North Truro. 📞 **508/487-1019.** www.theterraluna.com. Reservations recommended. Main courses $14–$20. AE, MC, V. Late May to mid-Oct daily 5:30–10pm. Closed mid-Oct to late May.

SWEETS & TAKEOUT

Jams (Finds)   Seeing as this deli/bakery/grocery is basically the whole enchilada in terms of downtown Truro, and seasonal to boot, it's good that it's so delightful. It's full of tantalizing aromas: fresh, creative pizzas; rotisserie fowl sizzling on the spit; or cookies straight from the oven. The pastry and deli selections deserve their own four-star restaurant, but they are all the more savory as part of a picnic.

14 Truro Center Rd. (off Rte. 6, in the center of town). 📞 **508/349-1616.** July–Aug 6:30am–6pm; call for off-season hours. Closed early Sept–late May.

---

4 PROVINCETOWN ★★★

---

56 miles NE of Sandwich; 42 miles NE of Hyannis

You made it all the way to the end of the Cape: one of the most interesting, rewarding spots on the Eastern seaboard. Throughout history, the place has thrilled just about everyone who's come here. Explorer Bartholomew Gosnold was surely pleased in 1602, when he and his crew happened upon a "great stoare of codfysshes" here (it wasn't quite the gold they were seeking but valuable enough to warrant changing the peninsula's name). The Pilgrims, of course, were overjoyed when they slogged into the harbor 18 years later: Never mind that they'd landed several hundred miles off course—it was a miracle they'd made it around the treacherous Outer Cape at all. Portuguese fishing and whaling crews from the Azores came here on purpose, found the sea generous, and built a life.

The painter Charles Hawthorne "discovered" the near-derelict fishing town in the late 1890s. Besotted by the "jumble of color in the intense sunlight accentuated by the brilliant blue of the harbor," he introduced the place to New York City's Greenwich Village intelligentsia. He'd probably be aghast at the commercial circus that rolls into town each summer, but he'd no doubt be proud that the Provincetown Art Association & Museum, which he helped found in 1914, is still going strong.

Every so often Provincetown has had an off year or dull stretch, but the town is wholeheartedly dedicated to creative expression, both visual and verbal, and right now it's on a roll. Some would ascribe the inspiration to the quality of the light (and it is particularly lovely—soft and diffuse) or the solitude afforded by long, lonely winters. But the general atmosphere of open-mindedness plays at least as pivotal a role, allowing a very varied assortment of individuals to pull together in pushing the cultural envelope. That same warm embrace of different lifestyles accounts for Provincetown's ascendancy as a gay and lesbian resort. During peak season, Provincetown's streets are a celebration of individual freedom and of the right to be as out as imagination allows.

The very traditional, devout Portuguese-American community still plies the maritime trades in Provincetown, and you might think that such a conservative culture would clash with free-spirited gays and artists. In fact, "family values" enjoy a very broad definition in this isolated settlement founded by the adventurous. Those who have chosen Provincetown (affectionately referred to as "P-town") know they live in a very special place, and in that, they have something precious in common.

ESSENTIALS

GETTING THERE   After crossing the Sagamore Bridge (see section 3, "Getting There & Getting Around," in chapter 3), head east on Route 6 or 6A to Orleans, and then north on Route 6.

If you plan to spend your entire vacation in Provincetown, you don't need a car, because everything is within walking or biking distance. And because parking is a hassle in this tiny town, consider leaving your car at home and taking a boat from Boston or Plymouth. Another advantage is that you'll get to skip the horrendous Sagamore Bridge traffic jams and arrive like the Pilgrims did.

Bay State Cruises (© 877/783-3779; www.provincetownfastferry.com) makes round-trips from Boston, daily from May to early October.

The high-speed *Provincetown Express* boat takes 90 minutes and makes three round-trips daily from mid-May to mid-October. It leaves 200 Seaport Blvd., at Boston's World Trade Center, at 8:30am, 1pm, and 5:30pm. On the return trip, it leaves Provincetown at 10:30am, 3pm, and 7:30pm. Tickets on the high-speed boat cost $49 one-way, $79 round-trip for adults. Seniors are $44 one-way and $73 round-trip. Children 3 to 12 are $32 one-way, $58 round-trip. Reservations are recommended.

The regular 3-hour boat, called *Provincetown II,* leaves from dockside at Boston's World Trade Center on Saturdays at 9am and arrives in Provincetown at 12:30pm. At 3:30pm, the boat leaves Provincetown, arriving in Boston at 6:30pm. On the slow boat, round-trip fare is $44 for adults and free for children through age 12 .

Boston Harbor Cruises (© 877/733-9425 or 617/227-4321; www.bostonharbor cruises.com) runs fast ferries from Boston's Long Wharf, next to the aquarium, to Provincetown's MacMillan Wharf. It's a 90-minute trip. In high season there are two or three round-trips a day from Boston, leaving at 9am and 2pm, with an additional 6:30pm trip Thursdays to Sundays. The boat leaves from Provincetown at 11am and 4pm, with an additional 8:30pm trip on Thursdays through Sundays. In the shoulder season, beginning in late May to mid-June and from early September to mid-October, there are one or two trips a day. Ferry tickets cost $79 round-trip for adults. Tickets for seniors cost $69 round-trip; tickets for children cost $58 round-trip. Bikes cost $6 each way. Reservations are a must on this popular boat.

Capt. John Boats (© 800/225-4000 or 508/747-2400; www.provincetownferry. com) connects Plymouth and Provincetown daily, weather permitting, mid-June through Labor Day; Tuesday, Wednesday, Saturday, and Sunday in September; and weekends only from late May to mid-June. The 90-minute boat ride leaves the state pier in Plymouth at 10am; it leaves Provincetown at 4:30pm. The adult round-trip fare is $40, seniors $35, children 11 and under $30; bikes are $5 extra.

You can also fly into Provincetown (see section 3, "Getting There & Getting Around," in chapter 3). **Cape Air/Nantucket Airlines** (© 800/352-0714 or 508/771-6944; www. flycapeair.com) offers flights from Boston in season. The trip takes about 25 minutes and costs $200 to $250 round-trip.

As far as getting around once you're settled, you can enjoy the vintage fleet of the **Mercedes Cab Company** (© 508/487-3333). There's also **Jody's Taxi** (© 508/487-0265). They charge only $7 per person to take passengers from MacMillan Pier to just about anywhere in town. Provincetown is such a funky place that it seems perfectly ordinary to use **Ptown Pedicabs** (© 508/487-0660) for your transportation needs. These cheerful bikers will ferry you up and down Commercial Street for about $1 per minute with a $5 minimum, plus extra for baggage. If you need to get from a gallery opening in the east end to dinner in the west end, this is the best way to do it.

VISITOR INFORMATION   Contact the **Provincetown Chamber of Commerce,** 307 Commercial St., Provincetown, MA 02657 (© **508/487-3424;** fax 508/487-8966; www.ptownchamber.com), open late May to mid-September daily from 9am to 5pm (call for off-season hours); the gay-oriented **Provincetown Business Guild,** 3 Freeman St., P.O. Box 421, Provincetown, MA 02657 (© **800/637-8696** or 508/487-2313; fax 508/487-1252; www.ptown.org), open Monday to Friday from 9am to noon and 12:30 to 2pm; or the **Cape Cod Chamber of Commerce** (see "Visitor Information," under "Eastham," earlier in this chapter).

GETTING AROUND

Parking is at a premium in Provincetown. Illegally parked cars are ticketed (even on Sun), and repeat offenders will be towed. If your inn provides parking, you may want to keep your car there and get around on foot, bicycle, or shuttle. **Provincetown's Summer Shuttle** (© **800/352-7155**) loops through town daily every 20 minutes late June to mid-September from 7am to 12:30am, traveling all along Bradford Street, to MacMillan

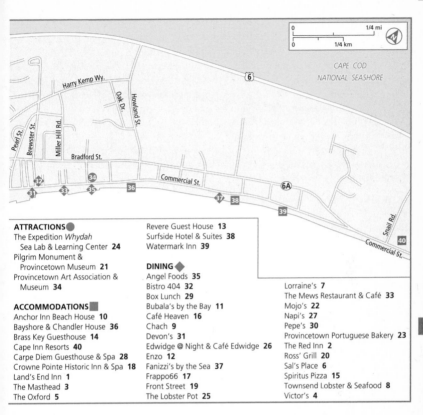

ATTRACTIONS ●
The Expedition *Whydah*
 Sea Lab & Learning Center **24**
Pilgrim Monument &
 Provincetown Museum **21**
Provincetown Art Association &
 Museum **34**

ACCOMMODATIONS ■
Anchor Inn Beach House **10**
Bayshore & Chandler House **36**
Brass Key Guesthouse **14**
Cape Inn Resorts **40**
Carpe Diem Guesthouse & Spa **28**
Crowne Pointe Historic Inn & Spa **18**
Land's End Inn **1**
The Masthead **3**
The Oxford **5**

Revere Guest House **13**
Surfside Hotel & Suites **38**
Watermark Inn **39**

DINING ◆
Angel Foods **35**
Bistro 404 **32**
Box Lunch **29**
Bubala's by the Bay **11**
Café Heaven **16**
Chach **9**
Devon's **31**
Edwidge @ Night & Café Edwidge **26**
Enzo **12**
Fanizzi's by the Sea **37**
Frappo66 **17**
Front Street **19**
The Lobster Pot **25**

Lorraine's **7**
The Mews Restaurant & Café **33**
Mojo's **22**
Napi's **27**
Pepe's **30**
Provincetown Portuguese Bakery **23**
The Red Inn **2**
Ross' Grill **20**
Sal's Place **6**
Spiritus Pizza **15**
Townsend Lobster & Seafood **8**
Victor's **4**

Wharf off Commercial Street, and all the way to North Truro. The beach loop travels to Herring Cove every 20 minutes from 9am to 7pm. Riders may flag down the bus at any intersection on Bradford Street. Service continues through October in Provincetown only, without the Truro stops. All rides cost $1 for adults, 50¢ for seniors and kids 6 to 17.

If you do drive into town, most inns have space for one car per room. Additional cars need to be parked on the street (and moved on "trash day"). Free street parking spaces can be almost impossible to find in high season. There are also several public and private parking lots throughout town that charge metered and day rates.

BEACHES & RECREATIONAL PURSUITS

BEACHES   With nine-tenths of its territory (basically, all but the "downtown" area) protected by the Cape Cod National Seashore (CCNS), Provincetown has miles of beaches. The 3-mile bay beach that lines the harbor, though certainly swimmable, is not all that inviting compared to the magnificent ocean beaches overseen by the National Seashore. The two official access areas (see below) tend to be crowded; however, you can always find a less densely populated stretch if you're willing to hike.

Note: Local beachgoer activists have been lobbying for "clothing-optional" beaches for years, but the rangers, fearful of voyeurs trampling the dune grass, are firmly opposed and routinely issue tickets, so stand forewarned (and fully clothed).

- **Herring Cove** ★★★ and **Race Point** ★★★: Both National Seashore beaches are spectacular, with long stretches of pristine sand, and they are very popular. Herring Cove, facing west, is known for its spectacular sunsets; observers often applaud. Race Point, on the ocean side, is rougher, and you might actually spot whales en route to Stellwagen Bank. Calmer Herring Cove is a haven for same-sex couples, who tend to sort themselves by gender. Parking costs $15 per day, $45 per season.
- **Long Point:** Trek out over the breakwater and beyond by catching a water shuttle to visit this very last spit of land, capped by an 1827 lighthouse. Locals call it "the end of the earth." Shuttles run hourly from 9am to 5pm in July and August—$8 one-way, $12 round-trip; hourly in season, or by demand off-season—from Flyer's Boat Rental (see "Boating," below), located at slip 2 on MacMillan Wharf.

BICYCLING North of town, nestled amid the Cape Cod National Seashore preserve, is one of the more spectacular bike paths in New England, the 7-mile **Province Lands Trail** ★★, a heady swirl of steep dunes (watch out for sand drifts on the path) anchored by wind-stunted scrub pines. With its free parking, the **Province Lands Visitor Center** ★ (© 508/487-1256; www.nps.gov/caco) is a good place to start: You can survey the landscape from the observation tower to try to get your bearings before setting off amid the dizzying maze. Signs point to spur paths leading to Race Point or Herring Cove beaches. The most centrally located bike rental store is **Arnold's Where You Rent The Bikes** (© 508/487-0844), at 329 Commercial St., near MacMillan Wharf. Bike rentals are also offered May through October at **Gale Force Bikes,** at 144 Bradford St. (© 508/487-4849; www.galeforcebikes.com), in the West End. The Province Lands Trail begins nearby. The Beach Market, on-site at Gale Force Bikes, offers delicious sandwiches and wraps (think Thanksgiving dinner—complete with roast turkey, stuffing, and fresh cranberries—in a wrap) and other picnic fare for your ride. It's also an easy jaunt from town, where you'll find plenty of good bike shops—such as **Ptown Bikes,** at 42 Bradford St. (© 508/487-8735; www.ptownbikes.com), where you should reserve several days in advance during high season. Bike rentals cost $20 for 24 hours.

BOATING In addition to operating a Long Point shuttle from its own dock (see "Beaches," above), **Flyer's Boat Rental,** at 131A Commercial St., in the West End (© 508/487-0898; www.flyersboats.com)—established in 1945—offers all sorts of crafts, from kayaks ($30–$50 half-day for singles and tandems) to various sailboats ($40–$75 for a half-day).

FISHING Surf-casting is permitted at Herring Cove Beach (off Rte. 6) and Race Point Beach (near the Race Point Coast Guard Station); many people drop a hand-line or light tackle right off the West End breakwater. For low-cost deep-sea fishing via party boat, board the *Cee Jay* (© 508/487-4330); it makes two 4-hour trips a day and costs $35 for adults and $25 for children. Both depart from MacMillan Wharf.

FITNESS For days when the weather forces your workouts indoors, the **Provincetown Gym,** at 81 Shank Painter Rd. (© 508/487-2776; www.ptowngym.com), has the usual equipment and promises a nonintimidating atmosphere. Day passes cost $15. The **Mussel Beach Health Club,** 35 Bradford St. (© 508/487-0001; www.musselbeach.net), attracts a rather buff clientele. Day passes are $20. For post-workout pampering, book a

massage or herbal wrap at the **West End Salon & Spa,** 155 Commercial St. (© 508/
487-1872; www.westendsalon.com).

NATURE TRAILS Within the Province Lands (off Race Point Rd., ½ mile north of
Rte. 6), the **Cape Cod National Seashore** maintains the 1-mile, self-guided **Beech For-est Trail** ★, a shaded path that circles a shallow freshwater pond blanketed with water
lilies (also look for sunning turtles) before heading into the woods. You can see the shift-ing dunes (much of this terrain is soft sand) gradually encroaching on the forest.

A walk along the **West End breakwater** ★★ and out to the end of **Long Point,** about
5 miles round-trip, is for hearty hikers. Walking just to the end of the wide breakwater,
located at the end of Commercial Street, next to the Provincetown Inn, is quite popular
and takes about 30 minutes each way. You'll see all ages maneuvering the layered boul-ders. If you want to continue to Long Point, the very tip of Cape Cod, it's about an 1½
hours across soft sand to the end of the point. At low tide the distance can be shortened
by cutting across the salt flats. **Wood End Lighthouse** is directly across the spit of sand
near the breakwater. **Long Point Lighthouse** is at the end of the point. Hikers deter-mined to reach the end of Long Point will want to bring a hat, water, and sunscreen for
this intense trek along the beach. The outside of the arm, where you look out on Cape
Cod Bay, tends to be the more scenic route for contemplative hikers; the inside of the
arm has views of Provincetown and Provincetown Harbor and a couple of shipwrecks.
The **Long Point Shuttle** runs from Flyer's Boat Rental in the West End across to Long
Point for $15 round-trip. Service is continuous in season.

TENNIS Three public courts are located at Motta Memorial Field, at the top of Win-slow Street (near the Provincetown Monument); for details, contact the **Provincetown
Recreation Department** (© **508/487-7097**). Open mid-May to mid-October, the
Provincetown Tennis Club, at 288 Bradford St. (© **508/487-9574;** www.province
towntennis.com), has seven courts—two asphalt, five clay—tucked amid tall trees. Court
time is $24 to $34 an hour. If you plan to visit the courts several times during your stay,
it may pay to get the season pass, $80 per person for unlimited play.

ORGANIZED TOURS

Art's Dune Tours ★★ In 1946, Art Costa started driving sightseers out to ogle the
decrepit "dune shacks," where such transient luminaries as Eugene O'Neill, Jack Kerouac,
and Jackson Pollock found their respective muses; in one such hovel, Tennessee Williams
cooked up the steamy *A Streetcar Named Desire.* The park service wanted to raze these
eyesores, but luckily saner heads prevailed: They're now National Historic Landmarks.
The tours conducted by Art's son and others, via Chevy Suburban, typically take about
1 to 1½ hours and are filled with wonderful stories of local literati and other characters.
Don't forget your camera for the views of this totally unique landscape. Additional tours
offered include a sunset clambake dune tour ($85 adults, $60 children) and a barbecue
tour ($75 adults, $55 children).

At the corner of Commercial and Standish sts. (in the center of town). © **800/894-1951** or 508/487-
1950. www.artsdunetours.com. Tickets $25 adults, $17 children 6–11. Sunset tours $38 adults, $24 chil-dren. Call for schedule and reservations.

Bay Lady II ★ In sightseeing aboard this 73-foot reproduction gaff-rigged Grand
Banks schooner, you'll actually add to the scenery for onlookers on shore. The sunset trip
is especially spectacular.

Whale-Watching: A Prime P-town Pastime

In 1975, 4 years after the U.S. government—fearing the species' extinction—called an official halt to whaling, fisherman Al Avellar noticed that they seemed to be making a comeback in the Stellwagen Bank feeding area, 8 miles off Provincetown. Together with marine biologist Charles "Stormy" Mayo of the Center for Coastal Studies, he came up with the notion of a new kind of hunt, spearheaded by tourists bearing cameras. An immediate success, their **Dolphin Fleet/Portuguese Princess** ★★, which works with the Center for Coastal Studies and uses their naturalists on the trips, on MacMillan Wharf (✆ **800/826-9300** or 508/240-3636; www.whalewatch.com), was widely copied up and down the coast. These are still the prime feeding grounds, however, which is why all the whale-watching fleets can confidently "guarantee" sightings—they offer a rain check should the cetaceans fail to surface. Prices for whale-watching trips are $39 for adults, $34 for seniors, $31 for children 5 to 12, and free for children 4 and under. Discounts of $3 off are available for AAA memberships and by using coupons available at the chamber of commerce.

Another good Cape Cod whale-watch organization is **Capt. John Boats,** which operates 4-hour trips daily in season out of Plymouth Harbor in Plymouth, about 20 miles north of the Sagamore Bridge (✆ **800/242-2469** or 508/746-2643; www.captjohn.com). Prices are $40 for adults, $34 for seniors, and $20 for children 12 and under.

On most cruises, running commentary is provided by naturalists with various qualifications. The naturalists aboard the *Portuguese Princess* are Center for Coastal Studies scientists who do research crucial to the whales' survival. Part of the *Princess'* tourist proceeds go to the center's efforts. Serious whale aficionados can take a daylong trip to the Great South Channel, where humpbacks and finbacks are likely to be found by the dozen.

Some tips for first-timers: Dress very warmly, in layers (it's cold out on the water), and definitely take along a windbreaker, waterproof if possible. The weather is capricious, and if you stand in the bow of the boat, the best viewing point, you can count on getting drenched. Veteran whale-watchers know to bring a spare set of dry clothes, as well as binoculars—although if the whales seem to be feeling friendly and frisky, as they often are, they'll play practically within reach of the boat. And last but not least, if you're prone to seasickness, bring along some motion-sickness pills: It can get pretty rough out there.

MacMillan Wharf (in the center of town). ✆ **508/487-9308.** www.sailcapecod.com. Tickets $20–$25 adults, $12–$20 children 12 and under. Mid-May to mid-Oct, 4 2-hr. sails daily at 10am, 12:30pm, 3:30pm, and 7pm; call for reservations. Closed mid-Oct to mid-May.

PROVINCETOWN MUSEUMS

The Expedition *Whydah* Sea Lab & Learning Center (Overrated Though the subject matter here is fascinating, this site is a bit of a tourist trap. Cape Cod native Barry Clifford made headlines in 1984 when he tracked down the wreck of the 17th-century pirate ship *Whydah* (pronounced *Wid*-dah, like Yankee for "widow") 1,500 feet off the coast of Wellfleet, where it had lain undisturbed since 1717. Only 10% excavated to date, it has already yielded over 100,000 artifacts, including 10,000 gold and silver coins, plus its namesake bell, proving its authenticity. In this museum/lab, visitors can supposedly observe the reclamation work involving electrolytic reduction, though it's unusual to see scientists or scholars actually at work removing barnacles. Some of the loot, like a surprisingly small man's boot, is displayed in cases.

MacMillan Wharf (just past the whale-watching fleet). $\textcircled{C}$ **508/487-8899.** www.whydah.com. Admission $10 adults, $8 seniors and children 6–12. June–Sept daily 10am–7pm; Oct–Dec and mid-Apr to May Sat–Sun only 10am–5pm. Closed Jan to mid-Apr.

Old Harbor Lifesaving Museum ★ (**Moments**) One of 13 lifesaving stations mandated by Congress in the late 19th century, this shingled shelter with a lookout tower was part of a network responsible for saving some 100,000 lives. Before the U.S. Life-Saving Service was founded in 1872 (it became part of the Coast Guard in 1915, once the Cape Cod Canal was in place), shipwreck victims lucky enough to be washed ashore were still doomed unless they could find a "charity shed"—a hut supplied with firewood—maintained by the Massachusetts Humane Society. The six valiant "Surfmen" manning each lifesaving station took a more active approach, patrolling the beach at all hours, sending up flares at the first sign of a ship in distress and rowing out into the surf to save all they could. When the breakers were too high to breach, they'd use a Lyle gun to shoot a line to be secured to the ship's mast, and over this, one by one, the crew would be pulled to shore astride a "breeches buoy"—like a lifesaving ring fitted out with canvas BVDs. All the old equipment is on view at this museum, and Thursday evenings at 6pm in season, rangers reenact a breeches-buoy rescue.

Race Point Beach (off Race Point Rd., about 2 miles northwest of the town center). $\textcircled{C}$ **508/349-3785.** www.nps.gov/history/maritime/park/oldhbrls.htm. Free admission; parking fee for Race Point is $15. July–Sept daily 2:30–5pm; call for off-season hours. Closed Nov–Apr.

Pilgrim Monument & Provincetown Museum ★★ You can't miss it: Anywhere you go in town, this granite tower looms, ever ready to restore your bearings. Climb up the 60 gradual ramps interspersed with 116 steps—a surprisingly easy lope—and you'll get a gargoyle's-eye view of the spiraling coast and, in the distance, Boston against a backdrop of New Hampshire's mountains. Definitely devote some time to the curious exhibits in the museum at the monument's foot, chronicling P-town's checkered past as both fishing port and arts nexus. Among the memorabilia you'll find polar bears brought back from MacMillan expeditions and early programs for the Provincetown Players. The museum now also houses the collection of the former Provincetown Heritage Museum, which includes a replica dune shack, furniture made by artist Peter Hunt, and paintings by Provincetown artists.

High Pole Hill Rd. (off Winslow St., north of Bradford St.). $\textcircled{C}$ **508/487-1310.** www.pilgrim-monument. org. Admission $7 adults, $5 seniors and students, $3.50 children 4–14. July to mid-Sept daily 9am–7pm; off-season daily 9am–5pm. Last admission 45 min. before closing. Closed Dec–Mar.

Province Lands Visitor Center of the Cape Cod National Seashore ★ Though much smaller than the Salt Pond Visitor Center, this satellite also does a good job of explicating this special environment, where plant life must fight a fierce battle to maintain its hold amid shifting sands buffeted by salty winds. After perusing the exhibits, be sure to circle the observation deck for great views of the parabolic dunes. A variety of ranger-guided tours and programs is offered daily in July and August, and frequently during the shoulder seasons. Inquire about special events, such as family campfires (reservations required).

There are also canoe programs ($15 adults, $9 children) and surf-casting programs ($12), both with equipment provided.

Race Point Rd. (about 1¹/₂ miles northwest of the town center). © **508/487-1256.** www.nps.gov/caco. Free admission. Mid-Apr to late Nov daily 9am–5pm. Closed late Nov to mid-Apr.

Provincetown Art Association & Museum ★★ (Moments This extraordinary cache of 20th-century American art began with five paintings donated by local artists, including Charles Hawthorne, the charismatic teacher who first "discovered" this picturesque outpost. Founded in 1914, only a year after New York's revolutionary Armory Show, the museum was the site of innumerable "space wars," as classicists and modernists vied for square footage; an uneasy truce was finally struck in 1927, when each camp was accorded its own show. In today's less competitive atmosphere, it's not unusual to see an acknowledged master sharing space with a less skilled upstart. Juried members' shows usually accompany the in-depth retrospectives, so there are always new discoveries to be made. Nor is there a hard and firm wall between creators and onlookers. Fulfilling its charter to promote "social intercourse between artists and laymen," the museum sponsors a full schedule of concerts, lectures, readings, and classes, in such disciplines as dance, yoga, and life drawing.

460 Commercial St. (in the East End). © **508/487-1750.** www.paam.org. Admission $7. July–Aug Mon–Thurs 11am–8pm, Fri 11am–10pm, Sat–Sun 11am–5pm; call for off-season hours.

KID STUFF

Kids love going out on whale-watching trips, where sightings are guaranteed. To really tire them out, climb the **Provincetown Monument,** which is located just a couple blocks from Commercial Street, just north of town hall, in the center of town. Toddlers will also enjoy the story hour held Wednesday and Saturday at 10:30am in the newly renovated **Provincetown Public Library** (© 508/487-7094), at 356 Commercial St. Kids will marvel at how the second-floor children's room is built around a 66½-foot-long half-scale replica of the *Rose Dorothea* schooner, which captured the Lipton Cup in 1907 in the famous sailboat race from Boston to Gloucester.

SHOPPING

If you want to stay one step ahead of the fashion-victims' pack, you have come to the right place. Many mavens visit off-season just to stock up on markdowns that are still well ahead of the curve. Of the several dozen art galleries in town, quite a few (noted below) are reliably worthwhile. For the largest concentration of galleries, wander down to the east end of town. (For in-depth coverage of the local arts scene, look to *Provincetown Arts,* a glossy annual sold at the Provincetown Art Association & Museum shop.) In season, most of the galleries and even some of the shops open around 11am, and then take a suppertime siesta from around 5 to 7pm, reopening and greeting visitors up to as late as 10 or 11pm. Shows usually open Friday evening, prompting a "stroll" tradition spanning the many receptions.

Antiques/Collectibles

Remembrances of Things Past, 376 Commercial St. (© **508/487-9443;** www.thingspast.com), is a kitsch-fest, with a jumble of 20th-century nostalgia ranging from Bakelite bangles to neon advertising art to vintage *True Confessions.*

At **Small Pleasures,** 359 Commercial St. (© **508/487-3712**), proprietor Virginia McKenna (also known as "Ginny Jewels") stocks fine estate jewelry, ranging from romantic Victorian settings to sleek silver for the 1920s-era male.

Showing the work of Provincetown's past and current luminaries, **Albert Merola Gallery,** 424 Commercial St., in the East End (📞 **508/487-4424;** www.albertmerolagallery. com), is simply one of the best galleries in town. Each summer, such respected figures as Michael Mazur *(Dante's Inferno)* and Helen Miranda Wilson deliver their latest musings. Closed mid-October to March.

Berta Walker is a force to be reckoned with, having nurtured many top artists through her association with the Fine Arts Work Center before opening her own gallery in 1990. At **Berta Walker Gallery,** 208 Bradford St., in the East End (📞 **508/487-6411;** www. bertawalker.com), the historic holdings span Charles Hawthorne, Milton Avery, and Robert Motherwell. Whoever has Berta's current attention, such as figurative sculptor Romolo Del Deo, warrants watching. Closed late October to late May.

Founded in 1994 by artist and publishing scion Nick Lawrence, **DNA (Definitive New Art) Gallery,** 288 Bradford St., above the Provincetown Tennis Club, in the East End (📞 **508/487-7700**), has risen to the top tier. It has attracted such talents as photographer Joel Meyerowitz, Provincetown's favorite portraitist, known for such tomes as *Cape Light;* sculptor Conrad Malicoat, whose free-form brick chimneys and hearths can be seen and admired about town; and painter Tabitha Vevers, who devises woman-centered shrines and "shields" out of goatskin vellum and gold leaf. Another contributor is local conceptualist/provocateur Jay Critchley. It's a very lively bunch, appropriately grouped under the rubric "definitive new art," and readings by cutting-edge authors add to the buzz. Closed mid-October to late May.

The **Fine Arts Works Center** displays weekly shows that are always worth checking out in its **Hudson D. Walker Gallery,** 24 Pearl St., in the center of town (📞 **508/487-9960;** www.fawc.org). The center is the heart of creativity in town, as it supports a crew of creative artists and writers on fellowships in residence every year.

Julie Heller started collecting early P-town paintings as a child—and a tourist at that. She chose so incredibly well, her roster at **Julie Heller Gallery** ★★, 2 Gosnold St., on the beach in the center of town, and at 465 Commercial St., across from the Provincetown Art Association and Museum (📞 **508/487-2169;** www.juliehellergallery.com), reads like a who's who of local art. Hawthorne, Avery, Hofmann, Lazzell, Hensche—all the big names from Provincetown's past are here, as well as some contemporary artists. Closed weekdays January to April. Open winter weekends by chance or appointment.

The work of Anne Packard and her daughters, Cynthia and Leslie, are displayed in the **Packard Gallery** ★, 418 Commercial St., in the East End (📞 **508/487-4690;** www. packardgallery.com), a majestic former church. Anne Packard's large canvases tend to depict emotive land- and seascapes, with the horizon as a focus. Cynthia's colorful figurative work has Fauvist elements, and Leslie's watercolors capture Provincetown landscapes. Closed mid-October to mid-June.

At **Rice/Polak Gallery** ★, 430 Commercial St., in the East End (📞 **508/487-1052;** www.ricepolakgallery.com), you'll find art with a decorative bent, which is not to say that it will match anyone's sofa, only that it has a certain stylish snap. Several gallery artists have fun with dimensions—such as painter Tom Seghi with his mammoth pears, and sculptor Larry Calkins with his assemblages of undersize, antique-looking dresses. Peter Plamondon's oil paintings capture still lifes with exquisite clarity. Closed December to April.

Schoolhouse Gallery ★, 494 Commercial St., in the East End (📞 **508/487-4800;** www.schoolhouseprovincetown.com), is an impressive setup, with two galleries, studios, arts programs, and an events series. The Driskel Gallery features photography and fine

THE OUTER CAPE

8

PROVINCETOWN

objects, while the **ArtStrand Gallery** ★ (© **508/487-1153;** http://artstrand.com), in the back of the building, shows the work of nine of the town's most prominent artists.

William-Scott Gallery, 439 Commercial St., in the East End (© **508/487-4040;** www.williamscottgallery.com), can be counted on to showcase the work of local emerging artists, as well as several who seem to have made it. In the latter category is John Dowd. Still quite young, his patrons include the Schiffenhaus brothers, who inherited the Hoppers' Truro house. Other selections, such as John DiMestico's Cape landscapes on paper, Dan Rupe's bold portraits in oil, and Will Klemm's lush and mysterious pastel landscapes, augur well for an influential future. Closed December to late May.

Books

Now Voyager, 357 Commercial St., in the East End (© **508/487-0848;** www.now voyagerbooks.com), offers both new and collectible gay and lesbian books and serves as an informal social center. There is also a large section of mystery and suspense books.

Provincetown Bookshop, 246 Commercial St. (© **508/487-0964**), has the most complete selection in town. You'll find all the bestsellers, as well as books about the region and local lore.

Discount Shopping

Marine Specialties ★, 235 Commercial St., in the center of town (© **508/487-1730;** www.ptownarmynavy.com), is packed to the rafters with useful stuff, from discounted Doc Martens to cut-rate Swiss Army knives and all sorts of odd nautical surplus whose uses will suggest themselves to you eventually. Be sure to look up: Hanging from the ceiling are some real antiques, including several carillons' worth of ships' bells.

Erotica

The dirtiest (and I don't mean dusty) store in Provincetown is **Shop Therapy,** 346 Commercial St. (© **508/487-9387;** www.shoptherapy.com), a store with wild murals (or is it graffiti?) filled with all manner of erotica. You'll want to wander in just for the sheer outrageousness of it all. Tall people beware; there's stuff hanging from the low ceiling that you might not want near your face.

Fashion

Giardelli/Antonelli Studio Showroom, 417 Commercial St., in the East End (© **508/ 487-3016**), is filled with Jerry Giardelli's unstructured clothing elements—shells, shifts, and palazzo pants—in vibrant colors and inviting textures. They demand to be mixed, matched, and perhaps offset by Diana Antonelli's statement jewelry.

Want to try on new identities? **Mad as a Hatter** ★, 360 Commercial St. (© **508/487-4063**), may be your best bet, with hats to suit every style and inclination, from folksy to downright diva-esque. Closed January to mid-February.

Moda Fina, 349 Commercial St. (© **508/487-6632;** www.shopmodafina.com), specializes in women's clothing and accessories, including shoes and lingerie, and a variety of unique summer dresses.

Silk & Feathers, 377 Commercial St., in the East End (© **508/487-2057;** www. silkandfeathers.com), has seasonal styles, and the lingerie they sell is almost too pretty to cover up. Other indulgences include seaweed soaps and statement jewelry.

Gifts/Home Decor

A breath of fresh contemporary design, **Utilities,** 393 Commercial St., in the center of town (© **508/487-6800;** www.utilitieshome.com), is a kitchenware/tabletop shop that features sleek and colorful essentials.

A study in beiges and blacks, **Wa** ★, 220 Commercial St., in the West End ((℃ **508/ 487-6355;** www.waharmony.com)—its name means "harmony" in Japanese—specializes in decorative home accessories that embrace a Zen aesthetic. This might mean a trickling stone fountain or Chinese calligraphy stones.

Toys

Take advantage of the Cape's strong winds and wide-open beaches by shopping at **Outer Cape Kites,** 277A Commercial St., at Ryder Street Extension, near MacMillan Wharf ((℃ **508/487-6133).** Closed mid-October to March.

WHERE TO STAY
Very Expensive

Brass Key Guesthouse ★★★ Brass Key Guesthouse, a compound of six buildings, is *the* place to stay in Provincetown. With Ritz-Carlton-style amenities and service in mind, the innkeepers have created a paean to luxury. They are the kinds of innkeepers who think of everything: goose-down pillows (choose yours from the pillow menu), showers with wall jets, and gratis iced tea and lemonade delivered poolside in season. Although all rooms share top-notch amenities, such as Bose radios, decorative styles vary according to the building. In the center is the extensively landscaped multilevel patio area, with an outdoor heated pool and a large (17-ft.) whirlpool. The inn has partnered with a local spa to offer in-room massages and other body treatments. There are two wheelchair-accessible rooms. In high season, the clientele here is primarily gay men, though all are made to feel welcome. In 2009, the owners added a lobby bar, **The Shipwreck Lounge,** which serves a menu of classic cocktails and signature drinks daily during the summer, and weekends during the off-season starting at about Happy Hour every day, along with international, domestic and local wines (many by the glass).

67 Bradford St. (in the center of town), Provincetown, MA 02657. (℃ **800/842-9858** or 508/487-9005. Fax 508/487-9020. www.brasskey.com. 42 units. Summer $400–$500 double. Rates include continental breakfast and afternoon wine-and-cheese hour. AE, DISC, MC, V. Closed late Nov–early Apr. No children 16 and under **Amenities:** Bar, 17-ft. hot tub; outdoor heated pool. *In room:* A/C, TV/DVD, fridge, hair dryer, Wi-Fi.

Crowne Pointe Historic Inn and Spa ★★ This property—an inn, restaurant, and spa—perched high on Bradford Street, is a deluxe lodging option. It is a particularly good place to stay in the off-season, when package specials offer some terrific bargains. Some prefer one of the many lodging houses on Commercial Street, though others like the appeal of a property that's a bit further away from the hurlyburly of Provincetown's main drag. Rooms here are spacious, and some of the deluxe rooms and suites have fireplaces, wet bars, and whirlpool spas. All rooms have such luxuries as down pillows, 300-count linens, thick cotton robes, and gourmet chocolates. The in-house spa has full-service treatment rooms for massages, facials, manicures, and pedicures; as well as a steam room, mineral soaking tub, and sauna, use of which is free for guests. The restaurant, the **Bistro at Crowne Pointe,** which is open nightly in season, offers a light menu, as well as fine-dining choices, with suggestions on wine pairings. You'll also get a cooked full breakfast served in the morning as well as a complimentary wine-and-cheese reception each evening.

82 Bradford St. (in the center of town), Provincetown, MA 02657. (℃ **877/CROWNE1** (276-9631) or 508/487-6767. Fax 508/487-5554. www.crownepointe.com. 35 units. Summer $299–$529 double. Rates include full breakfast, afternoon tea and cookies, and wine-and-cheese hour. AE, MC, V. **Amenities:** Bar, restaurant (dinner only); 2 10-person outdoor Jacuzzis; heated outdoor pool; spa w/steam room, mineral soaking tub, and sauna. *In room:* A/C, TV/DVD/VCR, CD player, fridge, hair dryer, Wi-Fi.

Anchor Inn Beach House ★★   This waterfront property, centrally located on Commercial Street, is exquisitely decorated with fine furniture and deluxe amenities. Each guest room has a wet bar with sink and fridge, as well as luxury bathroom amenities, including a robe. Many of the rooms feature deluxe showers, whirlpool tubs, and fireplaces. Sixteen rooms have balconies overlooking the harbor. Four rooms have separate entrances through private porches complete with wicker furniture.

175 Commercial St. (in the center of town), Provincetown, MA 02657. © **800/858-2657** or 508/487-0432. Fax 508/487-5115. www.anchorinnbeachhouse.com. 23 units. Summer $275–$385 double; $400 suite. Rates include continental breakfast. AE, MC, V. Closed Jan–Feb. *In room:* A/C, TV/VCR, CD player, fridge, hair dryer.

Land's End Inn ★★★ (Finds)   Enjoying a prime 1-acre perch atop Gull Hill, in the far West End of Commercial Street, this magical, whimsical 1907 bungalow is bursting with rare and often outlandish antiques. The two-bedroom loft suite, entered through an armoire (very *Narnia*), must be one of the most unusual and spectacular lodging spaces on the Cape. There's also a wonderful octagonal tower room, with windows wrapping halfway around, bay-view decks on two sides, and a cobalt glass turret. Though the inn caters predominantly to gay couples, cosmopolitan visitors will feel welcome. The staff is top-notch here; and the breakfast, an elaborate continental spread, features fresh fruits and homemade baked goods.

22 Commercial St. (in the West End), Provincetown, MA 02657. © **800/276-7088** or 508/487-0706. Fax 508/487-0755. www.landsendinn.com. 16 units. Summer $305–$420 double; $430–$480 tower rooms. Rates include continental breakfast and wine-and-cheese hour. AE, MC, V. Closed Nov–late May. *In room:* A/C, no phone.

The Oxford ★ (Value)   British innkeepers Stephen Mascilo and Trevor Pinker run this 1853 house in the far West End, which is one of the nicest B&Bs in town. Rooms are decorated in an English country style and are very comfortable. An extensive continental breakfast is served in the morning, when the inn fills with the scrumptious aroma of home-baked breads and coffeecake. You may want to take your coffee outside on the veranda overlooking the courtyard's fountain and pond.

8 Cottage St. (in the West End), Provincetown, MA 02657. © **888/456-9103** or 508/487-9103. www.oxfordguesthouse.com. 7 units, 2 with shared shower-only bathroom. Summer $159–$199 double with shared bathroom; $229–$319 double with private bathroom. Rates include continental breakfast. AE, DC, DISC, MC, V. *In room:* A/C, TV/DVD, CD player, fridge, hair dryer.

Watermark Inn ★★ (Kids)   If you'd like to experience P-town without being stuck in the thick of it (the carnival atmosphere can get tiring at times), this contemporary inn, at the peaceful edge of town, is the perfect choice. Resident innkeeper/architect Kevin Shea carved this beachfront manor into 10 dazzling suites; the prize ones, on the top floor, have peaked picture windows and sweeping water views from their decks. All have kitchenettes that include dishwashers. This inn is a favorite with families.

603 Commercial St. (in the East End), Provincetown, MA 02657. © **508/487-0165.** Fax 508/487-2383. www.watermark-inn.com. 10 units. Summer $205–$470 suite; weekly $1,310–$2,300. AE, MC, V. *In room:* TV, kitchenette.

Moderate

Bayshore and Chandler House ★★   This cherished beachfront complex in the far east end of town continues to be a popular lodging choice. It's a short walk to the center of P-town, but being in the East End means quiet nights. A second property, at 77 Commercial St., on the far West End of town, has two additional one-bedroom units. All of the apartments have improvised charm, such as a few select antiques, and salvaged architectural details. Rooms have private entrances and kitchenettes, including microwave ovens and dishwashers. The prize rooms at the east-side property surround a flower-lined lawn, with pride of place going to a cathedral-ceilinged loft right over the water. From late June to early September, rooms are available on a weekly basis only.

493 Commercial St. (in the East End), Provincetown, MA 02657. (C)/fax **508/487-9133.** Fax 508/487-0520. www.bayshorechandler.com. 25 units, 20 with tub/shower combination, 5 with shower. Summer $1,400 weekly studio, $1,350–$2,150 weekly 1-bedroom, $3,295 weekly 2-bedroom; shoulder season daily $120 studio, $140–$199 1-bedroom, $240–$299 2-bedroom. AE, DISC, MC, V. Dogs allowed with advance notice. *In room:* A/C (some units), TV/VCR, kitchenette.

Cape Inn Resort ★ This waterfront motel is a good choice for first-timers not quite sure what they're getting into. It's a no-surprises, pool-equipped motel at the far eastern edge of town. Guests in waterfront rooms get a nice view. There are free movies in the restaurant/lounge shown on a 70 sq. ft. screen in season. Though this motel is a bit of a hike from the town's center, an in-season town shuttle will whisk you down Commercial Street or to the beaches for $1 a ride.

698 Commercial St. (at Rte. 6A, in the East End), Provincetown, MA 02657. (C) **800/422-4224** or 508/487-1711. Fax 508/487-3929. www.capeinn.com. 78 units. Summer $140–$200 double. Rates include continental breakfast. AE, DC, DISC, MC, V. Closed Nov–Apr. Dogs allowed. **Amenities:** Restaurant; outdoor pool. *In room:* A/C, TV, fridge, hair dryer.

Carpe Diem Guesthouse & Spa ★★★ This guesthouse has always been top shelf, but, in recent years, it has been transformed by its three owners—a trio of hip German men—into one of the finest boutique hotels in Provincetown. With the addition of a new building, there are also four new suites and new common rooms and patios. The state-of-the-art **Namaste spa** here has to be one of the most deluxe in town, with a large hydrojet spa tub, Finnish dry sauna, Provincetown's largest steam room, and massage rooms. The full breakfast, prepared by the inn's French manager, features homemade French-influenced pastries.

12–14 Johnson St. (in the center of town), Provincetown, MA 02657. (C) **800/487-0132** or 508/487-4242 (also fax). www.carpediemguesthouse.com. 18 units. Summer $225–$245 double; $305–$365 suites; $385–$425 cottage. Rates include full breakfast and wine-and-cheese hour. AE, DISC, MC, V. **Amenities:** 6-person hot tub. *In room:* A/C, TV/DVD, fridge (in most).

The Masthead ★★ (Value) (Kids) This is the best-priced waterfront lodging option in Provincetown. The cottages are fun, some with net stair railings, wicker furniture, and hand-painted antique furniture by Peter Hunt, as well as full (if tiny) kitchens, which include microwave ovens. Two rooms are accessible to travelers with disabilities. In season, the cottage units rent weekly, but the rather generic motel units rent nightly. In some water-view rooms, with their 7-foot picture windows overlooking the bay and Long Point, you may feel like you're onboard a ship.

31–41 Commercial St. (in the West End), Provincetown, MA 02657. (C) **800/395-5095** or 508/487-0523. Fax 508/487-9251. www.themasthead.com. 21 units, 2 with shared bathroom, 3 with tub/shower combination, 16 with shower; 4 cottages. Summer $99 double with shared bathroom; $125–$312 double; $213–$333 efficiency and 1-bedroom; $489 2-bedroom apt; $2,541–$2,919 cottage weekly. AE, DC, DISC, MC, V. *In room:* A/C, TV, fridge.

Revere Guest House ★★ Nineteenth-century charm plus modern amenities prevail at this recently updated guesthouse on a quiet side street between Commercial and

Bradford streets. Owner Gary Palochko has created a restful place, from the back garden blooming with lilacs and roses to the multijet Jacuzzi on the patio and the outdoor shower, that classic summertime amenity. The rooftop deck has a 360-degree view of P-town. Rooms range from small ones that share bathrooms to large suites with whirlpool tubs.

14 Court St., Provincetown, MA 02657. (© 508/487-2292 or 508/487-2292. www.reverehouse.com. 10 units, 2 w/shared bathroom. Summer $175 shared bathroom; $195–$295 double; $280–$355 suite. Rates include continental breakfast. MC, V. **Amenities:** 5-person spa. *In room:* A/C, TV/DVD, minifridge, Wi-Fi.

Surfside Hotel and Suites ★   This motel on the far East End of Commercial Street, with one building on the water side and one across the street, has recently undergone a freshening up in decor that brings it up a level in comfort. But the reasonable prices make it a good bet for inexpensive lodging, particularly for busy weekends, when more stylish options are booked. The beds and bedding are top-notch. Rooms with views of the waterfront are prized; second best are the ones facing the rear, for quiet nights. Ones facing the street/pool can be noisy.

543 Commercial St. (in the East End), Provincetown, MA 02657. (© 508/487-1726. Fax 508/487-6556. www.surfsideinn.cc. 88 units. Summer $114–$169 double; $450 suite. AE, DC, DISC, MC, V. Pet-friendly. **Amenities:** Outdoor pool. *In room:* A/C, TV, fridge, hair dryer.

WHERE TO DINE
Very Expensive
Bistro 404 ★ NEW AMERICAN   The buzz is good on this expensive restaurant that replaced Chester, on the East End of town. Come to this restaurant expecting fine dining, with prices and service to match. Expect to wait a bit between courses, the better to appreciate the flavors. The menu changes nightly, but among the highlights are the niçoise salad with lobster. Look for the fresh-fish specialty prepared in a creative style; you can't go wrong.

404 Commercial St. (© 508/487-5404. http://bistro404.com. Reservations required. Main courses $31–$41. AE, DC, DISC, MC, V. Mid-June to early Sept daily 6–9:30pm; call for off-season hours.

The Red Inn ★★ NEW AMERICAN   Nothing beats the view from the floor-to-ceiling windows of this restaurant seemingly at the end of the earth, the far East End of Provincetown. This is the type of place where you might feel like beginning your meal with a glass of champagne and ending it with a soufflé. It's fine dining on the calorie-rich side, with such entrees as grilled thick pork chops with tomatillo salsa, and pepper-crusted filet mignon with truffle mashed potatoes and Jack Daniels sauce. Fresh fish and vegetarian main courses are also always on the menu.

15 Commercial St. (© 508/487-7334. www.theredinn.com. Reservations required. Main courses $21–$38. AE, DC, DISC, MC, V. Mid-June to early Sept daily 5:30–9:30pm, Thurs–Sun 10am–2:30pm; call for off-season hours.

Expensive
Devon's ★★★ NEW AMERICAN   You can tell which one is Devon. He's seating people, acting as line cook, busing tables, taking reservations, and chatting with customers. The restaurant itself, a former boat shack, is tiny, with fewer than 10 tables inside—all next to the open kitchen. In good weather the choice seats are on the patio out front. Service is professional here. The food is elegantly prepared and presented with special touches. The menu changes often but features wonderful fish, steak, chicken, and vegetarian preparations. One night we were there, patrons were raving over the sole that was

prepared with a wonderfully simple beurre blanc sauce. This is a romantic option, but you definitely need a reservation. It's also a good choice for breakfast, for those staying in the far East End of town.

401½ Commercial St. (in the East End). ℂ 508/487-4773. www.devons.org. Reservations recommended. Main courses $18–$25. DISC, MC, V. June–Sept Thurs–Tues 8am–1pm and 5:30–10pm; call for off-season hours. Closed Nov–Apr.

Edwidge @ Night and Café Edwidge ★★★ NEW AMERICAN

Dinner and breakfast are run by two different teams at this second-floor restaurant, long a favorite with locals. For seating, you have a choice: inside where wooden booths, rafters, and close-set tables provide a casual feel, or outside on a narrow, breezy patio that offers more private dining. Outstanding menu items include tuna tartare or lobster dumplings as appetizers, and for the main course, filet mignon with a blue-cheese fritter or *moqueca,* a Brazilian seafood dish. Breakfast here is a favorite with locals and visitors alike, so arrive early if you expect to get a table.

333 Commercial St. ℂ 508/487-2008. Reservations recommended. Main courses $18–$29. MC, V. June–Sept daily 8–11am and 6–10pm; call for off-season hours.

Front Street ★★ MEDITERRANEAN FUSION/ITALIAN

For years, this restaurant has delivered consistently high-quality food and service, and locals consider it a favorite, dependable locale. Located in a below-ground space on Commercial Street, in the center of town, this cozy restaurant feels most comfortable in the chilly days of spring and summer. The decor is very romantic, with antique booths and low lighting. Chef Donna Aliperti is constantly improving her menu, inspired by trips to Italy and southern France. The fusion menu, available in season, has such creative items as soft-shell crabs with corn-studded risotto, and Chinese five-spice grilled duckling. There is also a traditional Italian menu, with pastas available every night.

230 Commercial St. ℂ 508/487-9715. www.frontstreetrestaurant.com. Reservations recommended. Main courses $18–$25. DISC, MC, V. June–Sept Wed–Mon 5:30–9pm; call for off-season hours.

Lorraine's ★★ (Finds) MEXICAN/NEW AMERICAN

Located in the far West End of Commercial Street, Lorraine's has long been considered one of the town's top dining spots. Even those who shy away from Mexican restaurants should try Lorraine's; chef/ owner Lorraine Najar brings a certain daring to bear on the cuisine she learned at her grandmother's knee. Abandon all caution and begin with *chile relleno de queso,* which is fresh chili peppers stuffed with the chef's choice nightly, rolled in cornmeal and corn flour, and lightly fried. Maryland soft-shell crabs are lightly dusted in flour with Chimayo chile powder and pan-sautéed and served with a jalapeño aioli. For a main course, consider *viere verde*—sea scallops sautéed with tomatillos, flambéed in tequila, and cloaked in a green-chili sauce. For a treat, check out the extensive tequila menu; shots are served with a wonderful tomato-juice-based chaser.

133 Commercial St. (in the West End). ℂ 508/487-6074. www.lorrainesrestaurant.com. Reservations suggested. Main courses $17–$26. DISC, MC, V. June–Sept Mon–Fri 6–10pm, Sat–Sun 9am–1pm and 6–10pm; call for off-season hours.

The Mews Restaurant & Cafe ★★ INTERNATIONAL/AMERICAN FUSION

Bank on fine food and suave service at this beachfront restaurant, an enduring favorite since 1961. Upstairs is the cafe, with its century-old carved mahogany bar. The dining room downstairs sits right on the beach—and is practically of the beach, with its sand-toned walls warmed by toffee-colored Tiffany table lamps. The best soup in the region is the Mews' scrumptious summertime special, chilled cucumber miso bisque with curry shrimp timbale. Perennial pleasures include the Marsala-marinated portobello mushrooms and a mixed-seafood carpaccio. Desserts and coffees are delectable.

429 Commercial St. ☎ **508/487-1500.** www.mews.com. Reservations recommended. Main courses $18–$29. AE, DC, DISC, MC, V. Mid-June to early Sept daily 6–10pm, Sun brunch 10am–1:30pm; early Dec to mid-Feb daily 6–10pm; call for off-season hours.

Ross' Grill ★★★ NEW AMERICAN BISTRO Tucked on the second floor in the back of the Whalers' Wharf, don't make the mistake of overlooking this place, which some consider to be serving the best food in Provincetown. This is the place to go when you are in the mood for a very special, intimate dinner. The dining room, with subdued lighting and decorated with an urban feel, has large windows overlooking the waterfront. With 75 wines available by the glass, this is also the place to come for wine aficionados. Menu items of note include the steak frites with hand-cut french fries; the roasted free-range chicken with panzanella salad; and the shellfish risotto, a delightful mixture of fresh provender from the sea.

237 Commercial St. (in the Whaler's Wharf). ☎ **508/487-8878.** www.rossgrillptown.com. Reservations recommended. Main courses $22–$40. MC, V. May to mid-Sept Mon and Wed–Sat 11:30am–3pm and 5:30–9:30pm, Sun noon–3pm and 5:30–9pm; call for off-season hours.

Moderate

Bubala's by the Bay ★ BREAKFAST/AMERICAN This trendy bistro—with a gaudy yellow paint job and Picasso-esque wall murals—promises "serious food at sensible prices." And that's what it delivers, from buttermilk waffles with real maple syrup to lobster tarragon salad to creative focaccia sandwiches to fajitas, Cajun calamari, and pad thai. This is a big operation for Provincetown, and the huge outdoor patio facing Commercial Street means it's popular, particularly for breakfast. This is the only place on Cape Cod that serves ostrich. They're raised in Pennsylvania and served with a grilled-pepper crust and a caramelized-onion-and-balsamic glaze. In season, there's entertainment nightly from 10pm to 1am.

183 Commercial St. (in the West End). ☎ **508/487-0773.** www.bubalas.com. Reservations not accepted. Main courses $10–$21. AE, DISC, MC, V. Mid-Apr to late Oct daily 11am–11pm. Closed late Oct to mid-Apr.

Enzo ★ NORTHERN ITALIAN Run by the owners of the popular Bubala's (see above), across the street, this West End restaurant is one of the newer places on the Provincetown scene. Named after Enzo Ferrari, it has a sleek look that brings to mind modern Italian style. The menu features Italian classics, such as *osso buco* and *linguini con l'araguota,* a favorite dish of linguini with lobster. Inside are several serene dining rooms and a bar area; outside, two levels of patio seating are perfect for people-watching. Still working to build a clientele, Enzo is a good choice in the crowded summer months, when it is a challenge to secure a table at many Provincetown hot spots. The downstairs bar, Grotta, offers live entertainment most nights in season, and an upstairs inn has five elegant guest rooms.

186 Commercial St. (in the West End). ☎ **508/487-7555.** www.enzolives.com. Reservations not accepted. Most items $12–$28. AE, DISC, MC, V. July–Aug daily 6–10pm; call for off-season hours. Closed Feb–May.

Fanizzi's By The Sea ★★ ITALIAN/SEAFOOD This waterfront restaurant in the far East End of town is the perfect place to get away from all the hustle and bustle in the center of town. The beauty of this casual restaurant is that you can have a burger and fries,

enjoy such comfort food as Mom's best meatloaf, or splurge on shrimp scampi, and it's all
very reasonably priced. The view seen here through large wraparound plate-glass windows
is among the best in town. The $13 buffet brunch, served 'til 2pm on Sundays, is a good
deal.

539 Commercial St. © **508/487-1964.** www.fanizzisrestaurant.com. Reservations recommended. Main
courses $9–$21. AE, MC, V. Mid-June to mid-Sept Mon–Sat 11:30am–10pm, Sun 10am–9pm; call for off-
season hours.

Frappo66 ★ CAFETERIA It's a new dining concept: the fine-dining cafeteria. And
it works. Tucked into the lobby of the Art House theater, this is the place to go for a
reasonably priced gourmet meal, where you save time and money by serving yourself.
Besides soups, salads and sandwiches, there is always a special—such as filet of sole with
lobster mushroom stuffing—and you get to choose three "sides"—such as broccoli with
tofu or pasta salad, for example. This is the perfect place to go for a light meal after a
show.

214 Commercial St. (in the center of town). © **508/487-9066.** www.frappo66.com. Reservations not
accepted. Main courses $9–$21. MC, V. Mid-June to mid-Sept daily 8am–10pm, call for off-season hours.

The Lobster Pot ★ SEAFOOD Snobbish foodies might turn their noses up at a
venue so flagrantly Olde Cape Cod-ish, but for Provincetown regulars, no season seems
complete without at least one pilgrimage. You may feel like a long-suffering pilgrim waiting to get in: The line, which starts near the aromatic, albeit frantic, kitchen, often snakes
into the street. While waiting, check out the hand-painted bar stools, which provide an
architectural history of Provincetown. A lucky few will make it all the way to the outdoor
deck; however, most tables, indoors and out, afford nice views of MacMillan Wharf.
Spring for a jumbo lobster—boiled or broiled, sauced or simple. And definitely start off
with the chowder, a perennial award-winner.

321 Commercial St. (in the center of town). © **508/487-0842.** www.ptownlobsterpot.com. Reservations
not accepted. Main courses $15–$25. AE, DC, DISC, MC, V. Mid-June to mid-Sept daily 11:30am–10:30pm;
mid-Apr to mid-June and mid-Sept to Dec daily 11:30am–9:30pm. Closed Jan to mid-Apr.

Napi's ★★ INTERNATIONAL Restaurateur Napi Van Dereck can be credited with
bringing P-town's restaurant scene up to speed—back in the early 1970s. His namesake
restaurant still reflects that zeitgeist, with its rococo-hippie carpentry, select outtakes
from his sideline in antiques, and some rather outstanding art, including a crazy quilt of
a brick wall by local sculptor Conrad Malicoat. The food is truly international, with
dumplings from China; falafel from Syria; and, from Greece, shrimp feta flambéed with
the Greek liquors ouzo and *Metaxa*. The lower-priced tavern menu available on week-
nights ranges from $5 to $11. The restaurant has its own parking lot (around back),
which is unusual (and much welcome) in Provincetown.

7 Freeman St. (at Bradford St.). © **800/571-6274.** www.napis-restaurant.com. Reservations recommended. Main courses $14–$26. DISC, MC, V. May to mid-Sept daily 5–10pm; mid-Sept to Apr daily
11:30am–4pm and 5–9pm.

Pepe's ★★ AMERICAN This is a great lunch spot set on a deck on the beach overlooking Provincetown Harbor. Go elsewhere for dinner when the terrific first-floor patio
area here is closed. On the menu are burgers, salads, grilled paninis, fried-fish sandwiches, and lobster rolls—perfect summer food. Also fun, in a more honky-tonk way, is
the second floor tiki-style bar overlooking the beach, where the near-constant rumble of
a blender making frozen drinks is the background for conversations.

371 Commercial St. (center of town). ✆ **508/487-8717.** Reservations recommended. Main courses $14–$26 (lunch mostly under $15). DISC, MC, V. May to mid-Sept daily 11:30–10pm; call for off-season hours.

Sal's Place ★ (**Finds**) SOUTHERN ITALIAN   Sit in the front room, close to the street, in this authentic Italian restaurant. With its red-checkered tablecloths, chianti basket bottles hanging from the ceiling, and vintage photos on the walls, it feels like a place in Boston's North End. There is also an open-air deck in the rear with a harbor view, a good spot to sit on very hot nights. There is nothing subtle about this hearty Italian food, huge portions of traditional pasta dishes such as homemade manicotti, eggplant parmigiana, and spaghettini with sausage.

99 Commercial St. (in the West End). ✆ **508/487-1279.** www.salsplaceofprovincetown.com. Reservations recommended. Main courses $13–$23. MC, V. Apr–Oct daily 5:30–10pm; call for off-season hours.

Townsend Lobster & Seafood ★★ (**Finds**) (**Kids**) SEAFOOD   Insiders know to head off the beaten track, down Shank Painter Road, to find the best seafood platter deals in town. This is off-the-boat seafood, the freshest in town, caught by Capt. Chris, who is also the owner of the restaurant. Their goal is a family-friendly place to get good seafood, and on both counts, they have succeeded.

85–87 Shank Painter Rd. (off Bradford St.). ✆ **508/487-5161.** www.townsendseafood.com. Reservations recommended. Main courses $10–$23. MC, V. Apr–Oct daily 11:30–9pm; call for off-season hours.

Victor's ★★ (**Finds**) NEW AMERICAN TAPAS   This relatively new restaurant, a bit out of the way on Bradford Street, is gaining a reputation as a great place to go for an upscale meal of *tapas,* which are small plates of food meant for sharing. The dining room is attractive with a soaring cathedral ceiling and a large stone fireplace. Portions are such that two people can order three tapas plates—try the lobster spring rolls, with a chili-lime sauce, or the barbecue oysters—for about $15 apiece and have a very complete meal for less than two entrees would cost at other fine-dining establishments in town. There is a raw bar from 3 to 10pm nightly.

175 Bradford St. Ext. (in the West End, near W. Vine). ✆ **508/487-1777.** www.victorsptown.com. Reservations recommended. Tapas (small plates) $9–$15. MC, V. Apr–Oct Wed–Mon 8am–2pm; daily 5–10pm; call for off-season hours.

Inexpensive

Cafe Heaven ★ AMERICAN   Prized for its leisurely country breakfasts (served 'til midafternoon, for reluctant risers), this modern storefront—adorned with big, bold paintings by acclaimed Wellfleet artist John Grillo—also turns out substantial sandwiches, such as avocado and goat cheese on a French baguette. The salads are appealing as well—especially the "special shrimp," lightly doused with dilled sour cream and tossed with tomatoes and grapes. This casual cafe is a popular place in the evenings, especially late night, when a limited, light dinner menu, including hamburgers and a wonderful grilled ahi tuna sandwich, is served until 11pm.

199 Commercial St. (in the West End). ✆ **508/487-9639.** Reservations not accepted. Most items $8–$15. No credit cards. Late June–Aug daily 8am–2pm and 6–10pm; call for off-season hours. Closed Feb–May.

Chach ★ (**Finds**) DINER   A diner run by a chef, instead of a cook, means the omelets are divine, the BLTs are heavenly, and all kinds of little surprises are on the menu. It's a little off the beaten track, but it's worth seeking out Chach for reasonably priced dining, without the crowds you find on Commercial Street.

73 Shank Painter Rd. (off Bradford St., a few blocks south of town). ℂ **508/487-1530.** Most items under $10. No credit cards. Reservations not accepted. Apr–Feb Thurs–Tues 8am–2:30pm. Closed Mar.

Mojo's (Kids) SEAFOOD   This fried-seafood shack is known for its lightly breaded fried fish. French fries are hand-cut daily. There are also kid-friendly hot dogs and hamburgers, subs, veggie burgers, burritos, pizza, and chicken tenders. Eat at one of the six picnic tables on the patio or take it to the beach.

5 Ryder St. Ext. (near Fisherman's Wharf). ℂ **508/487-3140.** All items under $15. No credit cards. Early May to mid-Oct daily 11am–11pm. Closed mid-Oct to early May.

Spiritus Pizza PIZZA/ICE CREAM   A local landmark, Spiritus is an extravagant pizza parlor known for post-last-call cruising: It's open until 2am. The pizza's good, as are the fruit drinks, specialty coffees, and four brands of premium ice cream, from Emack & Bolio's to Coconut Joe's. For a peaceful morning repast—and perhaps a relaxed round of bocce—check out the little garden in back.

190 Commercial St. (in the center of town). ℂ **508/487-2808.** www.spirituspizza.com. All items under $15. No credit cards. Apr–Oct daily 11:30am–2am. Closed Nov–Mar.

Ice Cream

Not only a good spot to satisfy any ice-cream cravings (how about a 20-scoop "Vermonster"?), **Ben & Jerry's Scoop Shop** ★, 258 Commercial St., in the center of town (ℂ **508/487-3360**), is also handy for refueling midstroll with a fresh-fruit drink.

Takeout & Picnic Fare

Angel Foods, 467 Commercial St., in the East End (ℂ **508/487-6666;** www.angelfoods. com), is a gourmet takeout shop offering Italian specialties and other scrumptious prepared foods to go.

The rollwiches—pita bread packed with a wide range of fillings—at **Box Lunch,** 353 Commercial St., in the center of town (ℂ **508/487-6026;** www.boxlunch.com), are ideal for a strolling lunch.

One thing you absolutely have to do while in town is peruse the cases of *pasties* (meat pies) and pastries at **Provincetown Portuguese Bakery,** 299 Commercial St., in the center of town (ℂ **508/487-1803**). Point to a few and take your surprise package out on the pier for delectation. Though perhaps not the wisest course for the whale-watch-bound, it's the best way to sample the scrumptious international output of this beloved institution. Closed November to early April.

PROVINCETOWN AFTER DARK

The Club Scene

The Atlantic House   The "A-house"—the nation's premier gay bar—also welcomes straights of both sexes, except in the leather-oriented Macho Bar upstairs. Late in the evening, there's usually plenty going on in the Big Room dance bar. In the little bar downstairs—warm up at the fireplace—check out the Tennessee Williams memorabilia, including a portrait of the playwright *au naturel;* there's more across the street in the restaurant, Grand Central. 6 Masonic Place (off Commercial St., 2 blocks west of Town Hall). ℂ **508/487-3821.** www.ahouse.com. Cover for the Big Room $5–$10.

Crown & Anchor   The specialty bars at the large complex span leather ("The Vault"), disco, comedy, drag shows, and cabaret. Facilities include a pool bar and game room. Call for a schedule. Closed November to April. 247 Commercial St. (in the center of town). ℂ **508/487-1430.** www.onlyatthecrown.com. Admission to shows $20–$22.

Post Office Café and Cabaret   One of P-town's top clubs, the Post Office, despite its cramped space, can be depended on for amusing drag and comedy shows. In recent years, the B-Girlz (Hard Kora, Barbie-Q, and Belle Bottom) have been the featured act. Call for a schedule. Closed November to April. 303 Commercial St. (in the center of town). ℂ 508/487-0006. Cover $28.

Vixen   This chic women's bar occupies the lower floors of a former hotel. On the roster are jazz, blues, and comedy acts. There are also pool tables. Call for a schedule. Closed November to April. Pilgrim House, 336 Commercial St. (in the center of town). ℂ 508/487-6424. Cover $20 for shows.

The Bar Scene

Cafe Mews   This venue, with its bay view and vintage mahogany bar, is one of the few nightspots in town to lend itself well to the art of conversation. The jazz piano enhances rather than intrudes. A light cafe menu, in addition to the dining-room menu, is available. At The Mews (see "Where to Dine," earlier in this chapter), 429 Commercial St. ℂ 508/487-1500. www.mews.com.

Governor Bradford   It's a good old bar, featuring pool tables, drag karaoke (summer nights at 9:30pm), and disco. Call for a schedule. 312 Commercial St. (in the center of town). ℂ 508/487-2781.

Patio   A large outdoor seating area right on Commercial Street makes this a terrific place to sip summer cocktails and people-watch. A favorite for decades as Café Blasé, the renamed, remade watering hole now serves tasty appetizers, desserts, light fare, and even whole dinners. The updated interior holds a sleek, attractive bar. 328 Commercial St. (in the center of town). ℂ 508/487-4003.

Performance

Art House   This theater in a former cinema mounts avant-garde productions, such as a drag *Romeo and Juliet*, presenting four shows a night in season. While you wait for the show to begin, you can sip a latte and order main courses and yummy dessert crepes from the cafe's large menu. Performances are offered mid-May to mid-September from 7 to 10pm. Films are shown in the off-season, and there are occasional live performances and community activities from trivia contests to Wii bowling. 214 Commercial St. (in the center of town). ℂ 508/487-9222. www.ptownarthouse.com. Tickets $12–$30.

Meetinghouse Theatre and Concert Hall   In season, this glorious space is given over to a wide range of performances, from plays to opera to cabaret. Upstairs is an acoustically superb concert hall with a restored 1929 Steinway concert grand piano. Downstairs is an intimate theater. The season is usually capped off by a series of concerts by The Flirtations, a gay a cappella ensemble. A highlight in season is the Sunday at 5 music series, with a variety of performers, costing $10. At the Unitarian-Universalist Meetinghouse, 236 Commercial St. (in the center of town). ℂ 508/487-9344. Ticket prices vary.

The Provincetown Theater   With both Eugene O'Neill and Tennessee Williams as one-time residents, Provincetown went far too long without a state-of-the-art theater. The town had no dedicated theater from 1977, when the venerable Playhouse on the Wharf was destroyed by fire, until 2004, when this 200-seat venue was completed. The home of the New Provincetown Players, the building also serves as a concert hall, dance studio, cinema, and meetinghouse, and books in traveling shows and festivals. Credit cards are accepted at the theater, which is open year-round. Tickets can be purchased from Ptown Tix (located at 209 Commercial St., at the Aquarium Marketplace), at the

box office, or online. 238 Bradford St. (2 blocks east of Howland St.). ✆ **508/487-7487** (800/791-
7487 or 508/487-9793 for box office). www.provincetowntheater.com or www.ptowntix.com.
Ticket prices vary.

Low-Key Evenings

Fine Arts Work Center   Drawing on its roster of visiting artists and scholars, FAWC
offers exceptional readings and talks (some serve as fundraisers) year-round. Call for a
schedule. 24 Pearl St. (off Bradford St., in the center of town). ✆ **508/487-9960.** www.fawc.org.
Most events free.

Provincetown Art Association & Museum   Concerts, lectures, and readings
attract an intellectually inclined after-hours crowd. Call for a schedule. 460 Commercial
St. (in the East End). ✆ **508/487-1750.** www.paam.org. Admission varies.

Nantucket

In his classic novel, *Moby-Dick*, Herman Melville wrote, "Nantucket! Take out your map and look at it. See what a real corner of the world it occupies; how it stands there, away off shore . . ." More than 100 years later, this tiny island 30 miles off the coast of Cape Cod still defines itself, in part, by its isolation. At only 3½ by 14 miles in size, Nantucket is smaller and more insular than Martha's Vineyard. But charm-wise, Nantucket stands alone—all the creature comforts of the 21st century wrapped in an elegant 19th-century package.

The island has long appealed to wealthy visitors, and the ultrarich are more visible than ever. Locals shake their heads over the changing demographics. "If they can't get a reservation at a restaurant, they buy the restaurant," one islander said. Neverthe-less, this is still a terrific spot for a family vacation or a romantic retreat. After all, window-shopping at the island's exclusive boutiques and soaking up the sunshine on the pristine beaches are both free of charge.

The Nantucket we see today is the result of a dramatic boom and bust that took place in the 1800s. The whaling capital of the world, the Nantucket of Melville's time was a bustling international port whose wealth and sophistication belied its size. But the discovery of crude oil spelled doom for the whale-oil industry. Nantucket sank into a severe economic depression until the tourism industry revived it at the end of the 19th century. Stringent regulations have preserved the 19th-century character of Nantucket Town, and today 36% of the island (and counting) is maintained as con-servation land.

Nantucket Island's one town, also called Nantucket, hugs the yacht-filled harbor. This sophisticated burg bursts with boun-tiful stores, quaint inns, cobblestone streets, interesting historic sites, and pris-tine beaches. Scores of shops and galleries occupy wharf shacks on the harbor. The rest of the island is mainly residential, but for a couple of notable villages. Siasconset (nicknamed 'Sconset), on the east side of the island, is a tranquil community with picturesque, rose-covered cottages and a handful of businesses, including a pricey French restaurant. Sunset aficionados head to Madaket, on the west coast of the island, for the evening spectacular.

The lay of the land on Nantucket is rolling moors, heaths, cranberry bogs, and miles of exquisite public beaches. The vis-tas are honeymoon-romantic: an operating windmill, three lighthouses, and a skyline dotted with church steeples. Although July and August are still the most popular times to visit the island, Nantucket's tour-ist season has been lengthened consider-ably by several popular festivals: the Daffodil Festival in April, Nantucket Har-vest Weekend in October, and the month-long Nantucket Noel, the granddaddy of all holiday celebrations in the region. Off-season, a vacation can be more tranquil, and certainly less expensive. The "Grey Lady's" infamous fog is liable to swallow you whole, but you may well learn to rel-ish the moody, atmospheric weather.

1 ESSENTIALS

GETTING THERE

BY FERRY   The two companies that offer ferry service from Hyannis to Nantucket are the **Steamship Authority** and **Hy-Line Cruises.** Their terminals are on opposite sides of Hyannis Harbor. Tickets on the Steamship Authority are less expensive than tickets on the Hy-Line by about $10. Parking in the Steamship Authority lots is also a couple dollars less expensive.

From the South Street Dock in Hyannis, the **Steamship Authority** (✆ **508/477-8600,** or 508/228-3274 in Nantucket; www.steamshipauthority.com) operates year-round ferry service (including cars, passengers, and bicycles) to Steamboat Wharf in Nantucket using both **high-speed** ferries—which get you there in 1 hour—and **conventional** ferries, which take 2 hours and 15 minutes and cost about half the price.

Only the conventional ferries have space for cars, but there is no need to bring a car to the island because of its small size and superior public transportation and taxicab system.

Steamship Authority high-speed ferry: The Steamship Authority's **fast ferry to Nantucket, MV *Iyanough*** (✆ **508/495-3278**), is for passengers only (no cars). It takes 1 hour and runs five to six times a day in season. Tickets in season cost $33 one-way ($65 round-trip) for adults, $25 one-way ($49 round-trip) for children 5 to 12, and it is free for children 4 and under. Parking costs $12 to $15 per day. Passenger reservations are highly recommended.

Steamship Authority conventional ferry: For passengers, a one-way ticket on the Steamship Authority traveling on the conventional ferry (with or without cars) is $17 ($33 round-trip) for adults, $8.50 ($17 round-trip) for children 5 to 12, and $12 extra round-trip for bikes. Remember that Steamship Authority parking costs $12 to $15 per day in season; you do not need to make parking reservations.

Bringing a car to Nantucket: A round-trip fare, if you are bringing a car, costs a whopping $380 to $430 (depending on the length of the car) from mid-May to mid-October; during the off-season, from mid-October to mid-May, it's $260 to $300. (Do you get the impression they don't want you to bring a car?)

If you must bring a car to the island, you need to reserve *months in advance* to secure a spot on the conventional ferry, as only six boats make the trip daily in season (three boats daily off-season). Before you call, have alternative departure dates. When bringing a car to the island, remember to arrive at least 1 hour before departure to avoid your space being released to standbys. If you arrive without a reservation and plan to wait in the standby line, there is no guarantee you will get to the island that day. There is a $10 processing fee for canceling reservations 14 days in advance of the trip; no refunds are issued if the cancellation is made less than 14 days before the trip.

No advance reservations are required for passengers traveling without cars.

Note: The Steamship Authority charges different rates for different length cars. You will need to specify the make and model of your car when you place your reservation.

Car rates do not include drivers or passengers; you must get tickets for each person going to the island.

(Tips) Parking on the Mainland

You don't need a car on Nantucket, so plan to park your car in Hyannis before boarding a ferry to the island. For all **Hy-Line** ferry services, either go to the Ocean Street Dock, or call ✆ **800/492-8082;** or visit www.hy-linecruises.com), In July and August, it's a good idea not only to reserve ferry tickets in advance, but also to reserve a parking spot ahead of time. The all-day parking fee is $17 per calendar day in season; $10 in the shoulder seasons. If the Hy-Line lot is full, there are two competing lots next to the Hyannis Harbor Motel. *Note:* Choose the one where the attendants are wearing yellow shirts (not yellow jackets!)—they have the more reliable rates. Travelers on **Steamship Authority** (✆ **508/477-8600;** www.steamshipauthority.com) vessels do not need a parking reservation. Be sure to arrive at least 1 hour before sailing time to allow for parking. Parking at the Steamship Authority lots costs $12 to $15 per day in season. When the lot at the terminal and the nearby lot on Lewis Bay Road across from Cape Cod Hospital are full, there are parking lots several blocks away on Yarmouth Road and a couple miles away on Brooks Road. From the outlying lots, you access the ferry terminal via a free shuttle bus. In season, watch signs on Route 6, or tune in to radio station 1610 AM for up-to-the-minute ferry parking information.

Also from Hyannis, passenger ferries to Nantucket's Straight Wharf are operated by **Hy-Line Cruises,** Ocean Street Dock (✆ **888/778-1132** or 508/778-2600; for high-speed ferry reservations, call ✆ **800/492-8082** or 508/778-0404; www.hy-linecruises.com).

Hy-Line Cruises fast ferry: Hy-Line offers year-round service with its high-speed passenger catamaran, the *Grey Lady,* which makes five to six hourly trips per day. The cost of a one-way fare is $39 for adults ($75 round-trip), $29 for children 5 to 12 ($51 round-trip), and $6 extra for bicycles ($12 round-trip). It's best to reserve in advance for your ferry ticket and for a parking space. Pets are allowed on the *Grey Lady.*

Hint: It pays to buy a round-trip ticket on the Hy-Line fast ferry. It's a few dollars cheaper than buying two one-way tickets.

Hy-Line Cruises conventional ferry: From early May through October, Hy-Line's standard 1-hour-and-50-minute ferry service is also offered. Round-trip tickets are $43 for adults ($22 one-way), $22 for children 5 to 12 ($11 one-way), and $12 extra for bikes. On busy holiday weekends, you may want to order tickets in advance; otherwise, be sure to buy your tickets at least a half-hour before your boat leaves the dock.

The standard ferry also has a **first-class section** with a private lounge, bathrooms, a bar, and a snack bar; a continental breakfast or afternoon cheese and crackers is also served onboard. No pets are allowed on the *Great Point* ferry in the first-class section. Tickets in the first-class section are $56 round-trip, for all ages.

Note: Hy-Line reserves the right to add a fuel surcharge onto all of its tickets. In the summer of 2008, the fuel surcharge was $6 per round-trip ticket. There was no fuel surcharge added in 2009.

Hy-Line's **Around the Sound** cruise is a 1-day round-trip excursion from Hyannis, with stops in Nantucket and Martha's Vineyard, that runs from mid-June to mid-September. The price is $84 for adults, $54 for children 5 to 12, and $18 extra for bikes.

Hy-Line runs one passenger-only high-speed ferry **from Oak Bluffs,** on Martha's Vineyard, to Nantucket, from mid-June to mid-September (there is no car-ferry service btw. the islands). The trip time from Oak Bluffs is 1 hour and 10 minutes. The one-way fare is $34 for adults, $21 for children 5 to 12, and $6 extra for bikes.

From Harwich Port: You can avoid the summer crowds in Hyannis and board one of **Freedom Cruise Line**'s (702 Rte., 28 in Harwich Port, across from Brax Landing; ℭ 508/432-8999; www.nantucketislandferry.com) passenger-only ferries to Nantucket. From mid-May to early October, boats leave from Saquatucket Harbor in Harwich Port. They make two or three trips a day in season and one trip per day in the shoulder season. The trip takes 1 hour and 10 minutes. A round-trip ticket is $68 for adults, $51 for children 2 to 11, $6 for children 1 and under, and $12 extra for bikes. Parking is free for day-trippers; it's $15 overnight. Advance reservations are highly recommended.

BY AIR You can also fly into **Nantucket Memorial Airport** (ℭ **508/325-5300**), which is about 3 miles south of Nantucket Road, on Old South Road. The flight to Nantucket takes about 30 to 40 minutes from Boston, 20 minutes from Hyannis, and a little more than an hour from New York City airports. Keep in mind, there is frequent shuttle bus service from Nantucket Airport terminal to town for $2.

Airlines providing service to Nantucket include: **Cape Air/Nantucket Airlines** (© 800/ 352-0714 or 508/771-6944; www.flycapeair.com), year-round from Hyannis ($109 round-trip, $55 one-way), Boston (about $300 round-trip, $127–$152 one-way), Martha's Vineyard ($44–$50 each way), and New Bedford ($61–$80 each way); **Continental Express** (© 800/525-0280; www.continental.com), seasonally from Newark (about $520 round-trip); **Island Airlines** (© 800/248-7779 or 508/775-6606; www.islandair. net), year-round from Hyannis ($94 round-trip); and **Colgan/US Airways Express** (© 703/368-8880; www.colganair.com), year-round from Boston ($383 round-trip) and LaGuardia Airport in New York City ($479 and up round-trip). Both **Delta Airlines** and **JetBlue Airways** run flights from JFK Airport in New York City to Nantucket. Delta charges $188 each way for a 1 hour and 20 minute flight. Jet Blue charges $109 each way for a 1 hour and 10 minute flight.

Island Airlines and Nantucket Airlines both offer year-round charter service to the island. Another recommended charter company is **Ocean Wings** (© 800/253-5039; www.flyoceanwings.com).

GETTING AROUND

Nantucket is easily navigated on bike, moped, or foot, and also by shuttle bus or taxi. If you're staying outside of Nantucket Town, however, or if you simply prefer to explore by car, you might want to bring your own car or rent one when you arrive. Adventure-minded travelers may even want to rent a jeep or other four-wheel-drive vehicle, which you can take out on the sand—a unique island experience—on certain sections of the coast (a permit is required—see "By Car & Jeep," below). Keep in mind that if you do opt to travel by car, in-town traffic can reach gridlock in the peak season, and parking can be a nightmare.

BY BIKE & MOPED　When I head to Nantucket for a few days, biking is my preferred mode of transportation. The island itself is relatively flat, and paved bike paths abound—they'll get you from Nantucket Town to Siasconset, Surfside, and Madaket. There are also many unpaved back roads to explore, which make mountain bikes a wise choice when pedaling around Nantucket.

A word of warning to bikers: One-way street signs and all other traffic rules apply to you, too! This law is enforced in Nantucket Town, and don't be surprised if a tanned but stern island policeman requests that you get off your bike and walk. Helmets are required for children 15 and under. Bikers should also remember not to ride on the sidewalks in town, which are busy with pedestrians strolling and exiting shops.

Mopeds and scooters are also prevalent, but watch out for sand on the roads. Be aware that local rules and regulations are strictly enforced. Mopeds are not allowed on sidewalks or bike paths. You'll need a driver's license to rent a moped, and state law requires that you wear a helmet. The following shops rent bikes and scooters (all are within walking distance of the ferries): **Cook's Cycle Shop, Inc.,** 6 S. Beach St. (© 508/228-0800), which rents bikes and mopeds; **Nantucket Bike Shop,** at Steamboat and Straight wharves (© 508/228-1999; www.nantucketbikeshop.com), which rents bikes and scooters; and **Young's Bicycle Shop,** at Steamboat Wharf (© 508/228-1151; www. youngsbicycleshop.com), rents bikes and also does repairs. Cook's has the lowest bike-rental rates. Bike rentals average $20 to $30 for a full day. Most places renting scooters or mopeds require a valid driver's license and the operator to be 18 or older. Rentals cost about $70 for a one-seater or $90 for a two-seater for 24 hours.

Affordable Rentals of Nantucket, 6 S. Beach St. (© **508/235-3500** http://affrentals. com), also rents scooters to people over 21, with a valid driver's license and credit card, for $60 for 4 hours and $80 for 24 hours for a one-person scooter. Two-person scooters are $80 for 4 hours and $100 for 24 hours.

BY SHUTTLE BUS   Inexpensive shuttle buses, with bike racks and accessibility for those with disabilities, make frequent loops through Nantucket Town and beaches, and to outlying spots. For routes and stops, contact the **Nantucket Regional Transit Authority** (© **508/228-7025;** www.shuttlenantucket.com), or pick up a map and schedule at the visitor center on Federal Street or the chamber of commerce office on Main Street (see "Visitor Information," below). The shuttle permits you to bring your clean, dry dog along, too. There's room for two bikes on a first-come, first-served basis. The cost is $1 to $2, and exact change is required. A 3-day pass can be purchased at the visitor center for $10.

Shuttle routes and fares are pretty simple. Downtown shuttle stops are located on the corner of Salem and Washington streets (for South, Miacomet, and Airport loops); on Broad Street, in front of the Foulger Museum (for Madaket Loop and Beach Express); and on Washington Street, at the corner of Main Street (for 'Sconset loops). Most shuttles run approximately every 30 minutes for most of the season, from July until Labor Day, the Mid-Island Loop runs every 15 minutes, and the Miacomet Loop every 20 minutes

- **Airport Loop** services Nantucket Airport to the center of town at Washington Street; every 30 minutes, on the hour and half-hour, from 10am to 6pm; the fare is $2.
- **South Loop** services the Surfside Beach, Hooper Farm Road, and Pleasant Street areas; every 15 minutes, from 7am to 11:30pm; the fare is $1.
- **Miacomet Loop** services the Fairgrounds Road, Bartlett Road, and Hummock Pond areas; every 30 minutes, from 7am to 11:30pm (more frequently during the business months of summer); the fare is $1.
- **Madaket Route** services Madaket (from Broad St. downtown) via Cliff Road and New Lane; every 30 minutes, from 7am to 11:30pm; the fare is $2 each way.
- **'Sconset Route 1** services 'Sconset via Polpis Road; every 80 minutes, from 10am to 6pm; the fare is $2 each way.
- **'Sconset Route 2** services 'Sconset via Old South/Nobadeer Farm and Milestone roads; every 60 minutes, from 7am to 11pm; the fare is $2 each way.
- **Beach Express** services Surfside and Jetties beaches (the in-town stop is on Broad St.); every 40 minutes for Jetties Beach, and every 30 minutes for Surfside Beach, from 10:am to 5:30pm; the fare is $2 each way to Surfside, $1 each way to Jetties.

BY CAR & JEEP   I recommend a car if you'll be here for more than a week or if you're staying outside Nantucket Town. However, there are no in-town parking lots; parking, although free, is limited to Nantucket's handful of narrow streets, which can be a problem in the busy summer months. Also, gas is much more expensive on Nantucket than it is on the mainland.

Four-wheel-drive vehicles are your best bet, as many beaches and nature areas are off sandy paths; be sure to reserve at least a month in advance, if you're coming in summer. If you plan on doing any four-wheeling in the sand, you need to get an **Over-Sand Permit** ($150) from the **Nantucket Police Department** (© **508/228-1212**). To drive in the **Coskata-Coatue** nature area, you need a separate permit from the **Trustees of Reservations,** at the gatehouse (© **508/228-0006**), which costs about $140 for a season pass, or a $35 gate fee for a day-rental four-wheel-drive that comes with the Over-Sand Permit. Dogs are not allowed, even in a car.

The following on-island rental agencies offer cars, Jeeps, and other four-wheel-drive vehicles: **Affordable Rentals of Nantucket,** 6 S. Beach St. (© **508/235-3500** http:// affrentals.com); **Hertz,** at the airport (© **800/654-3131** or 508/228-9421; www.hertz. com); **Nantucket Windmill Auto Rental,** at the airport (© **800/228-1227** or 508/228-1227; www.nantucketautorental.com); and **Young's 4×4 & Car Rental,** Steamboat Wharf (© **508/228-1151;** www.youngsbicycleshop.com). A standard car costs about $95 to $129 per day in season; a four-wheel-drive rental is about $175 to $249 per day (including an Over-Sand Permit).

BY TAXI   You'll find taxis (many are vans that can accommodate large groups or those traveling with bikes) waiting at the airport and at all ferry ports. During the busy summer months, I recommend reserving a taxi in advance to avoid a long wait upon arrival. Rates are flat fees, based on one person riding before 1am, with surcharges for additional passengers, bikes, and dogs. The most centrally located taxi stand is at the bottom of Main Street, in front of the Club Car restaurant. A taxi from the airport to Nantucket Town will cost about $15, plus $1 for each additional person. Reliable cab companies on the island include **Canty's Cab** (© **508/228-2888**); **Chief's Cab** (© **508/284-8497**), which is run by the island's former fire chief; **Lisa's Taxi** (© **508/228-2223**); and **Val's Cab Service** (© **508/228-9410**).

VISITOR INFORMATION

For information, contact the **Nantucket Island Chamber of Commerce,** at 48 Main St., Nantucket, MA 02554 (© **508/228-1700;** www.nantucketchamber.org).

When you arrive, you should also stop by the **Nantucket Visitors Service and Information Bureau,** in Nantucket Town, at 25 Federal St. (© **508/228-0925**), which is open 9am to 5pm daily from June to September, but closed on Sundays from October to May,. Visitor Services is where to call if you are having trouble finding an available room. They have the most up-to-date accommodations availability listings. They can also help with 1-night stays and special events listings.

There are also information booths at Steamboat and Straight wharves. Always check the island's newspapers, *The Inquirer & Mirror* (www.ack.net) and *The Nantucket Independent* (www.nantucketindependent.com), for information on current events and activities around town.

Nantucket Accommodations, P.O. Box 217, Nantucket, MA 02554 (© **508/228-9559;** www.nantucketaccommodation.com), a fee-based private service, can arrange advance reservations for 95% of the island's lodgings. Last-minute travelers can use the **Nantucket Visitors Service and Information Bureau** (© **508/228-0925**), a daily referral service, rather than a booking service. It always has the most updated list of available accommodations.

Automated teller machines (ATMs) can be difficult to locate on Nantucket. **Nantucket Bank** (© **508/228-0580**) has five locations: 2 Orange St., 104 Pleasant St., 1 Amelia Dr., the Hub on Main Street, and the airport lobby, all open 24 hours. **Pacific National Bank** has four locations: the A&P Supermarket (next to the wharves), the Stop & Shop (open 24 hr. seasonally), the Steamship Wharf Terminal, and the Pacific National Bank lobby (open during bank hours only).

In case of a **medical emergency,** the **Nantucket Cottage Hospital,** 57 Prospect St. (© **508/825-8100;** www.nantuckethospital.org), is open 24 hours.

2 BEACHES & RECREATIONAL PURSUITS

BEACHES   In distinct contrast to Martha's Vineyard, virtually all of Nantucket's 110-mile coastline is free and open to the public. Though the pressure to keep people out is sometimes intense (especially when four-wheel-drivers insist on their right to go anywhere, anytime), islanders are proud that they've managed to keep the shoreline in the public domain.

Each of the following areas tends to attract a different crowd.

- **Children's Beach ★:** This small beach is a protected cove just west of busy Steamship Wharf. Appealing to families, it has a park, a playground, restrooms, lifeguards, a snack bar (the beloved Downy Flake, famous for its homemade doughnuts), and even a bandstand for free weekend concerts.
- **Cisco Beach ★★:** About 4 miles from town, in the southwestern quadrant of the island (from Main St., turn onto Milk St., which becomes Hummock Pond Rd.), Cisco enjoys vigorous waves—great for the surfers who flock here, not so great for the waterfront homeowners. Restrooms are available and lifeguards are on duty.
- **Coatue ★:** This fishhook-shaped barrier beach, on the northeastern side of the island, at Wauwinet, is Nantucket's outback, accessible only by four-wheel-drive vehicles, watercraft, or the very strong-legged. Swimming is strongly discouraged because of fierce tides.
- **Dionis Beach ★★★:** About 3 miles out of town (take the Madaket bike path to Eel Point Rd.) is Dionis, which enjoys the gentle sound surf and steep, picturesque bluffs. It's a great spot for swimming, picnicking, and shelling, and you'll find fewer children than at Jetties or Children's beaches. Stick to the established paths to prevent further erosion. Lifeguards patrol here, and restrooms are available.
- **Jetties Beach ★★★:** Located about a half-mile west of Children's Beach, on North Beach Street, Jetties is about a 20-minute walk, or an even shorter bike ride, shuttle bus ride, or drive, from town (there's a large parking lot, but it fills up early on summer weekends). It's another family favorite, for its mild waves, lifeguards, bathhouse, and restrooms. Facilities include the town tennis courts, volleyball nets, a skate park, and a playground; watersports equipment and chairs are also available to rent. There is also The Jetties, an upscale concession stand, complete with bar, serving lunch and dinner. The Fourth of July fireworks are held here. Every August, Jetties hosts an intense sand-castle competition.
- **Madaket Beach ★★★:** Accessible by Madaket Road, the 6-mile bike path that runs parallel to it, and by shuttle bus, this westerly beach is narrow and subject to pounding surf and sometimes serious crosscurrents. Unless it's a fairly tame day, you might content yourself with wading. It's the best spot on the island for admiring the sunset. Facilities include restrooms, lifeguards, and mobile food service.
- **Siasconset ('Sconset) Beach ★★:** The eastern coast of 'Sconset is as pretty as the town itself and rarely, if ever, crowded, perhaps because of the water's strong sideways tow. You can reach it by car, by shuttle bus, or by a less scenic and somewhat hilly (at least for Nantucket) 7-mile bike path. Lifeguards are usually on duty, but the closest facilities (restrooms, grocery store, and cafe) are back in the center of the village.
- **Surfside Beach ★★★:** Three miles south of town via a popular bike/skate path, broad Surfside—equipped with lifeguards, restrooms, and a surprisingly accomplished little snack bar—is appropriately named and commensurately popular. It draws thousands of visitors a day in high season, from college students to families, but the free parking lot can fit only about 60 cars—you do the math, or better yet, ride your bike or take the shuttle bus.

BICYCLING   Several lovely, paved bike paths radiate from the center of town to outlying beaches. The **bike paths** run about 6¼ miles west to Madaket, 3½ miles south to Surfside, and 8¼ miles east to Siasconset. To avoid backtracking from Siasconset, continue north through the charming village and return on the Polpis Road bike path. Strong riders could do a whole circuit of the island in a day. Picnic benches and water fountains stand at strategic points along all the paths.

For a free map of the island's bike paths (it also lists Nantucket's bicycle rules), stop by **Young's Bicycle Shop,** at Steamboat Wharf (© **508/228-1151;** www.youngsbicycleshop.com). It's definitely the best place for bike rentals, from basic three-speeds to high-tech suspension models. In operation since 1931—check out the vintage vehicles on display—they also deliver to your door. See "Getting Around," above, for more bike rental shops.

FISHING   For shellfishing, you'll need a permit from the **harbormaster's office** at 34 Washington St. (© **508/228-7261**), which costs $25 for nonresidents for the season. You'll see surf-casters all over the island (no permit is required). Deep-sea charters heading out of Straight Wharf include Capt. Bob DeCosta's *The Albacore* (© **508/228-5074;** www.albacorecharters.com), Capt. Josh Eldridge's *Monomoy* (© **508/228-6867;** www.monomoychartersnantucket.com), and Capt. David Martin's *Absolute* (© **508/325-4000;** http://absolutesportfishing.com). On the *Monomoy* and the *Absolute,* 5-hour bass-fishing trips for up to 8 people cost $800 to $1,100.

FITNESS   Nantucket Health Club, at 10 Youngs Way (© **508/228-4750;** www.nantuckethealthclub.com), offers all the usual equipment and classes. Nonmembers pay $25 a day.

GOLF   Two pretty courses are open to the public: the 18-hole **Miacomet Golf Course,** 12 W. Miacomet Rd. (© **508/325-0333;** www.miacometgolf.com), and the 9-hole **Siasconset Golf Club,** off Milestone Road (© **508/257-6596**). You'll pay $125 for 18 holes at Miacomet. At Siasconset, playing 9 holes costs $35.

NATURE TRAILS   Through preservationist foresight, about one-third of Nantucket's 42 square miles are protected from development. Contact the **Nantucket Conservation Foundation,** at 118 Cliff Rd. (© **508/228-2884;** www.nantucketconservation.com), for a map of their holdings ($4), which include the 205-acre **Windswept Cranberry Bog** (off Polpis Rd.), where bogs are interspersed amid hardwood forests; and a portion of the 1,100-acre **Coskata-Coatue Wildlife Refuge,** comprising the barrier beaches beyond Wauwinet (see "Organized Tours," below). **The Maria Mitchell Association** (see "Museums & Historic Landmarks," below) sponsors guided birding and wildflower walks in season.

TENNIS   The town courts are located next to Jetties Beach, a short walk west of town; call the **Nantucket Parks and Recreation Commission** (© **508/325-5334**) for information. The town courts cost $20 an hour for singles and $25 an hour for doubles. Though it's not generally open to the public, the grand, turn-of-the-19th-century **Siasconset Casino,** New Street, Siasconset (© **508/257-6585;** www.siasconsetcasino.com), occasionally has courts available for rent for nonmembers from 1 to 3pm for $40 an hour.

WATERSPORTS   Jetties Sailing Center manages the concession at **Jetties Beach** (© **508/228-5358**), which offers lessons and rents out kayaks, sailboards, sailboats, and more. Rental rates for single kayaks are $20 to $25 per hour; sailboards $20 to $25 per hour; and Sunfish $35 per hour. **Sea Nantucket,** on tiny Francis Street Beach, off Washington Street (© **508/228-7499**), also rents kayaks; it's a quick sprint across the harbor to beautiful Coatue. Single kayaks rent for $40 and tandems rent for $70, for 4½ hours.

sailing.org) gives relatively low-cost private and group lessons from the Jetties pier for adults (16 and up) and children; a seasonal adult membership covering open-sail privileges costs $250 for 4 weeks. One 2-hour private lesson costs $125.

Gear for scuba-diving, fishing, and snorkeling is readily available at the souvenir shop **Sunken Ship,** on South Water and Broad streets, near Steamboat Wharf (☎ **508/228-9226;** http://sunkenship.com). Fishing gear costs $20 per day, snorkeling gear costs $15 per day, and scuba-diving gear costs $75 per day. Scuba-diving lessons are $550.

---

3 MUSEUMS & HISTORIC LANDMARKS

Hadwen House ★★   During Nantucket's most prosperous years, whaling merchant Joseph Starbuck built the "Three Bricks" (nos. 93, 95, and 97 Main St.) for his three sons. His daughter married successful businessman William Hadwen, owner of the candle factory that is now the Whaling Museum, and Hadwen built this grand Greek Revival home across the street from his brothers-in-law in 1845. Although locals (mostly Quakers) were scandalized by the opulence, the local outrage spurred Hadwen on, and he decided to make the home even grander than he had first intended. The home soon became a showplace for entertaining the Hadwens' many wealthy friends. The Historical Association has done a magnificent job of restoring the home and furnishing it with period furniture, fabrics, porcelains, wallpapers, and other decorative accessories thought to be original. The gardens are maintained in period style by the Nantucket Garden Club.

96 Main St. (at Pleasant St., a few blocks southwest of the town center). ☎ 508/228-1894. www.nha.org. Admission included in Nantucket Historical Association's History Ticket ($18 adults, $9 children); admission for historic sites only (not Whaling Museum) $6 adults, $3 children. June–Sept Mon–Sat 10am–5pm, Sun noon–5pm; call for off-season hours. Closed Dec–Mar.

Jethro Coffin House ★★   Built around 1686, this saltbox is the oldest building left on the island. A National Historical Landmark, the brick design on its central chimney has earned it the nickname "The Horseshoe House." It was struck by lightning and severely damaged (in fact, nearly cut in two) in 1987, prompting a long-overdue restoration. Dimly lit by leaded-glass diamond-pane windows, it's filled with period furniture such as lathed ladder-back chairs and a clever trundle bed on wooden wheels. Nantucket Historical Association docents will fill you in on all the related lore.

6 Sunset Hill Lane (off W. Chester Rd., about ¹/₂ mile northwest of the town center). ☎ 508/228-1894. www.nha.org. Admission included in Nantucket Historical Association's History Ticket ($18 adults, $9 children); admission for historic sites only (not the Whaling Museum) $6 adults, $3 children. Late May to mid-Oct Mon–Sat 10am–5pm; Sun noon–5pm. Closed mid-Oct to late May.

Maria Mitchell Association ★★ (Kids)   This is a group of six buildings organized and maintained in honor of distinguished astronomer and Nantucket native Maria Mitchell (1818–89). The science center consists of astronomical observatories, with a lecture series, children's science seminars, and stellar observation opportunities (when the sky is clear) from the **Loines Observatory,** at 59 Milk St. Ext. (☎ **508/228-9273**). The Loines Observatory is open July and August on Monday, Wednesday, and Friday at 9pm; September to June, it's open Friday at 8pm. There is no opportunity for viewing at the older **Vestal Street Observatory,** at 3 Vestal St. (☎ **508/228-9273**), which is open June to September from Tuesday through Saturday at 11am only, for a 1-hour lecture about the association's history in the field of astronomy.

The **Hinchman House Natural Science Museum** (✆ **508/228-0898**), at 7 Milk St. (at Vestal St.), houses a visitor center and offers evening lectures, bird-watching, wildflower and nature walks, and discovery classes for children and adults. The **Mitchell House** (✆ **508/228-2896**), at 1 Vestal St., the astronomer's birthplace, features a children's history series and adult-artisan seminars, and it has wildflower and herb gardens. The **Science Library** (✆ **508/228-9219**) is at 2 Vestal St., and the tiny, child-oriented **aquarium** (✆ **508/228-5387**) is at 28 Washington St., and is open Monday to Saturday 9am to 4pm.

4 Vestal St. (at Milk St., about ¹/₂ mile southwest of the town center). ✆ **508/228-9198.** www.mmo.org. Admission to each site $6 adults, $5 children; museum pass (for birthplace, aquarium, science museum, and Vestal St. Observatory) $10 adults, $8 children ages 6–12. Early June–late Aug Tues–Sat 10am–4pm; call for off-season hours.

Nantucket Shipwreck and Lifesaving Museum ★★ (Finds) Housed in a replica of the Nantucket Life-Saving Station (the original serves as the island's youth hostel), the museum has loads of interesting exhibits, including historic photos and newspaper clippings, as well as one of the last remaining Massachusetts Humane Society surf boats and its horse-drawn carriage. Two-hour children's programs (ages 6–10) are offered in the summer for $20, with one offering demonstrations of the breaches buoy lifesaving technique.

158 Polpis Rd. (3 miles east of town). ✆ **508/228-1885.** www.nantucketlifesavingmuseum.com. Admission $5 adults, $3 children. Mid-June to mid-Oct daily 10am–4pm.

Whaling Museum ★★★ (Kids) Reopened after a grand multimillion-dollar renovation, this museum is a showpiece in the region. Appropriately, it is housed in a former spermaceti-candle factory (candles used to be made from a waxy fluid extracted from sperm whales). Kids will love the awe-inspiring skeleton of a 43-foot finback whale (stranded in the 1960s), and adults will be fascinated by the exceptional collections of scrimshaw and nautical art. (Check out the action painting, *Ship Spermo of Nantucket in a Heavy Thunder-Squall on the Coast of California 1876,* executed by a captain who survived the storm.) A wall-size map depicts the around-the-world meanderings of the *Alpha,* accompanied by related journal entries. The admission price includes daily lectures on the brief and colorful history of the industry, such as the beachside "whalebecue" feasts that natives and settlers once enjoyed. Don't miss the gift shop on the way out.

13 Broad St. (in the center of town). ✆ **508/228-1894.** www.nha.org. Admission $15 adults, $8 children 5–14; admission also included in the Nantucket Historical Association's History Ticket ($18 adults, $9 children). Apr–Nov Mon–Wed and Fri–Sat 10am–5pm, Thurs 10am–8pm, Sun noon–5pm. Closed Dec–Mar.

4 ORGANIZED TOURS

Coskata-Coatue Wildlife Refuge Natural History Tour ★★★ (Kids) The Trustees of Reservations, a private statewide conservation organization that oversees the bulk of the Coskata-Coatue Wildlife Refuge, offers a 3-hour naturalist-guided tour twice a day. The trip is over sand dunes via Ford Expedition out to the **Great Point Lighthouse,** a partly solar-powered replica of the 1818 original. Those interested can also tour the inside of the lighthouse. During the trip through this rare habitat, you might spot snowy egrets, ospreys, terns, and oystercatchers. Call to make a reservation.

Departs from Wauwinet parking lot, 120 Wauwinet Rd. ✆ **508/228-6799.** $40 adults, $15 children 12 and under. Call for reservations. Mid-May to mid-Oct daily 9:30am and 1:30pm. Closed mid-Oct to mid-May.

ATTRACTIONS ●
Hadwen House **49**
Jethro Coffin House **5**
Maria Mitchell Association **50**
Whaling Museum **22**

ACCOMMODATIONS ■
Anchor Inn **9**
Beachside at Nantucket **1**
Brant Point Inn **2**
Brass Lantern Inn **12**
Centerboard Guest House **7**
Cliff Lodge **4**
The Cottages/Woof Cottages **44**
Jared Coffin House **15**
Martin House Inn **8**
Nantucket Whaler Guest House **21**
The Nesbitt Inn **20**
The Pineapple Inn **14**
The Ships Inn **47**
Summer House at India Street **13**

Union Street Inn **46**
Vanessa Noel Hotel & Hotel Green **16**
The Veranda House **11**
White Elephant **3**

DINING ◆
American Seasons **6**
Arno's **35**
Black Eyed Susan's **34**
Boarding House **31**
Brant Point Grill **3**
The Brotherhood of Thieves **18**
Cambridge Street **40**
Cap'n Tobey's Chowder House **41**
Centre Street Bistro **33**

Club Car **38**
Company of the Cauldron **32**
Corazon del Mar **28**
Dune **19**
Easy Street Cantina **24**
The Even Keel Café **36**
Figs at 29 Fair **48**
Fog Island Café **39**
Island Reef **10**
The Juice Bar **27**
Le Languedoc Bistro **17**
LoLa Burgers **25**
Nantucket Lobster Trap **45**
Òran Mór **23**
Queequeg's **26**
Ropewalk **43**
Ships Inn Restaurant **47**
Starlight Theatre & Café **37**
Straight Wharf **42**
Sushi by Yoshi **30**
Town **29**

Endeavor Sailing Excursions ★★ (**Moments**) The *Endeavor* is a spirited 31-foot replica Friendship sloop, ideal for jaunts across the harbor into Nantucket Sound. Skipper James Genthner will gladly drop you off at one of the beaches for a bit of sunbathing or beachcombing.

Slip 15, Straight Wharf. *©* **508/228-5585.** www.endeavorsailing.com. Reservations recommended. Rates $25–$35 for a 1¹/₂-hr. sail (highest rates July–Aug). Closed Nov–Apr.

Gail's Tours ★★ (**Value**) If you want to get some dirt on the island's colorful residents, Gail Nickerson Johnson—a seventh-generation native whose mother started a tour business back in the 1940s—has the inside track, and the charm, to keep a captive vanload rapt throughout a 2-hour circuit of island highlights, including lots of celebrity info.

Departs from the Nantucket Information Bureau, 25 Federal St., and from prearranged pickup sites. *©* **508/257-6557.** www.nantucket.net/tours/gails. Reservations required. Rates $25 adults, free for children 3 and under. July–Aug departures at 10am, 1pm, and 3pm; call for off-season hours.

Nantucket Historical Association Guided Walking Tours ★ Stroll along downtown's cobblestone streets on this Historical Association tour that spotlights the history and architecture of Nantucket. The tours are led by Nantucket Historical Association docents trained in Nantucket history.

Sign up for tour at the Whaling Museum, 13 Broad St. (in the center of town). *©* **508/228-1894.** www.nha.org. Admission included in Nantucket Historical Association's History Ticket ($18 adults, $9 children). Apr–Nov Mon–Sat 10:15am and 2:15pm. Closed Dec–Mar.

5 KID STUFF

The **Nantucket Parks and Recreation Commission** (*©* **508/228-7213**) organizes various free and low-cost activities for kids, such as tennis clinics, a concert series, and tie-dye workshops (bring your own T-shirt). The **Artists' Association of Nantucket** (*©* **508/228-0294**; www.nantucketarts.org) sponsors a variety of classes for children in different media, and the **Nantucket Island School of Design and the Arts** (*©* **508/228-9248**; www.nisda.org) offers all sorts of summer courses. The **Nantucket Atheneum** (*©* **508/228-1110**; www.nantucketatheneum.org) holds readings in its spiffy children's wing. The **Nantucket Historical Association** (*©* **508/228-1894**; www.nha.org) sponsors **Living History for Children,** 3- to 4-day camp adventures for children 6 to 12, which include grinding flour at the Old Mill, baking bread at the Oldest House, and trying your hand at knots and sailors' valentines. The cost is $120 to $140.

Little kids might like to get their hands on (and into) the touch tanks at the modest little **Maria Mitchell Aquarium,** at 28 Washington St. (*©* **508/228-5387;** www.mmo.org), which overlooks the harbor from whence the creatures came; the cost is $6 for adults and $5 for children. It's open June through mid-October Monday to Saturday from 10am to 4pm. For a real seafaring adventure, consider embarking on a treasure hunt aboard the *Endeavor* (*©* **508/228-5585**).

6 SHOPPING

Nantucket shopping is so phenomenal you'll be tempted to rent a U-Haul. It's as if all the best big-city buyers, from Bendel's to Brooks Brothers, got together and gathered their favorite stuff. True, some tourist dreck has managed to drift in, but most of what you'll find for sale is as high in quality as it is in price—everything from $6 boxes of chocolate-covered dried cranberries to $900 cashmere sweaters. There are also bargains, such as lightly used designer togs at the **Nantucket Cottage Hospital Thrift Shop,** at 17 India St. (© **508/228-1125;** www.nantuckethospital.org/ThriftShop/ThriftShop.html), and at the **Murray's Warehouse** outlet, at 7 New St. (© **508/228-3584**).

ART & CRAFTS   The **Artists' Association of Nantucket** has the widest selection of work by locals, and the gallery at 19 Washington St. (© **508/228-0294;** www.nantucket arts.org) is impressive. In February and March, it's open by appointment only.

The celebrated sculptor **David L. Hostetler** exhibits his work in one of the little galleries along Old South Wharf, 2 Old South Wharf (© **508/228-5152;** www.hostetler sculpture.com). Private viewing appointments are also available in his large showroom. His work in various media appears as spiritual icons expressed in the female form.

Exquisite art-glass pieces, as well as ceramics, jewelry, and basketry, can be found at **Dane Gallery,** 28 Centre St. (© **508/228-7779;** http://danegallery.com), where owners Robert and Jayne Dane show top-quality work. You'll be amazed at the colors and shapes of the glassware.

BOOKS   At **Mitchell's Book Corner,** 54 Main St. (© **508/228-1080;** www.mitchells bookcorner.com), Mimi Beman handpicks her stock, with an astute sampling of general-interest books and an entire room dedicated to regional and maritime titles. **Nantucket Bookworks,** 25 Broad St. (© **508/228-4000;** www.nantucketbookworks.com), is a charming bookstore, strong on customer service and with a central location.

CHOCOLATE   **Sweet Inspirations,** 26 Centre St. (© **508/228-5814**), has been satisfying sweet tooths on Nantucket since 1981. This is artisan chocolate, carefully crafted on site. Even better, the beautiful Nantucket-themed packaging makes this a great place to come for gifts. The Rainbow Fleet tin containing chocolate scallop shells, clipper-ship medallions, and Nantucket mints, among other chocolates, is a delight.

FASHION   Eco-fashionista **Cheryl Fudge,** 23 Federal St. (© **508/228-9159**), sells what she calls up-cycled clothing, turning scarves into halter tops, for instance. Her funky dresses and vintage jewelry and ACK Green line of organic clothing are developing a passionate following. **Current Vintage,** 4 Easy St.; (© **508/228-5073;** http://current vintage.com), is one of the most original shops to open in recent years. Beth English, who is known on the island for exquisite taste, sells gorgeous vintage gowns and accessories, such as antique bags and jewelry, as well as special wines from small wineries.

Hepburn, 3 Salem St. (© **508/228-1458**), sells ultrafashionable women's clothing and accessories, a cut above the usual fare.

Martha's Vineyard may have spawned "Black Dog" fever, but this island boasts the inimitable "Nantucket reds"—cotton clothing that starts out tomato-red and washes out to salmon-pink. The fashion originated at **Murray's Toggery Shop,** 62 Main St. (© **800/ 368-2134** or 508/228-0437; www.nantucketreds.com). Legend has it that the original duds were colored with an inferior dye that washed out almost immediately. However, customers so liked the thick cottons and instant aged look that the proprietor was forced to search high and low for more of the same fabric. Roland Hussey Macy, founder of Macy's, got his start here in the 1830s. Today's management also keeps up with current trends.

Preppy patterns and bright colors are back! You'll find **Lilly Pulitzer's In The Pink,** which has sensational minidresses, at 5 S. Water St. (© **508/228-0569**).

Ralph Lauren's store, at 16 Main St. (☎ **508/228-9451**), scandalized Nantucketers when it first opened (there are no chains here, not even upscale ones), but now everyone is used to it. The store is stocked with high-end resort wear.

Zero Main, at 0 Main St. (☎ **508/228-4401**), has a limited but fine selection of elegant yet casual women's clothes, shoes, and accessories.

GIFTS/HOME DECOR **Nantucket Looms,** at 16 Federal St. (☎ **508/228-1908;** www. nantucketlooms.com), is the place to ogle exquisite brushed mohair chaise throws, and other handmade woven items. The weaving studio is upstairs, where they also make blankets and sweaters of cotton and cashmere.

Erica Wilson Needle Works, 25 Main St. (☎ **508/228-9881;** www.ericawilson. com), features the designs of its namesake, an islander since 1958 and author of more than two dozen books on needlepoint. The shop offers hands-on guidance for hundreds of grateful adepts, as well as kits and handiwork of other noteworthy designers.

The also eponymous **Claire Murray,** 11 S. Water St. (☎ **508/228-1913;** www.claire murray.com), is famous for its elaborate hand-hooked rugs. As a New York transplant running a Nantucket B&B in the late 1970s, Murray took up the traditional art of hooking rugs to see her through the slow season. She now runs a retail company grossing millions a year and is so busy creating new collections that she has hundreds of "hookers" (probably an old profession, but not the oldest) working for her around the world. Do-it-yourself kits ($100–$500) are sold in the shop here for about two-thirds the price of the finished rugs and come with complimentary lessons.

JEWELRY **Diana Kim England, Goldsmiths,** 56 Main St. (☎ **800/343-1468** or 508/ 228-3766; www.dianakimengland.com), is a team of five goldsmiths that have almost 70 years of combined experience in making jewelry. You'll find gold baskets and pearls, as well as unique custom pieces.

NEWSSTAND **The Hub,** 31 Main St. (☎ **508/325-0200**), offers a selection of newspapers, magazines, and books, as well as greeting cards by local artists.

SEAFOOD **Sayle's Seafood,** 99 Washington St. Ext. (☎ **508/228-4599;** www.sayles seafood.com), sells fresh seafood from Nantucket waters and a menu of takeout seafood platters. This is a great place to get a huge, steaming plate of fried clams to go.

TOYS **The Toy Boat,** 41 Straight Wharf (☎ **508/228-4552;** www.thetoyboat.com), is keen on creative toys that are also educational. In addition to the top commercial lines, owner Loren Brock stocks lots of locally crafted, hand-carved playthings, such as "rainbow fleet" sailboats, part of the Harbor Series that includes docks, lighthouses, boats, and everything your child needs to create his or her own Nantucket Harbor. There are also stackable lighthouse puzzles replicating Nantucket's beams.

---

7 WHERE TO STAY

Most visitors to Nantucket will wish to stay in the center of town. There's no need for a car here; in fact, parking can be a real problem in season. Everything is within walking distance, including beaches, restaurants, and the finest shopping in the region. Unless otherwise stated, hotels are open year-round.

Free parking is available at many Nantucket lodging establishments and at all large establishments. Some small inns have limited parking and it is best to check with the inn about how many cars they have room for. Fortunately, all the lodging establishments

listed here are within walking distance to the center of town or provide shuttle service. **241**
Cars are not needed on Nantucket as there is very good public bus service and numerous taxi companies.

VERY EXPENSIVE

Cliffside Beach Club ★★★ (Finds)   Right on the beach and within walking distance (about 1 mile) of town, this is the premier lodging on the island. There's a sublime beachy-ness to the whole setup, from the simply decorated rooms, the cheerful, youthful staff, the sea of antique wicker in the clubhouse, and of course, the blue, yellow, and green umbrellas lined up on the beach. All rooms have such luxuries as French milled soaps and exceptional linens. A very good continental breakfast is served in the large clubhouse room, its beamed ceilings draped with colorful quilts. The restaurant, **The Galley,** recently renovated, is one of the island's finest.

46 Jefferson Ave. (about 1 mile from town center), Nantucket, MA 02554. ℭ **508/228-0618.** Fax 508/325-4735. www.cliffsidebeach.com. 25 units, 1 cottage. Summer $450–$710 double; $875–$2,500 suite; $900 3-bedroom apt; $1,085 cottage. There is a 5.3% service charge in addition to taxes. Rates include continental breakfast. AE. Closed mid-Oct to late May. **Amenities:** Restaurant (The Galley, see p. 246); babysitting; concierge; exercise facility (Cybex equipment and a trainer on staff); steam saunas; indoor hydrotherapy spa. *In room:* A/C, TV/VCR, fridge, hair dryer.

Nantucket Whaler Guest House ★★   This lodging option, an 1850s Greek Revival sea captain's house, is unique in that all of the rooms are suites with their own entrance and kitchen facilities. Compared to other B&Bs on the island, this one has a particularly private feel, almost like having your own apartment. Many of the rooms have decks or patios. All rooms are comfortably outfitted with cottage-y furnishings, including overstuffed couches and stacks of games and books. Those guests who would prefer not to whip up their own breakfast and want to eat in can order up a customized continental breakfast basket for $40 per person.

8 N. Water St. (in the center of town), Nantucket, MA 02554. ℭ **508/228-6597.** Fax 508/228-6291. www.nantucketwhaler.com. 12 units, 8 with tub/shower combination, 4 with shower only. Summer $325–$460 double; $650–$795 2-bedroom. AE, DC, MC, V. Closed mid-Dec to late Apr. No children 12 and under. *In room:* A/C, TV/VCR, CD player, hair dryer.

Vanessa Noel Hotel (VNH) and Hotel Green (Overrated)   Shoe designer Vanessa Noel has two centrally located inns side by side. VNH has eight rooms with such boutique hotel features as Philippe Starck fixtures, queen-size feather beds with custom Frette linens, Bulgari toiletries, robes, slippers, 15-inch flatscreen plasma televisions, and minibars stocked with the hotel's bottled water. But most of the rooms in this historic building are tiny, though there are two, including an attic space, that are comfortably spacious. There is also the problem that there is virtually no lobby space. **Vanessa Noel Hotel Green,** 33 Centre St. (nearby, same phone number), which has an ecological theme, uses organic cottons for bedding and eco-friendly toiletries. It also has small rooms and no lobby.

5 Chestnut St. (in the center of town), Nantucket, MA 02554. ℭ **508/228-5300.** Fax 508/228-8995. www.vanessanoelhotel.com. 16 units. Summer VNH $300–$480 double; Green Hotel $250–$900 double. AE, DISC, MC, V. *In room:* A/C, TV, hair dryer, minibar.

The Wauwinet ★★   This ultradeluxe beachfront retreat is Nantucket's only Relais & Châteaux property. The inn is at the tip of a wildlife sanctuary and is nestled between the Atlantic Ocean and Nantucket Bay. All the rooms—some are on the small side—have pine armoires, Audubon prints, handsome fabrics, and an array of antique accessories. Extras include Egyptian cotton bathrobes and bottled water. Additional perks include a personalized set of engraved note cards. It's fun and romantic to order breakfast in your room here; the steward sets it up with a snowy white tablecloth and fine china. There is complimentary van service into town (12 trips daily).

120 Wauwinet Rd. (P.O. Box 2580, about 8 miles east of Nantucket center), Nantucket, MA 02584 ℂ **800/426-8718** or 508/228-0145. Fax 508/325-0657. www.wauwinet.com. 25 units, 10 cottages. Summer $680–$1,250 double; $1,020–$1,450 1- and 2-bedroom cottages. Rates include full breakfast and afternoon wine and cheese. AE, DC, DISC, MC, V. Closed mid-Oct to mid-May. Children 12 and older only. **Amenities:** Fine-dining restaurant (Topper's at The Wauwinet; see review below); mountain bikes on loan; bocce ball on loan; concierge; croquet lawn; room service; spa; 2 clay tennis courts w/pro shop and teaching pro; rowboats, sailboats, sea kayaks on loan. In room: A/C, TV/DVD and movie library, CD player, hair dryer, Wi-Fi.

White Elephant ★★★ This luxury property, right on the harbor, is the ultimate in-town lodging. Rooms are big and airy (the most spacious rooms on Nantucket), with country-chic decor and most with harbor views. Rooms are in the main hotel building as well as in 12 smaller "cottages," some of which contain two or three units. About half the rooms have working fireplaces. The hotel has pleasant common rooms, including a cozy library with a large fireplace.

50 Easton St. (P.O. Box 1390), Nantucket, MA 02554. ℂ **800/445-6574** or 508/228-2500. Fax 508/325-1195. www.whiteelephanthotel.com. 52 units, 11 cottages, 61 with tub/shower combination, 2 with shower only. Summer $615–$775 double; $680 1-bedroom cottage; $1,850 2-bedroom cottage; $1,430 3-bedroom cottage. Rates include full breakfast. AE, DC, DISC, MC, V. Closed Nov–Mar except for 1 week during Christmas Stroll, in early December. **Amenities:** Restaurant (lobster and steakhouse, serving lunch and dinner daily, plus an afternoon raw bar); concierge; exercise room; room service; spa. In room: A/C, TV/DVD and movie library, fridge, hair dryer.

EXPENSIVE

Beachside at Nantucket ★ No ordinary motel, the Beachside's 90 air-conditioned bedrooms and lobby have been lavished with Provençal prints and handsome rattan and wicker furniture; the patios and decks overlooking the central courtyard, with its heated pool, have been prettified with French doors and latticework. This place has very inexpensive deals in the shoulder season, with rooms as cheap as $110 per night!

30 N. Beach St. (about ³/₄ mile west of the town center), Nantucket, MA 02554. ℂ **800/322-4433** or 508/228-2241. Fax 508/228-8901. www.thebeachside.com. 90 units. Summer $355–$505 double; $425–$750 suite. Rates include continental breakfast. AE, DC, DISC, MC, V. Closed late Oct–late Apr. **Amenities:** Heated outdoor pool. In room: A/C, TV, fridge, hair dryer, Wi-Fi.

The Cottages/Woof Cottages ★★ These small apartments have the best location on the island, stacked up on a wharf that juts out into Nantucket Harbor. If you are looking for a place on Nantucket where you can bring your pooch, these one- and two-bedroom cottages are the perfect choice. All cottages are fresh and sparkling—floors polished, walls painted—and each has an eat-in kitchen and cozy living-room area. Dogs get a welcome basket of treats and a Nantucket bandanna. Guests have privileges at the White Elephant spa at a sister property.

24 Old South Wharf (in the center of town), Nantucket, MA 02554. ℂ **866/838-9253** or 508/325-1499. Fax 508/325-1173. www.harborviewcottages.com. 33 units. Summer $490–$750 studio and 1-bedroom; $750–$1,145 2-bedroom; $1,090–$1,240 3-bedroom. AE, MC, V. Closed mid-Oct to May. Pet-friendly. In room: TV/VCR, CD player, hair dryer, kitchenette, Wi-Fi.

The Pineapple Inn ★★ The graceful Quaker entrance of the 1838 home bespeaks the hospitality to come. Rooms are spacious and decorated in a colonial style with fine reproductions and antiques, including handmade Oriental rugs, marble bathrooms, and many four-poster canopy beds. Five large king bedrooms feature tiger maple beds. The smaller, less expensive rooms are on the third floor. The garden patio, with climbing roses, is a fine place to enjoy an afternoon cocktail and contemplate dinner plans. This inn is owned by the same owners as the Summer House, and guests can take a jitney ride to 'Sconset to enjoy the pool at that oceanfront property.

10 Hussey St. (in the center of town), Nantucket, MA 02554. ⓒ **508/228-9992.** Fax 508/325-6051. www.pineappleinn.com. 12 units, 8 with tub/shower combination, 4 with shower only. Summer $230–$375 double. Rates include continental breakfast. AE, MC, V. Closed early Dec to mid-Apr. No children 8 or under. *In room:* A/C, TV, hair dryer.

Summer House at India Street ★   There are five Summer House properties, four in town and the original property, the Summer House cottages, in 'Sconset. The India Street property is the most centrally located and is a handsome, restored historic house with top-notch amenities. Rooms are equipped with robes and deluxe toiletries. Most of the rooms are on the small side; bathrooms are former closets. Guests have access to complimentary jitney service to the Summer House beachfront property in 'Sconset (where rooms are $600 and up a night) and use of the pool there.

31 India St. (in the center of town), Nantucket, MA 02554. ⓒ **508/257-4577.** Fax 508/257-4590. www.thesummerhouse.com. 10 units. Summer $325–$395 double. Rates include continental breakfast. AE, MC, V. Closed Jan–Apr. *In room:* A/C, TV, hair dryer.

Union Street Inn ★★ (**Finds**)   Sophisticated innkeepers Deborah and Ken Withrow have a terrific location for their historic 1770s property, just steps from Main Street yet in a quiet, residential section. Many rooms have canopied or four-poster beds; half have working wood-burning fireplaces. The comfortable beds are made up with Egyptian cotton linens. Bathrooms are equipped with piqué-woven bathrobes and large terry bath towels.

7 Union St. (in the center of town), Nantucket, MA 02554. ⓒ **888/517-0707** or 508/228-9222. Fax 508/325-0848. www.unioninn.com. 12 units, 1 with tub/shower combination, 11 with shower only. Summer $295–$575 double; $545 suite. Rates include full breakfast. AE, MC, V. Closed Nov–Mar. *In room:* A/C, TV, hair dryer, no phone, Wi-Fi.

The Veranda House ★★ (**Finds**)   This stylish boutique inn is located in a quiet neighborhood a short walk from the center of town. It is perched on a hill, so rooms on the third floor have distant harbor views. Some of the more deluxe rooms have private balconies. All rooms have such extras as robes; beds are made with Frette linens and goose-down comforters. A continental breakfast is served, with great hospitality, on the ample front porch.

3 Step Lane (a few blocks from town center), Nantucket, MA 02554. ⓒ **877/228-0695** or 508/228-0695. Fax 508/374-0406. www.theverandahouse.com. 18 units. Summer $309–$449 double; $589 suite. Rates include continental breakfast. AE, MC, V. Closed mid-Oct to late May. *In room:* A/C, hair dryer, Wi-Fi.

MODERATE

Anchor Inn ★ (**Value**)   Innkeepers Ann and Charles Balas have a historic gem in this 1806 sea captain's home located next to the Old North Church. Authentic details can be found throughout both houses, in the antique hardware and paneling, wide-board floors, and period furnishings. Guests enjoy a continental breakfast with home-baked muffins at individual tables on the sunny enclosed porch or in the garden.

66 Centre St. (in the center of town), Nantucket, MA 02554. ⓒ **508/228-0072.** www.anchor-inn.net. 11 units, 2 with tub/shower combination, 9 with shower only. Summer $195–$229 double. Rates include continental breakfast. AE, MC, V. Closed Jan–Feb. *In room:* A/C, TV, hair dryer, Wi-Fi.

Brass Lantern Inn ★ (Value)   This reasonably priced historic inn just a short walk to the center of town is a great option for those traveling with children and/or pets. It is very close to Broad Street, where you'll find the Whaling Museum, good restaurants, and a convenient shuttle bus stop for the beach bus. The eight rooms in the front part of the inn are decorated with antiques, four-poster beds and Oriental rugs. Eight rooms in the back or garden wing area are more spacious and are decorated in a more cottage-y, contemporary style.

11 N. Water St. (in the center of town), Nantucket, MA 02554. ✆ **800/377-6609** or 508/228-4064. www.brasslanternnantucket.com. 16 units, 8 with tub/shower combination, 8 with shower only. Summer $325–$425 double; $600 2-bedroom suite. Rates include continental breakfast. AE, MC, V. Pet-friendly. *In room:* TV, hair dryer.

Brant Point Inn ★ (Value)   Thea and Pete Kaiser's two inn buildings, Brant Point and Atlantic Mainstap next door, offer relatively affordable accommodations in a good location, in between town and Jetties Beach. The inns are traditional post-and-beam style with country furnishings, such as quilts on the beds. The guest living room has exposed oak beams and a massive Belgian block fireplace. Pete is an experienced fishermen, and guests can arrange for fishing trips.

6 North Beach St. (a few blocks west of town), Nantucket, MA 02554. ✆ **508/228-5442.** Fax 508/228-8498. www.brantpointinn.com. 8 units. Summer $245 double; $225–$345 suite. Rates include continental breakfast. AE, MC, V. Closed Nov–Apr. *In room:* TV.

Centerboard Guest House ★ (Value)   This 1886 home is replete with parquet floors, Oriental rugs, lavish fabrics, plush feather mattresses, and lace-trimmed linens. The overall look is light, airy, and less cluttered than the original Victorian look. Of the inn's seven bedrooms, the first-floor suite is perhaps the most romantic, with a green-marble Jacuzzi and a private living room with fireplace. Other rooms and bathrooms are small, but all have bathrobes and minifridges.

8 Chester St. (in the center of town), Nantucket, MA 02554. ✆ **877/228-2811** or 508/228-9696. Fax 508/325-4798. www.centerboardguesthouse.com. 7 units. Summer $275–$450 double; $435 suite. Rates include continental breakfast. AE, MC, V. Closed Nov–Apr. *In room:* A/C, TV, fridge, hair dryer.

Cliff Lodge ★ (Finds)   A few blocks from the center of town, this charming 1771 whaling captain's house maintains its fresh, cozy-casual style. The cheerful guest rooms feature colorful quilts and splatter-painted floors. Rooms range from a first-floor beauty with king-size bed, paneled walls, and fireplace to the tiny third-floor rooms tucked into the eaves. The spacious apartment in the rear of the house is a sunny delight. Climb up to the widow's walk for a bird's-eye view of the town and harbor.

9 Cliff Rd. (a few blocks from the center of town), Nantucket, MA 02554. ✆ **508/228-9480.** Fax 508/228-6308. www.clifflodgenantucket.com. 12 units. Summer $155 single; $195–$320 double; $395 apt. Rates include continental breakfast. AE, MC, V. No children 10 and under. *In room:* A/C, TV.

Jared Coffin House ★ (Kids)   A little down on its heels, this three-story brick manse in the center of town was built in 1845 to the specs of the social-climbing Mrs. Coffin, who abandoned Nantucket for the big city after 2 years and left the house to boarders. The several buildings in the complex are awaiting a renovation by new owners, who also own the White Elephant (see review above) on the harbor. This inn's central location does have a drawback: The front rooms can be quite noisy.

29 Broad St. (at Centre St.), Nantucket, MA 02554. ✆ **800/248-2405** or 508/228-2400. Fax 508/228-8549. www.jaredcoffinhouse.com. 60 units, 52 with tub/shower combination, 8 with shower only. Summer $155–$175 single; $290–$470 double. AE, DC, DISC, MC, V. **Amenities:** Restaurant (Chinese); concierge. *In room:* TV, fridge, hair dryer, Wi-Fi.

9

NANTUCKET

WHERE TO STAY

Martin House Inn ★ (Value)   This is one of the lower-priced B&Bs in town but also one of the most stylish, with a formal parlor, dining rooms, and a spacious side porch. This historic 1803 mariner's home is kept shipshape; and because your innkeeper is an expert baker, it always smells yummy here. The four garret rooms, with a shared bathroom, are a bargain. Higher-priced rooms have four-posters and working fireplaces. The suite has such extras as a flatscreen TV, DVD player, and CD player.

61 Centre St. (btw. Broad and Chester sts., a couple blocks from town center), Nantucket, MA 02554. ✆ **508/228-0678.** Fax 508/325-4798. www.martinhouseinn.net. 13 units, 4 with shared bathroom, 4 with tub/shower combination, 5 with shower only. Summer $125 single with shared bathroom; $195 double with shared bathroom; $220–$385 double; $405 suite. Rates include continental breakfast. AE, MC, V. In room: A/C, no phone.

The Ships Inn ★ (Value)   This pretty, historic inn is on a quiet side street, just slightly removed—3 blocks—from Nantucket's center. Rooms are comfortable, spacious, and charming, and offer a good variety of bed arrangements, such as single rooms and twin beds. The **restaurant** downstairs holds its own (see "Where to Dine," below).

13 Fair St. (a few blocks from town center), Nantucket, MA 02554. ✆ **888/872-4052** or 508/228-0040. Fax 508/228-6524. www.shipsinnnantucket.com. 12 units, 2 with shared bathroom. Summer $135 single with shared bathroom; $275 double. Rates include continental breakfast. AE, DISC, MC, V. Closed late Oct to mid-May. **Amenities:** Fine-dining restaurant located in the basement. In room: A/C, TV, fridge, hair dryer.

INEXPENSIVE

Island Reef ★ (Value)   The inn, a historic Federal-style captain's house, has among the lowest rates around considering the rooms have private bathrooms. Many of the inn's 12 rooms have soaring ceilings, fireplaces, and four-poster beds. It is clean and comfortable.

20 N. Water St., Nantucket, MA 02554. ✆ **508/228-2156.** 12 units. Summer $150–$250 double. Rates include continental breakfast. MC, V. In room: A/C, TV, Wi-Fi.

The Nesbitt Inn ★ (Value)   The owners of this Victorian-style inn, one of the last of the old guesthouses with shared bathrooms, are slowly renovating the property, which has a great location in the center of town. The place still has an old-fashioned feel and is still a bargain. It is spotlessly clean and quite charming.

21 Broad St., Nantucket, MA 02554. ✆ **508/228-0156.** 15 units, 13 with shared bathroom. Summer $125 double with shared bathroom; $170 queen with private bathroom; $240/night, $1,600/week apt with bathroom. Rates include continental breakfast. MC, V. Small dog allowed. In room: No phone.

Robert B. Johnson Memorial Hostel (Value)   This Hostelling International youth hostel enjoys an almost perfect location. Set right beside Surfside Beach, the former "Star of the Sea" is an authentic 1873 lifesaving station, Nantucket's first. Where seven Surfmen once stood ready to save shipwrecked sailors, 49 backpackers now enjoy gender-segregated bunk rooms; the women's quarters, upstairs, still contain a climb-up lookout post.

31 Western Ave. (on Surfside Beach, about 3 miles south of Nantucket Town), Nantucket, MA 02554. ✆ **888/901-2084** or 508/228-0433. Fax 508/228-5672. http://capecod.hiusa.org. 49 beds. $32 to $35 for members; $35 to $38 for nonmembers; $178 private room. MC, V. Closed mid-Sept to mid-May.

8 WHERE TO DINE

Nantucket is filled with outrageously priced restaurants, in which star chefs create dazzling meals served in high style. Obviously you don't need this kind of treatment every night, but you'll probably want to try at least one deluxe place. Many of the best restaurants serve terrific lunches at half the price of their dinners. Thankfully, there are also a number of cafes scattered around town that serve reasonably priced lunches and dinners. Nantucket also has an old-fashioned drugstore soda fountain, **Island Pharmacy,** serving breakfast and lunch on upper Main Street, as well as the best smoothie on the island. It's really the best deli in town. If you dine in town, you may enjoy an evening stroll afterward, as many stores stay open late.

VERY EXPENSIVE

Brant Point Grill ★★ NEW AMERICAN   Recent renovations to the entire White Elephant complex on the harbor have converted this pretty dining room into a lobster, steak, and chops house. Many of the signature dishes, such as the cedar-planked Atlantic salmon and rotisserie of prime rib, are prepared on the Fire Cone grill, a 21st-century interpretation of a Native American technique that cooks food by radiant heat and imparts it with a smoky mesquite flavor. If you can't sit on the terrace, try to snag a seat near one of the windows, where you can watch the twilight fade over the harbor. The candlelight and white, airy dining room make for a perfectly romantic setting. Dinner at this establishment is an expensive proposition. However, the raw bar is open July through Labor Day from 4 to 7pm for light snacks, and a limited and less expensive all-day menu is served from 2:30 to 11pm. You may want to consider having lunch here, a perfect idea for a rainy day, when prices are more reasonable.

At the White Elephant, 50 Easton St. ✆ 508/325-1320. www.whiteelephanthotel.com/restaurant. Reservations strongly recommended. Collared shirt and long pants requested for gentlemen. Main courses $26–$39. AE, DISC, MC, V. Mid-Apr to early Dec daily 8–11am breakfast, 11:30am–3pm lunch, and 5:30–10pm dinner; all-day menu 2:30–11pm. Closed early Dec to mid-Apr.

The Club Car ★ CONTINENTAL   For decades, one of the top restaurants on Nantucket, this venue is coasting a bit on its reputation these days. Prices are sky-high, but quality is not as top-shelf as other venues in town. But this is still a fine place to come for lunch or, even better, the late-night piano-bar scene, both of which are in the antique first-class rail car. The menu at dinner has classic French influences, with the type of dishes, such as sautéed calf's brains and duck foie gras, that are rarely seen on the Cape and islands. The signature dish is Roast Rack of Lamb Club Car (with fresh herbs, honey-mustard glaze, and minted Madeira sauce).

1 Main St. ✆ 508/228-1101. www.theclubcar.com. Reservations recommended. Main courses $24–$45. AE, MC, V. July–Aug daily 11am–4pm and 6–9:30pm; call for off-season hours. Closed late Oct–Apr.

The Galley ★★★ (Moments) NEW AMERICAN   This beachfront restaurant with the coolest bar decor on the island is where you go if you want to feel like you are in a *Travel + Leisure* fashion spread. Given the setting, it's no surprise that the Galley specializes in seafood caught locally by island fishermen. Produce comes from the restaurant's own organic garden. The menu changes often, but noteworthy menu options include the restaurant's signature New England clam chowder with smoked bacon or the shrimp tempura served with Asian slaw. As a main course, there might be a luscious lobster risotto, native halibut with forest-mushroom strudel, Black Angus filet, or simply a 2-pound lobster with all the fixings. Desserts are made on-site by one of the island's finest pastry chefs. The Galley is also a good choice for lunch, when you can enjoy this delicious gourmet food at lower prices.

54 Jefferson Ave. ✆ 508/228-9641. Reservations required for dinner. Main courses $29–$39. AE, MC, V. Summer Mon–Fri noon–2:30pm and 6–10pm, Sat–Sun 10:30am–2:30pm and 6–10pm; call for off-season hours. Closed late Sept–late May.

Ship's Inn Restaurant ★★ NEW AMERICAN   In the brick-walled basement of a
12-room inn, this cozy hideaway is a short walk from Main Street down a quiet side street.
Professional and entertaining waitstaff make dining in the candlelit alcoves a real treat. The
menu features a variety of fresh fish, meat, and pasta dishes, including several lighter
options made without butter or cream. A flavorful starter is the Roquefort and walnut terrine with Asian pear. Popular main courses include the pan-roasted Muscovy duck breast
and the grilled yellowtail flounder. For a festive dessert, there's always the Grand Marnier
soufflé. The lengthy wine list, with a number of well-priced options, has won awards.

13 Fair St. ☎ **508/228-0040.** www.shipsinnnantucket.com. Reservations recommended. Main courses
$28–$38. AE, DISC, MC, V. July–Sept Wed–Mon 5:30–9:30pm; call for off-season hours. Closed Nov to
mid-May.

Straight Wharf ★★★ NEW AMERICAN   New chefs/owners Amanda Lydon and
Gabriel Frasca have turned long-established Straight Wharf into the must-get reservation
on the island. This is fine dining on the waterfront in the center of town. Make your reservation for 8pm on the outside deck so you can watch the sun set over the harbor. Straight
Wharf has long been known for its creative cuisine, and also as the place where the island's
top chefs hang out after their shifts. While the menu changes to reflect the best available
ingredients, one special item to look for is the watermelon gazpacho, which may be the
perfect chilled summer treat. Everyone loves Straight Wharf's "clambake," which includes
corn pudding, littlenecks, and lobster. In fact, you can't go wrong with seafood here (or just
about anything else on the menu), including the cherished smoked bluefish pâté.

6 Harbor Sq. (on Straight Wharf). ☎ **508/228-4499.** www.straightwharfrestaurant.com. Reservations
recommended. Main courses $34–$39. AE, MC, V. July–Aug Mon–Fri 11:30am–2pm and 5:30–9:45pm,
Sat–Sun 11am–2pm and 5:30–9:45pm; call for off-season hours. Closed late Sept–late May.

The Summer House ★★ (Finds) NEW AMERICAN   Old-school Nantucket atmosphere, 'Sconset-style, distinguishes this fine-dining experience from others on the island:
wicker and wrought iron, roses and honeysuckle. A pianist plays nightly—often Gersh-
win standards. The pounding Atlantic Ocean is just over the bluff. Service is wonderful,
and the food is excellent, though expensive. Specialties include fresh, locally caught seafood with island vegetables delicately prepared and stylishly presented. Tempting appetizers include the grilled portobello mushrooms served with a pungent Stilton-basil terrine,
and the house-smoked salmon *frisée* with avocado salsa. The distinctive main courses are
roast saddle of lamb with rosemary caponatina port and feta mashed potatoes; the
unusual and tasty lobster cutlets with coconut-jasmine risotto timbale and mint-tomato
relish; and the grilled rib-eye with wild mushrooms, foie gras, and cabernet. Desserts are
bountiful. Order the blueberry pie if it's in season. The Summer House also operates a
Beachside Bistro, next to its pool across the street, with views of the ocean. At lunch and
dinner the bistro serves such light fare as salads, specialty pizzas, burgers, and sushi. The
bistro is open 11:30am to 8pm in the summer.

17 Ocean Ave., Siasconset. ☎ **508/257-9976.** www.thesummerhouse.com. Reservations recommended.
Main courses $33–$39. AE, MC, V. July–Aug daily 6–10pm; May–June and Sept to mid-Oct Wed–Sun
6–9:30pm. Closed mid-Oct to Apr.

Topper's at The Wauwinet ★★★ REGIONAL/NEW AMERICAN   This 1850
restaurant—part of a secluded resort—is tastefully subdued, with wicker armchairs,
splashes of chintz, and a two-tailed mermaid to oversee a chill-chasing fire. Try to sit at
one of the cozy banquettes if you can. The menu features the finest regional cuisine:
Lobster is a major event (it's often sautéed with champagne beurre blanc); and be on the

9

WHERE TO DINE

lookout for unusual delicacies such as arctic char. Those are Gruyère-and-chive biscuits in the breadbasket, and you must try one. Other recommendable house specialties include the lobster-and-crab-cakes appetizer and the roasted Muscovy duck breast. Desserts are fanciful and fabulous: Consider the toasted brioche with poached pears and caramel sauce. The Wauwinet runs a complimentary launch service from mid-June to mid-September to the restaurant for lunch and dinner; it leaves from Straight Wharf at 11am and 5pm, takes 1 hour, and also makes the return trip.

120 Wauwinet Rd. (off Squam Rd.), Nantucket ℭ **508/228-8768.** www.wauwinet.com/restaurant.php. Reservations required for dinner and the launch ride over. Jacket requested for men. Main courses $34–$56. AE, DC, MC, V. May–Oct daily noon–2pm and 6–9:30pm. Closed Nov–Apr.

EXPENSIVE

American Seasons ★★ REGIONAL AMERICAN   This romantic little restaurant has a great theme: Choose your region (New England, Pacific Coast, Wild West, or Down South) and select creative offerings. You can mix or match your appetizers and main courses. For instance, begin with the Louisiana crawfish risotto with fire-roasted onion and fried parsnips in a sweet corn purée from Down South; then from the Pacific Coast, try an aged beef sirloin with caramelized shallot and Yukon potato hash, served with an Oregon blue-cheese salad with white-truffle oil and fried onions. A lighter *tapas* menu is available throughout the evening.

80 Centre St. (2 blocks from the center of town). ℭ **508/228-7111.** www.americanseasons.com. Reservations recommended. Main courses $24–$30. AE, MC, V. Mid-Apr to Nov daily 6–9:30pm; call for off-season hours. Closed early Dec to mid-Apr.

Boarding House ★★ NEW AMERICAN   This centrally located fine-dining restaurant doubles as one of the most popular bars in town. You can dine in the romantic lower-level dining room or upstairs in the hopping bar area. But on clear summer nights, you'll want to get one of the tables outside on the patio. The menu has definite Asian and Mediterranean influences in such dishes as the seared yellowfin tuna with sesame sushi rice cake and wasabi aioli. One of the best soups on Nantucket is the luxe double lobster chowder with fresh corn and truffle mousseline. But the signature dish is the classic grilled lobster tails with grilled asparagus, mashed potatoes, and champagne beurre blanc. The award-winning wine list offers a range of prices.

12 Federal St. ℭ **508/228-9622.** www.boardinghouse-pearl.com. Reservations recommended. Main courses $24–$35. AE, MC, V. July–Aug daily 5:30–10pm; call for off-season hours.

The Chanticleer ★★ FRENCH   The Chanticleer in the signature rose-covered cottage in 'Sconset has the atmosphere of a private club and beautiful garden seating. Owners Susan Handy and Chef Jeff Worster, who also own Black Eyed Susan's (see below), run this charming place as a "brasserie moderne." Wonderful inventions, such as cod beignets, and traditional appetizers, such as moules frites, share the menu with creative versions of steak au poivre and seared Nantucket sea scallops. *Tart au citron* is among the stellar desserts, but you can also end your meal with a plats fromage, with three types of succulent cheeses. How French!

9 New St., Siasconset (on the south side of the island). ℭ **508/257-4499.** www.thechanticleer.net. Reservations recommended. Main courses $24–$43. AE, MC, V. June–Aug Tues–Sun noon–2pm and 6–9:30pm; call for off-season hours. Closed mid-Oct to May.

Cinco Restaurant and Bar ★★ TAPAS   This exquisite restaurant specializes in *tapas*, those popular little Spanish-style plates of food. In this case, the dishes feature taste sensations

with cured meats, marinated vegetables, and grilled fish. Try the lovely lobster gazpacho, a
cool and luscious treat. The menu has been modified recently to include larger plates featuring steaks and chops, for those who would rather not just snack. There's a lively atmosphere here and much of it is due to the owner, Michael Sturgis, who is considered one of the top hosts on Nantucket. About two dozen tapas are on the menu; three or four per person would make a small meal, but you'll want to pass them around and share.

5 Amelia Dr. (¹/₄ mile from the rotary, just off South Rd.). *©* **508/325-5151**. www.cinco5.com. Reservations recommended. Tapas $5–$20; main courses $19–$27. AE, MC, V. Mid-June to Sept daily 6–10:30pm; call for off-season hours. Closed Jan–Mar.

Company of the Cauldron ★★★ CONTINENTAL This is one of the island's most romantic restaurants, run by one of the island's most creative chefs, Al Kovalencik. What is unusual here is the chef offers one distinctive three- to four-course fixed-price meal each night, so check the menu out front or by telephone before booking. In the candlelit dining room, classic American and Continental influences predominate; don't miss the soft-shell crab appetizer when it's offered. The main course could be a special swordfish preparation, rack of lamb, or beef Wellington. For dessert, there's always something exceptional, such as a chocolate soufflé cake. Because the fixed price includes three courses—an appetizer, main course, and dessert—and large portions, this restaurant is actually a fine-dining bargain on Nantucket. Several nights a week in season, a harpist serenades diners.

5 India St. (btw. Federal and Centre sts.). *©* **508/228-4016**. www.companyofthecauldron.com. Reservations required. Fixed-price dinner $55. MC, V. Early July–early Sept Tues–Sun 2 seatings 6:45 and 8:45pm, Mon 7pm seating only; call for off-season hours. Closed mid-Oct to mid-Apr, except Thanksgiving weekend and the first 2 weeks of Dec.

Corazon del Mar ★★ LATIN The newest restaurant from Seth and Angela Raynor, the husband-and-wife team who own the Boarding House and Pearl, is a Latin kitchen, featuring a ceviche, or seafood, and raw bar, as well as unusual and authentic tacos and a tequileria, or tequila bar. Early word on the restaurant is it offers exciting taste sensations that you can't get anywhere else on the island. Octopus glazed with olive oil is served with crushed potatoes and pepper; crispy codfish tacos come with an avocado and cabbage chili. But the portions are on the small side, and, with these prices, that means not a lot of bang for your buck.

21 S. Water St. *©* **508/228-0815**. www.corazonnantucket.com. Main courses $22–$32. AE, MC, V. July–Aug daily 5:30–10pm; call for off-season hours. Closed Jan–late Mar.

Dune ★★ NEW AMERICAN This chic bistro is one of the island's newer restaurants. The chef/owner, Michael Getter, who also started the restaurant American Seasons, is considered one of the island's most creative chefs. The interior is very modern, all sleek lines and neutral earth-tone colors. The food is made up of seasonal local produce, fish and meats from area farms. High-season choices that are light and summery might include a yellowfin tuna niçoise and a wonderful pan-seared striped bass with cucumber gazpacho.

20 Broad St. *©* **508/228-5550**. www.dunenantucket.com. Reservations recommended. Main courses $28–$38. AE, DISC, MC, V. July–Sept daily noon–2pm and 5:30–10pm; call for off-season hours.

Fifty-Six Union ★★ NEW AMERICAN This understated restaurant offers fine dining without pretensions: just good service, a pleasing contemporary atmosphere, and wonderful food. Diners can sit in the bar area, which tends to be loud and lively, or the quieter Garden Room or outdoor patio. Intriguing appetizers include a salad with prosciutto and grilled fig, and a crabmeat spring roll with a pepper *coulis*. Main-course choices could include anything from Javanese fried rice to risotto with wild mushrooms to a rack of Colorado lamb.

56 Union St. (¹/₂ mile from Main St.). ⓒ **508/228-6135.** www.fiftysixunion.com. Reservations recommended. Main courses $23–$32. AE, MC, V. Early July–early Sept daily 5:30–10pm; call for off-season hours.

Figs at 29 Fair by Todd English ★★ MEDITERRANEAN The owners of this historic restaurant, formerly the Woodbox, have brought in celebrity chef Todd English to create a new menu. The ambience is still the same: ancient rafters, exposed beams, and antique tables lit by very romantic candlelight. Mr. English calls his cuisine "rustic Mediterranean," and in this case, that means an array of pasta, such as spaghettini with large Tuscan meatballs, and pizzas with such unusual toppings as fig and prosciutto.

29 Fair St. ⓒ **508/228-7800.** www.thesummerhouse.com/29. Main courses $17–$27. AE, MC, V. Late Mar–early Jan Mon–Sat 6:30–9:30pm, Sun 10am–2pm and 6:30–9:30pm. Closed early Jan to mid-May.

Le Languedoc Bistro ★★ NEW AMERICAN/FRENCH This is Nantucket's most authentic French cafe. The atmosphere in this historic building is wonderful, and the prices are reasonable. There's also an expensive dining room upstairs, but locals prefer the casual bistro atmosphere downstairs and out on the terrace. There's a clubby feel here as diners come and go, greeting each other and enjoying themselves. Soups are superb, as are the Angus-steak burgers—which some call the best burgers in the world—with garlic french fries. More elaborate dishes include the roasted tenderloin of pork stuffed with figs and pancetta; *berlotti* bean stew; and the napoleon of grilled tuna, tapenade, and roasted vegetables with pesto sauce. Save room for classic French desserts, such as chocolate *pot du crème* and crème brûlée.

24 Broad St. ⓒ **508/228-2552.** www.lelanguedoc.com. Reservations not accepted for cafe; reservations recommended for dining room. Main courses $24–$44 (half-portions $15–$22). AE, MC, V. June–Sept Tues–Sun 5:30–9:30pm; call for off-season hours. Closed mid-Dec to mid-May.

Òran Mór Bistro ★★★ Ⓕ(inds) INTERNATIONAL This second-floor waterfront venue is one of the premier restaurants on the island. The menu changes nightly, and there are always surprising and unusual choices. Appetizer standouts are the Jonah crab and hearts of palm, and the braised rabbit ravioli with truffle butter sauce. Hearty entrees include grilled Wolf Neck Farm steak with cottage potatoes, and sautéed fluke with soft polenta. An excellent sommelier is on hand to assist wine lovers.

2 S. Beach St. (in the center of town). ⓒ **508/228-8655.** www.oranmorbistro.com. Reservations recommended. Main courses $22–$34. AE, MC, V. June to mid-Oct daily 6–9:30pm; mid-Oct to mid-Dec and mid-Apr to May Thurs–Tues 6–9pm. Closed mid-Dec to mid-Apr.

Ropewalk ★ SEAFOOD This open-air restaurant on the harbor is Nantucket's only outdoor raw bar, and it's where the yachting crowd hangs out after a day on the boat. While the food is a bit overpriced, the location is prime. The raw bar, serving littlenecks, oysters, and shrimp, is open daily from 3 to 10pm in high season and is a great place to go for a drink before dinner. This is also a good place to enjoy a light meal or appetizers, such as fried calamari, crab cakes, or fried oysters.

1 Straight Wharf. ⓒ **508/228-8886.** www.theropewalk.com. Reservations not accepted. Main courses $23–$33. AE, MC, V. May to mid-Oct daily 11am–10pm. Closed mid-Oct to Apr.

Town ★★ INTERNATIONAL Chef Neil Hudson's twist at this new restaurant is bringing international cooking styles from Africa, India, South America, and Asia to Nantucket's signature seafood dishes. For instance, there's a succulent Vietnamese pork spring roll and a lobster tandoori that gives an Indian flavor to the classic seared-lobster dish. There is a large outdoor patio and an inside dining room, but many people might want to sit at the bar, which is being manned by one of the island's more well-known bartenders, Graeme Fleming. The team behind this place has started several other very successful Nantucket restaurants, including Queequeg's.

4 E. Chestnut St. ✆ **508/325-TOWN** [8696]. www.townnantucket.com. Main courses $24–$32. Reservations recommended. AE, MC, V. July–Aug daily 5:30–10pm; Sept–June daily 6–10pm

MODERATE

Black Eyed Susan's ★★ (Finds) ASIAN/AMERICAN   This is supremely exciting food in a funky bistro atmosphere. The place is small, popular with locals, and packed. Reservations are accepted for the 6pm seating only, and they go fast. Others must line up outside the restaurant (the line starts forming around 5:30pm), and the hostess will assign you a time to dine. If you don't mind sitting at the counter, you'll have a better choice. Inside it may seem a bit too cozy, but that's all part of the charm. I always enjoy the spicy Thai fish cake when that is on the menu, and also the tandoori chicken with green mango chutney. There's usually a Southwestern touch, such as the Dos Equis beer-battered catfish quesadilla with mango slaw, hoppin' john, and jalapeño. You'll mop up the sauce with the delectable organic sourdough bread. There's no liquor license, but you can BYOB. The corking fee is $1 per person.

10 India St. (in the center of town). ✆ **508/325-0308.** www.black-eyedsusans.com. Reservations accepted for 6pm seating only. Main courses $12–$25. No credit cards. Apr–Oct daily 7am–1pm and Mon–Sat 6–10pm. Closed Nov–Mar.

Cap'n Tobey's Chowder House ★ SEAFOOD   This convenient eatery close to the harbor specializes in seafood obtained daily from local fishermen. Diners can choose between halibut, yellowfin tuna, Atlantic sea scallops, swordfish, and salmon, and have it grilled, baked, or blackened. Lobster is always on the menu. The raw bar features oysters, littlenecks, and shrimp. There is also a less expensive fried-fish menu, a good choice for families. Upstairs, called **Off Shore at Cap'n Tobey's,** there's live music in season.

20 Straight Wharf. ✆ **508/228-0836.** Reservations recommended. Main courses $17–$27. AE, DC, DISC, MC, V. Late June–Sept daily 11am–10pm; call for off-season hours. Closed Jan–Apr.

Centre Street Bistro ★★★ NEW AMERICAN   This tiny fine-dining restaurant in the center of Nantucket Town is owned and operated by Ruth and Tim Pitts, who are considered top chefs on the island. The dining room has only about eight tables and a few bar seats, though in the summer there is extra seating on the front patio. This cozy place features wonderful, creative cuisine at reasonable prices, especially compared to other island fine-dining restaurants. The menu is in constant flux, but high points have included the warm goat-cheese tart to start, and the Long Island duck breast with pumpkin and butternut-squash risotto as a main course. If the sautéed Nantucket Bay scallops are on the menu, you won't want to miss whatever clever preparations the Pitts have dreamed up. One dish featured these world-famous local scallops with wontons and a citrus-soy-and-spice glaze.

29 Centre St. ✆ **508/228-8470.** www.nantucketbistro.com. Reservations not accepted. Main courses $19–$25. No credit cards. Mon and Wed–Fri 11:30am–2pm and 6–9:30pm; Sat–Sun 8am–1pm and 6–9pm; call for off-season hours.

Nantucket Lobster Trap SEAFOOD   When only a bowl of chowder and a giant lobster roll will do, bring the whole family to this quintessential clam shack where the big game is usually on the TV behind the bar. Seating is on large picnic tables, and lobsters come straight from local waters. The mussels and clams served here are also from local waters, as are the world-renowned Nantucket Bay scallops. The prices are kept relatively affordable. There's also a kids menu.

23 Washington St. ✆ **508/228-4200.** www.nantucketlobstertrap.com. Reservations only for parties of 6 or more. Main courses $12–$30. AE, MC, V. June–Sept daily 5–10pm; call for off-season hours. Closed late Oct–early May.

Queequeg's ★★ NEW AMERICAN   A cozy bistro atmosphere and good value are the hallmarks of this small restaurant, which is tucked along a side street behind the Atheneum. Outside seating is available in good weather. As befits the *Moby-Dick* reference in the name, the specialty here is seafood. The menu offers a range from basics to fancier fare. For example, as an appetizer, you could have the New England clam chowder or tuna tartare. The rich and flavorful pan-seared halibut with Parmesan risotto is a favorite with locals. Meat lovers may enjoy chargrilled New Zealand lamb or New York strip sirloin. Vegetarians also have options.

6 Oak St. ✆ **508/325-0992.** www.queequegsnantucket.com. Reservations recommended. Main courses $18–$25. MC, V. June–Sept daily 6–9:30pm; call for off-season hours. Closed late Nov–late Apr.

Trattoria Sfoglia ★★★ NORTHERN ITALIAN   This rustic Italian eatery ranks near the top of many people's "my favorite" lists for Nantucket. Quirky and homespun, its style runs to mismatched glasses and fresh flowers in mason jars. The menu combinations are unusual in a familiar way—how about an antipasto of clams, salami, tomato, and fennel? There is a corn risotto with lobster and zucchini, and a roasted sausage accompanied by a plateful of *contorni* (tasty preparations of farm-fresh vegetables). Light eaters can ask for a half-order of pasta, which is enough to satisfy the average appetite. The kitchen turns out home-baked bread that some call the island's best, as well as desserts such as a fruit tart. They also make their own gelato. The only catch is that the restaurant is not in the center of town; you have to take a taxi.

130 Pleasant St. (across from the Stop & Shop). ✆ **508/325-4500.** www.sfogliarestaurant.com/nantucket. Reservations recommended. Main courses $16–$26. No credit cards. Apr to mid-Oct Mon–Sat 6–10pm; call for off-season hours.

INEXPENSIVE

Arno's ★★ (Kids) INTERNATIONAL   A storefront facing the passing parade of Main Street, this casual restaurant packs surprising style between its bare-brick walls. It also has a wine bar, offering close to 30 vintages by the glass and an extensive appetizer menu. The internationally influenced menu yields tasty, bountiful platters for breakfast, lunch, and dinner. Specialties include grilled sirloin steaks and fresh grilled fish. Generous servings of specialty pasta dishes, such as shrimp and scallop scampi Florentine, are featured nightly. The central location and relatively low prices make this a good choice for families.

41 Main St. ✆ **508/228-7001.** www.arnos.net. Reservations recommended. Main courses $9–$17. AE, DC, DISC, MC, V. Apr–Dec daily 8am–10pm. Closed Jan–Mar.

The Brotherhood of Thieves ★ PUB   This classic whaling bar housed in an early-19th-century brick building in the center of town is a Nantucket institution, though a recent renovation after a fire removed a lot of its former charm. In July and August, tourists line up for a table in the dark tavern downstairs to chow on burgers and hand-cut curly fries. An elaborate renovation added an upstairs dining room; there is also seating outside on a raised terrace. In the fall and winter, locals sit beside the cozy brick hearth

to enjoy decently priced dinner offerings such as chicken teriyaki and fried Cajun
shrimp. This place serves food later than anywhere else in town; you can order off the
late-night menu 'til midnight.

23 Broad St. ℂ **508/228-2551.** http://brotherhoodofthieves.com. Reservations not accepted. Main
courses $9–$18. No credit cards. Mar–Jan Mon–Sat 11:30am–midnight, Sun noon–10pm. Closed Feb.

Cambridge Street ★ INTERNATIONAL This funky little joint attracts a young
crowd, but the reasonably priced food and devil-may-care atmosphere also brings in
locals of all stripes. There are burgers and sandwiches, but the special dishes here are the
baba ghanouj, a Middle Eastern hummuslike spread served over a grilled pita, and the
veggie schwarma, which is grilled tofu with a spicy peanut sauce and sweet soy sauce.

12 Cambridge St. (btw. Easy St. and S. Water St.) ℂ 508/228-7109. www.cambridgestreetnantucket.
com. Reservations accepted. Main courses $9–$24. AE, DISC, MC, V. Tues–Sat 6–10pm.

Even Keel Cafe AMERICAN This low-key cafe in the heart of town serves breakfast,
lunch, and dinner both indoors and outside on the patio in the back. You'll find reasonable prices and nonexotic fare here, such as burgers and sandwiches. There are always
vegetarian choices as well as meat and fish dishes, everything from a cheeseburger to
grilled salmon to veal *osso buco*. There's also a kids menu, as well as high-speed Internet
access. This place has lots of off-season dining deals, such as half-price weekday breakfasts
and two-for-one dinners. On Sundays, they serve a hearty brunch. There is no alcohol
for sale here, but you can BYOB.

40 Main St. ℂ **508/228-1979.** www.evenkeelcafe.com. Reservations not accepted. Main courses $10–
$25. AE, MC, V. July–Aug daily 7am–9:30pm; call for off-season hours.

Fog Island Cafe ★ NEW AMERICAN You'll be wowed by the creative breakfasts
and lunches at this sassy cafe; they're reasonably priced, with super-fresh ingredients.
Homemade soups and salads are healthy and delicious. In season, they serve dinner, with
lots of choices for vegetarians.

7 S. Water St. ℂ **508/228-1818.** www.fogisland.com. Reservations not accepted. All items under $15.
MC, V. July–Aug Mon–Sat 7am–8pm, Sun 7am–1pm; call for off-season hours.

Starlight Theatre and Cafe ★ (Finds) (Kids) AMERICAN This small cafe/movie
theater is a convenient place to come either with kids or on a dinner date for a quick bite
before or after a film. It's simple fare such as salads, sandwiches, and burgers. For something a little different, try the lobster macaroni and cheese.

1 N. Union St. ℂ **508/228-4479.** http://starlightnantucket.com. Reservations not accepted. All items
under $15. AE, MC, V. July–Aug Mon–Thurs 11:30am–9pm, Fri–Sat 11:30am–11pm, Sun 9am–9pm; call for
off-season hours.

TAKEOUT & PICNIC FARE

Broad Street, located just steps from Steamboat Wharf, is the place to go for cheap takeout eats any time. Good choices are **Walters Deli,** 10 Broad St. (ℂ **508/228-0010**), for
sandwiches; and **Stubby's,** 8 Broad St. (ℂ **508/228-0028**), for burgers.

Bartlett's Farm ★★ You can get fresh-picked produce (in season, the tomatoes are
incomparable) right in town from Bartlett's traveling market, or head out to this seventh-
generation farm where, in June, you might get to pick your own strawberries. They also
sell sandwiches, quiches, pastries, pies, and more. Nearby are Cisco Brewery and East
Coast Seafood, to round out your picnic purchases.

33 Bartlett Farm Rd. ☎ **508/228-9403.** www.bartlettsfarm.com. Apr–Dec daily 7:30am–7pm. Truck parked on Main St., in season.

Cisco Brewery ★★   One friend likened this place to an amusement park for adults, and you do see a lot of smiling faces here. There are three shacks, with each selling a different homemade alcohol concoction: distilled liquor from Triple Eight Distillery (vodka, gin, and notch—short for "not scotch"), wine from Nantucket Vineyards (a 25-year-old vineyard using old-world techniques), and the signature beer from Cisco Brewers (of the eight types, Whale's Tale Pale Ale is the favorite). You can bring your beverage to tables outside and bring your own food to eat with it. You can also buy bottles to take home.

5 and 7 Bartlett Farm Rd. ☎ **508/325-5929.** www.nantucketvineyard.com. Apr–Dec Mon–Sat 10am–6pm; Sun noon–5pm. Closed Jan–Mar.

Easy Street Cantina ★   For cheap and yummy street food, just sidle up to this storefront on Broad Street and order yourself a hearty fish taco or cheese enchilada There are a couple of stand-up tables here, but you can just find a bench on Main Street and people-watch while eating the best bargain meal on the island.

2 Broad St. ☎ **508/228-5418.** All under $15. July–Aug daily 7:30am–10pm. Call for off-season hours

Lola Burger ★   The street-food version of the overpriced bistro down the street actually serves up some good burgers. Take yours over to the harbor and watch the yachting crowd come and go.

10 Broad St. ☎ **508/325-0282.** All under $15. July and August daily 11:30am–10pm. Call for off-season hours.

Something Natural ★★   A local institution and a terrific value, Something Natural turns out gigantic sandwiches, with fresh ingredients piled atop fabulous bread. Plan on sharing, so you'll have room for their addictive chocolate-chip cookies. It's a great place to stock up for a day at the beach, or you can eat your lunch at picnic tables on the grounds. This sandwich shop is a bit too far from town to walk to, unless you're in the mood for a hike. It's a great stop on a bike ride, though.

50 Cliff Rd. ☎ **508/228-0504.** www.somethingnatural.com. Apr to mid-Oct daily 8am–6:30pm. Closed mid-Oct to Mar.

Sushi by Yoshi ★★   This tiny place is Nantucket's best source of great sushi. The incredibly fresh local fish is artfully presented by Chef Yoshihisa Mabuchi, who also dishes up such healthy, affordable staples as miso or *udon* (noodle) soup. This is a busy place; in season, allow an hour for takeout.

2 E. Chestnut St. ☎ **508/228-1801.** www.sushibyyoshi.com. May to mid-Oct Sun–Thurs 11:30am–10pm, Fri–Sat 11:30am–10:30pm; mid-Oct to Apr Thurs–Sat 11:30am–9pm, Sun–Wed 5–9pm.

SWEETS

The Juice Bar ★★   This humble hole-in-the-wall scoops up some of the best homemade ice cream and frozen yogurt around, complemented by superb homemade hot fudge. Waffle cones are homemade, too. And, yes, you can also get juice—from refreshing lime rickeys to healthful carrot cocktails.

12 Broad St. ☎ **508/228-5799.** June–Aug Sun–Thurs 10am–11:30pm, Fri–Sat 10am–2am; mid-Apr to May and Sept to mid-Oct 11am–9pm daily. Closed mid-Oct to mid-Apr.

9 NANTUCKET AFTER DARK

Nantucket usually has an attractive crowd of bar-hoppers making the scene around town. The best part is that everything is within walking distance, so you don't have to worry about driving back to your inn. You'll find good singles scenes at the **Boarding House** and **The Club Car,** which are reviewed above as restaurants, or **Slip 14 on South Wharf** (*𝒞* **508/228-2033;** www.slip14.com). Live music comes in many guises on Nantucket, and there are a number of good itinerant performers who play at different venues. Meanwhile, it may be Reggae Night at **The Chicken Box,** 6 Daves St. (*𝒞* **508/228-9717;** www. thechickenbox.com), when the median age of this rocking venue rises by a decade or two. For a fun, not-too-fancy bar in town, try **Rose and Crown,** 23 S. Water St. (*𝒞* **508/ 228-2595;** www.theroseandcrown.com).

MOVIES
Nantucket has one first-run movie theater: **Starlight Theatre & Cafe,** 1 N. Union St. (*𝒞* **508/228-4435;** www.starlightnantucket.com). The **Siasconset Casino,** 10 New St., Siasconset (*𝒞* **508/257-6661**), shows films Tuesday, Thursday, and Sunday in season for $5.

NANTUCKET LITERATI
Nantucket Atheneum   Continuing a 160-year tradition, the Nantucket Atheneum offers readings and lectures for general edification year-round, with such local literati as Frank Conroy and Nathaniel Philbrick filling in for the likes of Henry David Thoreau and Herman Melville. The summer events are often followed by a charming garden reception. The library is open Monday through Saturday from 9:30am to 5pm, until 8pm on Tuesday and Thursday. Call for an event schedule. 1 India St. *𝒞* **508/228-1110.** www. nantucketatheneum.org. Free admission.

Nantucket's Theater Scene Makes a Comeback

The **Theatre Workshop of Nantucket** is back in business with a marquee name at the helm. Emmy Award-winning actor John Shea, a longtime Nantucket summer resident, has taken over as artistic director, and his appointment has served to rejuvenate the theater group, which lost its space at Bennett Hall at the First Congregational Church several years ago. That, combined with the demise of Actor's Theatre of Nantucket in 2004, meant the island's theater scene was in flux. Theatre Workshop moved to the basement space in the United Methodist Church at 2 Centre Street (formerly occupied by the Actor's Theatre), and it now produces a year-round slate of live theater that often includes the works of Broadway-quality writers and composers. Tickets are $10 to $25. See what's on next, and buy tickets online at **www.theatreworkshop.com**, or at the box office at the Methodist Church, 2 Centre Street, Nantucket (*𝒞* **508/228-4305**).

10

Martha's Vineyard

New England sea captains' houses, white picket fences, and ice-cream shops trim an authentic fishing village. Lighthouses pierce the fog with their signals. A Native American community preserves its identity amid miles of pristine beaches and rolling farmland. Martha's Vineyard is a picturesque island indeed.

Visit the Vineyard to bicycle the shaded paths that hug the coastline. Admire the regal mariners' homes in Edgartown and stop by the Edgartown Scrimshaw Gallery for a memento of the sea. Stroll down Circuit Avenue, in Oak Bluffs, with a Mad Martha's ice-cream cone and then ride the Flying Horses Carousel, said to be the oldest working carousel in the country. Don't miss the cheerful "gingerbread" cottages behind Circuit Avenue, where you can almost hear the echoes of 19th-century revival meetings in the imposing Tabernacle. Travel the country roads of West Tisbury and Chilmark, stopping at Allen Farm for sweaters made from the wool of their flock of over 200 sheep. Buy bread at the Scottish Bakehouse, in North Tisbury, and a lobster roll in the fishing village of Menemsha.

Unlike much of New England, Martha's Vineyard has long been a melting pot. In the tiny town of Aquinnah, the Wampanoag tribe is the only Native American tribe in the region to have official status in Washington, D.C. Once known as Gay Head, the red-clay cliffs of Aquinnah are a National Historic Landmark. The Wampanoags, 12th-generation Vineyarders, farm the land in Chilmark; and at Cronig's Market, they rub shoulders with posh Yankees from Edgartown.

In the late 19th century, the religious retreat community of Oak Bluffs was one of the first vacation spots for African Americans of means. Today this community includes such notables as film director Spike Lee and Washington power broker Vernon Jordan.

Unfortunately Martha's Vineyard has been discovered, in a big way. When the former First Family, the Clintons, chose to vacation on the island several years in a row, it only increased the worldwide fascination with this popular place. In 2009, President Obama and his family vacationed on the island for a week. In fact, the island is loaded with luminaries, but you are unlikely to see them, as they prefer private house parties. But don't come to this island on a star search: It's considered impolite to gawk and, like jaded New Yorkers, Vineyarders barely seem to notice the VIPs in their midst. Year-round locals and seasonal celebrity residents coexist in an almost effortless comfort, united in their protective attitude toward the island, their disapproval of traffic, and their criticism of the Steamship Authority.

There's always a lot of "hurry up and wait" involved in ferry travel to and from the Vineyard, so a weekend may not be enough time for a visit. If you're traveling from New York, take an extra day off, allowing a minimum of 3 days for this trip. Four days will feel more comfortable. One great way to shorten the journey from New York is to take the ferry from Rhode Island or New Bedford and avoid Cape traffic.

From Boston, a couple of days are fine (the drive from Boston to Woods Hole takes 1½ hrs. with no traffic), but beware of summer weekend bottlenecks (never aim for the last ferry). You really don't need to bring a car to get around this small

> **Fun Facts   Going Native on Martha's Vineyard**
>
> Down-island: If you *must* buy a Black Dog T-shirt, wait until you get home to wear it. Don't loiter at the Charlotte Inn. Have cocktails on the porch of the Harbor View Hotel. In Oak Bluffs, don't ask when Illumination Night is. (It's a secret.) Experience Edgartown on a snowy winter weekend or in spring when the lilacs are in bloom.
>
> Up-island: When in doubt, don't wear shoes. Sail a boat to a remote beach for a picnic. Don't view the rolling farmlands from a tour bus. By all means, bike. Kayak. Rent a cottage for a week or two. Don't be a day-tripper.

island, but if you absolutely must be accompanied by four wheels, you'll need a car reservation for the ferry (see "Getting There," below, for details).

Try to savor the 45-minute ferry ride to and from this pastoral place. The Vineyard's pace is decidedly laid-back—try to blend in with the ultracool attitude. The six towns on Martha's Vineyard have distinct identities, but they are either "down-island," referring to Vineyard Haven (officially called Tisbury), Edgartown, and Oak Bluffs; or "up-island," the towns of West Tisbury, Chilmark, and Aquinnah (formerly Gay Head).

If you can survive the hassles of getting to Martha's Vineyard, and can cope with the crowds and traffic once you arrive, you may just have the perfect vacation. Better yet, visit the island off-season, in May or October, when the weather is often mild and the crowds have cleared out.

1 ESSENTIALS

GETTING THERE

BY FERRY   Most visitors take the ferry service connecting the Vineyard and the mainland. If you're traveling via car or bus, you will most likely catch the ferry from Woods Hole in the town of Falmouth on Cape Cod; however, boats do run from Falmouth Inner Harbor, Hyannis, New Bedford, Rhode Island, and Nantucket. On weekends in season, the Steamship Authority ferries make over 25 trips a day to Martha's Vineyard from Woods Hole (2 other companies provide an additional 12 passenger ferries a day from Falmouth Inner Harbor). Schedules are available from the **Martha's Vineyard Chamber of Commerce** (© **508/693-0085;** fax 508/693-7589; www.mvy.com) or the Steamship Authority (see below).

The state-run **Steamship Authority** (www.steamshipauthority.com) runs the show in Woods Hole (© **508/477-8600** early Apr–early Sept daily 8am–5pm; or 508/693-9130 daily 8am–5pm) and operates every day, year-round (weather permitting). It maintains the only ferries to Martha's Vineyard that accommodate cars, in addition to passengers, and makes about 20 crossings a day in season. The large ferries make the 45-minute trip to Vineyard Haven throughout the year; some boats go to Oak Bluffs from late May to late October (call for seasonal schedules). During the summer, you'll need a reservation to bring your car to the island, and you must reserve *months in advance* to secure a spot. If you plan to bring your car over to the island, plan to get to the Woods Hole terminal at least 30 minutes before your scheduled departure.

Taking a Car to the Vineyard? Reservations Required!

Vehicle reservations are required to bring your car to Martha's Vineyard Friday through Monday from mid-June to mid-September. During these times, standby is in effect only on Tuesday through Thursday. Vehicle reservations are also required to bring your car to Martha's Vineyard on Memorial Day weekend. Technically, vehicle reservations can be made up to 1 hour in advance of ferry departure, but ferries in season are almost always filled with cars, and you cannot depend on a cancellation during the summer months. Also be aware that your space may be forfeited if you have not checked into the ferry terminal 30 minutes prior to sailing time. Reservations may be changed to another date and time with at least 24 hours' notice; otherwise, you will have to pay for an additional ticket for your vehicle.

If you arrive without a reservation on a day that allows standby in the summer, come early and be prepared to wait in the standby line for hours. The Steamship Authority guarantees your passage, if you're in line by 2pm on designated standby days only. For up-to-date **Steamship Authority** information, check out its website (**www.steamshipauthority.com**).

Many people prefer to leave their cars on the mainland, take the ferry (often with their bikes), and then rent a car, Jeep, or bicycle on the island. You can park your car at the Woods Hole lot (always full in the summer) or at one of the many lots in Falmouth and Bourne that absorb the overflow of cars during the summer months; parking is $10 to $12 per day. Plan to arrive at the parking lots in Falmouth at least an hour before sailing time to allow for parking, taking the free shuttle bus to the ferry terminal, and buying your ferry ticket. Free shuttle buses (some equipped for bikes) run regularly from the outlying lots to the Woods Hole ferry terminal.

The cost of a round-trip passenger ticket on the ferry to Martha's Vineyard is $15 for adults and $8 for children 5 to 12. (Kids 4 and under ride free.) If you bring your bike along, it's an extra $6 round-trip, year-round. You do not need a reservation on the ferry if you're traveling without a car, and no reservations are needed for parking. The cost of a round-trip car passage from April through October is $135 to $155 (depending on the size of your car); in the off-season it drops to $85 to $105. Car rates do not include drivers or passengers; you must buy tickets for each person going to the island.

Note: The Steamship Authority charges different rates for different length cars. You will need to specify the make and model of your car when you place your reservation.

Once you are aboard the ferry, you have won the right to feel relieved and relaxed. Now your vacation can begin. Ferries are equipped with bathrooms and snack bars. Your fellow passengers will be a gaggle of kids, dogs, and happy-looking travelers.

From Falmouth, you can board the *Island Queen* at Falmouth Inner Harbor (© 508/548-4800; www.islandqueen.com) for a 35-minute cruise to Oak Bluffs (passengers only). The boat runs from late May to mid-October; round-trip fare is $18 for adults, $9 for children 12 and under, and an extra $6 for bikes. There are seven crossings a day in

ACCOMMODATIONS
Beach Plum Inn **2**
The Captain R. Flanders House **6**
Hostelling International
  Martha's Vineyard **17**
Lambert's Cove Inn **8**
Menemsha Inn and Cottages **3**
The Winnetu Oceanside Resort **16**

DINING ◆
The Beach Plum Inn Restaurant **2**
The Bite **5**
Home Port **4**
Lambert's Cove Inn Restaurant **8**

ATTRACTIONS ●
Aquinnah Cliffs and Light **1**
Cape Pogue Wildlife Refuge **14**
Cedar Tree Neck Sanctuary **7**
East Chop Light **10**
Edgartown Light **13**
Felix Neck Wildlife Sanctuary **11**
Martha's Vineyard Museum **12**
Wasque Reservation **15**
West Chop Light **9**

0   2 mi
0   2 km

Nantucket Sound

Ferry to Hyannis (Year-round)
Ferry to Nantucket (Seasonal)
Ferry to Falmouth (Seasonal)
Ferry to Rhode Island (Seasonal)
Ferry to Falmouth (Seasonal)
Ferry to Woods Hole (Year-round)
Ferry to New Bedford (Year-round)

Cape Pogue Bay
East Beach (Wasque)
Dyke Bridge
Pocha Pond
Wasque Point
Chappaquiddick Island
Chappaquiddick Rd.
Litchfield Rd.
Norton Point
Katama Bay

Edgartown Harbor
Lighthouse Beach
Edgartown
Joseph A. Sylvia State Beach
Main St.
Herring Creek Rd.
W. Tisbury Rd.
Meeting House Rd.
Edgartown Great Pond
South Beach (Katama Beach)
Katama Rd.

Oak Bluffs Town Beach
Seaview Ave.
East Chop
Oak Bluffs
Owen Park Beach
Edgartown-Vineyard Haven Rd.
Edgartown-West Tisbury Rd.
Sengekontacket Pond
Lagoon Pond
Beach Rd.
Barnes Rd.
Edgartown-Oak Bluffs County Rd.

West Chop
Vineyard Haven
Main St.
Cove Rd.
Tashmoo Lake
Airport Rd.
MANUEL F. CORRELLUS STATE FOREST
Martha's Vineyard Airport
Old County Rd.
Oyster Pond
Tisbury Great Pond

Vineyard Sound
Lake Tashmoo Town Beach
Lambert's Cove
Lamberts Cove Rd.
North Tisbury
State Rd.
West Tisbury
South Rd.
North Rd.
Middle Rd.
Chilmark Pond

Menemsha Harbor
Menemsha Beach
Menemsha
Menemsha Pond
Chilmark
South Rd.
Lucy Vincent Beach (restricted to residents)
Squibnocket Beach (restricted to residents)
State Rd.
Squibnocket Pond
Lobsterville Beach
Aquinnah
Aquinnah Beach
Moshup Trail

ATLANTIC OCEAN

Beach
Ferry
Lighthouse
Popular Bike Trail

Cape Cod
Martha's Vineyard
Nantucket

season (eight on Fri and Sun), and no reservations are needed. Parking will run you $15 a day. Credit cards are not accepted.

The **Falmouth–Edgartown Ferry Service,** 278 Scranton Ave. (© **508/548-9400;** www.falmouthferry.com), operates a 1-hour passenger ferry, called the *Pied Piper,* from Falmouth Harbor to Edgartown. The boat runs from late May to mid-October, and reservations are required. In season, there are four crossings a day (more on Fri). Round-trip fares are $40 to $50 for adults (weekends are more expensive) and $25 to $30 for children 6 to 12. Bicycles are $10 round-trip. Parking is $25 per day.

From Hyannis, you can take the traditional **Hy-Line** ferry, Ocean Street Dock (© **800/492-8082;** www.hy-linecruises.com), to Oak Bluffs, early June through late September. They run three trips a day, and trip time is about 1 hour and 40 minutes; round-trip costs $43 for adults and $22 for children 5 to 12 ($10 extra for bikes).

Hy-Line also operates a year-round **fast ferry** from Hyannis to Martha's Vineyard. It departs five times daily in season and takes 55 minutes. Round-trip tickets cost $69 for adults, $48 for children.

From Nantucket, Hy-Line runs three passenger-only ferries to Oak Bluffs on Martha's Vineyard from early June to mid-September (there is no car-ferry service between the islands). The trip time is 2 hours and 15 minutes. The round-trip fare is $34 for adults, $21 for children 5 to 12, and $5 extra for bikes.

From New Bedford, Massachusetts, the fast ferry MV *Whaling City Express* travels to Martha's Vineyard in 1 hour. It makes six trips a day in season and is in service year-round, 7 days a week. A ticket costs $35 one-way and $70 round-trip for adults; $31 one-way and $62 round-trip for seniors; and $20 one-way and $40 round-trip for children 12 and under. Contact **New England Fast Ferry** for details (© **866/683-3779;** www.nefastferry.com).

Tip: Traveling to Martha's Vineyard from New Bedford is a great way to avoid Cape traffic and enjoy a scenic ocean cruise.

From **North Kingstown, Rhode Island,** to Oak Bluffs, Vineyard Fast Ferry runs its high-speed catamaran, *Millennium,* two to three round-trips daily from mid-June through October. The trip takes 90 minutes. The ferry leaves from Quonset Point, about 10 minutes from I-95, 15 minutes from T.F. Green Airport in Providence, and 20 minutes from the Amtrak station in Kingston. There is dockside parking. Rates are $69 round-trip for adults; $46 round-trip for children 4 to 12; and $12 round-trip for bikes. Parking next to the ferry port is $10 per calendar day. Reservations can be made by calling © **401/295-4040** or by visiting www.vineyardfastferry.com.

BY AIR You can fly into **Martha's Vineyard Airport,** also known as Dukes County Airport (© **508/693-7022**), in West Tisbury, about 5 miles outside Edgartown.

Airlines serving the Vineyard include **Cape Air/Nantucket Airlines** (© **800/352-0714** or 508/771-6944; www.flycapeair.com), which connects the island year-round with Boston (trip time 34 min., hourly shuttle service in summer about $127–$152 one-way); Hyannis (trip time 20 min.; cost $43 one-way); Nantucket (15 min.; $44–$50 one-way); Providence, Rhode Island (25 min.; $97 one-way); and New Bedford (20 min., $42 one-way). **US Airways** (© **800/428-4322;** www.usairways.com), flies from Boston for about $215 round-trip and also has seasonal weekend service from LaGuardia Airport, in New York City (trip time 1¼ hr.), which costs approximately $400 round-trip.

The only company offering year-round charter service is **Direct Flight** (© **508/693-6688;** flydirect@vineyard.net).

Peter Pan Bus Lines (© **888/751-8800** or 508/548-7588; www.peterpan
bus.com) connects the Woods Hole ferry port with South Station and Logan Airport, in
Boston, as well as with New York City and Providence, Rhode Island. The trip from
South Station takes about 1 hour and 35 minutes and costs about $26 one-way, $50
round-trip; from Boston's Logan Airport, the cost is $30 one-way, $55 round-trip; from
Providence, the 2½-hr. trip to Woods Hole costs $29 one-way or $56 round-trip; from
New York, the bus trip to Woods Hole takes about 6 hours and costs approximately $73
one-way or $121 round-trip.

BY LIMO **Falmouth Taxi** (© **508/548-3100**) also runs limo service from Boston and
the airport. It charges $195 including gratuity.

GETTING AROUND

The down-island towns of Vineyard Haven, Oak Bluffs, and Edgartown are fairly compact, and if your inn is located in the heart of one of these small towns, you will be within
walking distance of shopping, beaches, and attractions in town. Frequent shuttle buses
can whisk you to the other down-island towns and beaches in 5 to 15 minutes. To
explore the up-island towns, you will need to bike; it's possible to tour the entire island—
60-some odd miles—in 1 day. In season, you can also take the shuttle bus up-island.
Otherwise you will have to take a cab.

BY BICYCLE & MOPED You shouldn't leave without exploring the Vineyard on two
wheels, even if only for a couple of hours. There's a little of everything for cyclists, from
paved paths to hilly country roads (see "Beaches & Recreational Pursuits," below, for
details on where to ride), and you don't have to be an expert rider to enjoy yourself. Plus,
biking is a relatively hassle-free way to get around the island.

Mopeds are also a way to navigate Vineyard roads, but the number of accidents involving mopeds seems to rise every year, and many islanders are opposed to these vehicles. If
you rent one, be aware they are considered quite dangerous on the island's busy, narrow,
winding, sandy roads. Moped renting is banned in Edgartown.

Bike rental shops are clustered throughout all three down-island towns. Mopeds and
scooters can be rented in Oak Bluffs and Vineyard Haven only, and you will need a
driver's license. Bike rentals cost about $25 a day; mopeds cost $70 to $90 a day. For bike
rentals in Vineyard Haven, try **Martha's Bike Rentals,** Lagoon Pond Road (© **800/559-
0312** or 508/693-6593). For mopeds, try **Adventure Rentals,** Beach Road (© **508/693-
1959;** www.islandadventuresmv.com). In Oak Bluffs there's **Anderson's,** Circuit Avenue
Extension (© **508/693-9346**), which rents bikes only; and **Sun 'n' Fun,** 26 Lake Avenue
(© **508/693-5457;** www.sunnfunrentals.com), which also rents mopeds. In Edgartown,
you'll find bike rentals only at **R. W. Cutler Edgartown Bike Rentals,** 1 Main St. (© **800/
627-2763;** www.edgartownbikerentals.com); and **Wheel Happy,** with two locations at
204 Upper Main St. and 8 S. Water St. (© **508/627-5928**).

BY CAR If you're coming to the Vineyard for a few days and you're going to stick to
the down-island towns, it's best to leave your car at home, as traffic and parking on the
island can be brutal in summer. Also, it's easy to take the shuttle buses (see below) from
town to town, or you can simply bike your way around. If you're staying for a longer
period of time or you want to do some exploring up-island, you should bring your car
or rent one on the island—my favorite way to tour the Vineyard is by Jeep. Keep in mind
that car-rental rates can soar during peak season, and gas is much more expensive on the
island. Off-road driving on the beaches is a major topic of debate on the Vineyard, and

the most popular spots may be closed for nesting Piping Plovers at the height of the season. If you plan to do some off-road exploration, check with the chamber of commerce to see if the trails are open to vehicles before you rent. To drive off-road at Cape Pogue or Cape Wasque on Chappaquiddick, you'll need to purchase a permit from the **Trustees of Reservations** (www.thetrustees.org); the cost is $180 for the car and $3 per person. Keep in mind, if you drive a rental car off-road without permission from the rental company, you could be subjected to a $500 fine.

There are representatives of the national car rental chains at the airport and in Vineyard Haven and Oak Bluffs. Local agencies also operate out of all three port towns, and many of them also rent Jeeps, mopeds, and bikes. The national chains include **Budget** (✆ 800/527-0700 or 508/693-1911; www.budget.com) and **Hertz** (✆ 800/654-3131; www.hertz.com).

In Vineyard Haven, you'll find **Adventure Rentals,** Beach Road (✆ 508/693-1959; www.islandadventuresmv.com), where a Jeep will run you about $160 per day in season, and a regular car costs about $100 to $110 per day. In Edgartown, try **AAA Island Rentals,** 196 Main St. (✆ 508/627-6800); they're also at Five Corners in Vineyard Haven (✆ 508/696-5300).

BY SHUTTLE BUS & TROLLEY   In season, shuttle buses run often enough to make them a practical means of getting around. They are also cheap, dependable, and easy.

The **Martha's Vineyard Regional Transit Authority** (✆ 508/693-9440; www.vineyardtransit.com) operates shuttle buses year-round on about a dozen routes around the island. The buses, which are white with purple logos, cost about $2 to $5 depending on distance. The formula is $1 per town. For example, Vineyard Haven to Oak Bluffs is $2, but Vineyard Haven to Edgartown (passing through Oak Bluffs) is $3. A 1-day pass is $7, and a 3-day pass is $15. The Edgartown Downtown Shuttle and the South Beach buses circle throughout town or out to South Beach every 20 minutes in season. They also stop at the free parking lots just north of the town center—this is a great way to avoid circling the streets in search of a vacant spot on busy weekends. The main down-island stops are Vineyard Haven (near the ferry terminal), Oak Bluffs (near the Civil War statue, in Ocean Park), and Edgartown (Church St., near the Old Whaling Church). From late June to early September, they run more frequently—from 6am to midnight every 15 minutes or half-hour. Hours are reduced in spring and fall. Buses also go out to Aquinnah (via the airport, West Tisbury, and Chilmark), leaving every couple of hours from down-island towns and looping about every hour through up-island towns.

For a 2½-hour bus tour of the island, call **Island Transport** (✆ 508/627-8687 www.mvtour.com), or hop on one of the Island Transport buses that are stationed at the ferry terminals in Vineyard Haven and Oak Bluffs in the summer. Tours are $29 per person.

BY TAXI   Upon arrival you'll find taxis at all ferry terminals and at the airport, and there are permanent taxi stands in Oak Bluffs (at the Flying Horses Carousel) and Edgartown (next to the Town Wharf). Most taxi outfits operate cars as well as vans for larger groups and travelers with bikes. Cab companies on the island include **AdamCab** (✆ 800/360-8629 or 508/627-4462), **Accurate Cab** (✆ 508/627-9798; the only 24-hr. service), **All Island Taxi** (✆ 508/693-2929), **Vineyard Taxi** (✆ 508/693-8660), **Patti's Taxi** (✆ 508/693-1663), and **Atlantic Taxi** (✆ 508/693-7110). Rates from town to town in summer are generally flat fees based on where you're headed and the number of passengers on board. A trip from Vineyard Haven to Edgartown would probably cost around $23 for two people. Late-night revelers should keep in mind that rates double after midnight until 7am.

The **On-Time ferry** (© 508/627-9427; www.
chappyferry.net) runs the 5-minute trip from Memorial Wharf, on Dock Street in Edgartown, to Chappaquiddick Island from June to mid-October daily, every 5 minutes from 7am to midnight. Passengers, bikes, mopeds, dogs, and cars (3 at a time) are all welcome. A round trip is $3 per person, $10 for one car/one driver, $6 for one bike/one person.

VISITOR INFORMATION

Contact the **Martha's Vineyard Chamber of Commerce,** at Beach Road, Vineyard Haven, MA 02568 (© **800/505-4815** or 508/693-0085; fax 508/693-7589), or visit their website at **www.mvy.com**. Their office is just 2 blocks up from the ferry terminal in Vineyard Haven and is open Monday to Friday 9am to 5pm year-round, plus weekends in season. There are also information booths at the ferry terminal in Vineyard Haven; across from the Flying Horses Carousel, in Oak Bluffs; and on Church Street, in Edgartown. You'll want to poke your head into these offices to pick up free maps, tourist handbooks, and flyers on tours and events or to get answers to any questions you might have. Most inns also have tourist handbooks and maps available for guests.

Always check the two local newspapers, the **Vineyard Gazette** (www.mvgazette.com) and the free **Martha's Vineyard Times** (www.mvtimes.com), for information on current events.

In case of an **emergency,** call © **911** and/or head for the **Martha's Vineyard Hospital,** Linton Lane, Oak Bluffs (© **508/693-0410**), which has a 24-hour emergency room.

---

2 A STROLL AROUND EDGARTOWN

A good way to acclimate yourself to the pace and flavor of the Vineyard is to walk the streets of Edgartown. This walk starts at the Dr. Daniel Fisher House and meanders along for about a mile; depending on how long you linger at each stop, it should take about 2 to 3 hours.

If you're driving, park at the free lots at the edge of town (you'll see signs on the roads from Vineyard Haven and West Tisbury), and bike or take the shuttle bus (it costs only 50¢) to the **Edgartown Visitor Center,** on Church Street. Around the corner are three local landmarks: the Dr. Daniel Fisher House, Vincent House Museum, and Old Whaling Church.

The **Dr. Daniel Fisher House,** 99 Main St. (© **508/627-8017;** www.mvpreservation. org/fisher.html), is a prime example of Edgartown's trademark Greek Revival opulence. A key player in the 19th-century whaling trade, Dr. Fisher amassed a fortune sufficient to found the Martha's Vineyard National Bank. Built in 1840, his prosperous and proud mansion boasts such classical elements as colonnaded porticos, as well as a delicate roof walk. The only way to view the interior (now headquarters for the Martha's Vineyard Preservation Trust) is with a guided **Vineyard Historic Walking Tour** (© **508/ 627-8619**). This tour originates next door at the **Vincent House Museum,** off Main Street, between Planting Field Way and Church Street. The transplanted 1672 full Cape is considered the oldest surviving dwelling on the island. Plexiglass-covered cutaways permit a view of traditional building techniques, and three rooms have been refurbished to encapsulate the decorative styles of 3 centuries, from bare-bones colonial to elegant Federal. The tour also takes in the neighboring **Old Whaling Church,** 89 Main St., a magnificent 1843 Greek Revival edifice designed by local architect Frederick Baylies, Jr.,

ATTRACTIONS ●

Baptist Church **13**
Dr. Daniel Fisher House **6**
Federated Church **11**
Martha's Vineyard Museum **10**
North Water Street
    captains' homes **26**
Old Sculpin Gallery **20**
Old Whaling Church **8**
Vincent House Museum **7**
Vineyard Gazette **12**

ACCOMMODATIONS ■

Ashley Inn **3**
Charlotte Inn **15**
The Clarion, Martha's
    Vineyard **1**
Colonial Inn of
    Martha's Vineyard **23**
Edgartown Inn **25**
Harbor View Hotel &
    Resort **27**
The Hob Knob **4**
The Jonathan Munroe House **5**
The Victorian Inn **16**

DINING ◆

Alchemy **14**
Among the Flowers Cafe **18**
Atria **2**
Chesca's **23**
Détente **24**
Espresso Love **9**
L'etoile **17**
McPhail's Corner Cafe **19**
The Newes from America **22**
Seafood Shanty **21**
Water Street **27**

and built as a whaling boat would have been, out of massive pine beams. With its 27-foot windows and 92-foot tower, this is a building that knows its place in the community (central). Maintained by the Preservation Trust and still supporting a Methodist parish, the building is now primarily used as a performance site.

Continuing down Main Street and turning right onto School Street, you'll pass another Baylies monument, the 1839 **Baptist Church,** which, having lost its spire, was converted into a private home with a rather grand, column-fronted facade. Two blocks farther, on your left is the **Vineyard Museum,** 59 School St. (© **508/627-4441;** www.mvmuseum.org), a fascinating complex assembled by the Dukes County Historical Society. An absorbing display of island history, this cluster of buildings contains exhibits of early Native American crafts; an entire 1765 house; an extraordinary array of maritime art, from whalers' logs to WPA-era studies by Thomas Hart Benton; a carriage house to catch odds and ends; and the Gay Head Light Tower's decommissioned Fresnel lens.

Give yourself enough time to explore the museum's curiosities before heading south 1 block on Cooke Street. Cater-cornered across South Summer Street, you'll spot the first of Baylies's impressive endeavors, the 1828 **Federated Church.** One block left are the offices of the *Vineyard Gazette,* 34 S. Summer St. (© **508/627-4311;** www.mvgazette.com).

Operating out of a 1760 house, this exemplary small-town newspaper has been going strong since 1846; its 14,000 subscribers span the globe. If you are wandering by on a Thursday afternoon, you might catch a press run in progress.

Now head down Main Street toward the water, stopping in at any of the inviting shops along the way. Veer left on Dock Street to reach the **Old Sculpin Gallery,** 58 Dock St. (© 508/627-4881; late June to mid-Sept). The output of the Martha's Vineyard Art Association displayed here tends to be amateurish, but you might happen upon a find. The real draw is the stark old building itself, which started out as a granary (part of Dr. Fisher's vast holdings) and spent the better part of the 20th century as a boat-building shop. Keep an eye out for vintage beauties when you cross the street to survey the harbor from the deck at Town Wharf. It's from here that the tiny On-Time ferry makes its 5-minute crossing to **Chappaquiddick Island,** hauling three cars at a time and a great many more sightseers— not that there's much to see on the other side. However, the island does offer great stretches of conservation land that will reward the hearty hiker or mountain biker.

Mere strollers might want to remain in town to admire the many formidable captains' homes lining **North Water Street,** some of which have been converted into inns. Each has a tale to tell. The 1750 **Daggett House** (no. 59), for instance, expanded upon a 1660 tavern, and the original beehive oven is flanked by a secret passageway. Formerly an inn, the Daggett House is now a private home. Nathaniel Hawthorne holed up at the **Edgartown Inn** (no. 56) for nearly a year in 1789 while writing *Twice Told Tales*—and, it is rumored, romancing a local maiden who inspired *The Scarlet Letter.*

WINDING DOWN   After all that walking, you may need a refreshment. **The Newes from America,** at The Kelley House, 23 Kelley St. (just off N. Water St.; © 508/627-4397), is a classic old-world tavern with specialty beers and the best French onion soup on the island.

---

3 BEACHES & RECREATIONAL PURSUITS

BEACHES   Most down-island beaches in Vineyard Haven, Oak Bluffs, and Edgartown are open to the public and just a walk or a short bike ride from town. In season, shuttle buses make stops at **State Beach,** between Oak Bluffs and Edgartown. Most of the Vineyard's magnificent up-island shoreline, alas, is privately owned or restricted to residents, and thus off limits to transient visitors. Renters in up-island communities, however, can obtain a beach sticker (around $35–$50 for a season sticker) for those private beaches by applying with a lease at the relevant **town hall:** West Tisbury, © 508/696-0147; Chilmark, © 508/645-2100; or Aquinnah, © 508/645-2300. Also, many up-island inns offer the perk of temporary passes to residents-only beaches such as Lucy Vincent Beach (see below). In addition to the public beaches listed below, you might also track down a few hidden coves by requesting a map of conservation properties from the **Martha's Vineyard Land Bank** (© 508/627-7141; www.mvlandbank.com). Below is a list of visitor-friendly beaches.

- **Aquinnah Beach ★★★** (Moshup Beach), off Moshup Trail: Parking costs $15 a day (in season) at this peaceful half-mile beach just east (Atlantic side) of the colorful cliffs. Go early, as the lot is small and a bit of a hike from the beach. I suggest that all but one person get off at the wooden boardwalk along the road with towels, toys, lunches, and so on, while the remaining person heads back up to park. In season, you can also take the shuttle buses from down-island to the parking lot at the Aquinnah (formerly

Gay Head) cliffs and walk to the beach. Although it is against the law, nudists tend to gravitate here. Remember that climbing the cliffs or stealing clay for a souvenir here is against the law, for environmental reasons: The cliffs are suffering from rapid erosion. Restrooms are near the parking lot.

- **East Beach** ★★, Wasque (pronounced *Way*-squee) Reservation, Chappaquiddick: Relatively few people bother biking or hiking (or four-wheel-driving) this far, so this beach remains one of the Vineyard's best-kept secrets (and an ideal spot for bird-watching). You should be able to find all the privacy you crave. If you're staying in Edgartown, the Chappy ferry is probably minutes by bike from your inn. Biking on Chappaquiddick is one of the great Vineyard experiences, but the roads can be sandy and are best suited for a mountain bike. You may have to dismount during the 5-mile ride to Wasque. Because of its exposure on the east shore of the island, the surf here is rough. Pack a picnic and make this an afternoon adventure. Sorry, no facilities. The area is owned by the Trustees of Reservations. It costs $180 for a season pass for nonmembers to drive a four-wheel-drive vehicle out to the beach. Most people park their car near the Dyke Bridge and walk the couple hundred yards out to the beach. Admission is $3 per person.

- **Joseph A. Sylvia State Beach** ★★★, midway between Oak Bluffs and Edgartown: Stretching a mile and flanked by a paved bike path, this placid beach has views of Cape Cod and Nantucket Sound and is prized for its gentle and (relatively) warm waves, which make it perfect for swimming. The wooden drawbridge is a local landmark, and visitors and islanders alike have been jumping off it for years. Be aware that State Beach is one of the Vineyard's most popular; come midsummer, it's packed. The shuttle bus stops here, and roadside parking is also available—but it fills up fast, so stake your claim early. Located on the eastern shore of the island, this is a Nantucket Sound beach, so waters are shallow and rarely rough. There are no restrooms, and only the Edgartown end of the beach, known as Bend-in-the-Road Beach, has lifeguards.

- **Lake Tashmoo Town Beach** ★, off Herring Creek Road, Vineyard Haven: The only spot on the island where lake meets ocean, this tiny strip of sand is good for swimming and surf-casting but is somewhat marred by limited parking and often brackish waters. Nonetheless this is a popular spot, as beachgoers enjoy a choice between the Vineyard Sound beach with mild surf or the placid lake beach. Bikers will have no problem reaching this beach from Vineyard Haven; otherwise, you have to use a car to get to this beach.

- **Lobsterville Beach** ★★, at the end of Lobsterville Road, in Aquinnah (formerly Gay Head; restricted): This 2-mile beauty on Menemsha Pond boasts calm, shallow waters, which are ideal for children. It's also a prime spot for birding—just past the dunes are nesting areas for terns and gulls. Surf-casters tend to gravitate here, too. The only drawback is that parking is for residents only. This is a great beach for bikers to hit on their way back from Aquinnah and before taking the bike ferry over to Menemsha.

- **Menemsha Beach** ★★, next to Dutchers Dock, in Menemsha Harbor: Despite its rough surface, this small but well-trafficked strand, with lifeguards and restrooms, is popular with families. In season, it's virtually wall-to-wall colorful umbrellas and beach toys. Nearby food vendors in Menemsha—selling everything from ice cream and hot dogs to steamers and shrimp cocktails—are a plus here. *Tip:* This beach is the ideal place to watch a sunset. Get a lobster dinner to go at the famous **Home Port restaurant,** right next to the beach in Menemsha, grab a blanket and a bottle of wine, and picnic here for a spectacular evening. If you are staying at an up-island inn, Menemsha is a fun bike ride downhill. Energetic bikers can make it from down-island towns; plan to make it part of an entire day of scenic biking. Otherwise, you'll need a car to get here.

- **Oak Bluffs Town Beach,** Seaview Avenue: This sandy strip extends from both sides of the ferry wharf, which makes it a convenient place to linger while you wait for the next boat. This is an in-town beach, within walking distance for visitors staying in Oak Bluffs. The surf is consistently calm and the sand smooth, so it's also ideal for families with small children. Public restrooms are available at the ferry dock, but there are no lifeguards.

- **Owen Park Beach,** off Main Street, in Vineyard Haven: A tiny strip of harborside beach adjoining a town green with swings and a bandstand will suffice for young children, who, by the way, get lifeguard supervision. There are no restrooms, but this is an in-town beach, and a quick walk from most Vineyard Haven inns.

- **South Beach** ★★★ (Katama Beach), about 4 miles south of Edgartown, on Katama Road: If you have time for only one trip to the beach and you can't get up-island, go with this popular, 3-mile barrier strand that boasts heavy wave action (check with lifeguards for swimming conditions), sweeping dunes, and, most important, relatively ample parking space. It's also accessible by bike path or shuttle. Lifeguards patrol some sections of the beach, and there are sparsely scattered toilet facilities. The rough surf here is popular with surfers. *Tip:* Families tend to head to the left, college kids to the right.

- **Wasque Beach** ★★, Wasque Reservation, Chappaquiddick: Surprisingly easy to get to (via the On-Time ferry and a bike or car), this half-mile-long beach has all the amenities—lifeguards, parking, restrooms—without the crowds. Wasque Beach is a Trustees of Reservations property, and if you are not a member of this land-preservation organization, you must pay at the gatehouse (www.thetrustees.org). To park your car here and go to the beach, it is $3 per car plus $3 per person. To drive your car on to the beach, it's $30 for a day pass, plus $3 per person. For a season pass to drive on to the other beaches on Chappaquiddick, it's $100 for Norton Point and $180 for Cape Pogue.

BICYCLING   What's unique about biking on Martha's Vineyard is that you'll find not only the smooth, well-maintained paths indigenous to the Cape, but also long stretches of road with virtually no traffic that, while rough in spots, traverse breathtaking country landscapes with sweeping ocean views. Serious cyclists will want to do a 1-day **circle-the-island tour** through the up-island towns and out to Aquinnah, stopping in Menemsha before heading back down-island. You'll pass through all six Vineyard towns and encounter some unique off-the-beaten-track businesses.

For much of the trek, you'll travel country roads, so beware of sandy shoulders and blind curves. Avoid tour buses by taking routes outlined below, such as the Moshup Trail to Aquinnah, or the triangle of paved bike paths between the down-island towns. These bike paths, roughly 8 miles to a side, link the down-island towns of Oak Bluffs, Edgartown, and Vineyard Haven (the sound portion along Beach Rd., flanked by water on both sides, is especially scenic). From Edgartown you can also follow the bike path to South Beach (also known as Katama Beach). The bike paths are accessible off Edgartown–West Tisbury Road, in Oak Bluffs, West Tisbury, and Edgartown.

The up-island roads leading to West Tisbury, Chilmark, Menemsha, and Aquinnah are a cyclist's paradise, with sprawling, unspoiled pastureland, old farmhouses, and brilliant sea views reminiscent of Ireland's countryside. But the terrain is often hilly, and the roads are narrow and a little rough around the edges. Try **South Road** from the town of West Tisbury to Chilmark Center (about 5 miles). En route you'll pass stone walls rolling over moors, clumps of pine and wildflowers, verdant marshes and tide pools, and, every once in a while, an old Vineyard farmhouse. About halfway, you'll notice the road becoming hillier as you approach a summit, **Abel's Hill,** home to the **Chilmark Cemetery,** where comedian John Belushi is buried. A mile farther, don't miss the view of **Allen Farm,** an operating sheep farm amid picturesque pastureland. **Middle Road** is another lovely ride with a country feel and will also get you from West Tisbury to Chilmark. (It's usually less trafficked, too.)

My favorite up-island route is the 6-mile stretch from Chilmark Center out to Aquinnah via **State Road** and **Moshup Trail** ★. The ocean views along this route are spectacular. Don't miss the **Quitsa Pond Lookout,** about 2 miles down State Road, which provides a panoramic vista of Nashaquitsa and Menemsha ponds, beyond which you can see Menemsha, the Vineyard Sound, and the Elizabeth Islands—it's an amazing place to watch the sunset on a clear evening. A bit farther, just over the Aquinnah town line, is the Aquinnah spring, a roadside iron pipe where you can refill your water bottle with the freshest and coldest water on the island. At the fork after the spring, turn left on Moshup Trail—in fact, a regular road—and follow the coast, which offers gorgeous views of the water and the sweeping sand dunes. You'll soon wind up in Aquinnah, where you can explore the red-clay cliffs and pristine beaches. On the return trip, you can take the handy bike ferry ($7 round-trip) from Aquinnah to Menemsha. It runs daily in summer and weekends in May.

A word about Aquinnah: Almost every visitor to the Vineyard finds his or her way to the cliffs, and with all the tour buses lined up in the huge parking lot and the rows of tacky concession stands and gift shops, this can seem like a rather outrageous tourist trap. You're right; it's not the Grand Canyon. But the observation deck, with its view of the colorful cliffs, the adorable brick lighthouse, and the Elizabeth Islands beyond, will make you glad you bothered. Instead of rushing away, stop for a cool drink and a clam roll at the snack bar, with the deck overlooking the ocean.

The adventurous **mountain biker** will want to head to the 8 miles of trails in the **Manuel F. Correllus State Forest** (© 508/693-2540; www.mass.gov/dcr/parks/south east/corr.htm), a vast spread of scrub oak and pine smack-dab in the middle of the island that also boasts paved paths and hiking and horseback-riding trails. For those seeking an escape from the multitudes, the trails are so extensive that even during peak summer season it is possible to not see another soul for hours. On most of the conservation land on the Vineyard, however, mountain biking is prohibited, for environmental reasons.

Bike rental operations are ubiquitous near the ferry landings in Vineyard Haven and Oak Bluffs, and there are also a few outfits in Edgartown. For information on bike rental shops, see "Getting Around," earlier in this chapter.

A very good outfit out of Boston, called **Bike Riders** (© 800/473-7040; www.bike riderstours.com), runs 6-day island-hopping tours of Martha's Vineyard and Nantucket. The cost is $1,395 per person, plus $60 if you borrow one of their bikes. It's a perfect way to experience both islands.

The chamber of commerce has a great bike map available at its office on Beach Road, in Vineyard Haven (see "Visitor Information," earlier in this chapter).

BIRD-WATCHING **Felix Neck Wildlife Sanctuary,** Edgartown–Vineyard Haven Road, Edgartown (© 508/627-4850; www.massaudubon.org), is an easy 2-mile bike ride from Edgartown. A Massachusetts Audubon Property, it has a complete visitor center staffed by naturalists who lead bird-watching walks, among other activities. You'll see osprey nests on your right on the way to the center. Pick up a trail map at the center before heading out. Several of the trails pass Sengekontacket Pond, and the orange trail leads to Waterfowl Pond, which has an observation deck with bird-sighting information. While managed by the conservation group Sheriff's Meadow Foundation, the 300-acre **Cedar**

Tree Neck Sanctuary ★★★, in Tisbury was acquired with the assistance of Massachusetts Audubon Society. There are several trails, but you'll eventually arrive out on a picturesque bluff overlooking Vineyard Sound and the Elizabeth Islands. Check out the map posted at the parking lot for an overview of the property. The range of terrain here—ponds, fields, woods, and bog—provides diverse opportunities for sightings. The Sanctuary is on State Road. Follow State to Indian Hill Road, then to Obed Daggett Road, and follow signs (www.sheriffsmeadow.org). **Wasque Reservation** ★★★, on Chappaquiddick (see "Nature Trails," below), a sanctuary owned by the Trustees of Reservations and located on the easternmost reaches of the island, can be accessed by bike or four-wheel-drive vehicle (see "Getting Around," earlier in this chapter). The hundreds of untouched acres here draw flocks of nesting shorebirds, including egrets, herons, terns, and plovers.

FISHING   For shellfishing, you'll need to get information and a permit from the appropriate town hall (for the telephone numbers, see "Beaches," above). Popular spots for surf-casting include **Wasque Point** (Wasque Reservation), on Chappaquiddick (see "Nature Trails," below). Deep-sea excursions can be arranged aboard **Summer's Lease** (© 508/693-2880), out of Oak Bluffs. Up-island there is **North Shore Charters** (© 508/645-2993; www.bassnblue.com), out of Menemsha, locus of the island's commercial fishing fleet (you may recognize this weathered port from *Jaws*). Charter costs are about $500 to $600 for a half-day and $800 to $1,400 for a full day.

Cooper Gilkes III, proprietor of **Coop's Bait & Tackle,** at 147 W. Tisbury Rd., in Edgartown (© 508/627-3909; http://coopsbaitandtackle.com), which offers rentals as well as supplies, is another acknowledged authority. He's available as an instructor or charter guide and is even amenable to sharing hard-won pointers on local hot spots.

FITNESS   Gym addicts can get their workout fix at the **Health Club at the Mansion House Inn,** at 9 Main St., in Vineyard Haven (© 508/693-7400; www.mvmansion house.com), which accepts visitors for a $16 fee.

GOLF   The 9-hole **Mink Meadows Golf Course,** at 320 Golf Club Rd., off Franklin Street, in Vineyard Haven (© 508/693-0600; www.minkmeadowsgc.com), despite occupying a top-dollar chunk of real estate, is open to the general public. There is also the semiprivate, championship-level 18-hole **Farm Neck Golf Club,** off Farm Neck Way, in Oak Bluffs (© 508/693-3057). The Cafe at Farm Neck serves a wonderful lunch overlooking their manicured greens. In season, greens fees at Mink Meadows are $55 for 9 holes and $80 for 18 holes. In season, greens fees at Farm Neck are $145 (including cart) for 18 holes.

ICE-SKATING   The **Martha's Vineyard Ice Arena,** on Edgartown–Vineyard Haven Road, Vineyard Haven (© 508/693-4438; www.mvarena.com), offers public skating for $5 from mid-July to mid-April; call for details.

NATURE TRAILS   About a fifth of the Vineyard's landmass has been set aside for conservation, and much of it is accessible to energetic bikers and hikers. The **West Chop Woods,** off Franklin Street in Vineyard Haven, comprise 85 acres with marked walking trails. Midway between Vineyard Haven and Edgartown, the **Felix Neck Wildlife Sanctuary** (see "Bird-Watching," above) includes a 6-mile network of trails over varying terrain, from woodland to beach. Accessible by ferry from Edgartown, quiet Chappaquiddick is home to two sizable preserves. The **Cape Poge Wildlife Refuge** ★★★ and **Wasque Reservation** ★★★ (www.thetrustees.org), covering much of the island's eastern barrier beach, have 709 acres that draw flocks of nesting or resting shorebirds. Also on the island, 3 miles east on Dyke Road, is another Trustees of Reservations property, the distinctly poetic and alluring **Mytoi,** a 14-acre Japanese garden that is an oasis of textures and flora and fauna.

The 633-acre **Long Point Wildlife Refuge** ★★★, off Waldron's Bottom Road, in West Tisbury (gatehouse ✆ **508/693-7392;** www.thetrustees.org), offers heath and dunes, freshwater ponds, a popular family-oriented beach, and interpretive nature walks for children. In season, the Trustees of Reservations charges a $10 parking fee, plus $3 per person ages 16 and older. The 4,000-acre **Manuel F. Correllus State Forest** (www. mass.gov/dcr/parks/southeast/corr.htm) occupies a sizable, if not especially scenic, chunk midisland; it's riddled with mountain-bike paths and riding trails. This sanctuary was created in 1908 to try to save the endangered heath hen, a species now extinct. In season, there are free interpretive and birding walks.

Up-island, along the sound, the **Menemsha Hills Reservation,** off North Road, in Chilmark (✆ **508/693-7662**), encompasses 210 acres of rocks and bluffs, with steep paths, lovely views, and even a public beach. The **Cedar Tree Neck Sanctuary,** off Indian Hill Road, southwest of Vineyard Haven (✆ **508/693-5207**), offers some 300 forested acres that end in a stony beach (alas, swimming and sunbathing are prohibited). It's still a refreshing retreat.

Some remarkable botanical surprises can be found at the 20-acre **Polly Hill Arboretum,** 809 State Rd., West Tisbury (✆ **508/693-9426;** www.pollyhillarboretum.org). Horticulturist Polly Hill developed this property over the past 40 years and allows the public to wander the grounds Thursday to Tuesday from sunrise until sunset. There are guided tours at 2pm. The visitor's center and plant sale is open 9:30am to 4pm. This is a magical place, particularly mid-June to July when the Dogwood Allee is in bloom. Wanderers will pass old stone walls on the way to the Tunnel of Love, an arbor of bleached hornbeam. There are also witch hazels, camellias, magnolias, and rhododendrons. To get there from Vineyard Haven, go south on State Road, bearing left at the junction of North Road. The arboretum entrance is about a half-mile down, on the right. There is a requested donation of $5 for adults.

TENNIS Public courts typically charge a small fee and can be reserved in person a day in advance. You'll find clay courts on **Church Street,** in Vineyard Haven, and nonclay in Oak Bluffs' **Niantic Park;** West Tisbury's **grammar school,** on Old County Road; and the **Chilmark Community Center,** on South Road. Three public courts—plus a basketball court, softball field, and children's playground—are located at the **Edgartown Recreation Area,** on Robinson Road. You can also book a court (1 day in advance only) at a semiprivate club in Oak Bluffs: the **Farm Neck Tennis Club** (✆ **508/693-9728**). In season, expect to pay $24 per hour for court time.

WATERSPORTS **Wind's Up,** 199 Beach Rd., Vineyard Haven (✆ **508/693-4252;** www.windsupmv.com), rents out canoes, kayaks, and various sailing craft, including sailboards, and offers instruction on-site, on a placid pond; it also rents surfboards and boogie boards. Canoes and kayaks rent for $16 per hour, $45 for a half-day, and $55 for a full day.

4 MUSEUMS & HISTORIC LANDMARKS

Cottage Museum ★ Oak Bluffs' famous "Camp Meeting Grounds," a 34-acre circle with more than 300 multicolored, elaborately trimmed carpenter's Gothic cottages, looks

ATTRACTIONS ●
Cottage Museum 2
Flying Horses Carousel 12

ACCOMMODATIONS ■
The Dockside Inn 14
Isabella's Beach House 16
The Oak Bluffs Inn 4
Surfside Motel 13
Wesley Hotel 1

DINING ◆
Coup de Ville 15
Linda Jean's 8
Mad Martha's 10
Martha's Vineyard
   Gourmet Cafe & Deli 9
Murdick's Fudge 11
Oyster Bar Grill 6
Sharky's Cantina 7
Slice of Life 5
Sweet Life Café 3

0   1/8 mi
0   1/8 km

Oak
Bluffs
Harbor

ferries

Saco Ave.

Circuit Ave. Ext.

Northbluff Ave.

Pasque Ave.

Oak Bluffs Marina ▪

Oak Bluffs Ave.

Lake Ave.

Lake Ave.

Sunset
Lake

County Ave.

Rock Ave.

Central Ave.

Sea View Ave.

Cape Cod

Oak Bluffs

Martha's
Vineyard   Nantucket

▪ Oak Bluffs
Beach

Allen Ave.

4th Ave.

Pawtucket Ave.

Circuit Ave.

Kennebec Ave.

Ocean Ave.

OCEAN
PARK

Dukes County Ave.

Siloam Ave.

TRINITY
PARK

Trinity Park

Butler Ave.

Rural Ct.

Grove Ave.

Narragansett Ave.

Samoset Ave.

Roque Ave.

Victorian Park

Circuit Ct. Ext.

Circuit Ave.

Uncas Ave.

Pennacook Ave.

Massasoit Ave.

Tuckernuck Ave.

Niantic Ave.

Pequot Ave.

Naumkeag Ave.

Waban Ave.

MARTHA'S VINEYARD

10

MUSEUMS & HISTORIC LANDMAKRS

very much the way it might have more than a hundred years ago. These adorable little houses, loosely modeled on the revivalists' canvas tents that inspired them, have been handed down through the generations. Unless you happen to know a lucky camper, your best chance of getting inside one is to visit this homey little museum, which embodies the late-19th-century zeitgeist and displays representative artifacts: bulky black bathing costumes and a melodeon (a 19th-century organ) used for informal hymnal sing-alongs.

The compact architecture is at once practical and symbolic. The Gothic-arched French doors off the peak-roofed second-story bedroom, for instance, lead to a tiny balcony used for keeping tabs on community doings. The daily schedule was, in fact, rather hectic. In 1867, when this cottage was built, campers typically attended three lengthy prayer services daily. Today's denizens tend to blend in with the visiting tourists, though opportunities for worship remain at the 1878 Trinity Methodist Church within the park or, just outside, on Samoset Avenue, at the nonsectarian 1870 Union Chapel, a magnificent octagonal structure with superb acoustics (posted signs give the lineup of guest preachers and musicians).

At the very center of the Camp Meeting Grounds is the striking **Trinity Park Tabernacle** ★★. Built in 1879, the open-sided chapel is the largest wrought-iron structure in the country. Thousands can be accommodated on its long wooden benches, which are usually filled to capacity for the Sunday-morning services, in summer, as well as for community sings (Wed July–Aug) and occasional concerts. (See "Martha's Vineyard After Dark," later in this chapter.)

1 Trinity Park (within the Camp Meeting Grounds), Oak Bluffs. © 508/693-7784. www.mvcma.org/museum.htm. Admission $2 (donation). Mid-June to Sept Mon–Sat 10am–4pm. Closed Oct to mid-June.

Flying Horses Carousel ★★ (Kids) You don't have to be a kid to enjoy the colorful mounts adorning what is considered to be the oldest working carousel in the country. Built in 1876 at Coney Island, this National Historic Landmark maintained by the Martha's Vineyard Preservation Trust predates the era of horses that "gallop." Lacking the necessary gears, these merely glide smoothly in place to the joyful strains of a calliope. The challenge lies in going for the brass ring that entitles the lucky winner to a free ride. Some regulars, adults included, have grown rather adept—you'll see them scoop up several in a single pass. In between rides, take a moment to admire the intricate hand-carving and real horsehair manes, and gaze into the horses' glass eyes for a surprise: tiny animal charms glinting within.

33 Circuit Ave. (at Lake Ave.), Oak Bluffs. © 508/693-9481. www.mvpreservation.org/carousel.html. Tickets $1.50 per ride, or 8 rides for $10. Late May–early Sept daily 10am–10pm; call for off-season hours. Closed mid-Oct to mid-Apr.

Martha's Vineyard Museum ★ All of Martha's Vineyard's colorful history is captured here, in a compound of historic buildings. To acclimate yourself chronologically, start with the precolonial artifacts—from arrowheads to colorful Gay Head clay pottery—displayed in the 1845 **Captain Francis Pease House.**

The **Gale Huntington Reference Library** houses rare documentation of the island's history, from genealogical records to whaling-ship logs. The recorded history of Martha's Vineyard (the name has been attributed, variously, to a Dutch seaman named Martin Wyngaard, and to the daughter and/or mother-in-law of early explorer Bartholomew Gosnold) begins in 1642 with the arrival of missionary Thomas Mayhew, Jr., whose father bought the whole chain of islands, from Nantucket through the Elizabeths, for £40. Some extraordinary memorabilia, including scrimshaw and portraiture, are on view in the adjoining **Francis Foster Maritime Gallery.**

To get a sense of daily life during the era when the waters of the East Coast were the equivalent of a modern highway, visit the **Thomas Cooke House,** a shipwright-built colonial, built in 1765, where the Customs collector lived and worked. Further curiosities are stored in the nearby Carriage Shed. Among the vintage 19th-century vehicles are a painted peddler's cart, a whaling boat, a hearse, and a fire engine.

The Fresnel lens on display outside the museum was lifted from the Gay Head Lighthouse in 1952, after nearly a century of service.

59 School St. (corner of Cooke St., 2 blocks southwest of Main St.), Edgartown. © 508/627-4441. www.mvmuseum.org. Admission $7 adults, $4 children 6–15. Mid-June to mid-Oct Mon–Sat 10am–5pm; mid-Oct to late Dec and mid-Mar to mid-June Wed–Fri 1–4pm, Sat 10am–4pm; early Jan to mid-Mar Wed–Fri by appointment, Sat 10am–4pm.

5 ORGANIZED TOURS

Ghosts, Gossip, and Downright Scandal Walking Tours ★★ Laced with local lore and often led by the entertaining local historian Liz Villard, this 75-minute evening walking tour of Edgartown, by the Vineyard History Tours organization, gives a fun look at town history. Other 1-hour tours provide access to the interiors of the 1672 Vincent House (the island's oldest surviving dwelling), the 1840 Dr. Daniel Fisher House (an elegant Greek Revival mansion), and the splendid Old Whaling Church, a town showpiece built in 1843. There are also a variety of other van and walking tours, including "A-Whaling We Will Go," in Edgartown, and "Cottages, Campgrounds, and Flying Horses," in Oak Bluffs, which includes admission to the Cottage Museum and a ride on the Flying Horses.

From the Vincent House Museum, behind 99 Main St., Edgartown. ℂ 508/627-8619. Also from the Cottage Museum, 1 Trinity Park, Oak Bluffs, and at the Steamship Authority kiosk in Vineyard Haven. $10–$12 adults, free for children 12 and under. June–Sept Mon–Fri 11–3pm; call for off-season hours. Closed Nov–Apr.

Trustees of Reservations Natural History Tours ★★★ The Trustees, a statewide land-conservation group, offers several fascinating 2½-hour tours by safari vehicle or kayak around this idyllic nature preserve. The 2-hour Natural History kayak tour on Poucha Pond and Cape Poge Bay is designed for all levels. It costs $40 for adults and $18 for children. There are also tours of the Cape Poge lighthouse at 10am, noon, and 2pm. The cost is $25 for adults and $12 for children 15 and under. Call ℂ **508/693-7392** for details.

Cape Poge, Chappaquiddick Island. Meet at Mytoi on Chappaquiddick. ℂ **508/627-3599** for reservations. www.thetrustees.org. In season Mon–Fri 8:30am and 3pm. Closed mid-Oct to May.

6 KID STUFF

A must for tots to preteens is the unique **Flying Horses Carousel** in the center of Oak Bluffs (see "Museums & Historic Landmarks," above). For an atmospheric minigolf course, visit **Island Cove Mini Golf,** on State Road, outside Vineyard Haven (ℂ **508/693-2611;** http://islandcoveminigolf.com), a family-friendly setup with a snack bar serving Mad Martha's ice cream, an island favorite (see p. 285). A round costs $9 for adults, $8 for children 3 to 12. A climbing wall costs $5. Island Cove is closed October through March. On Tuesday to Sunday, from 10am to 3pm, children might enjoy visiting the **World of Reptiles and Birds,** off Edgartown–Vineyard Haven Road, on Bachelder Avenue, Edgartown (ℂ **508/627-5634;** www.reptilesandbirds.com), where they'll meet various snakes (including a 21-foot python), turtles, and even an alligator. There's also a bird park. Admission is $5. Call for hours. World of Reptiles is closed October through March. Nearby, the **Felix Neck Wildlife Sanctuary** (see "Beaches & Recreational Pursuits," earlier in this chapter), on Edgartown–Vineyard Haven Road, is always a popular destination with its exhibit room and self-guided trails. On Sundays in season, there are natural-history talks and activities geared to children. **Native Earth Teaching Farm,** 94 North Rd., Chilmark (ℂ **508/645-3304;** www.nativeearthteachingfarm.org), features rare ducks and other animals, and children can participate in the "chore of the day." It's open Wednesday, Saturday, and Sunday 10am to 6pm. Many families plan their vacations around the **Agricultural Society Annual Livestock Show and Fair** (ℂ **508/693-9549;** mvas.vineyard.net), in West Tisbury, in mid-August. It's an old-fashioned country fair with animals, food, and entertainment. An island event that your kids will always remember is **Illumination Night,** in Oak Bluffs, when all the cottages in the campground are lit up with Japanese lanterns. The exact date is a secret, but it's usually a Wednesday evening in late August, at 7:30pm.

7 SHOPPING

ARTS & CRAFTS A new little art gallery cluster called "The Arts District" in Oak Bluffs, just beyond the "gingerbread" cottage colony, is worth a visit. On Dukes County Avenue, there are six interesting shops: **Periwinkle Studio** (© 508/696-8304), an intriguing gallery; **Alison Shaw Gallery** (© 508/696-7429; www.alisonshaw.com), featuring the exquisite photographs of this artist; **Pik Nik Art & Apparel** (© 508/693-1366; www.piknikmv.com), a funky array of crafts, gifts, and clothing; **Dragonfly Gallery** (© 508/693-8877; www.mvdragonfly.com), showing a range of mediums; **Red Mannequin** (© 508/693-2858), with clothing, gifts, and artwork; and **Lucinda's Enamels** (© 508/696-7863; www.lucindasheldon.com), with fine-art jewelry.

No visit to Edgartown would be complete without a peek at the wares of scrimshander Thomas J. DeMont, Jr., at **Edgartown Scrimshaw Gallery,** at 43 Main St. (© 508/627-9439). In addition to DeMont's work, the shop carries the work of a number of the country's top scrimshaw artists. All the scrimshaw in the gallery is hand-carved using ancient mammoth ivory or antique fossil ivory.

The **Chilmark Pottery,** off State Road (about 4 miles southwest of Vineyard Haven), West Tisbury (© 508/693-6476), features tableware fashioned to suit its setting. Geoffrey Borr takes his palette from the sea and sky and produces serviceable stoneware with clean lines and a long life span. Summer pottery classes are available.

The **Field Gallery,** 1050 State Road (in the center of town), West Tisbury (© 508/693-5595; www.fieldgallery.com), set in a rural pasture, is where Marc Chagall meets Henry Moore and where Tom Maley's playful figures have enchanted locals and passersby for decades. You'll also find paintings by Albert Alcalay and drawings and cartoons by Jules Feiffer. The Sunday-evening openings are high points of the summer social season. Closed mid-October to mid-May.

Don't miss the **Granary Gallery at the Red Barn,** 636 Old County Road (off Edgartown–West Tisbury Rd., about one-quarter mile north of the intersection), West Tisbury (© 800/472-6279; www.granarygallery.com), which displays astounding prints by the late longtime summerer Alfred Eisenstaedt, dazzling color photos by local luminary Alison Shaw, and a changing roster of fine artists—some just emerging, some long since "discovered." A fine selection of country and provincial antiques is also sold here. Open April to December, and by appointment only January through March.

Another unique local artisans' venue is **Martha's Vineyard Glass Works,** 683 State Road, North Tisbury (© 508/693-6026; www.mvglassworks.com). World-renowned master glass blowers sometimes lend a hand at this handsome rural studio/shop just for the fun of it. The three resident artists—Andrew Magdanz, Susan Shapiro, and Mark Weiner—are no slouches themselves, having shown nationwide to considerable acclaim. Their output is decidedly avant-garde and may not suit all tastes, but it's an eye-opening array and all the more fascinating once you've witnessed a work in progress.

Etherington Fine Art, 71 Main St., second floor, Vineyard Haven (© 508/693-9696; www.etheringtonfineart.com), features estimable work, such as Vineyard- and Venice-inspired paintings by Rez Williams, nature collages by Lucy Mitchell, pastels and oils by Wolf Kahn, and the colorful iconographic sculpture by Sam Milstein that grace the front yard. Gallery owner Mary Etherington's selection is a giant step up from the usual seascapes and lighthouses offered by other Vineyard galleries.

BOOKS   **Bunch of Grapes Bookstore,** 44 Main St., Vineyard Haven (℃ **508/693-2291;** www.bunchofgrapes.com) has risen from the ashes after a fire destroyed the second floor a couple years ago. **Edgartown Books,** 44 Main St., Edgartown (℃ **508/627-8463;** www.edgartownbooks.net), has a lively presentation of timely titles highlighting local endeavors; inquire about readings and signings. Closed January to March.

FASHION   **The Great Put On,** Dock Street (in the center of town), Edgartown (℃ **508/627-5495**), dates back to 1969, but always keeps up with the latest styles, including lines by Vivienne Tam, Moschino, and BCBG. **Dream Weaver,** at 1 S. Water St., Edgartown (℃ **508/627-9683;** http://dreamweavercollection.com), has a very fine collection of contemporary women's apparel. **Saffron,** at 65 Main St., Edgartown (℃ **508/627-7088**), offers a hip selection of island ware. **Katydid** is another high-fashion option at 38 Main St., in Edgartown (℃ **508/627-1232**).

GIFTS/HOME DECOR   The owners of **Bramhall & Dunn,** 23 Main St., Vineyard Haven (℃ **508/693-6437**), have a great eye for the kind of chunky, eclectic extras that lend character to country homes. Expect to find the requisite rag rugs, rustic pottery, English country antiques, bed linens, and a large selection of sweaters.

My favorite place for gifts in Oak Bluffs is **Craftworks,** 149 Circuit Ave. (℃ **508/693-7463**), which is filled to the rafters with whimsical, colorful contemporary American crafts, some by local artisans.

Carly Simon owns a shop called **Midnight Farm,** 18 Water-Cromwell Lane, Vineyard Haven (℃ **508/693-1997;** www.midnightfarm.net), named after her popular children's book. This home store offers a world of high-end, carefully selected, and imaginative gift items starting with soaps and candles and including children's clothes and toys, rugs, furniture, books, clothes, and glassware.

Third World Trading Co., 52 Circuit Ave., Oak Bluffs (℃ **508/693-5550**), features well-priced clothing, accessories, and home accents gathered from around the globe.

JEWELRY   Stop by **C. B. Stark Jewelers,** 53A Main St., Vineyard Haven (℃ **508/693-2284;** www.cbstark.com), where proprietor Cheryl Stark started fashioning island-motif charms back in 1966.

SEAFOOD   Feel like whipping up your own lobster feast? For the freshest and biggest crustaceans on the island, head to the **Net Result,** 79 Beach Rd., Vineyard Haven (℃ **508/693-6071;** www.mvseafood.com). Run by the Larsen family, you'll find everything from shrimp, scallops, and swordfish to bluefish and tuna, as well as prepared foods, including sushi. If you're up-island, stop by **Larsen's Fish Market,** right on the docks at Menemsha Harbor.

8 WHERE TO STAY

When deciding where to stay on Martha's Vineyard, you'll need to consider the type of vacation you prefer. The down-island towns of Vineyard Haven, Oak Bluffs, and Edgartown provide shops, restaurants, beaches, and harbors within walking distance, and frequent shuttles to get you all over the island. But all three can be overly crowded on busy summer weekends. Vineyard Haven is the gateway for most of the ferry traffic; Oak Bluffs is a raucous town with most of the Vineyard's bars and nightclubs; and many visitors make a beeline to Edgartown's manicured Main Street. Up-island inns provide more peace and quiet, but you'll probably need a car to get around, including going to the beach. Nevertheless there are some wonderful places to stay on the Vineyard, and all of the following choices have something special to offer.

EDGARTOWN
Very Expensive

Charlotte Inn ★★   Owners Gery and Paula Conover have been tirelessly fine-tuning this cluster of 18th- and 19th-century houses (five in all, counting the carriage house, a replica) since 1971. Linked by formal gardens, each house has a distinctive look and feel, though the predominant mode is English country, with fascinating antiques, hunting prints, and quirky decorative accents. Bathrooms are luxurious, and some are enormous (bigger than most hotel rooms). This is one of only two Relais & Châteaux properties on the Cape and islands (the second is the Wauwinet, on Nantucket; p. 241)—a world-class distinction that designates excellence in hospitality. On-site is the **Terrace,** a fine-dining restaurant.

27 S. Summer St. (in the center of town), Edgartown, MA 02539. © **508/627-4151.** Fax 508/627-4652. www.relaischateaux.com/charlotte. 25 units. Summer $395–$695 double; $895–$1,000 suite. Rates include continental breakfast; full breakfast $15. AE, MC, V. No children 13 and under. **Amenities:** Restaurant. *In room:* A/C, TV, hair dryer.

Harbor View Hotel & Resort ★★   This grand 19th-century hotel is in the midst of a multiyear renovation, estimated to cost $77 million. Among the changes, 21 smaller hotel rooms have been converted into 13 luxury suites, some with private gardens and outdoor showers. The historic shingle-style complex started out as two Gilded Age waterfront hotels, later joined by a 300-foot veranda that overlooks Edgartown Harbor and the lighthouse. Behind the hotel, there's a large pool. The hotel is just far enough from "downtown" Edgartown to avoid the traffic, but close enough for a pleasant walk past regal captains' houses. **Water Street** (p. 283) serves three meals in an elegant setting, and **Henry's** is a cozy barroom.

131 N. Water St. (about ½ mile northwest of Main St.), Edgartown, MA 02539. © **800/225-6005** or 508/627-7000. Fax 508/627-8417. www.harbor-view.com. 124 units. Summer $369–$625 double; $1,200 1-bedroom suite; $1,500 2-bedroom suite; $1,800–$2,100 3-bedroom suite. AE, DC, MC, V. **Amenities:** 2 restaurants (fine dining; more casual bar open daily for lunch and dinner); babysitting; concierge; fitness center; heated outdoor pool; room service (seasonal only, breakfast, lunch, and dinner) spa. *In room:* A/C, TV, fridge, hair dryer, Wi-Fi.

The Hob Knob ★★★   Owner Maggie White has reinvented this 19th-century building as an exquisite destination now vying for top honors as one of the Vineyard's premier luxury boutique hotels. She also wants to stay eco-friendly and that ideal extends to all aspects of the inn, from recycling and composting to an organic breakfast menu. All rooms are equipped with plush bathrobes and fine Aveda toiletries, as well as flatscreen TVs. Maggie and her attentive staff will pack a splendid picnic basket ($20 per person), plan a charter fishing trip on Maggie's 27-foot Boston Whaler, or organize windsurfing lessons. The full farm breakfast is a delight and is served at beautifully appointed individual tables in the sunny, brightly painted dining rooms or outside on the terrace.

128 Main St. (on Upper Main St., in the center of town), Edgartown, MA 02539. © **800/696-2723** or 508/627-9510. Fax 508/627-4560. www.hobknob.com. 17 units, 3-bedroom and 4-bedroom cottage. Summer $420–$545 double; weekly rates $8,000–$20,000 weekly for cottages. Rates include full breakfast and afternoon tea. AE, MC, V. No children 6 and under. **Amenities:** Rental bikes ($20 per day); exercise room; spa; room service. *In room:* A/C, TV/DVD, hair dryer, minifridge, Wi-Fi.

The Winnetu Oceanside Resort ★★   One of the island's most full-service resorts, this large luxury hotel sits on 11 acres overlooking South Beach, in Katama. Guests can walk down a 250-yard path to get to the private beach. A 3-mile bike path links the inn to Edgartown. Most rooms are two- and three-bedroom suites with kitchenettes. Some have ocean views and such conveniences as a washer/dryer. Many have private decks or patios. The rooms are decorated in a cozy beach-house style. The inn offers a number of amenities at an extra charge, including rental of beach cabanas, bicycle delivery service, grocery delivery service, and Wednesday-evening family-style clambakes in season. With giant chess pieces, outdoor Ping-Pong, foosball, the pool, and the putting green, there are many on-site amusements for kids. The inn's fine-dining restaurant, **Lure,** is top-notch (see "Where to Dine," later in this chapter). Several wheelchair-accessible rooms are available.

South Beach, Edgartown, MA 02539. ℂ 866/335-1133 or 508/310-1733. Fax 508/310-7900. www. winnetu.com. 48 units. Summer $320 double; $770–$1,200 1-bedroom suite; $920 2-bedroom suite; $1,600 3-bedroom suite. AE, MC, V. Closed Dec to mid-Apr. **Amenities:** Fine-dining restaurant; children's program (late June–early Sept complimentary 9am–noon; fee in evenings for children 3 through pre-teens); concierge; fitness room; general store; outdoor heated pool; putting green; tennis courts with pro (6 Har-Tru, 4 all-weather). *In room:* A/C, TV/VCR, kitchenette, Wi-Fi.

Expensive

Ashley Inn ★   Located on Upper Main Street, in Edgartown, this attractive B&B is just a short walk to the many shops and restaurants on Main Street and the picturesque Edgartown Harbor. Innkeepers Fred and Janet Hurley have decorated the bedrooms in the 1860 captain's house with period antiques and quilts, and some rooms have canopy or four-poster beds. There are thoughtful extras at this B&B, such as a little box of Chilmark Chocolates left on your pillow. There's also a carriage house offering suites with a kitchen and whirlpool bath. In the morning, breakfast is served at individual tables in the dining room.

129 Main St., Edgartown, MA 02539. ℂ 508/627-9655. Fax 508/627-6629. www.ashleyinn.net. 10 units. Summer $255–$285 double; $310–$315 suites; $575–$600 2-bedroom suite. Rates include full breakfast. MC, V. *In room:* A/C, TV.

The Clarion Martha's Vineyard ★   For those who like a more generic lodging choice, this large motel on Upper Main Street, in Edgartown, might fit the bill. It has been recently renovated and refurbished, and it is about a 10-minute walk to the center of Edgartown's historic village center. The shuttle bus also travels past the inn, and you can flag down the bus. The inn is also along the bike path that runs between Edgartown and Oak Bluffs.

227 Upper Main St., Edgartown, MA 02539. ℂ 800/922-3009 or 508/627-5161. Fax 508/627-3444. www. clarionmv.com. 34 units. Summer $289–$399 double. Rates include continental breakfast. AE, MC, V. **Amenities:** Restaurant. *In room:* A/C, TV.

Colonial Inn of Martha's Vineyard ★★ (Kids)   Built in 1911, this four-story inn in the center of Edgartown has been kept up-to-date, making it a fine modern hotel. Its lobby serves as a conduit to the Nevins Square shops beyond, and two good restaurants are also on the premises. The 28 rooms, decorated in soothing, contemporary tones (with pine furniture, crisp fabrics, hardwood floors, wainscoting, and four-poster beds), offer all you could want in the way of "affordable luxury." Guests whose rooms lack harbor views can wander onto one of the four common harbor-view decks to have a cocktail and enjoy the scenery. Two rooms are accessible to guests with disabilities.

38 N. Water St., Edgartown, MA 02539. ☏ **800/627-4701** or 508/627-4711. Fax 508/627-5904. www. colonialinnmvy.com. 28 units. Summer $245–$425 double; $595 and up suite or efficiency. Rates include continental breakfast. AE, MC, V. Closed Dec–Mar. Pets allowed in designated rooms for $30 per day. **Amenities:** 2 restaurants (including Chesca's; see "Where to Dine," below); fitness room; spa. *In room:* A/C, TV, hair dryer.

The Victorian Inn ★★   In the center of Edgartown, the Victorian Inn is a freshened-up version of those old-style hotels that used to exist in the center of every New England town. There are enough rooms here so you don't feel like you are trespassing in someone's home, yet there's a personal touch. Several rooms have canopy beds and a balcony with a harbor view. Each year innkeepers Stephen and Karen Caliri improve and refine the inn, and they are always quick to dispense helpful advice with good humor.

24 S. Water St. (in the center of town), Edgartown, MA 02539. ☏ **508/627-4784.** www.thevic.com. 14 units, 2 with tub/shower combination, 12 with shower only. Summer $245–$425 double. Rates include full breakfast and afternoon tea. MC, V. Closed Nov–Mar. *In room:* A/C, TV, hair dryer, no phone.

Moderate

The Arbor Inn ★ (**Value**)   This 1880 farmhouse is at the far end of town, but it is still within walking distance from the center. The inn has a lovely cathedral-ceilinged living room with lots of comfortable seating for guests. Rooms range from tiny to spacious, but all are nicely appointed with antiques and reproductions. In the morning, baked goods are served in the dining room or outside in the garden. The rates are quite reasonable here compared to other Edgartown B&Bs.

222 Main St., Edgartown, MA 02539. ☏ **888/748-4383** or 508/627-8137. Fax 508/627-9104. www. arborinn.net. 10 units, 2 with shared bathroom. Summer $195–$225 double. Rates include continental breakfast. MC, V. Closed Dec–Apr. *In room:* A/C, TV, no phone.

Edgartown Inn ★ (**Value**)   This centrally located historic inn offers perhaps the best value on the island. Nathaniel Hawthorne holed up here for nearly a year, and Daniel Webster also spent time here. Rooms are no-frills but pleasantly traditional; some have TVs. Breakfast, which is open to the public, is available in the dining room for an extra charge of $5.50 to $8.50. Some rooms in the front of the house have harbor views and two have private balconies. Modernists may prefer the two cathedral-ceilinged quarters in the annex out back, which offer lovely light and a sense of seclusion.

56 N. Water St., Edgartown, MA 02539. ☏ **508/627-4794.** Fax 508/627-9420. www.edgartowninn.com. 20 units, 4 with shared bathroom. Summer $125 shared bathroom; $170–$275 double. No credit cards. Closed Nov–Mar. No children 6 and under. *In room:* A/C, TV (some units), no phone.

The Jonathan Munroe House ★★ (**Finds**)   With its graceful wraparound and colonnaded front porch, the Jonathan Munroe House stands out from the other inns and captains' homes on this stretch of Upper Main Street. Guest rooms are immaculate, antiques-filled, and dotted with clever details. Many rooms have fireplaces and tubs with whirlpool jets. At breakfast don't miss the homemade waffles and pancakes, served on the sunny porch. Wine and cheese are served in the evening. Request the garden cottage, with its flowering window boxes, if you are in a honeymooning mood.

100 Main St., Edgartown, MA 02539. ☏ **877/468-6763** or 508/939-6004. Fax 508/627-5536. www. jonathanmunroe.com. 7 units, 1 cottage. Summer $215–$250 double; $325 cottage. Rates include full breakfast and wine-and-cheese hour. AE, MC, V. No children 11 and under. *In room:* A/C, hair dryer.

OAK BLUFFS

If you're looking for a basic motel with a central location, you'll want to stay at **Surfside Motel** across from the ferry dock at 7 Oak Bluffs Avenue, in Oak Bluffs (② **800/537-3007** or 508/693-2500; www.mvsurfside.com). Summer rates are $160 to $215 double, $250 to $310 for suites. Rooms are equipped with air-conditioning, TVs, and mini-fridges. It is open year-round, and well-behaved pets are allowed.

Expensive

Isabelle's Beach House ★   This grand 19th-century home, across the street from the ocean in Oak Bluffs, has been recently renovated. Some of the rooms are on the small side, but they are light and airy, with crisp bedding. You'll love sitting out on the veranda, rocking away as the sea breeze cools the air.

83 Seaview Ave. (on the sound), Oak Bluffs, MA 02557. ② **800/674-3129** or 508/693-3955. Fax 508/693-2729. www.isabellesbeachhouse.com. 11 units. Summer $275 double; $300–$395 suite. Rates include continental breakfast. AE, DISC, MC, V. Closed late Oct–early May. *In room:* A/C, TV, minifridge, hair dryer.

The Oak Bluffs Inn ★ (Value)   This homey Victorian inn has a fun location at the top of Circuit Avenue, Oak Bluff's main drag. The inn stands out with its whimsical, colorful Victorian paint scheme and its prominent cupola, from which guests can enjoy a 360-degree view of Oak Bluffs. As is typical in a house of this vintage, some of the rooms are a tad on the small side, but others are spacious and even have comfortable seating areas. All rooms have ceiling fans.

64 Circuit Ave. (at the corner of Pequot Ave.), Oak Bluffs, MA 02557. ② **800/955-6235** or 508/693-7171. Fax 508/693-8787. www.oakbluffsinn.com. 9 units. Summer $215–$300 double. Rates include continental breakfast. AE, MC, V. Closed Nov–Apr. *In room:* A/C, hair dryer, no phone.

Moderate

The Dockside Inn ★ (Kids)   Set close to the harbor, the Dockside is perfectly located for exploring the town of Oak Bluffs and is geared toward families. Because it is so close to the harbor and several restaurants, it is also somewhat noisy late at night and early in the morning. A number of the apartments and suites have kitchenettes, allowing you to prepare your own meals and save money. Most of the standard-size rooms have either a garden or harbor view; they're decorated cheerfully in pinks and greens. Besides kitchenettes, some of the suites and apartments have private decks. There are two wheelchair-accessible rooms.

9 Circuit Ave. Ext. (P.O. Box 1206), Oak Bluffs, MA 02557. ② **800/245-5979** or 508/693-2966. Fax 508/696-7293. www.vineyardinns.com. 22 units. Summer $200–$250 double; $350 suite. Rates include continental breakfast. AE, DISC, MC, V. Closed late Oct–early Apr. Pets allowed. **Amenities:** 6-seat hot tub; free access to computer w/Internet. *In room:* A/C, TV, hair dryer.

Wesley Hotel ★ (Value)   Formerly one of the grand hotels of Martha's Vineyard, this imposing 1879 property, right on the harbor, is now a solid entry in the good-value category. The only drawback here can be the noise from revelers on the boats in the harbor or traffic on busy Lake Avenue. Most of the rooms are fairly compact and basic. Many have easy access to the wraparound decks on all three floors of the inn. The Wesley Arms, behind the main building, contains 33 air-conditioned rooms. Five rooms are equipped for travelers with disabilities. *Note:* Reserve early to specify harbor views, which do not cost more than regular rooms. This is also one of the few Vineyard hotels that does not require a minimum stay in season.

MARTHA'S VINEYARD

10

WHERE TO STAY

70 Lake Ave. (on the harbor), Oak Bluffs, MA 02557. ✆ **800/638-9027** or 508/693-6611. Fax 508/693-5389. www.wesleyhotel.com. 95 units, all with shower only. Summer $230–$260 double; $310 suite. AE, DC, MC, V. Closed late Oct–Apr. *In room:* A/C, TV, no phone.

VINEYARD HAVEN (TISBURY)
Expensive
The Mansion House Inn ★   After a fire burned down the 200-year-old Tisbury Inn several years ago, the owners decided to rebuild, making this one of the Vineyard Haven's most full-service inns. The building, occupying a prominent corner location in Vineyard Haven, is now a community hub, with a restaurant, health club, and shops. The rooms range in size from cozy to spacious, and prices vary accordingly. Many have kitchenettes, plasma-screen televisions, and extra-large bathtubs. Some have harbor views and gas fireplaces. One of the most unique features of the inn is the 75-foot mineral spring (no chlorine) swimming pool in the inn's basement. A full gourmet breakfast is served buffet-style at **Zephrus,** the hotel's restaurant (see review p. 286).

9 Main St., Vineyard Haven, MA 02568. ✆ **800/332-4112** or 508/693-2200. Fax 508/693-4095. www.mvmansionhouse.com. 32 units. $299–$309 double; $399–$559 suite. Rates include full buffet breakfast. AE, MC, V. **Amenities:** Restaurant; health club; room service; spa w/75-ft. pool. *In room:* A/C, TV, fridge, hair dryer, Wi-Fi (additional charge).

CHILMARK (INCLUDING MENEMSHA), WEST TISBURY & AQUINNAH
Very Expensive
Beach Plum Inn ★★ (Finds   This 8-acre property is tucked away in Menemsha yet is within walking distance of the harbor. There's a croquet course and Nova Grass tennis court on the grounds, plus bikes to take exploring (extra charge). The well-kept rooms are in the main inn and in four cottages, which contain six additional rooms. The room decor is predominantly cottage-y, though some rooms lean toward elegance. Linens are exceptional. Half the rooms have whirlpool baths. Most have decks or patios, some with views of Menemsha Harbor. One room is wheelchair-accessible. Inn guests get beach passes to the private up-island beaches. The inn's **restaurant** is one of the best fine-dining spots on the island (see "Where to Dine," below).

50 Beach Plum Lane (off North Rd., ¹⁄₂ mile northeast of the harbor), Menemsha, MA 02552. ✆ **508/645-9454.** Fax 508/645-2801. www.beachpluminn.com. 11 units. Summer $425–$575 double or cottage. Rates include full breakfast in season, continental off-season. AE, DC, DISC, MC, V. Closed Jan–Apr. **Amenities:** Restaurant; babysitting by arrangement; croquet court; tennis court; private beach passes. *In room:* A/C, TV, fridge, hair dryer.

Expensive
Lambert's Cove Inn ★★   Set far off the main road and surrounded by apple trees and lilacs, this secluded estate suggests an age when time was measured in generations. Rooms have been recently updated and are exceedingly comfortable. You'll find an all-weather tennis court on the grounds, and the namesake beach 1 mile away. The inn's **restaurant** (see review on p. 288) is known for New American dinners prepared by one of the island's best chefs.

90 Manaquayak Rd., (off State Rd., about 5 miles west of Vineyard Haven), Vineyard Haven, MA 02568. ✆ **866/526-2466** or 508/693-2298. Fax 508/693-7890. www.lambertscoveinn.com. 15 units. Summer $225–$550 double. Rates include full breakfast. AE, MC, V. Closed early Dec to mid-Mar. **Amenities:** Restaurant (dinner only); tennis court; private beach passes. *In room:* A/C, TV/DVD and movie library, CD player, high-speed Internet access, hair dryer.

Menemsha Inn & Cottages ★★ This 11-acre compound is about a half-mile walk through a wooded path to the beach at Menemsha Harbor. There's no restaurant—just a restful breakfast room. There are regular rooms, suites, and cottages, which have outdoor showers, barbecue grills, and kitchenettes. Guests have access to complimentary passes and shuttle-bus service to the Lucy Vincent and Squibnocket private beaches.

12 Menemsha Rd. (about ¹/₂ mile northeast of the harbor), Menemsha, MA 02552. ℂ **508/645-2521.** Fax 508/645-9500. www.menemshainn.com. 15 units, 12 cottages. Summer $355–$385 double; $450–$815 suite; $4,800 per week 2-bedroom cottage. Rates include continental breakfast for rooms and suites. AE, DISC, MC, V. Closed Dec to mid-Apr. **Amenities:** Fitness room (step machine, treadmill, exercise bike, and free weights); tennis court; beach passes. *In room:* TV/DVD; hair dryers.

Moderate

The Captain R. Flanders House ★ (Finds) Set amid 60 acres of rolling meadows crisscrossed by stone walls, this late-18th-century farmhouse, built by a whaling captain, has remained much the same for 2 centuries. This is a working farm, so there's no time for posing. Two countrified modern cottages overlooking the pond have living rooms but not kitchenettes. After fortifying yourself with homemade muffins, island-made honey, and jam at breakfast, you are free to fritter the day away. The owners will provide you with a coveted pass to nearby Lucy Vincent Beach, or perhaps you'd prefer a long country walk.

440 North Rd. (about ¹/₂ mile northeast of Menemsha), Chilmark, MA 02535. ℂ **508/645-3123.** www. captainflandersinn.com. 5 units, 2 with shared bathroom; 2 cottages. Summer $190 double with shared bathroom; $225 double with private bathroom; $300 cottage. Rates include continental breakfast. AE, MC, V. Closed Nov–early May. **Amenities:** Private beach pass; shuttle bus to beach. *In room:* No phone.

Inexpensive

Hostelling International Martha's Vineyard The first "purpose-built" youth hostel in the United States, this homey cedar-shake saltbox set at the edge of a vast state forest is still a front-runner. The hallways are plastered with notices of local attractions (some stores offer discounts to hostellers), and the check-in desk also serves as a tourist information booth. Outside there's a volleyball court and a sheltered bike rack. By bike, the hostel is a little more than 7 miles from the Vineyard Haven ferry terminal; shuttle buses also make the rounds in summer.

525 Edgartown–West Tisbury Rd. (about 1 mile east of the town center), West Tisbury, MA 02575. ℂ **888/901-2087** or 508/693-2665. Fax 508/693-2699. http://capecod.hiusa.org. 76 beds, 1 family room. $32 for members; $35 for nonmembers; $150–$200 private room. MC, V. Closed mid-Oct to mid-May. *In room:* No phone.

9 WHERE TO DINE

Restaurants tend to be expensive on the Vineyard, but the stiff competition has produced a bevy of places that offer excellent service, evocative settings, and creative cuisine. *A note on spirits:* Outside Oak Bluffs and Edgartown, all of Martha's Vineyard is "dry," including Vineyard Haven, so BYOB; some restaurants charge a small fee for uncorking. **Great Harbour Gourmet & Spirits,** 40 Main St., Edgartown (ℂ **508/627-4390**), has a very good wine selection. There's also **Jim's Package Store,** at 27 Lake Ave., in Oak Bluffs (ℂ **508/693-0236;** http://jimspackagestore.com).

Very Expensive

Atria ★★★ NEW AMERICAN   This fine-dining restaurant set in an 18th-century sea captain's house on Upper Main Street, in Edgartown, gets rave reviews for its gourmet cuisine and high-caliber service. Pronounced with the emphasis on the second syllable (ah-*tre*-ah), the name refers to the brightest of three stars forming the Southern Triangle constellation. You can sit in the elegant dining room, the rose-covered wraparound porch, or the brick cellar bar downstairs for more casual dining. Chef/owner Christian Thornton's menu has influences from around the world, with stops in the Mediterranean, Middle East, and Asia. It features organic island-grown produce, off-the-boat seafood, local shellfish, and aged prime meats. Popular starters include miso soup with steamed crab dumplings. A must-try is the wok-fried Martha's Vineyard lobster. *Tip:* It's not on the menu but this place makes the best burger and fries on the island. If you order it, they'll make it.

137 Main St. (a short walk from the center of town). © **508/627-5850.** www.atriamv.com. Reservations recommended. Main courses $30–$48. AE, MC, V. June–Aug daily 5:30–10pm; call for off-season hours.

L'étoile ★★★ CONTEMPORARY FRENCH   Chef Michael Brisson, one of the Vineyard's most acclaimed chefs, creates an ever-evolving menu devoted to local produce and seafood, along with delicacies flown in from the four corners of the earth. Sevruga usually makes an appearance—perhaps as a garnish for chilled leek soup. An étouffée of lobster with lobster, cognac, and chervil sauce might come with littlenecks, bay scallops, and roasted corn fritters; or roasted pheasant breast in a cider, apple-brandy, and thyme sauce may be accompanied by apple, sun-dried cherry, and mascarpone-filled wild-rice crepes.

22 N. Water St. (off Main St.). © **508/627-5187.** www.letoile.net. Reservations recommended. Main courses $36–$49; chef's tasting menu $115. AE, MC, V. July–Aug 6–10pm; call for off-season hours. Closed Dec–Apr.

Expensive

Alchemy ★★ FRENCH BISTRO   Chef/owners Scott Caskey and Michael Presnol serve up a little slice of Paris on Edgartown's Main Street. Such esoteric choices as oyster brie soup and Burgundy Vintners salad share the bill with escargot-and-chanterelle fricassee and *lapin moutarde spatzle* (yes, that's rabbit). As befits a true bistro, there's a large selection of cocktails, liqueurs, and wines. In addition to lunch and dinner, a bar menu is served from 2:30 to 11pm. This choice isn't for everyone, but sophisticated diners will enjoy the Continental flair.

71 Main St. (in the center of town). © **508/627-9999.** http://alchemymv.com. Reservations recommended Main courses $22–$33. AE, MC, V. June–Nov Mon–Sat noon–2:30pm lunch, daily 5:30–10pm dinner, daily 2:30–11pm bar menu; call for off-season hours.

Chesca's ★ (Finds) ITALIAN   This modern-decor restaurant at the Colonial Inn is a solid entry, with yummy food at reasonable prices. You're sure to find such favorites as paella (with roasted lobster and other choice seafood), risotto (with roasted vegetables), and ravioli (with portobello mushrooms and asparagus). Smaller appetites can fill up on homemade soup and salad.

At the Colonial Inn, 38 N. Water St. © **508/627-1234.** www.chescasmv.com. Reservations recommended only for parties with 6 or more. Main courses $22–$36. AE, MC, V. Late June–early Sept daily 5:30–10pm; call for off-season hours. Closed Nov–Mar.

Lure Grill ★★ NEW AMERICAN   This elegant restaurant on the second floor of the **283**
Winnetu Resort near Katama Beach, a few miles from Edgartown, is making a name for
itself as a wonderful place for dinner. Those fortunate to get a window seat or a spot on
the deck in good weather can watch the sun set as they enjoy the fine cuisine and professional service. Menu selections make the most of local produce and seafood. You might
begin with local Katama oysters or seared foie gras. For a main course, there are such
unique choices as poached lobster with pea ravioli or wild king salmon with crabmeat-
and-artichoke risotto. Homemade desserts, such as the caramelized apple Charlotte, are
inspired. A restaurant for families with children, **Minnows,** is also on-site.

At the Winnetu Oceanside Resort, Katama (South Beach). ✆ **508/627-3663.** www.luremv.com. Reservations recommended. Main courses $24–$37. AE, MC, V. July–Aug daily 6:30–9:30pm; call for off-season
hours. Closed Dec to mid-Apr.

Restaurant Détente ★★ NEW AMERICAN   In high season, it's difficult to get a
reservation at this small and cozy restaurant, which takes its name from the French word
for relaxation and good relations. But fans of fine-dining may want to be persistent. The
theme for the menu here is seasonal specials, featuring foods from local farms and markets. For starters, you can go light, with a spring watercress and spiced pecan salad, or
heavy, with island lobster ravioli. The main courses are similarly varied, from pesto-
marinated rack of lamb to orange curry-crusted monkfish. The wine list is extensive, with
numerous intriguing choices available by the glass.

Off Winter St. (in Nevin Sq., behind the Colonial Inn). ✆ **508/627-8810.** www.detentewinebar.com.
Reservations recommended. Main courses $29–$35. AE, MC, V. June–Aug daily 6–10pm; call for off-season hours. Closed Feb–Mar.

Water Street ★★ NEW AMERICAN   This is a terrific place to have a drink or to
dine, with its exquisite view of Edgartown Harbor and the lighthouse. The long and
elegant bar is particularly smashing. The menu is simple but stylish. To start there's soft-
shell crab with arugula and teardrop tomatoes. As a main course, try the caramelized sea
scallops with a salad of Asian pear and apple. Service is excellent; these are trained waiters, not your usual college surfer dudes. At the end of your meal, you may want to sit on
the rockers on the Harbor View Hotel's (see "Where to Stay," earlier in this chapter)
wraparound porch and watch the lights twinkling in the harbor. **Henry's** is a dark-paneled bar also in the hotel.

At the Harbor View Hotel, 131 N. Water St. ✆ **508/627-3761.** www.kelley-house.com/dining_water_
street.asp. Reservations recommended. Main courses $22–$30. AE, MC, V. June–Aug Mon–Sat 7–11am,
noon–2pm, and 6–10pm, Sun 11:30–2:30 and 6–9pm; call for off-season hours.

Moderate

Among the Flowers Cafe ★★ (Value) AMERICAN   Everything's fresh and appealing at this small outdoor cafe near the dock. Sit under the awning, and you'll just catch
a glimpse of the harbor. The breakfasts are the best around, and all the crepes, waffles,
and eggs are also available at lunch. The comfort-food dinners (chicken-and-black-pep-
per sauté over pasta; butter-and-crumb-crusted baked haddock with a sautéed lobster-
and-shallot-butter cream) are among the most affordable options in this pricey town.
There's almost always a wait, not just because it's so picturesque, but because the food is
homey, hearty, and kind on the wallet.

17 Mayhew Lane. ✆ **508/627-3233.** www.mvol.com/menu/amongtheflowers. Main courses $10–$18.
Reservations not accepted. AE, DC, DISC, MC, V. July–Aug daily 8am–9:30pm; May–June and Sept–Oct
daily 8am–4pm. Closed Nov–Apr.

The Seafood Shanty ★ (Finds) SEAFOOD   This casual restaurant overlooking Edgartown Harbor features outdoor dining and cheerful service by college kids. This is a great place for lunch with a water view. Good lunch choices are the lobster roll or the cold poached salmon. For dinner, options include a classic bouillabaisse-seafood stew or a prime-rib plate. There is also a children's menu. The restaurant has a convenient **walk-up counter** in a shack on Dock Street in front of the restaurant, where virtually the entire menu is available to go.

31 Dock St. ☎ **508/627-8622.** www.theseafoodshanty.com. Reservations recommended. Lunch $9–$17; dinner $17–$35. AE, MC, V. June–Aug daily 11am–10pm; call for off-season hours. Closed Nov to mid-May.

Inexpensive

Espresso Love ★★ (Finds) (Value) AMERICAN   Hidden behind a parking lot, this little gem is not only a great place to stop for breakfast (blueberry scones, fresh-baked muffins) and lunch (big sandwiches), but, in the summer, there is also dinner served outside on the patio, where the wholesome recipes of Carol McManus, the owner, rule the evening. Ms. McManus has even written a cookbook with her favorite recipes, and you'll find many of them here. This is very casual and affordable, with sandwiches and thin-crust pizza, in addition to tasty specials, such as her luscious lobster cakes.

17 Church St. (off Main St., behind the courthouse). ☎ **508/627-9211.** http://espressolove.com. Main courses $12–$18. AE, MC, V. July–Aug daily 6:30am–10pm; off-season 6:30am–6pm.

MacPhail's Corner Cafe DINER   This small diner near the harbor is the place to stop in the morning for fresh-squeezed orange juice and a home-baked muffin, washed down with fair-trade organic coffee. For lunch there are lobster rolls, grilled sandwiches, and chowder.

18 Dock St. (near the harbor). ☎ **508/939-3090.** Reservations not accepted. All items under $15. AE, MC, V. July–Aug daily 6:30am–10pm.

The Newes from America ★★ (Finds) PUB GRUB   The food is better than average at this subterranean tavern, built in 1742. The decor may be more Edwardian than colonial, but those who come to quaff don't seem to care. Locals love the French onion soup. Beers are a specialty here. Try a rack of five esoteric brews, or let your choice of food—from a wood-smoked oyster "Island Poor Boy" sandwich with linguiça relish to an 18-ounce porterhouse steak—dictate your draft; the menu comes handily annotated with recommendations. Don't miss their seasoned fries, accompanied by a savory Southwestern dipping sauce.

At The Kelley House, 23 Kelley St. ☎ **508/627-4397.** www.kelley-house.com/dining_news_from_america. asp. Reservations not accepted. Main courses $7–$10. AE, MC, V. Daily 7am–11pm.

OAK BLUFFS

Expensive

Oyster Bar Grill ★★ STEAK/SEAFOOD   Occupying a large space on Circuit Avenue, this restaurant, with a huge oak bar, is a hip venue for the 30-something crowd. Specializing in seafood and—unusual for Martha's Vineyard—steak, this place serves wonderful food, including a variety of its namesake oysters. Staff are particularly knowledgeable about food here. In season, there is live music and the scene is hopping.

57 Circuit Ave. ☎ **508/693-6600.** Reservations recommended. Main courses $19–$39. AE, MC, V. May–Nov daily 5–11pm; call for off-season hours.

Sweet Life Cafe ★★ FRENCH/AMERICAN   Locals are crazy about this pearl of a restaurant, set in a restored Victorian house on upper Circuit Avenue. In season, the most popular seating is outside in the garden. Fresh island produce is featured, with seafood specials an enticing draw. The menu changes often, and everything is terrific. Expect such yummy soups as vegetable white-bean pistou, and main courses such as roast lamb loin with ratatouille. There are also always vegetarian entrees on the menu.

63 Circuit Ave. ℂ **508/696-0200.** www.sweetlifemv.com. Reservations recommended. Main courses $32–$40. AE, DISC, MC, V. Mid-May to Aug daily 5:30–9:30pm; Apr to mid-May and Sept–Oct Thurs–Mon 5:30–9:30pm. Closed Nov–Mar.

Inexpensive

Coop de Ville ★ SEAFOOD   Of the several open-air harborfront choices in Oak Bluffs, this one has the best service and food. This outdoor fried-seafood shack serves up tasty beer-battered shrimp, grilled swordfish, lobster salad, and "world-famous" chicken wings. Wing connoisseurs can choose from mild to suicide to Three Mile Island, as well as Cajun, mango, and Maryland style, among others. It's a fun place to people-watch on sunny summer days, as boaters cruise around the harbor.

Dockside Market Place. ℂ **508/693-3420.** www.coopdevillemv.com. Reservations not accepted. Most items $9–$20. MC, V. June–Aug daily 11am–10pm; call for off-season hours. Closed mid-Oct to Apr.

Linda Jean's DINER   A great place to bring kids or just to have a low-key meal with no pretensions, Linda Jean's has excellent breakfast, lunch, and even dinner selections on its all-American-type menu of omelets, salads, sandwiches, and burgers. At breakfast, the line starts forming early here.

25 Circuit Ave. ℂ **508/693-4093.** Reservations not accepted. Most items under $15. MC, V. June–Aug daily 8am–8pm; call for off-season hours.

Sharky's Cantina ★ MEXICAN   A swinging Mexican joint right on Circuit Avenue is the hot spot in Oak Bluffs. Stretching from one end of the restaurant to the other, the large bar is packed five deep (with mostly young people) in the summer. It's within yelling distance of the dining area, where the margaritas wash down a standard array of quesadillas, tacos, enchiladas, and burritos. Although typical for a Mexican restaurant, the menu is an inexpensive rarity on the Vineyard. This well-run establishment is a solid entry on the Oak Bluffs scene.

31 Circuit Ave. ℂ **508/693-7501.** www.sharkyscantina.com. Reservations recommended. Main courses $6–$15. MC, V. June–Aug daily 8am–10pm; call for off-season hours.

Slice of Life ★ (Finds) DELI   This deli at the upper end of Circuit Avenue is the place to head for gourmet sandwiches, salads, and soups. There are just a handful of tables inside and more out on the screened porch in front. The eclectic menu includes burgers and pizza. Sandwiches are made with bread baked on-site. Wine, beer, and specialty coffees are served.

50 Circuit Ave. ℂ **508/693-3838.** www.sliceoflifemv.com. Reservations not accepted. Most items under $10. MC, V. June–Aug daily 7am–10pm; call for off-season hours.

Sweets

Mad Martha's ★   Vineyarders are mad for this locally made ice cream, which comes in two dozen enticing flavors. You could opt for a restrained mango sorbet, which isn't to say you shouldn't go for a hot-fudge sundae. There's also a branch at 7 N. Water St., Edgartown. (ℂ **508/627-8761**).

117 Circuit Ave. (in the center of town). ℂ **508/693-9151.** Daily 10am–1am. Closed Oct–Apr.

Martha's Vineyard Gourmet Cafe & Bakery ★ (Moments) This is where you go anytime from 9pm 'til 1am for the famous **Back Door Donuts,** hot and fresh-out-of-the-oven donuts, apple fritters, cinnamon buns, croissants, and other baked goods. You go to the back door of this bakery and one of the bakers will come over and sell you baked goods. During regular hours, you enter the bakery by the front door, in Post Office Square, off Circuit Avenue. But nothing beats Back Door Donuts. There's also a branch at 19 N. Water St., Edgartown. (© **508/627-5880**).

5 Post Office Sq. (in the center of town). © **508/693-3688.** Daily 8am–6pm. Back Door Donuts 9pm–1am.

Murdick's Fudge Since 1887, the Murdick family has been serving up homemade fudge, brittle, clusters, and bark. Bring the kids and watch the candy-makers. In addition to the location on Circuit Avenue, there's a branch at and 21 N. Water St., in Edgartown.

5 Circuit Ave. © **508/627-8047.** http://murdicks.com/fudge. Summer daily 9:30am–11pm; call for off-season hours.

VINEYARD HAVEN (TISBURY)

Expensive

Le Grenier ★★ FRENCH If Paris is the heart of France, Lyon is its belly—and that's where chef/owner Jean Dupon grew up on his *maman*'s hearty cuisine. Dupon has the Continental moves down, as evidenced by such classics as steak au poivre, calf's brains Grenobloise with *beurre noir* and capers, and lobster Normande flambéed with Calvados, apples, and cream. Despite the fact that Le Grenier means (and, in fact, is housed in) an attic, the restaurant is quite romantic, especially when aglow with hurricane lamps. *Remember:* You must BYOB here.

96 Main St. (in the center of town). © **508/693-4906.** www.legrenierrestaurant.com. Reservations recommended. Main courses $22–$32. AE, DC, DISC, MC, V. Daily 5:30–9pm.

Zephrus at the Mansion House Inn ★ INTERNATIONAL At this stylish restaurant at the Mansion House Inn in the center of Vineyard Haven, seating is at the sidewalk cafe on Main Street or inside by the hearth in view of the open kitchen. Menu items are creative at this high-energy venue, and portions are generous. For starters, you might try the snow crab cakes or the spicy mussels. Main-course winners are pan-roasted pork tenderloin served with sweet tater tots, and shrimp and *farfalle* pasta. Though the menu is in constant flux, there is always a good vegetarian choice such as the delicious vegetable risotto with truffle vinaigrette. Because the restaurant is BYOB, you'll want to bring your favorite wine. The corkage fee is $5 per table.

9 Main St. © **508/693-3416.** www.mvmansionhouse.com/zephrus.html. Reservations recommended. Main courses $20–$28. AE, DC, DISC, MC, V. July–Aug Mon–Sat 11:30am–3pm and 5:30–10pm, Sun 5:30–9:30pm; call for off-season hours.

Moderate

Black Dog Tavern ★ NEW AMERICAN How does a humble harbor shack come to be a national icon? Location helps. So do cool T-shirts. Soon after *Shenandoah* captain Robert Douglas decided, in 1971, that this hardworking port could use a good restaurant, influential vacationers stuck waiting for the ferry began to wander into this saltbox to tide themselves over with a bit of "blackout cake" or peanut-butter pie. The smartest marketing move was the invention of the signature "Martha's Vineyard whitefoot," a black Lab whose stalwart profile now adorns everything from babies' overalls to golf balls and needlepoint kits.

Still, tourists love this rough-hewn tavern, though it's mostly hype that keeps them happy. The menu is heavy on the seafood, of course (including grilled swordfish with banana, basil, and lime; and bluefish with mustard-soufflé sauce)—and the blackout cake has lost none of its appeal.

Beach St. Ext. (on the harbor). (✆) **508/693-9223.** www.theblackdog.com. Reservations not accepted. Main courses $14–$27. AE, MC, V. June–early Sept Mon–Sat 7–11am, noon–4pm, and 5–10pm; Sun 7am–noon, 1–4pm, and 5–10pm; call for off-season hours.

Saltwater ★★ NEW AMERICAN   With big picture windows, this new restaurant takes full advantage of its very pretty location overlooking the Lagoon Pond in Vineyard Haven. With this view, seafood is, of course, a specialty—try the day-boat scallops with curry coconut broth—but there are a number of special island-inspired dishes on the menu, particularly among the salads, made with island-grown produce.

79 Beach Rd. (at Tisbury Marketplace; 10 min. walk from Main St.). (✆) **508/338-4666.** www.saltwater restaurant.com. Reservations recommended. Main courses $$25–$35. AE, MC, V. July–Aug Mon–Sat 11:30am–3pm and 5:30–9:30pm, Sun 10am–3pm and 5:30–9:30pm; call for off-season hours.

Inexpensive

Art Cliff Diner ★★ DINER   Expect the best food you've ever had at a diner at this quirky establishment. It's a short walk from the center of Vineyard Haven. Be aware that the hours are a little unreliable, especially off-season, and you should call to be sure it is open before making the trek. The food here is scrumptious, whether you are having the (just caught) fish of the day served with herbs from the chef's garden, or a simple burger that is cooked just right. Desserts are homemade, of course. A new addition recently is that the chef/owner, Gina Stanley, parks a food truck in the restaurant parking lot on Thursday through Sunday evenings in summer and serves burgers, hand-cut fries, and falafels straight from a portable grill. There are also such desserts as fresh strawberries and cream, and Nutella doughnuts with chocolate sauce.

39 Beach Rd. (a short walk from Main St.). (✆) **508/693-1224.** Reservations not accepted. Main courses all under $15. No credit cards. July–Aug Thurs–Tues 7am–2pm; call for off-season hours. Closed Nov–Apr.

Takeout & Picnic Fare

Black Dog Bakery ★   In need of a snack at 5:30am? That's when the doors to this fabled bakery open; from midmorning on, it's elbow room only. The selection of freshly baked breads, muffins, and desserts can't be beat. Don't forget homemade doggie biscuits for your pooch.

Water St. (near the harbor). (✆) **508/693-4786.** www.theblackdog.com. Summer daily 5:30am–8pm; winter daily 5:30am–5pm.

CHILMARK (INCLUDING MENEMSHA) & WEST TISBURY

Very Expensive

The Beach Plum Inn Restaurant ★★★ INTERNATIONAL   This jewel of a restaurant is located in an inn that sits on a bluff overlooking the fishing village of Menemsha. Extensive renovations and attention to quality have made this one of the island's top dining venues. Guests can dine inside in the spare, but elegant, dining room, or outside on the tiled patio. Either way, diners enjoy sunset views of the harbor. The most popular dishes include hazelnut-encrusted halibut with Marsala wine beurre-blanc sauce and Alaskan king salmon, grilled over Peruvian blue mashed potatoes with a morel mushroom sauce and crabmeat timbale. For dessert, you'll flip for the chocolate quadruple-layer cake made with white and dark chocolate mousse and Chambord.

At the Beach Plum Inn, 50 Beach Plum Lane (off North Rd.), Menemsha. $\textcircled{C}$ **508/645-9454.** www.beach pluminn.com/restaurant.htm. Reservations required. Main courses $32–$40; 4-course fixed-price menu $68; off-season-only fixed-priced menu $50. AE, MC, V. Mid-June to early Sept daily seatings 5:30–6:45pm and 8–9:30pm; call for off-season hours. Closed Dec–Apr.

Expensive

Home Port ★★ SEAFOOD   Johnny Graham is a well-known chef in these parts, and when word spread that he was taking over the kitchen of the beloved Home Port in Menemsha, people began making the trek to the far end of the island to see what was up. The Home Port has always been known for lobster and sunsets; you get your order and bring it to the nearby beach. Don't forget the bevvies; it's BYOB in these parts. In addition to the usual seafood, the menu now has Johnny's special ribs and fish tacos. The restaurant is also serving brunch, with a range of interesting choices, including the grilled salmon club with bacon. Perhaps best of all, there is now a delivery cart stationed at the pick-up window that will ferry your dinner out to you on the beach.

512 North Rd., Menemsha. $\textcircled{C}$ **508/645-2679.** www.homeportmv.com. Reservations recommended. Complete dinners $30–$50. MC, V. July–Aug Mon–Sat 5–9pm, Sun 10am–2pm and 5–9pm; call for off-season hours. Closed Labor Day to mid-May.

Lambert's Cove Inn Restaurant ★★ (Finds) NEW AMERICAN   One of the Vineyard's favorite chefs, Joe Silva, runs the kitchen at this romantic country inn. If you are staying in one of the down-island towns such as Edgartown or Oak Bluffs, driving through the wooded countryside to this secluded inn feels like an expedition to an earlier time. The interior of the restaurant is set up with crisp white tablecloths and antique furniture. In good weather, you can dine alfresco on a deck surrounded by flowering trees and shrubs. The menu features fresh seafood, island produce, and meats. You might start with a crab and asparagus Napoleon, or simply a luscious cream of mushroom soup. Special dinner entrees include grilled marinated duck-breast casserole baked in a sherry lobster cream sauce. Desserts are homemade delicacies. Don't forget: The town of West Tisbury is "dry," so you must bring your own alcoholic beverages.

90 Manaquayak Rd. (about 3 miles west of Vineyard Haven) $\textcircled{C}$ **508/693-2298.** www.lambertscoveinn. com/restaurant.html. Reservations recommended. Main courses $24–$32. AE, MC, V. July–Aug daily 6–9pm; call for off-season hours.

Moderate

The Bite ★★ (Finds) SEAFOOD   It's places like The Bite that you crave when you think of New England. This is your quintessential "chowdah" and clam shack, flanked by picnic tables. Run by two sisters using their grandmother's recipes, The Bite makes superlative chowder, potato salad, fried fish, and so forth. The food comes in graduated containers, with a jumbo portion of shrimp topping out at around $26.

29 Basin Rd. (off North Rd., about ¼ mile northeast of the harbor), Menemsha. $\textcircled{C}$ **508/645-9239.** Main courses $18–$30. No credit cards. Reservations not accepted. July–Aug daily 11am–8pm; call for off-season hours. Closed late Sept to mid-May.

Takeout & Picnic Fare

Alley's General Store (Finds)   That endangered rarity, a true New England general store, Alley's—in business since 1858—nearly foundered in the profit-mad 1980s. Luckily the Martha's Vineyard Preservation Trust interceded to give it a new lease on life, along with a much-needed structural overhaul. The stock is still the same, though: basically, everything you could possibly need, from scrub brushes to fresh-made salsa. Best of all, the no-longer-sagging front porch still supports a popular bank of benches, along with a blizzard of bulletin-board notices. For a local's-eye view of noteworthy activities and events, this is the first place to check.

State Rd. (in the center of town), West Tisbury. ℂ **508/693-0088.** Summer daily 7am–7pm; winter Mon–Sat 7am–6pm, Sun 8am–5pm.

West Tisbury Farmers' Market (Finds) This seasonal outdoor market, open Wednesday from 2:30 to 5:30pm and Saturday from 9am to noon, is among the biggest and best in New England, and certainly the most rarefied, with local celebrities loading up on prize produce and snacking on pesto bread and other international goodies. The fun starts in June and runs for 18 Saturdays and 10 Wednesdays.

Old Agricultural Hall, West Tisbury. ℂ **508/693-9561.** www.westtisburyfarmersmarket.com.

10 MARTHA'S VINEYARD AFTER DARK

PUBS, BARS, DANCE CLUBS & LIVE MUSIC

The Lampost/The Dive Bar Young and loud are the watchwords at this pair of clubs; the larger features live bands or DJs and a dance floor, the smaller (down in the basement), acoustic acts. This is where the young folk go, and the performers could be playing blues, reggae, R&B, or '80s music. Call for a schedule. Closed November to March. 111 Circuit Ave. (in the center of town), Oak Bluffs. ℂ **508/696-9352.** Cover $1–$5.

Offshore Ale Company (Finds) In 1602, the first barley in the New World was grown on Martha's Vineyard. A few years ago, the Vineyard's first and only brewpub opened, featuring eight locally made beers on tap ($2.75–$5). It's an attractively rustic place, with high ceilings, oak booths lining the walls, and peanut shells strewn on the floor. There's a raw bar, and late-night munchies are served 'til 10pm, featuring pizza and hamburgers, among other offerings. Local acoustic performers entertain 6 nights a week in season. Open June to September daily, noon to midnight; call for off-season hours. 30 Kennebec Ave., Oak Bluffs. ℂ **508/693-2626.** www.offshoreale.com. Cover $2–$3.

Nectar's The dance club at the airport features top musicians, comedy, theme nights, and teen nights. Doors open on show nights at 7pm. Food is served until 11pm. Open April to mid-January. At Martha's Vineyard Airport (take West Tisbury/Edgartown Rd. to the airport). ℂ **508/693-1137.** www.nectarsmv.com. Tickets $10–$30.

The Ritz Café ★ (Moments) Locals and visitors alike flock to this down-and-dirty hole-in-the-wall that features live music every night in season and on weekends year-round. The crowd—a boozing, brawling lot—enjoy the pool tables in the back. Call for a schedule. 4 Circuit Ave., Oak Bluffs. ℂ **508/693-9851.** Cover $3.

The Sand Bar & Grille This cool-cat bar is the place to hang out in Oak Bluffs near the harbor to listen to the latest local bands. 6 Circuit Ave. (in the center of town), Oak Bluffs. ℂ **508/693-7111.**

LOW-KEY EVENINGS

Old Whaling Church ★★ This magnificent 1843 Greek Revival church functions primarily as a 500-seat performing-arts center offering lectures and symposiums, films, plays, and concerts. Such Vineyard luminaries as the actress Patricia Neal have taken their place at the pulpit, not to mention Livingston Taylor and Andre Previn, whose annual gigs always sell out. It's also the Edgartown United Methodist Church, with a 9am service on Sundays. Call for a schedule. 89 Main St. (in the center of town), Edgartown. © 508/627-4442. www.mvpreservation.org/whale.html. Ticket prices vary.

THEATER & DANCE

Vineyard Playhouse In an intimate (112-seat) black-box theater, carved out of an 1833 church-turned-Masonic lodge, Equity professionals put on a rich season of favorites and challenging new work, followed, on summer weekends, by musical or comedic cabaret in the gallery/lounge. Children's theater selections are performed on Saturdays at 10am. Townspeople often get involved in the outdoor Shakespeare production, a 3-week run, starting in mid-July, at the Tashmoo Overlook Amphitheatre, about 1 mile west of town. Tickets for the 5pm performances Tuesday to Sunday run only $5 to $10. Master-Card and Visa are accepted. Open June to September Tuesday to Saturday at 8pm, Sunday at 7pm; call for off-season hours. 24 Church St. (in the center of town), Vineyard Haven. © 508/696-6300; www.vineyardplayhouse.org. Tickets $15–$30.

MOVIES

The **Entertainment Cinemas,** at 65 Main St. (© **508/627-8008**), in Edgartown, has two screens. There are also vintage Art Deco movie theaters: **Island Theater,** at the bottom of Circuit Avenue, Oak Bluffs; the **Capawock,** in Vineyard Haven; and **The Strand,** Oak Bluffs Avenue Extension, Oak Bluffs. Call © **508/627-6689** for movie times.

ONLY ON THE VINEYARD

Gay Head Lighthouse (Moments) Though generally closed to the public, this 1856 lighthouse opens its doors on summer-weekend evenings to afford an awe-inspiring view of the sunset over the Devil's Bridge shoals. The light has been automated since 1952 (the original lens lights up the night sky in Edgartown), but the experience continues to be romantic. Tour time varies nightly. It begins 1½ hours before sunset and ends a half-hour past sunset. Tours run from late June to late September, Friday to Sunday 7 to 9pm. Off State Rd., Aquinnah. © 508/645-9954. www.mvmuseum.org/lighthousetours.php. Admission $2 adults, free for children 11 and under.

Trinity Park Tabernacle ★★ Designed by architect J. W. Hoyt, of Springfield, Massachusetts, and built in 1879, for just over $7,000, this open-air church, now on the National Register of Historic Places, is the largest wrought-iron-and-wood structure in America. Its conical crown is ringed with a geometric pattern of amber, carmine, and midnight-blue stained glass. Old-fashioned community sings take place Wednesday at 8pm, and concerts are scheduled irregularly on weekends. James Taylor and Bonnie Raitt have regaled the faithful here, but usually the acts are more homespun. Open July to August on Wednesdays at 8pm and occasional weekend evenings. Call for a schedule. Trinity Park (within the Camp Meeting Grounds), Oak Bluffs. © 508/693-0525. Free admission and $20 community tours.

11

Fast Facts, Toll-Free Numbers & Websites

1 FAST FACTS: CAPE COD & THE ISLANDS

AMERICAN EXPRESS The **American Express Travel Service** office is at 1600 Falmouth Rd., in Centerville (© **800/937-1255** or 508/778-2310), and is open Monday to Friday from 9am to 5:30pm.

AREA CODES The telephone area code for the Cape and islands is **508.** You must always dial © 1 and this area code first, even if you are making a call within the same town.

ATM NETWORKS See section 4, "Money & Costs," in chapter 3.

AUTOMOBILE ORGANIZATIONS Auto clubs will supply maps, suggested routes, guidebooks, accident and bail-bond insurance, and emergency road service. The **American Automobile Association (AAA)** is the major auto club in the United States. If you are an international visitor and belong to an auto club in your home country, inquire about AAA reciprocity before you leave. You may be able to join AAA even if you're not a member of a reciprocal club; to inquire, call AAA (© **800/222-4357**). AAA is actually an organization of regional auto clubs, so look under "AAA Automobile Club," in the white pages of the telephone directory. AAA has a nationwide emergency road service telephone number (© **800/AAA-HELP** [222-4357]). Use your AAA to get discounts at many Cape and islands hotels.

BUSINESS HOURS Business hours in public and private offices are usually Monday to Friday from 8 or 9am to 5pm. Most stores are open Monday to Saturday from 9:30 or 10am to 5:30 or 6pm; many are also open on Sunday from noon to 5pm or earlier. The exception is Provincetown, where many stores are open until 10 or 11pm. Most every town has some kind of convenience store carrying food, beverages, newspapers, and household basics; and the larger communities have supermarkets, which generally stay open as late as 10 or 11pm, or even 24 hours.

CAR RENTALS See section 3, "Getting There & Getting Around," in chapter 3.

CURRENCY For information see section 4, "Money & Costs," in chapter 3.

DRINKING LAWS The legal age for purchase and consumption of alcoholic beverages is 21; proof of age is required and often requested at bars, nightclubs, and restaurants, so it's always a good idea to bring ID when you go out.

Bars are allowed to stay open until 1am daily, with last call at 12:30am. Beer and wine are sold at grocery as well as package stores, hard liquor at package stores only. A few towns on Martha's Vineyard are dry by choice or tradition (no alcohol can be sold or served), but at most establishments lacking a liquor license, you're welcome to bring your own wine or beer; if in doubt, call ahead.

Do not carry open containers of alcohol in your car or in any public area that isn't zoned for alcohol consumption. The police can fine you on the spot. And nothing will ruin your trip faster than getting a citation for DUI ("driving under the influence"), so don't even think about driving while intoxicated.

DRIVING RULES   See section 3, "Getting There & Getting Around," in chapter 3.

ELECTRICITY   Like Canada, the United States uses 110 to 120 volts AC (60 cycles), compared to 220 to 240 volts AC (50 cycles) in most of Europe, Australia, and New Zealand. Downward converters that change 220to 240 volts to 110 to 120 volts are difficult to find in the United States, so bring one with you if you're visiting from overseas. Wherever you go, bring a **connection kit** of the right power and phone adapters, a spare phone cord, and a spare Ethernet network cable—or find out whether your hotel or B&B supplies them.

EMBASSIES & CONSULATES   All embassies are located in the nation's capital, Washington, D.C. Some consulates are located in major U.S. cities, and most nations have a mission to the United Nations in New York City. If your country isn't listed below, call for directory information in Washington, D.C. (✆ **202/555-1212**), or log on to **www.embassy.org/ embassies**.

The embassy of **Australia** is at 1601 Massachusetts Ave. NW, Washington, DC 20036 (✆ **202/797-3000;** http://australia. visahq.com). There are consulates in New York, Honolulu, Houston, Los Angeles, and San Francisco.

The embassy of **Canada** is at 501 Pennsylvania Ave. NW, Washington, DC 20001 (✆ **202/682-1740;** www.canada international.gc.ca/washington). Other Canadian consulates are in Buffalo (New York), Detroit, Los Angeles, New York, and Seattle.

The embassy of **Ireland** is at 2234 Massachusetts Ave. NW, Washington, DC 20008 (✆ **202/462-3939;** www.embassy ofireland.org). Irish consulates are in

Boston, Chicago, New York, San Francisco, and other cities. See the website for a complete listing.

The embassy of **New Zealand** is at 37 Observatory Circle, Washington, DC 20008 (✆ **202/328-4800;** www.nz embassy.com). New Zealand consulates are in Los Angeles, Salt Lake City, San Francisco, and Seattle.

The embassy of the **United Kingdom** is at 3100 Massachusetts Ave. NW, Washington, DC 20008 (✆ **202/588-6500;** http://ukinusa.fco.gov.uk). Other British consulates are in Atlanta, Boston, Chicago, Cleveland, Houston, Los Angeles, New York, San Francisco, and Seattle.

EMERGENCIES   In an emergency, call ✆ **911.**

GASOLINE (PETROL)   The cost of U.S. gasoline (also known as gas, but never petrol), varies widely. Cape Cod has some of the highest prices in the country, averaging at about $2.70 per gallon, with the islands of Martha's Vineyard and Nantucket even higher. Taxes are already included in the posted price. One U.S. gallon equals 3.8 liters or .85 imperial gallons. Fill-up locations are known as gas or service stations.

HOLIDAYS   Banks, government offices, post offices, and many stores, restaurants, and museums are closed on the following legal national or state holidays: January 1 (New Year's Day), the third Monday in January (Martin Luther King, Jr., Day), the third Monday in February (Presidents' Day), the third Monday in April (Patriots' Day, a state holiday), the last Monday in May (Memorial Day), July 4 (Independence Day), the first Monday in September (Labor Day), the second Monday in October (Columbus Day), November 11 (Veterans' Day/Armistice Day), the fourth Thursday in November (Thanksgiving Day), and December 25 (Christmas). The Tuesday after the first Monday in November is Election Day, a federal government holiday in presidential-election years (held every 4 years, most recently in 2008).

For more information on holidays, see "Calendar of Events," in chapter 3.

HOSPITALS The **Cape Cod Hospital,** at 27 Park St., Hyannis (℃ **508/771-1800**), offers 24-hour emergency medical service and consultation, as does the **Falmouth Hospital,** at 100 Ter Heun Dr. (℃ **508/548-5300**). On the islands, contact the **Martha's Vineyard Hospital,** on Linton Lane, in Oak Bluffs (℃ **508/693-0410**), or **Nantucket Cottage Hospital,** at 57 Prospect St. (℃ **508/825-8100**).

INSURANCE One thing to keep in mind when visiting the Cape and islands is that there are no refunds for bad weather. Fortunately, there are a number of things to do when you are stuck with a run of cloudy or rainy days. Most hotels and inns in the region give details about their cancellation policies when you book. Some will refund your money if you cancel more than a month before the trip and they are able to rebook the room. Some people would rather rely on travel insurance.

Medical Insurance: Although it's not required of travelers, health insurance is highly recommended. Most health insurance policies cover you if you get sick away from home—but check your coverage before you leave.

International visitors to the U.S. should note that unlike many European countries, the United States does not usually offer free or low-cost medical care to its citizens or visitors. Doctors and hospitals are expensive, and in most cases will require advance payment or proof of coverage before they render their services. Good policies will cover the costs of an accident, repatriation, or death. Packages, such as **Europ Assistance's "Worldwide Healthcare Plan,"** are sold by European automobile clubs and travel agencies at attractive rates. **Worldwide Assistance Services, Inc.** (℃ **800/777-8710;** www.

worldwideassistance.com) is the agent for Europ Assistance in the United States.

Though lack of health insurance may prevent you from being admitted to a hospital in a nonemergency, don't worry about being left on a street corner to die: The American way is to fix you now and bill the daylights out of you later.

If you're ever hospitalized more than 150 miles from home, **MedjetAssist** (℃ **800/527-7478;** www.medjetassistance.com) will pick you up and fly you to the hospital of your choice in a medically equipped and staffed aircraft, 24 hours day, 7 days a week. Annual memberships are $225 individual, $350 family; you can also purchase short-term memberships.

Canadians should check with their provincial health plan offices or call **Health Canada** (℃ **866/225-0709;** www.hc-sc.gc.ca) to find out the extent of their coverage and what documentation and receipts they must take home in case they are treated in the United States.

Travelers from the **U.K.** should carry their European Health Insurance Card (EHIC), which replaced the E111 form as proof of entitlement to free/reduced cost medical treatment abroad (℃ **0845/606-2030;** www.ehic.org.uk). Note, however, that the EHIC only covers "necessary medical treatment," and for repatriation costs, lost money, baggage, or cancellation, travel insurance from a reputable company should always be sought (www.travelinsuranceweb.com).

Travel Insurance: The cost of travel insurance varies widely, depending on the destination, the cost and length of your trip, your age and health, and the type of trip you're taking, but expect to pay between 5% and 8% of the vacation itself. You can get estimates from various providers through **InsureMyTrip.com.** Enter your trip cost and dates, your age, and other information, for prices from more than a dozen companies.

U.K. citizens and their families who make more than one trip abroad per year may find an annual travel insurance policy works out cheaper. Check **www.money supermarket.com**, which compares prices across a wide range of providers for single- and multitrip policies.

Most big travel agencies offer their own insurance and will probably try to sell you their package when you book a holiday. Think before you sign. **Britain's Consumers' Association** recommends that you insist on seeing the policy and reading the fine print before buying travel insurance. **The Association of British Insurers** (© 020/7600-3333; www.abi.org.uk) gives advice by phone and publishes *Holiday Insurance*, a free guide to policy provisions and prices. You might also shop around for better deals: Try **Columbus Direct** (© 0870/033-9988; www.columbusdirect. net).

Trip-Cancellation Insurance: Trip-cancellation insurance will help retrieve your money if you have to back out of a trip or depart early, or if your travel supplier goes bankrupt. Trip-cancellation insurance traditionally covers such events as sickness, natural disasters, and Department of State advisories. The latest news in trip-cancellation insurance is the availability of **expanded hurricane coverage** and the **"any-reason"** cancellation coverage—which costs more but covers cancellations made for any reason. You won't get back 100% of your prepaid trip cost, but you'll be refunded a substantial portion. **TravelSafe** (© 888/523-8020; www.travelsafe. com) offers both types of coverage. Expedia also offers any-reason cancellation coverage for its air-hotel packages. For details, contact one of the following recommended insurers: **Access America** (© 800/284-8300; www.accessamerica.com); **Travel Guard International** (© 800/826-4919; www.travelguard.com); **Travel Insured International** (© 800/243-3174; www. travelinsured.com); and **Travelex Insurance Services** (© 888/457-4602; www.travelex-insurance.com).

INTERNET ACCESS Most Cape and island towns have at least one cybercafe; check with your innkeeper or the local chamber of commerce to find the closest one. In addition, almost all libraries have free Internet access.

LEGAL AID If you are "pulled over" for a minor infraction (such as speeding), never attempt to pay the fine directly to a police officer; this could be construed as attempted bribery, a much more serious crime. Pay fines by mail, or directly into the hands of the clerk of the court. If accused of a more serious offense, say and do nothing before consulting a lawyer. Here the burden is on the state to prove a person's guilt beyond a reasonable doubt, and everyone has the right to remain silent, whether he or she is suspected of a crime or actually arrested. Once arrested, a person can make one telephone call to a party of his or her choice. International visitors should call their embassy or consulate.

LOST & FOUND Be sure to tell all of your credit card companies the minute you discover your wallet has been lost or stolen and file a report at the nearest police precinct. Your credit card company or insurer may require a police report number or record of the loss. Most credit card companies have an emergency toll-free number to call if your card is lost or stolen; they may be able to wire you a cash advance immediately or deliver an emergency credit card in a day or two. **Visa's** U.S. emergency number is © 800/847-2911 or 410/581-9994. **American Express** cardholders and traveler's check holders should call © 800/221-7282. **MasterCard** holders should call © 800/307-7309 or 636/722-7111. For other credit cards, call the toll-free number directory at © 800/555-1212.

If you need emergency cash over the weekend when all banks and American Express offices are closed, you can have money wired to you via **Western Union** (ℂ **800/325-6000;** www.westernunion. com).

MAIL At press time, domestic postage rates were 28¢ for a postcard and 44¢ for a letter. For international mail, a first-class letter of up to 1 ounce costs 94¢ (72¢ to Canada and Mexico); a first-class postcard costs 94¢ (72¢ to Canada and Mexico). For more information, go to **www.usps. com** and click on "Calculate Postage."

If you aren't sure what your address will be in the United States, mail can be sent to you, in your name, c/o **General Delivery** at the main post office of the city or region where you expect to be. (Call ℂ **800/275- 8777** for information on the nearest post office.) The addressee must pick up mail in person and must produce proof of identity (driver's license, passport, and so on). Most post offices will hold your mail for up to 1 month, and are open Monday to Friday from 8am to 6pm and Saturday from 9am to 3pm.

Always include zip codes when mailing items in the U.S. If you don't know your zip code, visit **http://zip4.usps.com**.

MEASUREMENTS See the chart on the inside front cover of this book for details on converting metric measurements to nonmetric equivalents.

MEDICAL CONDITIONS If you have a medical condition that requires **syringe-administered medications,** carry a valid signed prescription from your physician; syringes in carry-on baggage will be inspected. Insulin in any form should have the proper pharmaceutical documentation. If you have a disease that requires treatment with **narcotics,** you should also carry documented proof with you—smuggling narcotics aboard a plane carries severe penalties in the U.S.

For **HIV-positive visitors,** requirements for entering the United States are somewhat vague and change frequently. For up-to-the-minute information, contact AIDSinfo (ℂ **800/448-0440,** or 301/519-0459 outside the U.S.; www.aidsinfo.nih. gov) or the **Gay Men's Health Crisis** (ℂ **212/367-1000;** www.gmhc.org).

NEWSPAPERS & MAGAZINES The Enterprise Newspaper Group publishes the *Barnstable Enterprise, Falmouth Enterprise, Bourne Enterprise, Sandwich Enterprise* and *Mashpee Enterprise,* good resources for travelers visiting those towns. The *Cape Cod Times* is published daily and runs regular supplements on arts and antiques, events and entertainment, and restaurants. In addition, several other towns have their own weekly local paper. Martha's Vineyard has two weekly papers, the *Martha's Vineyard Times* and the *Vineyard Gazette,* each offering insight into regional issues. Nantucket also has one: *The Nantucket Inquirer and Mirror* (nicknamed "the Inky"). *Cape Cod Life* is a glossy bimonthly, with beautiful photography of the area. Each island has its own glossy. *Provincetown Arts,* published yearly, is a must for those interested in local arts and letters. In addition, a great many summer-guide magazines are available (don't expect much new information), and free booklets with discount coupons are ubiquitous; the nicest of these, with a friendly tone and a lot of useful information, is the *Cape Cod Guide.*

PASSPORTS The websites listed provide downloadable passport applications as well as the current fees for processing applications. For an up-to-date, country-by-country listing of passport requirements around the world, go to the "International Travel" tab of the U.S. Department of State website at **http://travel.state.gov**. International visitors to the U.S. can obtain a visa application at the same website. *Note:* Children are required to present a passport when entering the United States at airports. More information on obtaining a passport for a minor can be found at **http://travel.state.gov**. Allow plenty of time before your trip to apply for a passport; processing normally takes 4 to 6 weeks (3 weeks for expedited service) but can take longer during busy periods (especially spring). And keep in mind that if you need a passport in a hurry, you'll pay a higher processing fee.

For Residents of Australia: You can pick up an application from your local post office or any branch of Passports Australia, but you must schedule an interview at the passport office to present your application materials. Call the **Australian Passport Information Service** at ✆ **131-232,** or visit the government website at www.passports.gov.au.

For Residents of Canada: Passport applications are available at travel agencies throughout Canada or from the central **Passport Office,** Department of Foreign Affairs and International Trade, Ottawa, ON K1A 0G3 (✆ **800/567-6868;** www.ppt.gc.ca). *Note:* Canadian children who travel must have their own passport. However, if you hold a valid Canadian passport issued before December 11, 2001, that bears the name of your child, the passport remains valid for you and your child until it expires.

For Residents of Ireland: You can apply for a 10-year passport at the **Passport Office,** Setanta Centre, Molesworth Street, Dublin 2 (✆ **01/671-1633;** www.foreignaffairs.gov.ie). Those 17 and under must apply for a 5-year passport. You can also apply at 1A South Mall, Cork (✆ **21/494-4700**), or at most main post offices.

For Residents of New Zealand: You can pick up a passport application at any New Zealand Passports Office or download it from their website. Contact the **Passports Office** at ✆ **0800/225-050** in New Zealand, or 04/474-8100; or log on to www.passports.govt.nz.

For Residents of the United Kingdom: To pick up an application for a standard 10-year passport (5-yr. passport for children 16 and under), visit your nearest passport office, major post office, or travel agency or contact the **United Kingdom Passport Service** at ✆ **0300/222-0000,** or search its website at www.ips.gov.uk.

POLICE   For police emergencies, call ✆ **911.**

SMOKING   In the past few years, 14 out of 15 Cape Cod towns have gone "smoke-free" to some extent. The towns of Falmouth, Barnstable, Yarmouth, Dennis, Brewster, Chatham, Orleans, Eastham, Wellfleet, Truro, and Provincetown, and the islands of Martha's Vineyard and Nantucket, have all passed some variation on laws forbidding smoking in public places as a way to protect nonsmokers from secondhand smoke. This means that in the majority of restaurants and bars in these towns, you cannot light up. A few bars have installed a ventilation system and/or a separate area where smoking is allowed, but these are few and far between. While some large hotels set aside rooms for smokers, the vast majority of lodging establishments on Cape Cod are non-smoking. There is one establishment in Barnstable where smoking is currently allowed. At **Puff the Magic,** 649 Main St., Hyannis (✆ **508/771-9090**), a cigar bar where no food is served, you can smoke to your heart's discontent.

On Martha's Vineyard, all restaurants are smoke-free except those in Oak Bluffs and Edgartown that have separately enclosed and ventilated bar areas. Because the other four towns on the Vineyard are "dry," meaning no alcohol can be sold, there are no bars in those towns and, therefore, no smoking at all in restaurants. There is also no smoking allowed in the common areas of inns on the Vineyard. There may be some inns where certain rooms are designated for smokers, and visitors wishing to smoke should inquire when they book their rooms.

TAXES   In Massachusetts, the state sales tax is 5%. This tax applies to restaurant meals (but not to food bought in stores) and all goods, with the exception of clothing items priced lower than $175. All of the 15 Cape Cod towns plus the towns on Martha's Vineyard and Nantucket have the same hotel tax, a combination of state and local taxes that totals 9.7%. The United States has no value-added tax (VAT) or other indirect tax at the national level. Every state, county, and city may levy its own local tax on all purchases, including hotel and restaurant checks and airline tickets. These taxes will not appear on price tags.

TELEPHONES Many convenience groceries and packaging services sell **prepaid calling cards** in denominations up to $50; for international visitors these can be the least expensive way to call home. Many public pay phones at airports now accept American Express, MasterCard, and Visa credit cards. **Local calls** made from pay phones in most locales cost either 25¢ or 35¢ (no pennies, please). Most long-distance and international calls can be dialed directly from any phone. **For calls within the United States and to Canada,** dial 1 followed by the area code and the seven-digit number. **For other international calls,** dial 011 followed by the country code, city code, and the number you are calling.

Calls to area codes **800, 888, 877,** and **866** are toll-free. However, calls to area codes **700** and **900** (chat lines, bulletin boards, "dating" services, and so on) can be very expensive—usually a charge of 95¢ to $3 or more per minute, and they sometimes have minimum charges that can run as high as $15 or more.

For **reversed-charge or collect calls,** and for person-to-person calls, dial the number 0 then the area code and number; an operator will come on the line, and you should specify whether you are calling collect, person-to-person, or both. If your operator-assisted call is international, ask for the overseas operator.

For **local directory assistance** ("information"), dial ℭ **411;** for long-distance information, dial 1, then the appropriate area code and ℭ **555-1212.**

TELEGRAPH & FAX **Telegraph and telex services** are provided primarily by Western Union (ℭ **800/325-6000;** www. westernunion.com). You can telegraph (wire) money, or have it telegraphed to you, very quickly over the Western Union system, but this service can cost as much as 15% to 20% of the amount sent.

Most hotels have **fax machines** available for guest use (be sure to ask about the charge to use it). Many hotel rooms are wired for guests' fax machines. A less expensive way to send and receive faxes may be at stores such as the **UPS Store.**

TIME Cape Cod and the islands are in the Eastern Standard Time zone. The continental United States is divided into **four time zones:** Eastern Standard Time (EST), Central Standard Time (CST), Mountain Standard Time (MST), and Pacific Standard Time (PST). Alaska and Hawaii have their own zones. For example, when it's 9am in Los Angeles (PST), it's 7am in Honolulu (HST), 10am in Denver (MST), 11am in Chicago (CST), noon in New York City or Provincetown (EST), 5pm in London (GMT), and 2am the next day in Sydney.

Daylight saving time is in effect from 1am on the second Sunday in March to 1am on the first Sunday in November, except in Arizona, Hawaii, the U.S. Virgin Islands, and Puerto Rico. Daylight saving time moves the clock 1 hour ahead of standard time.

TIPPING Tips are a very important part of many workers' income, particularly workers in the service industry on Cape Cod and the islands, and gratuities are the standard way of showing appreciation for services provided. (Tipping is certainly not compulsory if the service is poor!) In hotels, tip **bellhops** at least $1 per bag

($2–$3 if you have a lot of luggage), and tip the **chamber staff** $1 to $2 per day (more if you've left a disaster area for him or her to clean up). Tip the **valet-parking attendant** $1 every time you get your car.

In restaurants, bars, and nightclubs, tip **service staff** 15% to 20% of the check, tip **bartenders** 10% to 15%, tip **checkroom attendants** $1 per garment, and tip **valet-parking attendants** $1 per vehicle.

As for other service personnel, tip **cab drivers** 15% of the fare; tip **skycaps** at airports at least $1 per bag ($2–$3 if you have a lot of luggage); and tip **hairdressers** and **barbers** 15% to 20%.

TOILETS Public toilets or "restrooms" are relatively rare on the Cape and Islands, but they can be found in the most touristy areas. Falmouth, Hyannis, Chatham, and Provincetown have public restrooms located on their main streets. Falmouth's public restrooms are in Peg Noonan Park near the library and Hyannis's are behind the JFK Hyannis Museum near town hall. Provincetown's are on Macmillan Pier and Chatham's are on Main Street near the central parking area. There are public restrooms at all transportation facilities, like ferry terminals (Hyannis, Woods Hole, Nantucket; Oak Bluffs and Vineyard Haven on Martha's Vineyard), bus terminals (Hyannis and Falmouth), and airports (Hyannis, Martha's Vineyard, Nantucket, Provincetown). Edgartown on the Vineyard has a restroom in its visitor center on Church Street off Main Street. In addition, many chambers of commerce have restrooms available for visitors. You will find fast food restaurants on main thoroughfares of a number of Cape towns (on Route 132 in Hyannis, for example) and those restrooms are open to the public, though you may need to make a small purchase. The Cape Cod Mall in Hyannis

also has restrooms, as do a number of large stores in Hyannis. Using the restrooms in bars and restaurants is usually reserved for patrons, but if you buy something (even a soft drink or snack), you can usually use the facilities. Some gas stations also have public restrooms.

USEFUL PHONE NUMBERS U.S. Department of State Travel Advisory: ℂ 202/647-5225 (manned 24 hrs.). **U.S. Passport Agency:** ℂ 202/647-0518. **U.S. Centers for Disease Control International Travelers' Hotline:** ℂ 404/332-4559.

VISAS For information about U.S. visas go to **http://travel.state.gov** and click on "Visas." Or go to one of the following websites:

Australian citizens can obtain up-to-date visa information from the **U.S. Embassy Canberra,** Moonah Place, Yarralumla, ACT 2600 (ℂ **02/6214-5600**), or by checking the U.S. Diplomatic Mission's website at **http://canberra.us embassy.gov/consular.**

British subjects can obtain up-to-date visa information by calling the **U.S. Embassy Visa Information Line** (ℂ **0891/200-290**), or by visiting the "Visas to the U.S." section of the American Embassy London's website at **www. usembassy.org.uk.**

Irish citizens can obtain up-to-date visa information through the **Embassy of the USA Dublin,** 42 Elgin Rd., Dublin 4 (ℂ **353/1-668-8777**), or by checking the website at **http://dublin.usembassy.gov.**

Citizens of **New Zealand** can obtain up-to-date visa information by contacting the **U.S. Embassy New Zealand,** 29 Fitzherbert Terrace, Thorndon, Wellington (ℂ **644/472-2068**), or get the information directly from the website at **http:// newzealand.usembassy.gov.**

2 AIRLINE, HOTEL & CAR-RENTAL WEBSITES

MAJOR DOMESTIC/ BUDGET AIRLINES

AirTran Airways
www.airtran.com

American Airlines
www.aa.com

Cape Air
www.flycapeair.com

Continental Airlines
www.continental.com

Delta Air Lines
www.delta.com

JetBlue Airways
www.jetblue.com

Midwest Airlines
www.midwestairlines.com

Nantucket Airlines
www.nantucketairlines.com

Northwest Airlines
www.nwa.com

Southwest Airlines
www.southwest.com

Spirit Airlines
www.spiritair.com

United Airlines
www.united.com

US Airways
www.usairways.com

Virgin America
www.virginamerica.com

MAJOR HOTEL & MOTEL CHAINS

Best Western International
www.bestwestern.com

Clarion Hotels
www.clarionhotel.com

Comfort Inn
www.comfortinn.com

Courtyard by Marriott
www.marriott.com/courtyard

Days Inn
www.daysinn.com

Doubletree Hotel
http://doubletree1.hilton.com

Econo Lodge
www.econolodge.com

Embassy Suites
http://embassysuites1.hilton.com

Hampton Inn
http://hamptoninn1.hilton.com

Hilton
www.hilton.com

Holiday Inn
www.holidayinn.com

Howard Johnson
www.hojo.com

Marriott
www.marriott.com

Quality Inn
www.qualityinn.com

Radisson Hotels & Resorts
www.radisson.com

Ramada Worldwide
www.ramada.com

Red Roof Inn
www.redroof.com

Renaissance
www.renaissancehotels.com

Rodeway Inn
www.rodewayinn.com

Sheraton Hotels & Resorts
www.starwoodhotels.com/sheraton

Super 8
www.super8.com

300 Travelodge
www.travelodge.com

Wyndham Hotels & Resorts
www.wyndham.com

CAR-RENTAL AGENCIES

Advantage
www.advantage.com

Alamo
www.alamo.com

Avis
www.avis.com

Budget
www.budget.com

Dollar
www.dollar.com

Enterprise
www.enterprise.com

Hertz
www.hertz.com

National
www.nationalcar.com

Payless
www.paylesscar.com

Rent-A-Wreck
www.rentawreck.com

Thrifty
www.thrifty.com

INDEX

See also Accommodations and Restaurant indexes, below.

Safety concerns, 50–51
Saffron, 275
Sailing. *See* Boating
Salt Pond Visitor Center, 22, 183–185, 187, 191
The Sand Bar, 145
The Sand Bar & Grille, 289
Sandcastle and Sculpture Day, 35
Sand Dollar Bar and Grill, 145
Sand Pond, 156
Sandwich, 7, 18, 74–85
    accommodations, 82–84
    beaches and recreational pursuits, 77
    restaurants, 84–85
    shopping, 81–82
    traveling to, 76
    visitor information, 76
    walking tour, 76–77
Sandwich Antiques Center, 81
Sandwich Auction House, 81
Sandwich Boardwalk, 78
Sandwich Boardwalk Celebration, 35
Sandwich Glass Museum, 76, 80
Sandwich Mini Golf, 81
Sandy Neck, 114
Sandy Neck Beach, 4–5, 77
Sayle's Seafood, 240
Scargo Lake, 137
Scargo Pottery, 139–140
Scargo Tower, 139
Schoolhouse Gallery, 213–214
The 1869 Schoolhouse Museum, 184–185
Science Library, 236
Scorton Creek, 114
Seafood, fresh
    Bourne, 89
    Brewster, 151
    Hyannis, Barnstable, and environs, 120
    Martha's Vineyard, 275
    Nantucket, 240
    Orleans, 179
    Sandwich, 82
    Wellfleet, 197–198
Seagull Beach, 131
Seal-watching, 26, 165
Seaside Trail, 165
Seasons, 30–32
Senior travel, 51–52
Seymours Pond, 156

Shawme-Crowell State Forest, 78
Shining Sea Bikeway, 6, 94
Shopping
    best, 12–13
    Bourne, 89
    Dennis, 139
    Harwich, 158
    Martha's Vineyard, 274–275
    Mashpee, 109–110
    Nantucket, 238–240
    Orleans, 175–176
    Provincetown, 31, 212–215
    Sandwich, 81–82
    Wellfleet, 193–194
    Yarmouth, 132–133
Shop Therapy, 214
Shoulder seasons, 31
Siasconset ('Sconset) Beach, 233
Siasconset Casino, 255
Silk & Feathers, 214
Skaket Beach, 173
Slip 14 on South Wharf, 255
Small Pleasures, 212
Small Swamp Trail, 191, 201
Smitty's Homemade Ice Cream, 107
Smoking, 296
Soccer, 132
Soft Earth, 98
South Beach, 164, 267
South Cape Beach, 109
South Cape Beach State Park, 109
South Road, 267
South Trail, 148
The Spectrum, 151
Spohr Gardens, 96
Spring, 32
Spruce Hill Conservation Area, 148
Stage Stop Candy, 144
Starlight Theatre & Cafe, 255
State Beach, 265
State Road, 268
St. Barnabas Strawberry Festival, 33
Steve's Pizzeria & More, 106
Stony Brook Grist Mill, 148
Stony Brook Grist Mill and Museum, 150
The Strand, 290
Stubby's, 253
Student travel, 52
Summer, 31–32
Sundae School, 144, 179
Sundancers, 145
Sun exposure, 48–49

Sunken Meadow Beach, 183
Surf Drive Beach, 94, 95
Surfing
    Eastham, 184
    Orleans, 174
Surfside Beach, 233
The Susan Baker Memorial Museum, 201–202
Sustainable tourism, 53–55
Sweet Inspirations, 239
Sweets (ice cream, desserts, pastries)
    Brewster, 154–155
    Chatham, 170–171
    Dennis, 144
    Eastham, 187
    Falmouth, 106–107
    Harwich, 160–161
    Hyannis, Barnstable, and environs, 119, 126–127
    Martha's Vineyard, 285–286
    Nantucket, 239, 254
    Orleans, 179
    Provincetown, 223
    Sandwich, 85
    Truro, 204
    Wellfleet, 198
Sydenstricker Glass, 151

Takeout and picnic fare
    Eastham, 187
    Falmouth, 106
    Hyannis, Barnstable, and environs, 127
    Martha's Vineyard, 287–289
    Nantucket, 253–254
    Orleans, 179
    Provincetown, 223
    Truro, 204
    Wellfleet, 197
Tao Water Art Gallery, 117–118
Taxes, 296–297
Taxis, 46
Telegraph and telex services, 297
Telephones, 56–57, 297
Tennis
    Bourne, 87
    Brewster, 149
    Chatham, 165
    Dennis, 138
    Eastham, 184
    Falmouth, 96
    Harwich, 157
    Martha's Vineyard, 270
    Nantucket, 234
    Orleans, 174